27th Ibero-American Conference on Software Engineering (CIbSE 2024)

Curitiba, Brazil
6 - 10 May 2024

ISBN: 979-8-3313-0043-2

Printed from e-media with permission by:

Curran Associates, Inc.
57 Morehouse Lane
Red Hook, NY 12571

Some format issues inherent in the e-media version may also appear in this print version.

CIbSE - IberoAmerican Conference on Software Engineering
c/o Luca Cernuzzi
Universidad Católica "Nuestra Seóra de la Asunción",
Campus Universitario, Asunción
Barrio Santa Ana, C.C.1683, C.P. 1364
Asunción - Paraguay

Phone: +595 21 334650
Fax: +595 21 310587

lcernuzz@uca.edu.py

Additional copies of this publication are available from:

Curran Associates, Inc.
57 Morehouse Lane
Red Hook, NY 12571 USA
Phone: 845-758-0400
Fax: 845-758-2633
Email: curran@proceedings.com
Web: www.proceedings.com

TABLE OF CONTENTS

CIbSE2024

XXVII Congreso Iberoamericano en Ingeniería de Software
XXVII Congresso Ibero-Americano en Engenharia de Software
XXVII Ibero-American Conference on Software Engineering

PROGRAM COMMITTEE CHAIRS

Edson OliveiraJr (State University of Maringá, Brazil)

Ignacio García Rodríguez de Guzmán (University of Castilla-La Mancha, Spain)

DOCTORAL SYMPOSIUM CHAIRS

Claudia P. Ayala (Universitat Politècnica de Catalunya, Spain)

Leonardo Murta (Universidade Federal Fluminense, Brazil)

JOURNAL FIRST CHAIRS

Monalessa Perini Barcelos (Federal University of Espírito Santo, Brazil)

Isabel Sofia Sousa Brito (Instituto Politécnico de Beja, Portugal)

EIbAIS CHAIRS

Adolfo Neto (Federal University of Technology - Paraná, Brazil)

Pedro Valderas (Universitat Politècnica de València, Spain)

INDUSTRY TALKS CHAIRS

Marco Paludo (Pontifícia Universidade Católica do Paraná, Brazil)

GENERAL CHAIRS

Sheila Reinehr (Pontifícia Universidade Católica do Paraná (PUCPR), Brazil)
Andreia Malucelli (Pontifícia Universidade Católica do Paraná (PUCPR), Brazil)

PROCEEDINGS CHAIR

Jose Antonio Cruz-Lemus (University of Castilla-La Mancha, Spain)

Preface

On behalf of the CIbSE 2024 Organizing Committee, we proudly present the proceedings of the 27th Iberoamerican Conference on Software Engineering (CIbSE 2024). CIbSE has provided a forum to present recent advances in the practices for engineering software-intensive systems since 1998. This year, the conference was hosted by the Pontifical Catholic University of Paraná, Brazil, which was a perfect scenario for making this high-quality event possible.

In a society that increasingly relies on software systems for our daily activity (e.g., in communication, finance, healthcare, and transport), the use of adequate engineering practices in the form of methods, processes, and tools throughout the lifecycle of these systems becomes essential to ensure their suitability. In this context, CIbSE is the leading Software Engineering (SE) research forum in Ibero-America. It promotes high-quality scientific research and, thus, supports the researchers in this community in publishing and discussing their work. In addition, the conference fosters collaboration and cross-fertilization among academics, students, and practitioners from the industry.

Eighty-four papers were submitted for this edition of the conference. Each submission was reviewed by at least three members of the Program Committee (formed by qualified experts), and followed by a leading review. After carefully peer-reviewing, 30 papers were finally selected (35% acceptance rate). Five distinguished papers were invited to submit an extended version to the Science of Computer Programming journal, and the best paper received an award certificate. In addition to the 18 original papers, 2 papers were accepted in the Journal First category, offering an opportunity for the authors to discuss their work with the community and enrich the CIbSE technical program, and 2 posters were presented. Finally, 6 papers were accepted in the new submission category entitled "Articles on applied R&D projects or contracts with companies", which present ongoing research projects and experiences in research transference.

CIbSE 2024 hosted the Doctoral Symposium, which aims at bringing together doctoral students working on foundations, techniques, tools, and applications of Software Engineering and allowing them to present and discuss their research in a constructive and international atmosphere where a board of experts discuss with the students to suggest new perspectives and improvements to the PhD theses. Two ongoing doctorate research projects were presented. Moreover, prof. Tayana Conte. (Federal University of Amazonas (UFAM), Brazil) presented the keynote "Getting in the Game - A Conversation with Those Truly Eager to Be Researchers".

CIbSE 2024 also hosted the 7th edition of the Ibero-American School on Software Engineering (EIbAIS). EIbAIS aims to promote a forum for discussions regarding Software Engineering, its related technologies, and theoretical foundations, allowing the participation of practitioners, undergraduate and graduate students, and researchers. This year, EIbAIS presented three tutorials, discussing general and specific topics of Software Engineering together with cross-fertilization with other technology disciplines:

- Process Mining: fundamentals, applications, and tools. Contributions to process modeling in requirements, quality assessment, and evidence-based improvement (Andrea Delgado).
- Machine Learning-Enabled Systems Requirements Elicitation and Specification (Marcos Kalinowski).
- Design thinking at stage zero: user requirements and needs (Rodrigo Gonzatto).

CIbSE 2024 included the Industry Talks, which aims at providing the industry and practitioners with means to discuss and work together in exploring how Software Engineer processes, methods, techniques, and tools can provide the industry with better solutions. Seven experts from the industry shared their experience with the CIbSE audience.

The conference had three important and trending keynotes:

- Advancing Leadership and Strategic Advantage in Software Engineering, presented as a "panel keynote". Anita Carleton (Carnegie Mellon University Software Engineering Institute) led, as panel chair, the discussion of Doug Schmidt (U.S. Department of Defense), John Robert (Software Engineering Institute), and Ipek Ozkaya (Software Engineering Institute) as speakers. The keynote panel discussed the evolution of software engineering and the use of AI to enhance software development, testing, and maintenance. Based on the study "Architecting the Future of Software Engineering" and collaboration with the NITRD program, they highlighted essential technologies and research areas. They focused on three main areas: AI-augmented software development, ensuring software assurance in continuously evolving systems, and constructing predictable software systems from modular components. The session explored these critical topics and their impact on the future of software engineering.
- Paving the Way for Tomorrow's Software Revolution. Jordi Cabot (Luxembourg Institute of Science and Technology - LIST). The talk addressed the growing demand for intelligent software, such as natural language interfaces, recommender systems, and client classification tools. Given the shortage of skilled developers, the speaker argued that hyperautomation is the

solution. Hyperautomation, which combines low-code and generative AI techniques, enables faster and more cost-effective application development. The talk demonstrated how these techniques work, their benefits and risks, and discussed the development of an open-source AI-enhanced low-code platform in Luxembourg.

- AI-Driven Business Transformation: Engineering Effective Machine Learning and LLM-Enabled Systems. Marcos Kalinowski (Pontifical Catholic University of Rio de Janeiro - PUC-Rio). The keynote combined practical experience and academic innovation to outline AI Engineering. It featured real-world systems from ExACTa PUC-Rio, highlighting effective business solutions and international patents. The academic insights came from recent AI research and publications. The presentation covered agile approaches to developing AI systems, focusing on the full development lifecycle and aligning business expectations. It addressed engineering software with ML and LLM components, offering practical advice and setting the stage for future research.

Finally, we would like to thank all people who contributed to making this event possible. The quality of the technical program is a result of the dedication of the members of the Program Committee and additional reviewers. We would also like to thank all members of the organizing committee, authors, keynotes, panelists, instructors, session chairs, and all the participants for their collaboration in making CIbSE 2024 a success. We express our gratitude to the CIbSE Steering Committee for their great support, particularly to Marcela Genero, Guilherme Horta Travassos, and Beatriz Marín. We would also like to express our gratitude to Giovanni Andrés Giachetti Herrera and Breno Bernard Nicolau de França (CIbSE 2023 Program Chairs) for their expertise and advice. We are thankful for the opportunity to serve as chairs for this conference.

Ignacio García Rodríguez de Guzmán and Edson OliveiraJr
CIbSE 2024 PC Chairs

Main Conference

PC Chairs

Ignacio García Rodríguez de Guzmán (University of Castilla-La Mancha, Spain)

Edson OliveiraJr (State University of Maringá, Brazil)

Program Committee

Leandro Antonelli (LIFIA, Facultad de Informática, UNLP, Argentina)

Hernan Astudillo (Universidad Tecnica Federico Santa María, Chile)

Claudia P. Ayala (Universitat Politècnica de Catalunya, España)

Clara Ayora (Universidad de Castilla la Mancha, España)

Monalessa Barcellos (UFES, Brazil)

María Cecilia Bastarrica (Universidad de Chile, Chile)

Pablo Becker (GIDIS_Web, Engineering School, UNLPam, Argentina)

Beatriz Bernárdez Jiménez (University of Seville, España)

Regina Braga (UFJF, Brazil)

Antonio Brogi (Università di Pisa, Italia)

Daniel Calegari (Instituto de Computación, Facultad de Ingeniería, Uruguay)

Valter Camargo (Federal University of São Carlos, Brazil)

Juan Pablo Carvallo (Universidad del Azuay, Ecuador)

Luca Cernuzzi (DEI - Universidad Católica, Chile)

Carlos Cetina (San Jorge University, España)

Nelly Condori-Fernández (Universidad Santiago de Compostela, España)

Tayana Conte (UFAM, Brazil)

Heitor Costa (Federal University of Lavras, Brazil)

Jose Antonio Cruz-Lemus (University of Castilla-La Mancha, España)

Felipe Curty (BNDES, Brazil)

Jose Luis de la Vara (University of Castilla-La Mancha, España)

Rafael de Mello (UFRJ, Brazil)

Andrea Delgado (Instituto de Computación, Facultad de Ingeniería, Universidad de la República, Uruguay)

Cláudio Farias (Universidade Federal do Rio de Janeiro, Brazil)

Eduardo Figueiredo (Federal University of Minas Gerais, Brazil)

Awdren Fontão (Federal University of Mato Grosso do Sul, Brazil)

Kelly Garces Pernett (Universidad de los Andes, Colombia)

Ignacio García (University of Castilla-La Mancha, España)

Jesus Garcia-Molina (Universidad de Murcia, España)

Antonio Garmendia (Universidad Autónoma de Madrid, España)

Alejandra Garrido (LIFIA-Facultad de Informatica-UNLP, Argentina)

Gustavo Gatica (Universidad Andrés Bello - Universidad de Santiago de Chile, Chile)

Marcela Genero (University of Castilla-La Mancha, España)

Giovanni Giachetti (Universidad Andrés Bello, Chile)

Enyo Gonçalves (Universidade Federal do Ceará, Brazil)

Laura González (University of the Republic, Uruguay)
Miguel Goulão (NOVA LINCS, Departamento de Informática, Faculdade de Ciências e Tecnologia, Universidade Nova de Lisboa, Portugal)
Renata Guizzardi (University of Twente, Países Bajos)
Graciela Dora Susana Hadad (Universidad Nacional del Oeste, Argentina)
Guilherme Horta Travassos (COPPE/UFRJ, Brazil)
Emanuel Irrazábal (Universidad Nacional del Nordeste, Argentina)
Marcelo Jenkins (University of Costa Rica, Costa Rica)
Marcos Kalinowski (Pontifical Catholic University of Rio de Janeiro (PUC-Rio), Brazil)
Miguel Katrib (Professor, Doctor)
Uirá Kulesza (UFRN, Brazil)
Maria Lencastre (Universidade de Pernambuco, Brazil)
Lidia Lopez (Universitat Politècnica de Catalunya, España)
Marcia Lucena (UFRN, Brazil)
Ivan Machado (UFBA - Federal University of Bahia, Brazil)
Beatriz Marin (Universidad Politecnica de Valencia, España)
Johnny Marques (Instituto Tecnológico de Aeronáutica (ITA), Brazil)
Silverio Martínez-Fernández (UPC-Barcelona Tech, España)
Santiago Matalonga (University of the West of Scotland, UK)
Denisse Muñante (ENSIIE & SAMOVAR, Francia)
Leonardo Murta (Universidade Federal Fluminense (UFF), Brazil)
Elisa Yumi Nakagawa (University of São Paulo, Brazil)
Vânia Neves (UFF, Brazil)
Breno Bernard Nicolau de França (UNICAMP, Brazil)
Toacy Oliveira (COPPE/UFRJ, Brazil)
Edson Oliveirajr (State University of Maringá, Brazil)
Luis Olsina (GIDIS_Web, Engineering School, UNLPam, Argentina)
Jose Ignacio Panach Navarrete (Universitat de València, España)
Marisa Daniela Panizzi (Universidad Nacional de Hurlingham, Argentina)
Oscar Pastor (Universidad Politécnica de Valencia, España)
Ernesto Pimentel (University of Malaga, España)
Claudia Pons (Universidad Nacional de La Plata, Argentina)
Carme Quer (Universitat Politècnica de Catalunya, España)
Christian Quesada-López (Universidad de Costa Rica, Costa Rica)
Sheila Reinehr (PucPR, Brazil)
Marcela Ridao (INTIA UNICEN, Argentina)
Luis Jorge Enrique Rivero Cabrejos (UFAM, Brazil)
Marcela Ruiz (Zurich University of Applied Sciences, Suiza)
Daniela S. Cruzes (NTNU, Noruega)
Victor Santander (Universidad Estadual do Oeste do Paraná, Brazil)
Gleison Santos (UNIRIO, Brazil)
Juliana Saraiva (Federal University of Paraiba, Brazil)
Estefanía Serral (KU Leuven, Bélgica)
Elvys Soares (Federal Institute of Alagoas, Brazil)

Sergio Soares (Informatics Center - CIn/UFPE, Brazil)
Isabel Sofia (Instituto Politécnico de Beja, Portugal)
Martin Solari (Universidad ORT Uruguay, Uruguay)
Simone R. S. Souza (ICMC/USP, Brazil)
Vitor E. Silva Souza (Federal University of Espírito Santo, Brazil)
Pedro Valderas (Universitat Politècnica de València, España)
Natasha Malveira Costa Valentim (UFPR - Universidade Federal do Paraná, Brazil)
Diego Vallespir (Facultad de Ingeniería, Universidad de la República, Uruguay)
Davi Viana (Federal University of Maranhão, Brazil)
Talita Vieira Ribeiro (UERJ, Brazil)
Jéssyka Vilela (Universidade Federal de Pernambuco, Brazil)

Doctoral Symposium

DS Chairs

Claudia P. Ayala (Universitat Politècnica de Catalunya, Spain)

Leonardo Murta (Universidade Federal Fluminense, Brazil)

DS Committee

Luca Cernuzzi (DEI - Universidad Católica, Chile)
Eduardo Figueiredo (Federal University of Minas Gerais, Brazil)
Marcela Genero (University of Castilla-La Mancha, España)
Guilherme Horta Travassos (Federal University of Rio de Janeiro, Brazil)
Luis Olsina (GIDIS_Web, Engineering School, UNLPam, Argentina)
Óscar Pastor (Universidad Politécnica de Valencia, España)
Sergio Soares (Informatics Center - CIn/UFPE, Brazil)
Isabel Sofia (Instituto Politécnico de Beja, Portugal)
Pedro Valderas (Universitat Politècnica de València, España)

Panel Experts

Luca Cernuzzi (DEI - Universidad Católica, Chile)
Marcela Genero (University of Castilla-La Mancha, España)
Óscar Pastor (Universidad Politécnica de Valencia, España)
Pedro Valderas (Universitat Politècnica de València, España)

Migration of Monolithic Systems to Microservices using AI: A Systematic Mapping Study

Ana Martínez Saucedo[1,2,3] and Guillermo Rodríguez[2,3]

[1]Universidad Argentina de la Empresa (UADE), Instituto de Tecnología (INTEC)
Buenos Aires, Argentina

[2]CONICET
Buenos Aires, Argentina

[3]ISISTAN Research Institute (CONICET - UNICEN)
Tandil, Buenos Aires, Argentina

anmartinez@uade.edu.ar, guillermo.rodriguez@isistan.unicen.edu.ar

Abstract. *The popularity of microservices architecture has been increasing considerably because of its capacity to alleviate monolithic architecture issues. Nonetheless, the migration of monolith systems to microservices is a complex task. This work aims to analyze and characterize the state of the art on migrating monolithic applications towards microservices (semi-) automatically using Artificial Intelligence (AI) techniques by applying a systematic mapping methodology. Results showed that clustering is the preferred IA technique to decompose a monolith, cited by 63% out of the 22 reviewed studies. Moreover, the most prevailing input type used in migration techniques was source code (36.4%).*

1. Introduction

The monolithic architecture is based on the integral encapsulation of the functionalities of a single application executed by a single process [Koschel et al. 2017]. This has been the most predominant architecture in the scope of software development due to the fact a monolithic application is easy to implement and deploy [Koschel et al. 2017]. Nonetheless, the problems of monolithic architecture appear as the application increases its size [Fritzsch et al. 2019b, Koschel et al. 2017], causing high code coupling, difficulties in comprehending code, arduous maintenance, slow compilation process, and increased communication effort among project's stakeholders [Li et al. 2019]. Therefore, the microservice architecture was designed to provide solutions for the drawbacks of monolithic architecture. The main components of such an architecture are the microservices, which are defined by several authors as small, independent, and autonomous services that are capable of efficiently performing a clearly defined task [Fowler and Lewis 2014, Newman 2015]. In this context, applications built according to microservice architecture have several advantageous aspects, mainly module-level scalability, faster delivery, and maintenance [Jamshidi et al. 2018]. This is why several companies, such as Netflix, SoundCloud, and Amazon, have chosen to migrate from monolithic architecture to microservice architecture [Li et al. 2019]. However, migration from monolithic to microservices architectures fails to be classified as a simple process, since it involves complex issues that require strategies to be solved [Balalaie et al. 2015, Christoforou et al. 2017].

This work aims to characterize the migration of monolithic systems to microservices using Artificial Intelligence (AI) techniques based on the state of the art. The information for carrying out this work was acquired through a systematic mapping study: we selected 22 studies from an initial set of 855 papers to answer questions that analyze the identification of microservices techniques. The main results of this work are:

- Migration of monolithic systems to microservices is complex and techniques to achieve migration are varied in terms of supported programming languages, types of input, and granularity;
- Clustering is the most addressed AI technique in the literature to migrate monolithic applications towards microservices.

The remainder of the article is organized as follows. Section 2 describes related work. In Section 3, the research method is presented. In Section 4, the results are presented based on the research questions. Section 5 discusses the findings of this study. Threats to Validity are described in Section 6. Finally, Section 7 concludes the article with remarks and future work.

2. Related Work

The migration of monolith applications to microservices has been reviewed from different perspectives. Most of the studies have focused on migration techniques or activities and factors that motivate migrating toward a microservice architecture. From the perspective of the migration process, Fritzsch et al. [Fritzsch et al. 2019b] address monolith's dissociation, which consists of fragmenting the monolithic application into small services. This is a substantial and high-level task in terms of complexity, which is the reason why it can be considered the most important task for migration. Thus, the authors perform a systematic literature review in order to collect techniques available in the literature to identify microservices, in which ten main techniques were found. Similarly, Ponce et al. [Ponce et al. 2019] reached a classification of migration approaches through a rapid review: model-driven, static and dynamic analysis of code.

In the same direction, Fritzsch et al. [Fritzsch et al. 2019a] investigate the migration process adopted in the industry, outlining the lack of a semi-automated process to support migration. Therefore, companies rely on non-systematic approaches or manual functional decomposition approaches to perform migration. For this reason, Lapuz et al. [Lapuz et al. 2021] gather from the literature dynamic data collection tools that were (or could be) employed to assist in the migration of monolithic applications to microservices through dynamic analysis. Finally, Di Francesco et al. [Di Francesco et al. 2018] focus on the industry as well by conducting an industrial survey that aims to characterize the activities and challenges faced by practitioners when migrating towards microservices.

However, to our knowledge, no work has focused on analyzing and characterizing migration techniques that have used AI techniques to support monolith decomposition. Considering the complexity involved in migrating towards a microservice architecture, the automation of (most of) the migration process would alleviate practitioners in the task of identifying loosely coupled and highly cohesive microservices.

3. Research Method

The purpose of this work is to analyze and characterize the state of the art on migrating monolithic applications towards microservices (semi-) automatically using AI techniques.

To do so, we performed a systematic mapping study. To assist in the execution of the research protocol, the tool StArt[1] was used, which tracks and documents each decision made throughout each phase of the protocol.

The research objective was defined using part of the model GQM (Goal-Question-Metric) [Basili and Weiss 1984]: the objective is to analyze migration from monolithic applications to microservices cases, with the purpose of characterizing, with respect to microservice identification techniques, from the researchers' point of view, in the context of theoretical and applied research.

With the purpose of complying with the protocol, criteria detailed by PICO (Population, Intervention, Comparison, and Outcome) were determined [Schugerl et al. 2009]. Since this work aims for characterization, only the attributes Population, Intervention, and Outcome were used, thus a PICO extract is shown in Table 1. Therefore, two research questions (Q) were designed as follows:

RQ1 – Which AI techniques are used to migrate monolithic applications to microservices?

RQ2 – Which aspects of a monolithic application are processed as inputs by AI models?

PICO criteria	Description
Population	Microservices, Monolith
Intervention	Decomposition, Migration, Transformation, Move, Modernization, Refactoring
Comparison	Not applicable
Outcome	Process / Technique / Model / Method / Approach / Features / Characteristics

Table 1. PICO criteria.

3.1. Sources Selection

The selection of the sources used for the execution of this work was made through a series of criteria and guided by the works of Petersen et al. [Petersen et al. 2015] and Kitchenham et al. [Kitchenham and Brereton 2013]. The criteria set out to select database and index systems were a) being a relevant scientific database in software engineering, and b) content access availability. A total of 855 studies were retrieved between 2015 and 2023 and composed the initial pool. The selected sources were: ACM (23.3%), IEEE Xplore (4.9%), Scopus (11.2%), SpringerLink (55%), and Science Direct (5.6%).

3.2. Search Strategy

The search strategy aims to find clauses that meet the main questions suggested in the research. First, the search was automated on the sources already established. For the development of this work, there was no restriction on the publication date of the bibliographic materials analyzed.

The search strategy is divided into the following steps:

(i) Criteria declaration, search clause extraction, and search execution. A total of 855 studies were included;

[1] `https://www.lapes.ufscar.br/resources/tools-1/start-1`

(ii) Removal of duplicates, in which 764 studies were kept;
(iii) Execution of the first qualitative analysis of the results based on the inclusion and exclusion criteria. As a result, a total of 158 studies were kept;
(iv) Snowballing activity by extracting for each study its relevant references, 7 studies were added;
(v) Conduction of the second qualitative analysis based on the analysis of the results, keeping 163 studies;
(vi) Data extraction to solve the research questions proposed, in which 22 out of 163 studies addressed migration answered the questions by a) presenting a migration technique and the steps needed to perform it, and b) the migration technique is based on an AI algorithm.

3.3. Search Terms

The search terms were gathered according to the following keywords: microservices, microservice, microservice architecture, monolith, monoliths, decomposition, migration, transform and move. These were used in a search string, which is a set of keywords combined with boolean operators that will execute the search.

The search string used to perform this search was:

(((microservices ***OR*** *microservice* ***OR*** *"microservice architecture")* ***AND*** *(monolith* ***OR*** *monoliths))* ***AND*** *(decomposition* ***OR*** *migration* ***OR*** *transform* ***OR*** *move* ***OR*** *legacy* ***OR*** *modernization* ***OR*** *refactoring))*

Since the exclusion criteria define that only studies in English are accepted, the terms used were written in English only. To provide the best result possible, two logical tests were applied to the string. In addition, metadata specification could have been applied. However, since the vocabulary is very particular to the Computer Science subject, it was disregarded to define it as the subject of the search.

3.4. Study Selection Criteria

For the selection of the bibliography resulting from the search, a series of inclusion and exclusion criteria were defined. It is important to note that there was no restriction on the search time. The inclusion and exclusion criteria adopted in this review are described below.

Inclusion criteria

- IC01: Study analyses the migration of monolithic systems to microservices
- IC02: Study presents an AI technique to identify microservices.

Exclusion criteria

- EC01: Duplicated study.
- EC02: Study is not written in English.
- EC03: Study published only as abstracts or prefaces of journals and events.
- EC04: Study is not available for download.
- EC05: Study is not peer-reviewed.
- EC06: Study is not related to the migration of monolithic systems to microservices.

3.5. Studies Selection Procedure

Titles and abstracts of the retrieved studies were analyzed to verify whether they are suitable for this work. From the analysis performed, it was possible to classify the studies with the assistance of the StArt tool as accepted, rejected, or duplicated. It was found 158 (18%) accepted, 606 (71%) rejected, and 91 (11%) duplicates.

Afterward, full texts of accepted studies were read to find answers to the questions made in the research protocol. It is important to notice that all accepted studies conform to the inclusion criteria and contribute to answering the questions.

4. Results

Migration techniques classification schema

In order to evaluate the works reviewed and make a comparative description among them, we have identified common criteria regarding relevant issues in the field of monolith to microservices migration:

- AI technique. This feature represents the AI technique used to decompose a monolith.
- Language support. This criterion deals with the monolith programming language that is supported by each migration technique.
- Input type. This feature evaluates which aspects of a monolithic application are required to perform migration, such as source code, log traces, and requirements, among others.
- Granularity. This criterion evaluates the unit of analysis used by each technique to approach migration, attempting to discover the quality of each decomposition obtained in terms of granularity.

A total of 22 studies were reviewed and characterized according to the aforementioned criteria as described in Table 2.

Table 2. Migration techniques.

Study	AI technique	Input type	Language support	Granularity
[Al-Debagy and Martinek 2019]	Clustering Word Embeddings	Documentation based (O)	Agnostic	API
[Baresi et al. 2017]	Clustering	Documentation based (O)	Agnostic	API
[Kamimura et al. 2018]	Clustering	Static	Java Cobol	Class
[Nunes et al. 2019]	Clustering	Static	Java	Class
[Pigazzini et al. 2019]	Topic Detection	Static	Java	Class
[Sellami et al. 2022]	Clustering	Static	Agnostic (Java)	Class
[Trabelsi et al. 2022]	Clustering SVM Word Embeddings	Static	Agnostic (Java)	Class

Table 2. Migration techniques (continued).

Study	AI technique	Input type	Language support	Granularity
[Nitin et al. 2022]	Label propagation	Static	Java	Class
[Brito et al. 2021]	Clustering Topic Detection	Static	Agnostic (Java)	Class
[Mathai et al. 2022]	Graph Neural Network	Static	Agnostic (Java)	Class
[Li et al. 2022]	Clustering	Documentation based (O) Dynamic Static	Agnostic (Java)	Method
[Kalia et al. 2021]	Clustering	Dynamic	Java	Class
[Liu et al. 2022]	Genetic algorithm	Dynamic	Agnostic (Java)	Class
[Jin et al. 2021]	Genetic algorithm	Dynamic	Agnostic (Java)	Class
[Bajaj et al. 2020]	Clustering	Dynamic	Agnostic	URI
[Eski and Buzluca 2018]	Clustering	Source control based Static	Agnostic	Class
[Mazlami et al. 2017]	Clustering	Source control based Static	Agnostic	Class
[Gysel et al. 2016]	Label propagation Clustering	Documentation based (A&D)	Agnostic	Nanoentity
[Ren et al. 2018]	Clustering	Dynamic Static	Agnostic (Java)	Method
[Cao and Zhang 2022]	Clustering	Dynamic Static	Agnostic (Java)	Method
[Matias et al. 2020]	Clustering	Data based Dynamic Static	Python	Class
[De Alwis et al. 2018]	Clustering	Data based Dynamic Static	PHP	Class

Research questions results

In order to answer RQ1 and RQ2, we have analyzed the criteria as mentioned above independently as described below.

By AI technique Among the AI-based techniques, a wide variety of algorithms have been employed to migrate towards microservices (Table 3). Nevertheless, clustering has been the most popular AI technique (63%) to identify microservices. Yet, varying clustering algorithms have been proposed for the decomposition problem, which is described below according to the classification presented by Xu et al. [Xu and Tian 2015]:

- Affinity propagation-based: Affinity Propagation [Al-Debagy and Martinek 2019]
- Density-based: ϵ-DBSCAN [Sellami et al. 2022]
- Graph theory-based: heuristics based [De Alwis et al. 2018] and MST-based [Mazlami et al. 2017]
- Hierarchical-based: Girven-Newman [Gysel et al. 2016, Matias et al. 2020], Louvain [Brito et al. 2021, Li et al. 2022], Fast Community [Eski and Buzluca 2018], Hierarchical K-means [Ren et al. 2018], Leiden [Cao and Zhang 2022], SArF [Kamimura et al. 2018] and SLINK [Kalia et al. 2021]
- Partitioning-based: Fuzzy C-means [Trabelsi et al. 2022] and K-means [Bajaj et al. 2020]
- Unclassified: [Nunes et al. 2019, Baresi et al. 2017]

Considering unsupervised techniques, the NSGA-II genetic algorithm is employed by the two studies in the category [Liu et al. 2022, Jin et al. 2021], while topic detection algorithms such as LDA [Pigazzini et al. 2019, Brito et al. 2021] or SLDA [Pigazzini et al. 2019] are used to group lexical and structural information from the monolith. The Word Embeddings models chosen in the reviewed studies are Word2Vec [Al-Debagy and Martinek 2019, Trabelsi et al. 2022], FastText [Al-Debagy and Martinek 2019] and CodeBERT [Trabelsi et al. 2022]

AI Technique	**Algorithm**	**Studies**	**Percentage**
Unsupervised	Clustering	[Al-Debagy and Martinek 2019, Kamimura et al. 2018, Nunes et al. 2019, Kalia et al. 2021, Gysel et al. 2016, Matias et al. 2020, Ren et al. 2018, Sellami et al. 2022, Brito et al. 2021, Li et al. 2022, Bajaj et al. 2020, Trabelsi et al. 2022, Eski and Buzluca 2018, Cao and Zhang 2022, Mazlami et al. 2017, De Alwis et al. 2018, Baresi et al. 2017]	63.0%
	Genetic algorithms	[Liu et al. 2022, Jin et al. 2021]	7.4%
	Topic detection	[Brito et al. 2021, Pigazzini et al. 2019]	7.4%
	Graph Neural Network	[Mathai et al. 2022]	3.7%
Self-supervised	Word Embeddings	[Al-Debagy and Martinek 2019, Trabelsi et al. 2022]	7.4%
Semi-supervised	Label propagation	[Nitin et al. 2022, Gysel et al. 2016]	7.4%
Supervised	SVM	[Trabelsi et al. 2022]	3.7%

Table 3. AI technique classification of AI-based migration techniques.

By input type All migration techniques need one or more aspects of a monolithic application to obtain microservices candidates. Nonetheless, the reviewed studies have used as input different outputs of a software development cycle. Consequently, a characterization of input types is proposed in Table 4.

Input type	Development phase
Documentation based (A&D)	Analysis & Design
Data based, Static	Implementation
Documentation based (O), Dynamic, Source control based	Operation

Table 4. Input type classification.

In the Analysis and Design (A&D) phases of an application, documentation is the principal output. However, several types of documentation might be used to migrate a monolithic application towards microservices, namely use cases [Gysel et al. 2016], design documents [Li et al. 2022, Gysel et al. 2016], and Entity-Relationship design models [Li et al. 2022, Gysel et al. 2016]. During the Implementation phase, source code (referred to in this study as Static) is developed and databases and tables (referred to in this study as Data based) are created and set up.

Finally, in the Operation (O) phase, the monolith application is deployed and running. In this phase, operation documentation such as OpenAPI specifications [Al-Debagy and Martinek 2019, Baresi et al. 2017] and hardware resource dependencies [Li et al. 2022] might be required as input to perform the migration. On the other hand, a dynamic aspect of a running monolith might be represented as log traces [Kalia et al. 2021, Liu et al. 2022, Jin et al. 2021, Ren et al. 2018, Cao and Zhang 2022, Matias et al. 2020, De Alwis et al. 2018], hardware utilization metrics [Li et al. 2022] or web access logs [Bajaj et al. 2020]. Source control-based inputs include repositories and Git history of commits.

As described in Table 5, in the reviewed studies the static aspect of a monolithic application is preferred when performing migration, followed by the dynamic aspect. To use source code as input to a migration technique is required to have access to those files. Therefore, when source code is not available, other migration techniques rely on the dynamic facet of an application, which corresponds to outputs generated when the application is up and running.

To rely on the static or dynamic aspect of a monolith application only has advantages and disadvantages. On the one hand, there are tools to support the static analysis of a monolith through source code. On the other, analyzing a monolith dynamically allows the identification of dead code and cyclic dependencies, which could affect the performance of the proposed microservices architecture. Nonetheless, the static facet of an application may not be sufficient to understand the true nature of dependencies in runtime. Conversely, to analyze the dynamic aspect of an application a complete runtime log traces from each operation performed by a user is needed, which generally conforms to the application test suite. In this case, high test coverage is fundamental to encompass most functionalities.

Due to the aforementioned impediments of focusing on a single aspect of an application to perform migration, 45.4% of the studies propose a multi-facet analysis in which the static aspect is always included. The most prevalent aspect to supplement the static aspect is source control: by analysing code repositories and change history it is allowed to identify code partitions that change together in time. However, it is important to note that source control on its own has not been used as input to obtain microservices candidates.

Other studies incorporated documentation into the analysis to reflect the true purpose of an application, which may diverge during the Implementation and Operation development phases. No studies include data as the only input to guide migration.

Input type	**Studies**	**Percentage**
Static	[Brito et al. 2021, Kamimura et al. 2018, Mathai et al. 2022, Nitin et al. 2022, Nunes et al. 2019, Pigazzini et al. 2019, Sellami et al. 2022, Trabelsi et al. 2022]	36.4%
Dynamic	[Bajaj et al. 2020, Jin et al. 2021, Kalia et al. 2021, Liu et al. 2022]	18.2%
Data based + Dynamic + Static	[De Alwis et al. 2018, Matias et al. 2020]	9.1%
Documentation based (O)	[Al-Debagy and Martinek 2019, Baresi et al. 2017]	9.1%
Dynamic + Static	[Cao and Zhang 2022, Ren et al. 2018]	9.1%
Source control based + Static	[Eski and Buzluca 2018, Mazlami et al. 2017]	9.1%
Documentation (A&D) + Dynamic + Static	[Li et al. 2022]	4.5%
Documentation based (A&D)	[Gysel et al. 2016]	4.5%

Table 5. Input type classification of migration techniques.

By language support Although the majority of the reviewed techniques are designed to support a monolith developed in any programming language (65.2%), a subset of them (53.3%) currently support Java monoliths due to the fact those techniques rely on tools that are only available for the Java language, for instance Wala [Ren et al. 2018] and Java Call Graph [Cao and Zhang 2022].

21.7% of the studies migrate Java monoliths to microservices, thus becoming Java the most popular monolith language to develop migration techniques. However, varied frameworks technologies are supported apart from Vanilla Java [Pigazzini et al. 2019]: Spring Framework [Kamimura et al. 2018], Java EE [Nitin et al. 2022, Kalia et al. 2021] and Fenix Framework used in conjunction with Spring Framework [Nunes et al. 2019].

By granularity When obtaining microservices candidates, each technique suggests migrating different types of elements to compose a microservice. Granularity denotes the unit of the element to be migrated, and the reviewed studies propose varying levels as described in Table 6.

Similarly to the aforementioned classification criteria, migration techniques consider levels of granularity that correspond to different phases in the software development lifecycle. During the Analysis & Design phase no code is available. In this phase, Nanoentities [Gysel et al. 2016] are proposed as migration elements that encode not only functionality but also data and its stores.

However, the vast majority of migration elements correspond to components that are available in the Implementation phase (81.7%): classes and methods. Choosing method level granularity when migrating towards microservices implies that methods of different or the same classes will compose a microservice. In the same fashion, class granularity involves moving whole classes to a microservice candidate.

While method granularity might be the most accurate unit of migration to choose in order to obtain cohesive and low coupled microservices, adjustments and merging needed to perform due to incorporating methods from different classes may take much effort considering the few tools available to semi-automatically support the process. On the contrary. the task of processing and analyzing classes might be alleviated thanks to tools available to perform, for example, call graph generation. This may explain why class granularity is the most chosen among migration techniques.

The second minority of studies (13.7%) has focused on elements made available during the Operation development phase. Those elements include URIs and APIs, which generally convey user-relevant functionality.

Studies	**Granularity level**	**Associated development phase**	**Percentage**
[Brito et al. 2021, Kalia et al. 2021, Liu et al. 2022, Jin et al. 2021, Eski and Buzluca 2018, Mazlami et al. 2017, Matias et al. 2020, Kamimura et al. 2018, Nunes et al. 2019, Pigazzini et al. 2019, Sellami et al. 2022, Trabelsi et al. 2022, Nitin et al. 2022, De Alwis et al. 2018, Mathai et al. 2022]	Class	Implementation	68.1%
[Li et al. 2022, Ren et al. 2018, Cao and Zhang 2022]	Method		13.6%
[Gysel et al. 2016]	Nanoentity	Analysis & Design	4.6%
[Bajaj et al. 2020]	URI	Operation	4.6%
[Al-Debagy and Martinek 2019, Baresi et al. 2017]	API		9.1%

Table 6. Granularity classification.

5. Discussion

This work aims to characterize the migration of monolithic systems to microservices by analyzing the identification of microservices techniques that are supported by AI models. Similarly to [Fritzsch et al. 2019b], we present a characterization of techniques that have been addressed in the literature. However, instead of proposing a technique classification that considers which aspects of a monolith may aid in the migration (static code, metadata, workload data, and runtime environment), we also defined language support and granularity criteria to decompose a monolith to provide for finer-granularity analysis.

Results show that techniques proposed in the literature are varied and have tradeoffs in terms of technological limitations or the need for manual intervention in the process. In effect, to uniformly assess the quality of a monolith decomposition, each technique would require the usage of an industrial and/or academic accepted metric against which decompositions could be evaluated. In the field of monolith to microservices migration, little consensus has been identified concerning how to evaluate a candidate microservices decomposition: whether decomposition should be evaluated against cohesion and coupling metrics only or include performance or even organizational metrics depends on the study focus. For this reason, it is difficult to assess if different AI algorithms perform better in terms of cohesion, coupling, performance, or organizational improvements.

Unsupervised techniques have been widely adopted to address monolith to microservices migration (81.5%) and in particular clustering algorithms that rely on a graph representation of the monolithic application are the most used in the literature, perhaps due to being a natural representation of the underlying software structure. While Natural Language Processing (NLP) algorithms have not been as widely researched as clustering algorithms, the exploration of the ability of Large Language Models (LLM) to identify cohesive and loosely coupled microservices based on the underlying domain knowledge represented by classes and methods could be addressed without prior input preparation by prompting source code directly to a code-specific LLM such as Code Llama. In this sense, this type of LLM would remove the need to focus on a specific programming language, as these models support a wide range of programming languages out of the box. Moreover, monolith knowledge coming from design documents or operational logs could be wired into these models by incorporating Retrieval Augmented Generation. Nonetheless, practitioners should consider the costs associated with running LLM locally, both due to licenses or appropriate hardware acquisition, as well as LLM challenges such as bias, information hallucinations, and explainability, among others [Zhao et al. 2023].

In line with the variety of metrics used to evaluate the performance of AI algorithms for the monolith decomposition task, and related to the lack of practical systems for benchmarking microservice-based architectures reported in [Di Francesco et al. 2019], the scarcity of a variety of open source projects in terms of size and complexity to validate results should be considered by researchers who want to propose new approaches to migrate monolithic systems to microservices. In this sense, the incorporation of synthetic projects created by LLM could also alleviate the task of evaluating migration techniques on monolithic applications of different sizes and domains.

6. Threats to Validity

We have considered the most common threats to validity of systematic literature reviews in Software Engineering reported in [Zhou et al. 2016] to account for how we mitigated them.

Construct validity To mitigate the threat of using inappropriate or incomplete search terms in the automatic search, we have tested our search string before executing the research protocol to ensure results were relevant. Moreover, we have included multiple databases and the StArt tool, which executes queries on the different sources to reduce subjective errors during the search phase and ensure replicability. We have also complemented our search results by including the snowballing method.

Internal validity To reduce bias in study selection and data extraction, two researchers performed these tasks independently and then cross-analyzed decisions made about each study suitability. Moreover, we have documented each accept/reject decision.

External validity To ensure the generalizability of our results, we have automated our search and complemented it with the snowballing method. Moreover, we have included peer-reviewed papers only, and have not restricted the publication date of bibliographic materials analyzed.

Conclusion validity To allow for replicable results, we have defined a protocol that was cross-validated by two researchers. Each researcher worked independently and individual findings were discussed and cross-validated.

7. Final Remarks

In this work, an analysis of studies referring to the current state of the art regarding migration from monolithic systems to microservices using AI techniques is presented. In addition, this work proposed a characterization of migration techniques in terms of AI technique, input type, language support, and granularity. Results show that no single technique is completely effective when migrating to microservices: aspects of a monolith to feed into AI models or technologies constraints make it difficult to obtain a general migration process which could be applied to any monolith system regardless of the technologies it was developed with or the domain it is contained. Notwithstanding the wide range of AI-based migration techniques supported, clustering is the preferred one to obtain candidate microservices decompositions, although little consensus is identified in the selected studies considering the inputs required by each technique.

Considering the vast amount of peer-reviewed papers addressing monolithic systems to microservices migration analyzed in this work, as future work we are further advancing our research by incorporating works that include gray literature, such as blogs and websites, among other sources, in order to extend it as a multivocal literature review.

Acknowledgments

We acknowledge the financial support provided by CONICET and UADE under doctoral grant id 14120210200034CO and project PIP no.11220200100430.

References

Al-Debagy, O. and Martinek, P. (2019). A New Decomposition Method for Designing Microservices. *Periodica Polytechnica Electrical Engineering and Computer Science*, 63(4):274–281. Number: 4.

Bajaj, D., Bharti, U., Goel, A., and Gupta, S. C. (2020). Partial migration for re-architecting a cloud native monolithic application into microservices and faas. In Badica, C., Liatsis, P., Kharb, L., and Chahal, D., editors, *Information, Communication and Computing Technology*, pages 111–124, Singapore. Springer Singapore.

Balalaie, A., Heydarnoori, A., and Jamshidi, P. (2015). *Migrating to Cloud-Native Architectures Using Microservices: An Experience Report.*

Baresi, L., Garriga, M., and De Renzis, A. (2017). Microservices Identification Through Interface Analysis. In De Paoli, F., Schulte, S., and Broch Johnsen, E., editors, *Service-Oriented and Cloud Computing*, Lecture Notes in Computer Science, pages 19–33, Cham. Springer International Publishing.

Basili, V. R. and Weiss, D. M. (1984). A Methodology for Collecting Valid Software Engineering Data. *IEEE Transactions on Software Engineering*, SE-10(6):728–738. Conference Name: IEEE Transactions on Software Engineering.

Brito, M., Cunha, J., and Saraiva, J. a. (2021). Identification of microservices from monolithic applications through topic modelling. In *Proceedings of the 36th Annual ACM Symposium on Applied Computing*, SAC '21, page 1409–1418, New York, NY, USA. Association for Computing Machinery.

Cao, L. and Zhang, C. (2022). Implementation of domain-oriented microservices decomposition based on node-attributed network. In *2022 11th International Conference on Software and Computer Applications*, ICSCA 2022, page 136–142, New York, NY, USA. Association for Computing Machinery.

Christoforou, A., Garriga, M., Andreou, A. S., and Baresi, L. (2017). Supporting the Decision of Migrating to Microservices Through Multi-layer Fuzzy Cognitive Maps. In Maximilien, M., Vallecillo, A., Wang, J., and Oriol, M., editors, *Service-Oriented Computing*, Lecture Notes in Computer Science, pages 471–480, Cham. Springer International Publishing.

De Alwis, A. A. C., Barros, A., Polyvyanyy, A., and Fidge, C. (2018). Function-Splitting Heuristics for Discovery of Microservices in Enterprise Systems. In Pahl, C., Vukovic, M., Yin, J., and Yu, Q., editors, *Service-Oriented Computing*, Lecture Notes in Computer Science, pages 37–53, Cham. Springer International Publishing.

Di Francesco, P., Lago, P., and Malavolta, I. (2018). Migrating Towards Microservice Architectures: An Industrial Survey. In *2018 IEEE International Conference on Software Architecture (ICSA)*, pages 29–2909.

Di Francesco, P., Lago, P., and Malavolta, I. (2019). Architecting with microservices: A systematic mapping study. *Journal of Systems and Software*, 150:77–97.

Eski, S. and Buzluca, F. (2018). An automatic extraction approach: transition to microservices architecture from monolithic application. In *Proceedings of the 19th International Conference on Agile Software Development: Companion*, XP '18, pages 1–6, New York, NY, USA. Association for Computing Machinery.

Fowler, M. and Lewis, J. (2014). Microservices.

Fritzsch, J., Bogner, J., Wagner, S., and Zimmermann, A. (2019a). Microservices migration in industry: Intentions, strategies, and challenges. In *2019 IEEE International Conference on Software Maintenance and Evolution (ICSME)*. IEEE.

Fritzsch, J., Bogner, J., Zimmermann, A., and Wagner, S. (2019b). From Monolith to Microservices: A Classification of Refactoring Approaches. volume 11350, pages 128–141. arXiv:1807.10059 [cs].

Gysel, M., Kölbener, L., Giersche, W., and Zimmermann, O. (2016). *Service Cutter: A Systematic Approach to Service Decomposition*. Pages: 200.

Jamshidi, P., Pahl, C., Mendonça, N. C., Lewis, J., and Tilkov, S. (2018). Microservices: The journey so far and challenges ahead. *IEEE Software*, 35(3):24–35.

Jin, W., Liu, T., Cai, Y., Kazman, R., Mo, R., and Zheng, Q. (2021). Service Candidate Identification from Monolithic Systems Based on Execution Traces. *IEEE Transactions on Software Engineering*, 47(5):987–1007. Conference Name: IEEE Transactions on Software Engineering.

Kalia, A. K., Xiao, J., Krishna, R., Sinha, S., Vukovic, M., and Banerjee, D. (2021). Mono2micro: a practical and effective tool for decomposing monolithic java applications to microservices. In *Proceedings of the 29th ACM Joint Meeting on European Software Engineering Conference and Symposium on the Foundations of Software Engineering*. ACM.

Kamimura, M., Yano, K., Hatano, T., and Matsuo, A. (2018). Extracting Candidates of Microservices from Monolithic Application Code. In *2018 25th Asia-Pacific Software Engineering Conference (APSEC)*, pages 571–580. ISSN: 2640-0715.

Kitchenham, B. and Brereton, P. (2013). A systematic review of systematic review process research in software engineering. *Information and Software Technology*, 55(12):2049–2075.

Koschel, A., Astrova, I., and Dötterl, J. (2017). Making the move to microservice architecture. In *2017 International Conference on Information Society (i-Society)*, pages 74–79.

Lapuz, N., Clarke, P., and Abgaz, Y. (2021). Digital transformation and the role of dynamic tooling in extracting microservices from existing software systems. In Yilmaz, M., Clarke, P., Messnarz, R., and Reiner, M., editors, *Systems, Software and Services Process Improvement*, pages 301–315, Cham. Springer International Publishing.

Li, S., Zhang, H., Jia, Z., Li, Z. E., Zhang, C., Li, J., and Gao, Q. (2019). A Dataflow-Driven Approach to Identifying Microservices from Monolithic Applications. *Journal of Systems and Software*, 157.

Li, Z., Shang, C., Wu, J., and Li, Y. (2022). Microservice extraction based on knowledge graph from monolithic applications. *Information and Software Technology*, 150:106992.

Liu, B., Xiong, J., Ren, Q., Tyszberowicz, S., and Yang, Z. (2022). Log2ms: a framework for automated refactoring monolith into microservices using execution logs. In *2022 IEEE International Conference on Web Services (ICWS)*, pages 391–396.

Mathai, A., Bandyopadhyay, S., Desai, U., and Tamilselvam, S. (2022). Monolith to microservices: Representing application software through heterogeneous graph neural network.

Matias, T., Correia, F. F., Fritzsch, J., Bogner, J., Ferreira, H. S., and Restivo, A. (2020). Determining microservice boundaries: A case study using static and dynamic software analysis.

Mazlami, G., Cito, J., and Leitner, P. (2017). Extraction of Microservices from Monolithic Software Architectures. In *2017 IEEE International Conference on Web Services (ICWS)*, pages 524–531.

Newman, S. (2015). *Building Microservices: Designing Fine-Grained Systems*. O'Reilly Media, 1st edition.

Nitin, V., Asthana, S., Ray, B., and Krishna, R. (2022). Cargo: Ai-guided dependency analysis for migrating monolithic applications to microservices architecture.

Nunes, L., Santos, N., and Rito Silva, A. (2019). From a monolith to a microservices architecture: An approach based on transactional contexts. In Bures, T., Duchien, L., and Inverardi, P., editors, *Software Architecture*, pages 37–52, Cham. Springer International Publishing.

Petersen, K., Vakkalanka, S., and Kuzniarz, L. (2015). Guidelines for conducting systematic mapping studies in software engineering: An update. *Information and Software Technology*, 64:1–18.

Pigazzini, I., Arcelli Fontana, F., and Maggioni, A. (2019). Tool support for the migration to microservice architecture: An industrial case study. In Bures, T., Duchien, L., and Inverardi, P., editors, *Software Architecture*, pages 247–263, Cham. Springer International Publishing.

Ponce, F., Márquez, G., and Astudillo, H. (2019). Migrating from monolithic architecture to microservices: A Rapid Review. In *2019 38th International Conference of the Chilean Computer Science Society (SCCC)*, pages 1–7. ISSN: 1522-4902.

Ren, Z., Wang, W., Wu, G., Gao, C., Chen, W., Wei, J., and Huang, T. (2018). Migrating Web Applications from Monolithic Structure to Microservices Architecture. In *Proceedings of the 10th Asia-Pacific Symposium on Internetware*, Internetware '18, pages 1–10, New York, NY, USA. Association for Computing Machinery.

Schugerl, P., Rilling, J., Witte, R., and Charland, P. (2009). A Quality Perspective of Software Evolvability Using Semantic Analysis. In *2009 IEEE International Conference on Semantic Computing*, pages 420–427.

Sellami, K., Saied, M. A., and Ouni, A. (2022). A hierarchical-dbscan method for extracting microservices from monolithic applications.

Trabelsi, I., Abdellatif, M., Abubaker, A., Moha, N., Mosser, S., Ebrahimi-Kahou, S., and Guéhéneuc, Y.-G. (2022). From legacy to microservices: A type-based approach for microservices identification using machine learning and semantic analysis. *Journal of Software: Evolution and Process*, n/a(n/a):e2503.

Xu, D. and Tian, Y. (2015). A comprehensive survey of clustering algorithms. *Annals of Data Science*, 2.

Zhao, W. X., Zhou, K., Li, J., Tang, T., Wang, X., Hou, Y., Min, Y., Zhang, B., Zhang, J., Dong, Z., Du, Y., Yang, C., Chen, Y., Chen, Z., Jiang, J., Ren, R., Li, Y., Tang, X., Liu, Z., Liu, P., Nie, J., and rong Wen, J. (2023). A survey of large language models. *ArXiv*, abs/2303.18223.

Zhou, X., Jin, Y., Zhang, H., Li, S., and Huang, X. (2016). A map of threats to validity of systematic literature reviews in software engineering. In *2016 23rd Asia-Pacific Software Engineering Conference (APSEC)*, pages 153–160.

Estudio de la Percepción de Ingenieros de Requisitos al Entrevistar y Modelar

Graciela D.S. Hadad[1], Jorge H. Doorn[1,2], María C. Elizalde[1]

[1]Instituto de Ingenierías y Nuevas Tecnologías – Universidad Nacional del Oeste
Córdoba 1055 – (1722) – Merlo – Buenos Aires – Argentina
[2]Universidad Nacional de Tres de Febrero – Buenos Aires – Argentina

{ghadad,jdoorn,melizalde}@uno.edu.ar

Abstract. *Studies in Requirements Engineering have revealed that the natural language models that are built largely depend on the people involved, resulting in significant differences between versions of the same model built by different authors. Furthermore, the manner in which information is obtained from the application context influences the modeling process. To understand the nature of this dependency, surveys included in a controlled experiment were conducted with requirements engineers. They independently used a natural language model construction process and participated as interviewers and modelers. The surveys were designed to analyze engineers' perception of the activity carried out and their relationship with their models. This allowed us to outline preliminary guidelines for the development of interviews and the use of natural language modeling processes, aimed at mitigating the of engineers' biases in their work.*

Resumen. *Estudios en Ingeniería de Requisitos han revelado que los modelos en lenguaje natural que se construyen dependen en gran medida de las personas intervinientes, habiéndose notado significativas diferencias entre versiones del mismo modelo construidas por distintos autores. Además, el cómo se elicita información del contexto de aplicación condiciona el modelado. Para entender la naturaleza de esa dependencia, mediante un experimento controlado, se realizaron encuestas a ingenieros de requisitos que aplicaron de manera independiente un proceso para construir un modelo en lenguaje natural, ocupando roles de entrevistadores y modeladores. Las encuestas se diseñaron con el fin de analizar la percepción de los ingenieros en la actividad desarrollada y la relación con sus modelos. Esto permitió establecer algunas pautas preliminares para el desarrollo de entrevistas y el uso de procesos de modelado en lenguaje natural, que permitan mitigar el sesgo de los ingenieros en su labor.*

1. Introducción

La Informática es usualmente percibida como una disciplina fuertemente orientada a las áreas técnico-científicas. Esta es una noción muy difundida en la sociedad en general, pero también suele ser parte de la cultura de los profesionales que la practican y de los centros educativos. Esto tiene un fuerte componente histórico, ya que los primeros computadores fueron utilizados en aplicaciones muy influenciadas por las matemáticas y la física, tales como la criptografía [1, pág. 58] y los modelos numéricos [2].

Cualquiera sea la naturaleza de un sistema de software, siempre hay un ser humano involucrado, utilizando sus resultados o efectos. Obviamente, el involucramiento de los seres humanos se ha incrementado notoriamente desde sus inicios, tanto en cantidad como en profundidad. Hoy día, más que nunca, un sistema de software bien concebido debe brindar los servicios que correspondan en forma coherente con las peculiaridades de las personas con las que se relaciona.

Planificar un sistema exige el acuerdo de los clientes y los usuarios. De los clientes, porque se deben atender los objetivos por los que se planifica construir ese sistema y de los usuarios, porque se debe lograr que su uso sea adecuado, considerando la manera habitual de desempeñarse y la comodidad, entre muchos otros aspectos.

Cualquiera sea la solución que se adopte, es necesario que los ingenieros de requisitos conozcan acabadamente la realidad actual, para poder proyectar los cambios posibles en el contexto de uso del sistema y especificar los requisitos coherentes con las peculiaridades de los usuarios en ese contexto.

Para que clientes y usuarios, por un lado, e ingenieros de requisitos, por el otro, se entiendan es necesario que ambas partes hablen el mismo lenguaje. Los informáticos usualmente se expresan utilizando modelos gráficos de diversa naturaleza. Los clientes y usuarios se expresan en lenguaje natural, aunque habitualmente desarrollan un conjunto de términos con un significado específico en el contexto donde se desempeñan. Es casi inevitable que el ingeniero de requisitos deba comprender ese vocabulario y representar sus propuestas utilizándolo. Esto lleva a que suelan emplear modelos escritos en lenguaje natural, utilizando el vocabulario de clientes y usuarios.

Obtener información acerca del contexto de desempeño y registrarla en modelos fácilmente entendibles por los clientes y usuarios no es una tarea sencilla, por los errores que se cometen en ambas actividades. En trabajos realizados por diferentes autores [3-9] comparando modelos construidos por distintas personas, se han encontrado defectos y diferencias significativas entre ellos, indicando una falta de comprensión del contexto estudiado con una fuerte dependencia de quien modelaba. Un factor preponderante son los sesgos de los propios ingenieros de requisitos [10], no contemplados en las técnicas utilizadas [7], como así también las falencias y sesgos de los clientes y usuarios [11].

Estos antecedentes llevaron a realizar un experimento controlado donde se puso a prueba la elicitación mediante una entrevista, grabándola y transcribiéndola, y un proceso de modelado, que incluía guías específicas destinadas a reducir los efectos producidos por los sesgos cognitivos de los participantes. Conjuntamente se realizaron encuestas a los ingenieros de requisitos intervinientes, con el objetivo de detectar la percepción de estos sobre el desarrollo de la entrevista y del modelado, de manera de evaluar el nivel de dependencia de los resultados (el modelo) respecto del proceso y del rol de los participantes. El presente trabajo se aboca a analizar los resultados de la evaluación de las encuestas realizadas, en el marco de los datos cuantitativos obtenidos. Esto ha permitido establecer guías para mitigar el sesgo de los ingenieros de requisitos al entrevistar y modelar en lenguaje natural.

En la siguiente sección se describe el uso de entrevistas en otras disciplinas y el uso de modelos en lenguaje natural en la Ingeniería de Requisitos. En la sección 3 se describe el experimento, en la sección 4 se presentan los datos cuantitativos obtenidos, mientras que en la sección 5 se describen las experiencias de los entrevistadores y modeladores respectivamente, en función de las encuestas realizadas. En la sección 6 se discuten dichas experiencias, dando algunas pautas generales, y finalmente en la sección 7 se presentan conclusiones y trabajos futuros.

2. Marco Conceptual

Toda consideración acerca de las entrevistas debe hacerse reconociendo que es una técnica que la Ingeniería de Requisitos ha importado de las Ciencias Sociales, las que tienen una experiencia abundante sobre ellas [12]. En estas ciencias es normativo que toda entrevista sea grabada y transcripta, y se indique el origen de cada conclusión mediante el marcado de las partes de la transcripción que la soportan [13-15]. Esto permite evitar en gran medida el grado de subjetividad inmerso inexorablemente en la elaboración de conclusiones a partir de información textual [16, 17].

Se optó por estudiar la técnica de entrevista considerando que es la técnica de recolección de información más ampliamente difundida en la literatura en Ingeniería de Requisitos [18-20] y la más utilizada en la práctica [11, 21, 22].

Un somero examen de las indicaciones sobre el manejo de entrevistas en la literatura de la Ingeniería de Requisitos [11, 20, 23, 24] muestra que estas suelen ser excesivamente básicas, ofreciendo solo guías acerca de la selección de entrevistados, el tipo de entrevista, la preparación y desarrollo de la entrevista, mencionando ocasionalmente la toma de notas y/o su grabación y la elaboración de resúmenes o actas de entrevistas. Sin embargo, no se dan pautas sobre cómo asegurarse que las preguntas sean entendibles por el entrevistado, sin inducir respuestas, cómo evitar distracciones o perder de vista el objetivo de la entrevista, entre otros aspectos. Además, a diferencia de las Ciencias Sociales, no se prescribe la necesidad de un procesamiento posterior lo más objetivo posible de la información obtenida; en la Ingeniería de Requisitos casi no se menciona la idea de transcribir las entrevistas [25].

Bano et al. [21] realizaron dos estudios sobre entrevistas con estudiantes sin experiencia, donde detectaron ciertos errores por parte de los estudiantes, referidos principalmente a preguntas mal formuladas (vagas, técnicas, irrelevantes, incorrectas), preguntas omitidas sobre el contexto, falta de orden en las preguntas, falta de habilidades de comunicación e interacción no adecuada (no empatizar, interrumpir, influenciar). A partir de esos estudios, elaboraron una lista general de 9 sugerencias para entrevistar. Thew y Sutcliffe [25] proponen principalmente el uso de entrevistas, y su transcripción en caso de ingenieros novatos o el uso de notas para expertos. Solo dan pautas sobre tópicos a tratar en la entrevista para detectar puntos de vista y emociones de los entrevistados, con el fin de mejorar la negociación de requisitos.

En lo que se refiere al impacto de los sesgos cognitivos de los participantes existen también escasos estudios en el área de la Ingeniería de Requisitos, destacándose el trabajo de Zalewski et al. [26] quienes clasifican los sesgos de un trabajo de 41 estudiantes de grado quienes realizaron la definición de los requisitos de un sistema interno de la universidad en base a sus propios conocimientos. En ese trabajo se utilizaron 8 sesgos básicos coincidentes con los utilizados por Mohanani et al. [27] en otra área de la Ingeniería de Software.

Por otro lado, cabe notar que existe una profusión de métodos en la Ingeniería de Requisitos que usan modelos escritos en lenguaje natural por su cercanía a los usuarios, los que facilitan validar y negociar, tales como casos de uso, escenarios e historias de usuario [28-32]. Sin embargo, estos métodos no ofrecen pautas precisas de cómo elaborar la información obtenida para trasladarla a modelos, evitando subjetividades.

3. Método de Trabajo Empleado

Se reformuló un proceso de construcción de un modelo específico en lenguaje natural, el Léxico Extendido del Lenguaje [29], introduciendo heurísticas de carácter lingüístico-cognitivo, detalladas en [8], que sintéticamente se refieren a:

- Identificación y selección de grupos acotados de conceptos[1] a modelar en cada iteración, para centrar la atención en una cantidad razonable de elementos.
- Reglas de modelado para conceptos y sus relaciones (sinónimos, homónimos, relaciones taxonómicas, relaciones mereológicas, vocabulario restringido), dada la variedad en las expresiones del lenguaje natural.
- Uso de la técnica de copiar y pegar desde la información obtenida al modelo, evitando malinterpretaciones del ingeniero en la traducción al modelo o interpretaciones basadas en su conocimiento previo.
- Manejo de iteraciones en el modelado con criterios de parada precisos. para reducir los sesgos personales al establecer el nivel de detalle del modelo.

El propósito del experimento fue establecer, si las heurísticas introducidas en el proceso de modelado junto con el tratamiento de la entrevista atemperaban los problemas detectados, y tener una retroalimentación sobre la entrevista y sobre el proceso, mediante encuestas a los sujetos participantes, que ayudara a detectar causas de los problemas persistentes, no identificables directamente del análisis de los modelos.

En el protocolo del experimento se establecieron los criterios de selección de sujetos, los roles a cubrir por los sujetos, la modalidad de entrenamiento, el caso a utilizar, las variantes en el modelado, y las encuestas a realizar. La Figura 1 muestra cómo se llevó a cabo el experimento en función del protocolo establecido.

Para la selección de los sujetos se usaron los siguientes criterios: experiencia en entrevistas (solo para entrevistadores) y experiencia en el modelo a construir. Los sujetos recibieron un documento con la descripción del proceso de modelado (47 páginas con ejemplos) y un instructivo de las tareas a cumplir. Hubo sesiones individuales para consultas sobre el proceso, y la ejecución del experimento se inició una vez que fueron evacuadas las dudas. Se asignaron los roles a los sujetos: dos ingenieros de requisitos participando como entrevistadores y modeladores, un ingeniero participando como revisor de la transcripción y modelador, y un ingeniero actuando solo como modelador. También hubo variantes en la fuente de entrada para el modelado: i) texto transcripto de la entrevista, o ii) audio de la entrevista.

La entrevista se desarrolló en el lugar de trabajo de la entrevistada, perteneciente a una organización privada. En ella participaron dos sujetos (Sujeto 1 y Sujeto 2), quienes grabaron la entrevista con previo consentimiento. Los entrevistadores habían recibido un documento preliminar de objetivo general y alcance del sistema. Se trató de una entrevista abierta para tener una primera aproximación al contexto de aplicación.

[1] Se utiliza la palabra *conceptos* en lugar de *términos* o *símbolos* para evitar incluir detalles sintácticos específicos del modelo utilizado [29].

Posteriormente, la entrevista fue transcripta usando una herramienta gratuita de reconocimiento automático de voz y el revisor (Sujeto 3) hizo mejoras al texto incorporando gestos verbales (subida de tono de voz, interrupciones, pausas, entre otras), mediante una herramienta de desarrollo propio de índole académico.

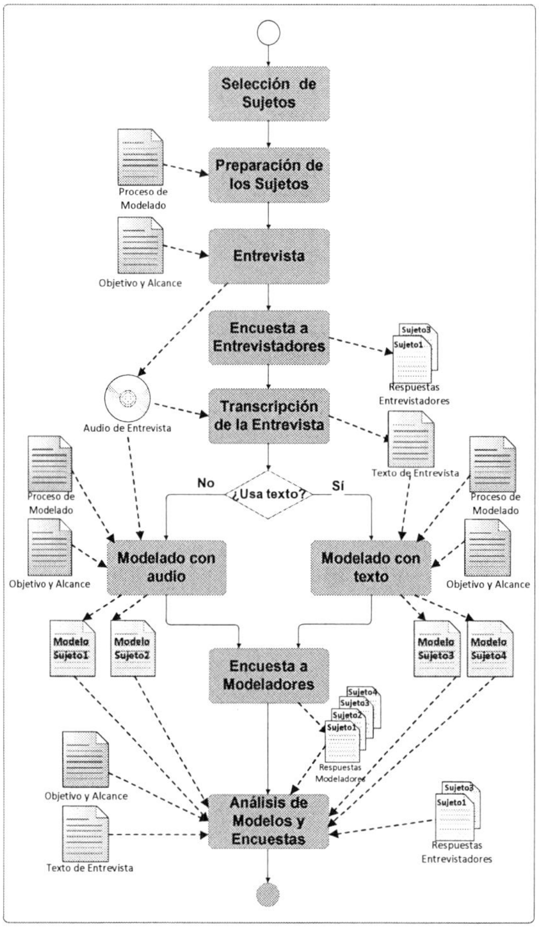

Figura 1. Ejecución del experimento

El modelado fue realizado en forma individual por los entrevistadores y por otros dos sujetos. El Sujeto 1 (entrevistador y modelador) y el Sujeto 3 (revisor y modelador) recibieron el texto transcripto de la entrevista, mientras que los otros Sujeto 2 (entrevistador y modelador) y Sujeto 4 (solo modelador) recibieron el audio de la entrevista. Con lo cual se cubrieron cuatro variantes de intervención en el experimento.

En la Figura 1, se muestran además otras dos actividades referidas a recabar información sobre la experiencia de los sujetos en la elicitación y en el modelado, mediante encuestas. Se realizaron tres encuestas, una referida a la entrevista y otras dos independientes referidas al modelado. Hubo dos tipos de encuestas, una del tipo autoevaluación basada en metacognición [33, 34] para detectar los factores que influyeron en los resultados obtenidos con base en el cumplimiento de objetivos, tanto de los entrevistadores como de los modeladores, y el otro tipo de encuesta multiple-choice para evaluar el propio proceso de modelado.

El uso de una encuesta de autoevaluación surge de la existencia de una cierta analogía entre el aprendizaje autorregulado basado en estrategias metacognitivas en la Educación Superior [34] y las actividades de elicitación, modelado y análisis en un proceso de Ingeniería de Requisitos. Ello se debe a que tienen fines bastante semejables, ya que el ingeniero de requisitos debe aprender las peculiaridades del contexto de aplicación para poder proponer una solución y establecer si cumple con los objetivos de los clientes y usuarios. Obviamente, estas similitudes son parciales ya que, durante la elicitación, los clientes y usuarios no cumplen un efectivo desempeño como docentes, y no siempre el conocimiento que transmiten está organizado ni elaborado. Sin embargo, el parecido entre esas actividades es suficiente para considerar la posibilidad de incorporar los beneficios que los enfoques metacognitivos [33, 34] han aportado en el dominio de la educación.

Las estrategias metacognitivas se basan en planificar la actividad para lograr los objetivos establecidos, controlar la actividad mientras se desarrolla y autoevaluar los resultados alcanzados en función de los objetivos a cumplir [33]. Un elemento inherente al aprendizaje autorregulado es el factor *reflexión consciente* [33], el cual se manifiesta primordialmente en la autoevaluación. Por tal motivo, se utilizó en este trabajo encuestas del tipo autoevaluación reflexiva, pero con un fin diferente, poner de manifiesto fortalezas y debilidades acaecidas en las actividades de entrevistar y modelar.

La última actividad del experimento se dedicó al análisis de la calidad de los modelos y de los resultados de las encuestas, la cual estuvo a cargo de dos evaluadores, quienes diseñaron el proceso de construcción del modelo y el experimento.

Validez del Experimento.

Ningún sujeto había utilizado previamente este proceso de modelado. Todos ellos ya habían utilizado una versión anterior [29] en varias oportunidades. Los sujetos recibieron el mismo tratamiento y material para su capacitación en el proceso. Cabe mencionar que ningún sujeto fue capacitado sobre el domino de aplicación. Ningún modelador tuvo contacto con los otros, evitándose el intercambio de consultas, dudas o experiencias. Las encuestas fueron entregadas para responder una vez concluida cada actividad, evitando influenciar en dicha actividad a raíz de las preguntas a responder. Ninguno de los participantes conoció los resultados de la evaluación de sus modelos con anterioridad a responder las encuestas.

Los resultados obtenidos refieren a una muestra específica de sujetos, con amplia experiencia en entrevistar y modelar. Además, se realizó una única entrevista en un caso de mediana complejidad. Esto lleva a que las conclusiones obtenidas no puedan generalizarse, pero permiten presentar indicios que pueden ser de cierta utilidad para encarar la realización de entrevistas y el modelado en lenguaje natural.

4. Análisis Cuantitativo del Modelo

Los evaluadores, previo a estudiar cada modelo resultante, elaboraron una lista de los conceptos relevantes que el modelo debía contener, estableciendo 28 conceptos. Este valor se tomó como base para ponderar los modelos construidos por los cuatro sujetos.

Los resultados cuantitativos preliminares[2] de cada versión se presentan en la Tabla 1. En ella se detallan la cantidad de conceptos modelados por cada sujeto, la cantidad de conceptos considerados relevantes o correctos (coincidentes con los establecidos por los evaluadores), la cantidad de conceptos incorrectos por ser irrelevantes o inventados, y la cantidad que se omitieron modelar (conceptos establecidos por los evaluadores, pero no modelados por el sujeto). Se denominan conceptos inventados a aquellos que no tienen correlato con la entrevista realizada.

Tabla 1. Datos cuantitativos

Roles cumplidos:	**Entrevistador y Modelador**		**Revisor y Modelador**	**Solo Modelador**
	Sujeto 1	**Sujeto 2**	**Sujeto 3**	**Sujeto 4**
Medio de Entrada:	Texto	Audio	Texto	Audio
conceptos modelados	**18**	**25**	**15**	**61**
conceptos modelados correctos	**17**	**21**	**13**	**21**
conceptos modelados irrelevantes	**0**	**1**	**2**	**16**
conceptos modelados inventados	**1**	**3**	**0**	**24**
conceptos omitidos	**11**	**7**	**15**	**7**
% conceptos incorrectos	**5,6%**	**16,0%**	**13,3%**	**65,6%**
% omisiones	**39,3%**	**25,0%**	**53,6%**	**25,0%**
Tiempo promedio de modelado por concepto (minuto)	**30**	**36**	**17**	**35**

Se observa que los Sujetos 1 y 3 que utilizaron como entrada el texto transcripto de la entrevista incluyeron muy pocos conceptos irrelevantes, pero tuvieron un número alto de omisiones. Por otro lado, los Sujetos 2 y 4 que utilizaron el audio de la entrevista modelaron más conceptos que los otros sujetos. En el caso del Sujeto 4 que no participó de la entrevista modeló una cantidad excesiva de conceptos, siendo el 66% incorrectos, mientras que el Sujeto 2 que participó de la entrevista tuvo muchos menos conceptos irrelevantes (16%). Es razonable esperar que quien tiene exceso de información modelada tenga bajas omisiones, aunque ello no implica en una mejor comprensión del modelo, por el contrario, puede ser contraproducente. Respecto a los tiempos, se puede atribuir el valor notablemente bajo del Sujeto 3 a que había escuchado el audio más de una vez antes del modelado durante la revisión de la transcripción automática.

5. Análisis de Encuestas

Las encuestas de autoevaluación para entrevistadores y para modeladores, contenían 4 preguntas abiertas. Para los entrevistadores, fueron:

1) ¿Logré cumplir con el objetivo planteado para la entrevista?
2) En caso de no cumplimiento o cumplimiento parcial, ¿cuál considero que fueron los motivos?
3) ¿Qué acciones positivas realicé en la entrevista?
4) ¿Qué podría mejorar para una próxima entrevista? ¿Cómo podría llevar a cabo esas mejoras?

La autoevaluación de modeladores incluyó preguntas de naturaleza similar a las

[2] Se encuentra en proceso de evaluación, a nivel fino, las oraciones de cada versión del modelo, en cuanto a cantidad de oraciones irrelevantes, omitidas, incorrectas e inventadas, y respecto al texto transcripto la cantidad de porciones útiles y no útiles modeladas y cantidad de porciones útiles omitidas en el modelo.

de los entrevistadores, donde la primera pregunta se amplió a: ¿Logré cumplir con el objetivo planteado para la actividad de modelado en un tiempo adecuado, con una calidad acorde a la información elicitada y siguiendo el proceso establecido?

La encuesta sobre el proceso de modelado constó de 10 preguntas, cada una incluía una selección de opciones y la posibilidad de una respuesta abierta en función de la opción elegida. Este cuestionario incluyó preguntas referidas a los niveles de dificultad para detectar conceptos, para establecer diversas relaciones entre conceptos, para identificar el fin de cada iteración y el fin del proceso, para realizar los pasos del proceso, y sobre beneficios y obstáculos del proceso.

A continuación, se describen las experiencias de los ingenieros de requisitos según los roles cumplidos en el experimento, en base a las encuestas realizadas.

5.1. Experiencia de los Entrevistadores

Ambos entrevistadores coincidieron en que el ambiente de la entrevista no era el adecuado, dado que la entrevistada estaba con mucho trabajo, debiendo interrumpir la sesión en más de una ocasión por demandas de trabajo, provocando falta de concentración en la entrevista por ambas partes.

Además, ambos entrevistadores expresaron como falencia su falta de conocimiento sobre el dominio. Uno de ellos expresó su necesidad de haberlo estudiado previamente. El otro consideró que tener conocimiento previo les hubiera permitido tener preparadas algunas preguntas generales para dar un orden a la entrevista en cuanto a la información obtenida de manera de facilitar la comprensión de los temas.

En el análisis posterior de la entrevista se notó esa falta de orden, tales como: el mismo tema tratado en distintos momentos ampliando o repitiendo información, varios temas tratados confusamente en una misma respuesta, respuestas vagas y algunas fuera del objetivo de la entrevista. Por ejemplo, uno de los entrevistadores informó: "*Traté de poder hacer preguntas/repreguntas sobre las cuestiones que había hablado de forma libre. Y de las respuestas de ella me di cuenta de que había cosas que no nos estaba contando referidas al contexto que nos interesa. Y estoy seguro de que hay bastantes más*". El otro entrevistador mencionó: "*Pensamos en una entrevista sin preguntas planificadas. Hubiese sido útil pensar algunas preguntas generales especialmente para dar un orden a la información obtenida*".

Como aspectos positivos expresaron el haber logrado empatía con la entrevistada, pudiendo cubrir varios temas, teniendo la posibilidad de repreguntar y quedando abierta la realización de futuras entrevistas.

Asimismo, en el análisis de las preguntas y respuestas de la entrevista, se observó ciertos problemas derivados de las preguntas, tales como, uso de palabras o frases confusas para la entrevistada o que interpretó con otro significado, preguntas sin relación con respuestas anteriores sino basadas en la propia experiencia, o falta de repreguntas frente a narrativas extensas de la entrevistada que cubrían varios temas con vaguedad, entre otras. Estos problemas derivaron en la obtención de información confusa, ambigua, superficial e incluso fuera del alcance establecido.

5.2. Experiencia de los Modeladores

Se abordaron dos cuestiones sobre la actividad de modelado: cuestiones generales de modelado mediante una encuesta de autoevaluación con preguntas abiertas y una encuesta detallada sobre tópicos específicos del proceso utilizado. Esta segunda encuesta tenía, por cada pregunta, una escala de cinco valores a elegir (Muy ato, Alto, Medio, Bajo, Muy bajo) y la posibilidad de explicar el valor elegido.

Primero se entregó a los modeladores la autoevaluación y una vez recibidas las respuestas, se entregó el cuestionario sobre el proceso, con el fin de evitar sesgos en las respuestas de autoevaluación en función de las preguntas del segundo cuestionario.

A continuación, se resumen los hallazgos identificados en ambas encuestas.

5.2.1. Encuesta de Autoevaluación a Modeladores

Los cuatro modeladores coincidieron en que seguir el proceso detallado les facilitó la tarea, obligando a prestar atención a ciertos aspectos importantes del modelo.

Los dos modeladores que usaron el audio como entrada señalaron que el modelado les llevó un excesivo esfuerzo y tiempo (demoras por re-escuchar varias veces el audio, no poder usar la técnica de copiar y pegar). Por ejemplo, uno de ellos mencionó: "*El esfuerzo de escuchar el audio (avanzando y retrocediendo) por cada duda que tuve me resultó agotador*". Además, ambos refirieron a dificultades para decidir utilizar o desechar información. Uno de ellos citó: "*Creo que lo que no hice correctamente fue que descarté conceptos que debería haberse incorporado como 'en proceso'.*", mientras que el otro señaló que necesitó categorizar los motivos de descarte de información para tomar sus decisiones al respecto.

Los dos modeladores que no participaron de la entrevista indicaron que no era suficiente la información obtenida de la entrevista, mencionando además su falta de conocimiento previo del dominio. Sin embargo, el modelador encargado previamente de la revisión de la transcripción (Sujeto 3) mencionó: "*Puedo destacar que, al haber revisado la transcripción del texto, más o menos ya sabía cuáles podrían o no ser conceptos que podrían integrar el modelo*". Esto fue acompañado por una baja tasa de información incorrecta. Además, este mismo sujeto, señaló que marcar el texto a medida que lo usaba le facilitó la tarea, evitando relecturas. Esto no solo le ahorró esfuerzo, sino que pudo colaborar en que no inventó información. Notablemente es el que incurrió en más omisiones.

Retornando al tema de atención requerida para realizar la actividad, para dos modeladores (Sujetos 2 y 3) ello fue positivo para alcanzar un mejor resultado. Uno de ellos que usó texto transcripto se predispuso a lograr un ambiente y momento tranquilo para realizar la actividad, y citó: "*Realizar el modelado sin tener otras tareas pendientes, sin distracciones, hizo que pueda estar atento a seguir adecuadamente el proceso establecido*". El otro que usó audio señaló que el proceso lo obligó a concentrase, aunque las re-escuchas lo demoraron. Sin embargo, un tercer modelador (Sujeto 4), que también usó el audio, refirió a su cansancio al requerir prestar mucha atención, observando esto como algo negativo.

A partir de esta encuesta, surgieron algunos aspectos de la conducta de los sujetos. El Sujeto 1 indicó su ansiedad en realizar el modelado, que lo llevó a seguir el proceso en líneas generales, pero no en detalle, con el fin de finalizar más rápidamente la tarea. Esto lo llevó a construir un modelo con pocos conceptos y poca información, aunque correcta, es decir, tuvo muchas omisiones. El Sujeto 3 logró un modelo de características similares, sin embargo, destacó su necesidad de concentración para dedicarse a seguir el proceso paso a paso. En el Sujeto 2 prevaleció también la concentración, lo que lo llevó a distinguir correctamente conceptos relevantes de irrelevantes y omitir poca información, logrando un modelo de buena calidad. Surge a partir de las expresiones del Sujeto 4, su minuciosidad al trabajar, yendo más allá de lo establecido en el proceso, categorizando los motivos de descarte de información y generando registros intermedios. Esto puede adjudicarse, en gran medida, a utilizar el audio. Sin embargo, su meticulosidad lo llevó a incluir en el modelo exceso de información irrelevante, mucha de ella no rastreable a la entrevista, es decir, inventada.

5.2.1. Encuesta sobre el Proceso

Tres modeladores respondieron que tuvieron escasos inconvenientes en identificar un conjunto reducido de conceptos a modelar en cada iteración del proceso. Por el contrario, el Sujeto 4 con exceso de conceptos irrelevantes modelados informó su dificultad en la identificación debido a no tener claro el objetivo perseguido y su falta de conocimiento en el dominio.

Los cuatro modeladores no tuvieron problemas en establecer el fin de cada iteración, como tampoco el fin del proceso. A ninguno se les presentaron situaciones que no pudieran resolver con los pasos o las consideraciones descriptas en el proceso.

Quienes utilizaron el audio (Sujetos 2 y 4) indicaron una cierta dificultad en decidir la incorporación o no de conceptos al modelo. Ellos también tuvieron inconvenientes para establecer relaciones taxonómicas y mereológicas entre conceptos, distinguir entre jerarquías y estados, e identificar sinónimos y homónimos.

Todos los modeladores reportaron que el proceso utilizado les aportó más beneficios que la versión anterior. Citaron como aportes: i) resultados más predecibles y menos fallas humanas; ii) heurísticas más precisas; y iii) mejor calidad del modelo.

Sin embargo, esto no se vio tan reflejado en todos los modelos construidos, pues continuaron valores no aceptables de omisiones, y hubo conceptos incorrectos, aunque menos, salvo en el Sujeto 4, persistiendo los inventados. En este último caso, se observó una baja significativa respecto a estudios anteriores donde 10 equipos de trabajo de 15 tuvieron entre un 20 % y un 40 % de conceptos inventados [7].

Por otro lado, los dos modeladores que usaron el audio (Sujeto 2 y Sujeto 4), a pesar de las ventajas del proceso, consideraron que este tenía un mayor grado de complejidad respecto al anterior, y mencionaron: i) proceso con muchos pasos a seguir; algunos engorrosos; ii) no siempre es posible utilizar la técnica de copiar y pegar; dar pautas más claras sobre en qué situaciones aplicarla o no y cómo; y iii) no es suficientemente claro el criterio para incluir o descartar información.

6. Discusión

Se destaca lo acertado de lo reportado por los entrevistadores, sobre la necesidad de un ambiente tranquilo, sin interrupciones externas, para la sesión de la entrevista de manera de aprovechar al máximo el tiempo disponible y lograr una adecuada concentración de todos los participantes.

Se debe mencionar la relevancia de que el entrevistado sepa el objetivo de la entrevista, es decir, qué se pretende obtener a partir de ella, y que también el entrevistador lo tenga presente. Esto redunda tanto en una reducción del tiempo de la entrevista como del número de futuras entrevistas. Aunque pareciera una obviedad, enfocarse en el objetivo a cumplir no resulta sencillo, ello se evidenció en algunas preguntas de los entrevistadores. Ello lleva a reforzar algunas pautas básicas a considerar antes de iniciar la entrevista.

Los entrevistadores observaron como de sumo interés lograr empatía con el entrevistado, lo cual confirma lo que la literatura suele destacar [12, 13, 25].

Tanto los entrevistadores como los modeladores que no participaron de la entrevista manifestaron la necesidad de poseer conocimiento previo sobre el tema a tratar. Esa afirmación es claramente antagónica con el hecho que el conocimiento previo induce a los entrevistadores y a los modeladores a intentar adaptar la realidad observada a ese conocimiento previo. Sin embargo, en [21] se reafirma la idea que el conocimiento previo evita muchos errores en la formulación de preguntas, a diferencia de lo expresado en [35]. En una entrevista no estructurada como la estudiada es esencial evitar tanto como se pueda el denominado sesgo de confirmación [36, 26], donde la persona interpreta la información recibida bajo sus propios preconceptos, lo que suele impedirle comprender correctamente la información que está procesando. En el caso de los dos entrevistadores, esto expresa resistencia a participar de una entrevista no estructurada, en la deben dedicarse a atender el discurso del entrevistado minimizando sus intervenciones. Esta necesidad de adaptar la información recibida a su conocimiento previo se manifiesta tanto en las encuestas como en los modelos ya que estos contienen información no rastreable a la fuente de información.

En cuanto a la actividad de los modeladores, todos coincidieron en que seguir un proceso bien detallado organiza el trabajo, obliga a concentrar la atención y además mitiga el desatender situaciones poco habituales en el modelo.

Es indudable y esperable que el uso del texto transcripto haya facilitado la tarea de los modeladores, en contraste con el esfuerzo que les insumió a los otros modeladores el uso del audio para capturar información y trasladarla al modelado siguiendo el proceso. Por otro lado, el modelador que usó texto y se encargó de revisar la transcripción automática, señaló que esa tarea le facilitó el reconocimiento de conceptos relevantes, lo que se vio reflejado en su modelo, como también en la reducción del tiempo de modelado. Esto es algo habitual en las Ciencias Sociales; el propio entrevistador realiza la transcripción manual y la elaboración de conclusiones. Sin embargo, en la práctica de la Ingeniería de Requisitos, es frecuente el trabajo en equipo donde varios ingenieros entrevistan y modelan colaborativamente. Esto requiere ponderar: i) el esfuerzo de la revisión frente a las ventajas de usar la transcripción, y ii) el impacto cognitivo que produce revisar la transcripción sobre el modelado posterior.

Basado en lo dicho por un modelador sobre el ahorro de esfuerzo al marcar el texto fuente utilizado, esto podría también tener impacto en la calidad del modelo, ya que, podría facilitar la detección de información no utilizada, pero podría ocultar porciones de texto con más de un concepto especialmente en los últimos identificados.

Se considera de interés la propuesta de un modelador en catalogar motivos de rechazo de conceptos dudosos de modelar. Es un tema recurrente, surgido en experimentos y estudios de caso previos [3, 4, 6-8], que los ingenieros de requisitos suelen tener dificultades en discernir sobre la relevancia de la información a modelar.

Respecto del proceso de modelado, las ventajas de utilizar la transcripción van más allá del esfuerzo adicional por los avances y retrocesos en el audio. El tratamiento de cada situación posible es mucho más eficiente cuando se utiliza el texto. Además, los modeladores plantearon algunos problemas puntuales que son factibles de mejora: criterio de inclusión/exclusión de información al modelo, casos de aplicación de la técnica de copiar y pegar (se detectó que no siempre es útil), y facilitar el seguimiento de los pasos del proceso.

En resumen, se bosquejan algunas pautas iniciales, básicas, para realizar entrevistas, algunas de ellas son novedosas y otras confirman lo expuesto en la literatura, por lo que deberían reforzarse al realizar la actividad:

- Grabar y transcribir la entrevista, para mitigar posteriores sesgos del modelador.
- Prestar atención al vocabulario utilizado por el entrevistado, de manera de usarlo en eventuales preguntas, o para indagar sobre sus peculiaridades.
- Evitar el uso de terminología relacionada con el dominio, pero no utilizada por el entrevistador.
- Concentrarse en la entrevista, interrumpiendo lo mínimo necesario, para darle continuidad o para centrarla en el objetivo establecido.
- Preguntar ordenadamente por los temas, para evitar retomar lo ya tratado.

En las sugerencias de Bano et al. [21], no se menciona la posibilidad de grabar la entrevista sino la elaboración de minutas; sí se menciona hacer las preguntas correctas y no hacer preguntas técnicas, lo cual está relacionado justamente con el vocabulario utilizado en las preguntas; también se señala la necesidad de ordenar las preguntas según el contexto, y de entablar una buena relación con el entrevistado, lo que no lograron gran parte de sus estudiantes, probablemente por su inexperiencia.

Para el modelado en lenguaje natural, se pueden esbozar preliminarmente las siguientes pautas considerando disponer de texto fuente de la elicitación:

- Evitar basarse en la memoria, especialmente cuando se ha participado en la entrevista.
- Procesar la información obtenida de manera más objetiva, usando el copiar y pegar al modelo en los casos recomendados, y elaborando información a partir del texto fuente que la avala.
- Tener presente el objetivo establecido para evitar incluir información no relevante y focalizarse en lo necesario.
- Evitar apartarse de las guías de modelado, según las establecidas para el modelo a construir. Tenerlas a mano para repasarlas, de ser necesario.

7. Conclusiones

Las actividades con intensa intervención humana suelen especificarse mediante heurísticas, lo que lleva a ciertas imprecisiones o vaguedades en su práctica. Este es el caso de gran parte de las actividades involucradas en un proceso de requisitos. En tales casos es necesario que las heurísticas incluyan guías que ayuden a tratar el factor humano. Esta necesidad se evidenció en estudios previos donde fue notoria la variabilidad en la calidad de los modelos obtenidos [3-5, 7, 8]. En el presente trabajo se capturó y estudió la percepción de los ingenieros de requisitos al realizar actividades de elicitación y modelado. Esta información resultó valiosa para comprender mejor las razones que subyacen bajo la variabilidad detectada en estudios anteriores.

A partir de los resultados del experimento, se han podido identificar indicios de las causas de algunos problemas (omisiones, ambigüedades, información artificiosa), los que dan un punto de partida para establecer pautas generales iniciales. El análisis realizado dio algunos resultados confirmatorios de lo que la literatura recomienda, tal como prestar atención, empatizar, enfocarse en el objetivo perseguido y evitar subjetividades y distorsiones de la memoria, entre otros. Sin embargo, la literatura de Ingeniería de Requisitos poco menciona el grabar la entrevista y menos aún transcribirla para usarla como fuente para la elaboración de modelos, así como tampoco el cómo reducir la inclusión de información irrelevante e inventada.

Uno de los aspectos que definitivamente requiere ser evaluado cuidadosamente es la insistencia de los participantes en afirmar que el conocimiento previo hubiera resultado beneficioso. Este es un aspecto que deberá estudiarse con cuidado y que no es tratado adecuadamente en la literatura, encontrándose propuestas enfrentadas [21, 35].

Otro aspecto para estudiar con más profundidad es si quien entrevista y luego modela puede distinguir con mayor facilidad o no qué información es relevante de aquella poco útil para modelar, dado que ello no quedó evidenciado en el experimento.

Los resultados obtenidos sugieren que revisar la transcripción de la entrevista tiene influencia sobre la calidad del modelo. Si bien esta influencia parece beneficiosa no se tiene suficiente información que permita descartar otros impactos cognitivos. En otras palabras, es importante determinar si es preferible que la revisión sea llevada a cabo por alguien que luego construye el modelo o es justamente lo opuesto.

En la siguiente etapa del trabajo de investigación se replicará el experimento usando las pautas bosquejadas, reforzándose el estudio de la combinación de roles y utilizando sujetos con y sin experiencia en entrevistas y modelado.

Referencias

[1] Campbell-Kelly, M., y Aspray, W. (1996). Computer: A History of the Information Machine, New York: Basic Books.

[2] Winsberg, E. (2010). Science in the Age of Computer Simulation, Chicago: University of Chicago Press.

[3] Ridao, M.N., y Doorn, J.H. (2006) "Estimación de Completitud en Modelos de Requisitos Basados en Lenguaje Natural", 11th Workshop on Requirements Engineering, Río de Janeiro, pp. 146-157.

[4] Hadad, G.D.S., Litvak, C.S., y Doorn, J.H. (2014) "Problemas y Soluciones en la Completitud de Modelos en Lenguaje Natural", II Congreso Argentino de Ingeniería, Tucumán, Argentina, T366.

[5] Martínez, S.N., Oliveros, A., Zuñiga, J.A., Corbo, S., y Forradelas, P. (2014) "Aprendizaje de la elicitación y especificación de requerimientos", XX Congreso Argentino de Ciencias de la Computación, Buenos Aires.

[6] Sebastián, A., Hadad, G.D., y Robledo, E. (2017) "Inspección centrada en Omisiones y Ambigüedades de un Modelo Léxico", XX Congreso Iberoamericano en Ingeniería de Software (CIBSE), Buenos Aires, pp. 375-388.

[7] Doorn, J.H., Hadad, G.D.S., Elizalde, M., García, A., y Carnero, L. (2019) "Críticas Cognitivas a Heurísticas Orientadas a Modelos", 22nd Workshop on Requirements Engineering, Recife.

[8] Elizalde, M.C., Hadad, G.D.S., y Doorn, J.H. (2021) "Incorporación de heurísticas lingüístico-cognitivas en el Proceso de Requisitos", 9° Congreso Nacional de Ingeniería Informática / Sistemas de Información, Mendoza, Argentina, pp. 312-320.

[9] Doorn, J.H., Hadad, G.D.S., Elizalde, M.C., Ridao, M.N., Casafuz, D., Sebastián, A., y Riera, G.A. (2022) "Impacto del Proceso de las Entrevistas en la Calidad de los Modelos", 10° Congreso Nacional de Ingeniería Informática / Sistemas de Información, Entre Ríos, Argentina.

[10] Sternberg, R.J., y Sternberg, K. (2009). Cognitve Psicology, 6ta. edición, CENGAGE Learning, Boston, pp. 185-227.

[11] Ferrari, A., Spoletini, P., y Gnesi, S. (2016) "Ambiguity and tacit knowledge in requirements elicitation interviews", Requirements Engineering Journal, Springer, 21, 3, pp. 333-353.

[12] Edwards, R., y Holland, J. (2013) "What is qualitative interviewing?", Blomomsbury Academic, Londres, pp. 43-52.

[13] Rands, M.L., y Gansemer-Topf, A.M. (2016) "Phenomenography: A Methodological Approach for Assessing Student Learning in Student Affairs", The Journal of Affairs Inquiry, 1, 2, pp. 1-22.

[14] Mann, S. (2016). The Research Interview Reflective Practice and Reflexivity in Research Processes, Palgrave Macmillan, Basingstoke, pp. 199-211.

[15] Buriro, A.G., Awan, J., y Lanjwani, A. (2017) "Interview: A Research Instrument for Social Science Researchers", International Journal of Social Sciences, Humanities and Education, 1, pp. 1-14.

[16] Dortins, E. (2002) "Reflections on phenomenographic process: Interview, transcription and analysis", Research and development in higher education: Quality conversations, 25, pp. 207-213.

[17] Roulston, K. (2010). Reflective interviewing: A guide to theory and practice, Sage Publications, Londres.

[18] Coulin, C., y Zowghi, D. (2005) "Requirements Elicitation for Complex Systems: Theory and Practice", en: Requirements Engineering for Sociotechnical Systems, Maté, J.L., Silva, A. (eds.), Information Science Publishing, Hershey, pp. 37-52.

[19] Carrizo, D., Dieste, O., y Juristo, N. (2008) "Study of elicitation techniques adequacy", 11th Workshop on Requirements Engineering, Barcelona, pp. 104-114.

[20] Wiegers, K., y Beatty, J. (2013) Software Requirements, 3ra. ed., Microsoft Press.

[21] Bano, M., Zowghi, D., Ferrari, A., Spoletini, P., y Donati, B. (2019) "Teaching requirements elicitation interviews: an empirical study of learning from mistakes", Requirements Engineering Journal, Springer, 24, pp. 259-289.

[22] Oliveros, A., y Antonelli, L. (2015) "Técnicas de elicitación de requerimientos", XXI Congreso Argentino de Ciencias de la Computación, Junín, Argentina.

[23] Alexander, I.F., y Beus-Dukic, L. (2009). Discovering Requirements: How to Specify Products and Services, John Wiley & Sons, Chichester, pp. 261-274.

[24] Ferrari, A., Spoletini, P., Bano, M., y Zowghi, D. (2020) "SaPeer and ReverseSaPeer: teaching requirements elicitation interviews with role playing and role reversal", Requirements Engineering Journal, Springer, 25, 4, pp. 417-438.

[25] Thew, S., y Sutcliffe, A. (2018) "Value-based requirements engineering: method and experience", Requirements Engineering Journal, Springer, 22, 4, pp. 443-464.

[26] Zalewski, A., Borowa, K., y Kowalski, D., (2020) "On Cognitive Biases in Requirements Elicitation", en: Integrating Research and Practice in Software Engineering, Jarzabek, S., Poniszewska-Marańda, A., Lech Madeyski, L., (eds.), Springer, Cham, pp. 111-124.

[27] Mohanani, R., Salman, I., Turhan, B., Rodríguez, P., y Ralph, P.: (2018) "Cognitive biases in software engineering: a systematic mapping study", IEEE Trans. Softw. Eng., 46, 12, pp. 1318-1319.

[28] Jacobson, I., Spence, I., y Bittner, K. (2011). Use Case 2.0 The Guide to Succeeding with Use Cases, Ivar Jacobson International.

[29] Hadad, G.D.S., Doorn, J.H., y Kaplan, G.N. (2009) "Creating Software System Context Glossaries", en: Encyclopedia of Information Science and Technology, 2da ed., IGI Global, Hershey, EE.UU., pp.789-794.

[30] Seyff, N., Maiden, N., Karlsen, K., Lockerbie, J., Grünbacher, P., Graf, F., y Ncube, C. (2009) "Exploring how to use scenarios to discover requirements", Requirements Engineering Journal, Springer, 14, 2, pp. 91-111.

[31] Antonelli, L., Delle Ville, J., Dioguardi, F., Fernández, A., Tanevitch, L., y Torres, D. (2022) "An iterative and collaborative approach to specify scenarios using natural language", 25th Workshop on Requirements Engineering, Natal.

[32] Dalpiaz, F., y Brinkkemper, S. (2018) "Agile Requirements Engineering with User Stories", 26th IEEE International Requirements Engineering Conference, Banff, Canadá, pp. 506–507.

[33] Klimenco, O., y Alvares, J.L. (2009) "Aprender cómo aprendo: la enseñanza de estrategias metacognitivas", Educación y Educadores, 12, 2, pp. 11-28.

[34] Roque Herrera, Y., Valdivia Moral, P.Á., Alonso García, S., y Zagalaz Sánchez, M.L. (2018) "Metacognición y aprendizaje autónomo en la Educación Superior", Educación Médica Superior, 32, 4, pp. 293-302.

[35] Niknafs, A., y Berry, D. (2017) "The impact of domain knowledge on the effectiveness of requirements engineering activities", Empirical Software Engineering, 22, 1, pp. 80-133.

[36] Nickerson, R.S. (1998) "Confirmation bias: a ubiquitous phenomenon in many guises", Review of General Psychology, Educational Publishing Foundation, 2, 2, pp. 175-220.

Supporting Technology Independent Interoperability between Business Processes and IoT Devices

Pedro Valderas

PROS Research Centre, Universitat Politècnica de València, Spain

pvalderas@pros.upv.es

Abstract. *The Internet of Things allows digital business processes to use physical devices to automate and improve the execution of some of their tasks. A business process is executed by a process engine, which usually provides built-in mechanisms to interact with IoT devices through REST APIs. However, IoT devices are technologically heterogeneous by nature. If they are not based on REST, the native support provided by process engines is not enough to interact with them. In addition, in case IoT devices have REST APIs, built-in mechanisms of process engines provide technologically coupled solutions since the engine must be configured with the connection data of each specific device. Thus, time-consuming adaptation tasks are required to update the process engine if IoT devices need to be replaced due to changes in business requirements. In this work, we provide a solution to improve these problems based on ontologies, BPMN, and microservices. First, IoT devices are abstractly described by means of the notions proposed by the SAREF ontology. Then, executable BPMN models that use the ontological descriptions of IoT devices are defined to implement a business process. Finally, microservices are used as instantiations of the IoT devices defined with the SAREF ontology, playing the role of gateways between the process engine and the real IoT devices, providing a high level of technological independence between both.*

1. Introduction

The Internet of Things (IoT) enables the connection of the physical world to digital business processes (BP). BPs use IoT devices as digitalised physical resources that participate as actors to automate and improve the execution of some of their tasks (Beverungen et al., 2020). For instance, during the execution of a BP, robotic bridges can be automatically opened upon the arrival of a ship, or a CO2 sensor can be accessed to know the CO2 level of an environment at a specific time. The BPs that make use of IoT devices are known as IoT-enhanced BPs (Torres et al., 2020).

IoT devices are heterogeneous by nature. They differ regarding communication protocols, interaction paradigms, data formats, and computing and storage power. For instance, there are commercial CO2 sensors that save the measures into their cloud server and provide an API REST to access them, while others allow a direct wireless connection through the MQTT protocol[1]. BPs are executed by a process engine, which is responsible

[1] See as representative examples these two commercial CO2 sensors that provide a cloud-based REST API and wireless MQTT-based communication, respectively: (1) https://www.disruptive-technologies.com/products/wireless-co2-sensor, (2) https://envira.global/nanoenvi-iaq/

for instantiating and controlling their execution (Weske, 2012). Currently, the most used BP engines are those based on the Business Process Model and Notation standard (BPMN, 2010), and there is a myriad of different commercial options (e.g., Camunda[2], Bonita[3], Bizagi[4], Siganvio[5], etc.).

Most of the existing BPMN engines provide built-in mechanisms to access external resources through REST APIs, which can be used to interact with IoT devices that support this communication model. However, these solutions require configuring the BPMN engine with the connection data of the IoT devices (protocol (HTTP or HTTPS), IP, port, path, HTTP method, input data, output data, etc.), which creates coupled implementations of IoT-enhanced BPs. If IoT devices need to be replaced due to changes in business requirements after an IoT-enhanced BP is deployed, time-consuming adaptation tasks are required to update the BPMN engine accordingly. On the other hand, if the BPMN engine needs to interact with IoT devices supported by other technologies, such as MQTT-based communication, complex bridges need to be implemented and integrated into the engine, which, in addition, also creates coupled implementations.

Thus, the integration of BPMN engines with IoT devices in order to implement IoT-enhanced BPs is not an easy task since different technological restrictions must be considered depending on the devices' underlying technology. This is still more complex if we need an IoT-enhanced BP implementation decoupled from the IoT technology in such a way that changes in the IoT devices do not require the adaptation of the BPMN engine after an IoT-enhanced BP has already been deployed.

We think this problem can be improved with the use of microservices, ontologies, event-based communication, and the proper development tools. In our previous work (Valderas et al., 2022), we proposed an architecture based on microservices to support the development of IoT-enhanced BPs. In (Valderas et al., 2023), we demonstrate how this architecture can support interdisciplinary development teams. However, this solution introduces technological dependencies among the architectural elements, which produce interoperability problems when some of them need to be replaced to support new technological requirements. In (Valderas & Torres, 2023), we improved this problem by introducing a bottom-up (i.e., from IoT devices to the BPMN engine) event-based communication that allows IoT devices to inject data into the BPMN engine in a decoupled way. In this work, we complement all the previous work by supporting a decoupled top-down (i.e., from the BPMN engine to the IoT devices) ontology-based communication in such a way a BPMN engine can ask an IoT device for the execution of a task without requiring knowing the underlying technology of the device.

The rest of the paper is organised as follows: Section 2 introduces a motivation example in order to understand the problem faced in this work properly. Section 3 presents an approach based on ontologies, BPMN and microservices to develop IoT-Enhanced BPs, and Section 4 introduces an architecture to support their deployment and execution. Section 5 analyses the related work, and conclusions and further work are commented on in Section 6.

---

[2] https://camunda.com/

[3] https://www.bonitasoft.com/

[4] https://www.bizagi.com/

[5] https://www.signavio.com/

2. Motivation Example

In this section, we present a motivation example to understand better the challenge we face in this work. Let's consider the IoT-enhanced BP presented in Figure 1, which describes the process of managing the CO2 level in a smart library. It is defined in BPMN by applying the modelling guidelines presented in (Valderas et al., 2022). In a nutshell: (1) A pool is used to represent the whole IoT-enhance BP within an organisation; (2) each IoT device that participates in the process is represented by a lane within this pool; (3) each IoT device's action required by the BP is defined as a Service Task in the corresponding lane; and (4) data autonomously injected by the IoT devices into the process is represented by means of message flows drawn between a pool that represents the physical world and the pool that represents the IoT-enhance BP. These message flows are labelled with the IoT device that injects the data.

According to the process shown in Figure 1, we have a CO2 sensor informing the BP about the CO2 level periodically (let's suppose every ten minutes). When the CO2 level is lower or equal to 2000 ppm, the BP does nothing. However, if the CO2 level is greater than this value, an emergency protocol is executed. First, an emergency air renewal system is started, and the notification of CO2 levels is stopped in the sensor. After waiting for five minutes, the BP directly requests the current level of CO2 to the CO2 Sensor. If it is lower or equal to 1500 ppm, the emergency air renewal system is stopped, and the sensor notifications are configured every ten minutes again. Otherwise, the BP asks the CO2 Sensor to notify the CO2 level every minute, an alarm is activated to warn people who are inside the library that they must leave, and access to the library is forbidden. Once the library is empty, the alarm is stopped. Regarding the CO2 level, the BP waits until it is lower or equal to 1000 ppm. At this moment, the emergency air renewal system is then stopped, CO2 notifications are configured every 10 minutes, and access is allowed again.

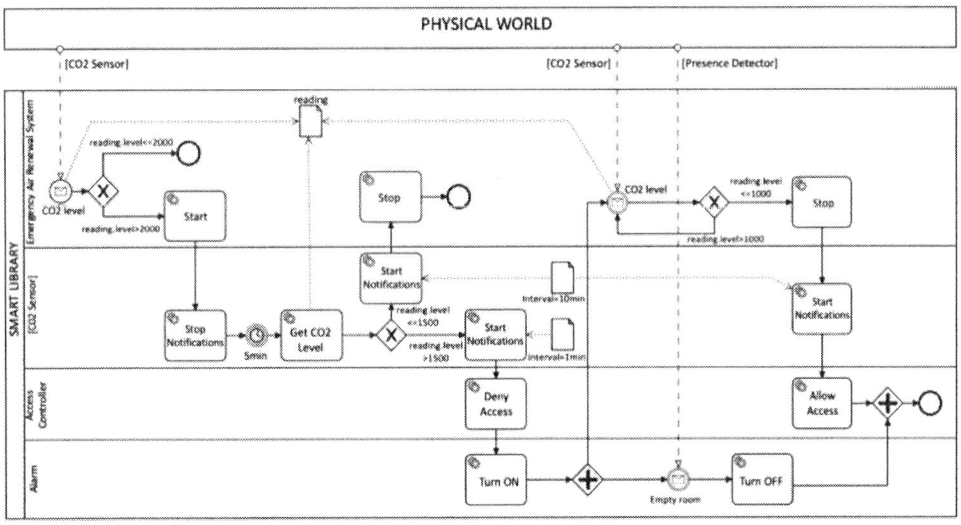

Figure 1. An IoT-enhanced BP for controlling CO2 level

How IoT devices autonomously inject data such as the CO2 level or the detection of presence into the process (i.e., message flows of the above-introduced BPMN model) was already faced in (Valderas & Torres, 2023). Thus, this challenge is out of the scope of this paper. In the current work, we face how a BP engine that executes the BPMN model in Figure 1 can interact, for instance, with the CO2 sensor in order to explicitly ask for the CO2 level (Service Task `Get CO2 Level` defined in the lane `CO2 Sensor`) or with the access controller to deny the access of people (Service Task `Deny Access` defined in the lane `Access Controller`) in a decoupled and independent way from the underlying technology of these IoT devices.

In order to see how current commercial BPMN engines support the interaction with external resources, let's analyse two of the most used open-source platforms: Camunda and Bonita. Regarding **REST APIs**, Camunda provides different solutions to do so, including the delegation to Java code, scripts, or connectors (Deehan et al., 2022). All of these solutions need either to hard-code the connection data of IoT devices in a specific piece of code or use the modeller interface to configure it. For simplicity purposes, Figure 2A only shows how a connector can be configured through the modeller interface in order to interact with a CO2 sensor that publishes a REST API. In the same way, Bonita allows connecting to a REST API either through a custom connector[6] implemented in Java, Groovy or Kotlin, which requires to hard-code the connection data, or using the REST built-in connector and configuring it through a wizard (as shown in Figure 2B). Regarding **other technologies**, such as the MQTT protocol, Camunda provides two solutions: either to implement a Java module that manages the interaction with the message broker or to use an external library that must be integrated into the commercial tool (Zambroski & Pohl, 2016). In Bonita, a custom connector should be implemented by using the above-commented programming languages.

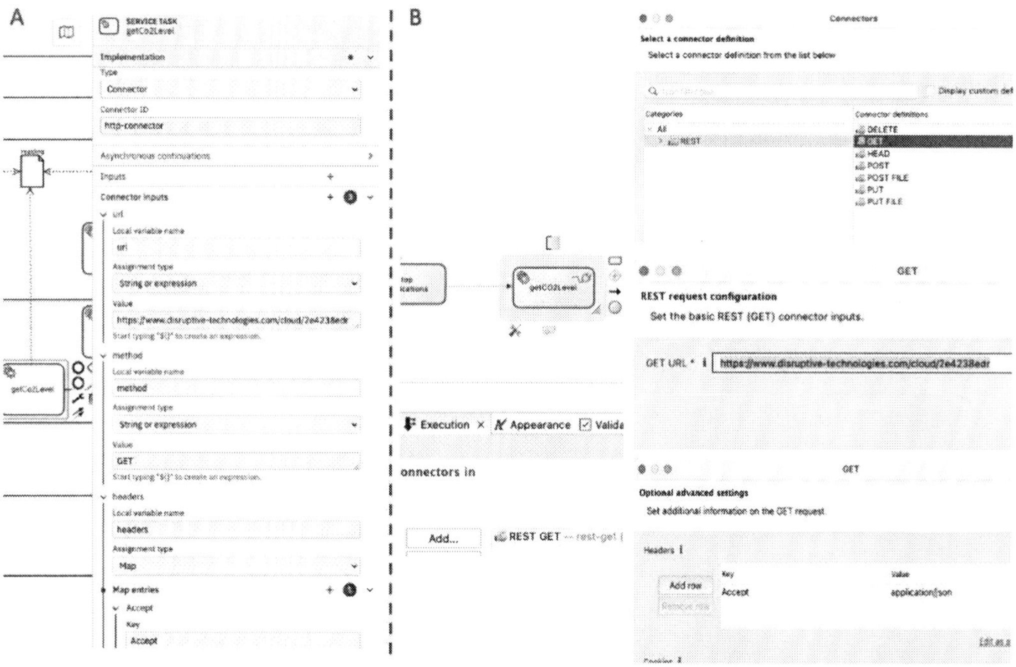

Figure 2. Connection of Camunda (A) and Bonita (B) with a REST API

Camunda and Bonita are only two representative examples of commercial BPMN engines. However, the rest of the engines that we can currently find in the market provide

[6] https://documentation.bonitasoft.com/bonita/latest/process/connector-archetype-tutorial

analogous solutions. Note that these solutions make the execution of the BPMN model that defines an IoT-Enhanced BP totally dependent on the technology that supports the IoT devices. Thus, changes in these devices require complex adaptations in the BPMN engine. For instance, consider that we initially configured the IoT-enhanced BP in Figure 1 to use a CO2 sensor that provides a REST API. We needed to create a configuration like the one shown in Figure 2 for each Service Task defined in the `CO2 Sensor` lane. Consider, also, that time after the deployment of the process, the CO2 Sensor needs to be replaced by another model that supports a communication based on MQTT. In this situation, time-consuming tasks of programming and re-configuration in the BPMN engine are needed in order to work with the new underlying technology. In addition, note that the CO2 sensor used in the IoT-enhanced BP in Figure 1 provides three operations through its REST API: `Get CO2`, `Start Notifications` and `Stop Notifications`. The newly deployed CO2 sensor should also provide these operations, or the logic of the process should be redefined.

To conclude this section, we can see that changing an IoT device when an IoT-enhanced BP is already deployed can be a complicated task if the BPMN engine that executes it directly interacts with the participant devices. In this work, we propose a solution based on the integration of BPMN and ontological descriptions of IoT devices in order to improve this problem.

3. Developing ontology-based IoT-Enhanced BPs

The solution we present in the work is a development process for IoT-Enhanced BPs based on the SAREF ontology, BPMN, and microservices. This process includes the following three stages:

1. IoT Device Ontological Description: In this stage, we propose to use the SAREF (Smart Appliances REFerence) ontology (Daniele et al., 2017) in order to describe IoT devices in an abstract way, totally independent from any manufacturer or technology. There are other ontologies that represent IoT concepts, such as SOSA[7] SensorML[8] or SAO[9]. We used SAREF because its concepts facilitate the description of the different functional capabilities that are provided by IoT Devices (actuating, meter, and sensing), which helps us to integrate them into a business process properly.
2. IoT-Enhanced BP Design: This stage consists of creating a BPMN model that describes the logic of the process that must be implemented. This BPMN model includes references to the abstract IoT devices defined in the previous stage.
3. IoT Device Microservice Implementation: As we explain in Section 4, the BPMN model defined in the previous stage is deployed in an architecture in which microservices play the role of gateway between the BPMN engine and the physical IoT devices. In this stage of the process, these microservices must be implemented as instances of the abstract descriptions of the IoT devices defined in the first stage. We use microservices because this architectural solution was proposed to create systems as a composition of highly decoupled independent business components and the main goal of this work is providing a high level of decoupling between BPMN engines and IoT Devices.

[7] https://www.w3.org/TR/vocab-ssn/
[8] https://www.ogc.org/standard/sensorml/
[9] http://iot.ee.surrey.ac.uk/citypulse/ontologies/sao/sao

Next, we introduce additional details about each stage through the motivating example. For replicability purposes, the ontology, BPMN model, and software artefacts developed to implement the motivating example can be found in a GitHub repository[10].

3.1. Ontological Description of IoT Devices

SAREF[11] is a reference ontology for smart devices that provides an important contribution to enabling semantic interoperability in the IoT. Among the different concepts defined in this ontology, we use the following: (1) *Device*, a tangible object designed to accomplish a particular task by means of one or more functions; (2) *Actuating Function*, a function that allows transmitting data to a device, such as level settings (e.g., temperature) or binary switching (e.g., open/close, on/off); (3) *Sensing Function*, a function that allows a device transmitting data autonomously, such as measurement values (e.g., temperature) or sensing data (e.g., occupancy); (4) *Meter Function*, a function that allows getting data from a device at a specific time such as current meter reading or instantaneous demand. The SAREF ontology also introduces concepts to describe the data structure that is managed by each function. However, this issue is left as further work.

As a representative example, Figure 3A graphically shows the SAREF description of the CO2 sensor used in the motivating example. This device is defined with one Sensing Function (`CO2 Level Sensing`), which is the one focused on autonomously transmitting the CO2 level; two Actuating Functions (`Start Notifications` and `Stop Notifications`), which allow to configure whether or not the CO2 level must be transmitted autonomously by the sensor and the periodicity; and one Metter Function (`getCO2Level`), which allows to get the CO2 level from the sensor at a specific instant.

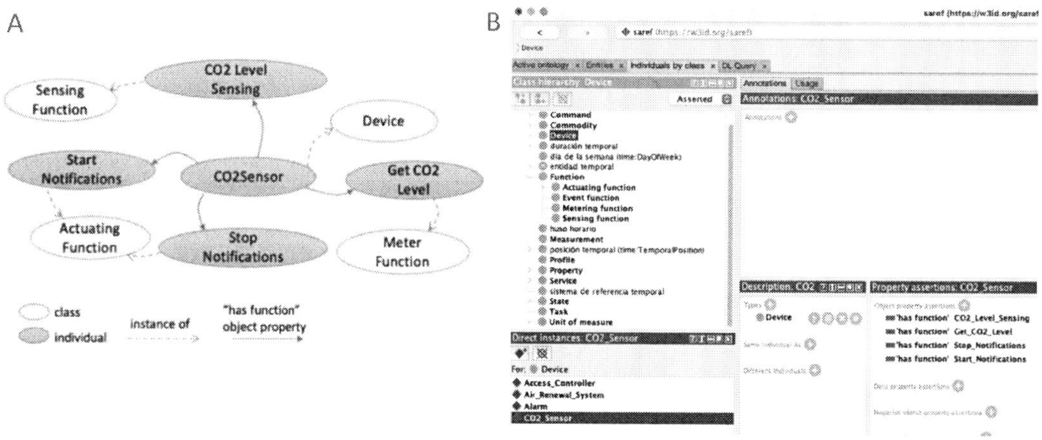

Figure 3. SAREF ontological description of a CO2 Sensor (left) created in Protégé (right)

Currently, there are many tools and languages that can be used to create ontologies (Slimani, 2015). In this work, we used Protégé[12] (see Figure 3B), which is a very popular open-source tool in the field of semantic web and computer science research. In order to

[10] https://github.com/pvalderas/pvalderas-iot-enhanced-bp-saref

[11] https://w3id.org/saref

[12] https://protege.stanford.edu/

integrate the semantic description of IoT devices with the BPMN modeller presented below, it was exported as an OWL file.

3.2. BPMN Modelling

In order to define the BPMN model that represents an IoT-Enhanced BP, we use the modelling approach presented in (Valderas et al., 2022), which has been summarised when introducing the motivating example in Section 2.

In our previous work, we created a web modelling tool[13] that allow us to apply this modelling approach to create BPMN models of IoT-Enhanced BPs. However, this tool includes specific data of the IoT devices into the BPMN models to make them executable, which links these models with the devices, creating a coupled solution. In this work, we have extended the web modelling tool in order to create BPMN models associated with ontological descriptions of IoT devices. This is complemented by the microservice architecture presented in Section 4, which allows the discovery of IoT devices that fit an ontological description and the interaction with them by means of decoupled event-based communication.

A SAREF OWL parser[14] has been developed and integrated into the tool to load ontological descriptions of IoT devices. As commented in Section 2, our modelling approach proposes to include IoT devices as BPMN lanes and the actions of these devices as service tasks. Thus, the extended version of the tool, once a SAREF ontology is loaded, allows the modeller to link each BPMN lane with one of the IoT devices defined in the SAREF ontology (see Figure 4A) and link the Service Tasks with the SAREF Actuating or Meter functions defined for the device (see Figure 4B). Note that Sensing functions are not provided in this wizard since they define the autonomous behaviour of the devices instead of operations that can be called by an external system.

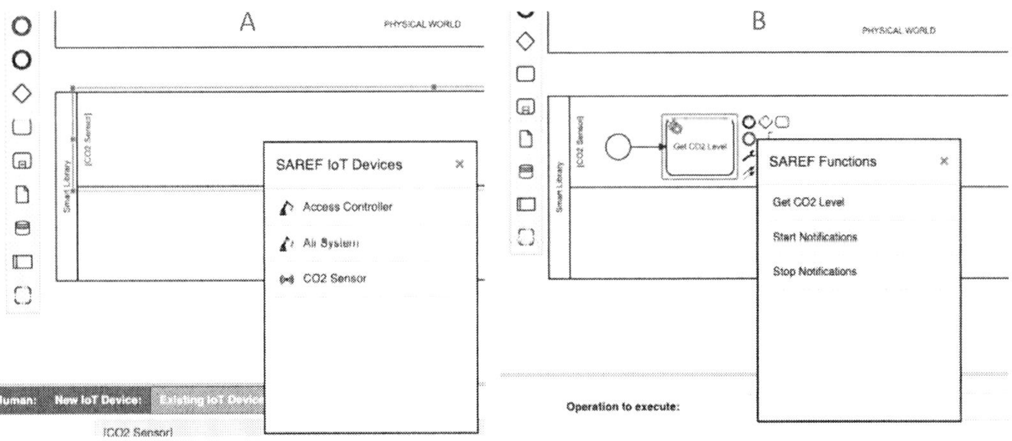

Figure 4. Snapshots of the web modelling tool

The BPMN model created by this tool is totally independent of the data required to interact with IoT devices. It only includes the names of the SAREF devices associated with BPMN lanes and the name of the SAREF functions associated with Service Tasks.

[13] http://pedvalar.webs.upv.es/iot-enhanced-bp-modeller/

[14] The reader can test the parser by uploading the OWL file available in the GitHub repository (or a analogous one) from the menu option 'IoT System->Create an IoT System from an Ontology'

How this definition is transformed into the actual execution of an operation in a real IoT device is achieved by means of the implementation of the proper microservices, as we explain next.

3.3. Microservice Implementation

The last stage in the process proposed to develop IoT-Enhanced BPs is the implementation of microservices that play the role of instantiations of the devices described through the SAREF ontology in stage 1. These microservices must implement the code required to interact with a real IoT device in order to support the functions defined in the ontological descriptions.

As we explain in the next section, the BPMN engine that executes the BPMN model of an IoT-Enhanced BP will interact with these microservices through an event-based bus. This means that these microservices must react by executing a specific operation in the real IoT device as a response to an event published in a bus by the BPMN engine. These events will represent the request for the execution of an operation in terms of the SAREF ontology.

```
@SpringBootApplication
@SAREFDevice(name="CO2 Sensor")
public class CO2Sensor {
    public static void main(String[] args) {
        SpringApplication.run(CO2Sensor.class, args);
    }
}
@Component
public class CO2SensorController {
    @SAREFMeterFunction(name="Get CO2 Level",
                description="Return the Level of CO2 when requested",
                resultType=CO2Level.class)
    public CO2Level getCO2() {
        return Backend.getCurrentInstance().getCO2Level();
    }

    @SAREFActuatingFunction(name="Start Notifications",
            description="Turns the automatic measurement of CO2 ON",
            resultType=Boolean.class)
    public Boolean startNotifications(String interval) {
        return Backend.getCurrentInstance().startNotications(interval);
    }

    @SAREFActuatingFunction(name="Stop Notifications",
            description="Turns the automatic measurement of CO2 OFF",
            resultType=Boolean.class)
    public Boolean stopNotifications() {
        return Backend.getCurrentInstance().stopNotications();
    }
}
```

Figure 5. Example of IoT Microservice implementation

In order to support this event-based reactive behaviour and facilitate the implementation of the proposed microservices, we have implemented a library based on the Java Spring Boot framework. Inspired by a solution we already used in our previous work (Valderas et al., 2023), this library provides a set of Java annotations that allow microservice developers to semantically annotate the Java code according to the IoT device descriptions done with the SAREF ontology. This library uses reflection mechanisms to detect these annotations and inject the functionality required to respond to the event-based requests performed by the BPMN engine. As a representative example, the code that is shown in Figure 5 implements the microservice that is in charge of managing a CO2 sensor. Note how the main class is annotated with `SAREFDevice` and the methods that implement the interaction with IoT devices are annotated with

SAREFActuatingFunction or SAREFMeterFunction. These two last annotations link the name of a SAREF function to a specific Java method in such a way that when the BPMN Engine publishes an event requesting the execution of a function (e.g., Get CO2 level), the functionality injected by the library is able to know the Java method that must be executed. The code that implements each of these methods depends on the underlying technology of the IoT device, which is out of the scope of this paper. Further details about the event-based reactive behaviour that is supported by this library are presented in the next section.

4. Supporting microservice architecture

The previous section has introduced how IoT-Enhanced BPs are developed by means of the SAREF ontology, BPMN models, and microservices. In this section, we introduce a microservice architecture that integrates these software artefacts in order to execute this type of process in a technology-independent way. This architecture improves the one presented in (Valderas et al., 2022) by supporting event-based communication between BPMN engines and IoT devices. It is shown in Figure 6.

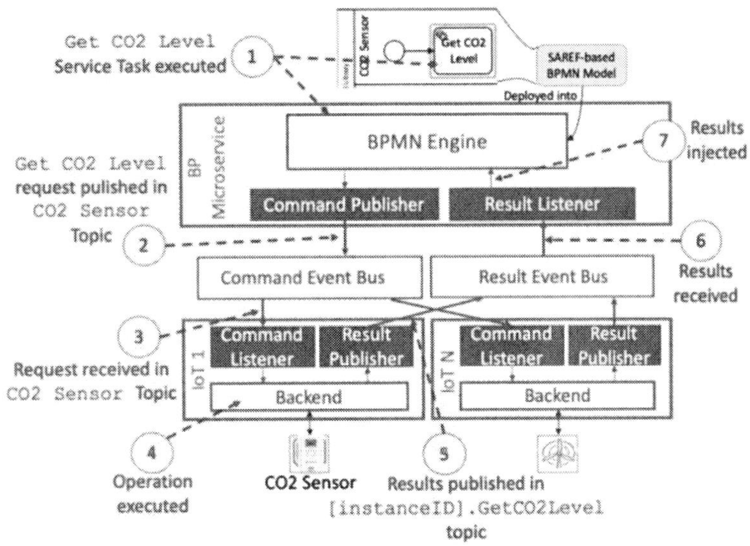

Figure 6. Microservice-based architecture to execute SAREF-based BPMN models of IoT-Enhanced BPs

The microservices included in the proposed architecture are the following:

(1) *BP microservice*, which is endowed with a BPMN engine that oversees executing IoT-enhanced BPs such as the one presented in Figure 1. In addition, the communication adapters *Command Publisher* and *Result Listener* are also deployed into this microservice. These adapters support event-based communication with IoT microservices (presented below). The tasks they perform to achieve this communication are introduced below in more detail. Note that this is an infrastructure microservice that can be used to deploy several IoT-enhanced BPs independently from their domain.

(2) An *IoT microservice* for each IoT device, which supports each SAREF device by implementing a backend that is in charge of managing the interaction with the real device in order to execute operations. This backend is implemented according to the

technology used by the device. Two communication adapters are also included in these microservices to support event-based communication with the BP microservice: *Command Listener* and *Result Publisher*. These adapters contain the functionality that is automatically injected when IoT microservices are implemented by using the Java library presented in Section 3.3.

The communication between the BP microservice and the IoT microservices is asynchronously done through topic-based event buses, which implement publish-subscribe communication (Eugster et al., 2003) through message queues. Publish-subscribe communication allows for the decoupling of producers and consumers, enabling scalability and a loosely coupled architecture. Message queuing ensures reliable and asynchronous communication with features like load balancing and message persistence. In addition, we use these event buses to implement the Command pattern (Dupire & Fernandez, 2001), which is a behavioural pattern used in object-oriented programming. A request is wrapped under an object as a command and passed to an invoker object. The invoker object looks for the appropriate object which can handle this command and passes the command to it to be executed. We adapt this pattern so that the request is created by the BP microservice and published to a topic-based *Command Event Bus* (see Figure 6). This request asks for the execution of a SAREF function. IoT microservices are subscribed to the *Command Event Bus* in such a way the request is handled by the appropriate microservice, which executes the corresponding operation in the IoT device. Once the operation is executed, the obtained result is published by the microservice into a topic-based *Result Event Bus*. The BP microservice is subscribed to this bus in such a way it obtains the results of executing the requested SAREF function.

4.1 Command-based communication in detail

Let's explain in more detail how the request to execute a SAREF function by the BP microservice is transformed into the execution of the operation of a real IoT device by applying the Command pattern (see execution steps depicted in red in Figure 6). A BPMN model such as the one presented in Figure 1 is executed by the BPMN engine deployed into the BP microservice. For each BPMN Service Task that is associated with a SAREF function (step 1), the BP microservice creates a request that asks for the execution of this function in the context of a specific running instance. This request is defined in JSON format by the *Command Publisher* adapter (step 2), and it is published in the topic-based *Command Event Bus*. The topic in which the request is published is the name of the IoT device that must execute it. An example is shown below, which asks for the execution of the `Get CO2 Level` function. This request is published on the `CO2 Sensor` topic. Note how the IoT device that defines the topic and the function included in the request are defined according to the description done with the SAREF ontology. They are obtained by the *Command Publisher* adapter from the name of the Service Task that is being executed by the BPMN engine and the name of the lane in which the task is defined (see the BPMN model in Figure 1). The name of the process is obtained from the BPMN pool. The name of the device is also included in the request for validation purposes.

```
{
  "process": "Smart Library",
  "instance": "582b8617-bcf5",
  "device": "CO2 Sensor",
  "function": "Get CO2 Level"
}
```

Once the request is published, the BP microservice, which is subscribed to the *Result Event Bus*, waits for the publication of the response by the corresponding IoT microservice. IoT microservices are subscribed to the *Command Event Bus* and are waiting for requests published in the topics associated with their name. For instance, the CO2 Sensor microservice is waiting for requests published on the `CO2 Sensor` topic (step 3 in Figure 6). Once a request is published on this topic, the *Command Listener* adapter of this IoT microservice oversees executing the Java method that corresponds to the SAREF function included in the request (step 4). These methods are identified by using the annotations presented in Section 3.3.

Once the Java method that corresponds to the requested SAREF function is executed, the result is managed by the *Result Publisher* adapter of the IoT microservices, which contains the functionality required to publish them into the topic-based *Result Event Bus* (step 5). The BP microservice is subscribed to this bus in order to receive the results of the requested function (step 6), which are managed by the *Result Listener* adapter in order to be injected into the BPMN engine (step 7). In this case, the topic used to communicate the IoT microservices and the BP microservice is defined by a string made up of the process instance ID and the function name. For instance, the response to the previous request is published in the topic `582b8617-bcf5.GetCO2Level` in such a way the BP microservice is able to obtain the response for the execution of a function for a specific running process instance. The response constructed by the *Result Publisher* adapter of each IoT microservice is also based on the SAREF ontology. However, details about this issue are omitted due to space restrictions.

4.2 Proof of concept validation

According to Völter (2006), a way of preliminary evaluating the proposal of a new architecture is through developing a prototype. Next, we introduce a realisation of the above-introduced architecture as a prototype involving mapping technology choices onto the solution concepts.

The main goal of the proposed microservice architecture is to facilitate decoupled interoperability among BPMN engines and IoT devices when the former needs to execute operations of the latest. Thus, in addition to developing a prototype with specific technology choices, we faced changing a participant IoT device in order to analyse the adaptation tasks that are required.

The implemented prototype. For the development of the initial prototype, we considered the running example presented in this paper, and we take as a basis the technology choices we made in previous work (Valderas et al., 2022):

- The event buses were implemented by means of the RabbitMQ Message broker.
- The BP microservice was supported by a Windows system with the community version of the Camunda 7 engine. We also deployed the *Command Publisher* and the *Result Listener* adapters.
  - The *Command Publisher* was developed as a Java library integrated into Camunda in order to manage the execution of each Service Task. This library also contains configurable functionality to facilitate the publication of messages into the *Command Event Bus*. Currently, the RabbitMQ message broker is supported.

- The *Result Listener* adapter was developed as a Java library that contains configurable functionality to facilitate the subscription to the *Result Event Bus* (currently, RabbitMQ) in order to process the results published by the IoT microservices. This library also includes the functionality required to inject the results obtained after the execution of an operation into the corresponding process instance.

- IoT microservices were implemented in Java by using the library introduced in Section 3.3. Their backends were initially implemented to interact with IoT devices that provide a REST API. Each of these microservices was deployed into Windows systems. The *Command Listener* and *Result Publisher* adapters were also deployed into each microservices. These adapters were developed as Java libraries that contain configurable functionality to facilitate the interaction with RabbitMQ in order to both receive the commands published into the *Command Event Bus* and publish the operation results in the *Result Event Bus*, respectively.

Replacement of an IoT device. Once this prototype was developed, we analysed its correctness through the execution of the BPMN model of the running example and the analysis of logs. Afterwards, we replaced the CO2 Sensor based on REST with an analogous one that uses an MQTT queue to publish data. To support this change, we just needed to reimplement the backend of the IoT microservice that manages the interaction with the CO2 Sensor in order to work with an MQTT queue instead of accessing a REST API. The communication adapters of this microservice did not require any modification since the communication with the event buses is totally decoupled from the backend. Also, no other microservice in the architecture requires an adaptation, neither the BP microservice nor the IoT microservices that manage other devices.

Discussion. The proposed architectural solution was shown to facilitate adaptation when an IoT device is replaced by another with a different technology. The decoupled communication model based on the Command pattern and event-based buses provided a high level of independence among the BPMN engine and the IoT devices. Also, this architectural solution facilitated the simultaneous interaction of the BPMN engine with IoT devices that are technologically different. For instance, once the initial REST-based CO2 Sensor was replaced by the MQTT-based version, Camunda interacted with IoT devices supported by two different technologies (i.e., the CO2 Sensor based on MQTT and the other devices based on REST). However, this was totally transparent for the engine. On the other hand, the use of microservices as gateways between the BPMN engine and the IoT devices allows for providing a common interface for all the IoT devices (based on the defined SAREF functions), although they do not support some operations natively. For instance, the CO2 sensor defined in the SAREF ontology provided three operations: Get CO2, Start Notifications and Stop Notifications. As the newly deployed MQTT-based sensor did not support the start and stop of notifications, we could implement some code that emulates them in the microservices' backend, maintaining a correct interaction with the BPM engine. Note that although some coding tasks were required to replace one IoT device with another, they were totally decoupled from the BPMN engine, and it was not necessary to stop the BPMN engine, adapt the BPMN model, and redeploy it.

5. Related Work

How to deal with the design and implementation of IoT-enhanced BPs has already been addressed in the literature by different authors. In this section, we provide an overview of some of these works and the architecture they present but also consider other works more focused on cyber-physical systems in general and how they deal architectonically with the heterogeneity and changing nature commonly found in this type of systems.

Regarding the specification and execution of IoT-enhanced BPs, most of the proposals we find in the literature (Mandal et al., 2017; Mottola et al., 2019; Suri et al., 2017) focus on providing a supporting infrastructure to specify and execute this type of BP properly. However, none of them addresses the technology decoupling issues along the whole architecture as we do, meaning that we always find solutions that are tight to the underlying technology. These solutions extend existing modelling notations (e.g., BPMN) to represent specific aspects of an IoT system (e.g., a sensor, an actuator, an event triggered by the physical world, etc.) as well as the interaction with them. Thus, BP engines need to be extended to be able to execute such extensions, turning proposals into highly coupled solutions with the BP engine. Our solution, in contrast, can be used with any commercial BPMN engine without the need to extend it to support new constructors.

To decouple all the infrastructure required to specify and execute such systems, other works make a clearer separation between the different layers of their proposed architecture (Kim et al., 2014; Sasirekha & Swamynathan, 2016; Schönig et al., 2018)). For example, Kim et al. (2014) propose to achieve the integration between BPs and IoT devices by means of adapters. In the proposal, there is a four-layer division that separates BPs (BP layer), software services (SW Service layer), adapters (Adaptation layer), and IoT services (IoT Service layer). While the BP layer directly invokes services from the SW Service layer and the Adaptation layer, there is no direct interaction with the IoT Service layer. In fact, this interaction is performed through the Adaptation layer, which includes adapters that respond to services requested by BPs and invoke IoT services in response to such requests. Besides this, IoT services are described according to the SensorML modelling language. Sasirekha & Swamynathan (2016) also propose an architecture of four layers: the BP layer, the semantic service layer, the web service layer, and the device layer, where BPs are specified in BPEL, services using semantic web languages, i.e., ontologies, and IoT devices are represented by means of an ontology which is defined as the integration of a defined domain ontology and the SSN ontology. Finally, Schönig et al. (2018) propose an architecture composed of three layers: the IoT layer, which contains sensors and wearable devices of human participants; the IoT infrastructure and communication middleware; and the BPMS. Besides this architecture, this work proposes to extend BPMN with Data variables to enrich BP models with data obtained from physical objects (e.g., machine status or actor position) and to specify how and where connected IoT devices influence the process. All these approaches try to achieve a more decoupled architecture, although the different layers communicate with each other through direct calls. We improve these solutions by achieving a more decoupled interaction based on the Command pattern and the use of asynchronous event buses based on a publish/subscribe communication.

Regarding the field of cyber-physical systems, we find the works developed by Cao et al. (2021) and Gómez et al. (2021), which propose the use of event-driven architectures (EDA) together with other architectonical solutions to overcome the technology decoupling challenge of such systems. On the one hand, Gómez et al. (2021) propose an architecture based on SOA, microservices, and Complex Event Processing (CEP) to offer a flexible service catalogue that allows them to connect to the system on any kind of device and interact in different scenarios. On the other hand, Cao et al. (2021) propose the use of an ontology model in an event-driven architecture to make sure that the event-driven services provided by organisations follow the organisational event access rules. Specifically, the ontology model is used to define the domain-specific concepts related to events. Although these works propose a similar solution to ours, the use of the Command pattern based on the SAREF ontology provides a higher level of decoupling, in addition to the fact that these solutions do not consider the specification of IoT-enhanced BPs.

6. Conclusions

This work has presented an approach to improve interoperability issues when implementing IoT-Enhanced BPs. It is based on the use of BPMN, the SAREF ontology and a microservice architecture that implements the Command pattern through asynchronous event buses.

Unlike current solutions of commercial BPMN engines, which are technology-coupled since they insert the connection data of IoT devices into the BPMN models, our approach allows an implementation of IoT-Enhanced BPs in which BPMN engines can interact with IoT devices without knowing their underlying technology. This makes it easier to replace IoT devices when requirements change since the BPMN engine and the deployed models do not need to be modified.

As further work, we plan to extend this approach by introducing goal-oriented modelling techniques in such a way the BPMN engine can execute the tasks of an IoT-Enhanced BP by using the IoT devices that better help achieve the specific goals in terms of, for instance, non-functional properties such as performance, energy consumption, user experience, and so on.

Acknowledgement

This work is part of the R&D&I project PID2020-114480RBI00 funded by MCIN/AEI/10.13039/501100011033

References

BPMN. (2010). *Business Process Model and Notation Concepts*. http://www.omg.org/spec/BPMN/20100501

Cao, H., Yang, X., & Deng, R. (2021). Ontology-Based Holonic Event-Driven Architecture for Autonomous Networked Manufacturing Systems. *IEEE Transactions on Automation Science and Engineering*, *18*(1), 205–215.

Daniele, L., García-Castro, R., Lefrançois, M., & Poveda-Villalon, M. S. (2017). *The Smart Applications REFerence Ontology*.

Deehan, N., Lea, N., Richtsmeier, I., Wulf, J., Graham, A., Ruecker, B., Oliver, R., & Ausley, C. (2022). *Make REST calls from Camunda Platform 7 Example*. https://github.com/camunda-community-hub/Make-Rest-Calls-From-Camunda-7-Example

Dupire, B., & Fernandez, E. B. (2001). The Command Dispatcher Pattern. In *8th Conference on Pattern Languages of Programs*. https://hillside.net/plop/plop2001/accepted_submissions/PLoP2001/bdupireandebfernandez0/PLoP2001_bdupireandebfernandez0_1.pdf

Eugster, P. T., Felber, P. A., Guerraoui, R., and Kermarrec, A.-M. (2003). The many faces of publish/subscribe. ACM computing surveys (CSUR), 35(2):114–131.

Gómez, H. D., Garcia-Rodriguez, J., Azorin-Lopez, J., Tomás, D., Fuster-Guillo, A., & Mora-Mora, H. (2021). IA-CPS: Intelligent architecture for cyber-physical systems management. *Journal of Computational Science*, *53*, 101409.

Kim, S. D., Lee, J. Y., Kim, D. Y., Park, C. W., & La, H. J. (2014). Modeling BPEL-based collaborations with heterogeneous IoT devices. *Proceedings - 2014 World Ubiquitous Science Congress: 2014 IEEE 12th International Conference on Dependable, Autonomic and Secure Computing, DASC 2014*, 289–294.

Mandal, S., Hewelt, M., & Weske, M. (2017). A framework for integrating real-world events and business processes in an IoT environment. *Lecture Notes in Computer*, *10573 LNCS*, 194–212. https://doi.org/10.1007/978-3-319-69462-7_13

Mottola, L., Picco, G. P., Oppermann, F. J.,…., Tranquillini, S., & Voigt, T. (2019). MakeSense: Simplifying the Integration of Wireless Sensor Networks into Business Processes. *IEEE Trans. on Software Engineering*, *45*(6), 576–596.

Sasirekha, S., & Swamynathan, S. (2016). Collaboration of IoT devices using semantically enabled resource oriented middleware. *ACM International Conference Proceeding Series*, *21-24-Sept*, 98–105.

Schönig, S., Ackermann, L., Jablonski, S., & Ermer, A. (2018). An integrated architecture for IoT-aware business process execution. *Lecture Notes in Business Information Processing*, *318*, 19–34.

Slimani, T. (2015). Ontology Development: A Comparing Study on Tools, Languages and Formalisms. *Indian Journal of Science and Technology*, *8*(24).

Suri, K., Gaaloul, W., Cuccuru, A., & Gerard, S. (2017). Semantic framework for internet of things-aware business process development. *Proceedings - 2017 IEEE 26th International Conference on Enabling Technologies: Infrastructure for Collaborative Enterprises, WETICE 2017*, 214–219.

Torres, V., Serral, E., Valderas, P., Pelechano, V., & Grefen, P. (2020). Modeling of IoT devices in Business Processes: A Systematic Mapping Study. *Proceedings - 2020 IEEE 22nd Conference on Business Informatics, CBI 2020*, *1*, 221–230.

Valderas, P., & Torres, V. (2023). Towards a Semantic Interoperability in IoTEnhanced Business Processes. An Event-Driven Solution based on Microservices. *2023 19th International Conference on Intelligent Environments, IE 2023 - Proceedings*.

Valderas, P., Torres, V., & Serral, E. (2022). Modelling and executing IoT-enhanced business processes through BPMN and microservices. *J. of Systems and Software*, *184*.

Valderas, P., Torres, V., & Serral, E. (2023). Towards an Interdisciplinary Development of IoT-Enhanced Business Processes. *Business & Information Systems Engineering*, 1–24.

Völter, M. (2006). Software architecture: A pattern language for building sustainable software architectures. In *EuroPLoP 2006 - 11th European Conference on Pattern Languages of Programs* (pp. 31–66). Mar.

Weske, M. (2012). Business process management: Concepts, languages, architectures, second edition. *Business Process Management: Concepts, Languages, Architectures, Second Edition*, 1–403.

Zambroski, S., & Pohl, T. (2016). *MQTT Camunda BPMN*.

A Qualitative Study on Requirements Engineering Practices in an Artificial Intelligence Unit of the Brazilian Industrial Research and Innovation Company

Mariana Crisostomo Martins, Taciana Novo Kudo, Renato F. Bulcão-Neto

[1]Instituto de Informática – Universidade Federal de Goiás (UFG)
Goiânia – GO – Brazil

Abstract. *In recent years, there has been a focus shift from software development in general to the construction and training of machine learning (ML) models integrated into a software product. This movement has raised challenges in ML systems' requirements engineering (RE) theory and practice. This paper investigates RE practices in ML systems research, development, and innovation projects carried out by an Artificial Intelligence (AI) Unit of the Brazilian Industrial Research and Innovation Company. Our methodology includes semi-structured interviews with leaders of 21 projects and data analysis through the grounded theory method. We identified the predominance of RE methods, techniques, and tools applied ad hoc and uncoordinatedly. This result corroborates the literature reports on RE for ML systems, especially those involving innovation projects.*

1. Introduction

Recent research has demonstrated a shift in focus from artificial intelligence (AI) algorithms supporting requirements engineering (RE) activities to RE approaches for AI-based software systems [Villamizar et al. 2021]. However, the literature has also pointed out the complexity of the RE process for these systems. For instance, RE professionals convey unrealistic expectations in AI-based software projects [Alves et al. 2024], it is not clear which RE techniques and tools have been used in practice, and whether well-established RE methods should or could be adapted [Villamizar et al. 2021].

In this paper, we report our findings about RE practices in research, development, and innovation projects carried out by an Artificial Intelligence (AI) Unit of the Brazilian Industrial Research and Innovation Company, called CEIA (Center of Excellence in Artificial Intelligence)[1]. We planned and conducted semi-structured interviews with leaders of 21 projects implementing AI algorithms for several application domains, such as health, entertainment, marketing, and the automobile industry. We performed a qualitative analysis based on Grounded Theory [Stol et al. 2016] and the method proposed by [Glaser and Strauss 2017].

As a result, we conclude that in this particular scenario, with such heterogeneous AI projects, there is a lack of a methodology for RE activities. The majority of coordinators who participated in the research reported that they do not possess any RE specialists on their team, and acknowledge the significance of the activity and the necessity of implementing a systematic process for it.

[1]https://ceia.ufg.br/

This paper is organized as follows: Section 2 outlines related work; Sections 3 and 4 describe our method and present our results, respectively; Section 5 discusses our results; Section 6 summarizes our study's threats to validity; and Section 7 brings our conclusions and future work.

2. Related Work

Interviews with 278 software engineering (SE) professionals with machine learning (ML) knowledge were carried out in [Ishikawa and Yoshioka 2019]. The goal is to verify the current state of ML applications from the perspective of SE activities and identify how ML is perceived by the SE community. The authors sought to understand respondents' experience in SE and ML, identify projects they had previously worked on, and identify perceived obstacles and distinctive features of ML. Among the challenges highlighted are understanding expectations, unrealistic customer expectations, the uncertain nature of the domain, the impossibility of guarantees, and the need for continuous engineering.

In [Silva and Canedo 2022], ER challenges and techniques for chatbot development were identified. The survey obtained 22 responses from Brazilian professionals in the chatbot industry. The authors investigated the nature of the respondents' organizations, the roles they assumed in the projects, the methodologies used for development, the elicitation and documentation techniques, and the tools used for elicitation. Most respondents work for private companies, practice Scrum, elicit requirements through brainstorming, and document using conversational flow. Most of the respondents believe that NFR and the ER process are neglected.

In recent work [Habibullah et al. 2023], the authors interviewed ten engineers specializing in functional and non-functional requirements to gain knowledge about the current state of the art and challenges associated with RE for ML. In addition to demographic factors, such as the professional profile of the interviewees, the authors also identified how non-functional requirements were addressed and evaluated in the projects in which these professionals participated. The authors highlighted among their findings that domain uncertainty and data selection are the central challenges.

Vogelsang and Borg also interviewed data scientists to get RE practice in ML development [Vogelsang and Borg 2019]. The scientists pointed out that they typically use interviews for elicitation. They highlighted the importance of having a legal specialist involved in obtaining needs. They also highlighted the importance of handling data and performance requirements and emphasized the importance of monitoring and the possibility of a checklist.

We advocate that our work complements those mentioned above since we aim to discover how RE practices have been carried out in 21 AI-based research, development, and innovation projects by interviewing project coordinators from different domains.

3. Method

3.1. Interviews

Our main goal is to obtain the state of RE practice in ML-based RDI projects in the CEIA Unit. We used the GQM (Goal-Question-Metric) goal definition template to define the following research objectives:

- **Object of study.** [What will be analyzed?]: the RE practice in CEIA innovation projects.
- **Purpose.** [Why will the object be analyzed?]: to characterize the state of RE practice in CEIA AI innovation projects.
- **Quality focus.** [Property of the object that will be analyzed]: the process, methodologies, and artifacts characteristics related to the RE phase.
- **Point of view.** [Who will use the collected data?]: CEIA innovation projects leaders (researchers).
- **Environment.** [What is the context in which the analysis is carried out?]: an Artificial Intelligence (AI) Unit of the Brazilian Industrial Research and Innovation Company at the Federal University of Goiás (CEIA-EMBRAPII-UFG), Brazil.

3.1.1. Hypotheses

- H01 - It does not carry out good traditional or agile elicitation practices in its projects.
- H02 - It does not implement good traditional or agile analysis practices.
- H03 - It does not implement good traditional or agile specification practices.
- H04 - It does not carry out good traditional or agile validation practices.
- H05 - It does not implement good traditional or agile management practices.
- H06 - Non-functional requirements are neglected.
- H07 - Coordinator's profile affects the adoption of good RE practices.
- H08 - Team's profile affects the adoption of good RE practices.

3.1.2. Research Questions

1. How are RE phases performed in AI projects?
2. How are non-functional requirements handled in AI projects?
3. Are better RE practices in projects achieved because of their leaders with more experience or greater knowledge of RE?
4. Are better RE practices in projects achieved because of their teams with more experience or greater knowledge of RE?
5. What RE challenges are faced in these projects?
6. What has generally been neglected from the RE phase in these projects?

The research questions guided the questions in the interview guide available in the repository of this article.

3.1.3. Characteristics

We conducted semi-structured interviews, in person or with recording via web conferencing for transcription (1h, on average). Interviews have three dimensions:

1. Temporal dimension: synchronous and interactive;
2. Spatial dimension: remote or in-person;
3. Structural dimension: scripted, classified as a semi-structured interview.

In this protocol, the interview candidates are RDI project coordinators. Initially, any coordinator could be invited, later we gave preference to people who had more than one project under their coordination. This is an exploratory study about the state of RE practice in AI/ML projects carried out at CEIA located at the Informatics Institute (INF) of the Federal University of Goiás (UFG).

This work was submitted to the Ethics Committee on 02/28/23 and approved under CAAE: *67531823.4.0000.5083*.

3.1.4. Data Collection

Coordinators of 21 AI systems projects were invited to answer the interview. More details about the interview setup are available at the survey link on Zenodo[2]. The research context and the application of the Free and Informed Consent Form (ICF) were explained during the interview. The questions organized in a script were asked based on the participant's answers. An interview was then carried out with authorized recording. The script was divided into 9 profile questions, 15 questions about the project, and 41 remaining about RE practice in these projects.

3.2. Data Analysis

Data analysis was carried out based on the Grounded Theory (GT) method [Glaser and Strauss 2017] that aims to generate theories rather than test or validate the existing theory. Widely used in qualitative data analysis and more recently widely used in software engineering research [Stol et al. 2016].

We follow the Straussian approach for GT [Glaser 1992]. In this approach, the research question is open and defined based on the literature. Literature is consulted throughout the process to understand concepts and information that may be useful throughout data analysis. The coding process is determined by the open, axial, and selective phases, which generate categories and relationships. Finally, the results are analyzed.

Open coding begins with detailed reading and searching for important information in documents. Subsequently, fragments are associated with quotations and codes are assigned that represent a certain phenomenon. For axial coding, the aim is to find categories that bring together several grouped and related codes. Finally, in selective coding, the central category is generated that represents the main finding of the research. This procedure is performed iteratively until theoretical saturation is reached [Corbin and Strauss 2014]. However, we did not reach theoretical saturation because we thought we would need more interviews and investments for different scenarios.

The interview process started in June 2023 and finished in December 2023. Some interviews needed to be divided into two parts due to participants' time availability. While conducting interviews, we realized transcribing and data coding. A follow-up interview was conducted with the coordinator after he had taken on more projects and gained more experience. For each interview record, we uploaded them to the *Reshape* tool, which automatically transcribes and edits texts with transcription problems. We downloaded the documents and uploaded them to the *Atlas.TI* tool.

[2]https://zenodo.org/records/10580470

For each document referring to an interview, we carried out coding. The document was read in its entirety, marking items that referred to a specific question in the answers. The idea was to identify similarities between the coordinators to group the coded items and establish what the RE practice was like in these projects, testing the hypotheses defined for this research. open, axial, and selective coding procedures were carried out by the first author. The second and third authors reviewed the codings weekly and discussed partial results.

The discussion helped to avoid inconsistencies, seeking completeness of responses by checking code nomenclature and relationships. For the 10 interviews, 838 citations were generated from which 249 codes and 39 groups of codes emerged, synthesized into 4 networks that address different aspects of the interviews, such as coordinator, project, practice requirements, and RE to AI.

4. Results

We conducted the interviews with ten coordinators and then transcribed them using the *Reshape* tool. A total of 555 minutes were written down. The interviews in the media lasted slightly less than 60 minutes.

4.1. Characterization

4.1.1. Project

Concerning the project, we distinguished teams with varying numbers of members. Teams of six to twenty-five people with varying degrees of training and expertise comprised the groups. The contributions made by the AI teams varied as well; on some teams, only 16% of the team worked on AI-related tasks, while on others, 100% of the team was directly involved with the AI solution. It is imperative to emphasize that teams exhibit volatility throughout a project, contingent upon the requirements of individual teams, project phases, and participant counts.

Technology Readiness Levels (TRL) represent a type of measurement system to determine the degree of maturity (from 1 to 9) of a specific technology [Dunbar 2017]. TRL levels for the projects consulted ranged from 3 to 7, with level 6 being the most typical. Technical coordinators, who oversaw smaller teams tasked with completing particular project tasks, assisted the coordinators under interview. Each project had one to three technical coordinators. About the agile approach used in research, most of the coordinators said they employed adapted Scrum and Kanban and a combination of agile approaches in their projects. No coordinator acknowledged using non-agile methods. While most of the project domains are in health, there is also AI research in business, industrial management, process improvement in organizations, law, and agribusiness.

Most of the projects use supervised and unsupervised learning approaches. We also find examples of reinforcement learning and semi-supervised learning. Prediction is the most common ML task in those projects. But, we also found other tasks such as recognition, diagnosis, regression, signal processing, robot navigation, prescription, and recommendation. There are not many participants in most projects who are requirements engineering experts. Most of the RE and SE experts are project coordinators or technical coordinators. Project information is in Table 1. In the task column, we represent acronyms

Coord.	Team	AI Team	TRL	Domain	Learning	Task	SE expert	RE expert
C1	17	25%	3	health	S	P	yes	no
C2	22	40%	6	health, industry	U and SS	P and D	yes	yes
C3	10	20%	6	business, HR	S	P	no	no
C4	20	80%	5	health, legal, energy	S, U and SS	P, D, RS and SA	no	no
C5	11	45%	7	health	S	IR	yes	yes
C6	18	80%	4	robotics	S	P, IR, RN	no	no
C7	10	30%	5	business	S and U	P, D, RS and SA	yes	yes
C8	13	60%	3	health	S and U	IR and RN	no	no
C9	12	50%	7	agribusiness and market	S, U and R	P and RS	no	no
C10	14	35%	7	industry	S	P	yes	yes

Tabela 1. Project characterization.

for prediction (P), diagnosis (D), recommendation (R), image recognition (IR), robot navigation (RN), and sentiment analysis (SA). Similarly, in the learning type column, with supervised (S), unsupervised (U), reinforcement (R), and semi-supervised (SS).

4.1.2. Coordinator

The majority of coordinators work on one or two projects. Half of the coordinators have prior experience working on AI projects in the industry with two to eighteen years of experience. Three coordinators reported experience of one to thirteen years of coordination in previous AI projects. Information regarding the profile of each coordinator can be seen in Table 2: the coordinator's identifier (ID), SE and RE knowledge, the number of current projects (CP), AI project development time (in years), industry experience in AI (in years), and SE experience, respectively.

ID	SE Knowledge	RE Knowledge	CP	AI Coord.	AI Industry	SE Exp.
C1	very understanding	understand	1	1	2	Since 2005
C2	very understanding	very understanding	2	1	-	Since 2005
C3	alguma experiência	understand	3	-	15	
C4	little understanding	middle understanding	5	13	18	
C5	very understanding	very understanding	2	1		Since 2018
C6	understand	middle understanding	1	13	14	Since 2009
C7	understand	understand	1	1	4	Since 2013
C8	little understanding	little understanding	2	10	2	Since 2010
C9	do not understand	little understanding	2	10	-	
C10	middle understanding	middle understanding	1	-	-	Since 2006

Tabela 2. Profile of the coordinators interviewed.

4.2. RE Practice

All coordinators carried out requirements elicitation, seven performed requirements analysis, five applied requirements validation techniques, and only one interviewed claimed he practiced some requirements management technique. Table 3 presents codification obtained with interviews regarding the RE practice in projects.

4.2.1. Elicitation

One coordinator said not to apply a specific method to elicitation, eight realized meetings, one made business analysis and another one realized documents analysis. Five coordinators realized brainstorming, two had done interviews and the other two realized prototyping. One realized observation and the other one realized paper analysis. Four coordinators consulted clients as stakeholders, two consulted users and one consulted expert domain. *Google Meet*, *Google Docs*, and *Figma* are examples of tools used to support requirements elicitation.

4.2.2. Analysis

In response to questions about the analysis, two coordinators said they had done requirements classification; one coordinator cited modeling, another coordinator said they had done prioritization, and a third coordinator said they had done grouping. According to the coordinator responsible for prioritization, he used *Google Meet* to hold a meeting with the client. Other coordinators emphasized the team's and the client's participation in the analysis stage. One coordinator had done use cases and the other one made use of flowcharts as analysis tools.

4.2.3. Specification

Regarding the specification, four coordinators reported using different approaches: one based on natural language, another on an approach based on ISO/IEC/IEEE 29148:2018, and two coordinators wrote requirements as user stories. One coordinator stated that he will use the ML Canvas, while another will apply team-generated reports.

About the attributes identified for requirements specification by the coordinators, we found the task description, author record, and identifier (ID). One coordinator claimed to be responsible for requirements specification. *Google Docs*, *Discord*, *Google Sheets*, *Clickcopy*, and *Gitscrum* were used for requirements specification. We realized that, even when requirements are not registered in an organized manner, the organization's project management tools already assist in doing so.

ID	Elicitation	Analysis	Specification	Validation	Management	Agile M.	NFR	Quality evaluation	Progress evaluation	Changing manag.	Lessons learned
C1	brainstorming, prototype and meet client	priorization, classification and modeling	user stories in docs & figma; ISO/IEC 29148 based	review, prototype	-	scrum	usability	usability and acceptance criteria	big commit	docs, gitscrum, weekly meet	yes
C2	documental analysis and meet client	priorization and classification	user stories in docs & Jira	review	-	scrum and kanban	usability	validation with client	work plan	weekly meet	no
C3	brainstorming, documental analysis and process analysis	-	in ML Canva, gitscrum	-	-	scrum	data exploration	proof of concept	weekly meet and big commit	-	no
C4	-	-	-	-	-	scrum and kanban	RGPD and data security	accuracy	weekly meet and big commit	weekly meet	no
C5	interview, meet client and brainstorming	fluxogram	-	prototype	-	scrum		-	-	weekly meet	no
C6	meet client, documental analysis	priorization	-	simulation, review	-	kanban	accuracy	accuracy	weekly meet	weekly meet	no
C7	meet client	use case	clickcopy	prototype	spreadsheets	scrum	model quality	satisfaction questionnaire	weekly meet	weekly meet	yes
C8	observation, brainstorming, paper and meet client	priorization	in spreadsheet and gitscrum	prototype	-	scrum	accuracy and image quality	accuracy	big cocmmit	-	yes
C9	brainstorming and meet clint	-	-	review, prototype	-	scrum	accuracy, scalability and sustainability	accuracy and response time	big commit	-	no
C10	interview, brainstorming and prototype	-	-	-	-	scrum	performance	paper metrics	big commit	weekly meet	yes

Tabela 3. RE Practice in the CEIA projects.

4.2.4. Validation

Regarding requirements validation, prototyping is the most mentioned method by five people. Only one coordinator uses simulation, and another uses peer review. Six coordinators affirm they consult the client to validate the requirements. *Google Docs* and *Discord* were mentioned as supporting tools for requirements validation.

4.2.5. Management

Only one coordinator interviewed performed the requirements management activity in his project. For this, he used the *Google Sheets* tool.

4.2.6. Other Questions

Six coordinators reported holding meetings regarding change management. Typically, the coordinator chooses whether or not to include the team in meetings that are with clients. Changes are tracked using the *Gitscrum* and *Google Docs* tools, where requirements are frequently documented.

Regarding the team's comprehension of the tasks that need to be completed and the project's anticipated outcomes, all the coordinators reported holding meetings with the team to align them. Three of them keep a weekly schedule for these meetings. Additionally, one coordinator reported that he validated the team's comprehension with *Gitscrum* tool.

All coordinators realized an evaluation of the project's advancement. Seven coordinators said they conducted the assessment based on macro deliveries, while three coordinators said they held weekly meetings to ensure that the progress was in line with the plan. Three coordinators gauge the project's progress by looking at the accuracy of their models, while two coordinators said they have a work plan and regularly review it to check if the project is not meeting expectations.

It was revealed by six of the coordinators that they failed to document the lessons they had learned from the project. Four coordinators, on the other hand, said they documented the lessons they had learned. The team was involved in this registration by two of these coordinators.

Concerning the evaluation of quality, these activities were found to be described by a few techniques, such as weekly meetings and macro deliveries with client participation. Only one coordinator cited other evaluations of quality activities which included response time, model evaluation, customer acceptance criteria, and satisfaction questionnaire. Two coordinators also said they did not conduct any quality assessments due to a lack of knowledge of software quality metrics.

The coordinators focused on two non-functional requirements: model accuracy and performance. Response time, data security, privacy, and usability were cited more than one time. Sustainability, model scalability, data exploration, ease of use, and data requirements appeared just one time.

Coord.	Better elicitation and spec.	Beter data req. and RNF	Difficulty in project	Reduce difficulties
C1	yes, extension process and methods	yes, estabilsh metrics	quality commit and discovery process to develop	process RE4ML
C2	yes, do not know how maybe extension process and methods and knowledge RE and patterns	not sure know acoording TRL	obtaining data and lack of experience	process RE4ML, specification forms
C3	no, adapted for RDI	no	team and infraestructure and RDI nature	document for communication
C4	yes, adapted for agile maybe extension process and other RE methods	yes aligning data to objective	team and infraestructure and obtaining data	RE agile and process RE4ML
C5	yes, other RE methods	yes, efficiency model and aligning data to objective	obtaining data	-
C6	yes, extension process	yes aligning data to objective	team and infraestructure and expectations clients	RE agile
C7	yes, use model cards	yes, model cards	financial and expectations clients and obtaining data	document for communication
C8	not sure know, adapted for agile	not sure know simplified method	time management and communication with team and RDI nature	process RE4ML
C9	yes, adapted for agile and extension of methods	yes, simplified method	obtaining data and expectations clients	document for communication and validation forms
C10	yes, knowledge RE and extension of methods	yes aligning data to objective	team, obtining data, expectations clients	document for communication

Tabela 4. RE aspects that can be improved in ML projects at CEIA.

4.3. RE for AI

We summarize responses from coordinators who face difficulties in projects that may be related to the lack of RE practice. About how to mitigate these difficulties. In Table 4, we present codification obtained with interviews about how RE practice can be better in AI projects.

4.3.1. Difficulties in ML Projects at CEIA

Seven coordinators responded that data gathering was the biggest challenge they encountered. Three coordinators cited the challenge of acquiring the infrastructure required for projects, and four coordinators characterized managing customer expectations as challenging. According to two coordinators, RDI projects have additional challenges, e.g., the coordinator's lack of experience with this kind of project, understanding of the development process, finances, team communication, process management, commit quality, and technical knowledge, etc.

As measures to lessen challenges that arise during project requirements documents, according to five coordinators, would facilitate communication. According to four coordinators, project management can be aided by implementing a RE process for machine learning. According to two coordinators, specifications can aid in project management and help in client negotiation to get additional time for task completion. According to one coordinator, innovative validation techniques can lessen project challenges.

4.3.2. RE Process

To gauge the coordinator's level of importance regarding the existence of a requirements engineering process for machine learning, we provided them with a Likert scale. Only one coordinator indicated that it was important, while eight coordinators said it was very important.

Concerning the lack of RE in AI, two coordinators believe this lack has to be in the ML domain. Others two coordinators believe that the challenges are due to the characteristics of RDI projects. All these four coordinators feel that the RE process needs to be adjusted to be more dynamic. Another coordinator stated that, in his opinion, cyclical reviews are necessary for the RE process in ML to comply with the data-based construction process. In response, three coordinators said they were unsure of how NFR can be adapted to the AI domain.

4.3.3. RE Improvements

We questioned coordinators about how they thought RE could be enhanced to handle NFR and accomplish AI domain-specific elicitation and specification.

According to five coordinators, better elicitation and specification for the AI domain can be achieved through the extension of diagrams, techniques, and tools. According to four coordinators, improving the requirements engineering process can lead to better specifications and elicitation as well as increased usability in real-world industrial settings. Six coordinators are unaware of the adaptability of requirements engineering. Two coordinators and additional RE methods for AI ought to be suggested. Two more think that better elicitation and specification for this domain can be achieved with increased requirements analyst knowledge. While some coordinators think requirements patterns can be helpful in this area, others think projects can use the model cards approach.

Four coordinators think linking data to the goal during the RE process will ensure better NFR handling. Two coordinators emphasized the challenges in defining metrics to improve NFR care. Additionally, two coordinators think implementing a simplified method in projects can ease specifying NFR. According to a coordinator, NFR ought to be addressed differently based on the TRL of the project. Three coordinators don't know how to specify NFR in AI projects. One coordinator thinks that assessing model efficiency can be a useful tool for identifying non-functional requirements for AI. Another coordinator thinks that the model cards approach can assist in managing NFR. Furthermore, according to one coordinator, requirements engineering cannot assist in obtaining improved NFR for artificial intelligence.

All these aspects synthesize the data obtained from interviews with machine learning project coordinators regarding requirements engineering practice. In the next section (see 5) we will present how this data validated our hypotheses and answered the research questions.

5. Discussion

We created a few hypotheses to accomplish the study's goal of characterizing the state of requirements engineering practice in an industrial setting involving RDI projects. Conventional requirements elicitation techniques, including brainstorming, prototypes, and meetings, are presented by the consulted unit. Customers, users, and domain experts are the stakeholders in this situation. There was no indication of any pertinent data scientist participation. Elicitation activities have been supported by the use of online meetings, project management software, and document creation tools.

Concerning the analysis stage, we observed that coordinators lack a systematic method for categorizing requirements. Typically, requirements are often modeled based on categorization and prioritization according to functionality and the project's main delivery. We were unable to locate a shared set of modeling methods and resources.

The coordinators declared documented the requirements for the practice of defining requirements. Usually, requirements include a date, an identifier, and an explanation of the activity. Requirements were recorded using spreadsheets, online document creation tools, and project management software. The project coordinator is the one in charge of registration. The coordinators stated struggled to decide which methods and resources would work best for documenting needs.

Numerous coordinators claimed to have performed some kind of validation. The interviewees stated that meetings, peer validation, and prototype use are the methods used for validations. There were no found processes, metrics, or tools to assist with the validation process. To validate partial deliveries, the customer is consulted.

Single coordinator is said to oversee and management requirements. Modifying the specification document's requirement is how this kind of management is done. As a result, not a single coordinator mentioned using a management procedure that addresses artifact traceability.

Agile development methods, mostly centered on Scrum, are used on all projects. The coordinators gave evidence that they had taken care of a few non-functional requirements aimed at the model, including usability, accuracy, and response time. We do point out that this is an uncommon and poorly established practice. We also found that coordinators meet with the team to make sure everyone is aware of the tasks and deliverables, and that requirement documentation typically acts as a record of what is done rather than directing the development process.

It has come to our attention that coordinators recognize the value of the requirements engineering process in the development of AI systems. Furthermore, they acknowledge that defining the process and artifacts can aid in development. The coordinators confirmed that traditional requirements engineering would not likely be successful in the unit if it were used, but they also stated that they did not know how this could be accomplished due to the nature of RDI projects and the feature of experimentation-based AI development.

Lastly, coordinators with more experience with requirements engineering and software engineering also showed a greater concern for requirements-related aspects of their projects. The application of these activities in projects is not supported by the involvement of SE or RE specialists unless this specialist is involved in requirements practices, which is not frequent in the projects consulted.

Regarding related work, we identified some similarities with the state of practice in our study. Such as the adoption of the agile scrum methodology, elicitation practices with brainstorming and interviews, and forms of documentation based on natural language. Another similarity is that there is the treatment of non-functional requirements, however it is poorly structured and the biggest concern is with the performance of the models. Concern with the RE process for the development of AI systems is also common in the works.

The null hypotheses of this study were all validated. From H01 to H05 we noticed that the unit does not present an appropriate method or process for practices in each of the requirements engineering phases. Each project adopts a practice and we realize that the analysis, validation and management phases are overcome in almost all projects. Traditional elicitation and specification approaches are typically applied, but without adequate registration or which makes traceability difficult. Regarding hypothesis H06, non-functional requirements are also neglected in projects, normally not addressing aspects of fairness, reliability and transparency that are so important for artificial intelligence systems. We realize that the absence of the requirements engineering professional on the team can impact specific or insufficient team decisions and execution of the requirements engineering process on projects or that affect the quality of the product [Chemuturi 2013, Hussain and Mkpojiogu 2016]. The same goes for when the coordinator has little knowledge about software engineering without adequate support from the requirements engineering professional to direct the requirements engineering process.

6. Threats to validity

Descriptive validity refers to the possibility an interviewer may not gather all pertinent information during the interview. We recorded the interviews in video and storage on a computer and Google Drive to mitigate this threat. We annotated the transcripts using the Reshape tool and we reviewed the transcripts. The interviews were conducted with a strict adherence to a precise and objective protocol. We aimed to entice project coordinators to engage in the research, which was non-obligatory and lacked benefits, but to evaluate the outcomes through the execution of the activities. It is posited that the semi-structured nature may potentially introduce biases in the research. Pilot testing of the questionnaires was conducted with the assistance of a project coordinator to anticipate and address potential issues in the interpretation of the questionnaires. There were no modifications made to the substance of the inquiries. Only the structuring was reformulated, and the issues began to be enumerated. The planning and execution of the evaluation were conducted following the planning presented by Wohlin in his book Experimentation for Software Engineering [Wohlin et al. 2012].

Concerning interpretation validity, i.e., the possibility of misunderstandings between interviewees and researchers, we mitigate this potential risk by communicating the study objective to the participants at the beginning of each interview. We explained the RE concepts to the participants. The interview guide was reviewed to improve its reliability. The concepts of researcher bias and theoretical validity pertain to the researcher's bias towards interpreting interviews in a manner that aligns with their objectives or initial theory. As this is our initial investigation in this particular domain, we do not possess a specific research methodology we wish to promote. We were very open to the outcomes of the interviews.

The term 'reactivity' refers to the possibility that interviewees may exhibit divergent behavior due to the interviewer's presence. It is not feasible to eliminate reactivity, however, we are cognizant of its potential impact on the observed phenomena. We attempt to mitigate this threat by highlighting the significance of the study and the potential for enhancements within the organization by identifying real needs.

Additionally, a threat to validity was the execution of the research in a single

Brazilian unit. We had limitations regarding the feasibility of carrying it out in other places, but we suggest that this research be replicated in other settings so that it can become more complete and broader.

7. Conclusions

To understand how the most complex activity in the development of ML-based AI systems has been developed in practice and what are the opportunities for improvement and research. We have conducted a qualitative interview study to understand the perception of and practices for RE in development projects of AI systems in the RDI scenario.

In general, coordinators believe that:

- requirements activities can be improved in projects,
- traditional RE and already known artifacts would hardly be successful in the unit,
- do not know how to apply RE practices to RDI projects involving AI,
- the treatment of NFR can be improved in projects,
- a requirements document can help in communicating projects
- the RE process adapted to ML development can improvement quality of deliveries and stakeholders satisfaction.

Based on the results of our research, we conclude that it is complementary to what already exists regarding the state of RE practice for ML. Although we do not address specific types of requirements or a specific category in the domain, we interviewed project coordinators with different knowledge and experiences. RE practices change but challenges remain similar.

We think that combining artifacts appropriate for the AI domain with a requirements engineering process can help mitigate challenges found during project development, resulting in higher-quality deliveries and the verification of these qualities. Additionally, it can act as a guide for team members who are unfamiliar with this kind of system's requirements practice.

The primary constraint on this research was its examination within a restricted context at the Embrapii facility. However, we think the findings apply to other organizations that similarly do RDI projects. Additional research is required to look into other RDI units and apply methods, techniques, and tools in these kinds of situations by combining agile approaches with ad hoc approaches and research proposals.

8. Acknowledgments

This study was financed in part by the Coordenação de Aperfeiçoamento de Pessoal de Nível Superior – Brasil (CAPES) – Finance Code 001.

Referências

Alves, A. P. S. et al. (2024). Status quo and problems of requirements engineering for machine learning: Results from an international survey. In Kadgien, R., Jedlitschka, A., Janes, A., Lenarduzzi, V., and Li, X., editors, *Product-Focused Software Process Improvement*, pages 159–174, Cham. Springer Nature Switzerland.

Chemuturi, M. (2013). *Requirements Engineering and Management for Software Development Projects*. Springer New York, 1st edition.

Corbin, J. and Strauss, A. (2014). *Basics of Qualitative Research: Techniques and Procedures for Developing Grounded Theory*. SAGE Publications, 4th edition.

Dunbar, B. (2017). National aeronautics and space administration (nasa). technology readiness level. https://esto.nasa.gov/trl/.

Glaser, B. G. (1992). *Basics of grounded theory analysis: Emergence vs forcing*. Sociology Pr.

Glaser, B. G. and Strauss, A. L. (2017). *The Discovery of Grounded Theory: Strategies for Qualitative Research*. Routledge.

Habibullah, K. M., Gay, G., and Horkoff, J. (2023). Non-functional requirements for machine learning: understanding current use and challenges among practitioners. *Requirements Engineering*, 28(2):283–316.

Hussain, A. and Mkpojiogu, E. O. C. (2016). Requirements: Towards an understanding on why software projects fail. *AIP Conference Proceedings*, 1761(1):020046.

Ishikawa, F. and Yoshioka, N. (2019). How do engineers perceive difficulties in engineering of machine-learning systems? - questionnaire survey. In *IEEE/ACM Joint International Workshop on Conducting Empirical Studies in Industry and International Workshop on Software Engineering Research and Industrial Practice*, pages 2–9.

Silva, G. R. S. and Canedo, E. D. (2022). Requirements engineering challenges and techniques in building chatbots. In *International Conference on Agents and Artificial Intelligence*.

Stol, K.-J., Ralph, P., and Fitzgerald, B. (2016). Grounded theory in software engineering research: A critical review and guidelines. In *2016 IEEE/ACM 38th International Conference on Software Engineering (ICSE)*, pages 120–131.

Villamizar, H., Escovedo, T., and Kalinowski, M. (2021). Requirements engineering for machine learning: A systematic mapping study. In *2021 47th Euromicro Conference on Software Engineering and Advanced Applications (SEAA)*, pages 29–36.

Vogelsang, A. and Borg, M. (2019). Requirements engineering for machine learning: Perspectives from data scientists. *2019 IEEE 27th International Requirements Engineering Conference Workshops (REW)*, pages 245–251.

Wohlin, C., , et al. (2012). *Experimentation in Software Engineering*. Springer Berlin Heidelberg.

The Project Management Ontology called ProjectCO: Architectural Aspects, Concepts, and Usefulness

Luis Olsina, Pablo Becker, and María Fernanda Papa

GIDIS_Web, Facultad de Ingeniería, UNLPam, General Pico, LP, Argentina

{olsinal, beckerp, pmfer}@ing.unlpam.edu.ar

Abstract. *This paper presents the concepts, relationships, constraints, and verification issues of the project management ontology called ProjectCO. Its concepts represent key concerns of the conceived world for project management, embracing particular things (or entities) and their relations, as well as assertions that deal with them. ProjectCO is placed at the core level in the context of a five-tier ontological architecture, which considers foundational, core, top-domain, low-domain, and instance layers. A given ontology is located in this architecture according to the level of generality/specificity of its concepts, which in turn depend on the established development goal and scope. Therefore, since we aim for ProjectCO concepts to be cross-cutting, domain-independent concerns of any specific discipline, its scope is limited to core terms that need to be reused and specialized at lower domain levels. Note that many definitions and labels of ProjectCO terms were adopted or adapted from four well-known standard glossaries, as well as from a previous project management ontology. To showcase its usefulness, this work discusses enriched and harmonized concepts for a top-domain ontology for measurement and evaluation projects.*

1. Introduction

The ISO 704 (2022) standard establishes that the vocabulary or terminology of an area or field of science is not an arbitrary collection of concepts. The relevant concepts – designated by terms– constitute a coherent concept system based on the relations existing between them. Concept systems can be represented and formalized from lower to higher structural richness, from glossaries and taxonomies to ontologies. While a glossary includes terms that designate concepts and their definitions –and occasionally synonyms, acronyms, references, and additional notes–, an ontology is a concept system with a richer structure than a glossary since it represents not only defined terms for concepts in a given subject field or subfield but also taxonomic and non-taxonomic relationships and constraints. Glossaries are well-known knowledge/information resources used in academia and industry to support the human consultation, understanding, and learning of frequently used concepts in a given field. Ontologies also support human understanding and learning in addition to other benefits such as structuring and representing knowledge in a more reusable, extensible, and interoperable way, supporting tools with semantic processing capabilities, and semantic annotation of information resources, among other features.

For example, for the project area, several different initiatives have developed glossaries and ontologies for project management. On one hand, just to mention a couple of glossaries, most professionals in this field are familiar to some extent with glossaries such as PMBOK (2021), which stands for Project Management Body of Knowledge, and APM (2021), which stands for Association for Project Management. According to Becker et al. (2023), the former has 350 primary terms while the latter has 753. This large number of terms can hinder the human understanding and learning process, mainly if the terms designate concepts at different levels of generality/specificity, e.g., at the core and domain levels. Furthermore, in a comparative analysis of four project management glossaries, these authors showed problems of syntactic and semantic consistency, as well as problems of semantic correctness, since, for instance, their definitions are rarely linked explicitly and correctly through the use of hypernym-hyponym relations, when necessary. On the other hand, just to mention a couple of ontologies, Rivera et al. (2016) built the first version of a project management ontology, which adopted and adapted some labels and/or definitions of terms from PMBOK (2013). This ontology was reduced in the number of included terms and therefore in its scope. Also, it does not represent the generality/specificity of terms considering domain and core levels in the framework of a multitier architecture. More recently, Bastos et al. (2018) developed SPMO, the Software Project Management Ontology, with the aim of establishing a common conceptualization of the software project management field, initially focusing on software project planning and monitoring. SPMO does consider core and domain terms, but its scope is limited to the software field and project planning and monitoring concepts in terms of scope, time, and cost. As the authors recognize, concepts related to techniques or methods, among others, applied to project management are left out of the conceptualization of the SPMO.

The main contribution of this work is the discussion of ProjectCO, which is a Project management Core Ontology built considering updated standard glossaries and an ontology in this area. D'Aquin and Gangemi (2011) establish a set of principles or characteristics that must be taken into account when building 'beautiful ontologies'. They claim that international terminological standards for a given domain should be considered as sources when building an ontology. Another principle is that the designed ontology elements should be grounded in a foundational ontology. Additionally, the designed ontology should be modular, extensible, and reuse already developed related ontologies, as suggested by the characteristic of beautiful ontologies of being modular or integrated into a modular framework or architecture.

Regarding the first principle, ProjectCO is based on definitions and labels of glossary terms coming from PMBOK, APM, IAPM (2021), which stands for International Association of Project Managers, and PRINCE2 (2017), which stands for PRojects IN Controlled Environments. To do this, ProjectCO takes into account the comparative analysis carried out by Becker et al. (2023), which recommends a set of lists of common terms to be adopted or adapted from these four glossaries that evidenced higher to lower levels of syntactic/semantic consistency. In addition, ProjectCO also considers some ontology terms and definitions made by Rivera et al. (2016).

Regarding the second principle, ProjectCO is based on the foundational ontology called ThingFO (Olsina, 2023), which represents the world with three generic concepts such as the particular thing (and instances), universal thing (or categories of things), and human assertions that deal with these two concepts and their relationships. Having ontologies for different application domains that inherit the same core and foundational basis allows terms and relationships with similar semantics to have a common background or conceptual foundation. Lastly, ProjectCO, which is conceived as an ontological component at the core level that has domain-independent concepts and relationships for project management, reuses terms and relationships from developed ontologies at the same level such as ProcessCO (Becker et al., 2022) and can be extended at domain levels for different types of project management regarding development, evaluation, and testing, among others. All these ontologies are placed in the framework of an ontological architecture called FCD-OntoArch (Olsina, 2023), which stands for Foundational, Core, Domain, and instance Ontological Architecture.

As a result, the ProjectCO conceptualization includes 45 core terms –each semantically enriched with terms reused from other core ontologies, or with terms extended from ThingFO–, 10 properties, 20 taxonomic relationships, 33 defined non-taxonomic relationships, as well as constraints. Finally, as functional requirements, we defined 27 competency questions to be answered by ProjectCO. The ontology development approach followed was Methontology (Fernández-López et al., 1997).

The remaining sections are organized as follows: Section 2 provides an overview of FCD-OntoArch, in which ProjectCO and other ontologies are placed. Section 3 discusses the goal, scope, and additional requirements of the proposed project management core ontology and its conceptualization. Section 4 illustrates the usefulness of ProjectCO for enriching concepts and relationships of a domain ontology. Section 5 analyzes related work and Section 6 outlines the conclusions and future work.

2. Location of ProjectCO in a Multi-level Ontological Architecture

One motivation for this research lies in the updating of a previously developed project management ontology (Rivera et al., 2016) since it was limited in the number of represented concepts –and therefore in its scope– and there was no clear separation of concerns considering the domain and core levels when placing generic/specific project management terms into modules in the context of a multi-level architecture. Hence, keeping this goal in mind, the new ProjectCO module or component is placed at the core level in the context of FCD-OntoArch as shown in Fig. 1. It should be noted that this ontological architecture was conceived in 2019 after the development of the first version of the project management ontology which was in 2016. More details about guidelines and rules of this ontological architecture can be found in Olsina (2023).

To provide an identification of the ontological components in FCD-OntoArch, ontologies that belong to a certain level of generality/specificity have a designation associated with their location within it. For example, an ontology at the foundational level is called Foundational Ontology (FO for short); ontologies at the core level are called Core Ontologies (CO); ontologies at the top-domain level are called Top-Domain Ontologies (TDO), and so forth. On the left side of Fig. 1, the five levels of generality/specificity are depicted. It also shows the domain-independent and domain-dependent layers. The components located on the right side of the figure correspond to the ontologies already built in the architecture and harmonized with ThingFO.

At the foundational level, ThingFO is the only necessary ontology, which has the three generic concepts mentioned in the Introduction Section. It represents the world through particular Things, universal Things, and Assertions. These are the unique concepts (plus their related terms) that specialize in the lower components.

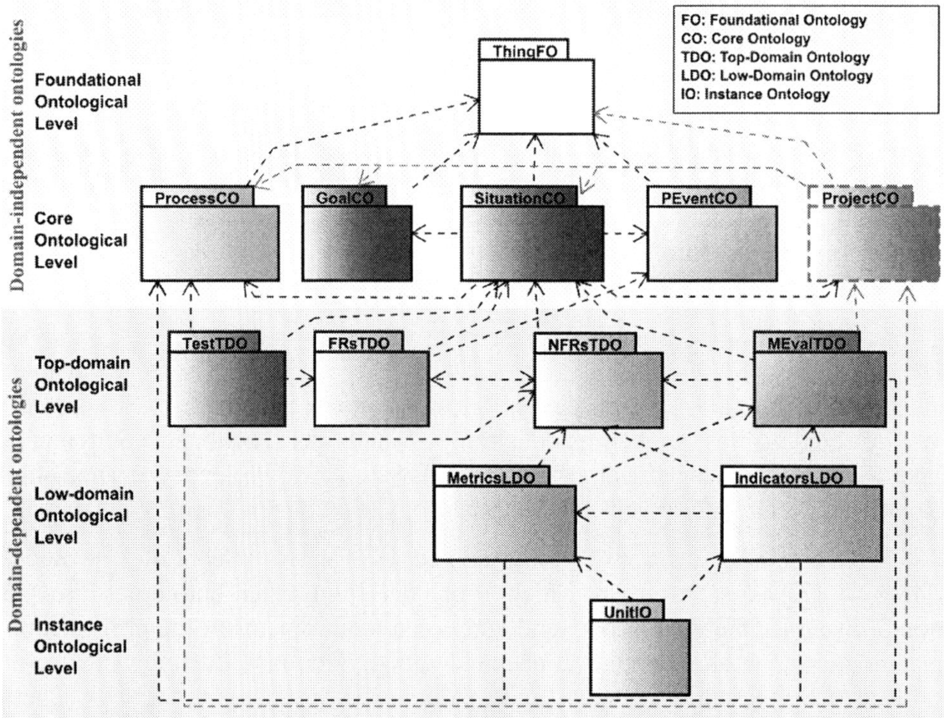

Figure 1. Allocating the new ProjectCO component in the context of the ontological architecture called FCD-OntoArch

At lower levels of the above architecture, the ontologies already updated are: i) at the core level: ProcessCO, GoalCO, SituationCO, and PEventCO (Particular Event); ii) at the top-domain level: TestTDO, FRsTDO (Functional Requirements), NFRsTDO (Non-Functional Requirements), and MEvalTDO (Measurement and Evaluation); and iii) at the low-domain level: MetricsLDO and IndicatorsLDO. Note also that Fig. 1 depicts components shaded in grey that will not be mentioned later in this paper.

As said, the former project management ontology should be updated and harmonized in light of other abovementioned foundational and core ontologies, resulting in ProjectCO. Fig. 1 shows with red dashed lines not only the location of the ProjectCO component to be updated but also the dependency relationships with other ontological components. Therefore, some ProjectCO terms should be semantically enriched with ThingFO terms and others should reuse the semantics of ProcessCO, GoalCO, and SituationCO terms. In turn, ontologies at the top-domain domain level, such as MEvalTDO and TestTDO (Tebes et al., 2021) specialize, for example, the term "Project", which is now a core term. Thus, in MEvalTDO the specialized term is "Evaluation Project" and in TestTDO it is "Test Project", which are specific to the measurement/evaluation and testing domains respectively.

Consequently, since the ProjectCO component is now finalized, the MEvalTDO and TestTDO ontologies must be revised to realign and harmonize them with the new or updated core terms of ProjectCO. In Section 4, we will discuss the usefulness of ProjectCO to semantically enrich and harmonize some terms and relationships from the previously developed MEvalTDO ontology.

3. Discussion of ProjectCO Scope, Concepts, and Relationships

As commented in the Introduction Section, the ProjectCO module includes 45 core terms –each semantically enriched with generic terms reused from other core ontologies, or with terms specialized from ThingFO. Therefore, at first glance, it is a more complete ontology than the previous project management ontology (Rivera et al., 2016) which included only 16 terms mixing top domain and core terms in the same component. Next, in subsection 3.1, we discuss the goal of ProjectCO, as well as its scope or functional requirements, defining a collection of 27 categorized competency questions (CQs). Then, in subsection 3.2, we depict the resulting ProjectCO conceptualization and analyze a set of concepts and relationships that will be used in Section 4. Finally, in subsection 3.3, we show an excerpt from the ProjectCO terms, relations, and properties verification matrix considering CQs.

3.1. Definition of Competency Questions

ProjectCO's development goal statement can be briefly formulated as "Build a project management ontology at the core level –primarily considering terms from recognized and up-to-date project management glossaries– where its domain-independent concepts can be specialized into domain levels for different disciplines and, as benefits, can be used as a reference vocabulary for understanding, learning, and communication for stakeholders in both academia and industry, as well as providing semantic processing capabilities". It should be noted that ProjectCO concepts can be specialized by different disciplines, not only for the field of software engineering but also for civil, mechanical, and biomedical engineering, among many others.

Before building ProjectCO, we conducted an exploratory study to perform a comparative analysis of the syntactic and semantic consistency of terms from four selected project management glossaries and then to provide recommendations for core terms. We did so by considering glossary terms that belong to categories related to the organizational entity, intentionality/goal, situation/event, work process, work product, and project resources such as strategy/approach, method/technique, and agent/role. These terminological-semantic categories turned out useful for identifying conceptual blocks or patterns and specifying the scope of the new project management ontology at the core level in the context of FCD-OntoArch, which was described in Section 2.

As a result, 5 CQs belong to the Organizational Entity category, 2 to the Project Goal, 3 to the Project Situation, 6 to the Project Work Process, 3 to the Project Work Product, and 8 CQs are included in the Project Resource category. For example, below, CQ2 is included in the Organizational Entity category, CQ9 is a CQ related to the Project Situation category, CQ13 is a CQ related to the Project Work Process, and CQ20 belongs to the Project Resource category.

- **CQ2**. What are the entities through which an organization organizes work and resources together?
- **CQ9**. Are a project's situation, objectives, and requirements related in any way?
- **CQ13**. What are the processes that are integrated into a project process?
- **CQ20**. What are the types of resources that a project has?

The reader can find the rest of the categorized CQs in Appendix B of the document at https://bit.ly/ProjectCO_Appendices.

As a final observation, Monfardini et al. (2023) reported on a survey that provides data on how CQs have been used in ontology engineering. This study shows that CQs have been considered useful and have mainly helped to define the scope of a given ontology and verify its conceptualization. We fully adhere to these perceptions of usefulness, both to help define the scope and to verify and validate the conceptualization.

3.2. ProjectCO's Conceptualization

As noted in the Introduction Section, the four project management glossaries selected and analyzed are PMBOK, APM, IAPM, and PRINCE2, which were the main glossary sources for recommending the core terms to be included in ProjectCO. For example, the term Project is a common term in all four glossaries, i.e., it has a frequency of occurrence of 4. This term label was then recommended and adopted, as well as the terminological-semantic category of Organizational Entity, which was common in the definitions of the four terms. At the same time, this term was also available in Rivera et al. (2016), so we adapted its definition as shown in Table 1, which is somewhat similar to the definitions given in all glossaries, now explicitly having the type of particular thing or entity. However, the term Program was not available in this cited ontology, while it has an occurrence frequency of 4 in the glossaries, so we adapted its definition from the PMBOK. The same goes for the term Project Management Office.

Fig. 2 depicts the resulting conceptualization of ProjectCO specified in UML. It shows 45 core terms, which are semantically enriched with stereotyped terms reused from other core ontologies, or with extended terms from ThingFO, among other elements. It is worth mentioning that the ontologies of this work use the stereotype as a mechanism to reuse, enrich, and align terms semantically. What does it mean that the concepts of an ontology at one level can be semantically enriched by other higher-level ontology concepts? It means that a given concept (usually designated by one or more terms) of an ontology at a certain level (e.g., core or top-domain) can inherit the semantics of the corresponding more general concept and then specialize it. The same procedure can be used to enrich a term from terms of other components at the same level. For example, in Fig. 2 we observe that the term Plan has the semantics of Artifact, which is a term defined in ProcessCO. In turn, the term Artifact inherits the semantics of the term Thing. In Becker et al. (2022), authors argued that stereotypes can reduce model complexity, also promoting understandability and communicability.

For the sake of brevity, looking at Fig. 2, we can see that an Organization establishes a Project Goal and arranges work by means of a Project. In turn, a Project operationalizes a Project Goal, which is derived in Project Requirements and implies a Project Situation.

The term (concept of) Project mandatorily has a Project Process and Project Resources. In turn, the Project Process necessarily has two work processes that are labeled Project Management Process and Engineering Process. These three terms for processes are enriched with the stereotype <<Work Process>>, which is a term defined in ProcessCO. Also, the Project Management Process produces a Project Management Plan, which is a Plan that has the semantics of <<Artifact>>. In ProcessCO, the term Artifact is a kind of Work Product and, in turn, the term Work Product has the semantics of a particular Thing, which is one of the three concepts included in ThingFO.

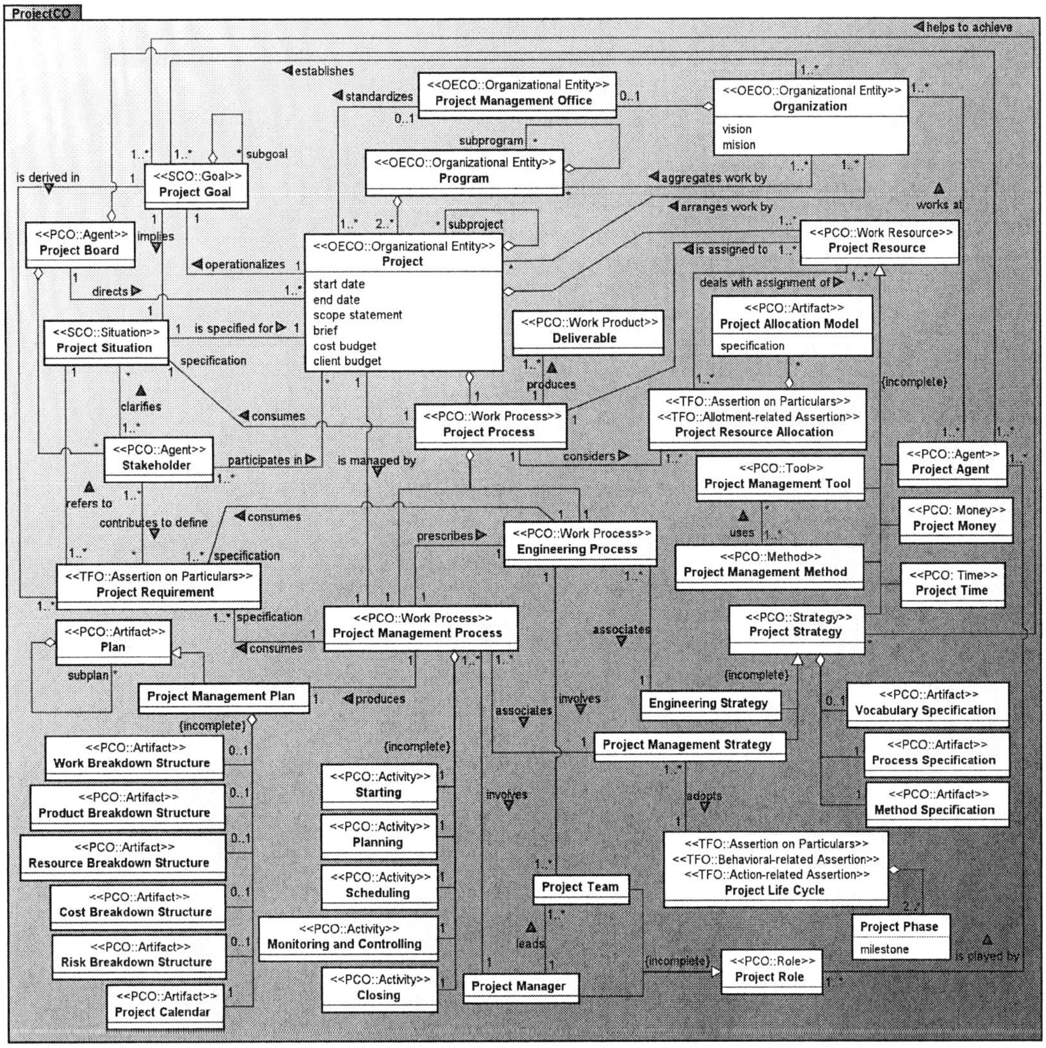

Figure 2. Project management ontology, which is located at the core level of FCD-OntoArch in Figure 1. Note that TFO stands for Thing Foundational Ontology, PCO for Process Core Ontology, SCO for Situation Core Ontology, and OECO for Organizational Entity Core Ontology (yet to be developed)

Table 1. Excerpt from ProjectCO v2.0's particular concepts

Term	Definition
Deliverable	It is a Work Product that can add other Work Products, which is produced by the Project Process and delivered as agreed to an internal or external involved Agent. Note 1: The internal and external involved Agents are Stakeholders and Project Agents. Note 2: A Deliverable can be an Artifact, a Service, or an Outcome. The term Work Product and its subtypes viz Artifact, Service, and Outcome are defined in ProcessCO.
Engineering Process	It is a Work Process including a set of technical Activities intended to produce the agreed Work Products to be delivered to certain Stakeholders.
Engineering Strategy	It is a Project Strategy that helps to achieve the engineering (technical) purpose of a Project Goal.
Organization	It is an Organizational Entity, generally under a defined legal form, comprising people and other resources that is structured and managed to establish and pursue

	organizational Goals and is affected by and affects its environment or context.
Organizational Entity	It is a Thing comprising Work Processes and human and non-human resources that are structured and managed to establish and pursue primary or subsidiary organizational Goals and purposes and is affected by and affects its environment or context.
Process Specification	It is an Artifact that represents a model which relates a set of process elements such as Activities, tasks, inputs and outputs, pre- and post-conditions, Artifacts, and Roles, amongst others. Note: A Process Specification can consider different process perspectives such as functional, behavioral, informational, and organizational.
Program	It is an Organizational Entity representing a strategic goal-oriented, temporary endeavor made up of related Projects, subsidiary programs, and program activities and resources that are managed in a coordinated manner to obtain benefits not available from managing them individually.
Project	It is an Organizational Entity representing a goal-oriented, temporary endeavor with defined *start* and *end dates*, which considers a managed set of interrelated Activities, tasks, and Project Resources aimed at producing, modifying, and delivering unique Work Products (i.e., Artifacts, Services, or Outcomes) to meet the needs of certain Stakeholders.
Project Goal (synonym: **Project Objective)**	It is a Goal that the Organization intends to achieve through a specific Project. Note: In SituationCO, the term Goal says, "It is an Intention-related Assertion, that is, the statement of the aim to be achieved by the Organization which considers the propositional content of a Goal's purpose in a given Situation and time frame".
Project Management Process	It is a Work Process including a set of managerial Activities intended to achieve the Project Goal operationalized by a Project. Note: The Project Management Process is usually composed of five interrelated Activities, namely: Starting (Initiating), Planning, Scheduling, Monitoring and Controlling, and Closing.
Project Process	It is a Work Process representing the entire process that is composed of two interrelated sub-processes, namely, the Project Management Process and the Engineering Process, which leads to the delivery of the project Work Products considering the Project Situation, Project Requirements, and Project Resources.
Project Requirement	It is an Assertion on Particulars that states managerial, engineering (technical), and contextual aspects of the Project and its Work Products to be delivered considering the needs of certain Stakeholders. Note: See the definition of the term Assertion on Particulars in ThingFO.
Project Situation	It is a Situation that the Stakeholders and ultimately the Project Board define for the Project. Note: In SituationCO, the term Situation says, "It is a Situation-related Assertion that explicitly states and specifies the combination of circumstances, episodes and relationships/events embracing particular entities and their surroundings, [...], which is of interest and relevant to be represented by a Human Agent/Organization with an established Goal".
Project Strategy (synonym: **Project Approach)**	It is a Strategy as a Project Resource that includes principles and integrated properties such as a Vocabulary Specification, a Process Specification, and a Method Specification to help achieve the purpose of a Project Goal.
Stakeholder	It is an Agent, such as individuals or groups, that has an interest and participation in the Project or is impacted by it. Note: A Project Agent as an internal interested party may be a Stakeholder but not necessarily.

Lastly, the term Project Situation (see definition in Table 1) is not available in the four glossaries or in Rivera et al. (2016). The stereotyped term Situation is borrowed from SituationCO and has the semantics of <<Assertion>>, which is another concept included in ThingFO. Instead, Project Life Cycle –defined as "*It is an Assertion on Particulars, specifically, a Behavioral- and Action-related Assertion that defines the series of phases that a Project passes through from its inception to its closure*"– is a semantically enriched term directly from ThingFO, as represented in Fig. 2. The reader can find the rest of the definitions for terms, properties, and non-taxonomic relationships in Appendix A at https://bit.ly/ProjectCO_Appendices.

As a final observation, we would like to point out again that the 45 ProjectCO terms are cross-cutting concerns and independent of the domain of any specific discipline. For this reason, the scope of ProjectCO is limited to core terms that must be reused and specialized at lower domain levels by any discipline, not only for the software engineering domain but also for fields such as civil, electrical, and biomedical engineering, among others. In contrast, SPMO (Bastos et al., 2018) is mainly intended for the software engineering field.

3.3. Verification Matrix for the ProjectCO's Conceptualization

Verification and Validation (V&V) are two key approaches to the artifact construction process. V&V entails activities, methods, tools, and ultimately strategies for ensuring quality when developing artifacts. An ontology as an artifact can be conceptualized and/or implemented. Tebes et al. (2021) have applied five V&V methods for the TestTDO conceptualization and implementation.

In the present paper, due to the current state of ProjectCO development, we only show the static verification of its conceptualization against the CQs, which represent the scope-related requirements, as commented in subsection 3.1. The goal purpose is to verify that all CQs were addressed by some of the terms, properties, and relationships. In this direction, we generated a verification matrix as shown in Table 2 using a specification-based (black-box) method. To design the verification matrix, we used as a test basis the 27 CQs and the elements that any ontology has such as terms, relationships, and/or properties. Thus, this matrix is a checklist that contains one row per CQ, in which we record what elements of the conceptualization help answer the CQ. After iterations, at the end of the ProjectCO conceptualization process, we ensured that each CQ passed.

Note that Table 2 represents an excerpt from the ProjectCO verification matrix. The entire verification matrix with all checked CQs can be accessed in Appendix C at https://bit.ly/ProjectCO_Appendices.

Just to highlight a few aspects, in the right column of Table 2, we see taxonomic and non-taxonomic relationships with underlined text. For example, for CQ2, the association between the terms Organization and Program is defined in Appendix A as "*An Organization aggregates work by means of none or more Programs*". Note that the UML cardinalities in Fig. 2 act as constraints, as well as the `{incomplete}` label for the subtypes of the term Project Resource. Even if we represent commonly used terms for project resources (see answers for CQ20), we could include, for example, the term Project Knowledge Base as a subtype.

Additionally, in the glossaries analyzed the term Project Objective is used more frequently than Project Goal. But the latter is the term adopted in our previously developed ontologies, which is why we indicate in CQ9 that Project Objective is synonymous with Project Goal. Besides, we use the non-taxonomic relationship has the semantics of to express the dependency between a given term and the term which enrich it, as is seen in the CQ13. Finally, we show the two well-known taxonomic relationships such as is part of and is a, for example, in CQ20.

Table 2. Excerpt from the ProjectCO verification matrix

Competency Question	Verification of Terms, relationships, and *properties*
CQ2. What are the entities through which an organization organizes work and resources together?	An Organization arranges work by Projects
	An Organization aggregates work by Programs
CQ9. Are a project's situation, objectives, and requirements related in any way?	Project Objective is a synonym of Project Goal
	A Project Goal implies a Project Situation
	A Project Goal is derived in Project Requirements
	A Project Requirement refers to a Project Situation
CQ13. What are the processes that are integrated into a project process?	A Project Management Process is a type of (has the semantics of) Work Process
	A Project Management Process is part of a Project Process
	An Engineering Process is a type of (has the semantics of) Work Process
	An Engineering Process is part of a Project Process
CQ20. What are the types of resources that a project has?	A Project Resource is part of a Project
	A Project Agent is a Project Resource
	Money is a Project Resource
	Time is a Project Resource
	A Project Management Tool is a Project Resource
	A Project Management Method is a Project Resource
	A Project Strategy is a Project Resource

4. ProjectCO's Usefulness

In the sequel, we highlight how some MEvalTDO terms are aligned and harmonized with the new ProjectCO ontology. It is important to note that this article will not discuss the content of the MEvalTDO ontology, but rather the resulting enrichment and reuse of terms, properties, and relationships. Fig. 3 shows a fragment of the updated MEvalTDO ontology with some elements semantically enriched or reused from ProjectCO. The complete updated conceptualization can be found at http://bit.ly/updatedMEvalTDO.

MEvalTDO is a top-domain ontology that addresses measurement and evaluation (ME) activities and methods in general, while MetricsLDO and IndicatorsLDO are ontologies at the low-domain level (see Fig. 1), which address, in particular, measurement and evaluation activities and methods based on metrics and indicators, respectively. Note that MEvalTDO can also be specialized by other low-domain ontologies such as QuestionsLDO, i.e., a Questionnaire-based Measurement Low-Domain Ontology to be developed. It is important to say that since MEvalTDO is for ME activities and methods, only the minimum and necessary ProjectCO terms have been considered. Thus, for example, terms related to the activities involved in the evaluation project management process are not explicitly included in this updated version of MEvalTDO.

In the previous version of MEvalTDO (which can be found at http://bit.ly/MEvalTDO) there was the term called Evaluation with the stereotype <<Work Process>> (from ProcessCO) to designate the concept of the evaluation process and the term called Evaluation Management with the stereotype <<Project Management>> (from the Rivera et al. (2016) ontology) to designate the evaluation project management process. However, the term Project Management in the old version of the project ontology was not enriched with any stereotypes. Thanks to the new ProjectCO, in the updated MEvalTDO the term Evaluation is now renamed Evaluation

Process (see Fig. 3) and is stereotyped as <<Engineering Process>> (from ProjectCO, which in Fig. 2 is enriched with <<Work Process>> from ProcessCO). Also, the old term Evaluation Management is now renamed as Evaluation Project Management Process and stereotyped as <<Project Management Process>> (also enriched with <<Work Process>> in Fig. 2). Consequently, it is now clearer that an Evaluation Project has an Evaluation Project Process composed of engineering and management processes.

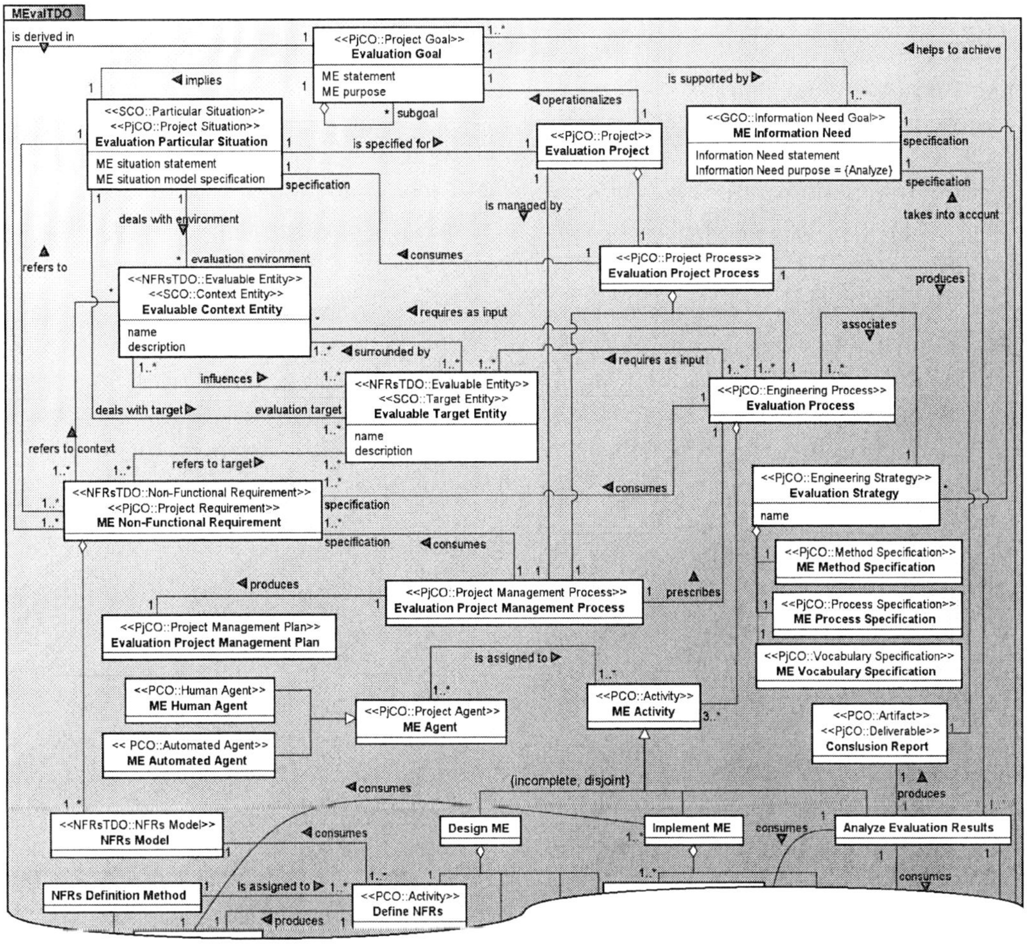

Figure 3. Excerpt from the conceptualization of the Measurement and Evaluation Top-Domain Ontology (MEvalTDO), which is aligned and harmonized with the new ProjectCO. Note that ME stands for Measurement and Evaluation, PjCO for Project management Core Ontology, PCO for Process Core Ontology, SCO for Situation Core Ontology, GCO for Goal Core Ontology, and NFRsTDO stands for Non-Functional Requirements Top-Domain Ontology

Furthermore, in ProjectCO, an Engineering Process associates an Engineering Strategy that helps to achieve a Project Goal. MEvalTDO is now aligned with this conceptual pattern since an Evaluation Process associates an Evaluation Strategy (stereotyped <<Engineering Strategy>>) that helps to achieve an Evaluation Goal (stereotyped <<Project Goal>>). The concept of Evaluation Strategy in the previous MEvalTDO was enriched with the concept of Strategy (from the Rivera et al. (2016) ontology) and was defined as "*It is a work resource that encompasses principles and integrated capabilities such as domain conceptual bases, the specification of ME process perspectives, and methods for helping to achieve an Evaluation Project's goal purpose*". As the reader can surmise, the stereotype and this definition do not allow us to distinguish whether an Evaluation Strategy is an Engineering Strategy or a Project Management Strategy.

Fig. 3 shows that an Evaluation Strategy has an ME Method Specification, an ME Process Specification, and an ME Vocabulary Specification (which are new terms in MEvalTDO and specialized from ProjectCO). An example of ME process specification for the evaluation strategy called GOCAME (*Goal-Oriented Context-Aware Measurement and Evaluation*) (Olsina and Becker, 2017) is shown in Fig. 4. This process specification takes advantage of the MEvalTDO terminology represented by the ME Vocabulary Specification domain concept. Thus, the activity names in Fig. 4 are taken from terms of the updated MEvalTDO. Note that the specification in Fig. 4 shows only the process behavioral perspective, but other process perspectives are possible.

Besides, in the fragment shown in Fig. 3, Analyze Evaluation Results produces a Conclusion Report, which is stereotyped as <<Artifact>> (a type of Work Product in ProcessCO) and <<Deliverable>> (from ProjectCO). Originally, the term Conclusion Report was defined as "*It is an Artifact that documents the analysis of all Measurement and Evaluation Values*", but thanks to the double enrichment it is now defined as "*It is an Artifact that documents the analysis of all Measurement and Evaluation Values and is delivered as agreed to an internal or external involved Agent*". Hence, this new Conclusion Report definition considers the idea of Deliverable (see this term definition in Table 1).

Previously, in MEvalTDO there was no direct relationship between the terms Evaluation Process (originally called Evaluation) and ME Non-Functional Requirement. But thanks to the new ProjectCO, there is now a relationship named consumes between both concepts since an Evaluation Process consumes the ME Non-Functional Requirements specification. Note that this conceptual pattern is modeled in ProjectCO by the more general Engineering Process and Project Requirement concepts. Finally, some properties are specialized considering ProjectCO. For example, the 'statement' and 'purpose' properties of the Evaluation Goal term have been renamed to 'ME statement' and 'ME purpose' to be more specific.

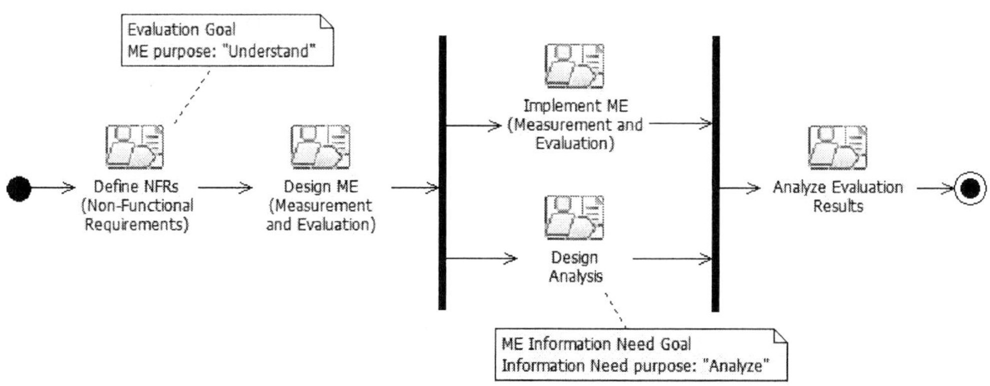

Figure 4. Measurement and Evaluation (ME) Process Specification for the Evaluation Strategy named GOCAME: A behavioral perspective

5. Related Work

In this Section, we discuss related work that simultaneously considers the three principles stated in the Introduction Section. They should be taken into account when building an ontology and are: i) the use of international terminological standards such as glossaries; ii) the use of the elements of a foundational ontology to specialize and align the newly developed elements; and iii) the designed ontology must be modular, extensible, and integrated into a multi-level ontological architecture or network.

Recently, Iatrellis et al. (2021) conducted a systematic literature review on software project management ontologies. Most of the reported ontologies do not satisfy the above three principles simultaneously. For example, we can mention the project management ontology called PMO (Ruiz Bertol and Dolado, 2008) and the one proposed by Aramo-Immonen (2009) that are based on previous versions of the PMBOK glossary. Moreover, the latter ontology, for its development, was also based on the knowledge of other standard terminologies. However, both do not satisfy the criterion of being aligned with the elements of a foundational ontology. It is important to note that PMO represents core terms (in the PM-Core component) that are expanded with the components called PM-Process, PM-Organization, PM-Cost, and PM-Planning.

The ontology that does meet the three principles is SPMO (Bastos et al., 2018). Regarding the principle i), the authors nourish SPMO from PMBOK (2013). Regarding principle ii), the authors align SPMO with the Unified Foundational Ontology (Guizzardi, 2005), which is made up of three foundational ontologies, namely: UFO-A (endurants), UFO-B (perdurants or events), and UFO-C (social entities, built on top of UFO-A and B). And taking into account principle iii), SPMO is in the context of an ontological architecture called SEON (Ruy et al. 2016), which locates ontologies organized in layers of generality/specificity.

Ultimately, ProjectCO also satisfies the three principles. Unlike SPMO, ProjectCO has a broader scope and nourishes most of its core concepts by making a comparative analysis of the syntactic and semantic consistency and recommending terms from the four project management glossaries mentioned in subsection 3.2. In addition, FCD-OntoArch includes only a foundational ontology instead of the three of UFO. ThingFO has only three foundational concepts, which facilitate specialization in lower-level ontologies. Finally, the project management ontology of Rivera et al. (2016) does not meet the three principles, as emphasized at the beginning of this paper.

6. Conclusions and Future Work

This paper has primarily discussed the goal, scope, and conceptualization of ProjectCO, which is a domain-independent ontology for project management concepts placed at the core level in the context of a five-tier ontological architecture. This architecture promotes a clear separation of concerns by considering ontological levels that allow for proper mapping of conceptual components (ontologies) and encourages modularity and consistent reuse and extension of ontological elements at all lower levels.

Since ProjectCO is at the core level, some ontologies at lower levels benefit from specializations of its core project management concepts. For example, to show the usefulness of ProjectCO, this paper has illustrated the semantically enriched terms of the MEvalTDO ontology at the top-domain level, as well as the reuse of its terminology in the process specification of the measurement and evaluation strategy called GOCAME.

As commented throughout the paper, many definitions and labels of ProjectCO terms were adopted or adapted from the PMBOK, APM, IAPM, and PRINCE2 glossaries, as well as from a previous project management ontology. Since these glossaries are well-known knowledge/information resources used in academia and industry to support the human consultation, understanding, and learning of frequently used concepts in this field, ProjectCO with 45 core terms can benefit the structuring of these glossaries that range from 197 to 753 intermixed core and domain terms. One can envision having a glossary section for core terms, including domain-independent terms that designate cross-cutting concepts. Then, we can design other related sections for specific domains such as agile project management and quality project management, among others. As an additional benefit, the terminologist can express hypernym-hyponym relationships between core and domain terms in their definitions. Rarely are the definitions of terms in the cited glossaries structured using the hypernym-hyponym relationship, which implies a lack of semantic correctness. Instead, we do this explicitly with the use of the expression 'is_a' in all definitions, as can be seen in Table 1.

In future work, we will discuss the updated MEvalTDO with ProjectCO in detail to showcase how its concepts impact the design and application of real-world evaluation strategies.

References

APM. (2021). Association for Project Management, APM Glossary, Available at: https://www.apm.org.uk/resources/glossary/. Accessed by November 15, 2023.

Aramo-Immonen, H. (2009). Project management ontology: the organizational learning perspective. Doctoral dissertation, Tampere University of Technology, Finland. ISBN 978-952-15-2330-4.

Bastos, E.C., Barcellos, M.P., Falbo, R. (2018). Using Semantic Documentation to Support Software Project Management. *Journal of Data Semantics* 7, pp. 107–132. https://doi.org/10.1007/s13740-018-0089-z.

Becker, P., Papa, M.F., Olsina L. (2024). Exploratory Study on the Syntactic and Semantic Consistency of Terms in Project Management Glossaries to provide Recommendations for a Project Management Ontology. *Science of Computer Programming Journal, SCICO_103094 (Special Issue from Selected Papers of CIbSE 2023)*, Elsevier, pp. 1–18, https://doi.org/10.1007/978-3-031-35923-1.

Becker, P., Papa, M.F., Tebes, G., Olsina L. (2022). Discussing the Applicability of a Process Core Ontology and Aspects of its Internal Quality, *Software Quality Journal*, Springer, 30:(4), pp. 1003–1038. https://doi.org/10.1007/s11219-022-09592-3.

D'Aquin, M., Gangemi, A. (2011). Is there beauty in ontologies? *Applied Ontology*, 6:(3), pp. 165–175.

Fernández-López, M., Gómez-Pérez, A., Juristo, N. (1997). Methontology: From Ontological Art Towards Ontological Engineering. Proceedings of the Ontological Engineering AAAI-97 Spring Symposium Series.

Guizzardi, G. (2005). Ontological foundations for structural conceptual models. PhD thesis, University of Twente, Enschede, The Netherlands, ISBN 90-75176-81-3.

IAPM. (2021). International Association of Project Managers, Project Managers' Guide and Agile Project Managers' Guide, Available at: https://www.iapm-cert.net/documents/glossary-en/a.html. Accessed by November 15, 2023.

Iatrellis, O., Fitsilis, P. (2021). A Review on Software Project Management Ontologies. In Information Resources Management Association (Ed.), *Research Anthology on Recent Trends, Tools, and Implications of Computer Programming*. IGI Global. pp. 27–46. https://doi.org/10.4018/978-1-7998-3016-0.ch002.

ISO 704. (2022). Terminology work – Principles and methods.

Monfardini, G.K.Q., Salamon, J.S., Barcellos, M.P. (2023). Use of Competency Questions in Ontology Engineering: A Survey. In: Almeida, J.P.A., et al. (eds) Conceptual Modeling. ER 2023. Lecture Notes in Computer Science, vol 14320. Springer, Cham. https://doi.org/10.1007/978-3-031-47262-6_3.

Olsina, L. (2023). The Foundational Ontology ThingFO: Architectural Aspects, Concepts, and Applicability. In: Fred, A., Aveiro, D., Dietz, J., Bernardino, J., Masciari, E., Filipe, J. (eds.) Knowledge Discovery, Knowledge Engineering and Knowledge Management. IC3K 2021. Communications in Computer and Information Science, vol 1718, Springer. Chapter 5, pp. 73–99.

Olsina, L., Becker, P. (2017). Family of Strategies for different Evaluation Purposes. In: 20th Conferencia Iberoamericana en Software Engineering (CIbSE'17) held in the framework of ICSE, CABA, Argentina, Curran Associates 2017, pp. 221–234.

PMBOK. (2021). PMBOK® Guide, A Guide to the Project Management Body of Knowledge. 7th Edition. Available at: https://www.pmi.org/pmbok-guide-standards/foundational/pmbok?sc_camp=D750AAC10C2F4378CE6D51F8D987F49D. Accessed by November 15, 2023.

PMBOK. (2013). A Guide to the Project Management Body of Knowledge. 5th Edition.

PRINCE2. (2017). PRINCE2®, 6th Edition Glossaries of Terms. Available at: https://www.axelos.com/resource-hub/glossary/prince2-6th-edition-glossaries-of-terms. Accessed by November 15, 2023.

Rivera, B., Becker, P., Papa, M.F., Olsina, L. (2016). A Holistic Quality Evaluation, Selection, and Improvement Approach driven by Multilevel Goals and Strategies. *CLEI Electronic Journal*, 19:(3), Paper 3, pp. 1–28, ISSN 0717-5000.

Ruiz Bertol, F. J., Dolado, J. (2008). Una ontología para la gestión del conocimiento de proyectos software. *REICIS. Revista Española de Innovación, Calidad e Ingeniería del Software*, 4:(1), pp. 6–22. Available in Spanish at: https://www.redalyc.org/articulo.oa?id=92240103.

Ruy, F.B., Falbo, R.A., Barcellos, M.P., Costa, S.D., Guizzardi, G. (2016). SEON: A Software Engineering Ontology Network. In: 20th Int'l Conference on Knowledge Engineering and Knowledge Management, Bologna, Italy, pp. 527–542.

Tebes, G., Olsina, L., Peppino, D., Becker, P. (2021). Specifying and Analyzing a Software Testing Ontology at the Top-Domain Ontological Level, *Journal of Computer Science & Technology*, 21:(2), pp. 126–145, https://doi.org/10.24215/16666038.21.e12.

An Exploratory Evaluation of Continuous Feedback to Enhance Machine Learning Code Smell Detection

Daniel Cruz , Amanda Santana , Eduardo Figueiredo

[1]Computer Science Department (DCC)
Federal University of Minas Gerais (UFMG)

{danielvsc, amandads, figueiredo}@dcc.ufmg.br

Abstract. *Code smells are symptoms of bad design choices implemented on the source code. Several code smell detection tools and strategies have been proposed over the years, including the use of machine learning algorithms. However, we lack empirical evidence on how expert feedback could improve machine learning based detection of code smells. This paper aims to propose and evaluate a conceptual strategy to improve machine-learning detection of code smells by means of continuous feedback. To evaluate the strategy, we follow an exploratory evaluation design to compare results of the smell detection before and after feedback provided by a service - acting as a software expert. We focus on four code smells - God Class, Long Method, Feature Envy, and Refused Bequest - detected in 20 Java systems. As results, we observed that continuous feedback improves the performance of code smell detection. For the detection of the class-level code smells, God Class and Refused Bequest, we achieved an average improvement in terms of F1 of 0.13 and 0.58, respectively, after 50 iterations of feedback. For the method-level code smells, Long Method and Feature Envy, the improvements of F1 were 0.66 and 0.72, respectively.*

1. Introduction

Code smells are symptoms of bad design choices implemented on source code [16]. They negatively affect software quality attributes [38], such as software comprehension [2] and robustness [22]. To detect code smells, several techniques and tools have been proposed [12, 20, 28, 29, 30, 32, 36]. In fact, these techniques present different types of detection strategies, such as software metrics, textual analysis, and AST analysis [11]. For the software metrics-based detection strategies, thresholds must be defined to identify code smells. Defining proper thresholds is a major drawback due to their innate complexity, being addressed by several studies that propose methods for threshold derivation [14, 17].

Several studies rely on machine learning algorithms to detect code smells have been proposed in the literature [3, 13, 20, 21, 26, 27]. For instance, Fontana et al. [15] provided an extensive comparison among different machine learning algorithms for detecting code smells, using the same data and evaluating them in the same way. In their study, almost all algorithms achieved good results for the code smell detection problem. However, a replication study conducted by Di Nucci et al. [10] found diverging results. Their study [10] indicates that the detection need to be improved for several algorithms and code smells. In a previous work [9], we built a dataset of code smells for twenty Java systems by using five code smell detection tools. In this dataset, we identified and analyzed four code smells: *God Class*, *Long Method*, *Feature Envy*, and *Refused Bequest*.

Based on this dataset, we also performed a comparative study of seven machine learning algorithms [9]: *Naive Bayes*, *Logistic Regression*, *Multilayer Perceptron*, *Decision Trees*, *K-Nearest Neighbors*, *Random Forest*, and *Gradient Boosting Machine*. We found a better performance for tree-based algorithms, such as *Random Forest*.

Despite the advances in machine learning algorithms, the quality of data is an important matter to obtain high-performance machine learning systems. In a supervised learning scenario, obtaining the labels for the training samples is one of the main concerns, and it can be very expensive. As the use of machine learning to resolve problems has become a trend, we can find the most diverse domains in which models are being developed. In this context, it is common to find actors with domain knowledge, that we named *experts*, to support the creation of high-quality data. Their knowledge can help improve the performance of the models by providing insights and understanding about the data being used. They also can provide the knowledge to define if some model's prediction is right, acting as a labeler or evaluator.

By relying on a service to simulate experts, this paper first proposes a conceptual strategy to improve the models' accuracy using expert feedback (Section 2). This feedback would be collected, for instance, after the detection being provided by a tool that uses a trained machine learning model. The feedback provided by the expert service can be used to update the initial model. We hypothesize that the model can keep evolving with a qualified feedback from the expert to improve its accuracy on the next detection. We then conduct an exploratory evaluation of the proposed conceptual strategy as follows (Section 3). We first evaluate the viability of the feedback as a source of improvement in the code smell detection and searched for parameters of the strategy to assess an optimal configuration for its application. We then evaluate the strategy by simulating 50 iterations of feedback and model training. We then compare results of the smell detection before and after feedback. We focus on four code smells, God Class, Long Method, Feature Envy, and Refused Bequest, detected in twenty Java systems. Our goal in this study is to quantitatively evaluate the performance improvement of the machine learning models after several iterations of expert feedback.

Our results indicated that machine learning models achieved an improvement on the detection of all code smells (Section 4). For instance, for the *Feature Envy* detection, the mean improvement was about 0.72 in F1, after all feedback cycles. We also found a consistent pattern of improvement for all code smells. That is, the detection performance presents a small variation between a few cycles, but in the long run, they all tend to improve. Thus, the contributions of this paper is twofold: (1) a conceptual strategy to continuously update a machine learning model aiming to improve the detection performance of code smells by means of continuous feedback and (2) an exploratory evaluation of this strategy, through a service that allowed us to simulate 50 iterations of expert feedback.

2. The Conceptual Feedback Strategy

Software development is in constant evolution as should be the tools to identify or to refactor quality issues, such as code smells. Given this scenario, we select a pre-trained model based on the Random Forest classifier to accomplish the code smell detection task. Our aim is to evolve this model for detecting code smells by means of expert feedback, aligned to the idea of continuous training the supervised machine learning system.

Figure 1 depicts the cyclic conceptual strategy proposed to improve the quality of the code smell detection. In a nutshell, the quality of the detection is improved by keeping the model updated; i.e., by means of the knowledge of *Software Engineer Experts*. The process is divided in three main routines. Each routine can be identified in Figure 1 by the numbers in the circles. The first routine consists of the execution of a detection tool by the *User* to perform the code smell detection. The detection results can be stored into the *Detection Storage* for a later analysis. The second routine deals with the feedback loop. First, the *Software Engineer Experts* have access to the *Detection Storage*. In fact, the *User* and the *Software Engineer Expert* can be the same person since a developer is also supposed to have knowledge about the software design. Experts can select as many detections as they want to analyze and provide feedback. This selection can be facilitated by explainable ML models, such as the SHAP results [7], and by the model's confidence. For instance, if one instance was detected as smelly, but the metrics that contributed more to this classification do not seem to make sense to the expert, they could seek to analyze the instance more deeply in the code. In our exploratory evaluation, we create a service to act as an expert by accessing the ground truth of our dataset (see Sections 3.3 and 3.4).

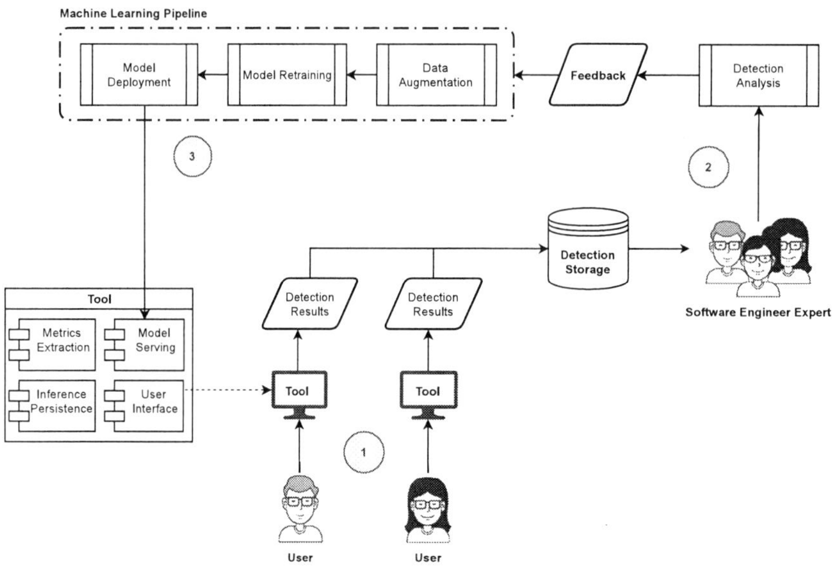

Figure 1. A Strategy to Detect Code Smells based on Continuous Feedback

After providing feedback for a set of instances, the third routine is triggered. The automated pipeline updates the model currently used by the tool. As the number of instances used for training is, in general, much larger than the set of feedback, it is necessary to provide some augmentation for the data, by prioritizing them and making them impact the retraining of the model. The model retraining, in this case, is done by merging the augmented data with the initial data. Finally, after retraining the model, we can finish the process by deploying the model.

We developed a prototype tool, named *FeedSniffer*, to support the proposed strategy with four essential modules described as follows. **Metrics Extraction**: The first module of *FeedSniffer* is responsible to calculate the software metrics for the source code. Since several tools are available to extract metrics [24], we integrated *FeedSniffer* with two existing tools: CK Metrics [4] and VizzMaintenance [5]. The software metrics extracted are used for training the models. **Model Serving**: The tool is also responsible to load the trained machine learning model into memory and use it to perform the detection. That is, it uses the pre-trained model to classify the target instance, labeling it as smelly or not. **User Interface**: An interface that helps the user to perform the detections, but in our case it has a command-line interface. That is, *FeedSniffer* outputs a CSV file listing all elements (classes and methods) of the project and their respective labels (i.e., 1 for smelly and 0 for non-smelly). **Inference Persistence**: This module of *FeedSniffer* is responsible to store the results in the *Detection Storage*. In case the user changes the label of an element (e.g., turn 1 into 0), the updated list can also be stored.

3. The Exploratory Study Design

Section 3.1 defines the research questions and the metrics used for evaluation. To answer the research questions, we followed five steps described in Sections 3.2 to 3.6.

3.1. Research Questions and Evaluation Metric

The first aspect to be considered is how the model retraining with the experts' feedback affects its performance. Therefore, before going into the evaluation of the entire process, RQ1 aims to evaluate how much the detection can be improved when the retraining occurs only once. We the evaluate with RQ2 the model performance after several cycles.

RQ1: How much the model's performance can be improved by one-time feedback?

RQ2: How much the model's performance can be improved by continuous feedback?

Evaluation Metric. Since the code smell datasets are highly imbalanced, we evaluated feedback strategy with *F-Measure* using the unitary weight (F1). F1 is the harmonic mean of Precision and Recall and a robust measurement of machine learning performance.

$$F1 = 2 * \frac{precision * recall}{precision + recall}$$

3.2. Dataset: Smells, Systems, and Metrics

Code Smells. In this work, we focused on four code smells: God Class, Refused Bequest, Long Method, and Feature Envy. God Class [16] consists of a class that accumulates several responsibilities. Refused Bequest [16] is also related to a class. It defines a class that inherits from another but does not even use the attributes and methods inherited. Long Method is related to a method and consists of a method with a large and complex behavior, providing multiple functionalities. Finally, Feature Envy is also related to a method and consists of a method that is more associated with another class than its own. We have selected these smells based on previous studies that analyzed the perception of code smells by developers [33, 34]. For instance, Palomba et al. [33] investigated how developers perceive the severity of the code smell. They have also investigated how often they identify them. Considering a range from 1 to 5, they found that God Class and Long Method were classified with the highest severity, with a median value of 5 and 4, respectively. For the Feature Envy and Refused Bequest smells, the degree of severity achieved a median value of 4. Other studies [34, 39] reported similar findings, but they mostly found Refused Bequest as harmful as God Class and Long Method.

Software Systems and Metrics. We created a dataset with 20 open source Java systems that contain instances of four code smells. The systems were mainly extracted from the *Qualita Corpus* [35], with most of them being used in other machine learning studies [15, 10]. Table 1 presents the complete list of 20 selected systems. The first column presents the name of the system, while the second column presents a brief classification according to its purpose [9, 35]. The third and fourth columns depict the size of the systems in terms of number of classes and number of methods, respectively. For every class and method in the dataset, we extracted 17 metrics for the class level and 13 metrics for the method level. The class level metrics were extracted using the tool VizzMaintenance [5]. This tool calculates known metric suites [6, 8, 18, 23]. The method level metrics were extracted by the CK Metrics tool [4]. The tool computes known metrics, such as *Weighted Method Count* and more experimental ones, like *Quantity of Assignments*. We selected these tools and metrics because (i) both tools export measurement data in a way we could integrate to *FeedSniffer* and (ii) these metrics have been used in previous work about machine learning detection of code smells [9]. The full list of extracted metrics can be found in our online replication package [1].

3.3. Ground Truth Creation

To create the ground truth of code smells, we combined the result of five automatic detection tools: PMD[1], JDeodorant [12], JSpirit [36], an implementation[2] of DECOR [30], and Organic [31]. We rely on the agreement among tools in a majority voting ensemble. It consists of comparing the results among the tools to determine the final outcome. These tools have some limitations, as each one can be used to detect only a small subset of code smells. Therefore, we have identified which tools could detect the same code smells. The goal was to have three different tools for every code smell. Thus, with this voting, an instance (class or method) is considered smelly if two or more tools detected the same smell. The result of this voting ensemble is also in our online replication package [1].

We evaluate the agreement between the tools' results and the human perception, since we know about the subjective nature of code smells detection [38]. The manual evaluation was performed by 10 software engineering researchers; i.e., PhD candidates and junior developers in our research lab. Due to the large size of the dataset, a complete evaluation was not feasible. Instead, we rely on statiscally sampling. First, for every code smell, we determined a sample size to meet a confidence level of 90% and a maximum error of 10%. Then, we randomly extracted the necessary sample size from our ground truth and grouped the samples by system. Finally, each researchers manually evaluated code smells of two systems. The agreement between tools and a manual evaluation was high enough for our purposes (above 80% for all systems).

3.4. Data Preparation

We defined four groups of datasets (one for each code smell) instead of only one dataset. The features are the set of software metrics used to characterize each instance (class or method) and the target is a binary variable indicating if the instance is smelly or non-smelly. It is worth mentioning that not every system in the dataset contains all four code smells. The God Class smell was found in all 20 systems, Feature Envy in 15 systems,

[1] pmd.github.io

[2] ptidej.net/publications/Keyword/CODE-AND-DESIGN-SMELLS.php

Table 1. Selected Systems

Name	Description	Classes	Methods
Checkstyle	IDE	511	2,620
Commons Codec	Tool	145	1,481
Commons IO	Tool	282	2,638
Commons Lang	Tool	642	5,947
Commons Logging	Tool	74	546
Hadoop	Middleware	3,703	18,111
Hibernate	Database	6,745	43,828
HtmlUnit	Testing	882	7,485
JasperReports	Data Viewer	1,642	14,880
JFreeChart	Tool	1,037	11,528
JHotDraw	3D/Graphics	732	6,641
JMeter	Testing	1,023	8,689
Lucene	Tool	4,353	20,135
Quartz	Middleware	268	2,495
Spring Framework	Middleware	5,935	30,321
SquirrelSQL	Database	73	550
Struts	Middleware	2,139	12,656
Tapestry	Middleware	1,957	9,276
Tomcat	Middleware	1,794	14,017
Weka	Tool	1,663	18,110
	Total	**35,600**	**231,954**

Long Method in 13 systems, and Refused Bequest in 11 systems. Furthermore, due to limited resources, we avoid an evaluation with a large group of actual experts to provide feedback for all experimental runs. As a result, we decide to create a service to act as an expert by accessing the ground truth of our dataset. Therefore, in the context of our experimental setup, we define Oracle as a service that represents the Software Engineer Expert. The Oracle is responsible for identifying the wrong detections, by accessing the ground truth available for a specific instance. From these wrong detections, the Oracle is able to provide a fraction of correct detections as feedback (e.g., 10%, 20%).

3.5. Single Training Evaluation (RQ1)

To compare the effect of updating the model with feedback from the experts, we designed two moments for the experimentation: before and after any feedback is provided. The evaluation process for each Target System Dataset (TSD) is defined as follows.

1. We train a model using TSD's training data and the Random Forest algorithm, including its hyperparameters, found as a good choice in previous work [9].
2. This trained model is used to detect the code smells on the test data, which consists of the instances of the target system.
3. The performance metric (F1) is calculated for the detection results.

In the second moment, we perform the following procedures to update the models with the feedback and evaluate their performance against the initial ones, obtained from the first moment. For each TSD:

1. We ask the Oracle for the feedback from the detection results obtained in the first moment. In this step, the amount of feedback requested varied. This amount is defined as the *Feedback Size (N)*.
2. We process the feedback data by duplicating them. In this step, the amount of oversampling applied varied and it is defined as the *Oversampling Ratio (K)*.

3. The initial training data is merged with the oversampled feedback data and is used to retrain the model, keeping the existing hyperparameters. We also remove from the initial test data the data provided as feedback, keeping the assessment fair.
4. The retrained model is used to detect the code smells on the test data.
5. The performance metrics are calculated again for the new detection results.

The *Feedback Size (N)* and *Oversampling Ratio (K)* provided by Oracle varied, as we intend to explore different values. The reason is because we do not know upfront a common value, requiring empirical evaluation. For *Feedback Size (N)*, we tried seven possible configurations: 10%, 20%, 30%, 40%, 50%, 60%, and 70%. For the *Oversampling Ratio (K)*, we defined eleven configurations: 1%, 5%, 10%, 15%, 20%, 25%, 30%, 35%, 40%, 45%, and 50%.

3.6. Continuous Training Evaluation (RQ2)

A key difference for this design is the control of the experimented variables. The first one, Feedback Size (N), was kept constant with the value of 10%. The reason is that our goal here is not to explore the effects of large amounts of feedback at once, as we expect it to be provided more incrementally. First, we have conducted a pilot to evaluate the execution of seven cycles of the strategy. The pilot was enough to make clear the potential of the strategy and then we have expanded the number of cycles to 50. As it is not guaranteed nor expected that after several cycles the detection to be perfect (i.e., it would achieve the maximum value of a performance metric) these fifty iterations were enough to demonstrate the effects of the model updating in the code smell detection.

The other important factor to consider, which was also defined, is the Oversampling Ratio (K). In this case, we defined a fixed value of 1% for two reasons. First, this value is not aggressive, which is quite important in the strategy context, since the model is updated more than one time. For higher values, the model could lose its generalization power, as the data from the other systems would begin to be overwhelmed by the duplicate data from the target system. Second, through the results of the pilot study, we found some quantitative indicators that most of the best results have used lower values for the oversampling configuration, in special, the value of 1%.

4. Results and Discussion

Section 4.1 reports the results regarding the single training evaluation, while Section 4.2 presents the results regarding the continuous training evaluation.

4.1. Single Time Feedback Results

Using the data collected before and after the feedback, we aim to understand for each system if any of the configurations were superior to the initial result. If so, what is the best K and N configuration to update the model. Thus, we extract the best results among the different configurations, and compare them with the initial model performance. Based on our results, we observed that the detection was not improved for only one system, and it was actually worsened. We also noticed that the farther from the line the marker is, the greater the difference in performance after the feedback. For instance, for one of the target systems, the base F1 was around 0.2 before feedback. However, after the feedback with one of the provided configurations, it reached an F1 of about 0.8. Nevertheless, to make sure they are significantly different, we have performed statistical tests to confirm it. Then, we state the following null hypotheses:

H_0: Updating the model with feedback has no effect on detection performance.

We perform the Shapiro-Wilk test for normality for each one of our experimental groups. We have selected this test because the normality tests are influenced by the sample size. As our samples are small (less than 30 units), this test will be less affected by Type I error (i.e., false positive). We found that for all smells except the God Class sample before feedback, the detection performances (i.e., measured by F1) follow a normal distribution with a significance level of 99%.

Since they follow a normal distribution, we applied the paired T-test for the samples of the code smells Long Method, Feature Envy, and Refused Bequest. For the samples of the God Class code smell, we applied the Wilcoxon signed-rank test, which is a non-parametric version of the paired T-test. Considering the following p-values obtained from the tests: 1.03×10^{-4} (God Class), 1.96×10^{-7} (Long Method), 6.06×10^{-7} (Feature Envy), 6.45×10^{-5} (Refused Bequest), we found that for all code smells, we could reject the null hypothesis. That is, updating the model with feedback affects detection performance, with a significance level of 99%.

As expected, we observed that the best results were achieved when the expert provides more feedback (i.e., N=70). Regarding oversampling, we found in most cases the best results provided by the configurations with the smallest oversampling ratio (i.e., K=1%). Due to space constraints, detailed results about the single training evaluation is available in our replication package [1].

Answering RQ1. The performance improvement varies according to the code smell, with a wide improvement space, reaching an increase of up to 0.63 in F1 for some systems. God Class detection presented an average improvement of 0.1 in F1. Feature Envy, Long Method, and Refused Bequest achieved an average improvement of 0.26 in F1.

4.2. Continuous Feedback Results

Figure 2 summarizes the model performance across the incremental feedback cycles for each code smell group. Each row in this figure is related to one code smell and it presents two charts divided into two columns. The chart in the left column presents the evolution of the F1 metric in the vertical axis across the feedback cycles displayed in the horizontal axis. We can observe two series: the black line represents the median value and the blue line represents the mean value for all systems evaluated. The chart in the right column presents the evolution of the F1 metric in the vertical axis across the feedback cycles displayed in the horizontal axis. However, as we performed ten repetitions when selecting the 10% feedback sample, we also present the 95% confidence interval for the scores, to avoid selection bias in the evaluation. Hence, the black lines also represent the mean value for the F1, while the shading outlines the confidence interval area. It is noteworthy that we plotted the mean twice to analyze two different perspectives. For the charts in the left column, we aim to analyze the distance between the mean and the median and to understand if there is more variance of the results across the different systems evaluated. For the charts in the right column, we aim to analyze the impact of the random shuffling of the feedback sample through the mean and the confidence interval.

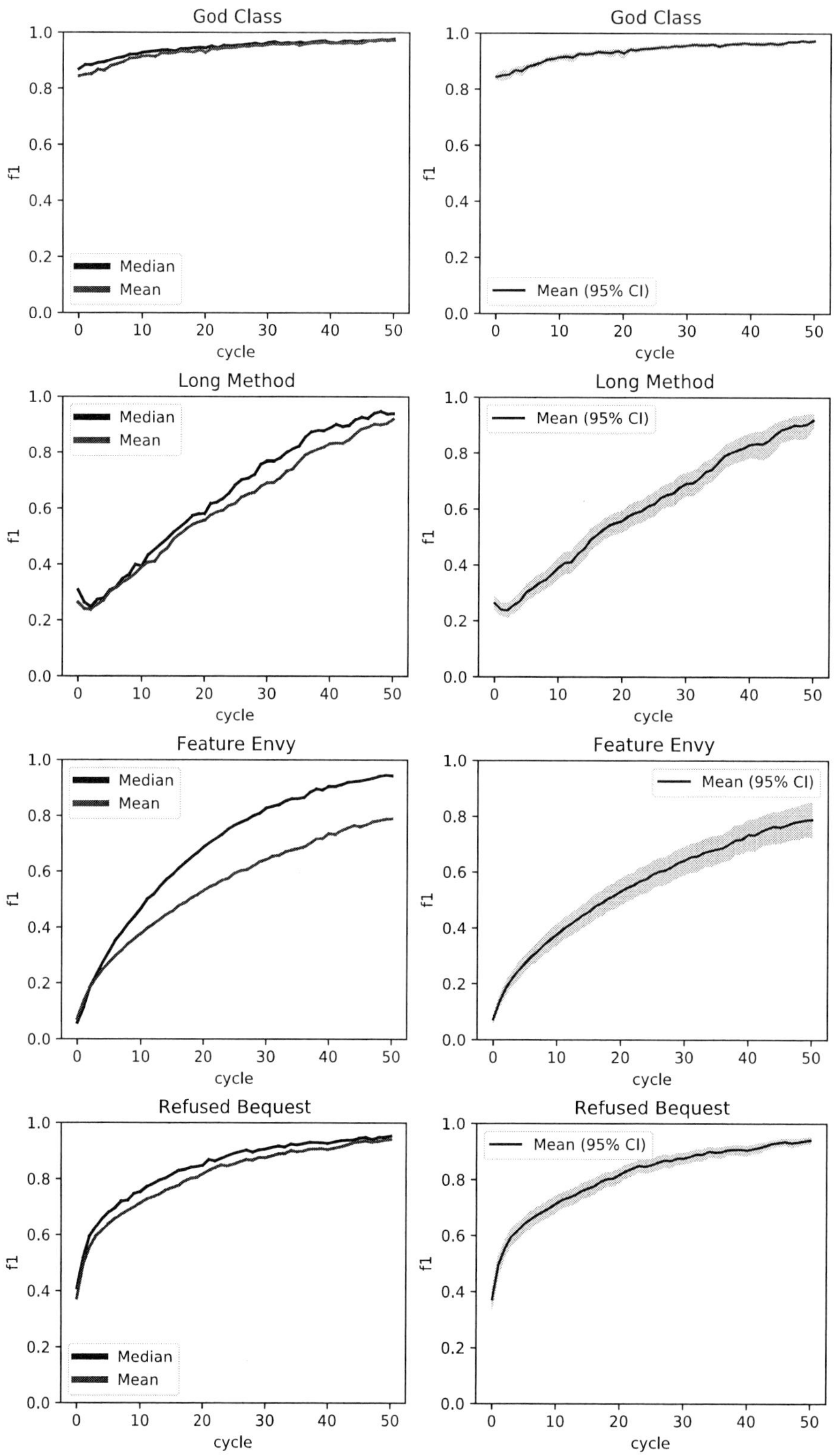

Figure 2. Continuous Feedback Results

For the first smell, God Class, we can observe similar results to the obtained on the previous design. In general, each cycle provides a small increase in F1. At a short pace, the performance is increased, but as it reaches a great F1 (above 0.9), it seems to reach an asymptote close to the maximum F1 possible. We can understand this behavior as there is a small space for improvement. As we discussed before in Section 3.6, we do not expect the F1 score to reach the maximum value, even though it can happen for some systems. Looking at the God Class chart on the left column, we can observe only a small difference between the systems and, in general, they behave the same. From the chart in the right column, we can observe that the selection of the feedback sample across the cycles does not affect the results, as the confidence interval is really small.

Regarding the detection of Long Method, we can observe a linear trend of performance increase. However, we first observe that both median and mean decrease in the first iterations with the feedback. This may be due to the random sample selection. After the first cycles, the performance starts to increase and stabilize when F1 reaches around 0.9. We can also observe a small difference between the mean and the median, as most of the systems behave the same, increasing only a little bit less than some others. From the chart in the right column, we can observe a larger band for the confidence interval. This means that, depending on the instances present in the feedback sample, the performance may vary between cycles. However, by looking at the broader perspective, we can observe a significant improvement between the fifty cycles. For instance, when looking for differences between the first cycle, without feedback, and after the last cycle, we found an improvement in F1 greater than 0.6. That is, F1 increased from an average of 0.26 to 0.92.

The Feature Envy detection presented an improvement behavior too, but not linear as the previous smell, Long Method. The first twenty cycles present a faster improvement, increasing from the average F1 of 0.08 to an average F1 of about 0.5. In the last thirty cycles, it kept increasing until reaching an average F1 of 0.79. However, observing the blue line of the left column chart, we can notice that the median presents a higher value. Investigating the results deeply, i.e., per system, we found that some systems did not perform well and had a very small increase, lowering the average value. However, in general the systems performed well as can be observed by the black line (median). For this code smell, we found two patterns of improvement. Most of the systems increased their performance since the first cycles. However, despite also improving, some systems follow a much slower pace until the end of the fifty cycles. Analyzing these systems, the main common attribute is the high number of methods. This suggests that F1 could further increase by executing more cycles. Looking at the chart in the right column, we can also observe that the confidence interval is well contained and does not seem to affect the overall result. However, we can observe that the band becomes broader in the last cycles, although in general, the improvement is clear when looking over all cycles.

Finally, we have the Refused Bequest smell. For this one, we can observe a behavior similar to Feature Envy, in which a trend of increase in detection performance is presented since the first cycles. However, differently from the Feature Envy detection, the two lines, representing the median and the mean of F1, remain close throughout the cycles. All systems evaluated had their performance increased. Worth noticing that after only ten cycles, the mean F1 has almost doubled, from 0.37 to 0.71, ending with an average F1 of 0.94. The selection of the feedback sample also did not impact the results in general, as we can see in the confidence interval band from the chart in the right column. Through these analyses, we can answer the RQ2 as follows.

Answering RQ2. The performance improvement varies according to the code smell. God Class detection presented the smaller average improvement, an increase of 0.13 in F1, as the initial performance was already high. The Long Method detection presented an average improvement of 0.66 in F1. For the Feature Envy and Refused Bequest detections, we found average improvements of 0.72 and 0.58 in F1, respectively.

5. Threats to Validity

Despite the careful design of our empirical study, some limitations may affect the validity of our results. In this section, we discuss some of those threats and our actions to mitigate them, organizing them by construct, internal, external, and conclusion validity [37].

Construct Validity. With respect to the number of instances used to evaluate the models after several cycles, it is important to note that the number of test instances does not drive the results. That is, as we remove the feedback samples from the test data to keep the evaluation fair, we also evaluated how many instances were removed and if the results could be impacted by a small number of instances left to be evaluated. First, we did not keep the cycles running after the number of feedback available had finished, avoiding increasing the performance for the last cycles. Then, we also evaluated how many instances from the initial set were removed from the initial amount. As we have tested the entire dataset through our systems cross-validation, we compare the initial size of the test data for each code smell, before and after the last cycles, for each system.

Internal Validity. Regarding the internal validity of the continuous training evaluation study, as we set the value of the feedback size, we also replicate the process, changing the 10% randomly selected for feedback from each cycle. We aim to mitigate the possibility of obtained results being influenced by the selection of the instances belonging to the feedback. For instance, if in the first cycle the majority of the feedback is related to false negatives, this could influence our model differently from if the majority of instances in the first cycle were false positives. Beyond the fact that we can estimate the error of our model, through these replications, we can obtain the confidence interval for our measurements. Our focus is not on obtaining a fixed F1 value, but a range, providing more confidence to our results, even if more systems were added to the model. In total, ten repetitions for each system/group were performed. Each repetition preserves the random seed for all code smells and systems on its execution.

External Validity. First, concerning the external validity of our studies, the systems evaluated may not represent all systems available, and they are all written in Java. However, the strategy itself and the experimental studies designed to evaluate it are not dependent on the programming language and could be performed in different datasets.

Conclusion Validity. Regarding the conclusion validity of the single training evaluation study, the results found could be based on the wrong choice of the statistical tests. To avoid it, we performed previous analyses regarding the normality of the samples and their dependency relation. Thus, we applied two tests separately to mitigate this threat. Another threat, for both studies, is the performance metric that drives our conclusion. As we have discussed in Section 3.1, the main metric selected to evaluate the performance is the F1 score. The main reason is that we do not want to prioritize neither precision nor recall. We also are dealing with heavily imbalanced data. Hence, we are focusing on the metrics related to the class that matters, the positive one that represents the presence of a smell.

6. Related Work

Several detection techniques and tools have been proposed in the literature. Recently, the adoption of machine learning techniques to detect code smells has became a trend [21, 26, 27, 3, 13, 15, 10]. For instance, Khomh et al. [20] proposed a Bayesian approach which initially converts existing detection rules to a probabilistic model to perform the predictions. Khomh et al. [21] later extended their previous work [20] by the introduction of Bayesian Belief Networks, improving the accuracy of the detection. Maiga et al. [26, 27] proposed an SVM-based approach that uses the feedback information provided by practitioners. Amorim et al. [3] presented an experience report on the effectiveness of Decision Trees for detecting code smells. They choose these classifiers due to their interpretability [3]. Thus, most of the proposed works focus only on one classifier. They were also trained in a dataset composed of few systems and, consequently, the results may be positive towards their approach due to overfitting.

Other studies [13, 15, 10, 9] evaluated and compared the performance of different machine learning algorithms on distinct sets of systems. For instance, Fontana et al. [13, 15] performed a larger comparison of classifiers [15]. The notorious impact of their work was the great performance reported. Even naive algorithms were able of achieving good results using a small training dataset. Di Nucci et al. [10] replicated the study and verified that the reported performance could be biased by the dataset and some procedures, such as unrealistic balanced data, in which one-third of the instances were smelly. Cruz et al. [9] contributed with further empirical evidences on the use of machine learning algorithms for code smells detection by using a larger dataset of curated systems.

Few studies address a feedback process to improve the detection of code smells as we do here. Hozano et al. [19] proposed a platform to consider the developer feedback, to create personalized rules for a rule-based detection technique. However, we did not found in their work how the rules evolve. Their evaluation was also performed only on two small systems and using only the accuracy metric. It may lead to an incorrect conclusion, without taking into consideration the data distribution. Liu et al. [25] proposed an automatic way to update the thresholds used to perform code smell detection. This technique is based on feedback provided by a software engineer. Their strategy focuses on making it possible to interact with the threshold definition by explicitly directing the detection regarding one metric, in their case, precision. However, different from our work, they focused on finding metrics thresholds to provide better detection. Meanwhile, our goal was to propose and evaluate a high abstraction strategy, aiming at providing a trained ML model with explicit feedback from a expert service.

7. Conclusion

Code smells are important indicators of quality improvement opportunities in the source code of a system. Although many techniques and tools have been proposed, we lack a continuous improvement alternative for the machine learning based detection of code smells. In this paper, we proposed a conceptual strategy to improve the code smell detection through a continuous feedback approach, in which a machine learning model is retrained over the iterations with a expert that provides feedback about the detection results. We also evaluated the strategy with an exploratory study in which we experimented different parameterizations and simulated the use of the strategy with fifty cycles of feedback in a dataset of 20 software systems. We found that by using the proposed strategy, code smell detection can be improved incrementally for all code smells. For the detection of *God Class*, a code smell with a detection performance initially good, we achieved an average improvement of 0.13 in terms of F1. For the other code smell related to a class, *Refused Bequest*, after all iterations of the strategy, we achieved an average improvement of 0.58 in terms of F1. For the method level code smells, *Long Method* and *Feature Envy*, we achieved an average improvement of 0.66 and 0.72 in terms of F1, respectively.

As future work, we foresee some opportunities to further improve the current strategy or its evaluation. For instance, a good topic to be investigated in future work would be to add noise to the feedback acquisition. That is, provide some wrong feedbacks to understand how the model deals with this noisy data. Another topic for future work is the possibility of prioritizing the instances to ask for feedback. As we observed in our results, the random selection of the group of 10% of instances to be given as feedback did not impact the detection's performance. However, there are other techniques from related fields (e.g., Active Learning), that could lead us to a way of selecting a set of instances that could make the performance of the detection improve faster (i.e., with fewer cycles). It is also important to expand the dataset to cover other code smells and more systems. Finally, it is worth mentioning as future work an experimental evaluation with humans; i.e., actual software experts. For this evaluation, our prototype tool could also be improved, for instance, with a friendly user interface.

Acknowledgements. This research was partially supported by Brazilian funding agencies: CAPES, CNPq, and FAPEMIG..

References

[1] An exploratory evaluation of continuous feedback to enhance machine learning code smell detection - online replication package, 2023. URL `https://zenodo.org/record/8122453`.

[2] M. Abbes, F. Khomh, Y. Gueheneuc, and G. Antoniol. An empirical study of the impact of two antipatterns, blob and spaghetti code, on program comprehension. In *European Conference on Software Maintenance and Reengineering (CSMR)*, 2011.

[3] L. Amorim, E. Costa, N. Antunes, B. Fonseca, and M. Ribeiro. Experience report: Evaluating the effectiveness of decision trees for detecting code smells. In *Int. Symposium on Software Reliability Engineering (ISSRE)*, pages 261–269, 2015.

[4] M. Aniche. *Java code metrics calculator (CK)*, 2015. Available in github.com/mauricioaniche/ck/.

[5] H. Barkmann, R. Lincke, and W. Löwe. Quantitative evaluation of software quality metrics in open-source projects. In *Int'l Conf. on Advanced Information Networking and Applications Workshops (AINA)*, pages 1067–1072, 2009.

[6] J. M. Bieman and BK. Kang. Cohesion and reuse in an object-oriented system. *Software Engineering Notes (SEN)*, 20:259–262, 1995.

[7] T. Chen and C. Guestrin. Xgboost: A scalable tree boosting system. In *Int'l Conf. on knowledge discovery and data mining (KDD)*, pages 785–794. ACM, 2016.

[8] S. R. Chidamber and C. F. Kemerer. A metrics suite for object oriented design. *Transactions on Software Engineering*, 20:476–493, 1994.

[9] D. Cruz, A. Santana, and E. Figueiredo. Detecting bad smells with machine learning algorithms: an empirical study. In *Proceedings of the 3rd International Conference on Technical Debt*, pages 31–40, 2020.

[10] D. Di Nucci, F. Palomba, D. A. Tamburri, A. Serebrenik, and A. De Lucia. Detecting code smells using machine learning techniques: are we there yet? In *Int'l Conf. on Software Analysis, Evolution and Reengineering (SANER)*, pages 612–621, 2018.

[11] E. Fernandes, J. Oliveira, G. Vale, T. Paiva, and E. Figueiredo. A review-based comparative study of bad smell detection tools. In *Proceedings of the Int'l Conf. on Evaluation and Assessment in Software Engineering (EASE)*, 2016.

[12] M. Fokaefs, N. Tsantalis, E. Stroulia, and A. Chatzigeorgiou. Jdeodorant: identification and application of extract class refactorings. In *Int'l Conf. on Software Engineering (ICSE)*, pages 1037–1039, 2011.

[13] F. Fontana, M. Zanoni, A. Marino, and M. V. Mäntylä. Code smell detection: Towards a machine learning-based approach (icsm). In *Int'l Conf. on Software Maintenance*, pages 396–399, 2013.

[14] F. Fontana, V. Ferme, M. Zanoni, and A. Yamashita. Automatic metric thresholds derivation for code smell detection. In *2015 IEEE/ACM 6th International Workshop on Emerging Trends in Software Metrics*, pages 44–53. IEEE, 2015.

[15] F. A. Fontana, M. V. Mäntylä, M. Zanoni, and A. Marino. Comparing and experimenting machine learning techniques for code smell detection. *Empirical Software Engineering*, 21(3):1143–1191, 2016.

[16] M. Fowler. *Refactoring: improving the design of existing code*. Addison-Wesley Professional, 1999.

[17] S. Herbold, J. Grabowski, and S. Waack. Calculation and optimization of thresholds for sets of software metrics. *Empirical Software Engineering*, 16(6):812–841, 2011.

[18] M. Hitz and B. Montazeri. *Measuring coupling and cohesion in object-oriented systems*. Citeseer, 1995.

[19] M. Hozano, H. Ferreira, I. Silva, B. Fonseca, and E. Costa. Using developers' feedback to improve code smell detection. In *Proceedings of the 30th Annual ACM Symposium on Applied Computing*, pages 1661–1663, 2015.

[20] F. Khomh, S. Vaucher, YG. Guéhéneuc, and H. Sahraoui. A bayesian approach for the detection of code and design smells. In *Int'l Conf. on Quality Software*, pages 305–314, 2009.

[21] F. Khomh, S. Vaucher, YG. Guéhéneuc, and H. Sahraoui. Bdtex: A gqm-based bayesian approach for the detection of antipatterns. *Journal of Systems and Software*, 84(4):559–572, 2011.

[22] F. Khomh, M. Di Penta, YG. Guéhéneuc, and G. Antoniol. An exploratory study of the impact of antipatterns on class change-and fault-proneness. *Empirical Software Engineering*, 17(3):243–275, 2012.

[23] W. Li and S. Henry. Object-oriented metrics that predict maintainability. *Journal of systems and software*, 23(2):111–122, 1993.

[24] R. Lincke, J. Lundberg, and W. Löwe. Comparing software metrics tools. In *Proceedings of the 2008 international symposium on Software testing and analysis*, pages 131–142, 2008.

[25] H. Liu, Q. Liu, Z. Niu, and Y. Liu. Dynamic and automatic feedback-based threshold adaptation for code smell detection. *IEEE Transactions on Software Engineering*, 42(6):544–558, 2015.

[26] A. Maiga, N. Ali, N. Bhattacharya, A. Sabané, Y. Guéhéneuc, and E. Aimeur. Smurf: A svm-based incremental anti-pattern detection approach. In *Working Conference on Reverse Engineering (WCRE)*, pages 466–475, 2012.

[27] A. Maiga, N. Ali, N. Bhattacharya, A. Sabané, Y. Guéhéneuc, G. Antoniol, and E. Aïmeur. Support vector machines for anti-pattern detection. In *Proceedings of Int'l Conf. on Automated Software Engineering (ASE)*, pages 278–281, 2012.

[28] C. Marinescu, R. Marinescu, P. F. Mihancea, and R. Wettel. iplasma: An integrated platform for quality assessment of object-oriented design. In *In ICSM (Industrial and Tool Volume)*, pages 77–80, 2005.

[29] R. Marinescu. Detection strategies: Metrics-based rules for detecting design flaws. In *Int'l Conf. on Software Maintenance (ICSM)*, pages 350–359, 2004.

[30] N. Moha, YG. Gueheneuc, L. Duchien, and AF. Le Meur. Decor: A method for the specification and detection of code and design smells. *Transactions on Software Engineering*, 36(1):20–36, 2009.

[31] W. Oizumi, L. Sousa, A. Oliveira, A. Garcia, A. B. Agbachi, R. Oliveira, and C. Lucena. On the identification of design problems in stinky code: experiences and tool support. *Journal of the Brazilian Computer Society*, 24(1), 2018.

[32] F. Palomba, G. Bavota, M. Di Penta, R. Oliveto, A. De Lucia, and D. Poshyvanyk. Detecting bad smells in source code using change history information. In *Int'l Conf. on Automated Software Engineering (ASE)*, pages 268–278, 2013.

[33] F. Palomba, G. Bavota, M. Di Penta, R. Oliveto, and A. De Lucia. Do they really smell bad? a study on developers' perception of bad code smells. In *International Conference on Software Maintenance and Evolution*, pages 101–110, 2014.

[34] D. Taibi, A. Janes, and V. Lenarduzzi. How developers perceive smells in source code: A replicated study. *Information and Software Technology*, 92:223–235, 2017.

[35] E. Tempero, C. Anslow, J. Dietrich, T. Han, J. Li, M. Lumpe, H. Melton, and J. Noble. The qualitas corpus: A curated collection of java code for empirical studies. In *Asia Pacific Software Engineering Conference (APSEC)*, pages 336–345, Nov 2010.

[36] S. Vidal, H. Vazquez, J. A. Diaz-Pace, C. Marcos, A. Garcia, and W. Oizumi. Jspirit: a flexible tool for the analysis of code smells. In *Int'l Conf. of the Chilean Computer Science Society (SCCC)*, pages 1–6, 2015.

[37] C. Wohlin, P. Runeson, M. Höst, M. Ohlsson, B. Regnell, and A. Wesslén. *Experimentation in software engineering*. Springer Science & Business Media, 2012.

[38] A. Yamashita and S. Counsell. Code smells as system-level indicators of maintainability: An empirical study. *J. of Systems and Software*, 86(10):2639–2653, 2013.

[39] A. Yamashita and L. Moonen. Do developers care about code smells? an exploratory survey. In *2013 20th working conference on reverse engineering (WCRE)*, 2013.

Validación del método de análisis de factibilidad del despliegue de sistemas de software: Estudios de caso

Leandro M. Moreno[1], Marisa Panizzi[1,2], Roberto Bertone[3]

[1] Programa de Maestría en Ingeniería en Sistemas de Información. Escuela de Posgrado. Universidad Tecnológica Nacional. Universidad Tecnológica Nacional. Facultad Regional Buenos Aires. Medrano 951, C.A.B.A, Argentina.
[2] Instituto de Tecnología e Ingeniería, Universidad Nacional de Hurlingham, Av. Vergara 2222 (B1688GEZ) - Villa Tesei - Bs. As. Argentina.
[3] Instituto de Investigación en Informática (III-LIDI). Facultad de Informática. Universidad Nacional de La Plata. Calle 50 y 120 - La Plata - Bs. As. – Argentina.

leandro.moreno@gmail.com, marisa.panizzi@outlook.com, pbertone@lidi.unlp.edu.ar

Resumen. *En este artículo se presenta la validación de la aplicabilidad de un método de análisis de factibilidad del despliegue de sistemas de software, que consiste en el análisis de las dimensiones Organización, Proceso, Personas, Producto y Prácticas, herramientas y técnicas del proceso de despliegue. Se realizaron dos estudios de caso en Pequeñas y Medianas empresas (PyMES) desarrolladoras de software de Argentina en los que se evaluaron las percepciones de los usuarios sobre el método. Se obtuvieron resultados que validan la facilidad, utilidad e intención de uso del método, con dimensiones del método muy bien valoradas excepto las dimensiones Personas y Organización que deberán tenerse en cuenta para refinar el método.*

1. Introducción

El proceso de despliegue de sistemas de software es un proceso crucial del ciclo de vida de su desarrollo. En sentido estricto, se circunscribe al momento en el que el sistema finalmente estará operativo para que el cliente pueda beneficiarse económicamente de su uso [Subramanian 2017]. La implementación de estándares existentes en el mercado frecuentemente se percibe costosa y compleja de realizar [Jansen y Brinkkemper 2006], por lo que las organizaciones más pequeñas deben enfrentar el desafío de hallar el equilibrio entre sus prácticas cotidianas horizontales y los procedimientos formales, definidos y documentados inherentes a la aplicación de procesos de mejora de software más avanzados [Subramanian 2017], [Paredes y Carvalho 2017]. Las fallas totales o parciales en los procesos de despliegue pueden ocasionar numerosos inconvenientes a nivel de proyecto y en la relación comercial con los clientes de una organización, ya sea por la negativa a recibir un software incompleto o con defectos. Esto puede ocasionar potenciales pérdidas económicas relacionadas al incumplimiento de objetivos y los retrasos experimentados en cada proyecto. En sentido contrario, los procesos exitosos de despliegue pueden aumentar sensiblemente la percepción de la calidad del software y, en consecuencia, sus expectativas comerciales [Jansen y Brinkkemper 2006]. Dado que aproximadamente el 80% de las organizaciones dedicadas al desarrollo de software en la Argentina son PyMES [Ministerio de Producción y Trabajo 2018]. los aportes realizados para este tipo de organizaciones contribuyen a la mejora continua de la industria del software.

Dada la relevancia del proceso de despliegue, los inconvenientes que conlleva un despliegue inadecuado más la necesidad de las PyMES de disponer de herramientas que las ayude a identificar los elementos del despliegue que requieren ajustes o revisiones para lograr la entrega satisfactoria, decidimos definir un método que permita analizar la factibilidad de despliegue de sistemas de software. Este método se basa en un análisis de cinco dimensiones que inciden directa o indirectamente sobre el proceso de despliegue: "Organización" (estructura organizacional en donde se desarrolla el proyecto de software), "Proceso" (flujo de trabajo del despliegue), "Personas" (factor humano que participa en el proceso de despliegue), "Producto" (sistema de software a desplegar) y "Prácticas, herramientas y técnicas" (abordajes sistematizados para llevar adelante el despliegue) [Petersen y Wohlin 2009]. A partir de la aplicación del método, se podrán identificar elementos del despliegue que requieran ajustes o revisiones para lograr un resultado exitoso, integrando una visión organizacional al análisis técnico, cuyo valor radica en la transversalidad de la evaluación que considera aspectos procedimentales, metodológicos y humanos, sumando mayor exhaustividad y permitiendo mejorar la calidad del proceso de toma de decisiones al momento de ejecutar cada despliegue.

En este artículo se presentan los resultados de la validación del método de análisis de factibilidad del despliegue de sistemas de software mediante dos estudios de caso que permitieron evaluar la percepción de los usuarios del método en PyMES desarrolladoras de software de Argentina para detectar las fortalezas y debilidades del método. Las tres variables de percepción tomadas del *Technology Acceptance Model* (TAM) [Davis 1989] son: "Facilidad de Uso Percibida" (en inglés, *Perceived Ease of Use* o PEOU), "Utilidad Percibida" (en inglés, *Perceived Usefulness* o PU) e "Intención de Uso" (en inglés, *Intention to Use* o ITU).

Para el diseño del método, realizamos el estado del arte mediante un mapeo sistemático de la literatura [Moreno *et al.* 2022] que nos permitió identificar la relevancia de las dimensiones "Organización", "Proceso", "Personas", "Producto" y "Prácticas, herramientas y técnicas" y logramos evidenciar que existe preponderancia de las dimensiones "Organización" y "Proceso" sobre las restantes, además de la ausencia de enfoques integrales en que se encuentren presentes las cinco dimensiones en un mismo análisis.

Posteriormente, construimos una primera versión del método considerando las dimensiones "Organización" y "Proceso", las cuales fueron validadas mediante un estudio de caso [Moreno *et al.* 2023]. Este estudio arrojó que el 93,3% del total de 60 preguntas del análisis sobre la factibilidad del despliegue de sistema de software del método fueron fáciles de comprender y relevantes. Asimismo, el 6,7% de dichas preguntas tuvieron deficiencias en la claridad y 3,35% en la precisión. Los resultados obtenidos de este estudio nos permitieron refinar y continuar con el desarrollo del método incorporando las tres dimensiones de análisis restantes (Personas, Producto, y Prácticas, herramientas y técnicas).

2. Descripción general del método

Para el diseño del método para analizar la factibilidad del despliegue de un sistema de software, se consideraron las dimensiones de análisis de los procesos de software propuestas por Petersen y Wohlin [Petersen y Wohlin 2009], estas son: "Organización", "Proceso", "Personas", "Producto" y "Prácticas, herramientas y técnicas".

El método propuesto se basa en el principio de los sistemas de inferencia difuso [Jang 1993] y recoge el formato de tabulación y cálculo de un modelo de evaluación de proyectos de explotación de información [Pytel 2014], aplicado en escenarios de medición de variables de origen multidimensional cuyo valor proviene de la interpretación de un usuario. Del mismo modo, el método de análisis de factibilidad de despliegue de un sistema de software propone la evaluación de dimensiones de análisis, a partir de la codificación de un conjunto limitado de valores lingüísticos para cada respuesta a preguntas contenidas en una plantilla. Cada una de las dimensiones seleccionadas se componen de categorías que abarcan diferentes conceptos sobre los que se realizan cada una de las preguntas de un cuestionario, cuyas respuestas representan un determinado nivel de certeza o completitud. Esto permite mitigar parcialmente potenciales desvíos producidos por la asignación de valores fijos, que podrían verse distorsionados de acuerdo con la percepción de cada usuario. Cada respuesta tiene un intervalo difuso asociado, con cuatro puntos de ruptura cuyos valores oscilan entre 0 al 10: "Nada" (0,01;0,01;1,2;2,2); "Poco" (1,2;2,2;3,4;4,4); "Regular" (3,4;4,4;5,6;6,6); Mucho (5,6;6,6;7,88;8); "Todo" (7,8;8,8;10;10). Asimismo, tomando en cuenta que el análisis de cada variable no tiene una relevancia constante dentro del método, se le brindó a cada pregunta un peso relativo y un umbral o valor mínimo esperado, cuyo incumplimiento no permite aprobar el puntaje mínimo requerido para dar por aprobado el análisis de factibilidad. Posteriormente, se obtiene el valor resultante por cada dimensión, y finalmente, el resultado total del método que consistirá en la igualación o superación de un umbral general.

En la Tabla 1, se presentan las categorías identificadas para cada una de las dimensiones definidas en el método. Por restricciones de espacio, la plantilla del cuestionario que conforma al método se encuentra detallada en un anexo [Moreno *et al.* 2024]. Para el cálculo del resultado del análisis de factibilidad del despliegue de software, se utiliza una planilla de cálculo que se presenta en el siguiente enlace: https://docs.google.com/spreadsheets/d/1PJuOTH1xhPYD83JdWNMLlcQT5RHYcUPB_wOyqYfy4SY.

Este método al realizarse en la instancia previa al despliegue del sistema de software permite identificar con los puntajes obtenidos a través de la observación de categorías contenidas en cada dimensión analizada, aquellas que requieran ajustes o revisiones para lograr un despliegue exitoso. Asimismo, cabe destacarse que el perfil indicado para llevarlo adelante es el de líder de proyecto, por ser el responsable ante el cliente que puede ser externo o interno. Tiene, además, conocimiento para solicitar cambios en caso de ser necesario y una visión transversal sobre cada dimensión estudiada. Finalmente, los puntajes parciales obtenidos en cada resultado de cada dimensión son sujetos a un cálculo global cuyo límite será traducido en una alerta visual representada por tres colores: a) Rojo: no factible; b) Amarillo: potencialmente no factible; c) Verde: potencialmente factible. Esto brindará insumos para evaluar qué dimensiones no cumplen individualmente el umbral de aprobación e identificar los elementos a observar, corregir y/o accionar.

Tabla 1. Dimensiones y categorías del método.

Dimensión	Categoría	Concepto	Descripción
Organización (OR)	Estructura organizacional	Flexibilidad y distribución	Adaptabilidad y flexibilidad de la organización [Nagappan *et al.* 2018].
	Gestión del conocimiento y comunicación	Capacitación, integración, conocimiento	Administración de los recursos intelectuales de la organización y flujo de información [Nagappan *et al.* 2018].
	Gestión del proyecto	Institucionalización, relevancia interna y asignación de recursos	Institucionalización de procesos, traducido en la adherencia de las prácticas previstas para su desarrollo [Nagappan *et al.* 2018].
	Estándares y regulación	Legislación, contrato, restricciones de la industria, restricciones internas	Restricciones y regulaciones que afectan el desempeño de las actividades [Nagappan *et al.* 2018].
Proceso (PR)	Institucionalización	Internalización, adherencia, madurez y proyección	Adherencia, internalización, madurez y proyección organizacional del proceso [CMMI Product Team 2018].
	Sistematicidad	Integridad, integralidad, prerrequisitos, verificabilidad, trazabilidad, métricas y roles	Integridad y satisfacción de requisitos necesarios para cumplir con el proceso de despliegue [CMMI Product Team 2018].
	Comunicación	Difusión	Publicidad del proceso de despliegue [CMMI Product Team 2018].
	Riesgo	Identificación y formalización	Acciones de identificación y mitigación de riesgos [CMMI Product Team 2018].
Personas (PE)	Recursos humanos y roles	Definición, involucramiento y dedicación	Generación de roles y perfiles adecuados en cada actividad [Nagappan *et al.* 2018].
Producto (PD)	Complejidad	Origen y tamaño	Multiplicidad o diversidad de orígenes y tamaño de los artefactos involucrados [Petersen y Wohlin 2009].
	Madurez	Evolución	Evolución para alcanzar un grado de madurez en la última versión, a partir del uso sostenido por parte de los usuarios finales, de acuerdo con el estándar ISO/IEC 25010 [ISO/IEC 2017].
	Mantenibilidad	Desarrollo, modularidad, código fuente, analizabilidad, capacidad de prueba	Criterios de mantenibilidad y escalabilidad, propuestos por los estándares ISO/IEC 25010 e ISO 5055 [ISO/IEC 2017] [ISO 2021] [Petersen y Wohlin 2009].
	Compatibilidad	Desarrollo	Coexistencia con otros sistemas en infraestructuras compartidas, según el estándar ISO/IEC 25010 [ISO/IEC 2017].
	Fiabilidad	Tolerancia a fallos	Capacidad para operar según lo previsto en presencia de fallos hardware

Dimensión	Categoría	Concepto	Descripción
			o software, según el estándar ISO/IEC 25010 [ISO/IEC 2017].
Prácticas, herramien-tas y Técnicas (PHT)	Monitorización	Monitorización de procesos y artefactos	Existencia de dispositivos que permitan visualizar y controlar el proceso de despliegue y sus componentes, propuesto por el estándar ISO/IEC 19770 [ISO/IEC 2017b].
	Mejora continua	Mejora continua	Mecanismos de retroalimentación sobre experiencias anteriores aplicables al proceso [CMMI Product Team 2018].
	Automatizaciones	Automatizaciones	Prácticas automatizadas ya sea para el despliegue como para la ejecución de pruebas, de acuerdo a los estándares ISO/IEC/IEEE 29119 e ISO/IEC/IEEE 32675 [ISO/IEC/IEEE 2022], [ISO/IEC/IEEE 2022b].
	Configuración	Gestión de la configuración	Prácticas de gestión de la configuración en el marco del proyecto, conforme a CMMI [CMMI Product Team 2018].
	Prácticas y técnicas	Prácticas, entrega continua e integración continua	Técnicas de replicación de ambientes, estrategias de rollback, despliegue continuo e integración continua como instrumentos para el despliegue, de acuerdo a la ISO/IEC/IEEE 32675 [ISO/IEC/IEEE 2022b].

3. Estudios de caso

En esta sección se presentan dos estudios de caso (EC1 y EC2) realizados en PyMES desarrolladoras de software de Argentina, con el propósito de validar el método de análisis de factibilidad de despliegue de sistema de software propuesto para detectar sus fortalezas y debilidades. En estos estudios se evaluaron las percepciones de las variables PEOU, PU e ITU tomadas como se mencionó anteriormente del *Technology Acceptance Model* (TAM) [Davis 1989]. Para la realización y reporte de los estudios de casos se siguieron las directrices propuestas por en [Runeson *et al.* 2012].

3.1. Objetivos y preguntas de investigación (PI) de los estudios de caso

En la Tabla 2 se presenta el objetivo de los estudios de caso siguiendo el paradigma Goal-Question-Metric [Basili *et al.* 1988].

Tabla 2. Objetivo de los estudios de caso.

Analizar	la aplicación del método de análisis de factibilidad para el despliegue de sistemas de software,
con el propósito de	evaluar la percepción de los usuarios,
con respecto a	la "Facilidad de Uso Percibida", "Utilidad Percibida" e "Intención de Uso",
desde el punto de vista	de profesionales de la industria del software,
en el contexto de	PyMES de Argentina.

Para lograr este objetivo se plantearon las siguientes preguntas de investigación (PI):

PI1: ¿Cuál ha sido la percepción de los profesionales de la industria del software al aplicar el método de análisis de factibilidad del despliegue de sistemas de software?

Para dar respuesta a esta pregunta, como se comentó anteriormente, se evaluaron tres variables de percepción tomadas de (TAM) [Davis 1989].

PI2: ¿Cuáles son las fortalezas y debilidades informadas por la organización al aplicar el método propuesto?

Con esta pregunta se busca indagar las fortalezas y debilidades del uso del método, y así indagar sobre qué aspectos sería necesario mejorar.

3.2. Contexto, caso y unidad de análisis (EC1 y EC2)

De acuerdo con la clasificación de Yin [Yin 2014] los dos estudios de caso son holísticos y de casos únicos caracterizados por los elementos que se presentan en la Tabla 3. Se utilizó la clasificación de PyMES en Argentina según la cantidad de empleados [Ministerio de Desarrollo Productivo 2018].

Tabla 3. Contexto: actores, contexto, caso y unidad de análisis de los estudios de caso (EC1, EC2).

Estudios de caso	Actores	Contexto	Caso	Unidad de análisis
EC1	**PyME mediana de tramo 1** de 46 empleados, ubicada en Argentina, que ofrece servicios del rubro financiero.	La empresa utiliza una metodología de desarrollo ágil, en la que se cumplen las etapas de recolección de requerimientos, análisis, codificación e implementación de los desarrollos dentro de cada sprint, finalizando con el proceso de despliegue en ambiente productivo.	Despliegue de un sistema web de gestión de accesos e identidad de clientes.	Aplicación del método de análisis de factibilidad de despliegue de sistema de software.
EC2	**PyME mediana de tramo 1** de 55 empleados, ubicada en Argentina, que ofrece servicios del rubro financiero.		Despliegue de un paquete de evolutivos para un sistema de enrolamiento con datos biométricos de una empresa del sector financiero.	

En la Tabla 4 se muestra el detalle de cada uno de los módulos involucrados en el despliegue para cada uno de los estudios de caso. Las fechas de despliegue (puesta en producción) y de capacitación han sido acordadas entre el cliente y las PyMES

Tabla 4. Módulos involucrados en el despliegue y su descripción.

Estudios de caso	Nombre del módulo	Descripción
EC1	Formularios de autenticación.	Identificador de origen de sesión Implementación de mecanismo de prevención de inyección de datos Look and Feel.
	Autogestión de identidad.	Edición de datos personales Look and Feel.
EC2	Dashboard de uso de reconocimiento facial.	Monitor actualizado en tiempo real con datos de transacciones sobre la aplicación.
	Dashboard histórico de conversiones.	Reporte histórico con datos de fechas pasadas que incluye enrolamientos.

3.3. Preparación para la recolección de los datos

En los estudios de caso participaron dos lideres de proyectos, uno de cada una de las PyMES a los cuales se les brindo una capacitación sobre el método propuesto, en dos sesiones de dos horas cada una de manera virtual a través de *Microsoft Teams*.

Para facilitar la recolección de los datos y dar respuesta a la primera pregunta de investigación (PI1), se utilizó un cuestionario basado en TAM, para evaluar la percepción de los usuarios una vez aplicado el método de análisis de factibilidad de despliegue dentro de sus respectivos procesos de despliegue (Ver Tabla 5). Este cuestionario contiene 20 ítems definidos para medir las dimensiones descritas anteriormente. Cada ítem se evalúa con una escala Likert de 5 puntos utilizando etiquetas lingüísticas. Las etiquetas lingüísticas utilizadas son: "Totalmente de acuerdo", "De acuerdo", "Parcialmente de acuerdo", "En desacuerdo" y "Totalmente en desacuerdo".

La estructura del cuestionario cuenta con un primer nivel con cada una de las dimensiones definidas en el método (Organización, Proceso, Personas, Producto y Prácticas, herramientas y técnicas). Cada una de éstas cuenta con un segundo nivel para cada una de las variables de percepción a medir (PEOU, PU y ITU). La variable PEOU se mide utilizando diez ítems de la encuesta (P1, P3, P5, P8, P9, P11, P13, P15, P17 y P19). La variable PU se mide con cinco ítems de la encuesta (P2, P7, P10, P14 y P18). Y la variable ITU se mide con cinco ítems (P4, P6, P12, P16 y P20). Además, en el cuestionario se plantearon algunos ítems de manera positiva y algunos ítems de manera negativa para mitigar los desvíos de un posible sesgo por parte del usuario al responder en serie. El cuestionario basado en TAM se envió a los Líderes de proyecto vía correo electrónico.

Tabla 5. Cuestionario basado en TAM.

Ítems del cuestionario	Variable a medir
Dimensión Organización	
P1.- Considero que las preguntas incluidas dentro de la dimensión Organización del método son claras y fáciles de entender.	PEOU

P2.- En general, encuentro útiles las preguntas propuestas para la dimensión Organización.	PU
P3.- Considero que las preguntas formuladas en la dimensión Organización son claras y fáciles de aplicar.	PEOU
P4.- Usaré la sección correspondiente a la dimensión Organización para futuros despliegues de sistemas de software	ITU
Dimensión Proceso	
P5.- Encuentro que los recursos propuestos en la dimensión Proceso son fáciles de aplicar.	PEOU
P6.- Usaré las preguntas de la dimensión Proceso para ejecutar el despliegue de sistemas de software.	ITU
P7.- Considero que las preguntas de la dimensión Proceso mejorarían el proceso de despliegue de sistemas de software.	PU
P8.- Las preguntas planteadas en la dimensión Proceso son fáciles de aplicar en el despliegue de software.	PEOU
Dimensión Personas	
P9.- Encuentro las preguntas del relativas a la dimensión Personas complejas y difíciles de responder.	PEOU
P10.- Considero que el proceso de elaboración de las respuestas en la dimensión Personas permitirían reducir problemas en el despliegue.	PU
P11.- Considero que la estructura del cuestionario en la dimensión Personas es confusa y difícil de entender.	PEOU
P12.- No tengo la intención de utilizar la dimensión Personas del método en los futuros despliegues de sistemas de software.	ITU
Dimensión Producto	
P13.- Encuentro las preguntas relativas a la dimensión Producto complejas y difíciles de responder.	PEOU
P14.- Considero que el proceso de elaboración de las respuestas en la dimensión Producto permitirían reducir problemas en el despliegue.	PU
P15.- Considero que tanto la estructura del cuestionario en la dimensión Producto es confuso y difícil de entender.	PEOU
P16.- No tengo la intención de aplicar la Dimensión Producto del método en los futros despliegues de sistemas de software.	ITU
Dimensión Prácticas, herramientas y técnicas	
P17.- Encuentro las preguntas relativas a la dimensión Prácticas, herramientas y técnicas complejas y difíciles de responder.	PEOU
P18.- Considero que el proceso de elaboración de las respuestas en la dimensión Prácticas, herramientas y técnicas permitirían reducir problemas en el despliegue.	PU
P19.- Considero que tanto la estructura en la dimensión Prácticas, herramientas y técnicas es confusa y difícil de entender.	PEOU
P20.- No tengo la intención de utilizar la dimensión Prácticas, herramientas y técnicas en los futuros despliegues de sistemas de software.	ITU

El tipo de recolección de datos definida en EC1 y EC2 se corresponde a la técnica de recolección de primer grado según la clasificación propuesta por Lethbridge *et al.* [Lethbridge *et al.* 2005].

La etapa de recolección de datos cualitativos en EC1 y EC2 se completa a través de codificación de las respuestas y la realización de los cálculos de las respuestas del cuestionario basado en TAM, en la planilla de cálculo ubicada en *https://docs.google.com/spreadsheets/d/1Z3j-iJaeAzvZtkB5uUZ6IGjQGsbs2HnD4Q2FFTWNyhE* . Con esto se obtuvo respuesta a la primera pregunta de investigación (PI1).

Posteriormente, para dar respuesta a la segunda pregunta de investigación (PI2), se realiza una entrevista semiestructurada a cada uno de los líderes de proyecto que aplicaron el método propuesto, con el objetivo de indagar sobre las fortalezas y debilidades de este. El cuestionario empleado en la entrevista se divide en tres categorías de preguntas. Para las preguntas de la primera categoría respecto a las preguntas demográficas (PE1 y PE2) se consideraron las preguntas del estudio HELENA [Kurmann *et al.* 2018] por tratarse de un estudio internacionalmente reconocido. Las restantes preguntas se focalizan en las dimensiones del método (PE3 y PE4) y finalmente, sobre la experiencia general del método que han aplicado los lideres de proyectos (PE5, PE6 y PE7). En la Tabla 6 se presentan las preguntas del cuestionario utilizado en la entrevista.

Tabla 6. Preguntas del cuestionario utilizadas en la entrevista de EC1 y EC2.

Categoría 1: Preguntas demográficas.
PE1.- ¿Cuál es su rol actual en la empresa?
PE2.- ¿Cuánto tiempo hace que trabaja en la industria del software?
Categoría 2: Preguntas sobre los instrumentos del método.
PE3.- ¿Completó todas las dimensiones definidas en el método (Organización, Proceso, Personas, Producto y Prácticas, herramientas y técnicas)?
PE4.- ¿Cuál es su opinión respecto al cuestionario del método?
Categoría 3: Preguntas sobre el método en general
PE5.- ¿Qué agregaría o quitaría al método?
PE6.- ¿Cuál es su valoración sobre su experiencia del uso del método? (Muy buena/Buena/Parcialmente buena/Regular/Mala).
PE7.- ¿Cómo valora el impacto de usar el método en la calidad de sus futuros despliegues? Alto/Medio/Bajo.

Los resultados de las entrevistas cuyo objetivo consiste en dar respuesta a la PI2 respecto a las fortalezas y debilidades descriptas por la PyME al aplicar el método se encuentran detallados en el Anexo [Moreno *et al.* 2024]. El tiempo empleado para entrevistar al líder de proyecto ha sido de aproximadamente 15 minutos. El desarrollo de la entrevista consistió en las siguientes fases:

- Fase 1: explicación del objetivo de la entrevista. En esta etapa se solicitó permiso para la grabación.
- Fase 2: en esta etapa se realizaron preguntas demográficas relacionadas a la experiencia profesional en la industria del software, rol que desempeña en la empresa (PE1, PE2).
- Fase 3: en esta etapa se realizaron las preguntas relacionadas a las dimensiones del método (PE3, PE4).
- Fase 4: en esta etapa se realizaron preguntas relacionadas con la experiencia general del uso del método (PE5, PE6 y PE7).

- Fase post entrevista: se realizó la transcripción de la entrevista y se validó con el entrevistado para asegurar la fiabilidad de las respuestas interpretadas.

Para facilitar el análisis de los datos recopilados en las entrevistas y realizar un registro sistemático de los datos se definió una planilla con un esquema de codificación de acuerdo con el enfoque de la plantilla [Runeson *et al.* 2012], que se encuentra en el Anexo [Moreno *et al.* 2024]. Esto permite satisfacer el requisito de formalismo y estructuración que garantizan la revisión entre los pares investigadores, la trazabilidad y la capacidad de replicación.

3.4. Análisis e interpretación de los datos de EC1 y EC2

En esta sección, en primer lugar, se presentan los resultados obtenidos del cuestionario TAM sobre las percepciones de los usuarios (lideres de proyectos) del método para dar respuesta a la PI1. En segundo lugar, se describen los resultados de las entrevistas realizadas a cada uno de los usuarios con el propósito de dar respuesta a la PI2 respecto a las fortalezas y debilidades del método.

En la Tabla 7 se presentan los resultados de las tres variables de percepción obtenidas de cada usuario.

Tabla 7. Variables de percepción del método (EC1 y EC2).

Estudio de caso	Usuarios	PEOU	PU	ITU
EC1	Líder de proyecto	92%	84%	52%
EC2	Líder de proyecto	76%	84%	84%

Para lograr los resultados de cada una de las variables de percepción para cada uno de los usuarios se realizaron los pasos obtenidos de [Panizzi 2022].

Las percepciones obtenidas del usuario Líder de Proyecto sobre el método para EC1 y EC2, se recoge un valor 92% y 76% para cada uno, respecto a la variable "Facilidad de Uso Percibida". Sobre la variable "Utilidad Percibida", 84% para ambos casos. Finalmente, para medir la percepción de la variable "Intención de Uso", se recogieron valores de 52% y 84% del método en futuros despliegues. Para lograr la descomposición porcentual de cada variable de percepción por cada una de las dimensiones del método se realizaron los siguientes pasos obtenidos de [Panizzi 2022]:

1) Para cada variable se calculó la percepción parcial por dimensión de la misma manera que se calcula la percepción total de la variable. Los valores para emplear en los cálculos se presentan en la Tabla 8.

Tabla 8. Cálculo de la variable de percepción (EC1 y EC2).

Cálculo de variable de percepción – Dimensión					
Total de Preguntas	Total de Respuestas	Puntuación Mínima posible	Puntuación Máxima Posible	Puntuación Total en la escala	% Percepción por dimensión

2) Una vez obtenidos los porcentajes para cada una de las dimensiones de una determinada variable de percepción, se realiza la sumatoria.

3) Para cada dimensión de una determinada variable de percepción se realiza el siguiente cálculo:

Porcentaje de la dimensión/Sumatoria de los porcentajes de todas dimensiones

De esta manera, se obtiene la descomposición porcentual de la variable para cada una de las dimensiones del método.

En Tabla 9 se presenta para cada uno de los casos (EC1 y E2) y variables de percepción (PEOU, PU e ITU), su composición en relación con las dimensiones propuestas en el método para el usuario objetivo.

Tabla 9. Percepción de cada dimensión del método (EC1 y EC2).

Dimensión	PEOU		PU		ITU	
	EC1	EC2	EC1	EC2	EC1	EC2
Organización	21,74%	5,26%	23,81%	23,81%	7,69%	23,81%
Proceso	21,74%	26,32%	23,81%	23,81%	38,46%	23,81%
Personas	21,74%	26,32%	4,76%	4,76%	7,69%	23,81%
Producto	21,74%	15,79%	23,81%	23,81%	38,46%	23,81%
Prácticas, herramientas y técnicas	13,04%	26,32%	23,81%	23,81%	7,69%	4,76%

Las transcripciones de las entrevistas realizadas a los líderes de proyecto fueron llevadas a cabo por uno de los investigadores y la codificación resultante fue examinada entre los tres autores para mitigar el riesgo de sesgo por parte del primero [Runeson *et al.* 2012]. El detalle de estas se encuentra en el anexo [Moreno *et al.* 2024].

3.5. Resultados de EC1

Los resultados obtenidos en EC1, llevado a cabo en una PyME de tramo 1 (46 empleados) desarrolladora de software de Argentina, relacionados con las preguntas de investigación son los siguientes:

PI1: ¿Cuál ha sido la percepción de los profesionales de la industria del software al aplicar el método de análisis de factibilidad del despliegue de sistemas de software?

A partir de la lectura de las variables de percepción del cuestionario realizado al líder de proyecto, se considera que el método tiene niveles de aprobación en las variables "Facilidad de uso percibida" (92%) y "Utilidad percibida" (84%). Asimismo, respecto a la variable "Intención de uso", el nivel fue notablemente menor (52%) que el resto.

Respecto a la representatividad de las dimensiones sobre cada variable, en primer lugar, con relación a las dimensiones Organización, Proceso, Personas y Producto, la variable "Facilidad de Uso Percibida" presenta el mayor valor (21,74%). El menor valor se presenta en la dimensión Prácticas, herramientas y técnicas. (13,04%). Con relación a la variable "Utilidad Percibida", presentan un porcentaje más elevado (23,81%) las dimensiones Proceso, Producto y Prácticas, herramientas y técnicas. En último lugar se ubica la dimensión Personas (4,56%). En relación con las dimensiones Proceso y

Producto, la variable "Intención de Uso" presenta un alto porcentaje (38,46%). Las restantes dimensiones Organización, Personas y Prácticas, herramientas y técnicas se registran un menor valor de representatividad (7,69%).

PI2: ¿Cuáles son las fortalezas y debilidades informadas por la organización al aplicar el método propuesto?

El usuario entrevistado cumple el rol de líder de proyecto y cuenta con 8 años de experiencia en la industria del software. Este usuario indica que la experiencia general de la aplicación del método ha sido positiva en tanto logró identificar a través de una alerta por bajo puntaje global en forma de semáforo rojo sobre el área de resultados de la plantilla utilizada para llevarlo adelante, elementos sobre la Dimensión Proceso a reforzar y sobre los cuales capacitar. Asimismo, asegura que incorporar este método impactaría medianamente en la calidad de los futuros despliegues de sistemas de software de la empresa. Por otra parte, indica que, si bien el cuestionario del método pudo ser respondido en su totalidad, algunas preguntas relativas a la composición de los roles sobre la dimensión Personas resultaron menos relevantes, mientras que carece de elementos para responder otras de la dimensión Organización sobre la distribución interna de recursos. Por este motivo, sostiene que se debería poder omitir algunas preguntas o bien, prescindirse.

3.6. Resultados de EC2

Los resultados obtenidos en EC2, llevado a cabo en una PyME de tramo 1 (55 empleados) desarrolladora de software de Argentina, relacionados con las preguntas de investigación son los siguientes:

PI1: ¿Cuál ha sido la percepción de los profesionales de la industria del software al aplicar el método de análisis de factibilidad del despliegue de sistemas de software?

De acuerdo a lo obtenido en la respuesta de las preguntas del cuestionario de la Encuesta TAM por parte del usuario líder de proyecto, se considera que el método tiene un alto nivel en las tres variables analizadas: "Facilidad de uso percibida" (76%), "Utilidad percibida" (84%) e "Intención de uso" (84%).Asimismo, respecto a la representatividad de las dimensiones, con relación a las dimensiones Proceso, Personas y Prácticas, herramientas y técnicas, la variable "Facilidad de Uso Percibida" presenta el mayor valor (26,32%). En segundo lugar, se encuentra la dimensión Producto (15,79%). En último lugar se encuentra la dimensión Organización (5,26%). Con relación a la variable "Utilidad Percibida", presentan el mayor porcentaje de representatividad (23,81%), las dimensiones Organización, Proceso, Producto y Prácticas, herramientas y técnicas. En último lugar se ubica la dimensión Personas (4,76%). En relación con las dimensiones, Organización, Proceso, Personas, Producto, la variable "Intención de Uso" presenta un alto porcentaje de representatividad (23,81%). La restante dimensión Prácticas, herramientas y técnicas se ubica con menor representatividad en la intención de uso (4,76%).

PI2: ¿Cuáles son las fortalezas y debilidades informadas por la organización al aplicar el método propuesto?

El usuario entrevistado cumple el rol de líder de proyecto y cuenta con 12 años de experiencia en la industria de software. Este usuario indica que la experiencia general de la aplicación del método ha sido muy buena al haber logrado ajustar elementos sobre la dimensión Proceso, así como revisar y accionar sobre otros de la dimensión Organización a través del trabajo en aspectos comunicacionales de la empresa. El método arrojó un puntaje parcial por debajo del umbral previsto en las dimensiones Organización y Proceso, por lo que el valor final fue representado por un indicador semáforo de color rojo sobre la sección de resultados. Por este motivo, argumenta que el potencial impacto en la calidad de los futuros despliegues de sistemas de software de la empresa es de nivel alto. Asimismo, desearía que pudieran omitirse ciertas preguntas relativas a las prácticas, herramientas y técnicas y/o considerar alguna forma de que se ignoren en la puntuación final. Particularmente, el usuario manifestó que las preguntas sobre el uso de herramientas de monitoreo y el desarrollo de automatizaciones no aplican ni podrían considerarse en su caso de despliegue y que sería conveniente poder eliminarlas o ignorarlas.

3.7. Amenazas a la validez

Para analizar las amenazas a la validez de EC1 y EC2 se tuvieron en cuenta los factores propuestos por Runeson *et al.* [Runeson *et al.* 2012].

- Validez del constructo. El cuestionario basado en TAM permitió evaluar la percepción de las tres variables y de todas las dimensiones que componen el método. Las entrevistas realizadas de manera personalizada permitieron comprender las preguntas por los usuarios (Lideres de proyectos). La formación impartida ha sido adecuada. Todas estas acciones realizadas nos permitieron mitigar este aspecto.
- Validez interna. Si bien la información obtenida a través del cuestionario basado en TAM y las entrevistas proviene de solo 2 Lideres de proyectos de 2 PyMES desarrolladoras de software en Argentina es importante resaltar que el método ha sido aplicado y evaluado en el contexto real y que se lograron responder las preguntas de investigación.
- Validez externa. El uso de un estudio de caso único y holístico puede limitar la generalización de los resultados. Encontramos que los dos lideres de proyectos coinciden en que el método les ha permitido identificar y evaluar accionables para la mejora de su proceso de despliegue, y basados en su experiencia, lo podrían extender a otros escenarios.
- Fiabilidad. Los datos de EC1 y EC2 fueron recopilados por un solo investigador. Aunque fueron analizados entre los tres autores, esto puede considerarse una amenaza para la investigación. Para agregar un mayor grado de confiabilidad, sería recomendable que otro investigador aplicara la estrategia del caso (cuestionario TAM y entrevista) en otros estudios de caso.

4. Conclusiones y trabajos futuros

En este artículo se han presentado dos estudios de caso en los que se aplicó el método de análisis de factibilidad en el despliegue de sistemas de software por parte de los respectivos líderes de proyecto sobre escenarios reales. Ambos estudios fueron realizados en dos PyMES desarrolladoras de software de Argentina, obteniendo retroalimentación sobre la percepción de su facilidad de uso, utilidad e intención de uso:

- En ambos estudios de caso (EC1 y EC2), se obtuvo una respuesta favorable sobre la Facilidad de Uso Percibida (76% y 92% respectivamente), lo que nos brinda un indicador positivo respecto al registro lingüístico y a la estructura del método.

- Los entrevistados, con experiencia en la industria del software de 8 y 12 años respectivamente, en ambos estudios de caso (EC1 y EC2) hicieron mención sobre el menor grado de representatividad de la dimensión Personas respecto a la variable Utilidad Percibida. El usuario de EC1 mencionó que la
- Los estudios de caso (EC1 y EC2) arrojaron diferentes resultados respecto a la intención de uso global del método para el futuro. En EC1, la intención global de uso arrojó un 52%, mientras que en EC2, fue de 84%. En ambos casos se observa la mayor representatividad de las dimensiones Producto y Proceso, lo que puede considerarse una fortaleza para el método propuesto ya que ponderan tanto la evaluación propuesta sobre los aspectos procedimentales del despliegue como las variables del artefacto desplegado. No obstante, se recogió que tanto las dimensiones Personas como Prácticas, herramientas y técnicas fueron evaluadas con menor utilidad e intención de uso, lo que las hace menos atractivas para la adopción del método. Los usuarios del método señalaron la incapacidad para evaluar algunos aspectos de las personas involucradas en el proyecto como también la irrelevancia de otras variables relativas a las tecnologías utilizadas.

Teniendo en cuenta los resultados obtenidos en los estudios de casos, el próximo paso en esta investigación será refinar el método revisando, simplificando o analizando la exclusión dinámica de ciertas preguntas de los cuestionarios de cada dimensión. Dada la diversidad de escenarios en los que se podría implementar el método, se introducirá la posibilidad de responder opcionalmente a través de la asignación de un valor residual del tipo "no aplica". Asimismo, se considerará el desarrollo de alguna herramienta que permita automatizar en mayor medida la aplicación del método de forma más sencilla y en menor tiempo.

Otras posibles líneas de trabajo futuro son: a) extender la evaluación del método por fuera del universo de las PyMES de Argentina y b) evaluar continuar el método propuesto y desarrollar una funcionalidad de salida de datos exportables para su uso y explotación.

5. Bibliografía

Basili V., Rombach D. (1988), The TAME project: towards improvement-oriented software environments. IEEE Transactions on Software Engineering, 14(6).

CMMI Product Team (2018), "CMMI for Development, Version 2.0," Software Engineering Institute, Carnegie Mellon University, Pittsburgh, Pennsylvania.

Davis F. (1989), Perceived Usefulness, Perceived Ease of Use and User Acceptance of Information Technology. MIS Quarterly 13, 13(3), pp. 319-340.

ISO/IEC. (2017), ISO/IEC 25010. Systems and software engineering. Systems and software Quality Requirements and Evaluation (SQuaRE)

ISO/IEC. (2017b), ISO/IEC 19770. Information technology - IT asset management

ISO/IEC/IEEE. (2022), ISO/IEC/IEEE 29119. Software Testing Standard.

ISO/IEC/IEEE. (2022b), ISO/IEC/IEEE 32675. Information technology — DevOps —

ISO. (2021), ISO 5055. Information technology. Software measurement.

Jang, J.S.R. (1993), ANFIS: Adaptive-Network-Based Fuzzy Inference System.

Jansen S., Brinkkemper S (2006), Definition and validation of the key process of release, delivery and deployment for product software vendors: *Turning the ugly duckling into a swan IEEE International Conference on Software Maintenance*, pp. 166-175.

Kurmann M., Tell P., Klünder J., Hebig R., Licorish S., MacDonell S. (2018), Complementing materials for the HELENA study.

Ministerio de Producción y Trabajo. (2018), "Informe Argentina Productiva", Presidencia de la Nación Argentina. Secretaría de la Transformación Productiva. - Economía del Conocimiento, https://biblioteca.produccion.gob.ar/buscar/?fid=16

Moreno L., Panizzi M., Bertone R. (2022), Revisión de la Literatura sobre el Análisis de Factibilidad del Despliegue de Sistemas de Software. En *10mo Congreso Nacional de Ingeniería Informática y Sistemas de Información*, CONAIISI 2022, pp. 731-738. Concepción del Uruguay, Entre Ríos, Argentina. https://rtyc.utn.edu.ar/index.php/ajea/article/view/1146/1059

Moreno L., Panizzi M., Bertone R. (2023), Refinamiento del método de análisis de factibilidad del despliegue de sistemas de software: Estudio de caso. En *XXIX Congreso Argentino de Ciencias de la Computación,* CACIC 2023*, Luján, Buenos Aires, Argentina*

Moreno L., Panizzi M., Bertone R. (2024), Anexo: Validación del método de análisis de factibilidad del despliegue de sistemas de software: Estudios de caso. https://doi.org/10.6084/m9.figshare.25093541

Panizzi M. (2022). *DepProMod*: Modelo de Proceso de Despliegue de Sistemas de Software. Tesis Doctoral. Universidad Nacional de La Plata. http://sedici.unlp.edu.ar/handle/10915/139509

Nagappan, N., Murphy, B., Basili, V. (2018), The influence of organizational structure on software quality.

Paredes I., Carvalho J. (2017), Research in Progress: Understanding the process of implantation IT Enterprise Applications in Small and Medium Enterprises (SMEs).

Petersen, K. Wohlin, C. (2009), Context in industrial software engineering research.

Pressman, R. S. (2010), Software Engineering: A Practitioner's Approach. 7th Edition. MacGraw Hill, New York

Pytel, P. (2014), Viabilidad y Estimación de proyectos de explotación de información. Tesis doctoral. Facultad de Informática. Universidad Nacional de La Plata. http://sedici.unlp.edu.ar/handle/10915/43572

Runeson P., Höst M., Rainer A., Regnell B. (2012), Case study research in software engineering: guidelines and examples. Wiley Publishing, Hoboken.

Subramanian N. (2017), The software deployment process and automation. pp. 28-34

Yin R. (2014), Case study research: design and methods. Fifth Edition. Sage Publications.

Metrics in Large-Scale Agile Software Development: A Multivocal Literature Review

Renato Menezes[1], **Marcelo Marinho**[1], **Suzana Sampaio**[1]

[1]Computer Department – Universidade Federal Rural de Pernambuco (UFRPE)
Recife – PE – Brazil

{renato.vmenezes, marcelo.marinho,suzana.sampaio}@ufrpe.br

Abstract. *Software development is widespread across various sectors. As large-scale projects increasingly adopt agile development practices, there arises a need for metrics to enhance team coordination, promote continuous improvement and monitor progress. This discussion focuses on the current state of metrics for large-scale agile software development, outlining the reasons for their adoption and showcasing the achieved results. The analysis involves a comprehensive literature review, exploring grey literature. A catalog of metrics applicable to scalable agile projects is presented, featuring examples such as 'Velocity', 'Business value per effort', and 'Defect rate'.*

1. Introduction

Coordinating multiple teams across different projects using agile methodologies represents a complex and crucial challenge in the software development environment [Marinho et al. 2021, Camara et al. 2021]. In this dynamic context, maintaining an adequate level of communication becomes more challenging [Philipp et al. 2023]. Large organizations struggle to use metrics effectively due to many influencing factors, such as lack of skill demanded, infrastructure and a lack of guidance, making efficient measurement complex [Korpivaara et al. 2021]. Therefore, for monitoring processes and projects, more than relying solely on qualitative feedback by regularly communicating with each agile team is required for program management decision-making [Philipp et al. 2023, Camara et al. 2021]. In such circumstances, metrics can enhance or replace qualitative feedback [Ertaban et al. 2018, Philipp et al. 2023].

Despite the fundamental importance of metrics in this context and repeated calls from researchers for documented knowledge, there is still a shortage in the scientific literature of dedicated studies to fill this gap [Dingsøyr and Moe 2014, Edison et al. 2021, Korpivaara et al. 2021, Philipp et al. 2023]. Therefore, it is essential to turn to grey literature to add more evidence to the academic literature on metrics used scaling agile, as discussed and presented by industry professionals and experienced academics.

This paper aims to contribute to the body of knowledge in large-scale agile methods, proposing a comprehensive approach that includes the compilation of metrics, an in-depth exploration of the justifications for their application, and an analysis of the results obtained. To do so, we systematically categorize metrics to provide continuous support to organizations in agile scaling and those exploring new work paradigms. We highlight how the judicious application of metrics can drive agility at scale, promoting substantial improvements in organizational practices and development team performance.

In addition to this introduction, Section 2 presents a background and related work. Sections 3 and 4 present the research methodology and results, respectively. Section 5 discusses the findings of this study. Section 6 exposes some threats to validity, and finally, Section 7 provides some conclusions and contributions of the work.

2. Background and Related Works

2.1. Software Metrics

In traditional software development, metrics assisted in project guidance and decision-making [Chloros et al. 2022]. With the popularization of agile values, different software development processes emerged, where metrics needed to adapt to changes in all development phases [Hossain et al. 2021, Leal et al. 2022]. Agile teams use metrics to improve agile processes, comply with agility protocols, enhance software quality during development, improve estimation and planning, and increase productivity [Chloros et al. 2022, Leal et al. 2022].

Metrics are measurements, variables to which a quantity is assigned due to measuring one or several entities [Fenton and Bieman 2014, Leal et al. 2022]. Due to their advantages, many agile metrics have been proposed or adapted to help measure various aspects of software development processes and products [Leal et al. 2022].

2.2. Large-Scale Agile Development

Most agile software development organisations are based on self-managed teams responsible for developing a subset of features [Camara et al. 2020, Marinho et al. 2021, Marinho et al. 2019]. Agile at scale is a way to manage processes beyond team-level software development using specific agile tools [Laanti 2014], also encompassing the implementation of agile methods and principles throughout the organisation [Dingsøyr and Moe 2014].

Dingsoyr *et al.* [Dingsøyr et al. 2014] categorize the scale of agile software development projects by team count. Small-scale projects consist of a single team, coordinating through standard agile practices. Large-scale projects involve 2 to 9 teams, requiring scaling methodologies for coordination. Projects with 10 or more teams are considered very large-scale, necessitating a scaling framework. This study follows Dingsoyr's definition of large-scale agile.

The organization's size, geographic distribution, team size, culture, system complexity, governance and business objectives are some aspects considered when scaling agile methods [Razzak et al. 2017, Shameem et al. 2017]. The main known agile scaling frameworks are: Scrum-at-Scale, Large Scale Scrum (LeSS), Scaled Agile Framework (SAFe), Disciplined Agile (DA), Spotify and Nexus [Shameem et al. 2017, Edison et al. 2021].Compared to SAFe, other agile frameworks (e.g., Scrum-at-Scale, LeSS, Nexus, Spotify) offer fewer native metrics, artifacts, roles and events beyond Scrum [Razzak et al. 2017].

2.3. Related Work

Among the related works, Edison et al. (2021) investigated the various known methods of large-scale agile development by comparing them through an SLR. The review did not present which metrics are used in some of the major existing frameworks [Edison et al. 2021]. Kišš and Rossi (2018) sought to understand the "Agile to Lean" transformation processes, covering benefits, challenges, and metrics in transformations at larger scales. Lead Time emerged as the most used metric to measure transformation progress among the metrics. However, metrics were presented only in that context [Kišš and Rossi 2018].

Britto et al. (2014) reported the evidence obtained from SLRs regarding effort estimation in software development in the global and agile context. Size metrics such as Function Points, Lines of Code, Use Case Points, and Story Points were presented. However, the work is focused only on effort estimation aspects [Britto et al. 2014].

3. Research Method

We conducted a Multivocal Literature Review (MLR) to gather and synthesize the limited information found in academic literature with other findings from grey literature, aiming to extract information about the metrics used within the context of large-scale agile development. This MLR followed the guidelines provided by [Garousi et al. 2019].

To specify the objective of this article, two research questions were formulated: **(RQ1)** What metrics are used in large-scale agile software development? And **(RQ2)** What are the reasons and results of using metrics in large-scale agile development?

We used the following databases to find relevant literature: ACM, IEEExplore, Springer-Link, Scopus and ScienceDirect to specifically locate academic literature. And Google search (http://www.google.com/) to find grey literature. To find evidence according to the research questions, the string used was as follows: **(Metric) AND (SAFe OR "Scaled agile framework" OR LeSS OR "Large scale scrum" OR "Scrum-at-Scale" OR "Scrum@Scale" OR DA OR "Disciplined agile" OR Spotify OR Scrum OR "Scaling agile" OR Nexus) AND ("Large-scale" OR Large OR Scaled)**.

We defined inclusion and exclusion criteria to ensure the inclusion of all relevant sources and the exclusion of sources outside the scope. We included: (i) literature that explicitly discusses the use of metrics related to large-scale agile projects, solutions, or adaptations of metrics in this scenario; (ii) conference papers, journals and pages about metrics of the related frameworks; (iii) literature published after 2001; (iv) first 10 pages of the Google search. We excluded: (i) inaccessible literature; (ii) results that Google search considers similar to other results; (iii) Google ads; (iv) articles and pages in a language other than English.

For academic literature, the period from January 2001 to December 2022 considers the entire period since the publication of the Agile Manifesto. A total of 3,479 articles were returned in the automatic selection. After removing 393 duplicate articles, 3,086 remained to be classified, of which no articles belonged to ScienceDirect since all duplicates came from this database.

The process of selecting studies began with analyzing titles and abstracts (phase 1), in which 3,027 articles were discarded for not meeting the inclusion criteria. Of these works, 59 were sent to phase 2, in which the introduction and conclusion of the articles were read, and then 34 articles were excluded. After reading the full text of the remaining 25, only 14 papers that met the inclusion criteria proceeded to extraction.

Before selecting results from grey literature, links from official pages available on metrics of recognized frameworks present in the string were separated in advance to ensure their inclusion in the research. Subsequently, the first ten links from search with string were considered, excluding Google ads. From the valid results, up to 2 cycles of forward snowballing were applied in the selection process. The search for grey literature was conducted in January 2023. After reading the titles and metatexts, 13 initial valid results were selected, considering the top ten links plus snowballing and three official framework pages. No links were academic articles. During the full-text reading, one page was added after snowballing. Applying the inclusion criteria to the 14 sources, five pages were eligible for the study. Table 1 summarizes and quantifies the results.

Table 1. Summary of research findings and selection for primary studies

Search mechanism	Initial results	Titles, metatext, abstracts, introductions, conclusions	Full texts
IEEEXplore	974	5	3
ACM	285	1	0
SpringerLink	184	14	7
Scopus	1643	5	4
ScienceDirect	0	0	0
Google	13	13	5

To enable peer review and study replicability, all methodology and research data is available as supplementary material (See in [Menezes et al. 2024b]).

3.1. Analysis

We consider the Software Development Life Cycle (SDLC) stages to address RQ1. The mapped metrics applied in the agile scaling environment will be linked to some SDLC stages. To do so, we will consider both information provided in the studies about the stages of the cycle in which they were applied and the descriptions and characteristics of the metrics themselves.

In addition, we will adopt the Goal Question Metric (GQM) approach to address RQ2, aiming to identify patterns in the transformations caused by the discovered metrics. The GQM approach provides tools for defining and interpreting software measurements guided by organizational goals, specifying a measurable objective refined into a set of quantifiable questions related to the objectives [Basili 1992]. As presented by the author, these questions, in turn, help define a set of metrics and data for collection.

Regarding the goal within the GQM approach, inspired by [Scrum@Scale 2022], it is observed that large agile organization seeks to improve and measure at least one of the following factors: customer responsiveness, value delivery, productivity, sustainability, and quality [Scrum@Scale 2022]. Therefore, the target metric model have the following objectives: to improve customer responsiveness, commercial value delivery, end-to-end productivity, sustainability of practices from both the organizational and customer perspectives and quality of the software development process. Based on these objectives, five questions were proposed: **Q1:** Are we more responsive to customers in the agile way of working? **Q2:** Do we deliver more value to customers in the agile way of working? **Q3:** Are we more productive working agile? **Q4:** Do we have better sustainability practices in the organizational environment? **Q5:** Do we have better product quality?

4. Results

4.1. Overview of academic studies

The included academic studies were classified according to research type aspects based on [Wieringa et al. 2006]. Regarding the contributions of the works, they were classified according to [Petersen et al. 2008], which include theory, model, framework, guideline, lessons learned, addendum, and tool. Table 2 overviews academic studies, research type, contribution aspects, publication year, and methods used.

Table 2. Overview of academic studies

Year	Research Type	Contribution	Study Method	Reference
2010	Experience	Lessons learned	Experience report	[Greening 2010]
2011	Experience	Lessons learned	Case study	[Brown 2011]
2012	Solution	Tool	Action research/literature review	[Staron et al. 2012]
2013	Experience	Tool	Experience report	[Tabib 2013]
2013	Solution	Guideline	Grounded theory/quasi-experiment	[Heidenberg et al. 2013]
2013	Solution	Tool	Action research	[Staron et al. 2013]
2014	Philosophical	Addendum	Grounded theory	[Laanti 2014]
2015	Experience	Lessons learned	Experience report	[Greening 2015]
2015	Experience	Lessons learned	Case study	[Tripathi et al. 2015]
2016	Validation	Framework	Case study	[Grimaldi et al. 2016]
2017	Experience	Framework	Observations	[Razzak et al. 2017]
2018	Experience	Lessons learned	Multiple case study/exploratory	[Stettina and Schoemaker 2018]
2020	Solution	Tool	Case study	[Thawaba et al. 2020]
2022	Validation	Framework	Experience report/experiment	[Tessarolo et al. 2022]

Table 3 presents information about the number of organizations (No. Org) referenced in the included literature. The symbol "+" in the column for organization size next to the term "large scale" represents a quantity of teams greater than or possibly greater than 9, and the term "large scale" represents a quantity between 2 and 9 teams [Dingsøyr et al. 2014]. In the column distribution, "Locally" is used when people are working remotely from the same city, "Nationally" working from cities within a single country, "Continentally" for working from different countries within the same continent and "Globally" for working from countries on different continents.

Table 3. Organizational context of the studies

No. Org	Size	Framework/ Method	Distribution	Industry	Reference
1	+ Large scale	Scrum+Kanban	Globally	IT	[Greening 2010]
1	+ Large scale	Scrum+XP	Continentally	Banking	[Brown 2011]
1	Large scale	Scrum	Globally	IT	[Tabib 2013]
-	Undefined	Scrum+Kanban	Undefined	IT	[Greening 2015]
1	Large scale	Scrum+Lean	Continentally	Healthcare	[Tessarolo et al. 2022]
1	+ Large scale	Agile+Lean	Nationally	Telecom	[Staron et al. 2012]
1	+ Large scale	Agile+Lean	Nationally	Telecom	[Staron et al. 2013]
1	Undefined	Agile	Nationally	IT	[Heidenberg et al. 2013]
-	Undefined	SAFe	Undefined	Undefined	[Laanti 2014]
1	Undefined	SAFe	Undefined	Telecom	[Grimaldi et al. 2016]
1	Large scale	SAFe	Globally	IT	[Razzak et al. 2017]
1	Undefined	SAFe	Undefined	Healthcare	[Thawaba et al. 2020]
5	Undefined	Scrum-of-scrums /SAFe/Spotify	Undefined	Telecom /Government	[Stettina and Schoemaker 2018]
2	Large scale	Kanban	Globally	Telecom	[Tripathi et al. 2015]
1	Large scale	LeSS	Continentally	Financial	[Korson 2015][1]

[1] *Grey literature sources.*

4.2. RQ1 - What metrics are used in large-scale agile software development?

Table 4 presents all the metrics found in this review. They are grouped by the primary studies in which they were mentioned or by the reference of the internet pages where they were mentioned and classified according to the agile framework/method in which they were applied or related. Metrics with identical names that appear repeatedly were identified in both types of literature and are equivalent.

Table 4. Metrics for large-scale agile software development (MLR)

Metrics	Framework/Method	Reference
Time to delivery first increment; Time to project closure; Velocity; Blocked tasks; Defect rate with severity; Process maturity level; Agile practices adoption rate; Function points per man-year; Burndown chart; Burnup chart; Agile Team Pulse (Adoption of iterative development; Two-level planning; Shared vision; Continuous integration and Team-based approach)	Scrum/XP	[Brown 2011]
Velocity; Velocity Deviation; Forecast Horizon; True Sprint Length; Dependency Count; Lead Time	Scrum/Kanban	[Greening 2015]
Net Present Value per effort	Scrum/Kanban	[Greening 2010]
Estimation accuracy delta; Effectiveness; Efficiency; Planned virtual hour cost; Real virtual hour cost; Waste; Impediments; Delta cost	SAFe	[Grimaldi et al. 2016]
Customer service response time; Functionality per work effort; Business value per effort; Commit Pulse; Flow distribution; Number of external problem reports; Open days and external problem reports; Lead Time; Cycle time per resource	Agile	[Heidenberg et al. 2013]
Net Promoter Score (NPS)	SAFe	[Laanti 2014]
SAFe practices adoption rate (Product Ownership Health, PI/ Release Health, Sprint Health, Team Health and Technical Health)	SAFe	[Razzak et al. 2017]
Measurement systems completeness indicator	Agile/Lean	[Staron et al. 2013]
Release readiness indicator	Agile/Lean	[Staron et al. 2012]
Planned velocity; Velocity	Scrum/Scrum of Scrums	[Stettina and Schoemaker 2018]
Team happiness	Scrum/Spotify	[Stettina and Schoemaker 2018]
Cycle time per resource; Velocity	Scrum/SAFe	[Stettina and Schoemaker 2018]
Code lines per user story; Number of files per user story; Code lines for refactoring; Number of developers per resource; Unit test coverage per user story; Unit test success per user story; Number of defects per user story	Scrum	[Tabib 2013]
Perceived effectiveness (Teamwork assessment; Requirement elicitation; Planning; Methodology quality; Culture; Knowledge sharing; General process perception; Team morale; Participant engagement and satisfaction)	Scrum/Lean	[Tessarolo et al. 2022]
Cost per function; Time per function; Remaining time; Time spent (all tasks); Remaining cost; Cost spent (all tasks); Remaining functions; Completed functions (all tasks); Remaining patterns; Achieved patterns (all tasks); Time Spent (main tasks using sub-task completion); Available time; Available cost	SAFe	[Thawaba et al. 2020]
Work In Progress; Lead Time	Kanban	[Tripathi et al. 2015]
Employee engagement; Flow distribution; Velocity; Flow time; Flow Load; Flow efficiency; Flow predictability; Deployment frequency; Wait time for changes; Time to restore service; Change failure rate; Business agility (Lean-Agile Leadership – Team and Technical Agility – Agile Product Delivery – Enterprise Solution Delivery – Lean Portfolio Management – Organizational Agility – Continuous Learning Culture); Core competencies (Team and Technical – Execution – Value Delivery – Organizational and Value Stream – Lean Portfolio and Strategy – Customer and Solutions – Quality Practices)	SAFe	[SAFe 2022][1]
Test pass rate; In-flow defect rate to out-flow defect rate; Release readiness	SAFe	[Copado 2022][1]
Value of business by effort; Team happiness; Function points per man-year; Defect rate; Service downtime	Scrum-at-scale	[Scrum@Scale 2022][1]
Predictability index; Technical debt; Acceleration	Agile/Lean	[Liyanage 2014][1]
Burnup chart; Work In Progress	LeSS	[Korson 2015][1]

[1]*Grey literature sources.*

Table 5 presents an overview of the metrics grouped by software development stage on the life cycle.

Table 5. Metrics linked to the Software Development Life Cycle

Stage	Metric	Reference
Product feasibility		
	Planned virtual hour cost; Estimation accuracy delta; Effectiveness; Real virtual hour cost; Waste; Efficiency; Impediments; Delta cost	[Grimaldi et al. 2016]
	Cost per function; Time per function	[Thawaba et al. 2020]
	Planned velocity	[Stettina and Schoemaker 2018]
	Number of developers per resource	[Tabib 2013]
	Flow predictability	[SAFe 2022]
Development		
	Velocity; Blocked tasks; Burndown chart; Burnup chart	[Brown 2011]
	Code lines per user story; Number of files per user story; Code lines for refactoring; Unit test coverage per user story; Unit test success per user story; Number of defects per user story	[Tabib 2013]
	Velocity; Dependency Count	[Greening 2015]
	Functionality per Work Effort; Commit Pulse	[Heidenberg et al. 2013]
	Velocity	[Stettina and Schoemaker 2018]
	Work In Progress	[Tripathi et al. 2015]
	Velocity; Flow Load	[SAFe 2022]
	Burnup chart; Work In Progress	[Korson 2015]
Testing		
	Defect rate with severity	[Brown 2011]
	Number of external problem reports; Open days and external problem reports	[Heidenberg et al. 2013]
	Number of defects per user story	[Tabib 2013]
	Release readiness indicator	[Staron et al. 2012]
	Remaining time; Time spent (all tasks); Remaining cost; Cost spent (all tasks); Remaining functions; Completed functions (all tasks); Remaining patterns; Achieved patterns (all tasks); Time spent (main tasks using subtask completion); Available time; Available cost	[Thawaba et al. 2020]
	Defect rate	[Scrum@Scale 2022]
	Test pass rate; In-flow defect rate to out-flow defect rate; Release readiness	[Copado 2022]
Deployment		
	Customer service response time	[Heidenberg et al. 2013]
	Net Promoter Score (NPS)	[Laanti 2014]
	Deployment frequency; Wait Time for Changes; Time to restore service	[SAFe 2022]
	Service downtime	[Scrum@Scale 2022]
Maintenance		
	Net Present Value per effort	[Greening 2010]
	Time to delivery first increment; Time to project closure; Process maturity level; Agile practices adoption rate; Agile team pulse; Function points per man-year	[Brown 2011]
	True Sprint Length; Lead Time; Velocity Deviation; Forecast Horizon	[Greening 2015]
	Perceived effectiveness	[Tessarolo et al. 2022]
	Measurement systems completeness indicator	[Staron et al. 2013]
	Lead Time; Cycle time per resource; Business value per effort; Flow distribution	[Heidenberg et al. 2013]
	SAFe practices adoption rate	[Razzak et al. 2017]
	Cycle time per resource; Team happiness	[Stettina and Schoemaker 2018]
	Employee engagement; Flow distribution; Flow time; Flow efficiency; Change failure rate; Business agility; Core competencies	[SAFe 2022]
	Business value per effort; Team happiness; Function points per man-year	[Scrum@Scale 2022]
	Predictability index; Technical debt; Acceleration	[Liyanage 2014]

4.3. RQ2 - What are the reasons and outcomes of using metrics in large-scale agile development?

The final step in GQM modeling was determining the 80 metrics in the multivocal literature (Table 4) to be used according to the raised questions. Some metrics related to each questions presented Q1, Q2, Q3, Q4 and Q5 are presented in Table 6, 7, 8, 9 and 10 respectively. Each table lists the metric name, descriptions (when necessary) and the formulas or data that quantify them (See all metrics in [Menezes et al. 2024a]).

Table 6. Are we more responsive to customers in the agile way of working?

Name	Description	Calculation Formula
Time to delivery first increment	Time spent from project initiation to delivery of the first increment	*Delivery date of the first increment - Project initiation date*
Time to project closure	Time spent from project initiation to project closure	*Project closure date - Project initiation date*
True Sprint Length		*Actual delivery date of the increment when greater than the previously defined sprint end date - Sprint initiation date*
Forecast Horizon	Sum of estimation points, h, from the top of the product backlog to a given point	If we know the estimated team velocity $\mu(V)$ and the standard deviation $\sigma(V)$, we can express the Forecast Horizon in sprints as $h/\mu(V) \pm \sigma(V) * h/\mu(V)$ for 68% confidence or $h/\mu(V) \pm 2\sigma(V) * h/\mu(V)$ for 95% confidence. If we know the sprint length l, we can express the Forecast Horizon in time units as $hl/\mu(V) \pm l\sigma(V) * h/\mu(V)$
Lead Time		*Completion date of a process - Start date of a process*
Customer Service Response Time	Measures the return of customer service requests	*Resolved customer service request date - Created customer service request date*
Cycle Time per Resource	Measures the cycle time for resources selected for development.	*Date of completion of resource readiness - Date when the resource was added to the backlog*
Flow Distribution	Measures the quantity of each type of work in the system over time	A simple measurement is counting the number of each type of work item at any given time. A more accurate measure may consider the size of each work item
Release Readiness Indicator	Predicts in which week the product release would be possible given the number of known defects up to that point, how many defects were removed on average in the last 4 weeks and how many defects were expected to be discovered	*#Defects / Defect_removal_rate - (Test_execution_rate - Test_pass_rate).* Where *#defects* is the number of open defects for the product, *defect_removal_rate* is the average amount of defects removed in the last 4 weeks, *test_execution_rate* is the average number of test cases executed in the last 4 weak points and *test_pass_rate* is the average number of test cases passed in the last 4 weak points
Time per Function		*Task duration time / Task function quantity*
Remaining Time	Remaining time to complete the task	*Task duration time / (Task test date - Task start date)*
Time Spent (All Tasks)	Time spent during task implementation	*((Task test date - Task start date) / Task duration time)* $*$ *100*
Available Time	Available time for sub-tasks or main tasks	*Time spent in sub-tasks - (Task test date - Task start date)*
Flow Time	Total time elapsed for all stages of a workflow	Measured by the average period of time it takes to complete a certain type of work item
Wait Time for Changes		Amount of waiting time to make a change

Table 7. Do we deliver more value to customers in the agile way of working?

Name	Description	Calculation Formula
Net Present Value per Effort	Profitability value by effort	*Net Present Value / Effort*
Functionality per Work Effort	How much functionality can be delivered relative to a certain work effort	*Test points / Person hours*
Business Value per Effort	Here it is indicated as more frequent major releases in relation to the work effort	*Number of major releases in a year / Hours per person*
Net Promoter Score	User/customer feedback	Calculated by asking customers if they would recommend the product to colleagues on a scale from 0 to 10. Responses are categorized as detractors (0-6), passives (7-8) and promoters (9-10). Finally, the total percentage of detractors is subtracted from the percentage of promoters to determine the NPS
Flow Efficiency	How much of the total flow time is spent on value-added work activities versus waiting between steps	*Total active time / Flow time*
Flow Predictability	Measures how well teams, Agile Release Trains (ARTs) and Solution Trains can plan and meet their Program Increment (PI) objectives	Ratio between planned business value achieved and actual business value delivered in a PI

Table 8. Are we more productive working agile?

Name	Description	Calculation Formula
Velocity		Quantity of story points completed for work items of a type over a period of time
Blocked Tasks		Number of tasks blocked during a specific time period
Function Points per Man-Year		Amount of work done by an individual throughout the year
Burndown Chart	Measures sprint progress and provides indicators of the team's work process	Marks the sprint days on the horizontal axis and the points planned to compose the sprint on the vertical axis, starting from the maximum points of the sprint (team velocity) to zero
Burnup Chart	Measures progress based on remaining hours or points from the top down. Measures release progress and provide indicators of the team's work process	Marks the sprint days on the horizontal axis and the points planned to compose the sprint on the vertical axis, starting from the maximum points of the sprint (team velocity) to zero
Velocity Deviation	Measures velocity stability	$\sigma(V)/\mu(V)$. Where $\mu(V)$ is the expected velocity (average velocity based on a certain number of previous sprints) and $\sigma(V)$ is the velocity standard deviation
Dependency Count	Dependency between teams where bugs and delays affect immediate dependents	Number of immediate dependents
Efficiency	Indicates how well we use the team compared to maximum capacity	*AH / C*. Where *AH* represents the actual hours spent producing tangible results and *C* is the ideal number of hours a team can deliver, depending on team size, number of teams, non-working days and days spent on ceremonies. $C = S*(DS-(NWD+(DS*KO/20)))*TS*DH)$, where *DS* is the sprint duration, *NWD* represents days off, *KO* stands for knowledge transfer/planning/estimation days, *TS* is the team size and *DH* is daily development capacity in hours
Impediments	Any 'time loss' due to a defect or obstacle that hampers productivity	Number of hours that do not produce tangible results
Commit Pulse	Measures how continuous integration is within sprints	Number of days between commits
Planned Velocity		Amount of work (story points) that a team expects to complete during a sprint
Cost per function		*Task cost / Number of task functions*
Remaining Cost	Measures the remaining cost for task completion	*Task cost - Expense cost*

In this MLR, among the academic studies, there are reports from large organizations that scaled Scrum to scale beyond software development teams, promoting agile thinking throughout the organization [Greening 2010], as well as to development teams working together [Brown 2011, Greening 2015], or situated in different geographical locations [Tabib 2013, Tessarolo et al. 2022], using metrics to address challenges and promote improvements. Purely agile management was referenced in the research in studies that addressed measurements more focused on aspects of organizational transformations [Heidenberg et al. 2013], improvement of workflow control [Staron et al. 2013], and organization performance goals [Staron et al. 2012]. The SAFe framework appears in research with proposals to enrich its native metrics to meet demands for speed in deliveries by measuring resources and costs in the process [Grimaldi et al. 2016] and improving confidence in developing critical security systems [Thawaba et al. 2020]. An efficient mechanism for measuring the adoption rate of SAFe practices in Small and Medium Enterprises (SMEs) wishing to adapt to scalable frameworks was also found [Razzak et al. 2017]. In [Stettina and Schoemaker 2018], performance, quality, progress and status metrics were mentioned in methodologies such as Scrum-of-scrums, SAFe and Spotify. The importance of Kanban in controlling and scaling workflows among teams using metrics such as work limits and wait times was highlighted [Greening 2010, Greening 2015, Tripathi et al. 2015].

In the grey literature, most findings are related to SAFe, which has a robust system

Table 9. Do we have better sustainability practices in the organizational environment?

Name	Description	Calculation Formula
Agile Team Pulse	Involves team's regular casual assessments to understand their views on adopting iterative development practices, two-level planning, shared vision, continuous integration and a team-based approach	Collected through informal surveys
SAFe Practices Adoption Rate	Self-assessment survey sent to participants. Each question includes a numeric rating (Likert scale) and an optional comment section	The Likert scale has six response options (from 'never' to 'always') to gauge the frequency of practice usage in areas like product ownership health, PI/release health, sprint health, team health and technical health
Measurement Systems Completeness Indicator	Assessment of measurement system completeness for workflow monitoring, as temporal and process dependencies are used between process activities	*(#Activities with measures or indicators / #Activities in total)* $*$ *100%*. The measurement system that provides measures or indicators for all activities of the monitored process is 100
Employee Engagement	Measures how motivated individuals feel and how actively engaged they are in supporting the organization's goals and values	Various methods exist to gauge employee engagement, and each organization should choose what suits them best. Some use an annual survey, while others rely on an Employee Net Promoter Score (eNPS), asking employees how likely they are to recommend their employer on a 10-point scale
Business Agility	High-level assessment summarizing how agile the business is at any given time	Two assessment methods are available: (i) Participants fill out assessments independently, followed by group discussion and analysis; (ii) All participants collectively discuss and agree on scores (1 to 5) for each statement. The assessment report includes visualizations tracking progress in SAFe's seven core competencies

of suggested metrics [SAFe 2022]. In addition to SAFe's native metrics, we found a proposal to add quality measurement to its flow monitoring in a DevOps environment [Copado 2022], a perspective currently not covered in [SAFe 2022]. Scrum-at-scale does not officially commit to a predefined metrics system but clearly emphasizes the need to monitor productivity, quality, value delivery and sustainability, directly influencing decision-making and promoting transparency [Scrum@Scale 2022].

The synergy between Agile and Lean is vital in improving agility in large-scale agile systems [Liyanage 2014]. In [Liyanage 2014], metrics to measure business agility based on predictability of development risks/costs, maintaining product reliability and adaptability to conditions impacting value delivery were presented and directly associated with Lean and Agile management principles. LeSS emerged in the research through a case study summary in which using the burnup chart as an indicator of scope increase and establishing a WIP limit for making corrections were essential for project progress and completion [Korson 2015]. No evidence was found regarding the metrics used to implement the Disciplined Agile scalable agile framework.

5. Discussion

Considering the small number of academic papers (14) it can be inferred that while the interest in agile software development is growing, the community likely still lacks comprehensive knowledge and understanding of this context, given the limited number of studies. Regarding the variety of research types, experience reports predominate [Brown 2011, Greening 2010, Greening 2015, Razzak et al. 2017, Stettina and Schoemaker 2018, Tabib 2013, Tripathi et al. 2015], followed by solution proposals [Heidenberg et al. 2013, Staron et al. 2012, Staron et al. 2013, Thawaba et al. 2020], with 7 and 4 occurrences, respectively. Only 2 validation studies

Table 10. Do we have better product quality?

Name	Description	Calculation Formula
Defect Rate with Severity	Measures the software defect rate	*Number of defects (severity 1 and 2) in production / 100*
Number of External Problem Reports	Measures the total number of external problem reports during a specific time period	Number of external problem reports originating from a particular version
Open Days and External Problem Reports	Measures the average number of days external problem reports have remained unresolved from creation to resolution	*Date of resolved problem reports - Date of problem reports created*
Code Lines per User Story		*Code Lines / User Story*
Number of Files per User Story		*Number of Files / User Story*
Code Lines for Refactoring		Quantity of code lines for refactoring
Number of Developers per Resource		*Number of Developers / Feature*
Unit Test Coverage per User Story		*Unit Test Coverage / User Story*
Unit Test Success per User Story		*Unit Test Pass Rate / User Story*
Number of Defects per User Story		*Number of Defects / User Story*
Change Failure Rate	Measures flow efficiency	Percentage of changes requiring remediation after going into production
Time to Restore Service	Flow time metric	Amount of wait time for service restoration
Test Pass Rate	Measures trends in approval rate for automated test suites	Percentage of approval rate for automated test suite
In-Flow Defect Rate to Out-Flow Defect Rate	Determines if the team can fix more bugs than just those discovered during testing	*In-Flow Defects / Out-Flow Defects*
Defect Rate		*Number of Defects / 100*
Service Downtime		Amount of time a particular service has been down

[Grimaldi et al. 2016, Tessarolo et al. 2022] and 1 philosophical study [Laanti 2014] were recorded. This reinforces the need for more relevant research addressing new metric proposals not yet implemented in practice and extensive evaluations of metric usage in daily operations using large-scale agility.

When separating metrics by lifecycle stages, it is concluded that 29 metrics were or could be used during the maintenance stage, defined as the last stage of the life cycle. 23 metrics were or could be used within the testing stage. The quantities of 15, 12, and 6 metrics were or could be applied for the development, product feasibility, and deployment stages. No metrics were found to be applied or specifically defined for the requirements and design stages.

For each question in the resulting metric model, there is a set of associated metrics out of the total 80 identified in this MLR. For Q1, related to monitoring customer responsiveness, 18 metrics were identified. Value delivered to customers metrics (Q2) has the smallest set, with only 6 metrics. This number may indicate the need to investigate the feasibility of additional value delivery measurement alternatives. The larger set (Q3), with 21 metrics, is related to team performance. There are 18 metrics evaluating sustainability in practices (Q4), and 17 measuring product quality (Q5).

Most works address metrics to support large organizations that strategically scaled Scrum to improve results or mitigate challenges in adverse situations [Brown 2011, Greening 2010, Greening 2015, Tabib 2013, Tessarolo et al. 2022]. Pure agile management was referenced in the research, along with metrics that supported flow control [Staron et al. 2013], organizational transformations [Heidenberg et al. 2013] and the pursuit of business agility [Staron et al. 2012, Liyanage 2014]. We found that SAFe has native metrics cited in articles as proposals to enrich its metrics to monitor resources and costs [Grimaldi et al. 2016], meet evaluating reliability [Thawaba et al. 2020] and quality demands [Copado 2022] and apply organizational model transformations [Razzak et al. 2017]. The relevance of Kanban in controlling and scaling workflows among teams using metrics such as limits and wait times was also noted [Greening 2010, Greening 2015, Tripathi et al. 2015]. The Scrum-at-scale framework suggests measurements to facilitate decision-making and promote transparency [Scrum@Scale 2022].

6. Threats to Validity

The main limitation of this study is that, apart from selecting academic articles, all other phases of the MLR were conducted solely by the first author and validated by other authors. To mitigate this challenge, we followed guidelines from Garousi et al. (2019) for incorporating grey literature and conducting a multivocal review in software engineering, which were adopted and validated.

Another limitation arises from our search string containing generic terms like "Metric", "DA" and "Scrum", resulting in a diverse and irrelevant initial dataset, making the initial literature selection phases challenging.

7. Conclusions

This study aimed to consolidate key findings on large-scale agility metrics, enhancing visibility and accessibility to this knowledge for the scientific community and agile teams. We identified 19 sources through a multivocal literature review, providing insights into metrics, motivations, and outcomes in scalable, agile processes. We considered the stages of the software development life cycle to map the identified metrics. Also, a curated set of 80 metrics was categorized using the GQM model. These metrics are linked to organizational goals, including delivering customer value, improving team productivity, ensuring product quality, and fostering sustainable practices. Notably, most metrics focus on monitoring overall process functionality and boosting productivity, with only a minority addressing value delivery measurement.

Using metrics in large-scale agile development is essential for assessing effectiveness, identifying challenges, promoting transparency, and guiding decision-making. Their analysis significantly impacts the improvement and success of enterprise agile initiatives, providing a clear view of progress, facilitating collaboration among teams, and ensuring consistency in deliveries. By providing valuable context for data-driven decision-making, these metrics represent a fundamental tool for the success and effectiveness of large-scale agile development. Considering the diverse outcomes, a company's selection and customization of metrics often hinge on factors such as organizational size and alignment with its business goals, operational framework, and specific requirements. The insights from this study will equip researchers and practitioners with the knowledge to delve deeper into metrics-related challenges within large-scale agile environments, fostering the development of more targeted solutions.

For future work, we consider conducting case studies in organizations implementing Disciplined Agile as a scalable agile framework to collect data on used metrics. Additionally, we highlight the relevance of surveying to solidify findings regarding metrics implemented in a scalable environment.

Referências

Basili, V. R. (1992). Software modeling and measurement: the goal/question/metric paradigm. Technical report.

Britto, R., Usman, M., and Mendes, E. (2014). Effort estimation in agile global software development context. In *Agile Methods. Large-Scale Development, Refactoring, Testing, and Estimation: XP 2014 International Workshops, Rome, Italy, May 26-30, 2014, Revised Selected Papers 15*, pages 182–192. Springer.

Brown, A. W. (2011). A case study in agile-at-scale delivery. In *International Conference on Agile Software Development*, pages 266–281. Springer.

Camara, R., Alves, A., Monte, I., and Marinho, M. (2020). Agile global software development: A systematic literature review. In *Proceedings of the XXXIV Brazilian Symposium on Software Engineering*, pages 31–40.

Camara, R., Marinho, M., and Moura, H. (2021). Agile tailoring with scaling agile frameworks in distributed large-scale settings. In *Anais Estendidos do XX Simpósio Brasileiro de Qualidade de Software*, pages 12–17. SBC.

Chloros, D., Gerogiannis, V. C., and Kakarontzas, G. (2022). Use of software and project management metrics in agile software development methodologies: A systematic mapping study. In *Proceedings of the 2022 European Symposium on Software Engineering*, pages 25–32.

Copado, T. (2022). How to optimize flow metrics quality in scaled agile framework (safe). `https://www.copado.com/devops-hub/blog/how-to-optimize-flow-metrics-quality`. (accessed 4 January 2023).

Dingsøyr, T., Fægri, T. E., and Itkonen, J. (2014). What is large in large-scale? a taxonomy of scale for agile software development. In *Product-Focused Software Process Improvement: 15th International Conference, PROFES 2014, Helsinki, Finland, December 10-12, 2014. Proceedings 15*, pages 273–276. Springer.

Dingsøyr, T. and Moe, N. B. (2014). Towards principles of large-scale agile development. In *International Conference on Agile Software Development*, pages 1–8. Springer.

Edison, H., Wang, X., and Conboy, K. (2021). Comparing methods for large-scale agile software development: A systematic literature review. *IEEE Transactions on Software Engineering*.

Ertaban, C., Sarikaya, E., and Bagriyanik, S. (2018). Agile performance indicators for team performance evaluation in a corporate environment. In *Proceedings of the 19th International Conference on Agile Software Development: Companion*, pages 1–3.

Fenton, N. and Bieman, J. (2014). *Software metrics: a rigorous and practical approach*. CRC press.

Garousi, V., Felderer, M., and Mäntylä, M. V. (2019). Guidelines for including grey literature and conducting multivocal literature reviews in software engineering. *Information and software technology*, 106:101–121.

Greening, D. R. (2010). Enterprise scrum: Scaling scrum to the executive level. In *2010 43rd Hawaii International Conference on System Sciences*, pages 1–10. IEEE.

Greening, D. R. (2015). Agile enterprise metrics. In *2015 48th Hawaii International Conference on System Sciences*, pages 5038–5044. IEEE.

Grimaldi, P., Perrotta, L., Corvello, V., and Verteramo, S. (2016). An agile, measurable and scalable approach to deliver software applications in a large enterprise. *International Journal of Agile Systems and Management*, 9(4):326–339.

Heidenberg, J., Weijola, M., Mikkonen, K., and Porres, I. (2013). A metrics model to measure the impact of an agile transformation in large software development organizations. In *Int. Conference on Agile Software Development*, pages 165–179. Springer.

Hossain, S. S., Ahmed, P., and Arafat, Y. (2021). Software process metrics in agile software development: A systematic mapping study. In *Computational Science and Its Applications–ICCSA 2021: 21st International Conference, Cagliari, Italy, September 13–16, 2021, Proceedings, Part IX 21*, pages 15–26. Springer.

Kišš, F. and Rossi, B. (2018). Agile to lean software development transformation: A systematic literature review. In *2018 Federated Conference on Computer Science and Information Systems (FedCSIS)*, pages 969–973. IEEE.

Korpivaara, I., Tuunanen, T., and Seppänen, V. (2021). Performance measurement in scaled agile organizations. In *Proceedings of the Annual Hawaii International Conference on System Sciences*. University of Hawai'i at Manoa.

Korson, T. (2015). Cash-in comfort. `https://less.works/case-studies/cash-in-comfort`. (accessed 4 January 2023].

Laanti, M. (2014). Characteristics and principles of scaled agile. In *International Conference on Agile Software Development*, pages 9–20. Springer.

Leal, S., Hauck, J., Bertan, M., and Vieira, G. (2022). How agile organizations use metrics: A systematic literature mapping. In *Proceedings of the XXI Brazilian Symposium on Software Quality*, pages 1–11.

Liyanage, J. R. (2014). Lean agile metrics for scaled agile systems. `https://www.methodsandtools.com/archive/leanagilemetrics.php`. (accessed 4 January 2023).

Marinho, M., Camara, R., and Sampaio, S. (2021). Toward unveiling how safe framework supports agile in global software development. *IEEE Access*, 9:109671–109692.

Marinho, M., Noll, J., Richardson, I., and Beecham, S. (2019). Plan-driven approaches are alive and kicking in agile global software development. In *2019 ACM/IEEE International Symposium on Empirical Software Engineering and Measurement (ESEM)*, pages 1–11. IEEE.

Menezes, R., Marinho, M., and Sampaio, S. (2024a). Complete metrics tables for "goal question metrics" modeling. `https://doi.org/10.7910/DVN/HTQTEE`.

Menezes, R., Marinho, M., and Sampaio, S. (2024b). Replication data for: Metrics in large-scale agile software development: A multivocal literature review. `https://doi.org/10.7910/DVN/8MJG8K`.

Petersen, K., Feldt, R., Mujtaba, S., and Mattsson, M. (2008). Systematic mapping studies in software engineering. In *12th International Conference on Evaluation and Assessment in Software Engineering (EASE) 12*, pages 1–10.

Philipp, P., Tobisch, F., Menzel, L., and Matthes, F. (2023). A method for metric management at a large-scale agile software development organization.

Razzak, M. A., Noll, J., Richardson, I., Canna, C. N., and Beecham, S. (2017). Transition from plan driven to safe®: periodic team self-assessment. In *International Conference on Product-Focused Software Process Improvement*, pages 573–585. Springer.

SAFe (2022). Measure and grow. `https://scaledagileframework.com/measure-and-grow/`. (accessed 4 January 2023).

Scrum@Scale (2022). The scrum at scale® guide. the definitive guide to the scrum@scale framework. `https://www.scrumatscale.com/scrum-at-scale-guide-online/`. (accessed 4 January 2023).

Shameem, M., Kumar, C., Chandra, B., and Khan, A. A. (2017). Systematic review of success factors for scaling agile methods in global software development environment: A client-vendor perspective. In *2017 24th Asia-Pacific Software Engineering Conference Workshops (APSECW)*, pages 17–24. IEEE.

Staron, M., Meding, W., and Caiman, M. (2013). Improving completeness of measurement systems for monitoring software development workflows. In *International Conference on Software Quality*, pages 230–243. Springer.

Staron, M., Meding, W., and Palm, K. (2012). Release readiness indicator for mature agile and lean software development projects. In *International Conference on Agile Software Development*, pages 93–107. Springer.

Stettina, C. J. and Schoemaker, L. (2018). Reporting in agile portfolio management: Routines, metrics and artefacts to maintain an effective oversight. In *International Conference on Agile Software Development*, pages 199–215. Springer, Cham.

Tabib, R. (2013). Need 4 speed: leverage new metrics to boost your velocity without compromising on quality. In *2013 Agile Conference*, pages 117–120. IEEE.

Tessarolo, F., Petsani, D., Conotter, V., Nollo, G., Conti, G., Nikolaidou, M., Onorati, G., Bamidis, P. D., and Konstantinidis, E. I. (2022). Developing ambient assisted living technologies exploiting potential of user-centred co-creation and agile methodology: the captain project experience. *Journal of Ambient Intelligence and Humanized Computing*, pages 1–16.

Thawaba, A. A., Ramli, A. A., Fudzee, M., Md, F., and Wadata, J. (2020). A mechanism to support agile frameworks enhancing reliability assessment for scs development: a case study of medical surgery departments. In *International Conference on Soft Computing and Data Mining*, pages 66–76. Springer.

Tripathi, N., Rodríguez, P., Ahmad, M. O., and Oivo, M. (2015). Scaling kanban for software development in a multisite organization: challenges and potential solutions. In *International Conference on Agile Software Development*, pages 178–190. Springer.

Wieringa, R., Maiden, N., Mead, N., and Rolland, C. (2006). Requirements engineering paper classification and evaluation criteria: a proposal and a discussion. *Requirements engineering*, 11:102–107.

Analyzing the adaptability of MoWebA to different environments

Magalí González T.[1]**, Luca Cernuzzi**[1]

[1]Departamento de Electrónica e Informática
Universidad Católica "Nuestra Señora de la Asunción" (UC) – Asunción – Paraguay

{mgonzalez,lcernuzz}@uc.edu.py

Abstract. *Some of the major challenges facing Web applications are those of portability, adaptability, and evolution, not only in the environment in which they run but also in the way in which they must be developed, often requiring different languages, frameworks, tools, environments, platforms, etc. MDD takes into account these issues. However, achieving portability, adaptability, and evolution depends to some extent on the degree of independence that the models adopt. This paper focuses on the Architecture Specific Model (ASM) of MoWebA (Model Oriented Web Approach). It analyses its impact on portability and adaptability across different architectures. A case study is presented to validate this issue by extending MoWebA to three different architectures. In such extensions, we analyze the grade of adaptability of MoWebA and automation of PIM-ASM, as well as the grade of independence of the PIM metamodel.*

1. Introduction

Current Web engineering methods center on developing techniques and/or models needed to define the design processes, and on providing tools to support them, following the MDD (Model Driven Development) approach in many cases [Brambilla et al. 2017]. Various quantitative and qualitative studies show how MDD practices contribute to increasing the efficiency and effectiveness in software development [Panach et al. 2021] [Farshidi et al. 2021], and others propose challenges that need to be addressed by the Web and MDE community [Bordeleau et al. 2017][Rossi et al. 2016].

The main challenges facing applications today include portability, adaptability, and evolution, not only in the environment in which they run but also in the way they need to be developed. This often requires different languages, frameworks, tools, environments, platforms, etc. MDD takes these issues into account. However, the degree of independence of the models is critical to achieving such desirable properties.

In previous studies, we proposed the MoWebA approach [González et al. 2016b] [González et al. 2016a]. Some of its features have a positive impact on the portability and adaptability problems. In particular, this study focuses on the analysis of the Architecture Specific Model (ASM), which corresponds to a level of abstraction between the Platform Independent Model (PIM) and the Platform Specific Model (PSM), encapsulating details related to the architecture the developed software will have. This encapsulation makes it possible to improve both the generalization of the modeling and its understanding (by separating concepts). Therefore, it keeps the portability of the PIM regarding the different architectures (e.g., RIA, SOA, Mobile) and facilitates the adaptability and evolution of the method to different architectures.

Different extensions of MoWebA have been presented for various architectures: MoWebA4RIA (extension of MoWebA for RIA functionalities) [Nuñez et al. 2018], MoWebAMobile4FC (extension of MoWebA for mobile applications for functions in the cloud) [Sanchiz et al. 2018], and MoWebAMobile4Persistence (Extension of MoWebA in mobile applications for the persistence layer) [Núñez et al. 2020]. MoWebA prescribes the definition of a new ASM for each extension, along with the respective PIM-ASM transformation rules and ASM-Code generation. Furthermore, each extension presented the validation of the proposal.

This study enriches the previous works by presenting a case study to analyze the role of the ASM phase, both for modeling and transformation processes, based on the three previous experiences. The aim is to determine the degree of adaptability and evolution of the MoWebA method, including the automation of PIM-ASM, as well as the grade of independence of the PIM metamodel, concerning the three different architectures.

The main findings are as follows. All three extensions were successfully developed from the same PIM metamodel with a reduced number of adaptations. Each extension has involved revising the elements defined in the PIM Metamodel and defining the ASM Metamodel for a specific architecture. The ASM-PIM transformation has been completed for the ASM elements that are derived from the PIM by inheritance, with a few manual adjustments.

The rest of the paper is structured as follows. Section 2 presents the related works. Section 3 provides a brief introduction to MoWebA, with some details on the ASM model. Section 4 focuses on the analysis of MoWebA's adaptability to different architectures. Finally, Section 5 concludes and outlines future work.

2. Related Works

The Model Driven Development approach provides various benefits in terms of portability, adaptability, and evolution [Brambilla et al. 2017]. Thus, several web methodologies follow the Model Driven Web Engineering approach [Rossi et al. 2016].

Moreover, several methodologies such as WebML and UWE propose extensions to consider emerging technologies and architectures. Such extensions are generally contemplated with new constructors that are introduced in the proposal's notation by UML stereotypes, or specific DSL included in the original notation for modeling so that the original proposal becomes an enriched one for the extension under consideration. In other words, the adaptation mechanism is based on the inclusion of notational elements in the models, thus reducing their independence from the platform or architecture. This is because the extensions are not defined as a separate modeling layer. The result of this extension mechanism is that the platform-independent modeling (PIM) stage contemplates elements of a specific platform or architecture, combining both concepts in a single final model. Other proposals decided to add architectural-specific information at the PSM level. In this case, architecture and platform details are included at the same modeling level, losing portability at the architectural level for different technologies where it can be implemented (e.g., UWA for RIA [Bernardi et al. 2014]). However, the WebRatio Mobile Platform [Brambilla et al. 2014], an extension of WebML, is the only one that considers an ASM to some extent. None of the others capture the requirements for specific architectures at a different level of abstraction, as proposed by MoWebA. As a counterpart, to offer a greater reusability of the PIM facilitating the architectural evolution of the Web applications, this mechanism of extension requires some additional effort, including the need for metamodels and the definition of the corresponding transformation rules, to achieve automatic transformations on the proposed architecture or platform. But with this separation, a clear distinction is made between what would be the problem space, presenting a model that is completely independent of the target architecture or platform; and the solution space, through the specific extension oriented to architecture, platform, and the final code.

For a more detailed analysis and discussion of the role of ASM in the portability, adaptability, and evolution of the methodology, we refer the interested reader to section 2.2.1 of [González 2022].

3. MoWebA at a Glance

Figure 1 presents the dimensions of MoWebA that cover its modeling and transformation processes. MoWebA adopts the MDA approach by identifying three different phases related to modeling and transformation activities (the *Phases* dimension): i) the problem space, covered by CIM (Computational-Independent Model), and PIM; ii) the solution space, covered by ASM, and PSM; and, iii) the source code definition, covered by the ISM (Implementation-Specific Model) and manual code adjustments.

The *Levels* dimension deals with complementary perspectives to be considered in every phase (content, business logic, navigation, presentation, users). Finally, the *Aspects* dimension addresses structural and behavioral considerations for each perspective [González et al. 2016b].

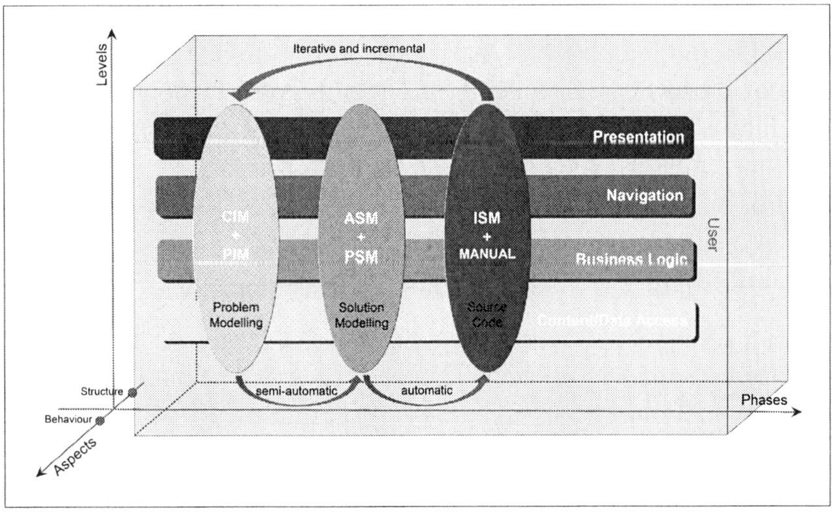

Figure 1. Dimensions of MoWebA that cover its modeling and transformation processes.

To develop applications, MoWebA defines two main complementary processes: the first related to modeling activities and the second one related to transformation activities. To formalize the modeling and transformation processes, it adopts the MOF language for the definition of the abstract syntax, and the UML profile extension for a precise definition of the modeling language (i.e., concrete syntax).

The ASM allows details related to the architecture to be moved out from the problem space (PIM) to an intermediate model in the solution space (ASM), preventing the PIM from containing such details and contributing to its so desired portability. Moreover, the ASM model can result in different PSM models, one per each implementation platform. Therefore, the ASM model enriches previous models with additional information related to the system architecture (e.g., Rich Internet Application (RIA), REST, mobile, among others).

In this line of thought, MoWebA can be extended to other architectures through the definition of the ASM, used to complement the PIM with information about a specific architecture. To utilize an ASM model, it must first be defined. This involves specifying the corresponding metamodel, among other steps. The ASM metamodel definition follows the recommendation of Brambilla et al. [Brambilla et al. 2017]. Furthermore, MoWebA complements the suggested process with additional steps that go from the definition of the concrete syntax until the generation of the final code of an application [González et al. 2016a]. The steps of this process are synthesized below:

1. Define the ASM metamodel using MOF, and corresponding UML Profile.
2. Specify the mapping rules from PIM elements to ASM elements.
3. Define transformation rules from PIM to ASM using standard transformation languages such as Atlas Transformation Language (ATL) or Query/View/Transformation (QVT).
4. Define transformation rules from ASM to PSM and PSM to code, or from ASM to code, using Model-to-Model (M2M) and Model-to-Text (M2T) transformation languages, respectively.

Indeed, the MoWebA approach requires some additional effort as a counterpart to improving the portability of the PIM and facilitating the architectural evolution of applications. This additional effort includes the need for the specification of ASM metamodels and the definition of the corresponding transformation rules, to achieve automatic transformations on the proposed architecture. In any case, it should be noted that these steps will only be executed once when targeting a new architecture for the first time.

Once the ASM for a specific architecture is defined, it can be used to develop an application for the selected architecture following these steps:

1. Define the MoWebA CIM and PIM diagrams following the modeling process.
2. Apply transformation rules to obtain the first version of the ASM model.
3. Make manual adjustments (if necessary) to complete the ASM model.
4. Generate the PSM models and the final code, applying transformation rules.
5. Include manual adjustments, if necessary.

Figure 2 illustrates the proposed process for the development of applications for a specific architecture. In the figure, we can see that the process begins with the PIM definition with the MagicDraw tool (http://www.nomagic.com/products/magicdraw.html) using the corresponding UML profiles. The PIM model is then exported to an XMI file, which is imported into the EMF (https://www.eclipse.org/modeling/emf/) tool, where, through the mapping of the defined M2M transformation rules, it is transformed into a new XMI with diagrams corresponding to the ASM. The new XMI is imported into the Acceleo tool. The latter uses the transformation rules to perform transformations from

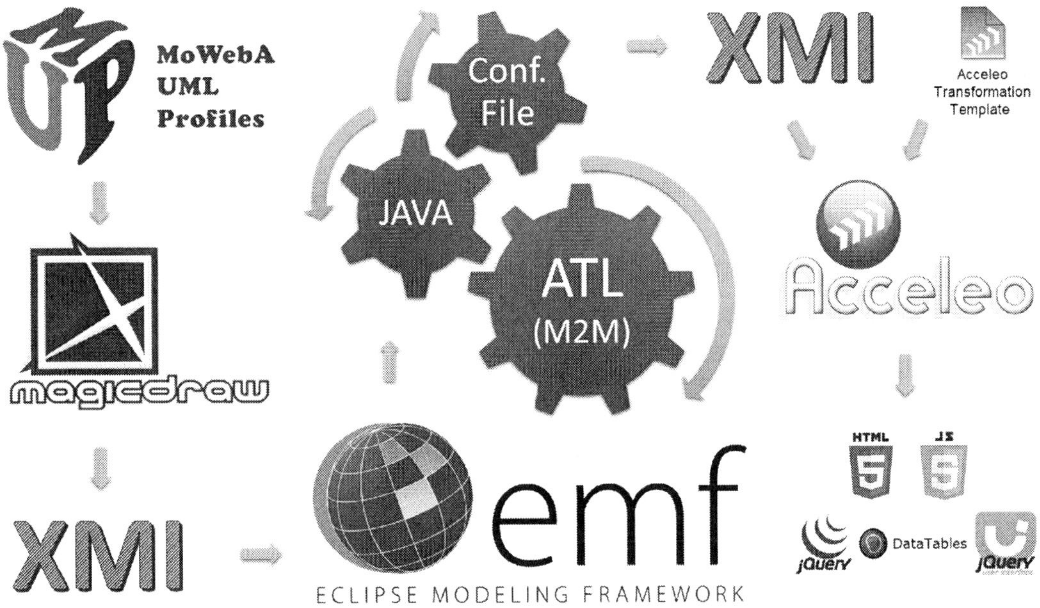

Figure 2. MoWebA development process

model to text, generating the code in different languages depending on the architecture specified.

We claim that the ASM extension mechanism proposed by MoWebA can improve the adaptability and evolution of MoWebA. To support this assertion, we present below a case study that aims to analyze this aspect.

4. Analyzing the Extension of MoWebA to other architectures

The focus of the study is on the ASM phase, both for modeling and transformation processes. The experience was structured taking into account a framework that Runeson et al. [Runeson et al. 2012] have defined for case studies. The case study was done as part of a research project at the Catholic University of Asuncion called "Mejorando el Proceso de Desarrollo de Software: Una propuesta basada en MDD" (https://www.dei.uc.edu.py/proyectos/mddplus/), Paraguay.

In this experience, the extensions were made to three different architectures: MoWebA4RIA (extension of MoWebA for RIA functionalities) [Nuñez et al. 2018], MoWebAMobile4FC (extension of MoWebA for mobile applications for functions in the cloud) [Sanchiz et al. 2018], and MoWebAMobile4Persistence (Extension of MoWebA in mobile applications for the persistence layer) [Núñez et al. 2020].

Using the GQM [Basili et al. 1994] template, the main purpose of this validation was described as follows: "**Analyze** the MoWebA method **for the purpose of** determining the grade of adaptability and evolution of the method **with respect to** the architecture **from the point of** view of the researcher **in the context of** a research project with students, professionals, trainee researchers, and MDD experts".

Based on this general objective, we propose the following research questions:

- **RQ1:** To what extent are the evolution and adaptability of the extension mechanism proposed by MoWebA achieved to incorporate new architectures?

- **RQ2:** How independent is the MoWebA PIM for use in the modeling stage before ASM?
- **RQ3:** To what extent automation can be obtained with MoWebA's model-to-model and model-to-code transformation rules?

This study was developed by a research team composed of 11 participants (five undergraduate students, one master's degree student, two PhD students, and three MDD PhD experts). The final-year undergraduate students involved in the project knew MDE and MDD, in addition to previous knowledge and experience with the MoWebA proposal. One of the undergraduate students was in charge of performing the PIM-ASM mappings and developing the M2M transformation rules from PIM to ASM and the others have worked independently in the definition of the metamodels and the code generation rules for each extension.

4.1. Design of validation

The follow-up of the development of the extensions was accompanied by weekly meetings of approximately 2 hours duration. The weekly meetings were held for one year (including a series of validation experiences for each extensions that are not included in this paper for reason of space). The meetings were oriented to follow the experiences done in the period, complemented with open interviews, observations, and focus groups.

The extension proposals have been divided into stages, considering the process proposed by MoWebA for ASM extension and other additional activities. The activities carried out for the development of the extensions are: i) Definition of the scope to be considered for extensions; ii) Revision and adjustments to the PIM taking into account the architecture established for the extension; iii) ASM metamodeling using MOF; iv) PIM-ASM mapping; v) PIM-ASM transformation rules definition with ATL; vi) Definition of code generation rules; vii) Proof of Concept development; viii) Validation of the extension. For each activity, we identified sources of data to be considered during the experience analysis stage.

In the following subsections, we will present a synthesis of the metamodels proposed for the three architectures, and then focus on items (iv), (v), (vi), and (viii). The details of each of the extensions can be found in the following articles [Nuñez et al. 2018] [Sanchiz et al. 2018] [Núñez et al. 2020].

4.1.1. ASM Metamodel and UML Profile Definition

The **MoWebA4Ria** metamodel incorporates the functionalities to model the features of client data, client business logic, and asynchronous communication between client and server. To save data in a web client, specifically in a web browser, there were created two concepts, a *ClientValueObject*, which extends the value object of the original MoWebA logic diagram, and a *ClientStaticObject*, which extends a static object, a new element introduced in the logic diagram to represent sets of statically defined values as properties of the class. In terms of processes executed on the client, there were created three elements considered in the presentation page, the *RichForm*, the *RichTextInput*, and the *RichTable*.

To allow asynchronous communications between client and server there were created the element called *AsynchronousCall*.

The **MoWebAMobile4FC** metamodel extends the logic diagram of MoWebA to enable the definition of logic processes. Network communication is viewed as a logic process. The logic diagram comprises the logic processes (i.e., *TProcesses* and the procedures for doing a specific task (i.e., *Services*). Also, the logic diagram has *ValueObjects*, which group attributes of entities and enable access to the entities' data. The extensions for obtaining the ASM are based on the REST architecture and the four types of network communication functions: CloudServer, ResourceInterface, RestProcess, and Request type (lightdata, download, upload, loadImage).

The **MoWebAMobile4Persistence** metamodel focuses on the data access level of mobile applications. The definition of the mobile ASM for persistence started with the extension of MoWebA's Entity Diagram at the PIM to take advantage of conceptual elements of the structural type. In this extension, we can define mobile applications with local data persistence and data provider components. Regarding data persistence, we introduce elements to identify what data will be stored on the device (*persistentEntity* tag value), and what type of persistence will be used (*persistentType* tag value). Concerning data providers, we introduce the following interfaces: *WebServiceInterface*, *HardwareDeviceInterface*, and *MobileAppDataInterface*, for the representation of external providers (via web-services), internal providers (through commonly supported sensors among platforms) and interoperability with other applications (data types defined for communication between applications), respectively.

4.1.2. PIM-ASM Mapping Rules

A visual analysis of the defined profile was used to perform the mapping. During the mapping phase, we noticed that, in general, when the relation between elements from source and target profiles is an inheritance, the transformation that allows us to obtain the corresponding target element is very simple and consists of the application of the correct stereotype.

In **MoWeba4Ria** mapping, we identified the following mapping: i) A *Table* element of the PIM, becomes a *RichTable* in the ASM; ii) A *Form* element of the PIM, becomes a *RichForm*; iii) A *TextInput* of the PIM, is transformed into a *RichTextInput*; iv) A *StaticObject* element of the PIM, becomes a *ClientStaticObject*; v) A *ValueObject* of the PIM, is transformed into a *RichValueObject*.

In **MoWebaMobile4FC** mapping, we identified the following mappings: *tProcess* from the PIM becomes a *restProcess* in the ASM, a *service* from the PIM becomes *cloudService* and a *valueObject* from the PIM becomes a *cloudValueObject*.

In **MoWebAMobile4Persistence** mapping, we could detect that a class Entity in the PIM model, becomes a *PersistentEntity* class in the ASM model and that property *entityProperty* in the PIM model is transformed into a *persistentEntityProperty* in the ASM model.

When the relation between two elements in one profile is not an inheritance, the mapping becomes a bit more difficult. In the case of the RIA profile, we found two relations of this type, one between the *ServiceState* and *AsynchronousCall* elements, and the other between the *ServiceState* and *RichTable* elements. Analyzing these relationships, we could conclude that the *AsynchronousCall* must be created when it is related to a *ServiceState*, which, in addition, must represent an asynchronous service. This condition can be detected automatically, allowing the automation of the transformation.

4.1.3. PIM to ASM Transformation Rules

For the definition of the M2M transformation rules, we have chosen ATL (http://www.eclipse.org/atl/) (Atlas Transformation Language) over QVT (http://www.omg.org/spec/QVT/About-QVT/). This choice was based, above all, on the fact that ATL is considered one of the most widely used transformation languages, both in academia and industry, and a mature tool support is available [Brambilla et al. 2017].

Another significant choice was the selection of the engine execution mode of the ATL transformation, which has two modes of execution: default and refining [García Rubio et al. 2013]. When the source and target metamodels are different, it is mandatory to use the default execution mode, but when the metamodels of the source and target models are the same you can opt for either of the two execution modes [García Rubio et al. 2013]. In our case, both, the metamodels of source and target models are the same because MoWebA's implementation is based on profiles [González et al. 2016b]. Moreover, the M2M transformation from PIM to ASM fits conceptually better to the refining mode, since the PIM is justly refined to obtain the ASM. For all this, we opted for the refining execution mode. This choice has greatly reduced the number of necessary transformation rules. However, this also led to some complications, since the application of profiles in ATL is performed in the imperative block and turns out this option when using refining mode. For the above reason, we were forced to change the compiler. The default compiler in Eclipse is the EMF-specific Virtual Machine (EMF-specific VM), but it also provides other compilers. We opted for the EMF Transformation Virtual Machine (EMFTVM). Although the main reason for this choice was that it allows the use of the imperative block in the refining mode, which is necessary to work with profiles, there are some other advantages. For example, its performance is roughly 80% better than the EMF-specific Virtual Machine, and allows us to invoke native Java methods.

Another important aspect of the transformation rules definition is the Configuration file. Configuration files allow the designer to control some transformation aspects, allowing the achievement of two important capabilities: on the one hand, the possibility of capturing specific design decisions of the system under design that would otherwise not be automated, and on the other hand, the possibility that the designer has some level of influence over the transformation rules. Two different configuration files have been considered. One that allows to indicate which elements of the model are transformed and which are not, called "ArchConfTransformacion.yaml", and another one that allows to specify some properties for the classes created automatically when executing the M2M transformation rules, called "ArchConfAsynchronousCall.yaml".

Among the challenges of the M2M transformation that have been tackled, we can mention:

1. The inability to work with profiles in the refining mode, forced us to use a compiler different from the one proposed by default.
2. The asynchronous services identification, is necessary for automating the creation of asynchronous classes.
3. The correct configuration of the IDE to access native Java methods was created expressly for the processing of the configuration files.

The *called rules* is another vital section of transformation rules. The called rule named *applyMobileStereoTypes* allows changing the stereotypes in the target model.

4.1.4. ASM to Code Generation

After the generation of the ASM of the application, it is possible to go through the process of generating code. To do this, we have defined transformation rules from model to text using the Acceleo tool for the three extensions.

These transformation rules follow a template-based approach in which text templates are specified with entries for data to be extracted from the model diagrams. The MTL (http://www.omg.org/spec/MOFM2T/1.0/) language was used for the definition of the templates, and OCL to make queries to the model. In addition, services defined in Java were used to extend MTL with greater functionalities.

In the case of **MoWebA4RIA**, these rules are responsible for transforming elements defined in the logic and content diagrams to HTML5, Javascript, jQuery, jQuery code, and Datatables libraries.

In **MoWebAMobile4FC** we have built a service in Java to extend the functions of the MTL. We have built the transformation rules based on the classes, properties, and operations characterized by the respective stereotypes, tag values, and enumerations defined in the ASM's profile. In this sense, such rules perform a mapping between the model elements defined and the target code to be generated. The generation for both sides, mobile and cloud, depends on each combination of a *CloudServer*, a *RestProcess*, *ResourceInterface* and *CloudRequestHandler*. The target code generated consists, on one side, of native mobile code written in Java for Android, in Swift for iOS, and on the other side, in open source code written in Javascript with Node.js for the Openshift and Amazon Web Services platforms. Additionally, our cloud implementation is based on Docker which is a container where an application runs. Moreover, Docker is an emerging method developed by the open-source community for easing the portability of cloud applications.

In **MoWebAMobile4Persistence**, the generated target codes for Android and Windows Phone are Java and C#, respectively. Additionally, GUI code is also generated for Android (XML) and Windows Phone (XAML). This generated code is ready to be executed for both mobile platforms, Android and Windows Phone, with previous compilation in their respective IDEs.

The tools defined for the three MoWebA extensions, which include the metamodels, UML profiles, PIM-ASM transformation rules, and ASM-code transformation rules, are available on the *MDD+ project* website (http://www.dei.uc.edu.py/proyectos/mddplus/herramientas/).

4.2. Data Collection

The data collection can be classified as first-degree since we were in direct contact with participants and we collected data in real-time using different methods. The main sources of data were results/outputs expected for each stage.

We considered as **information sources** for data collection:

1. the *project documentation*, which includes PIM metamodels, ASM metamodels, PIM-ASM transformation rules, ASM-Code generation, proof of concept, and all the documentation generated for each validation extension;
2. the work sessions' *timesheets* of each validation extension.

The **quantitative data** were collected from these information sources. On the other hand, the **qualitative data** were obtained from the comments and opinions of the participants.

In the first place, the **project documentation** allowed us to determine the success rate of the participants. Therefore, the **timesheets** permitted us to determine the completion time of each process in the validation extensions. Table 1. presents a summary of data collected during the experience.

Table 1. Summary of data collected during the experience.

Data Collection method	Materials	Outputs
1. Definition of the scope to be considered for extensions.		
Focus Group, Open, and semi-structured interviews	Scientific documentation (articles, proceedings, books)	Theoretical framework and state of the art related to each architecture; Document with scope definition.
2. Revision and adjustments to the PIM taking into account the architecture established for the extension.		
Observation (category 3); Archival data	Magic Draw; MoWebA specification; Internet	PIM metamodel modified; PIM modification report.
3. Metamodel and UML profile: definition of architecture metamodels, considering the Brambilla et al. framework [Brambilla et al. 2017]. Definition of UML profiles.		
Observation (category 3); Archival data	Magic Draw; Brambilla specification; UML profile specification	MOF definition for each architecture; UML profile definition for each architecture; Explanatory report
4. PIM-ASM mapping.		
Observation (category 3); Archival data	Magic Draw	Mapping rules identification
5. PIM-ASM transformation rules definition with ATL.		
Observation (category 3); Archival data	ATL tool	Transformation rules in ATL; Explanatory report
6. Definition of transformation rules from the ASM model to the final code. Generation of source code.		
Observation (category 3); Archival data	Acceleo tool	Transformation definition in Acceleo; Documentation

Table 1. Summary of data collected during the experience.

Data Collection method	Materials	Outputs
7. Proof of Concept development.		
Focus group; Open and semi-structured interviews	MagicDraw; ATL tool; Acceleo	PIM Models; ASM models, code generated

4.3. Data Analysis

The analysis carried out consists of a qualitative analysis and judgment for each research question, based on the data collected and the monitoring throughout the process. We begin the section with table 2, which presents a summary of the activities carried out and the achievements reached for each of the extensions.

Table 2. Resume of activities of ASM extensions development

Task	RIA	Mobile for Function and the Cloud	Mobile for Persistence
Scope for the extensions	client data, client business logic, and asynchronous communication between client and server	light-data, load-image, download-files, upload-files	data persistence mechanisms: databases, files, and key-value pairs providers: external, internal, and other applications
Modifications to the PIM metamodel	Logic Diagram: *staticObject* and *value* attribute. Content Diagram: *requestType* attribute of Form element, *name* attribute of List element, *submitButton* as a specialization of Button	none	Entity Diagram: *EntityProperty* element and *Datatype*
PIM Diagrams extended	Logic and Content Diagrams	Logic Diagram	Entity Diagram
PIM elements extended into the ASM metamodel	6 elements: *valueObject* and *staticObject* into the Client Data; *table*, *form* and *textInput* into the Client Business Logic; and *service* in the Asynchronous Communication)	3 elements: *valueObject*, *service* and *TProcess*	2 elements: *persistenceEntity* and *persistenceEntityProperty*
Number of elements defined in the ASM metamodel	11 elements: 3 for Client Data, 4 for Client Business Logic and 4 for Asynchronous Communication	18 elements: for Mobile Cloud Communications	17 elements: 5 for data persistence y 12 for data providers

Table 2. Resume of activities of ASM extensions development

Task	**RIA**	**Mobile for Function and the Cloud**	**Mobile for Persistence**
PIM-ASM Mapping	5 direct mapping elements from inheritance and 1 mapping from associations	3 direct mapping elements from inheritance	2 direct mapping elements from inheritance
PIM-ASM Transformation	ATL with refining mode and 2 configuration files	manually	ATL with refining mode and 1 configuration file
M2T Code Generation	**M2T Tool:** Acceleo **Final code:** HTML5, Javascript, jQuery, jQuery UI, and Datatables libraries	**M2T Tool:** Acceleo **Final Code:** Java (Android), Swift (iOS), Node.js , Docker	**M2T Tool:** Acceleo **Final Code:** Java (Android) and C# (Windows), GUI code in XML (Android) and XAML (Windows)

Below we discuss each of the research questions.

RQ1: To what extent are the evolution and adaptability of the extension mechanism proposed by MoWebA achieved to incorporate new architectures?

From the experience with the three different extensions, we can conduct the following analysis:

- All three extensions have been successfully developed, starting from the same PIM metamodel, with a reduced number of adjustments to the already defined PIM level. However, we had to make some decisions for the development of the extensions, which have involved some minor adjustments to the PIM metamodel, and changes in the environments to be used for the definition of the transformation rules (e.g. the ATL tool used for M2M transformations explained in section 4.1.3).
- The MoWebA proposal for adaptation to other architectures can be done by users with knowledge of MDD and the use of standards. This observation is made because the extensions have been developed by undergraduate students whose knowledge and experiences have been the fundamentals, tools, and standards of MDD. They have learned the MoWebA proposal during their degree studies and as part of the work carried out in the project.
- One aspect to consider is that the greater the number of elements of the ASM metamodel that are not related to elements of the PIM metamodel (either through inheritance or association), the degree of PIM-ASM automation decreases. Therefore, more effort is required in manual adjustments to the ASM model before code generation. However, the configuration files have allowed to introduction of design decisions before the transformation processes and thus increased the degree of automation.
- Finally, regarding the number of elements added in the ASM metamodels, we consider that it corresponds to a reasonable and manageable amount to include

new concepts in a methodological proposal (11 for RIA, 18 for Cloud Communications, and 17 for persistence). On the other hand, the fact of considering the modeling of a specific architecture (ASM) in a different level of abstraction is not mandatory and should be included only in case the architecture must be specified in the modeling process. Doing so, the PIM remains independent of the proposed extensions.

RQ2: How independent is the MoWebA PIM for use in the modeling stage before ASM?

The extensions made to MoWebA have involved revisions to the elements defined in the PIM metamodel and the definition of the ASM metamodel for a specific architecture. In some cases, these revisions implied a more detailed specification of certain existing elements, and in other cases the inclusion of new no contemplated elements into the PIM. In all three cases, the extensions were made based on diagrams already defined in the PIM, since each extension aims to consider aspects of an architecture that includes one or more layers of an application. It should be noted that for the three metamodels defined, there are elements that correspond to specializations of elements from the PIM (e.g. *richForm* is a specialization of *form* in the RIA metamodel, *CloudService* as a specialization of *Service* in the FC extension, or *persistenceEntity* as a specialization of *entity* in the persistence ASM).

Table 2 shows some details of how the extensions were made. From this Table we have conducted the following analysis:

- The first has to do with the extended diagrams. In this regard, it should be noted that the three extensions have been based on diagrams already existing in the PIM, which leads us to believe that the PIM has the necessary independent modeling elements to carry out these extensions.
- Another aspect worth mentioning is that specializations of existing concepts have also been made in the three extensions, i.e., elements have been redefined or specialized to orient the elements towards specific architectures. It gives us evidence that the generic or independent concepts are included in the PIM metamodel.
- In two of the three extensions, new elements have been proposed, or, existing elements have been redefined in the PIM metamodels. This is because, in addition to being required for the extensions, they have been considered as generic concepts, i.e., independent of the architecture, so we decided to include them in the PIM metamodels (e.g., the *staticObjects* identified in RIA, or *EntityProperty* added to the PIM during the persistence extension). It should be noted, however, that the number of new elements included in the PIM has been minimal (2 classes and 3 attributes in RIA, no elements in Cloud, 1 class and 1 enumeration in Persistence), which again confirms the fact that the PIM is independent enough to be extended, but at the same time has the necessary elements to PIM modeling.

RQ3: To what extent automation can be obtained with MoWebA's model-to-model and model-to-code transformation rules?

ASM-PIM transformation has been completed for ASM elements derived from PIM by inheritance.

In cases where additional information has been required from the user to include design decisions, the configuration files have allowed to enter such information before performing the transformations, thus improving the degree of automation.

The PIM-ASM transformation experiences described in [Núñez et al. 2020] have shown that although it is possible to include manual adjustments to the ASM models generated from the PIM, the configuration files have helped to reduce these percentages considerably.

It should also be noted that the following manual adjustments have been made by using the extensions: i) including certain elements in the ASM that could not be derived from the PIM; ii) modifying the final code related to the user interface of the applications and other adjustments for the generation of the application from the code generated in Acceleo; iii) modifying the final code and the models for validation purposes.

5. Conclusions and Future Works

The purpose of this study was to analyze the role of the Architecture Specific Model (ASM) phase in both modeling and transformation processes. Specifically, we examined its use in extending MoWebA for three different architectures: MoWebA4RIA (an extension for RIA functionalities), MoWebAMobile4FC (an extension for mobile applications with functions in the cloud), and MoWebAMobile4Persistence (an extension for mobile applications with a persistence layer). MoWebA prescribes the definition of a new ASM for each extension, along with the respective PIM-ASM transformation rules and ASM-Code generation. The development of the extensions was followed up through weekly meetings over one year. These meetings were complemented by open interviews, observations, and focus groups.

The results show that MoWebA provides an interesting degree of adaptability and automation to the PIM-ASM, as well as independence from the PIM meta model. Experience has shown that all three extensions were successfully developed from the same PIM metamodel with a reduced number of adaptations. Each extension has involved revising the elements defined in the PIM metamodel and defining the ASM metamodel for a specific architecture. Two of the extensions have included the PIM-ASM transformation rules with configuration files. While in the other extensions (i.e., (MoWebAMobile4FC), the PIM-ASM transformation required a few manual adjustments.

We identified several opportunities to improve and extend the proposal. In the modeling dimension, it is relevant the development of a modeling tool to simplify the use of MoWebA for PIM and ASM modeling, along with the revision and improvement of Model-to-Model and Model-to-Code transformation rules. Considering the need for adaptation of the methodologies, we envision the extensions to other environments and architectures. Finally, usability experiences with MoWebA and further validation of the proposal (e.g., formal experiments or case studies) in industrial or commercial contexts are necessary steps to consolidate the approach.

References

Basili, V. R., Caldiera, G., and Rombach, D. H. (1994). *The Goal Question Metric Approach*, volume I. John Wiley & Sons.

Bernardi, M. L., Lucca, G. A. D., and Distante, D. (2014). Model-driven fast prototyping of rias: From conceptual models to running applications. In *2014 International*

Conference on Advances in Computing, Communications and Informatics (ICACCI), pages 250–258.

Bordeleau, F., Liebel, G., Raschke, A., Stieglbauer, G., and Tichy, M. (2017). Challenges and research directions for successfully applying MBE tools in practice. In *Proceedings of 20th International Conference on Model Driven Engineering Languages and Systems (MODELS 2017), Austin, TX, USA, September, 17, 2017*, pages 338–343.

Brambilla, M., Cabot, J., and Wimmer, M. (2017). *Model-Driven Software Engineering in Practice, Second Edition*. Synthesis Lectures on Software Engineering. Morgan & Claypool Publishers.

Brambilla, M., Mauri, A., and Umuhoza, E. (2014). Extending the interaction flow modeling language (IFML) for model driven development of mobile applications front end. In *Mobile Web Information Systems - 11th International Conference, MobiWIS 2014, Barcelona, Spain, August 27-29, 2014. Proceedings*, pages 176–191.

Farshidi, S., Jansen, S., and Fortuin, S. (2021). Model-driven development platform selection: four industry case studies. *Software and Systems Modeling*, pages 1–27.

García Rubio, F. O., Vara Mesa, J. M., and Chicote, C. V. (2013). *Desarrollo de Software Dirigido por Modelos: Conceptos, Métodos y Herramientas*. Ra-Ma Editorial.

González, M., Cernuzzi, L., Aquino, N., and Pastor, O. (2016a). Developing web applications for different architectures: The moweba approach. In *Tenth IEEE International Conference on Research Challenges in Information Science, RCIS 2016, Grenoble, France, June 1-3, 2016*, pages 1–11. IEEE.

González, M., Cernuzzi, L., and Pastor, O. (2016b). A navigational role-centric model oriented web approach - MoWebA. *Int. J. Web Eng. Technol.*, 11(1):29–67.

González, M. (2022). *A Navigational Role-Centric Model Oriented Web Approach MoWebA*. Phd thesis, Polictecnic University of Valencia, Valencia, Spain.

Nuñez, G., Bonhaure, D., González, M., Aquino, N., and Cernuzzi, L. (2018). A model-driven approach to develop rich web applications. *CLEI Electron. J.*, 21(2).

Núñez, M., Bonhaure, D., González, M., and Cernuzzi, L. (2020). A model-driven approach for the development of native mobile applications focusing on the data layer. *J. Syst. Softw.*, 161.

Panach, J. I., Dieste, O., Marín, B., España, S., Vegas, S., Pastor, O., and Juristo, N. (2021). Evaluating model-driven development claims with respect to quality: A family of experiments. *IEEE Trans. Software Eng.*, 47(1):130–145.

Rossi, G., Urbieta, M., Distante, D., Rivero, J. M., and Firmenich, S. (2016). 25 years of model-driven web engineering: What we achieved, what is missing. *CLEI Electron. J.*, 19(3):1.

Runeson, P., Höst, M., Rainer, A., and Regnell, B. (2012). *Case Study Research in Software Engineering - Guidelines and Examples*. Wiley.

Sanchiz, E., González, M., Aquino, N., and Cernuzzi, L. (2018). Moweba mobile: Modeling and generation of the communication of mobile apps with their functions in the cloud. In *Proceedings of the XXI Iberoamerican Conference on Software Engineering, Bogota, Colombia, April 23-27, 2018*, pages 312–325.

UX evaluation of IoT-based applications for Smart Cities: a rapid systematic review

Joelma Choma[1] and Luciana Zaina[1]

[1]Federal University of São Carlos (UFSCar)
Sorocaba – SP – Brazil

jchoma@ufscar.br, lzaina@ufscar.br

Abstract. *The development of systems based on the Internet of Things (IoT) technologies is becoming increasingly popular in the context of Smart Cities. Recent research in Software Engineering (SE) has investigated the characteristics of these systems and the most appropriate approaches to their design and development. IoT-based applications are strongly characterized by the interaction among multiple devices, users, and services. These characteristics make these applications complex and difficult to evaluate, particularly in terms of User Experience (UX) design. In this study, we performed a rapid systematic review to examine the methods and practices commonly employed for evaluating the UX of IoT-based applications for Smart Cities. We analyzed 43 studies covering different types of IoT-based applications, most in the area of Smart Home. Our findings indicate that user testing questionnaire-based (e.g., SUS - System Usability Scale and UEQ - User Experience Questionnaire) and interviews are the most used methods to evaluate IoT applications, while few studies mentioned user testing based on automated measurement or expert-based reviews. This work contributes to SE research by revealing the need to explore UX evaluation methods based on usage data and the combination of methods for continuous UX evaluation in the context of IoT and Smart Cities.*

1. Introduction

Recent research in Software Engineering has increasingly focused on addressing challenges related to the design and development of systems based on the Internet of Things (IoT). IoT plays a key part in the development of Smart Cities platforms by allowing the integration of a wide range of devices and applications [Syed et al. 2021]. Applications based on IoT technologies have been used in the area of Smart Cities to make urban planning and infrastructure maintenance more efficient, monitor air quality, and reduce waste of water, energy, and other natural resources, focusing on boosting the living experience of their residents [Whaiduzzaman et al. 2022]. Regardless of how many aspects and dimensions are involved, IoT-based applications for Smart Cities are closely related to sensor networks, smart devices, real-time data, and information and communications technology integration in all aspects of human life [Cretu 2012].

IoT supplies the technological basis for continuous communication between devices, systems, and people through a combination of three main components: (i) smart devices (hardware) equipped with components to provide communication (sensors, chips, antennas, etc.); (ii) IoT applications (middleware) using computing technologies such as ML and AI for on-demand storage and analysis of data received from various devices; and

(iii) graphical user interfaces (mobile or web application) for management and control of smart devices and data visualization [Gubbi et al. 2013].

IoT-based applications offer novel ways for human-thing and thing-thing interactions. However, such interactions in smart environments involving multiple devices, users, and services make the IoT scenarios complex and difficult to evaluate software quality attributes such as User Experience (UX) [Andrade et al. 2017]. The concept of UX was introduced in the 90s by Donald Norman to describe all aspects of the end user's interaction with the company, its services, and its products [Norman and Nielsen 2020]. Over the years, a variety of definitions have been suggested to better understand the meaning of UX from different perspectives. From an industry perspective, ISO 9241-210 defines UX as *"the user perceptions and responses that result from the use and/or anticipated use of a system, product or service"* [ISO9241-210 2019]. From the perspective of evaluating experience, for Hassenzahl and Tractinsky [Hassenzahl and Tractinsky 2006], the idea of UX goes beyond providing an intuitive and functional *design* about software, emphasizing that experience is a phenomenon that emerges from the integration of action, perception, motivation, and emotion, which occur within a given space of time and place.

Due to the dynamic and temporal aspect of UX, experience information can be collected at different points in the product development cycle to include different experience episodes [Hassenzahl and Tractinsky 2006]. However, IoT-based applications for Smart Cities pose additional challenges for evaluating UX due to the nature of the interaction, which can change from explicit to implicit, encompass different interaction methods, and scale from one to many interactions [Stephanidis et al. 2019]. Furthermore, recent studies have highlighted the lack of generic and systematic approaches to evaluating UX in the IoT scenarios [Stephanidis et al. 2019] [Almeida et al. 2018].

In this study, we present a rapid review (RR) [Tricco et al. 2015] conducted to investigate UX evaluation methods commonly used in the context of IoT and Smart Cities to address a problem identified in practice. RR is a variant of the Systematic Literature Review (SLR) which simplifies some steps of the review procedures intended providing actionable insights for practice at a low cost and in less time [Cartaxo et al. 2018]. The question we are trying to answer with this research is: *Which methods are commonly applied for evaluating the UX of IoT-based applications?* By answering this question, this literature review contributes to an overview of UX evaluation in IoT for Smart Cities, highlighting some research gaps such as the lack of studies on evaluation methods based on usage data, automated measurements, and the combination of methods for continuous UX evaluation in this area.

The remainder of this paper is structured as follows: we present the background on IoT-based applications for Smart Cities and the existing literature on UX evaluation in this area, in Section 2. Section 3 presents the research method describing the RR context, planning, and execution. Section 4 shows the RR results on IoT layers, things and users involved, and UX methods applied in the Smart City context. We discuss our findings in Section 5 and conclude the paper in Section 6.

2. Background

This section provides the concepts covered in our study through an overview of studies on IoT-based applications for Smart Cities and UX evaluation in IoT applications.

2.1. IoT-based applications for Smart Cities

Considering the recent emerging technological trends for smart environments, several studies have pointed out challenges referring to IoT system design and structure [Whaiduzzaman et al. 2022], the management and analysis of large amounts of data collected from different sources [Reinfurt et al. 2017], users working with a set of heterogeneous devices and machines [Syed et al. 2021], and concerns on human aspects to understand context of use, users need, and business interests [Motta et al. 2023]. IoT research is recognized as a multidisciplinary domain that covers a range of topics from socio-technical to business. Motta et al. [Motta et al. 2018] identified seven facets to be taken into account in IoT software systems design by characterizing this multidisciplinary. Interactivity is one of the identified facets that refers to the involvement of humans, non-humans, and things in exchanging information and the degree to which this happens through connectivity and interoperability.

In the Smart City context, IoT systems involve the collection of data from sensors about the city's state to a central cloud, and the performing of data analytics operations to extract information to support policymakers and citizens [Syed et al. 2021]. IoT-based applications have been developed in Smart Cities for many purposes, including monitoring energy consumption, traffic control, pollution reduction, and solid waste management [Abdulsattar et al. 2022] [Ismail et al. 2019]. The eight components of a Smart City are: Smart Energy, Smart Homes, Smart Industry, Smart Infrastructure, Smart Agriculture, Smart Transportation, Smart Health, and Smart City Services [Syed et al. 2021]. A typical IoT architecture for Smart Cities consists of five layers: 1) *sensing layer* (i.e., sensors, actuators, mobile elements), 2) *network layer* (i.e., network technologies and topologies), 3) *middleware layer* (i.e., APIS, databases, security), 4) *applications layer* (i.e., applications, systems, and platforms), and 5) *business layer* (i.e. analytics, machine learning, optimization, deep learning) [Syed et al. 2021].

2.2. UX evaluation of IoT-based applications

The literature has investigated more effective methods for evaluating the UX of IoT applications. Shin [Shin 2017] theoretically conceptualized the notion of quality in the IoT, established a relationship between technical quality and users' perceived assessments, and proposed an approach to evaluating the quality of experience for IoT applications focused on content, hedonicity, coolness, affordance, system, and utility. Almeida et al. [Almeida et al. 2018] conducted an RSL on methods for evaluating UX in the IoT scenario and identified a predominance of the use of empirical methods, such as observation of user behavior and interviews. As challenges in conducting UX evaluation, they found that evaluation in the controlled environment may differ from the user's actual use environment, as well as in an environment with many IoT applications. In an exploratory study, Hacid et al. [Hacid et al. 2023] examined where IoT and UX meet for the benefit of users by associating conventional interaction design principles (i.e., Nielsen's usability heuristics [Nielsen 1994]) to challenges that IoT wider acceptance faces according to existing literature. The authors found that programmability and context sensitivity were the most evaluated aspects of IoT.

Mendoza et al. [Mendoza et al. 2023] conducted an SLR on evaluation in ubiquitous and pervasive technology scenarios of interactive installations (e.g., art installation, multimodal installation, and museum exhibition). They found that most studies adopted classical evaluation methods, such as interviews, video recordings, questionnaires, observation, system logs, and physiological measurements. Moreover, they identified three main groups of objects of evaluation addressed in selected studies: (1) people involved directly in their experience, behavior, learning, engagement, affective states, and social relations; (2) system-focused in its usefulness and design; and (3) an "in-between" human-technology relation, encompassing interaction, usability, usage, and overall scenario. Angeloni et al. [Angeloni et al. 2023] carried out a rapid review (RR) on assessments for quality in the use (QinU) of applications in smart environments. QinU refers to the overall quality of the system in its operational environment used by specific users (e.g., elderly or people with disabilities) for the execution of specific tasks (e.g., to help keep elderly people safe at home). Effectiveness, efficiency, freedom from risk, and satisfaction are the main QinU constructs. Commonly, QinU evaluations can be performed by observing the user's interaction with the application. However, this study revealed that the evaluation of applications in smart environments that consider the end user is often done by questionnaires after the use of the software system.

More recently, Ntoa et al. [Ntoa et al. 2021] proposed a conceptual and methodological framework named UXIE for the evaluation of UX in intelligent environments. Taking into account the various characteristics of intelligent environments, the UXIE framework provides concepts and concrete metrics from seven fundamental quality attributes, namely intuitiveness, unobtrusiveness, adaptability and adaptivity, usability, appeal and emotions, safety, and privacy, as well as technology acceptance and adoption. As a methodological tool, UXIE also provides recommendations on the methods to be used to acquire the specified metrics. In this framework, the evaluation methods were categorized into six categories: (1) user testing task-based, or think-aloud, (2) user testing questionnaire-based, (3) user testing through interviews, (4) field study or in-situ evaluation, (5) expert-based reviews; and (6) user testing using automated measurement. It is worth noting that the categorization of UX metrics and attributes is not part of the scope of this article.

Despite the relevance of the previously mentioned studies, to the best of our knowledge, no study has investigated UX evaluation from the perspective of IoT architecture layers and Smart Cities components. In this study, we adopted the classification provided in [Syed et al. 2021] to categorize studies according to five IoT architecture layers and eight Smart City components (see Section 2.1). The identification of UX methods considering the IoT architecture is useful to indicate the layers commonly evaluated, allowing us to identify more suitable methods for each of them or identify deficiencies in evaluation studies in one layer or another. Additionally, we categorized the UX evaluation methods applied in primary studies based on the categories proposed in the UXIE framework [Ntoa et al. 2021], as it is focused on intelligent environments.

3. Research Method

A Rapid Review (RR) study was performed to investigate how UX evaluation has been applied in the area of IoT and Smart Cities. This RR was motivated by an issue raised in an interaction of the researchers with software practitioners, aiming at investigating the challenges faced by software companies to improve product quality through UX design practices [Choma et al. 2022]. In one of the studied companies, practitioners mentioned a challenge regarding evaluating the UX of an IoT platform to support decision-making in the area of water and gas loss management developed for public and private companies. This IoT platform included three main components: 1) a device for remote noise collection (sensing layer), 2) a database and algorithms involving signal processing using artificial intelligence to capture different formats of data coming from different devices (middleware layer), and 3) a web application for data visualization (application layer). Given the researchers' and practitioners' interest in evaluating the UX of IoT platforms in the Smart City context, the following research question arose: *Which UX methods are commonly applied for evaluating the UX of IoT-based applications?* By answering this question, practitioners will be able to select the most appropriate methods to evaluate their applications and identify UX issues that need to be fixed and/or improved.

RR planning: RR is a lightweight variant of the systematic literature review widely used in medicine, focused on delivering evidence to practitioners on time [Tricco et al. 2015]. Cartaxo et al. introduced RRs into evidence-based software engineering, explaining that some steps of the review procedure are omitted or simplified to reduce costs and completion time [Cartaxo et al. 2018]. As a strategy, RRs can limit the literature search by sources or data, employ just one person to screen studies, eliminate the quality assessment step, and/or present the results succinctly and directly. According to them, RRs can be commissioned by professionals, policymakers, or researchers as long as they offer useful knowledge to support decision-making for a practical problem [Cartaxo et al. 2018]. In our RR, we developed a research protocol that can be seen in Table 1. As shown in this table, we performed a quality assessment on the selected primary studies by checking four criteria (i.e., C1 to C4), where each of them was assigned a value based on the response of "Yes" (weight= 1), "Partially" (weight= 0.5), or "No" (weight=0). In addition, we prepared an extraction form to retrieve the following information from the selected studies: research type, contribution type, study objective, things to be evaluated, target users/ stakeholders, IoT layers [Syed et al. 2021], Smart city areas [Syed et al. 2021], and UX evaluation methods to be categorized from concepts presented in UXIE framework [Ntoa et al. 2021] (see in Section 2).

RR execution: By following the guidelines suggested by [Cartaxo et al. 2018], we opted to limit the number of data sources and search period to reduce cost and completion time. We searched for studies in the three databases, in March 2023. We set a limit of the last five years for searches across all databases (i.e., from 2018 to 2022). Nevertheless, we considered selecting secondary studies in our sample to cover periods before 2018. The search string applied to the databases returned 666 studies. Figure 2 shows the number of studies retrieved per database. The Parsifal tool [1] was used to support the search, selection, and analysis activities. In the selection phase, the duplicate studies were eliminated (n=23). Secondly, the researcher analyzed the studies´ titles and abstracts excluding those that did not meet the selection criteria (n=439), resulting in 204 studies. Finally, the researcher analyzed the entire content of the remaining papers and eliminated 161 additional studies that did not meet the acceptance criteria, resulting in 43 articles for extracting and analyzing data. The searching, selection, data extraction, and analysis took around thirty days. Table 2 presents the selected papers. The selection procedure and data extraction are available at `http://tinyurl.com/cfz74xbt`.

[1] https://parsif.al/

Table 1. Rapid review protocol on UX evaluation of IoT-based applications

Objective	This review aims to investigate commonly used methods for evaluating the UX of IoT applications in the context of Smart Cities.
Search string	("user experience" OR "ux") AND("assessment" OR "evaluation" OR "measurement" OR "monitoring") AND ("IoT" OR "internet of things" OR "smart" OR "smart city")
Sources	ACM Digital Library (http://portal.acm.org) IEEE Digital Library (http://ieeexplore.ieee.org) Scopus (http://www.scopus.com)
Inclusion Criteria	(I1) Primary and secondary studies (I2) Studies addressing UX evaluation of IoT-based applications in Smart City.
Exclusion Criteria	(E1) Duplicated papers (E2) Not articles (title page and preface) (E3) Not fully accessible (E4) Not related to IoT or Smart City areas (e.g., medicine, health) (E5) Not related to UX research (E6) Not written in English (E7) Short papers (4-page long or less)
Quality Assessment Checklist	(C1) Is the research aim/objective clearly defined? (C2) Is the context of research well addressed? (C3) Are the findings clearly stated? (C4) Based on the findings, how valuable is the research to this study?

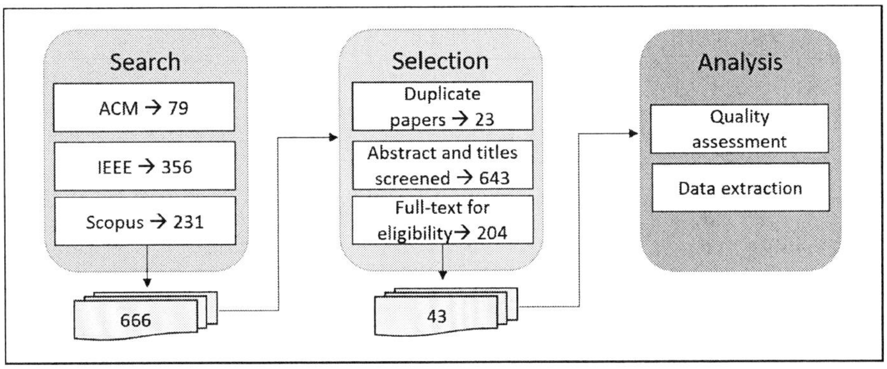

Figure 1. Selected papers process

4. Results

This section presents the results from the analysis of the 43 primary and secondary studies based on the research protocol (see Table 1). Section 4.1 presents an overview of the selected studies. IoT layers, target things, and target users addressed in the primary studies are presented in Section 4.2. Section 4.3 presents the UX evaluation methods commonly applied in IoT applications for Smart Cities. Section 4.4 describes the secondary studies. Finally, Section 4.5 discusses the threats to the validity of this study.

4.1. Overview

As shown in Figure 2-a, 65% of the selected studies (28 out of 43) were from journals, mostly long and complete manuscripts. About 35% of the studies presented proposals of models, frameworks, sensors, platforms, architecture, and guidelines, to name the most frequent ones. We found four studies about IoT and Smart City platforms for intelligent traffic control (S8), urban planning (S23), flood risk, the vulnerability of private properties (S26), and digital urban interfaces (S24). Regarding UX proposals, we found six primary studies proposing UX evaluation guidelines and checklist (S15 and S38), UX evaluation methodology (S24 and S41), and UX metrics (S29). Surveys and interviews were the other two most frequent research methods applied in the studies (Figure 2-b). Figure 2-c

Table 2. List of selected papers

ID	Title
S1	A Context-Aware Concept Evaluation Approach Based on User Experiences for Smart Product-Service Systems Design
S2	A continuous, semi-automated workflow: From 3d city models with geometric optimization and cfd simulations to visualization of wind in an urban environment
S3	A Critical Review of Smart Residential Environments for Older Adults With a Focus on Pleasurable Experience
S4	A generic user interface for energy management in smart homes
S5	A Novel Internet of Things-Based Plug-And-Play Multigas Sensor for Environmental Monitoring
S6	A QoE Model for Mulsemedia TV in a Smart Home Environment
S7	A Study of Smart Home User Personas Based on Context Theory
S8	Adaptive Interface Ecosystems in Smart Cities Control Systems
S9	Address and Command: Two-Handed Mid-Air Interactions with Multiple Home Devices
S10	Adoption of Environmental Information Chatbot Services Based on the Internet of Educational Things in Smart Schools
S11	Ambient intelligence in the living room
S12	An exploratory study on how Internet of Things developing companies handle user experience requirements
S13	An intrusion detection framework for non-expert users
S14	Autonomous parking system user interface – assessment of visual behavior
S15	CHASE: Checklist to Assess User Experience in IoT Environments
S16	Comparing Heuristic Evaluation and MALTU Model in Interaction Evaluation of Ubiquitous Systems
S17	Detecting Anomalies in Daily Activity Routines of Older Persons in Single Resident Smart Homes
S18	End-user Development for Smart Spaces: A Comparison of Block and Data-flow Programming
S19	Environment monitoring system of dairy cattle farming based on multi-parameter fusion
S20	Evaluating a workflow tool for simplifying scenario planning with the online whatif? Planning support system
S21	Evaluating Smart Home Services and Items: A Living Lab User Experience Study
S22	EVLibSim: A tool for the simulation of electric vehicles' charging stations using the EVLib library
S23	Experimental towards User Experience and User Interface in Smart Land Use Informatic Platform
S24	Having a smarter city through digital urban interfaces: An evaluation method
S25	I am not a number: Towards participatory IoT monitoring in the workplace
S26	Less is more? Evaluating technical aspects and user experiences of smart flood risk assessment tools
S27	Longitudinal User Experience Studies in the IoT Domain: A Brief Panorama and Challenges to Overcome
S28	Low-cost IoT remote sensor mesh for large-scale orchard monitorization
S29	Measuring User Experience Quality of Voice Assistants
S30	Mid-air gesture control of multiple home devices in spatial augmented reality prototype
S31	MorSocket: An Expandable IoT-Based Smart Socket System
S32	Multimodal Interface for Human–Robot Collaboration
S33	On User Experience in The Internet of Things
S34	ParlAmI: A Multimodal Approach for Programming Intelligent Environments
S35	QFD-Based Research on Sustainable User Experience Optimization Design of Smart Home Products for the Elderly
S36	Quality Provisioning in the Internet of Things Era: Current State and Future Directions
S37	Reshaping the Smart Home Research and Development in the Pandemic Era: Considerations around Scalable and Easy-to-Install Design
S38	Smart Co-housing for People With Disabilities: A Preliminary Assessment of Caregivers' Interaction With the DOMHO
S39	Ubiquitous Machinery Monitoring – A Field Study on Manufacturing Workers' User Experience of Mobile and Wearable
S40	User experience evaluation for a bus tracking apps in smart campus initiative
S41	User Experience Evaluation in Intelligent Environments: A Comprehensive Framework
S42	User Interface for the Creation of Smart Home Automation Rules
S43	UX Evaluation with Standardized Questionnaires in Ubiquitous Computing and Ambient Intelligence

shows the distribution of studies per year. When evaluating the quality of the articles, we obtained a score of 3.56 on average, which means a high degree of quality regarding rigor and relevance. We found only one article with a score below the cutoff line we established (i.e., <= 1.0), which was excluded from our analysis (see Figure 2-d).

4.2. IoT layers, target things and users

In general, the articles deal with more than one IoT layer in their proposals. The mapping of studies by IoT layers is presented in Table 3. About 77% of studies address the application layer, which uses the data through various API's and database management services to provide users with services [Syed et al. 2021], bridging the gap between the virtual world and the physical world [Hidalgo et al. 2022]. The sensing layer is the second most addressed layer, mentioned in 44% of studies. This layer is where the data is read and passed onward to the middleware layer using the networking layer through wireless net-

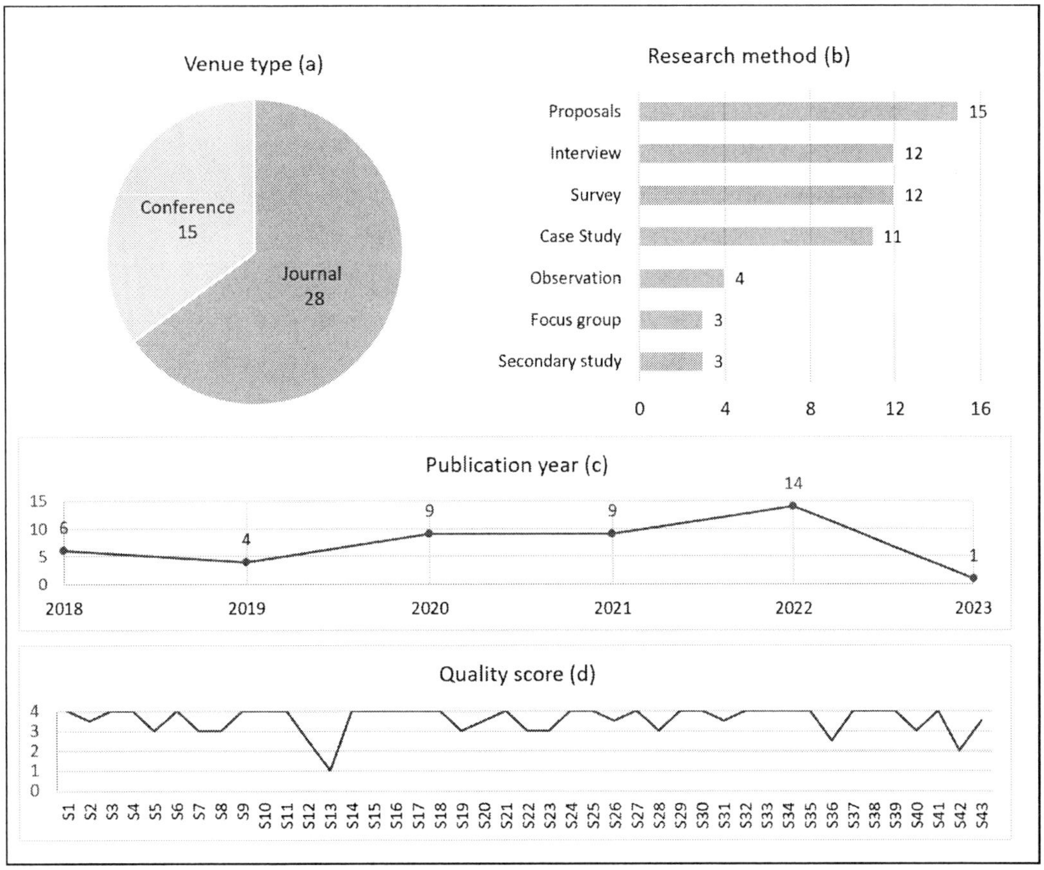

Figure 2. Selected papers overview

work technologies such as Wi-Fi, Bluetooth, etc [Syed et al. 2021]. Few studies mention the business layer in charge of developing strategies and rules that help manage the overall operation of the IoT system, which is attached to the application layer [Syed et al. 2021]. The studies address different types of applications and things, as shown in Figure 3. Regarding target users or stakeholders, smart home residents and UX experts are the focus of most studies (see Figure 3-b).

4.3. UX evaluation methods applied in Smart City

As explained in Section 2, we adopted concepts from UXIE framework [Ntoa et al. 2021] to categorize the UX evaluation methods applied in the studies. In this step, we excluded twelve studies from this analysis either because they did not mention the application of a UX evaluation method or because they were secondary studies. The UX methods identified in the remaining studies were mapped by Smart City areas, as shown in Figure 4. It is worth noting that we identified more than one method in some studies, as we can see in Figure 4. A third of the selected studies applied more than one evaluation method; with two studies applying 3 methods (S30 and S39) and one study applying 4 methods (S38). Also, in some studies, we identified more than one Smart City area covered. The areas most identified in studies are Smart Home and Smart City Services On the other hand, we found few UX evaluation studies in Smart Energy and Smart Agriculture. The most applied method is *user testing based on questionnaire*, which was identified in 57%

Table 3. IoT layers addressed in the studies

IoT Layer	N	Studies
Application layer: applications, systems, platforms	33	S2, S4,S6, S7, S8, S10, S11, S12, S14, S15, S16, S17, S18, S19, S21, S22, S23, S24, S26, S27, S29, S32, S33, S34, S35, S36, S37, S38, S39, S40, S41, S42, S43
Sensing layer: sensors, actuators, mobile elements (e.g., smartphones, cars)	19	S3, S6, S11, S14, S17, S19, S25, S27, S28, S29, S30, S31, S32, S33, S36, S37, S39, S41, S43
Middleware layer: APIs, databases, security	8	S3, S5, S13, S20, S23, S33, S36, S37
Business layer: data analytics, machine learning, optimization, deep learning	4	S1, S2, S9, S36

(a) target things (b) target users/ stakeholders

Figure 3. Target things and users/ stakeholders addressed in the studies

of studies (17 of 30). These questionnaires are often applied together with user testing task-based or think-aloud (S4, S9, S30, S32, S38), followed by interviews (S26, S30, S35, S38, S39), or in-field studies (S37, S38, S39). More than half of the studies (9 of 22 - 52%) applied standardized UX questionnaires such as SUS[2] (S4, S9, S30, S32, and S39), UEQ[3] (S9, S18, S29, and S30), meCUE[4] (S40), NASA-TLX[5] (S32), and UTAUT[6] (S10). The remaining eight studies applied non-standardized UX questionnaires (S6, S21, S22, S26, S33, S37, S38, and S35). Only four studies reported expert-based review and the other two reported user testing based on automated measurement. Expert-based reviews were identified in studies related to Smart Home (S15, S16, and S41), Smart City Services (S24), and Smart Health (S16); while user testing based on automated measurement appeared in studies related to Smart Industry (S1) and Smart City Services (S1 and S8).

[2]SUS - System Usability Scale [Brooke 2013]
[3]UEQ - User Experience Questionnaire [Laugwitz et al. 2008]
[4]meCUE - A modular questionnaire for recording the user experience [Minge et al. 2017]
[5]NASA-TLX - Task Load Index [Hart and Staveland 1988]
[6]UTAUT - Unified Theory of Acceptance and Use of Technology [Venkatesh et al. 2003]

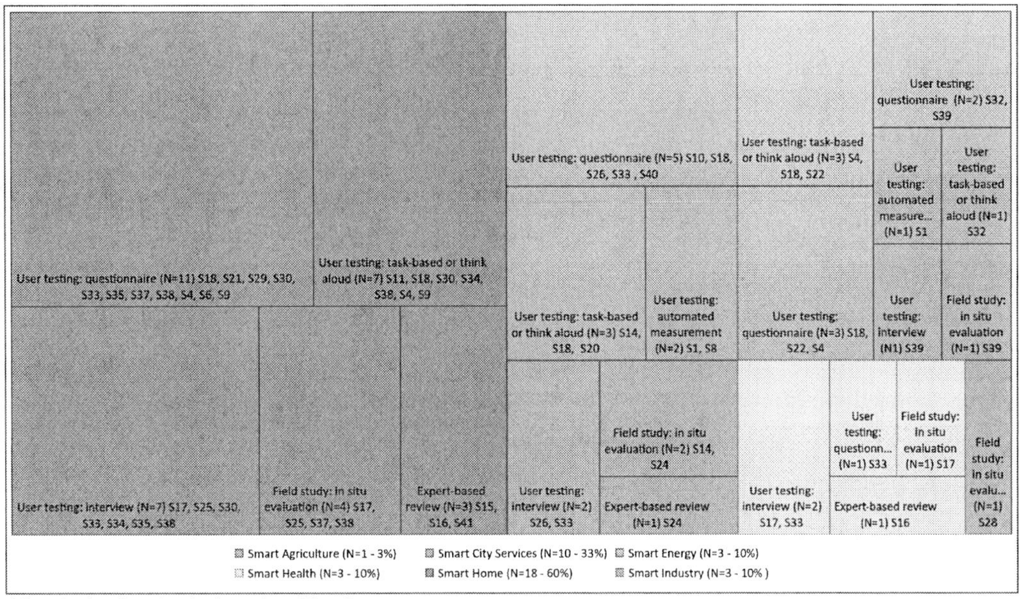

* the caption shows the number of studies covering each Smart City area.

Figure 4. Mapping of UX methods by Smart City areas

4.4. Secondary studies

Next, we describe three systematic literature studies that we selected in our RR (S3, S27, and S43). Lee and Kim [Lee and Kim 2020] (S3) conducted a critical review of smart residential environments aimed at supporting positive aging and pleasurable user experience in the architecture domain. From the study findings, the authors provide a framework to evaluate the well-being, independence, acceptance, and design of smart homes. The details covered in their framework are critical factors that should be considered in providing this type of environment, from the beginning stage of understanding the target user to the design and system evaluation stages.

Diáz-Oreiro et al. [Díaz-Oreiro et al. 2021] (S43) performed a systematic literature review to investigate the use of the three most recognized standardized questionnaires for UX evaluation, i.e., AttrakDiff [Hassenzahl et al. 2003], UEQ [Laugwitz et al. 2008], and meCUE [Minge et al. 2017], in studies involving ubiquitous computing, ambient intelligence, and nontraditional interfaces. They analyzed 132 studies evaluated with standardized questionnaires in the areas of ubiquitous computing and ambient intelligence studies, of which 36 studies on in-vehicle information systems, 28 studies on IoT and wearable sensors, and 27 studies on Smart Cities. As a result, the authors found that AttrakDiff has been the predominant questionnaire for studies of Smart Cities, including smart homes and in-vehicle information systems.

Melo et al. [Melo et al. 2022] (S27), firstly, performed the forward snowballing from a set of key studies to investigate UX evaluations in the IoT field, especially focused on long-term evaluation. Secondly, they conducted a systematic mapping to explore how longitudinal evaluations are done in IoT to understand the strategies used by researchers in this domain. Moreover, they also searched for UX theoretical constructs associated with the long-term adoption or rejection of IoT systems, to explore the opportunities, difficulties, and potentialities of conducting UX longitudinal studies in the IoT domain.

Due to privacy concerns about IoT devices, they found that users may tend not to want to participate in longitudinal studies with log collection when the usage information is exposed. Furthermore, they pointed out the difficulties of conducting longitudinal UX evaluations in real scenarios. Due to the cost of execution, many assessments are carried out in simulated environments which do not cover some situations that only occur in real contexts. Lastly, they highlighted the challenge of choosing appropriate UX constructs to evaluate IoT systems over time.

4.5. Threats to validity

As with any other empirical study, Rapid Reviews are also subject to limitations and threats to validity. However, due to lightweight methodology, RRs usually present more threats to validity than other systematic studies [Cartaxo et al. 2018]. To mitigate the threat of obtaining a limited number of primary studies, we applied our search string to three different databases, one of which (i.e., Scopus) indexes and searches several relevant digital libraries on Software Engineering. The search, selection, and data extraction steps were conducted by a solo researcher. To mitigate the selection and interpretation bias of the researcher, these steps were reviewed and discussed by a second researcher. To ensure the reliability of the evidence, we performed a quality assessment of the selected primary studies. Moreover, we adopted a research protocol based on [Cartaxo et al. 2018] to ensure the replicability of the study.

5. Discussion

Previous studies have been concerned with conceptualizing quality in the IoT and extending the conventional UX approach to the IoT context [Shin 2017], as well as developing practical tools to assist UX evaluation in the IoT scenario [Almeida et al. 2018]. Other studies have investigated related areas such as ubiquitous and pervasive technology scenarios of interactive installations [Mendoza et al. 2023] and more general themes such as assessments for quality in the use of applications in smart environments involving specific users [Angeloni et al. 2023]. The secondary studies selected in our review also addressed the UX evaluation of smart environments in a specific domain (i.e., smart homes from an architectural perspective, in-vehicle information systems, and wearable devices [Lee and Kim 2020] [Díaz-Oreiro et al. 2021]) and comprehensively the long-term UX assessment in the IoT domain.

Unlike the studies aforementioned, the primary studies selected in this review cover a broad range of IoT applications from different Smart Cities areas. We found several studies that covered research interests coming from domains outside the SE boundaries (e.g., Urban Planning, Psychology, Buildings, Technologies, and Machines), outlining the multidisciplinary nature of IoT technologies for the Smart Cities context. In SE, this multidisciplinary nature is already recognized, as the IoT paradigm encompasses many knowledge areas (e.g., ubiquitous domains, computing and cloud computing, and data analytics) which are integrated to create autonomous and intelligent software systems [Motta et al. 2018]. Regardless of the UX methods applied, our findings indicate that the UX attributes evaluated may vary depending on the domains and areas of interest. In this sense, we noticed that *the diversity of contexts and purposes in the Smart City area can lead to the combination of UX methods to encompass several constructs to be evaluated (e.g., usability, acceptance, trust, integration, privacy)* (see Section 4.3).

Although studies on the IoT application layer were found more frequently, we found a few studies on UX evaluation in Smart City platforms (see Section 4.1). Smart City platforms usually are based on a continuous workflow embracing data model implementation and analysis of different visualization schemes on urban activities to support different [Deininger et al. 2020]. However, we found a single study that was concerned with defining methodology and tools to evaluate user experience in the domain of digital urban interfaces [Aceves Gutierrez et al. 2019]. In this study, the authors defined a series of specific guidelines for evaluating urban interfaces based on the literature review and other characteristics of urban space such as physical location, use schedule, and citizen profile [Aceves Gutierrez et al. 2019]. Regardless a few studies have applied expert-based user testing methods, our findings indicate the need *to extend conventional guidelines for UX evaluation to encompass details on the characteristics of the context of use, user profile, and technologies involved in the application domain.*

The evidence on the application of non-standardized questionnaires obtained in this RR also reinforces the need *to develop new instruments or expand existing ones (e.g., SUS, UEQ, and meCUE) to cover UX constructs in applications involving IoT technologies and smart environments.* Díaz-Oreiro et al.'s study pointed out that the AttrakDiff [Hassenzahl et al. 2003] questionnaire was predominant for studies in Smart Cities and homes [Díaz-Oreiro et al. 2021]. Curiously, we found a single study mentioning this questionnaire (S15), perhaps due to the time frame set up in our RR (i.e., the last five years). On the other hand, our results can strengthen Díaz-Oreiro et al.'s findings, who had already noticed that UEQ was surpassing AttrakDiff in use since 2017. Thus, we argue that *a comparative analysis between these two instruments (i.e., UEQ and AttrakDiff) can provide insights to understand why the UEQ has gained ground in the evaluation of IoT systems.*

When investigating longitudinal studies in IoT systems, Melo et al. [Melo et al. 2022] reported that most UX evaluations were done in simulated environments. Unlike them, we identified long-term UX studies carried out in real-world environments, mainly field studies involving follow-up of the daily activities of smart home residents through interviews and questionnaires (S17, S25, and S38). Melo et al. argued that an automated collection of UX data in IoT systems could enable longitudinal studies in real contexts by reducing infrastructure and logistics costs. We also found only two studies that involved automated data collection in smart environments (S1, S8). Therefore, we also see the need for *methods and tools to facilitate remote and automated UX data collection that contribute to user engagement with the guarantee of privacy and foster the UX continuous evaluation in IoT and Smart City contexts.*

6. Conclusion and further work

The main contribution of this work is to provide scientific evidence on UX methods commonly applied to evaluate IoT-based applications in the context of Smart Cities to support both researchers and practitioners from the software industry. To respond and transfer scientific knowledge to practitioners at the company that develops an IoT system aimed at identifying water and gas leaks in the Smart City Services area, we are currently working on a report that summarizes the main conclusions and better fits their needs, as recommended by Cartaxo [Cartaxo et al. 2018].

The study contributions also extend to academia by pointing out takeaways that should drive further proposals of UX methods to cover attributes inherent to applications based on IoT technologies for Smart City environments. Further studies are needed to investigate actionable UX metrics and improve UX assessment methods for automated measurement in this area, which could leverage the sensing layer of the IoT structure. Furthermore, a comparative analysis of the use of standardized and non-standardized questionnaires can provide insights to recommend the application of these collection instruments according to IoT scenarios under evaluation. In future work, we will extend this review by mapping the UX attributes, metrics, and constructs that were evaluated in the primary studies, taking into account the methods, context of use, characteristics of applications, things, and users. So, we can deepen our understanding of how IoT layers or target things are linked with UX aspects.

Acknowledgments

This work is partially supported by the Coordenação de Aperfeiçoamento de Pessoal de Nível Superior - Brasil (CAPES) - Finance Code 001 and Conselho Nacional de Desenvolvimento Científico e Tecnológico (CNPq - Brazil), grant 309497/2022-1.

References

Abdulsattar, N. F., Abbas, A. H., Mutar, M. H., Hassan, M. H., Jubair, M. A., and Habelalmateen, M. I. (2022). An investigation study for technologies, challenges and practices of iot in smart cities. In *2022 5th International Conference on Engineering Technology and its Applications (IICETA)*, pages 554–557. IEEE.

Aceves Gutierrez, L. C., Martin Gutierrez, J., and Del-Rio-Guerra, M. S. (2019). Having a smarter city through digital urban interfaces: an evaluation method. *Applied Sciences*, 9(17):3498.

Almeida, R. L., Darin, T. G., Andrade, R. M., and de Araújo, I. L. (2018). Towards developing a practical tool to assist ux evaluation in the iot scenario. In *Anais Estendidos do XXIV Simpósio Brasileiro de Sistemas Multimídia e Web*, pages 91–95. SBC.

Andrade, R., Carvalho, R. M., Araújo, I. L. d., Oliveira, K. M., and Maia, M. E. (2017). What changes from ubiquitous computing to internet of things in interaction evaluation? In *Int. Conf. on Distributed, Ambient, and Pervasive Interactions*, pages 3–21.

Angeloni, M. P. C., Oliveira, K. M. d., Grislin-Le Strugeon, E., Duque, R., and Tirnauca, C. (2023). A review on quality in use evaluation of smart environment applications: What's next? In *Companion Proceedings of the 2023 ACM SIGCHI Symposium on Engineering Interactive Computing Systems*, pages 9–15.

Brooke, J. (2013). Sus: a retrospective. j. usability stud. 8 (2), 29–40.

Cartaxo, B., Pinto, G., and Soares, S. (2018). The role of rapid reviews in supporting decision-making in software engineering practice. In *Proceedings of the 22nd International Conference on Evaluation and Assessment in Software Engineering 2018*, pages 24–34.

Choma, J., Machado, L., de Souza, C. R., Sharp, H., Barroca, L., and Zaina, L. (2022). Towards understanding how software startups deal with ux from customer and user information. In *International Conference on Software Business*, pages 287–303. Springer.

Cretu, L.-G. (2012). Smart cities design using event-driven paradigm and semantic web. *Informatica Economica*, 16(4):57.

Deininger, M. E., von der Grün, M., Piepereit, R., Schneider, S., Santhanavanich, T., Coors, V., and Voß, U. (2020). A continuous, semi-automated workflow: from 3d city models with geometric optimization and cfd simulations to visualization of wind in an urban environment. *ISPRS International Journal of Geo-Information*, 9(11):657.

Díaz-Oreiro, I., López, G., Quesada, L., and Guerrero, L. A. (2021). Ux evaluation with standardized questionnaires in ubiquitous computing and ambient intelligence: a systematic literature review. *Advances in Human-Computer Interaction*, 2021:1–22.

Gubbi, J., Buyya, R., Marusic, S., and Palaniswami, M. (2013). Internet of things (iot): A vision, architectural elements, and future directions. *Future generation computer systems*, 29(7):1645–1660.

Hacid, H., Al-Shamaileh, O., and Maamar, Z. (2023). An exploratory study of rethinking user experience in the internet of things. *Computing*, 105(1):1–12.

Hart, S. G. and Staveland, L. E. (1988). Development of nasa-tlx (task load index): Results of empirical and theoretical research. In *Advances in psychology*, volume 52, pages 139–183. Elsevier.

Hassenzahl, M., Burmester, M., and Koller, F. (2003). Attrakdiff: Ein fragebogen zur messung wahrgenommener hedonischer und pragmatischer qualität. *Mensch & Computer 2003: Interaktion in Bewegung*, pages 187–196.

Hassenzahl, M. and Tractinsky, N. (2006). User experience-a research agenda. *Behaviour & information technology*, 25(2):91–97.

Hidalgo, A., Serif, T., Groenli, T.-M., and Ghinea, G. (2022). On user experience in the internet of things. In *2022 IEEE International Conference on Internet of Things and Intelligence Systems (IoTaIS)*, pages 31–37. IEEE.

Ismail, N. A., Majid, N., and Hassan, S. A. (2019). Iot-based smart solid waste management system a systematic literature review. *International Journal of Innovative Technology and Exploring Engineering*, 8(8):1456–1462.

ISO9241-210 (2019). Ergonomics of human-system interaction—part 210: Human-centred design for interactive systems. *ISO: Geneva, Switzerland.*

Laugwitz, B., Held, T., and Schrepp, M. (2008). Construction and evaluation of a user experience questionnaire. In *HCI and Usability for Education and Work: 4th Symposium of the Workgroup Human-Computer Interaction and Usability Engineering of the Austrian Computer Society, USAB 2008, Graz, Austria, November 20-21, 2008. Proceedings 4*, pages 63–76. Springer.

Lee, L. N. and Kim, M. J. (2020). A critical review of smart residential environments for older adults with a focus on pleasurable experience. *Frontiers in psychology*, 10:3080.

Melo, B., Andrade, R., and Darin, T. (2022). Longitudinal user experience studies in the iot domain: a brief panorama and challenges to overcome. In *Proceedings of the 21st Brazilian Symposium on Human Factors in Computing Systems*, pages 1–13.

Mendoza, Y. L. M., Duarte, E. F., de Queiroz, M. J. N., and Baranauskas, M. C. C. (2023). Evaluation in scenarios of ubiquity of technology: a systematic literature review on interactive installations. *Personal and Ubiquitous Computing*, 27(2):343–361.

Minge, M., Thüring, M., Wagner, I., and Kuhr, C. V. (2017). The mecue questionnaire: a modular tool for measuring user experience. In *Advances in Ergonomics Modeling, Usability & Special Populations: Proceedings of the AHFE 2016 International Conference on Ergonomics Modeling, Usability & Special Populations, July 27-31, 2016, Walt Disney World®, Florida, USA*, pages 115–128. Springer.

Motta, R. C., de Oliveira, K. M., and Travassos, G. H. (2018). On challenges in engineering iot software systems. In *Proceedings of the XXXII Brazilian symposium on software engineering*, pages 42–51.

Motta, R. C., de Oliveira, K. M., and Travassos, G. H. (2023). An evidence-based roadmap for iot software systems engineering. *Journal of Systems and Software*, 201:111680.

Nielsen, J. (1994). 10 usability heuristics for user interface design. `https://www.nngroup.com/articles/ten-usability-heuristics/`. Online accessed 08 Dec 2023.

Norman, D. and Nielsen, J. (2020). The definition of user experience (ux). `https://www.nngroup.com/`. Online accessed 08 May 2023.

Ntoa, S., Margetis, G., Antona, M., and Stephanidis, C. (2021). User experience evaluation in intelligent environments: A comprehensive framework. *Technologies*, 9(2):41.

Reinfurt, L., Breitenbücher, U., Falkenthal, M., Leymann, F., and Riegg, A. (2017). Internet of things patterns for devices: Powering, operating, and sensing. *International Journal on Advances in Internet Technology Volume 10, Number 3 & 4, 2017.*

Shin, D.-H. (2017). Conceptualizing and measuring quality of experience of the internet of things: Exploring how quality is perceived by users. *Information & Management*, 54(8):998–1011.

Stephanidis, C., Salvendy, G., Antona, M., Chen, J. Y., Dong, J., Duffy, V. G., Fang, X., Fidopiastis, C., Fragomeni, G., Fu, L. P., et al. (2019). Seven hci grand challenges. *International Journal of Human–Computer Interaction*, 35(14):1229–1269.

Syed, A. S., Sierra-Sosa, D., Kumar, A., and Elmaghraby, A. (2021). Iot in smart cities: A survey of technologies, practices and challenges. *Smart Cities*, 4(2):429–475.

Tricco, A. C., Antony, J., Zarin, W., Strifler, L., Ghassemi, M., Ivory, J., Perrier, L., Hutton, B., Moher, D., and Straus, S. E. (2015). A scoping review of rapid review methods. *BMC medicine*, 13(1):1–15.

Venkatesh, V., Morris, M. G., Davis, G. B., and Davis, F. D. (2003). User acceptance of information technology: Toward a unified view. *MIS quarterly*, pages 425–478.

Whaiduzzaman, M., Barros, A., Chanda, M., Barman, S., Sultana, T., Rahman, M. S., Roy, S., and Fidge, C. (2022). A review of emerging technologies for iot-based smart cities. *Sensors*, 22(23):9271.

A study about graphs in the representation of knowledge in discussion forums in Software Engineering

Patrick Rodrigo Da Silva[1], Érica Ferreira de Souza[1], Glaúcia Braga e Silva[2], Katia Romero Felizardo[1], Giovani Volnei Meinerz[1]

[1]Academic Department of Computing
Federal University of Technology - Paraná (UTFPR)- Cornélio Procópio, PR, Brazil

[2]Instituto de Ciências Exatas e Tecnológicas
Universidade Federal de Viçosa (UFV) - Florestal, MG, Brazil

patricksap@hotmail.com, ericasouza@utfpr.edu.br, glaucia@ufv.br, giovanimeinerz@utfpr.edu.br, katiascannavino@utfpr.edu.br

Abstract. *In the social web paradigm, discussion forums are effective tools to facilitate the knowledge transfer among developers. However, manually finding useful information in discussions on a particular topic is a complex task, making it a major challenge for knowledge management. The objective of this study is to explore the representation of knowledge supported by graphs generated from discussion forums in the context of Software Engineering. Firstly, graphs were built considering the discussion topics of the Stack Overflow forum. Visual analysis as well as analysis of thematic relevance of the graphs were performed. Next, an evaluation of the graphs generated through interviews with software industry professionals was also conducted in order to obtain a practical view of the study conducted. Using graphs generated from discussion forums can help the software industry identify useful information and new trends.*

Resumo. *No paradigma da web social, os fóruns de discussão são ferramentas eficazes para facilitar o compartilhamento de conhecimento entre os desenvolvedores. Contudo, encontrar manualmente informações úteis em discussões sobre um determinado tema é uma tarefa complexa, tornando-se um grande desafio para a gestão do conhecimento. O objetivo deste trabalho é explorar a representação do conhecimento apoiada em grafos gerados a partir de fóruns de discussão no contexto da Engenharia de Software. Primeiramente, foram construídos grafos de conhecimento considerando os tópicos de discussão do fórum Stack Overflow. Foram realizadas análises visuais e de relevância temática dos grafos gerados. Em seguida, também foi realizada uma avaliação dos grafos gerados por meio de entrevistas com profissionais da indústria de software, a fim de obter uma visão prática do estudo realizado. O uso de grafos gerados a partir de fóruns de discussão pode ajudar a indústria de software a identificar informações úteis e novas tendências.*

1. Introdução

No desenvolvimento de software, um grande volume de informação é gerado e tem se tornado um componente de grande capital intelectual. A Gestão do Conhecimento (GC) pode desempenhar um importante papel para representar e compartilhar o conhecimento gerado nas organizações (Silva et al. 2020). A transformação do conhecimento tácito em explícito para que esse possa ser compartilhado e difundido tem sido objeto de muito investimento, resultando em propostas metodológicas e tentativas práticas que focalizam a passagem do individual e pessoal para o coletivo/grupal (Nonaka and Krogh 2009).

O conhecimento tácito gerado a partir de uma discussão de grupo, por exemplo, pode ser um item de conhecimento valioso. O paradigma web social pode ser útil para compartilhar o conhecimento tácito através das tecnologias interativas e colaborativas, tais como redes sociais e fóruns de discussões (Abidi et al. 2009). Fóruns de discussão, em particular, são ferramentas eficazes para facilitar o compartilhamento de conhecimento tácito e informal entre desenvolvedores. Os fóruns de discussão tornam-se ferramentas importantes para a GC uma vez que o conhecimento útil pode ser gerado e capturado durante as discussões (Falbo et al. 2004). Além disso, por meio dos fóruns é possível fazer conversão do conhecimento tácito em explícito (Nonaka and Krogh 2009).

Os fóruns de discussão na área de desenvolvimento de software fornecem uma enorme quantidade de conteúdo valioso. A disponibilidade de uma grande quantidade de discussões de diferentes tópicos oferece amplas oportunidades para aquisição de conhecimento. No entanto, os fóruns na área de desenvolvimento de software contém muitos tópicos discutidos e encontrar manualmente informações úteis nas discussões de um determinado tópico é uma tarefa minuciosa (Gottipati et al. 2011), tornando-se um grande desafio para a GC. Dessa forma, sendo um fórum de discussão uma base com uma grande quantidade de dados textuais é possível que sejam realizadas análises visuais por meio da codificação desse conhecimento a fim de facilitar o entendimento. Algumas das abordagens existentes para codificar e representar o conhecimento são: mapas cognitivos, árvores de decisão, taxonomias de conhecimento e grafos (Dalkir 2005).

Os grafos, também conhecidos como grafos de conhecimento, representam os dados na forma de um grafo conectado (Paulheim 2016). A representação do conhecimento a partir de um grafo torna-se apropriada, pois as informações consideradas importantes são representadas por meio de conceitos e relações entre eles. Os vértices do grafo são os conceitos e as arestas representam a proximidade dos conceitos no texto (Azevedo 2011).

Considerando o contexto acima, o objetivo deste trabalho é explorar a representação do conhecimento apoiado em grafos gerados a partir de fóruns de discussão no contexto da Engenharia de Software. Para determinar qual fórum de discussão seria objeto deste estudo, um mapeamento sistemático foi conduzido em (Silva et al. 2020), e assim, foram construídos grafos de conhecimento considerando os tópicos de discussão do fórum *Stack Overflow*. Foram realizadas análises visuais e de relevância temática dos grafos gerados. A análise visual tem como objetivo identificar relações entre os conceitos do grafo que possam ser consideradas relevantes, já a análise de relevância temática mede a qualidade da comunicação e relevância da discussão em relação ao tópico selecionado (Azevedo et al. 2011). Por fim, também foi realizada uma avaliação dos grafos por meio de entrevistas com gestores de empresas desenvolvedoras de software, a fim de obter uma visão prática do estudo conduzido.

O restante deste artigo está estruturado da seguinte forma. A seção 2 apresenta os trabalhos relacionados. A seção 3 discute os passos para condução da pesquisa. Os resultados e discussões são apresentados na seção 4. Na seção 5 são apresentados impressões de profissionais da área. Por último, as considerações finais são apresentadas na Seção 6.

2. Trabalhos Relacionados

Diversos trabalhos têm surgido com o objetivo de representar o conhecimento por meio de grafos considerando dados oriundos da internet, como os fóruns de discussão e repositórios de código fonte. Em (Liu et al. 2017), por exemplo, foi apresentado um novo método de roteamento de perguntas no *Stack Overflow*, baseado em grafo de conhecimento, denominado *Knowledge Graph Question Routing framework* (KGQR). De acordo com os autores, quando surge uma nova pergunta, o KGQR fornece uma lista classificada de usuários mais adequados para respondê-la, com base em um modelo treinado. Em (Zhao et al. 2019), foi projetada uma ferramenta chamada GitGraph, que recebe como entrada um repositório do Sistema de Controle de Versões Distribuído (GIT) e constrói automaticamente um grafo associado ao repositório. Resultados experimentais preliminares mostraram que o GitGraph pode gerar corretamente grafos de conhecimento para projetos GIT e foram úteis para os usuários compreenderem os projetos.

No trabalho (Azevedo 2011), foi desenvolvida a ferramenta MineraFórum. A ferramenta visa auxiliar os professores na análise qualitativa das contribuições textuais registradas por alunos em fóruns de discussões educacionais. No trabalho, foram utilizadas técnicas de mineração textual e grafos de conhecimento. A partir da análise das postagens, o docente pode identificar quais alunos redigiram contribuições textuais que contemplam conceitos relativos ao tema da discussão, e quais discentes não o fizeram. Já em (Neto and Silva 2018), é apresentada a ferramenta ColMiner. A ferramenta ColMiner é capaz de medir a qualidade da comunicação em um ambiente de rastreamento de problemas, por meio do cálculo da relevância temática dos comentários do assunto para o tema principal da discussão. Seu objetivo foi identificar falhas no processo de comunicação. A abordagem da análise de comunicação também utilizou algumas técnicas de mineração de texto baseadas no uso de grafos para representar o conteúdo textual dos comentários.

Assim como os trabalhos relacionados mencionados anteriormente, este trabalho tem como objetivo explorar a representação do conhecimento por meio de grafos gerados a partir de fóruns de discussão. No entanto, o escopo deste trabalho contempla discussões na área de Engenharia de Software no fórum do *Stack Overflow*, com o intuito de obter uma visão prática sobre a geração de grafos de conhecimento e a possível detecção de informação útil que possa apoiar gerentes de projetos de software em uma organização.

3. Metodologia para geração dos grafos de conhecimento

Nesta seção, apresenta-se a metodologia definida para criação de grafos de conhecimento, composta por três etapas, conforme apresentado na Figura 1. A seguir, são apresentadas as etapas, bem como suas respectivas atividades.

Etapa 1 - Preparação dos dados. A etapa de preparação dos dados tem como objetivo importar os dados textuais de um fórum de discussão. Para determinar qual fórum seria considerado no estudo, um mapeamento sistemático da literatura foi conduzido (Silva et al. 2020). De acordo com os resultados do mapeamento, os desenvolvedores de software tem usado extensivamente o *Stack Overflow* para compartilhar conhecimento sobre desenvolvimento de software. Dessa forma, o repositório definido para construção dos grafos de conhecimento foi o *Stack Overflow*. Já para a escolha dos tópicos a serem

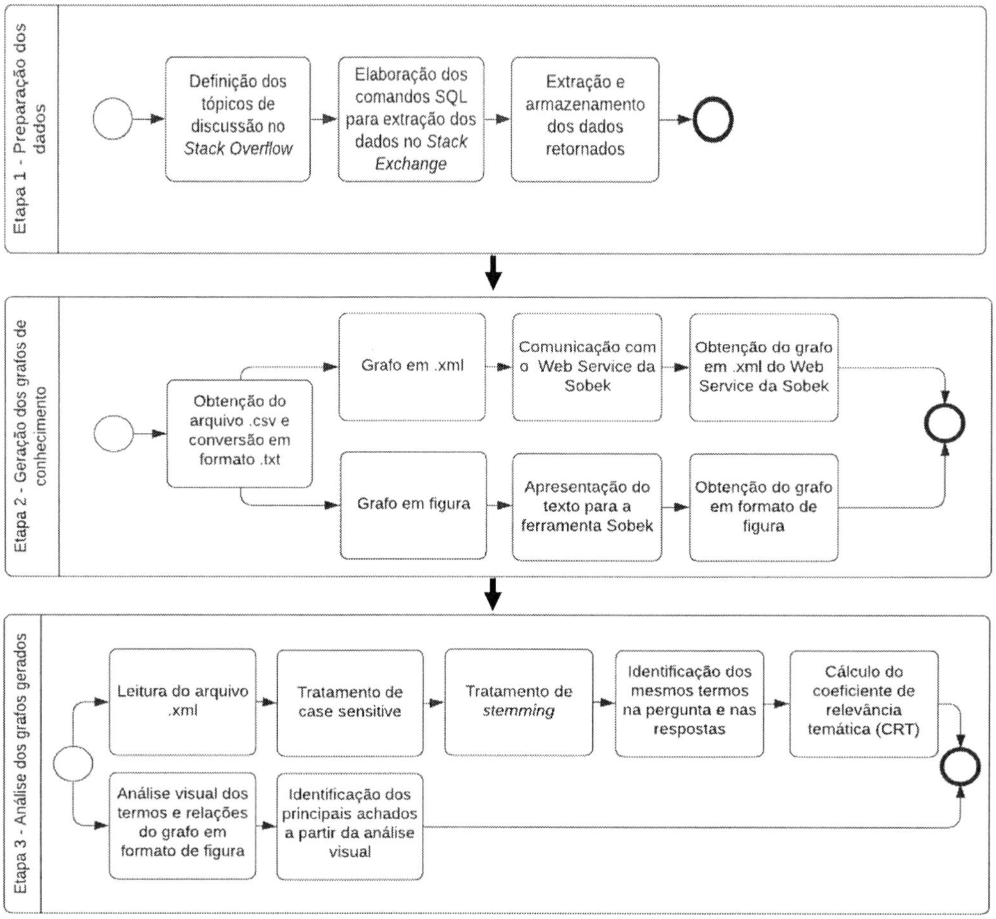

Figura 1. Etapas para criação do grafo de conhecimento

trabalhados foram considerados os seguintes parâmetros: aderência ao escopo de teste de software, devido ao conhecimento e à experiência dos autores deste artigo; e número de respostas registradas.

A segunda atividade é a extração dos dados textuais dos tópicos escolhidos no *Stack Overflow*. Cada tópico de discussão possui um identificador único (ID), por meio do qual é possível fazer pesquisas através de comandos SQL. Os comandos são executados no *Stack Exchange*[1], responsável por disponibilizar a consulta via comando SQL ao banco de dados do *Stack Overflow*. Vale destacar que duas consultas são necessárias; uma para a pergunta e outra para as respostas do tópico, pois no *Stack Overflow* são apresentadas em tabelas diferentes e relacionadas por um ID. Uma vez executadas as consultas SQL no *Stack Exchange*, o mesmo disponibiliza para download e armazenamento os dados em formato .CSV. Para geração dos grafos de conhecimento, foi necessário converter os arquivos .CSV para .txt e .xml.

Etapa 2 - Geração dos grafos de conhecimento. Para geração dos grafos, foi utilizada a Sobek[2], uma ferramenta de mineração textual que representa os dados encontrados em

[1]https://data.stackexchange.com/stackoverflow/query/new

[2]http://sobek.ufrgs.br/

formato de texto através de um grafo (Azevedo 2011). A ferramenta foi desenvolvida no Programa de Pós-Graduação em Informática na Educação, na Universidade Federal do Rio Grande do Sul (UFRGS). Foram utilizadas duas formas de representação de grafos utilizando a ferramenta Sobek: uma visual, por meio de uma figura; e uma textual, por meio de um arquivo .xml. A representação visual gera uma figura com o grafo de conhecimento contendo todo o conteúdo do tópico de discussão, a partir do qual é possível realizar uma análise visual dos nós (conceitos) e arestas (relacionamentos) do grafo. Já para a representação em arquivo .xml, utiliza-se o Web Service da ferramenta Sobek. A conversão do grafo em formato .xml torna-se necessária pois para ser realizado o cálculo de relevância temática é preciso ter acesso ao formato dos dados numéricos apresentados nos grafos, como, por exemplo, a quantidade de relacionamentos que um nó contém.

A Figura 2 apresenta um resumo do processo desde a extração dos dados até a geração dos grafos.

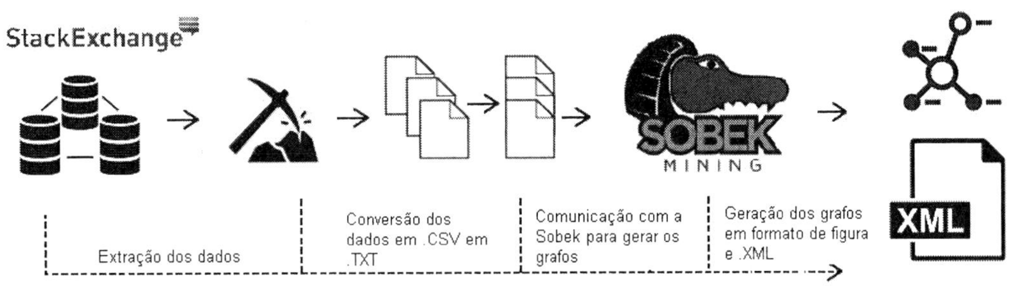

Figura 2. Processo da extração dos dados do tópico e geração dos grafos

Etapa 3 - Análise dos grafos. Uma vez gerados os grafos, tanto em formato de figura como em .xml, o objetivo desta etapa é a análise dos grafos. Duas análises foram consideradas neste estudo: análise visual e análise de relevância temática. A análise visual sobre a figura objetiva identificar conceitos e relações relevantes no grafo, como, por exemplo, novas tecnologias, *frameworks*, funcionalidades ou tendências. Já análise de relevância temática, foi conduzida a fim de medir a qualidade da comunicação e a relevância da discussão em relação ao tópico selecionado para análise. O termo "relevância temática", neste estudo, está sendo usado para representar a relevância das respostas em relação ao tema principal de uma discussão. A medição da relevância temática foi feita considerando o seguinte Cálculo da Relevância Temática (CRT) (Azevedo 2011):

$$CRT = NC + NA \tag{1}$$

Sendo, *NC* = número de conceitos relevantes utilizados no texto; e *NA* = número de relacionamentos entre os conceitos relevantes utilizados no texto. O valor mínimo para o CRT ser considerado relevante é 1. O valor mínimo indica que toda mensagem com valor de CRT maior ou igual a 1 é considerada relevante em relação ao tópico de discussão. O valor 1 é o menor número que pode ser calculado pela fórmula do CRT, situação alcançada quando $NC = 1$ e $NA = 0$. Os trabalhos (Azevedo 2011) e (Neto and Silva 2018) serviram como base para automatizar a realização do cálculo do CRT. Para este estudo foram criados diversos algoritmos em Python que apoiam todas as atividades da Etapa 3. Os algoritmos estão disponibilizados em *https://zenodo.org/records/10618628*.

Neste estudo, o algoritmo criado recebe os valores das tags (conceitos) retornadas no arquivo .xml. Em seguida, os valores da tags recebem tratamentos de *Case Sensitive* e *Stemming*. O tratamento de *Case Sensitive* foi aplicado para evitar que a mesma palavra que começa com maiúscula e outra com minúscula sejam consideradas diferentes. Já o tratamento de *Stemming*, foi realizado, pois, por muitas vezes o radical dos termos poderiam ser iguais. Uma vez efetuados os dois tratamentos nas tags, foram analisados os conceitos dos grafos (pergunta e resposta). Se um conceito da pergunta também constar na resposta, esse será contabilizado como conceito relevante. Do mesmo modo, se dois conceitos que constam na pergunta constarem também na resposta e tiverem um relacionamento entre si, esse relacionamento será contabilizado (Neto and Silva 2018). Esse processo de checagem (identificação e comparação) dos conceitos, também foi automatizado, ou seja, na checagem, leva-se em conta a comparação das listas de grafos das perguntas e das respostas do tópico a fim de identificar possíveis relações. Finalmente, o cálculo do CRT é realizado, conforme apresentado na Fórmula (1).

4. Resultados e Discussões

Para avaliar a metodologia definida neste estudo, três tópicos de discussão do *Stack Overflow* foram analisados considerando o escopo de "Teste de Software".

4.1. Tópico de Discussão 1

A Tabela 1 apresenta uma sumarização das principais características do primeiro tópico de discussão do *Stack Overflow* escolhido para análise.

Tabela 1. Características do Tópico de Discussão 1

Características	**Resultados**
Pergunta	*"What are unit tests, integration tests, smoke tests, and regression tests?"*
Tema	Teste de Unidade, Teste de Integração, Smoke e Teste de Regressão
Data de Criação	06 de fevereiro de 2009
Número de respostas	17
Número de visualizações	302.000
Número de caracteres	24.754
Número de palavras	4411
Número de frases	675
Número de parágrafos	242
SQL Criadas	Primeira extração: • Consulta do título e corpo do tópico: *select Title, Body FROM Posts WHERE Id=520064;* • Comentários feitos sobre o título: *select Text from Comments where PostId=520064;* • Respostas: *select Title,Body FROM Posts WHERE ParentId=520064;* • Comentários feitos sobre as respostas: *select DISTINCT Text from Comments inner join Posts on PostId = ParentId WHERE ParentId=520064;* Segunda extração: • Consulta do título e corpo do tópico: *select Title,Body FROM Posts WHERE Id=520064;* • Respostas: *select Title,Body FROM Posts WHERE ParentId=520064;*

A Figura 3 apresenta o grafo gerado para o Tópico de Discussão 1.

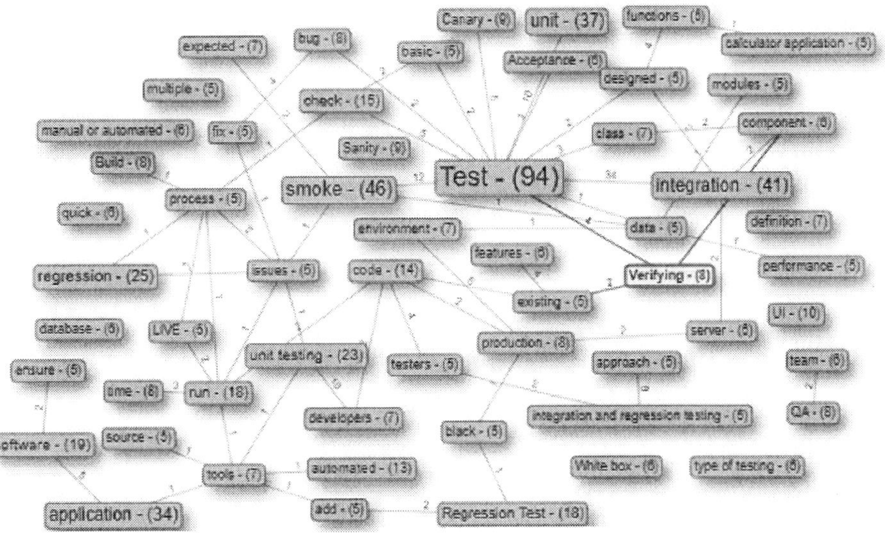

Figura 3. Grafo de conhecimento do Tópico de Discussão 1

(a) Análise Visual A seguir são apresentadas algumas interpretações e achados identificados no grafo do Tópico de Discussão 1 a partir de uma análise visual.

1. Relação entre os nós "*unit testing*" e "*developers*". Alinhado com o que é apresentado na literatura, a relação permite afirmar que o teste unitário é feito pelo próprio desenvolvedor quando testa pequenas partes de código fonte.
2. Relação entre os nós "*integration*", "*server*", "*designed*", "*component*" e "*test*". É possível inferir que o grafo gerado consegue demonstrar de forma visual relações que representam a finalidade do teste de integração, que é analisar o comportamento do software quando interage com outras aplicações ou processos.
3. Relação entre "*tools*"e "*automated*". A relação sugere que em vários momentos o assunto automação de teste entrou em discussão. Isso pode ser também notado em outras relações destacando técnicas de teste para automação.
4. Relação entre os nós "*canary*" e "*test*". A relação destaca um tipo de teste conhecido como "*canary test"* ou testes A/B. O teste canário consiste em habilitar novas funcionalidades apenas para um grupo controlado de usuários (os canários). De acordo com os respondentes do tópico, o teste canário é um teste automatizado e não destrutivo executado regularmente em um ambiente de produção, de forma que, se falhar, algo muito ruim acontecerá.
5. Relação dos nós "*smoke*" e "*test*". O *smoke test*, ou teste de fumaça, também está relacionado com a automação de teste. Esse tipo de teste compreende um conjunto não exaustivo de testes que visa garantir que as funções mais importantes funcionam. O resultado desse teste é usado para decidir se um software é estável o suficiente para prosseguir com testes adicionais.

(b) Relevância Temática A Tabela 2 apresenta os resultados do CRT para o Tópico de Discussão 1. Para o cálculo do CRT, foi gerado um grafo para cada resposta do tópico. Dessa forma, cada grafo gerado recebeu um ID, conforme apresentado na Tabela 2. Um cálculo do CRT é feito para cada grafo e depois uma média simples é apresentada.

Tabela 2. CRT para o Tópico de Discussão 1

ID	Quant. de Palavras	NC (N.º de Conceitos)	NA (N.º de Arestas)	CRT
1	263	4	1	5
2	63	2	0	2
3	41	1	0	1
4	191	2	1	3
5	106	4	1	5
6	173	4	1	5
7	118	3	1	4
8	171	2	1	3
9	64	4	3	7
10	59	1	0	1
11	179	4	3	7
12	148	2	0	2
13	664	2	0	2
14	109	2	1	3
15	28	1	0	1
16	56	1	0	1
17	83	2	1	3
Média	148	2	0,8	3

A seguir são apresentados as principais conclusões a partir da análise dos resultados do cálculo de CRT para o grafo do tópico de discussão 1.

1. O valor do CRT variou de 1 a 7, mostrando, assim, que todas as respostas continham relevância em comparação com a pergunta.
2. Quatro respostas do tópico (IDs 3, 10, 15 e 16) apresentaram valor igual a 1 para o CRT. Isso ocorreu, pois no grafo da resposta consta apenas um único conceito que existe no grafo da pergunta e sem nenhum relacionamento. A resposta 10, por exemplo, obteve valor de CRT igual a 1, pois o único conceito constante no grafo foi "*test*".
3. A resposta 13 contém o maior número de palavras (664 palavras) e obteve um valor de CRT igual a 2. Já a resposta 9, que contém 64 palavras, obteve o maior valor de CRT, sendo igual a 7. Isso mostra que não necessariamente uma resposta necessita conter muitas palavras para ter um valor de CRT alto.
4. Uma média simples dos resultados mostrou que a quantidade geral de palavras por resposta foi de 148, e o valor médio de CRT das respostas ficou em 3. Com isso pode-se concluir que as respostas do tópico têm uma boa relação com a pergunta, mostrando assim serem relevantes.

4.2. Tópico de Discussão 2

As principais características do segundo tópico de discussão analisado, encontram-se apresentadas na Tabela 3.

Tabela 3. Características do Tópico de Discussão 2

Características	Resultado
Pergunta	*"How to make junior programmers write tests?"*
Tema	Elaboração de testes por testadores iniciantes
Data de Criação	01 de Julho de 2015
Número de respostas	24
Número de visualizações	9.000

Número de caracteres	24.743
Número de palavras	4859
Número de frases	628
Número de parágrafos	162
SQL Criadas	Primeira extração: • Consulta do título e corpo do tópico: *select Title, Body FROM Posts WHERE Id=7252;* • Comentários feitos sobre o título: *select Text from Comments where PostId=7252;* • Respostas: *select Title,Body FROM Posts WHERE ParentId=7252;* • Comentários feitos sobre as respostas: *select DISTINCT Text from Comments inner join Posts on PostId = ParentId WHERE ParentId=7252;* Segunda extração: • Consulta do título e corpo do tópico: *select Title,Body FROM Posts WHERE Id=7252;* • Respostas: *select Title,Body FROM Posts WHERE ParentId=7252;*

A Figura 4 apresenta o grafo gerado para o Tópico de Discussão 2.

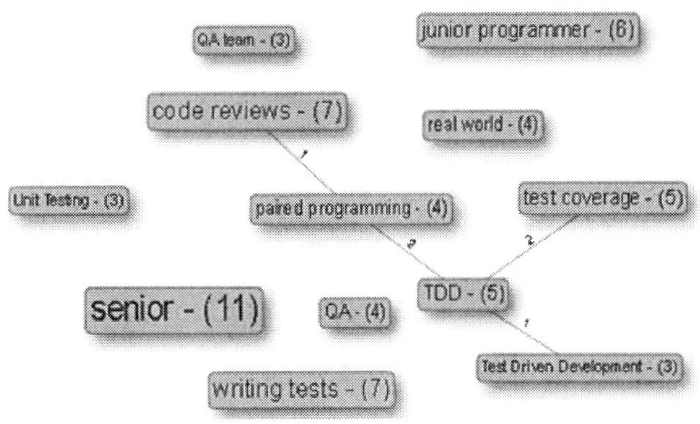

Figura 4. Grafo de conhecimento do Tópico de Discussão 2

(a) Análise Visual A seguir são apresentadas as principais interpretações e achados identificados a partir da análise visual do grafo do Tópico de Discussão 2.

1. Nó "*paired programming*". Programação em pares é uma prática utilizada pelo método ágil *eXtreme Programming*, e é indicada pelos respondentes como útil no aprendizado de testadores iniciantes.
2. Nó "*code reviews*". A revisão de código também é mencionada pelos respondentes como uma prática importante para aprendizado. Analisando as respontas dos respondentes, um deles mencionou que a adoção da práticas de revisão de código é muito eficiente quando aplicada com um intuito educativo e não punitivo.
3. Relação dos nós "TDD" e "*paired programming*". A prática *Test Driven Development* (TDD) tem como objetivo escrever os teste antes de desenvolver as funcionalidade do sistema. De acordo com o grafo gerado, TDD teve destaque em relação a testadores iniciantes. De acordo com um dos respondentes, a combinação entre TDD e programação em pares é desejável para um testador iniciante, pois melhora probabilidade de cobertura de teste.
4. Relação dos nós "TDD" e "*Test coverage*". A cobertura de teste é usada para medir o grau em que o código de um programa é executado (coberto) quando um determinado conjunto de testes é exercitado. A combinação de TDD e cobertura

de código também foi mencionada como boas práticas a serem utilizadas por testadores iniciantes.

(b) Relevância Temática A Tabela 4 apresenta os resultados do CRT para o Tópico de Discussão 2.

Tabela 4. CRT para o Tópico de Discussão 2

ID	Quant. de Palavras	NC (N.º de Conceitos)	NA (N.º de Arestas)	CRT
1	204	1	0	1
2	258	2	0	2
3	84	2	1	3
4	585	3	1	4
5	126	1	0	1
6	81	3	0	3
7	96	3	1	4
8	280	1	0	1
9	281	0	0	0
10	247	2	1	3
11	74	0	0	0
12	86	2	0	2
13	191	2	0	2
14	157	2	0	2
15	46	2	0	2
16	136	2	1	3
17	107	3	2	5
18	257	3	1	4
19	155	0	0	0
20	143	2	1	3
21	746	4	2	6
22	50	0	0	0
23	133	3	1	4
24	210	3	0	3
Média	188	1,91	0,5	2,41

As principais conclusões a partir da análise do CRT são apresentadas a seguir.

1. O valor de NC, variou de 0 a 4, e o valor de NA, ficou entre 0 e 2. O valor do CRT variou de 0 a 6. Das 24 respostas, apenas 3 tiveram o valor 1 (IDs 1, 5, 8), que é o mínimo para a resposta ser relevante.
2. Do total de 24 respostas, 4 tiverem o valor do CRT igual a 0 (IDs 9, 11, 19, 22), mostrando assim que nesses grafos não houve nenhum conceito nem aresta que constasse também no grafo da pergunta. Considerando o número total de respostas, o valor 4 foi um número considerável de respostas que não foram consideradas relevantes. A média geral do valor de CRT do tópico ficou em 2, mostrando que apesar de algumas respostas terem o resultado zero, a média geral teve um valor maior que 1 que é considerado o mínimo para ser relevante.
3. A resposta que obteve o maior valor de CRT foi a de ID 21, que teve o valor de 6. O número de palavras da resposta foi de 746 palavras.
4. As respostas que tiveram valor de CRT igual a zero, tiveram o número de palavras variando entre 50 e 281, por outro lado, a resposta que teve o menor número de palavras (ID 15), apresentou valor igual a 46, e obteve um valor de CRT igual a 2. Novamente, isso mostra que não necessariamente uma resposta com grande quantidade de palavras vai ter um número alto de CRT.
5. A média do valor de CRT foi de 2 e a média do número de palavras das respostas foi de 188.

4.3. Tópico de Discussão 3

A Tabela 5 apresenta as características do terceiro tópico de discussão do *Stack Overflow*.

Tabela 5. Características do Tópico de Discussão 3

Características	**Resultado**
Pergunta	*"A programming language designed to be testable?"*
Tema	É questionado no tópico se existe uma linguagem de programação que pode ser mais facilmente testada.
Data de Criação	28 de Outubro de 2014
Número de respostas	14
Número de visualizações	4.000
Número de caracteres	12.512
Número de palavras	2328
Número de frases	290
Número de parágrafos	74
SQL Criadas	Primeira extração: • Consulta do título e corpo do tópico: *select Title, Body FROM Posts WHERE Id=3371268;* • Comentários feitos sobre o título: *select Text from Comments where PostId=3371268;* • Respostas: *select Title,Body FROM Posts WHERE ParentId=3371268;* • Comentários feitos sobre as respostas: *select DISTINCT Text from Comments inner join Posts on PostId = ParentId WHERE ParentId=3371268;* Segunda extração: • Consulta do título e corpo do tópico: *select Title,Body FROM Posts WHERE Id=3371268;* • Respostas: *select Title,Body FROM Posts WHERE ParentId=3371268;*

A Figura 5 apresenta o grafo gerado para o Tópico de Discussão 3.

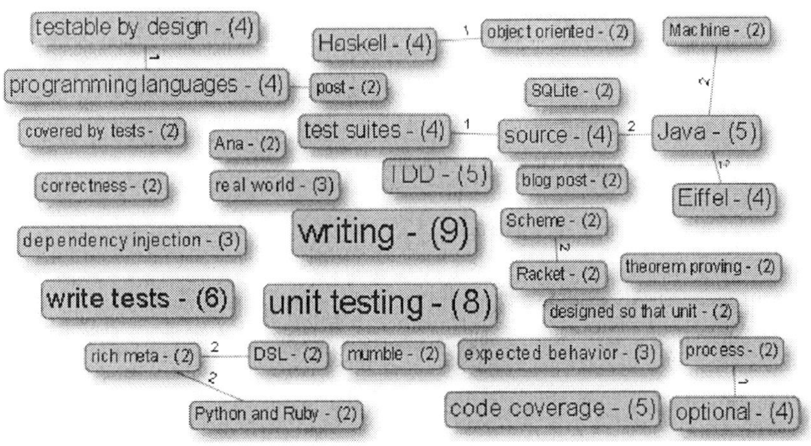

Figura 5. Grafo de conhecimento do Tópico de Discussão 3

(a) Análise Visual A seguir são apresentadas as principais interpretações identificadas no grafo a partir de uma análise visual.

1. Nó "*Eiffel*". A linguagem de programação *Eiffel* foi citada por um dos respondentes em relação a linguagens mais facilmente testáveis. De acordo com o res-

pondente, a linguagem encoraja o programador a colocar pré-condições e pós-condições em seu código, e elas são testadas.
2. Nó "*Racket*". De acordo com o respondente, se trata de uma linguagem de programação de pesquisa, e que na mesma, quando um teste falha, a linguagem informa não apenas a falha, mas também identifica em qual parte do código aconteceu a falha.
3. Nó "*Haskell*". De acordo com um dos respondentes, a *Haskell* é uma linguagem de programação puramente funcional, já que em tal linguagem as funções não têm efeitos colaterais e sempre produzirão os mesmos resultados com a mesma entrada, sendo assim, considerada uma linguagem com boas propriedades para condução de testes.
4. Nó "Ana". Onde o correto é "Anna", a linguagem é uma extensão da linguagem Ada e fornece anotações formais para todas as construções Ada. De acordo com um dos respondentes, a linguagem apoiou a elaboração de alguns testes, porém o mesmo não se aprofundou na explicação do porquê a linguagem apoiou testes. Segundo outro respondente, a linguagem Anna nunca passou da fase de pesquisa.
5. Outro achado foi a existência de linguagens mais comerciais como "Java", "Python" e "Ruby".
6. Um achado relevante para esse tópico foi a grande quantidade de nós com pouco ou nenhum relacionamento. Isso mostra que houve várias respostas interessantes, com bastante conteúdo, mas que não continham muitas relações entre si.

(b) Relevância Temática A Tabela 6 apresenta os resultados do CRT para o Tópico de Discussão 3, e a seguir são apresentadas as principais conclusões a partir da análise dos resultados do cálculo de CRT.

Tabela 6. CRT para o Tópico de Discussão 3

ID	Quant. de Palavras	NC (N.º de Conceitos)	NA (N.º de Arestas)	CRT
1	223	5	0	5
2	240	3	1	4
3	152	2	0	2
4	18	0	0	0
5	115	2	1	3
6	732	3	0	3
7	94	1	0	1
8	228	2	1	3
9	16	0	0	0
10	60	3	2	5
11	38	1	0	1
12	98	0	0	0
13	41	0	0	0
14	35	1	0	1
Média	149	1,64	0,35	3

1. O valor de NC variou entre 0 e 5, e o valor de NA, ficou entre 0 e 2. O valor de CRT variou entre 0 e 5.
2. Um achado que chamou a atenção deste tópico foi o grande número de grafos de respostas com valor de CRT igual a 0. Isso mostra que nesses grafos não houve nenhum conceito ou aresta que existisse também no grafo da pergunta. Foram 4 respostas com valor zero (IDs 4, 9, 12, 13).
3. A resposta que contém o menor número de palavras foi de 16 palavras (ID 9), obtendo um valor de CRT igual a 0. E a que obteve o maior valor de CRT, continha 223 palavras (ID 1).

4. A média geral de valor de CRT foi 2 e a média do número de palavras foi 149, mostrando assim que mesmo contendo um grande número de respostas com CRT igual a zero, na média geral, o valor de CRT ainda pode ser considerado relevante.

5. Visão prática de profissionais da área

Uma vez que os grafos foram criados e analisados, uma análise preliminar a partir da visão prática de profissionais da área também foi conduzida. Foram realizadas entrevistas semiestruturadas com dois profissionais de empresas de desenvolvimento de software. Os entrevistados possuem mais de 15 anos de experiência na indústria de software e com profundo conhecimento em teste de software. As entrevistas foram realizadas de forma síncrona por meio de videoconferência (via *Google Meet*) e gravadas. As perguntas realizadas na entrevista estão disponíveis em *https://zenodo.org/records/10618628*.

PRIMEIRA ENTREVISTA O primeiro profissional entrevistado é um diretor de tecnologia em uma empresa localizada na cidade de São Paulo-SP. Atualmente, é responsável por atividades de testes de software na empresa. A empresa tem como foco principal o desenvolvimento web, tendo como seguimento a criação de plataformas de incentivo de marketing para empresas. A empresa contém 106 funcionários distribuídos em todo o Brasil e adota metodologias ágeis em seus projetos.

Inicialmente, foram realizadas perguntas relacionadas às práticas de GC. De acordo com o entrevistado, a empresa utiliza um *Wiki* interno para registrar características dos produtos desenvolvidos e também uma prática de compartilhamento de erros. Também são utilizadas algumas ferramentas que permitem facilitar a troca e aquisição de conhecimento: *TEAMS*[3] e a *YAMMER*[4]. A ferramenta *TEAMS* permite a comunicação interna do time. Já a *YAMMER* permite desenvolver algumas práticas de GC. Por exemplo, existe uma função chamada "Quem sabe compartilha" que permite o time divulgar boas práticas e lições. O entrevistado também destacou que os desenvolvedores utilizam o fórum *Stack Overflow* para buscar conhecimento.

Na sequência, foi apresentado para o entrevistado o estudo conduzido neste artigo, e, em seguida, algumas perguntas foram feitas com intuito de coletar as impressões do profissional sobre uma possível utilização do uso de grafos na empresa. De acordo com o entrevistado, um grafo pode facilitar o entendimento de um tópico de discussão, pois mostra um resumo visual do tópico a ser analisado tornando possível inferir informações relevantes, visualizar comportamentos e mostrar tendências, como, práticas de teste mais utilizadas, por exemplo. Durante a entrevista, essa atividade de análise de conceitos nos grafos acabou sendo realizada junto com o entrevistado. O entrevistado também afirmou que utilizaria tais práticas na empresa. Ele mencionou que se o grafo mostrasse novas ferramentas, a chance dele fazer uma busca por estas depois, seria bem maior.

Por fim, ao ser questionado sobre uma possível desvantagem na utilização de grafos, o entrevistado apontou como desvantagem a possibiliade da fonte de dados ser viciada, inconsistente ou tendenciosa, pois não traria dados confiáveis para a análise.

SEGUNDA ENTREVISTA O segundo entrevistado assume o papel de *Product Owner* na empresa. A empresa fica localizada na cidade de Santo Antônio da Platina – PR e

[3]https://www.microsoft.com/pt-br/microsoft-teams/group-chat-software

[4]https://www.microsoft.com/pt-br/microsoft-365/yammer/yammer-overview

tem como principal produto um Sistema de Gestão Empresarial (*Enterprise Resource Planning* – ERP) para controle financeiro, estoque, vendas e área fiscal. A empresa adota práticas ágeis de desenvolvimento, principalmente relacionadas ao *framework Scrum*, e possui a certificação Melhoria de Processo do Software Brasileiro (MPS.BR).

Sobre as práticas de GC, o profissional respondeu que as mesmas não são aplicadas na empresa de forma explícita. De acordo com o entrevistado, o conhecimento adquirido fica com o indivíduo, e pode até ser compartilhado, porém de maneira informal durante os eventos de uma *Sprint*[5]. Além disso, a documentação da empresa hoje é considerada mínima. O entrevistado disse que a empresa possui um espaço no Wiki, mas não existe o hábito de registrar informações nesse espaço. Ele afirmou também que criar esse hábito será um grande desafio para a organização, e que entende como uma grande necessidade tornar explícito o conhecimento gerado.

Na próxima etapa da entrevista, foi apresentado para o entrevistado o estudo realizado neste artigo a fim de coletar impressões. De acordo com o entrevistado, um grafo facilitaria a interpretação de um tópico de discussão, pois auxiliaria na síntese e interpretação de tudo que é retornado em uma pesquisa online. O entrevistado mencionou que utilizaria grafos de conhecimento na empresa, inclusive ele destacou que o uso de tais práticas seriam vantajosas para mais áreas, além do desenvolvimento e teste de software, por exemplo, para os profissionais envolvidos com a área de suporte do software. Já em relação às desvantagens que o entrevistado visualiza, a resposta foi a possibilidade de o termo aparecer no grafo, mas não no contexto exatamente esperado. Por exemplo, uma técnica de desenvolvimento aparecer várias vezes no texto, tornar-se um conceito no grafo, mas não de forma positiva, e sim, uma técnica que não está sendo sugerida para ser utilizada no desenvolvimento. O grafo teria que ser inteligente o bastante para mostrar essa situação.

6. Conclusões

O objetivo geral deste trabalho foi explorar a representação do conhecimento apoiado em grafos gerados a partir de fóruns de discussão no contexto da Engenharia de Software. Considerando os resultados alcançados até o momento, é possível observar que os grafos de conhecimento podem auxiliar as empresas de desenvolvimento de software a identificarem informações úteis a partir de fóruns de discussão. Embora este estudo seja ainda preliminar, acredita-se que o uso de grafos possa auxiliar a indústria de software nas decisões de projeto, por exemplo, na identificação de novas tendências, ferramentas, *frameworks* ou práticas de desenvolvimento.

Algumas limitações foram encontradas neste trabalho. Na etapa de geração dos grafos, a principal limitação foi o processo manual de extração dos dados da base de dados do *Stack Overflow*. A criação de uma ferramenta para automatizar essa extração tornaria o processo mais rápido e menos trabalhoso. Já na condução das entrevistas, a principal limitação foi o número de profissionais entrevistados. Um número maior de entrevistas poderia melhorar a qualidade desta pesquisa; no entanto, dado o perfil dos entrevistados, acredita-se que as entrevistas realizadas trouxeram importantes contribuições para o estudo. Trabalhos futuros incluem a automatização do processo de captura dos dados do fórum de discussão através da criação de um *Web Crawler*; a análise de novos tópicos de

[5]Nome dado a um ciclo de desenvolvimento no Scrum.

discussão do *Stack Overflow*; e a realização de mais entrevistas com profissionais da área para a obtenção de uma visão mais ampla da aplicação da abordagem na indústria.

Referências

[Abidi et al. 2009] Abidi, S., Hussini, S., Sriraj, W., Thienthong, S., and Finley, A. (2009). Knowledge sharing for pediatric pain management via a web 2.0 framework. *Studies in health technology and informatics*, 150:287–91.

[Azevedo 2011] Azevedo, B. F. T. (2011). *Minerafórum: um recurso de apoio para análise qualitativa em fóruns de discussão.* PhD thesis, Universidade Federal do Rio Grande do Sul. Tese de Doutorado em Informática na Computação.

[Azevedo et al. 2011] Azevedo, B. F. T., Behar, P., and Reategui, E. (2011). Qualitative analysis of discussion forums. In *International Journal of Computer Information Systems and Industrial Management Applications.*, pages 671–678.

[Dalkir 2005] Dalkir, K. (2005). *Knowledge Management in Theory and Practice*. The MIT Press.

[Falbo et al. 2004] Falbo, R., Arantes, D., and Natali, A. (2004). Integrating knowledge management and groupware in a software development environment. volume 3336, pages 94–105.

[Gottipati et al. 2011] Gottipati, S., Lo, D., and Jiang, J. (2011). Finding relevant answers in software forums. In *26th IEEE/ACM International Conference on Automated Software Engineering*, page 323–332.

[Liu et al. 2017] Liu, Z., Li, K., and Qu, D. (2017). Knowledge graph based question routing for community question answering. In *Neural Information Processing*, pages 721–730, Cham. Springer International Publishing.

[Neto and Silva 2018] Neto, L. E. C. and Silva, G. B. e. (2018). Colminer: A tool to support communications management in an issue tracking environment. In *XIV Brazilian Symposium on Information Systems*, SBSI'18.

[Nonaka and Krogh 2009] Nonaka, I. and Krogh, G. (2009). Tacit knowledge and knowledge conversion: controversy and advancement in organizational knowledge creation theory. *Organization Science*, 30:635–652.

[Paulheim 2016] Paulheim, H. (2016). Knowledge graph refinement: A survey of approaches and evaluation methods. *Semantic Web*, 8.489–508.

[Silva et al. 2020] Silva, P. R., Santos, V. ; Souza, E. F., Meinerz, G. V., Felizardo, K. R., and Vijaykumar, N. L. (2020). Extraction of useful information from unstructured data in software engineering: A systematic mapping. In *XXIII Ibero-American Conference on Software Engineering (CIBSE)*, pages 1–14.

[Zhao et al. 2019] Zhao, Y., Wang, H., Ma, L., Liu, Y., Li, L., and Grundy, J. (2019). Knowledge graphing git repositories: A preliminary study. In *International Conference on Software Analysis, Evolution and Reengineering (SANER)*, pages 599–603.

Evaluating the Impact of Developer Experience on Code Quality: A Systematic Literature Review

Jefferson G. M. Lopes[1] **, Johnatan Oliveira**[2] **, Eduardo Figueiredo**[1]

[1]Department of Computer Science (DCC)
Federal University of Minas Gerais (UFMG)
Belo Horizonte – MG – Brazil

[2]Department of Computer Science (DCC)
Federal University of Lavras (UFLA)
Lavras – MG – Brazil

{jeffersonmoreira, figueiredo}@dcc.ufmg.br, johnatan.oliveira@ufla.br

Abstract. *The relationship between developer experience and code quality continues to provoke extensive debate and diverging interpretations in software engineering. To investigate this subject, we conducted a systematic literature review and identified 18 relevant papers from which we aim to answer an overarching research question: to what extent does developer experience impact on code quality? Our analysis reveals different definitions and dimensions for both developer experience and code quality, highlighting the complexity and multifaceted nature of their relationship. We also observed contradictory results on the impact of developer experience on code quality. This literature review contributes in two key ways. First, it synthesizes various perspectives on developer experience and code quality, offering a consolidated viewpoint of the current academic work. Second, it uncovers significant gaps in our understanding of the relationship between these two concepts, pinpointing areas for further research and emphasizing the needs for more focused studies to bridge these knowledge gaps.*

1. Introduction

In software engineering, the experience of developers may play a pivotal role in shaping the quality of the software they produce. A common belief is that increased individual experience correlates with enhanced competency [1]. This notion, seemingly straightforward, has driven numerous studies [2, 3] to explore the relationship between a developer's experience and the quality of code they create. However, empirical research in this area often yields conflicting results, underscoring the complexity in defining and measuring both experience and code quality in software development [2].

The concept of code quality itself is diverse, with aspects such as technical debt [4], bug frequency [5], and adherence to coding standards [6]. Additionally, there are a similar diversity while defining a developer's experience, that can relate to years worked in the field [7] or contributions made to a project [8]. Previous work [2, 3] in this field have yielded inconsistent findings. For example, Dieste et al. [2] conducted a study of the effects of different definitions of experience (academic background, programming experience, unit testing experience) on the performance of 126 programmers and they found that experience is not able to predict code quality and productivity. On the other hand, Alfayez et al. [3], after analyzing 38 Apache Java systems and applying multiple statistical analysis, concluded that more experienced developers introduce less technical debt. With many definitions of developer experience and code quality, different results and the lack of review studies, it is not clear how those two concepts relate.

Our paper aims to delve into this intricate relationship, providing a comprehensive analysis of the existing literature to shed light on the nuances that underlie the connection between developer experience and code quality. This paper provides two main contributions. First, a comprehensive review of the definitions of code quality and developer's experience used by previous studies. Second, an overview of the explored areas and gaps in our understanding of the relationship between the two concepts. To accomplish that, we defined a systematic literature review protocol and reviewed 1026 candidate studies to answer the research questions. With the results, we aim to offer valuable insights for both practitioners and researchers in software engineering. For practitioners, understanding this relationship can guide better team formation, project management, and training strategies. For researchers, our study provides a foundation for future investigations into the nuances of developer experience and its implications for software quality.

By conducting our systematic review protocol, we found and classified 7 distinct ways of measuring code quality and 5 distinct ways of accounting a developer's experience over the reviewed studies. Additionally, we show that exists a clear trend of previous work in defining a developer's experience as project experience and taking code quality as the number of bugs introduced. Other combinations of experience and code quality needs more investigation as there are contradictory results and unexplored areas.

Following this introduction, the paper is organized as follows: Section 2 presents our review protocol. Section 3 discusses the results of our review, focusing on the definitions of experience and code quality used in the studies and the relationship between them. Section 4 outlines potential threats to the validity of our findings. Section 5 reviews the related work, situating our study within the existing body of research. Finally, Section 6 concludes the paper with a summary of our findings and suggestions for future research directions.

2. Systematic Literature Review Protocol

This section explains the research process used in this study and the overall objectives of the initiative.

2.1. Study Goal and Research Questions

A systematic literature review in software engineering is an approach for collecting, analyzing, and interpreting all available research relevant to a specific research question, topic area, or phenomenon of interest [9]. Systematic reviews aim to present an unbiased evaluation of a research topic by employing a reliable, thorough, and auditable method [9]. They are distinct from traditional literature reviews in their commitment to comprehensiveness and in minimizing bias through exhaustive literature searches and explicit selection criteria [9, 10]. This systematic review adheres to the guidelines specified by Kitchenham and Charters [9], ensuring a detailed and replicable method. Furthermore, the search protocol was designed and a pilot study was conducted in a very similar way as previous work [11]. The review process involves defining research questions, establishing inclusion and exclusion criteria, searching for studies, assessing the quality of the included studies, extracting data, and synthesizing the findings.

The primary goal of this study is to explore how developer experience impacts on code quality in the field of software engineering. This investigation is driven by the ongoing debate and diverse perspectives within the academic and professional communities about this relationship. To achieve this goal, we created three research questions (RQs) to guide this systematic literature review.

RQ1: How is developer experience evaluated in the context of software engineering?

RQ2: What metrics or methods are used to evaluate software quality?

RQ3: How does developer experience relates to code quality?

Since developer experience and code quality have different and complex meanings, *RQ1* and *RQ2* are meant to be used in conjunction with *RQ3*. Our goal in doing this is to more thoroughly and correctly examine their relationship. It is anticipated that the study's conclusions improve comprehension of these ideas and provide guidance for future research in academia and industry.

2.2. Search String and Selection Criteria

We created a search string and particular selection criteria that are in line with our goal and research questions to gather an extensive and relevant set of literature papers. To ensure that as many relevant papers as possible were found, we ran a preliminary pilot search and then gradually improved the search string. We just used the search string on the metadata, which consists of keywords, abstracts, and titles. We define the search string as follows.

(developer AND (experience OR "years of experience" OR "programming experience" OR "career experience")) AND ("code quality" OR defect* OR "technical debt" OR bug* OR "code smell*")*

In order to include as many research as possible that addressed different aspects of code quality and developer experience, we considered the various terms we included in the search string. Three primary components make up the search string: first, it contains terms associated with developers; second, it contains common terms connected to experience, including years of experience and professional experience; and third, it looks for terms associated with quality, like technical debt and defects. We ensure a comprehensive review of pertinent literature by allowing research addressing related topics and variations to be included by utilizing asterisks (*) as wildcard characters.

Table 1 presents the Inclusion and Exclusion Criteria. With this set of criteria, we aim to highlight research that is both accessible and pertinent to the scope of our study. Our emphasis on Computer Science publications guarantees the technical applicability of the content. Furthermore, our language and format requirements are designed to make the review process easier to use and more reliable. To ensure that the publications addressed the range of our study topics, we only included those that directly compare a developer's experience with code quality. We exclude grey literature and purely theoretical papers to maintain the scientific rigor and empirical focus of the review. By limiting the scope to papers published after 2000, we ensure that the review is based on contemporary understandings and technologies relevant to current software engineering practices.

Table 1. Inclusion and Exclusion Criteria

Inclusion Criteria	Exclusion Criteria
Papers published in Computer Science.	Grey literature.
Papers written in English.	Papers published before 2000.
Papers that investigate the relationship between developer's experience and code quality.	Purely theoretical papers.

2.3. Data Sources and Search

Identifying the right data sources and crafting an effective search strategy are crucial steps in conducting a systematic literature review [9]. This section details the selection of data sources and the method employed in searching for relevant studies.

A search was conducted across multiple data sources to ensure a broad and diverse range of relevant studies. The selected databases are recognized for their extensive collections of scientific and technical papers, particularly in the field of Computer Science and Software Engineering. The following databases were used: ACM Digital Library, IEEE Xplore, Scopus, and Web of Science. These databases were chosen for their relevance on the field, peer-reviewed content, and indexing features, which are essential for conducting a thorough and effective literature review in software engineering. It was essential that the data sources allowed searches on metadata only (title, abstract, and keywords) and the use of logic operators.

We used Zotero [1] to manage the reference and metadata. One of the authors executed all the phases and constantly reviewed the results with the other authors in frequent meetings. When we started the search string was first run through all data sources, 1026 papers were found. After that, the reference manager downloaded the publications metadata. After the first extraction, this review was divided into four stages. Figure 1 shows these phases and overviews the paper extraction from the selected databases.

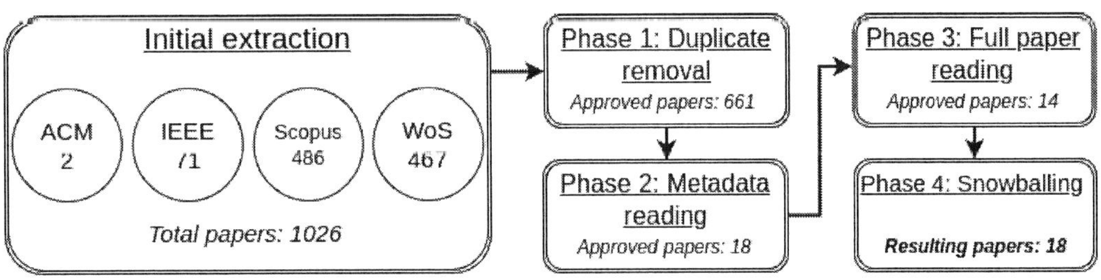

Figure 1. Paper selection and extraction

Phase 1: Duplicate Removal. We removed all duplicated papers from Zotero. After that, the list of studies were sorted by alphabetical order and checked one by one. This first phase removed 365 studies and 661 went to the next phase.

Phase 2: Metadata Reading. In this phase, we read the title and abstract of all 661 papers. We made this phase to verify its adherence to the research questions and to the inclusion/exclusion criteria. The title and abstract were available as part of the initial extraction (we removed 643 papers and 18 went to the next phase).

[1]https://www.zotero.org/

Phase 3: Full Paper Reading. We read the remaining papers. This analysis led to the removal of 4 papers, mainly because they did not adhere to the inclusion/exclusion criteria. The common reasons for exclusion were due to not directly comparing the developer's experience with code quality, or failing to generate measurable conclusions. Consequently, only 14 papers met the criteria and were approved in this phase.

Phase 4: Snowballing. This study analyzed all references from the previous 14 selected papers and triaged them based on their metadata, using the same review process from Phase 1 to Phase 3. After this procedure, the final count of papers found is 18. This step was composed only by a backward snowballing process.

2.4. Data and Metadata Analysis

To respond the research questions and extract information using our search string, we reviewed all pertinent data we had gathered. We looked at the years that the gathered papers were published in order to gain a better understanding of the activity and novelty in this field of study. The majority of the papers were released in 2018 (4), suggesting a lot of activity that year. Figure 2 shows the distribution of the research throughout time. Table 2 presents the 18 selected primary studies that compose this systematic literature review.

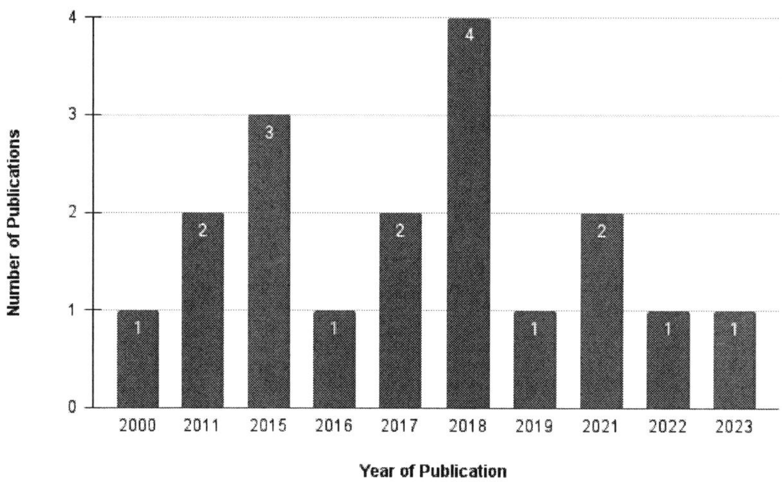

Figure 2. Distribution of the relevant studies by year of publication.

Considering the range of study methods, topics, and formats, we kept a spreadsheet to record the definition of code quality, experience, and corresponding findings of each publication. We classified their definitions of quality, experience, and research outcomes into more general ones based on accepted ideas in the literature so that the results from other studies could be compared. A thematic synthesis, based on the methods described by D. Cruzes et al. [26], was employed to construct dimensions and subdimensions that can represent the studies data.

Table 2. List of papers included.

Authors	Paper Title
González et al.	*A preliminary investigation of developer profiles based on their activities and code quality: Who does what?* [12]
Qiu et al.	*An Empirical Study of Developer Quality* [13]
Tufano et al.	*An empirical study on developer-related factors characterizing fix-inducing commits* [14]
Campos et al.	*An empirical study on the influence of developers' experience on software test code quality* [15]
Alfayez et al.	*An exploratory study on the influence of developers in technical debt* [3]
Piantadosi et al.	*Do attention and memory explain the performance of software developers?* [7]
Eyolfson et al.	*Do Time of Day and Developer Experience Affect Commit Bugginess?* [16]
Dieste et al.	*Empirical evaluation of the effects of experience on code quality and programmer productivity: an exploratory study* [2]
Tsunoda et al.	*Evaluating the work of experienced and inexperienced developers considering work difficulty in software development* [17]
Ando et al.	*How Does Defect Removal Activity of Developer Vary with Development Experience?* [18]
Salamea et al.	*Influence of Developer Factors on Code Quality: A Data Study* [19]
Hokka et al.	*Linking Developer Experience to Coding Style in Open-Source Repositories* [20]
Karimi et al.	*Links between the personalities, styles and performance in computer programming* [21]
Falcão et al.	*On Relating Technical, Social Factors, and the Introduction of Bugs* [22]
Rahman et al.	*Ownership, Experience and Defects: A Fine-Grained Study of Authorship* [23]
Kini et al.	*Periodic Developer Metrics in Software Defect Prediction* [8]
Mockus et al.	*Predicting Risk of Software Changes* [24]
Amanatidis et al.	*Who is Producing More Technical Debt? A Personalized Assessment of TD Principal* [25]

3. Results and Discussion

This section aims to answer RQ1, RQ2 and RQ3 while conducting a discussion over the results. Section 3.1 presents definitions of experience to answer RQ1. Section 3.2 presents definitions of code quality to answer RQ2. Section 3.3 discusses the relationship between experience and code quality found in the relevant studies to answer RQ3. Finally, a brief discussion of the results is included in Section 3.4.

3.1. Definitions of Experience

This section presents the results of our first research question (RQ1), defined as follows.

RQ1: How is developer experience evaluated in the context of software engineering?

Figure 3 illustrates the dimensions and sub-dimensions we identified, along with their respective counts. It is important to note that a study may employ multiple definitions of experience; as a result, the count in a given row can exceed 18. In this figure, each ellipse represents the number of papers we found in each dimension.

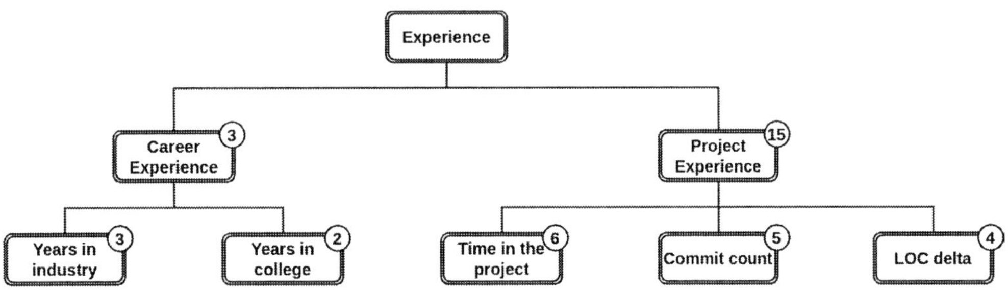

Figure 3. Dimensions and sub-dimensions of a developer's experience and a count of how many papers utilized it. A study can have more than one definition.

The literature frequently operationalizes experience as a theoretical construct in two ways [1, 27]. First, it defines experience as the duration of time spent in the field.

Second, it define it as particular skills and information acquired by active involvement in various tasks. Career Experience and Project Experience are two separate but related concepts that are captured by these operational definitions. We classify the primary studies into one of these two dimensions, notwithstanding the wide range of definitions of experience in the examined papers.

Career Experience is similar to the classic idea of experience as time-based in that it takes into account the chronological amount of time spent in the area [1]. A comprehensive understanding of the field and a depth of knowledge gained over years of working in numerous positions and technologies are correlated with this dimension of experience [28, 29]. This definition was used by three out of the studies in our review [2, 7, 21] . Project Experience, on the other hand, places more emphasis on the volume and variety of work involved in a given project. It reflects the specialized knowledge and problem-solving capabilities developed in real-world situations and includes the practical, hands-on skills gained via direct involvement in software projects [30, 31]. Most of the papers (15) used this concept, albeit they employed various methods for measurement.

Project Experience turns on the breadth and applicability of unique skills to tasks and projects, whereas Career Experience shows the long-term accumulation of knowledge. Understanding how experience appears in a software engineer's career path and how it affects their performance and project success is made possible in large part by this distinction. While some research used numerous sub-dimensions of a single dimension, the majority of studies used one dimension
with one sub-dimension.

Table 3 presents the sub-dimensions we defined in for comparison of results. To maintain comparable results, we restricted our study to only five sub-dimensions and two dimensions, despite the fact that the definitions and calculation techniques for the developer's experience vary greatly and may be further refined in granularity. For instance, the Project Experience sub-dimensions exhibit the most variation among these indicators. For example, some studies solely consider the experience on files that have defects, while others weight metrics based on the timestamp of changes.

Table 3. Comparison of Career and Project Experience Metrics

Career Experience	Project Experience
Years in industry–Refers to the total duration a developer has spent working in the software industry. A total of 3 papers utilized this metric and collected it via a questionnaire.	Time in the project– Tries to quantify the time a developer has been involved with a specific software project. The analyzed papers often calculated this metric using the difference between the date of the first commit and the last commit by a developer. A total of 6 studies utilized this metric.
Years in college– Represents the duration of formal education in software engineering or related fields. This metric was used by two papers.	Commit count– Refers to the number of code contributions (commits) a developer has made to a project's repository. This metric was used by five studies.
	LOC delta– Stands for lines of code delta, which measures the net change in lines of code a developer contributes to a project. The metric was used by 4 of the relevant studies.

RQ1 summary: In the context of software engineering, developer experience is primarily evaluated through 2 dimensions: Career Experience and Project Experience. Career Experience focuses on the chronological time spent in the field, reflecting a broad understanding and depth of knowledge, while Project Experience emphasizes the diversity and volume of work on specific projects, highlighting specialized skills and problem-solving capabilities.

3.2. Definitions of Code Quality

This section presents the results of our second research question (RQ2), defined as follows:

RQ2: What metrics or methods are used to evaluate software quality?

Figure 4 presents the different dimensions and sub-dimensions of code quality classified in the studies. Software quality in software engineering is multifaceted and evaluated using a range of metrics and methods. This systematic review categorizes these into three distinct areas: Technical Debt, Bug, and Code Style. Technical Debt [4] refers to the cost of additional work caused by choosing a faster approach in development rather than a more robust solution. It includes the idea of code smells and the effort required for remediation, reflecting the long-term impact of initial development choices [4].

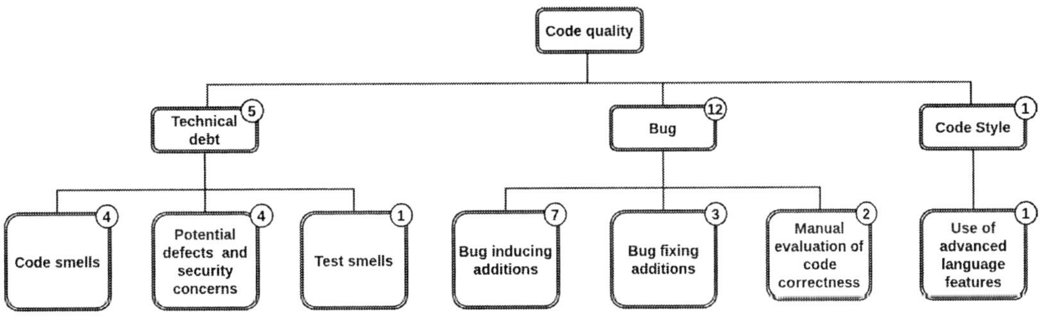

Figure 4. Dimensions and sub-dimensions of a developer's code quality. A study can have more than one definition.

Software quality is assessed through the frequency, severity, and types of software defects in the context of bugs [32]. Bugs indicate direct issues in the software, affecting its functionality and reliability [32]. This study only classified bugs as actual issues in software identified or verified by humans. This definition includes bug tickets in issue tracking systems, code additions considered buggy, or code additions to repair bugs. Possible bugs, such as those reported by static analysis tools or similar probabilistic software, were classified as technical debt as its indication is no certainty of a bug. This definition of bug avoids the well-known miss classification errors from static code analysis tools and restricts its use for actual confirmed problems in software.

Code Style pertains to coding practices that influence the maintainability and readability of the software. This includes adherence to coding standards and using advanced language features, contributing to the software's overall quality [33].

From each dimension of code quality, Table 4 shows the sub-dimensions to better understand and compare how the different studies measure quality. With those results, most of the studies try to quantify code quality by measuring defects or problems in the code and using that as an inverse measure of quality. With that, the higher the Bug count or Technical Debt count, the less quality a developer's code has. The exception was the study that performed a manual evaluation of code correctness and verified the use of advanced features in the code [20]. However, both alternatives often require expert revision and manual work to obtain.

Table 4. Comparison of Technical Debt, Bug, and Code Style Metrics

Technical Debt	Bug	Code Style
Code smells – Refers to certain structures in the code that suggest a violation of fundamental design principles. Used in four studies.	Bug-inducing additions – Changes in the code base that introduce errors. Used in 7 studies.	Code style– Adherence to coding standards and readability. Used in 1 study.
Potential defects and security concerns – Issues identified by static analysis tools. Considered technical debts in this review. Used in 4 studies.	Bug-fixing additions – Modifications aimed at correcting bugs. Used in 3 studies.	
Test smells – Characteristics in test code indicating potential issues. Used in 1 study.	Manual evaluation of code correctness – Manual code review process. Used in 2 studies.	

RQ2 summary: Software quality in engineering is evaluated through metrics and methods that can be categorized into Technical Debt, Bugs, and Code Style. Technical Debt assesses the long-term impact of initial development choices, Bugs focus on software functionality issues confirmed by human verification, and Code Style examines practices for maintainability and readability.

3.3. Relationship between Experience and Code Quality

After a clear understanding of the definitions of experience and code quality for the reviewed studies, we can answer the RQ3, defined as follows:

RQ3: How does developer experience relates to code quality?

The relevant studies reached different conclusions, and this systematic review classified them into three, as follows: more experience relates to better code quality; more experience relates to worst code quality; it is not possible to establish a relationship. As the classical claim that more experience leads to better performance is only hypothesized, it is imperative that we outline that the studies' empirical results only show evidence of a relationship, or correlation, between the variables experience and code quality. A statistical correlation does not automatically imply causation between the first and second variables [34], meaning that it is not possible to affirm that a developer produces code with high quality because of their experience. However, evidence that they are related is the basis of theoretical work that can potentially explain the observed phenomenon. As there are different dimensions and sub-dimensions for code quality and experience, we aggregated the results based on the type of experience to facilitate the comparison of results.

Career Experience and Code Quality. From the 3 studies that used career experience as a definition of experience, 2 concluded that more experience relates to better code quality [7, 21] and one did not find any evidence of a relationship between the two factors [2]. Interestingly, no study on this dimension used technical debt or code style as a metric of code quality, only bugs. Given that the experience was manually collected via questionnaire in all these studies, 2 also manually evaluated the code's correctness [2, 7]. Despite having no study pointing out that more years of experience relates to worst code quality, the evidence to support the contrary is sparse, with only 2 studies pointing the opposite and one with inconclusive results.

Project Experience and Code Quality. A majority of the analyzed studies used project experience as a metric for the developer's experience, with 15 studies using it. From those, 8 concluded that more experience relates to better code quality [3, 8, 13, 14, 16, 18, 20, 24], 3 concluded that more experience relates to worst code quality [12, 15, 19] and 4 were inconclusive [17, 22, 23, 25]. From the 8 studies that found more experience is related to better code quality, 6 used bugs [8, 13, 14, 16, 18, 24], and the remaining 2 used technical debt or code style as a metric for quality [3, 20]. The 3 studies that concluded more experience relates to worst code used technical debt [12, 15, 19]. Finally, 3 studies with inconclusive results used bugs [17, 22, 23] and one used technical debit as a metric for quality [25].

The results show a clear predominance in academia that, while using project experience as a measure of a developer's experience and the number of bugs as a metric of quality, the experience of the developer and its code quality are correlated. However, no clear indication of consensus can be drawn by using tech debt or code style as a metric of quality in the scope of project experience.

> *RQ3 summary: Studies on the relationship between developer experience and code quality show mixed results: some indicate that more experience improves quality, others suggest a negative impact, and a few find no clear link. Evidence highlights a correlation, not causation, between experience and code quality, with varied findings across different metrics of quality.*

3.4. Discussion

Figure 5 illustrates the overall findings of the study. The data obtained show conflicting findings - while certain studies identified a positive link between experience and code quality, others reported either a negative correlation or no significant relationship at all. This inconsistency may be attributed to the diverse ways in which experience and code quality are defined and measured across studies, suggesting that the impact of experience on code quality is not straightforward and is influenced by various nuanced factors.

Different types of experience, like career length and project involvement, appear to have distinct impacts on code quality. However, the results are mixed, especially regarding career experience, calling for further investigation into what aspects of experience most significantly affect code quality. Additionally, the varied methodological approaches and quality metrics used in these studies highlight the lack of standardization in this research area. Our study concludes that while a clear evidence exists regarding the positive impact of project experience on code quality, other aspects of the experience-code quality relationship remain ambiguous and asks further research to achieve a more comprehensive understanding about the subject.

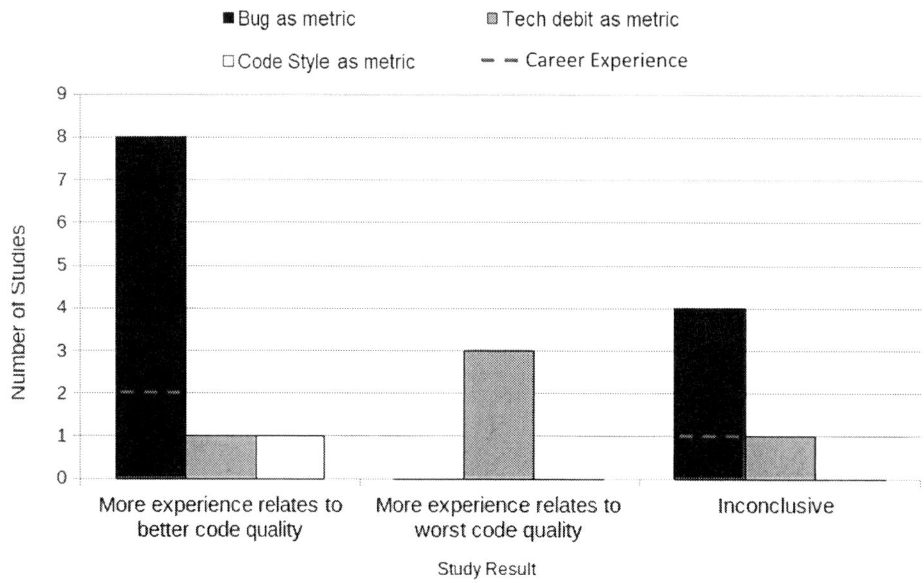

Figure 5. Overall relationship between experience and code quality.

4. Threats to Validity

Even with careful planning, some threats may affect the validity of our findings. This section discusses some threats and our actions to mitigate them, organizing by construct, internal, external, and conclusion validity [35].

Construct Validity: Construct validity concerns the mapping of the results of the study to the concept or theory [35]. For instance, the electronic database selected might not provide all relevant papers. To minimize this threat, we selected four different databases that aggregate papers from multiple publishers. Another threat refers to the search string used which may not return all relevant papers to answer our research questions. However, we tuned our search string by trying several combinations of different combination of terms in the digital libraries.

Internal Validity: Influences that can affect the independent variable to causality [35]. In our study, we favor internal validity by providing a detailed description of the search string, the search engines used, and the inclusion and exclusion criteria. However, one possible threat to internal validity may be related to the judgment and (sometimes subjective) selection of the relevant primary studies. To minimize this threat, the involved researchers have discussed all criteria and selected papers.

Conclusion Validity: Threats to the conclusion validity are concerned with issues that affect the ability to draw the correct conclusion between the treatment and the outcome [35]. In our context, the data summaries extracted from the literature represent the researchers' point of view. To minimize this conclusion threat, we documented all steps to allow replication from external researchers. Moreover, in case of missing or unclear data to answer the research questions, cross-discussions among the paper authors often took place to reach a common agreement.

External Validity: Threats to external validity are conditions that limit our ability to generalize the results of our paper [35]. For instance, this threat is related to the representativeness of the selected papers to answer our research questions. We used several digital libraries to support a broad representation of the selected papers, but other relevant papers may have been published elsewhere or indexed using unusual terms (not present in our search string). Our results may also not generalize to other perspectives of developer experience or code quality. Therefore, further studies can be performed to complement our findings and investigate possible gaps.

5. Related Work

The experience of the developers may have a direct impact on the software product quality. Besides the code they write, an experienced developer may define architectural solutions essential to the system's maintainability. Some works have studied the impact of developer experience and use metrics to study the relationship with the software maintainability and evolution [36, 37, 38]. R. Brasil-Silva et al. [38], for example, present a catalog of metrics that have been used to quantify developers' experience. They conducted a systematic mapping from 34 relevant papers. These metrics are classified by the type of experience they represent and the purpose of using them. The results showed that most of the selected studies used metrics based on counting developer activities in code. The main difference between this study and our work is that while they provide a comprehensive catalog of metrics for quantifying developers' experience, our study specifically focuses on the relationship between metrics of experience and the direct impact on code quality of developers.

E. Kalliamvakou et al. [36] describe the main challenges to be faced when mining software repositories and propose solutions to alleviate them. Instead, they do not classify nor organize existing papers in terms of such dimensions. Their goal is to help new researchers to conduct well-designed software mining studies rather than to provide a state-of-the-art of the current research in the field. The key distinction between their study and ours is that our research explicitly categorizes and analyzes the impact of developer experience on code quality, which is not the primary focus of Kalliamvakou et al.'s work [36].

T. Carvalho et al. [39] studied machine learning methods for predictive maintenance through a systematic literature review. Their review focused on two scientific databases and provided a valuable foundation for machine learning techniques and their main results, challenges, and opportunities. It also supports new research work in the predictive maintenance field. As a result, the authors identified that each proposed approach addressed specific equipment, making it more challenging to compare it to other techniques. The primary difference between their study and ours is the specific focus on machine learning techniques in predictive maintenance, whereas our study centers on the correlation between developer experience and code quality across various software engineering contexts.

J. Morales et al. [40] conducted a systematic literature review on the Programmer eXperience (PX) over the past ten years (January 2009 to October 2018). Initially, 977 papers were identified, which was refined to 73 relevant papers after applying selection criteria. They appoint key findings. The primary factors influencing PX are the motivation of programmers and the choice of tools they use, such as programming environments. A majority (59%) of the studies focused on evaluating the influence of Programmer eXperience, User Experience, and usability on programming environments. About 70% of the studies used usability tests and heuristic evaluation methods. Four sets of heuristics were identified for evaluating software development artifacts related to programming environments, languages, and application programming interfaces. The main difference between their study and ours lies in the focus; while Morales et al [40] delve into the broader aspects of Programmer eXperience and its tools, our study specifically targets the impact of this experience on the quality of code produced by individual developers.

6. Conclusion

We selected and reviewed 18 papers, out of a total of 1028, in a systematic manner. To better comprehend the relationship between experience and code quality, we grouped the definitions of each after classifying and evaluating the pertinent publications. Some research indicates that experience leads to better code quality, whereas other studies find no significant correlation or the contrary. This discrepancy most likely results from the different criteria and definitions applied to experience and code quality evaluations. These differences highlight how complex this relationship is, implying that code quality may not always be predicted only by experience.

When considering career and project experience separately, this review suggests they have different impacts on code quality. The inconsistency in findings, particularly with career experience showing limited evidence of a positive correlation, highlight the need for a more detailed understanding of "experience" when measured in years of work or study. This situation raises questions about the specific aspects of experience that influence code quality. These aspects may include the domain of work, the complexity of projects undertaken, or the development methodologies employed.

Finally, the results of this review point to a gap in the existing literature and suggest a direction for future work. Most research relies on bugs as a proxy for code quality, although a very small number of studies use other possible proxy measures. Comparably, few studies use years of experience as a criterion, even though the majority concentrate on project experience. As demonstrated, experience and code quality have a complex relationship that needs more research to effectively guide scholarly discourse and industrial practice. There is general agreement, according to this study, between increased project experience and higher-quality code. Other combinations of code quality and developer experience, however, produce contradictory findings and call for additional data to provide a more comprehensive general academic understanding.

Acknowledgments. This research was partially supported by Brazilian funding agencies: CAPES, CNPq, and FAPEMIG.

References

[1] K. A. Ericsson. *The Cambridge Handbook of Expertise and Expert Performance*. 2006.

[2] O. Dieste et al. Empirical evaluation of the effects of experience on code quality and programmer productivity: An exploratory study. In *Proceedings of the 2018 International Conference on Software and System Process*, pages 111–112, 2018.

[3] R. Alfayez et al. An exploratory study on the influence of developers in technical debt. In *Proceedings of the 2018 International Conference on Technical Debt*, pages 1–10, 2018.

[4] W. Cunningham. The wycash portfolio management system. In *ACM SIGPLAN OOPS Messenger*, volume 4, pages 29–30, 1992.

[5] E. Giger et al. Comparing fine-grained source code changes and code churn for bug prediction. 2011.

[6] Y. Wang et al. Complying with coding standards or retaining programming style: A quality outlook at source code level. *Journal of Software Engineering and Applications*, 01:88–91, 2008.

[7] V. Piantadosi et al. Do attention and memory explain the performance of software developers? *Empirical Software Engineering*, 2023.

[8] S. Kini et al. Periodic developer metrics in software defect prediction. In *2018 IEEE 18th International Working Conference on Source Code Analysis and Manipulation (SCAM)*, pages 72–81, 2018.

[9] B. Kitchenham et al. Guidelines for performing systematic literature reviews in software engineering. 2, 2007.

[10] P. Brereton et al. Lessons from applying the systematic literature review process within the software engineering domain. *Journal of Systems and Software*, 80:571–583, 2007.

[11] L. Olsina et al. Specifying the process model for systematic reviews: An augmented proposal. *Journal of Software Engineering Research and Development*, 7:7:1 – 7:23, Dec. 2019.

[12] C. González et al. A preliminary investigation of developer profiles based on their activities and code quality: Who does what? In *2021 IEEE 21st International Conference on Software Quality, Reliability and Security (QRS)*, pages 938–945, 2021.

[13] Y. Qiu et al. An empirical study of developer quality. In *2015 IEEE International Conference on Software Quality, Reliability and Security-Companion*, pages 202–209, 2015.

[14] M. Tufano et al. An empirical study on developer-related factors characterizing fix-inducing commits. *Journal of Software: Evolution and Process*, 29(1):e1797, 2017.

[15] D. Campos et al. An empirical study on the influence of developers' experience on software test code quality. In *Proceedings of the XXI Brazilian Symposium on Software Quality*, pages 1–10, 2022.

[16] J. Eyolfson et al. Do time of day and developer experience affect commit bugginess? In *Proceedings of the 8th Working Conference on Mining Software Repositories*, pages 153–162, 2011.

[17] T. Tsunoda et al. Evaluating the work of experienced and inexperienced developers considering work difficulty in software development. In *2017 18th IEEE/ACIS International Conference on Software Engineering, Artificial Intelligence, Networking and Parallel/Distributed Computing (SNPD)*, pages 161–166, 2017.

[18] R. Ando et al. How does defect removal activity of developer vary with development experience? In *SEKE*, pages 540–545, 2015.

[19] M. Salamea et al. Influence of developer factors on code quality: A data study. In *2019 IEEE 19th International Conference on Software Quality, Reliability and Security Companion (QRS-C)*, pages 120–125, 2019.

[20] H. Hokka et al. Linking developer experience to coding style in open-source repositories. In *2021 IEEE International Conference on Software Analysis, Evolution and Reengineering (SANER)*, pages 516–520, 2021.
[21] Z. Karimi et al. Links between the personalities, styles and performance in computer programming. *Journal of Systems and Software*, 111:228–241, 2016.
[22] F. Falcão et al. On relating technical, social factors, and the introduction of bugs. In *2020 IEEE 27th International Conference on Software Analysis, Evolution and Reengineering (SANER)*, pages 378–388, 2020.
[23] F. Rahman et al. Ownership, experience and defects: A fine-grained study of authorship. In *Proceedings of the 33rd International Conference on Software Engineering*, pages 491–500, 2011.
[24] A. Mockus et al. Predicting risk of software changes. *Bell Labs Technical Journal*, 5(2):169–180, 2000.
[25] T. Amanatidis et al. Who is producing more technical debt? a personalized assessment of td principal. In *Proceedings of the XP2017 Scientific Workshops*, pages 1–8, 2017.
[26] D. Cruzes et al. Recommended steps for thematic synthesis in software engineering. In *2011 International Symposium on Empirical Software Engineering and Measurement*, 2011.
[27] B. Curtis et al. A field study of the software design process for large systems. *Communications of the ACM*, 31(11):1268–1287, 1988.
[28] W. Chase et al. The mind's eye in chess. 1973.
[29] K. Ericsson et al. The role of deliberate practice in the acquisition of expert performance. *Psychological Review*, 100(3):363–406, 1993.
[30] R. Jeffries et al. The processes involved in designing software. 1981.
[31] K. McKeithen et al. Knowledge organization and skill differences in computer programmers. *Cognitive Psychology*, 13(3):307–325, 1981.
[32] M. Hamill et al. Common trends in software fault and failure data. *IEEE Transactions on Software Engineering*, 35:484–496, 2009.
[33] A. Mohan et al. Programming style changes in evolving source code. *Proceedings. 12th IEEE International Workshop on Program Comprehension, 2004.*
[34] N. Altman et al. Association, correlation and causation. *Nature Methods*, 12:799–800, 2015.
[35] C. Wohlin et al. *Experimentation in Software Engineering*. Heidelberg, 2012. ISBN 978-3-642-29043-5.
[36] E. Kalliamvakou et al. The promises and perils of mining github. In *Proceedings of the 11th Working Conference on Mining Software Repositories*, pages 92–101, 2014.
[37] K. Stol et al. Reporting empirical research in open source software: The state of practice. In *Open Source Ecosystems: Diverse Communities Interacting*, pages 156–169, 2009.
[38] R. Brasil-Silva et al. Metrics to quantify software developer experience: A systematic mapping. *Proceedings of the 37th ACM/SIGAPP Symposium on Applied Computing*, 2022.
[39] T. Carvalho et al. A systematic literature review of machine learning methods applied to predictive maintenance. *Computers Industrial Engineering*, 137, 2019.
[40] J. Morales et al. Programmer experience: A systematic literature review. *IEEE Access*, 7:71079–71094, 2019.

A Literature Study on Application Domains and IoT Software Systems Architectures Solutions Influencing Quality Requirements

Fernando N. R. da Silva, Bruno P. de Souza, Guilherme H. Travassos

PESC/COPPE - Federal University of Rio de Janeiro (UFRJ)
Rio de Janeiro – RJ – Brazil

{fernandonrs,bpsouza,ght}@cos.ufrj.br

Abstract. *The Internet of Things (IoT) enables the development of software systems using exclusively addressable objects. This literature study investigates IoT software systems' architectural models and quality requirements. The study reveals **28** architectural solutions in **four** application domains, influencing **seven** quality requirements and indicating best practices that can be used to support decision-making when engineering IoT software systems.*

Resumo. *A Internet das Coisas (IoT) permite o desenvolvimento de sistemas de software utilizando exclusivamente objetos endereçáveis. Este estudo da literatura investiga modelos arquiteturais e requisitos de qualidade necessários para sistemas de software IoT. O estudo revelou **28** diferentes soluções de arquitetura em **quatro** domínios de aplicação, influenciando **sete** requisitos de qualidade que podem apoiar a tomada de decisão sobre melhores práticas para a engenharia de sistemas de software IoT.*

1. Introduction

Throughout history, technological advancements such as steam power, electricity, and electronics have significantly transformed our daily lives and workplaces. We are in the midst of the fourth industrial revolution, which is characterized by integrating physical objects, sensors, actuators, and the Internet. This revolution is made possible by breakthroughs such as the Internet of Things (IoT) and software solutions.

IoT was introduced by Kevin Ashton in 1999 as the interconnection of sensing and actuating devices that share information through a unified network, as mentioned in [Gubbi et al. 2013]. Atzori et al. (2010) define IoT as the widespread presence of various objects that can interact and cooperate through unique addressing schemes. Motta et al. (2019) describe IoT as a paradigm that allows the composition of software systems from exclusively addressable objects that can communicate and cooperate to achieve a goal.

Atzori et al. (2010) have identified five primary application domains for IoT: transportation, healthcare, smart environments, personal/social, and futuristic. Gubbi et al. (2013) categorized IoT application domains as personal/home, enterprise, utilities, and mobile. These domains are significant in realizing IoT software projects.

The IoT paradigm capabilities offer opportunities for creating numerous software systems that can significantly enhance our quality of life in domains like homes, travel, work, healthcare, and sports activities. Architecture is a crucial asset that facilitates the development of intricate and high-quality software systems and mitigates potential design and implementation challenges. These interconnected systems operate intelligently based on the received information and require simplified architecture to handle diverse hardware and network protocols, ensuring smooth operation and high quality.

The quality of a software system is determined by the degree to which it meets its stakeholders' explicit and implicit requirements, thus providing value in terms of functionality, performance, security, and maintainability [ISO/IEC 25010 2023]. Architectural decisions for software systems aim to fulfill stakeholders' expectations through quality requirements (QRs) or attributes. However, these requirements are often neglected, leading to project failures, especially in IoT software systems.

However, *how do architecture IoT software systems take one or another QR into account?* Therefore, we decided to review the literature to comprehensively understand IoT software systems, exploring how various application domains and their distinct characteristics influence QRs. We want to understand architectural solutions and their impact on healthcare software projects. Our interest is driven by the need to identify the best software system arrangements. Our research question focuses on supporting software engineers in making these decisions. By analyzing the software architecture of different IoT software systems, we can gain insight into the factors contributing to their success. Therefore, it is vital to clearly understand the application domains and their corresponding software architectures to ensure the delivery of high-quality IoT software systems. Consequently, we conducted a literature study on architectural design solutions influencing QRs in IoT software systems to answer the following question:

"What application domains and characteristics of their IoT software systems architectures influence QRs?"

Our review of 28 primary studies provided a taxonomy of the most recent IoT software architectures and identified application domains, architectural solutions, and QRs. This paper offers insights and practices for engineering IoT software systems and raises research opportunities.

Besides this introduction, this paper comprises five more sections. In Section 2, related works are presented. Section 3 describes how our literature study was conducted. In section 4, the results of this study are shown. Next, section 5 shows the threats to validity. Finally, in section 6, the conclusions and future research are discussed.

2. Related Works

The ongoing study underscores the importance of continuous updates in guiding decisions for IoT software systems' architecture design. The significance of these two related works will significantly influence the research strategy. Firstly, Alreshidi and Ahmad (2019) focus on the architectural challenges in designing software systems for the Internet of Things (IoT). The authors highlight the difficulty in creating systems that can handle IoT systems' heterogeneity, dynamicity, and scalability. They also discuss the need for addressing security and privacy concerns in designing IoT systems. The article proposes a conceptual model for developing IoT software systems that integrate cloud services and open standards to overcome these architectural challenges. Also later, Razzaq (2020), presents a systematic review of software architectures for IoT systems focusing on adopting microservices architecture. The authors emphasize the need for IoT software systems to be scalable, flexible, and handle data diversity. They review traditional architectural patterns such as n-tier and service-oriented architectures and discuss their limitations in the context of IoT. The article then explores the potential benefits of microservices architecture in addressing the architectural challenges of IoT systems, such as achieving modularization, flexibility, and compatibility. Finally, the article proposes future research directions for adopting microservices architecture in IoT systems.

Besides, it is worth discussing IoT reference architectures. A reference architecture provides a flexible framework for developing and evaluating systems, especially in the industrial IoT. It is not tied to specific technologies or standards, offering adaptable structural guidance for networks, cloud services, and compatible hardware. Experts from various fields propose these architectures to transform industries using available technologies [Mirani et al. 2022]. Specifically, reference architectures offer a basic IoT software system design, showing the main elements, hardware, and software components and how they connect to ensure the functioning and operations of an IoT-based software system [Alreshidi and Ahmad 2019]. Reference architectures are usually created informally. However, establishing a systematic design approach guarantees quality, durability, and sustainability. At the same time, many reference architectures do not survive after their first release or publication in journals or scientific events [Nakagawa and Antonio, 2023].

2.1. Industrial Internet Reference Architecture (IIRA)

The Industrial Reference Architecture for the Industrial Internet of Things (IIoT), known as the IIRA, is a model that system architects can use to design IoT software systems. It is not a standard, but it is based on the Industrial Internet Architecture Framework (IIAF), which provides principles and guidelines for the consistent description of architectures in the IIoT context. The IIRA aims to promote a shared basis of understanding and improved interoperability across industrial sectors.

The IIRA adopts a generic, high-level abstraction approach for broad applicability in industry. It consists of three layers: the Edge Layer, the Platform Layer, and the Enterprise Layer. These layers are interconnected to create a Proximity Network that combines various devices, control systems, sensors, and assets. The IIRA aims to guide the development of standards and technologies needed for interoperability and applicability in different industrial contexts, thus providing a conceptual roadmap for designing and implementing IoT software systems [Mirani et al. 2022] [Nakagawa and Antonio 2023].

2.2 Reference Architectural Model (RAMI 4.0)

RAMI 4.0 is a Reference Architectural Model for Industry 4.0, developed in Germany to modernize manufacturing and industrial automation processes. RAMI 4.0 guidelines promote an interconnected network of products, distribution of functionalities throughout the network structure, and independent communication between participants, regardless of the system hierarchy. It is based on Service Oriented Architecture (SOA) to provide networking protocols for the system components, enabling the transformation of complex tasks into simpler processes based on independent technologies and products, with interdisciplinary collaborations among electronics, electrical, mechanical, and IT standards [Alreshidi and Ahmad 2019] [Mirani et al. 2022] [Nakagawa and Antonio 2023].

3. Literature Study

This study explores the areas where the features of IoT software system architectures emerge. The goal is to gather these projects' commonly observed QRs and comprehensively analyze the identified ones in the primary sources. These QRs encapsulate architectural challenges relevant to our IoT software projects, characterizing these IoT software systems regarding application domains and other QRs (such as security, performance, maintainability, and compatibility). This characterization is done from the perspective of software engineering researchers, drawing upon existing knowledge in technical literature related to architectural characteristics within the context of IoT software projects. Therefore, we have divided the primary research question (Section 1) into five parts to facilitate a deeper understanding (Table 1).

The research began with a Literature Search (LS) [Kuhrmann et al. 2017] to identify articles from 2019, due to Alreshidi and Ahmad (2019), in the technical literature addressing architectural design solutions influencing QRs in IoT software systems. An initial PICO-inspired search string (Table 1) was performed on Scopus (www.scopus.com) on December 22, 2022, returning 130 articles, with six selected to form the starting points for Snowballing (one level backward and forward) [Wöhlin 2014]. The result was an initial set of papers, with two being related and aligned with the objectives of our study. Subsequent searches and refinements, incorporating search terms (Table 1) from the related works [Alreshidi and Ahmad 2019] and [Razzaq 2020], led to a broad final search in Scopus in July 2023, producing 38 articles. Four articles from this set were appended to the initial set of papers, totaling ten, for executing a new Snowballing trial (one level backward and forward).

Table 1. Research Questions, Search Strings, Inclusion, and Exclusion Criteria.

RQs		**RQ1:** What are the application domains of IoT software systems?
		RQ2: What are the proposed IoT software system architectures?
		RQ2.1: What are the characteristics of these IoT software system architectures?
		RQ2.2: What are the QRs identified in these IoT software system architectures?
		RQ2.3: How are these QRs worked out in these IoT software system architectures?
Search String	**Initial**	("IoT" OR "Internet of Things") AND ("Quality Requirement" OR "Non-Functional" OR "architectural requirements") AND ("architecture" OR "architectural elements")
	Final	(software OR "Software Architect*") AND ("IoT" OR "Internet of Things") AND ("Quality Requirement" OR "Non-Functional" OR "Architectural Requirements") AND ("Architecture" OR "Architectural Elements" OR component OR design OR model OR framework) AND PUBYEAR > 2019 AND PUBYEAR < 2023
Criteria	**Inclusion**	The paper must be in the context of IoT software systems.
		The paper must report a primary study.
		The paper must provide data to answer most of the LS research questions.
		The paper must be written in the English language.
		The paper's publishing date must be from 2020 to 2022.

Exclusion	Duplicate publication/self-plagiarism.
	Register of proceedings.
	Papers that are not peer-reviewed.

Finally, the papers were chosen based on specific inclusion and exclusion criteria (Table 1). Subsequently, two researchers thoroughly examined the chosen sources to address each research question. A final researcher evaluated the selection process, in which 28 primary sources were identified and selected.

4. Results

At the end of the study, we anticipate identifying a set of IoT software systems domains and their primary architectures, describing them, and associating them with at least one QR [ISO/IEC-25010 2023], such as security, performance, and flexibility. Thus, we aim to provide a dataset for decision-making regarding architecture solutions when designing and developing IoT software systems focusing on QRs. A mapping categorizes the selected IoT application domains, QRs, and software systems architectures. Next, these solutions are described, focusing on the addressed QRs. Finally, the architectural features for each QR are organized into catalogs.

4.1. What are the application domains of IoT software systems?

The primary sources revealed similar IoT application domains with various terminologies. Therefore, we propose a classification of IoT application domains based on [Atzori et al. 2010], [Gubbi et al. 2013], and [Motta et al. 2019].

Our study identified 28 architectural solutions associated with IoT application domains or for generic use. Some of these solutions are versatile and can be applied across all domains called "Generic." It does not mean the others cannot be used in domains other than those proposed in the primary source. Subsequently, Figure 1 presents the statistical analysis of the application areas for these architectures.

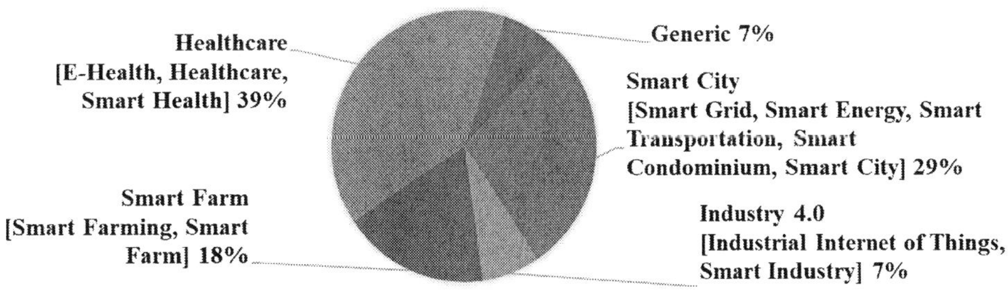

Figure 1. IoT Application Domains found in this study.

4.2. What are the proposed IoT software systems architectures?

Table 2 lists proposed IoT software systems architectures for applications such as healthcare, industry 4.0, smart cities, and smart farms. The architectures vary from cloud-based solutions to event-driven IoT, blockchain-based, geographic-based, layered, edge-computing fault-tolerant frameworks. These architectures are designed to address specific challenges related to the domain and the QR addressed. The variations reflect the complexity of IoT software systems and the need for customized solutions to ensure efficient and successful implementation.

Table 2. IoT Software Systems Architectures Solutions.

IoT Domain	Architecture Solution	Source (Appendix A)
Generic	SDN based	[SS4]
	Layered Blockchain-Based SDN	[SS27]
Healthcare	Layered	[SS2] [SS18]
	Cloud-based Secure Biometric	[SS19]
	Event-driven IoT	[SS16]
	Deep Learning based	[SS23]
	Fog Computing based	[SS3]
	Hybrid (Centralized and Distributed)	[SS5]
	Distributed Edge-Cloud	[SS25]
	Multi-layered Cloud-Edge	[SS20]
	Hybrid Cloud-Fog Computing	[SS10]
Industry 4.0	Industrial Internet of Things (IIoT)	[SS24]
	Layered	[SS22]
Smart City	Layered Blockchain and AI-enabled	[SS1]
	Blockchain-enabled	[SS26]
	Geographic-based	[SS14]
	Layered	[SS13]
	Cloud computing and the Internet of Things	[SS28]
	Distributed Blockchain-SDN based	[SS15]
	Edge Computing-based Fault Tolerant Framework	[SS12]
	SAPPARCHI	[SS21]
	Smart City	[SS17]
Smart Farm	Layered	[SS9] [SS11]
	LoRaWAN	[SS6]
	Microservices	[SS7]
	Agricultural IoT Reference Architecture (AITRA)	[SS8]

4.2.1. What are the characteristics of these IoT software system architectures?

To answer this question, we will briefly present all the IoT architecture software systems solutions, their characteristics, and how the QRs are addressed (Table 3).

Table 3. The characteristics of each IoT software systems architecture solution.

Layered Blockchain and AI-enabled [SS1]
The secure smart city infrastructure employs blockchain and AI **security** measures, IoT device authentication, and data encryption protocols. **Privacy** techniques, such as anonymization and data minimization, are also implemented while adhering to **data protection** regulations. **Real-time** threat detection and incident response mechanisms are incorporated for proactive **security**.
Layered [SS2]
The proposed healthcare monitoring framework uses wearable sensors and social networking data to monitor patients' health. It includes machine learning algorithms, cloud computing, and data analytics for real-time processing and analysis. The framework ensures **scalability**, **security**, and **high performance** using distributed processing, access control mechanisms, encryption, and secure communication protocols. It aims to improve patient care and outcomes by proactively warning patients and assisting physicians in delivering effective treatments.
Fog Computing based [SS3]
Fog-based architecture and **load balancing** can create efficient health monitoring systems. This approach uses fog nodes as intermediaries between the source and cloud and **distributes workload** across multiple nodes to maintain **efficiency under high loads**.

SDN based [SS4]
The Efficient Counter-Based DDoS Attack Detection Framework leverages SD-IoT for security and includes measures like distributed counters, access control, cryptography, and authentication. It addresses potential vulnerabilities with machine learning algorithms and incident response plans. It is a robust **security** solution for **protecting** IoT devices and networks from DDoS attacks.
Hybrid (Centralized and Distributed) [SS5]
A fog-cloud-assisted framework for the Internet of Healthcare Things (IoHT) includes a load-balancing mechanism that helps **distribute workload** across fog nodes for efficient resource utilization and system management. This mechanism plays a vital role in scaling the framework and ensuring **reliable operation** under different conditions.
LoRaWAN [SS6]
This paper presents a **cost-effective** LoRaWAN power switch architecture for smart farm applications. It includes a LoRaWAN module for wireless communication, a power switch circuit for power supply control, and user-defined inputs for customization. The architecture provides a cost-effective and enables real-time monitoring and management of farm operations.
Microservices [SS7]
The article proposes an AWS (Amazon Web Services) architecture for smart livestock monitoring. It is based on a microservices architecture pattern that includes AWS IoT services for managing and collecting sensor data, and AWS Lambda functions for processing data in real-time. The architecture provides **scalability, performance,** and flexibility for monitoring livestock in large-scale farms while incorporating **security** mechanisms such as AWS Certificate Manager and AWS Identity and Access Management (IAM) to ensure **data privacy**.
Agricultural IoT Reference Architecture (AITRA) [SS8]
The IoT architecture for agriculture prioritizes **reliability**, **security**, and **interoperability**. It supports real-time data processing and modular **scalability** for different use cases. The design emphasizes **data privacy** and **protection** against cyber-attacks, making it a secure framework for increasing productivity in the agricultural sector.
Layered [SS9]
The system uses Docker containerization for **interoperability and seamless maintenance**, open-source technologies for **cost-effectiveness**, and Debian OS for customization, **energy efficiency**, and **portability**. It has heterogeneous nodes, MQTT protocols, and AI-driven agro-weather analysis for flexibility. The user-friendly GUI layer follows a Multi-Agent System (MAS) approach to enable **scalable**, **reliable** services.
Hybrid Cloud-Fog Computing [SS10]
It is a software architecture for IoT-based healthcare systems that leverages cloud and fog computing to improve **availability**, **reliability**, **performance**, and **mobility**. The architecture uses machine learning algorithms and data analytics for predictive analysis and decision-making, providing a **scalable**, **reliable**, **high-performing** solution.
Layered [SS11]
The Smart Indoor Farms architecture enables a sustainable agricultural revolution through technological advancements. It ensures **scalability**, **security**, **privacy**, **safety**, **interoperability**, and **mobility**. The architecture **efficiently utilizes resources**, **integrates new technologies**, and adheres to regulatory standards. IoT sensors enable remote monitoring and control, while open standards facilitate **interoperability**.
Edge Computing-based Fault Tolerant Framework [SS12]
This paper presents an edge computing-based **fault-tolerant** framework for vehicular networks. It includes redundancy and distributed architecture to ensure **fault tolerance** and **availability**. The framework is designed to be scalable and flexible, providing a robust solution for enhancing fault tolerance, **portability**, and **availability** in vehicular networks.
Layered [SS13]

The proposed architecture has three layers: Data Acquisition, **Energy Efficient** Event Classification Fog, and Temporal Health Prediction with Geographic Mapping Cloud. IoT sensors collect data, and the Fog layer classifies it and optimizes transmission to the Cloud layer. The Cloud layer predicts future health states and prioritizes evacuations. The system employs intelligent data selection and dimensionality reduction techniques to contribute to **sustainability**.
Geographic-based [SS14]
SGeoL is a smart city architecture that prioritizes **Performance**, **Security**, **Interoperability**, and **Scalability**. It uses open protocols such as NGSI-LD, HTTP, and OAuth and provides developers with easy access through high-level RESTful APIs. The architecture includes SGeoL middleware and infrastructure layers, allowing efficient data storage and **flexible scalability**. SGeoL supports a range of data manipulation APIs, semantic support, storage formats, and advanced visualization.
Distributed Blockchain-SDN-based [SS15]
DistB-Condo is a **secure**, **load-balanced**, and blockchain-based model for smart condominiums. It incorporates IoT integration and software-defined networking (SDN) for centralized control, high **security**, high **reliability**, and **privacy** for IoT sensor data. It offers improved **efficiency**, advanced **security** measures, and a **balanced living experience**. Virtualization provides **load balancing**, **power saving**, and **cost-effectiveness** for smart condominiums.
Event-driven IoT [SS16]
This text describes an event-driven IoT architecture for **reliable** healthcare applications. It includes complex event processing for data analysis and various features integrated to handle data generated by sensors and devices. The architecture can improve healthcare applications by responding to **real-time** event triggers and analyzing data for better decision-making.
Smart City [SS17]
SmartGC proposes a garbage collection software architecture for smart cities that prioritizes **interoperability**, **security**, and **scalability**. It uses open standards and protocols for **interoperability**, cryptography for **protection**, and distributed elements for **scalability**. The result is a robust and **scalable** solution for efficient garbage collection and **secure** data management.
Layered [SS18]
This architecture prioritizes **security** and **privacy** through blockchain technology. It uses public and private blockchain mechanisms to secure small information units and ensure reliable and synchronized records. The fog layer enhances e-health system **performance**, allowing patients equipped with IoT sensors to transmit health data to the cloud for remote monitoring by doctors.
Cloud-based Secure Biometric [SS19]
The Health Data Management System in the healthcare cloud includes client, provider, and data center levels. Biometric authentication enhances **security**. The system uses dynamic signature features for user authentication, ensuring **energy and cost efficiency** through mobile devices. The Access Hierarchy based on user priority provides **fault tolerance**.
Multi-layered Cloud-Edge [SS20]
An architecture is proposed to secure smart healthcare systems using edge computing, which reduces the time and resources required to transfer patient data to the cloud. The framework includes encryption, access control, and identity management to ensure **data privacy** and **confidentiality**. This design enables efficient healthcare monitoring while maintaining patient data **security**.
SAPPARCHI [SS21]
SAPPARCHI is a **scalable** platform for Smart Cities that uses containerization technology to achieve horizontal **scalability**. This approach isolates application components and ensures that they can be scaled independently. The platform can efficiently handle increasing numbers of users, IoT devices, and sensors, making it a flexible solution for Smart City environments.
Layered [SS22]
The IoT system architecture uses sensor networks for **scalability**, standardized and modularized components for **maintainability**, access control and encryption for **security**, redundant components and distributed architectures for **availability**, and open and standardized protocols for **portability**.
Deep Learning based [SS23]

HealthFog system uses an ensemble deep-learning approach to diagnose heart diseases using patient data from various sensors. It ensures **data integrity**, **privacy**, **security**, **load balancing**, and **performance**. The system encrypts patient data when transmitted between IoT gateways, fog nodes, and cloud resources. It also includes a **load-balancing** mechanism and provisions for **data integrity**. Overall, it meets high-quality standards while ensuring the **security** and **privacy** of patient data and optimal **performance**.
Industrial Internet of Things (IIoT) [SS24]
The IIoT software architecture is designed to tackle industrial challenges focused on **scalability** and **interoperability**. It uses fog/edge computing to meet **real-time** and **low-latency** requirements. The architecture has four layers: Sensing/THINGS, Data Provider, Fog/Edge Computing, and Applications/Services. Each layer includes management and **security services** to address challenges such as **data security** and **real-time** capabilities. DDS middleware ensures **secure data transmission** over the Internet for a robust IIoT application **security** framework.
Distributed Edge-Cloud [SS25]
The paper proposes a secure healthcare monitoring framework integrating NDN with edge cloud technology. It includes encryption, authentication, and access control mechanisms to safeguard patient data. NDN allows **safe** data transfer, while edge cloud computing ensures real-time processing. These measures enable a **secure**, **scalable**, and **efficient** healthcare monitoring solution.
Blockchain-enabled [SS26]
The IoT architecture prioritizes **security** and **energy efficiency** using a cluster structure and distributed trust in the blockchain instead of traditional Proof of Work (POW) mechanisms. The SDN controller manages secure transactions and aims to create a resilient and **energy-efficient** IoT infrastructure by monitoring and blocking malicious nodes.
Layered Blockchain-Based SDN [SS27]
The paper proposes a secure routing architecture for SDN-enabled IoT networks that uses blockchain technology to ensure the **reliability** and **immutability** of data. The architecture includes an IoT gateway and SDN controller to facilitate **secure** communication between devices, offering a robust solution while maintaining **data integrity** and **reliability**.
Cloud computing and the Internet of Things [SS28]
The fog computing architecture integrates fog nodes with base stations, improving transmission efficiency. SDN facilitates a flexible and **scalable** fog node core network, optimizing network deployment flexibility. A layered fog computing model is introduced to address **data privacy** concerns in IoT, employing proxy virtual processors to analyze and categorize user data while protecting personal **privacy**. Two schemes for application virtual processor deployment, local and remote, offer flexibility based on the nature of data processing requirements.

4.2.2. What are the QRs identified in these IoT software system architectures?

Figure 2 shows the statistics about the QR found during the execution of this study. Each of them represents a challenge during the architecture design phase of an IoT software system. The solution for managing those QR codes is still emerging and needs to be identified and utilized as evidence of success for future developments. The graph (Figure 2) shows that security is the most present QR when designing IoT architecture software systems, influenced by performance and flexibility. The graph highlights the need for effective design features to address security concerns, such as cryptography, certificates, blockchain technology, and a layered approach to security.

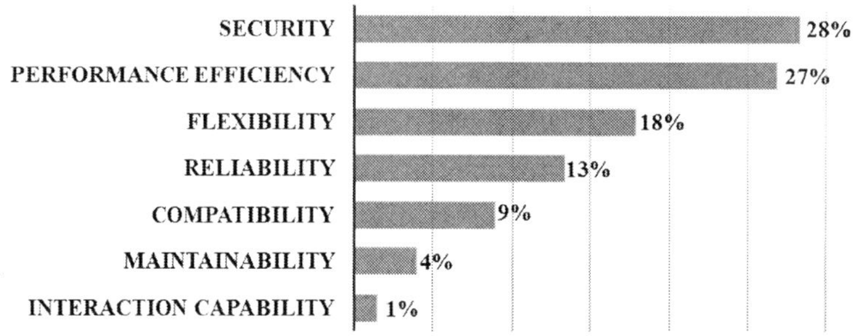

Figure 2. Statistics of the Quality Requirements found.

4.2.3. How are these QRs worked out in these IoT software system architectures?

The studied architectures have comprehensive design features (Table 5) addressing many QRs. Implementing these architectures uses technologies such as Kubernetes, PPSE, FogBus framework, blockchain technology, Docker, SDN, and others, resulting in a flexible and robust IoT software system design and implementation framework.

Table 4. Quality Requirement and Architectural Technologies.

Security		
Authenticity	- Authentication, authorization, and data access control. - IoT device authentication [Stojanov and Dobrilović 2021]. - Cloud-based biometric authentication [Shakil et al. 2020]. - OAuth protocol. - Amazon Simple Storage Service (Amazon S3).	[SS1] [SS2] [SS4] [SS8] [SS9] [SS11] [SS14] [SS15] [SS17] [SS18] [SS19] [SS20] [SS21] [SS22] [SS23] [SS24] [SS26]
Confidentiality	- Authentication, authorization, and data access control. - Searchable and encrypted edge-layer data (Privacy-Preserving Searchable Encryption - PPSE). - Blockchain technology. - Amazon Simple Storage Service (Amazon S3).	
Integrity	- FogBus framework [Tuli et al. 2019]. - Blockchain technology. - Hash.	
Resistance	- Counter-based DDoS Attack Detection (C-DAD) application for Software Defined Networks (SDN) [Bhayo et al. 2020]. - HTTP reverse proxy to protect REST services.	
Performance/Efficiency		
Resource Utilization	- Algorithm for Fog layer data selection (Data uniqueness and only important data) for transmission. - Wired communications. - Lightweight communications protocols (MQTT, HTTP, ZigBee, BLE, LoRaWAN, SigFox). - Hybrid energy design of the nodes (solar and AC power). - Network Function Virtualization (NFV). - Hypervisor (a virtual machine monitor, VMM, or virtualizer). - FogBus framework [Tuli et al. 2019]. - Load Balancing (LAB) scheme [Fan and Ansari 2020]. - Adapted Particle Swarm Optimization (APSO) [Chudhary and Sharma 2021] and Software Defined network (SDN). - Open-source technologies. - Long-Range Wide Area Network (LoRaWAN) technology. - Edge and Fog computing.	[SS3] [SS5] [SS6] [SS9] [SS13] [SS15] [SS23] [SS24]

Time Behaviour	- Data Distribution Protocol (DDS).	
Flexibility		
Adaptability	- Containerization technology (Docker). - Web-based applications. - Public/Subscriber protocols.	[SS2] [SS7] [SS9] [SS10] [SS12] [SS14] [SS21] [SS22] [SS25]
Scalability	- Multi-agent system (MAS) approach. - Amazon Simple Storage Service (Amazon S3). - Publish/Subscribe to standard messaging pattern. - Distributed computing architecture. - Infrastructure-as-a-service (IaaS). - Virtualization. - Software Defined Network (SDN). - Software Defined Virtual Private Network (SD-VPN). - Amazon Web Services (AWS). - Layered Architecture with loosely coupled components. - Serverless on Edge and Microservice in Fog. - Separated Databases (complex queries and simple queries).	
Reliability		
Availability	- Kubernetes framework (no single point of failure). - Separated Databases (complex queries and simple queries). - TCP-IP protocol on Client/Server architecture for data communication. - Reputation concept (Blockchain-based SDN-enabled network architecture) [Zeng et al. 2022]. - Software Defined Network (SDN). - Edge gateway. - Fog layer local data processing. - Data processing in the fog layer. - Multi-agent system (MAS) approach. - Fog layer in two levels: First Level – Intra mobility (User network): Nodes (Data transfer, device management, temporary local storage, notifications, and data consistency). Second Level – Extra mobility (Different domains): Smart Gateways (Local processing and database).	[SS9] [SS12] [SS15] [SS16] [SS21] [SS22] [SS27]
Fault Tolerance	- Kubernetes framework (no single point of failure).	
Compatibility		
Interoperability	- Containerization (Docker), separating the deployed software architecture from the hardware infrastructure. - RESTFul APIs. - Simple object access protocol (SOAP). - Publish/Subscribe to standard messaging pattern.	[SS9] [SS8] [SS10] [SS14] [SS22] [SS24]
Maintainability		
Modularity	- Layered Architecture with loosely coupled components.	[SS9] [SS21]
Reusability	- Containerization technology (Docker).	
Interaction Capability		
Operability	- Remote access to the deployed platform and its components (Web App and SSH).	[SS9]

4.3. What are the application domains and characteristics of their IoT software systems architectures that influence QRs?

By consolidating the data presented in the previous section, we obtain the key findings for our primary research question. The study identified 28 architectural solutions (See Table 2) corresponding to 21 QRs (See Figure 2). All architectural features were mapped to the QR (See Figure 2) and addressed as a reusable solutions catalog (See Table 4).

This study leverages the importance of the design phase when implementing an IoT software system. Overall, identifying the application domains and their characteristics is crucial in designing IoT software systems architectures that meet the specific QRs of each application domain and contribute to the successful deployment of IoT software systems in various fields, including healthcare.

5. Threats to Validity

Threats to validity in empirical studies always demand consideration. The first consideration is about the selection of the initial works. We used clear and objective inclusion and exclusion criteria (See Table 1) to compose the first papers from the Scopus database. Moreover, two related works (See section 2) were selected and used to refine our search procedure, reducing this threat and increasing reliability. Primary sources were identified, and inclusion and exclusion criteria, full reading, and snowballing techniques were performed for a concreted conclusive outcome.

Two researchers identified the articles to mitigate potential biases in the chosen papers and the interpretation bias among researchers, while another conducted a comprehensive review of the final set. The research protocol is designed to enhance the traceability of its data.

Finally, taxonomy bias was mitigated by referencing the works with the same objectives and theme (See section 2). The structure of these studies was considered and reused to map the goals of this work. Overall, every effort was made to conduct a secondary, well-conducted survey, aiming to reduce the threats to validity and increase the reliability and validity of the results.

6. Conclusion and Future Works

The development of IoT software systems architectures has been experiencing substantial growth, driven by increasing demand, adaptation requirements, and emerging challenges. Therefore, reusing successful cases in the software engineering process is crucial for supporting decision-making in designing IoT software systems architecture strategies. So, we collect data from primary sources to maintain the database of challenges and solutions, focusing on QRs. A list of IoT domain areas was introduced, an IoT architectures classification was demonstrated, and QRs architectural solutions were illustrated.

Based on what has been exposed, many software systems with cloud-based processing are observed to meet the requirements of energy efficiency and performance criteria, for example. The use of layers in architectures for a separation of concerns and good maintainability also remains a common decision in the design of the solutions. Security, leveraged by performance efficiency and flexibility, is the QR most considered when designing IoT software system architectures. Blockchain, cryptography, and SDN are very useful for mitigating these challenges.

More solutions and challenges must be added to this database for future research as continuous work. Furthermore, the data from related works and this study must be filtered and structured for application in a decision tree. This tool will aid in making decisions during the design phase of IoT software systems architecture development.

Acknowledgments

This work is partially supported by the Coordenação de Aperfeiçoamento de Pessoal de Nível Superior -Brasil (CAPES) -Finance Code 001 and by CNPq. Prof. Travasssos is a CNPq Researcher (305701/2022-3) and CNE FAPERJ (E-26/201.170/2021, which support this research.

References

Alreshidi, A. and Ahmad, A. (2019). Architecting software for the Internet of Things-based systems. Future Internet, v. 11, n. 7, p. 153.

Atzori, L., Iera, A. and Morabito, G. (2010). The Internet of Things: A survey. Computer Networks, v. 54, n. 15, p. 2787–2805.

Davami, F., Adabi, S., Rezaee, A. and Rahmani, A. M. (2021). Fog-based architecture for scheduling multiple workflows with high availability requirements. Computing, v. 104, n. 1, p. 169–208.

Fan, Q. and Ansari, N. (2020). Towards workload balancing in fog computing empowered IoT. IEEE Transactions on Network Science and Engineering, v. 7, n. 1, p. 253–262.

Gubbi, J., Buyya, R., Marusic, S. and Palaniswami, M. (2013). Internet of Things (IoT): A vision, architectural elements, and future directions. Future Generation Computer Systems, v. 29, n. 7, p. 1645–1660.

ISO/IEC-25010 (2023). ISO/IEC 25010. ISO 25010—Systems and Software Quality Requirements and Evaluation (SQuaRE)—System and software quality models. ISO.org. ISO/IEC Fdis 25010:2023. https://www.iso.org/obp/ui/en/#iso:std:iso-iec:25010:ed-2:v1:en. v. 2010, 2023.

Kuhrmann, M., Méndez, D. and Daneva, M. (2017). On the pragmatic design of literature studies in software engineering: an experience-based guideline. ESE, v. 22, n. 6, p. 2852–2891.

Mirani, A. A., Velasco-Hernandez, G., Awasthi, A. and Walsh, J. (2022). Key Challenges and Emerging Technologies in Industrial IoT architectures: A review. Sensors, v. 22, n. 15, p. 5836.

Motta, R. C., Silva, V. and Travassos, G. H. (2019). Towards a more in-depth understanding of the IoT Paradigm and its challenges. JSERD, v. 7, p. 3.

Nakagawa, E. and Antonio, P. [Eds.] (2023). Reference architectures for critical domains: Industrial Uses and Impacts. 1. ed. Springer Cham.

Razzaq, A. (20 oct 2020). A Systematic Review of software architectures for IoT systems and future direction to adopting a microservices architecture. SN Computer Science, v. 1, n. 6.

Tuli, S., Mahmud, R. and Buyya, R. (2019). FogBus: a blockchain-based lightweight framework for edge and fog computing. JSS, v. 154, p. 22–36.

Wöhlin, C. (2014). Guidelines for Snowballing in Systematic Literature Studies and a Replication in Software Engineering. EASE 14. p. 1–10.

Appendix A

Selected Studies

SS1	Ahmed, I., Zhang, Y., Jeon, G., et al. (2022). A blockchain- and artificial intelligence-enabled smart IoT framework for sustainable city. International Journal of Intelligent Systems, v. 37, n. 9, p. 6493–6507.
SS2	Ali, F., El–Sappagh, S., Islam, S. M. R., et al. (2021). An intelligent healthcare monitoring framework using wearable sensors and social networking data. Future Generation Computer Systems, v. 114, p. 23–43.
SS3	Asghar, A., Abbas, A., Khattak, H. A. and Khan, S. U. (2021). FOG-based architecture and load balancing methodology for health monitoring systems. IEEE Access, v. 9, p. 96189–96200.
SS4	Bhayo, J., Hameed, S. and Shah, S. A. (2020). An efficient Counter-Based DDOS attack detection framework leveraging software-defined IoT (SD-IoT). IEEE Access, v. 8, p. 221612–221631.
SS5	Chudhary, R. and Sharma, S. (2021). Fog-cloud assisted framework for Heterogeneous Internet of Healthcare Things. Procedia Computer Science, v. 184, p. 194–201.
SS6	Da Silveira, J. D. F., Da S Veloso, A. F., Reis, J. V. D., Soares, A. and Rabelo, R. a. L. (17 oct 2021). A new Low-Cost LORAWAN power switch for smart farm applications—2021 IEEE International Conference on Systems, Man, and Cybernetics (SMC).
SS7	Dineva, K. and Atanasova, T. (2021). Design of scalable IoT architecture based on AWS for smart livestock. Animals, v. 11, n. 9, p. 2697.
SS8	El-Basioni, B. M. M. and El-Kader, S. M. A. (2020). Laying the foundations for an IoT reference architecture for the agricultural application domain. IEEE Access, v. 8, p. 190194–190230.
SS9	Faid, A., Sadik, M. and Sabir, E. (2021). An agile AI and IoT-Augmented Smart Farming: a Cost-Effective cognitive weather station. Agriculture, v. 12, n. 1, p. 35.
SS10	Hajvali, M., Adabi, S., Rezaee, A. and Hosseinzadeh, M. (2021). Software architecture for IoT-based healthcare systems with cloud/fog service model. Cluster Computing, v. 25, n. 1, p. 91–118.
SS11	Hati, A. J. and Singh, R. R. (2021). Smart Indoor Farms: Leveraging technological advancements to power a sustainable agricultural revolution. AgriEngineering, v. 3, n. 4, p. 728–767.
SS12	Javed, A., Malhi, A. and Främling, K. (2020). Edge Computing-based Fault-Tolerant Framework: A Case Study on Vehicular Networks. International Wireless Communications and Mobile Computing (IWCMC),
SS13	Kaur, A., Sahil, S. and Sood, S. K. (2022). Cloud-FOG assisted Energy Efficient Architectural Paradigm for disaster evacuation. Information Systems, v. 107, p. 101732.
SS14	Pereira, J., Batista, T., Cavalcante, E., et al. (2022). A platform for integrating heterogeneous data and developing smart city applications. Future Generation Computer Systems, v. 128, p. 552–566.
SS15	Rahman, A., Islam, Md. J., Rahman, Z., et al. (2020). DISTB-ConDo: Distributed Blockchain-Based IoT-SDN model for smart condominium. IEEE Access, v. 8, p. 209594–209609.
SS16	Rahmani, A. M., Babaei, Z. and Souri, A. (2020). Event-driven IoT architecture for data analysis of reliable healthcare applications using complex event processing. Cluster Computing, v. 24, n. 2, p. 1347–1360.

SS17	Ramalho, M. S., Rossetti, R. J. F., Cacho, N. and Souza, A. S. (2020). SmartGC: a software architecture for garbage collection in smart cities. International Journal of Bio-inspired Computation, v. 16, n. 2, p. 79.
SS18	Safdar, Z., Farid, S., Qadir, M., et al. (2020). A novel architecture for the Internet of Things based E-Health systems. Journal of Medical Imaging and Health Informatics, v. 10, n. 10, p. 2378–2388.
SS19	Shakil, K. A., Zareen, F. J., Alam, M. and Jabin, S. (2020). BAMHealthCloud: A biometric authentication and data management system for healthcare data in the cloud. Journal of King Saud University - Computer and Information Sciences, v. 32, n. 1, p. 57–64.
SS20	Singh, A. and Chatterjee, K. (2021). Securing smart healthcare system with edge computing. Computers & Security, v. 108, p. 102353.
SS21	Souza, A., Cacho, N., Batista, T. and Ranjan, R. (2022). SAPPARCHI: an Osmotic Platform to Execute Scalable Applications on Smart City Environments. IEEE 15th International Conference on Cloud Computing (CLOUD).
SS22	Stojanov, Ž. and Dobrilović, D. (2021). Software architecture quality attributes of a layered sensor-based IoT system (short paper). Workshop Information Technologies: Algorithms, Models, Systems (ITAMS), p. 66–74.
SS23	Tuli, S., Basumatary, N., Gill, S. S., et al. (2020). HealthFog: An ensemble deep learning-based Smart Healthcare System for Automatic Diagnosis of Heart Diseases in integrated IoT and fog computing environments. Future Generation Computer Systems, v. 104, p. 187–200.
SS24	Ungurean, I. and Gaitan, N. C. (2020). A software architecture for the Industrial Internet of Things—A Conceptual model. Sensors, v. 20, n. 19, p. 5603.
SS25	Wang, X. and Cai, S. (2020). Secure healthcare monitoring framework integrating NDN-based IoT with edge cloud. Future Generation Computer Systems, v. 112, p. 320–329.
SS26	Yazdinejad, A., Parizi, R. M., Dehghantanha, A., Zhang, Q. and Choo, K. R. (2020). An Energy-Efficient SDN controller architecture for IoT networks with Blockchain-Based security. IEEE Transactions on Services Computing, v. 13, n. 4, p. 625–638.
SS27	Zeng, Z., Zhang, X. and Xia, Z. (2022). Intelligent Blockchain-Based secure routing for multidomain SDN-Enabled IoT networks. Wireless Communications and Mobile Computing, v. 2022, p. 1–10.
SS28	Zhang, C. (2020). Design and application of fog computing and Internet of Things service platform for smart city. Future Generation Computer Systems, v. 112, p. 630–640.

Avaliação Ergonômica de Interfaces Gráficas para Aplicações Mobile: Limites e Reflexões

Thiago Adriano Coleti[1], **Mayke Henrique Araújo do Amaral**[1]
Maria Renata de Mira Gobbo[1], **Marcelo Morandini**[2], **Clodis Boscarioli**[3]

[1]Universidade Estadual do Norte do Paraná
Bandeirantes – PR – Brasil

[2]Escola de Artes, Ciências e Humanidades da Universidade de São Paulo
São Paulo – SP – Brasil.

[3]Universidade Estadual do Oeste do Paraná
Cascavel – PR – Brazil

{thiago.coleti, mr.gobbo}@uenp.edu.br, maykedo.amaral@outlook.com

m.morandini@usp.br, boscarioli@gmail.com

Abstract. *Mobile applications are of strategic importance for companies as they enable easy access and greater proximity to their users. With this in mind, verifying that the interface components meet the design requirements is crucial to ensure the acceptance of these applications by the end user. This article examines the applicability of the Ergonomic Criteria developed in the 1990s to support usability testing of mobile devices by design and/or system evaluation teams. The empirical results show that, with some adaptations, they are also efficient for the inspection of mobile applications.*

Resumo. *As aplicações móveis têm uma importância estratégica para as empresas, pois viabilizam facilidade de acesso e maior proximidade com seus usuários. Com isso em mente, verificar se os componentes da interface atendem aos requisitos de design é fundamental para garantir a adoção facilitada dessas aplicações pelo usuário final. Este artigo explora a aplicabilidade dos Critérios Ergonômicos, desenvolvidos na década de 1990, para apoiar testes de usabilidade de dispositivos móveis por equipes de design e/ou avaliação de sistemas. Os resultados empíricos mostram que, com algumas adaptações, eles são também eficientes para inspeção de aplicativos móveis.*

1. Introdução

A evolução dos celulares para o conceito de *smartphone* promoveu mudanças no *design* das interfaces interativas para esses equipamentos, por terem telas menores, integração com sensores como GPS, acelerômetros e giroscópio, comandos de voz, gestos e telas *touchscreen*, além da possibilidade de manipulação de textos, vídeos, fotos, ambientes 3D e a combinação entre esses e outros mecanismos de interação [Neil 2014, Wroblewski 2011].

As empresas identificaram oportunidades para melhorar e/ou mudar suas estratégias de negócios, passando a disponibilizar produtos e serviços, como vendas, marketing, relações públicas entre outras, em aplicativos para *smartphone*. Tais aplicações implicaram na preocupação com a qualidade dessas interfaces a fim de garantir uma experiência apropriada ao usuário. Dentre as ações necessárias para essa finalidade está a inspeção ergonômica, que visa verificar se a interface está de acordo com guias, padrões de design ou critérios ergonômicos [Cybis et al. 2015].

Os Critérios Ergonômicos (CE) p por Dominique Scapin e Cristian Bastien na década de 1990 são uma composição de oito critérios e dezoito subcritérios que indicam ações que podem apoiar os projetos de interface a terem usabilidade [Scapin and Bastien 1997], e se referem à aparência e ao comportamento que componentes de interface devem dispor, uma vez que estes ajudam os desenvolvedores a selecionarem e configurarem seus projetos de forma mais assertiva.

Os critérios ergonômicos foram utilizados pela comunidade científica e empresarial no decorrer dos anos, em aplicações *desktop* e *web*, o que lhes garante um alto grau de eficiência e eficácia na avaliação de sistemas interativos. Embora amplamente utilizados, todo o seu desenvolvimento ocorreu em uma época na qual os padrões de interação e componentes de interface não eram voltados à aplicações *mobile*, pairando a interrogação sobre a eficácia desses critérios em sistemas interativos para *smartphone*, visto que estes possuem restrições que os sistemas *desktop* não possuem, a exemplo de tamanho de tela reduzido, interação realizada por toque na tela, entre outras.

Existem outras recomendações de interface, como as citadas por [Cybis et al. 2015]: Regras de Ouro de Sheiderman; Princípios de design do Android; Princípios de Diálogo da Norma ISSO/ABNT 9241:110. Tais normas e guias de estilos foram propostos por diferentes pesquisadores, empresas e fabricantes e, usualmente, são consideradas genéricas, pois se referem às interfaces em geral. Padrões de *design* para dispositivos móveis foram propostos por [Neil 2014], e critérios a serem atendidos foram apresentados por [Parente Da Costa et al. 2019] e por [Nascimento et al. 2016a], além das heurísticas de [Rocha et al. 2014], mas não abordam os critérios ergonômicos, de interesse neste estudo.

Neste contexto, o objetivo desta pesquisa foi o de realizar um estudo empírico para verificar se os CE podem ser aplicados para auxiliar a inspeção ergonômica em aplicativos para *smartphones* (Android e IOS), além de verificar se as questões disponíveis no ambiente ErgoList, um *website* desenvolvido para inspeçoes com base nos CE, para apoiar, também, inspeções em aplicativos móveis.Sobre o ErgoList[1], cabe destacar que é um compilado de 194 questões para auxiliar na quali e quantificação das características ergonômicas dos ambientes interativos, que têm o objetivo de estimular a investigação dos componentes das interfaces, e as questões que compõem esse questionário estão indexadas pelos Critérios Ergonômicos a que são relacionadas, motivos pelos quais foi utilizado.

Este artigo é conduzido a partir da seguinte questão básica: *O emprego dos Critérios Ergonômicos é adequado e suficiente para o projeto e avaliação das interações em aplicativos móveis de aparelhos celulares?* e, segue assim organizado: Na Seção 2 é apresentada a fundamentação teórica de sustentação da pesquisa; a Seção 3 traz os procedimentos metodológicos adotados; a Seção 4 contempla a análise dos dados produzidos nos experimentos realizados e, por fim, a Seção 5 abarca as considerações finais e perspectivas da pesquisa.

[1]Disponível em: https://usabilidade.github.io/

2. Aspectos teóricos e trabalhos relacionados

Esta seção apresenta aspectos teóricos que embasaram a pesquisa, como os conceitos de usabilidade e CE, padrões de *design*, e os trabalhos considerados como relacionados.

2.1. Usabilidade e Critérios Ergonômicos

A usabilidade é a principal característica de qualidade dos sistemas interativos. Segundo a ISO 25010 [Cybis et al. 2015], é a capacidade que sistemas computacionais proporcionam aos usuários de realizar tarefas específicas em contextos específicos com eficácia, eficiência e satisfação [Sobral 2019]. Por eficácia, entende-se a capacidade do usuário atingir seu objetivo ao utilizar a aplicação, já a eficiência é a capacidade do usuário de atingir seu objetivo com a melhor utilização de recursos, e, em relação à satisfação, trata-se das reações e emoções dos usuários na utilização da aplicação [Barreto et al. 2018].

A avaliação da usabilidade é fundamental no processo de *design* da Interação Humano-Computador (IHC), e pode ser conduzida por técnicas como: (a) avaliação heurística, na qual profissionais avaliam a interface e emitem parecer de valor de eventuais problemas que possam causar ruídos, barreiras ou bloqueios [Benyon 2011]; (b) inspeção de ergonomia, a qual visa garantir que a interface esteja de acordo com critérios ou *guidelines* ou boas práticas de IHC, como os CE, as Heurísticas de Nielsen e as Regras de Ouro de Shneiderman [Rocha et al. 2014] supracitadas; e (c) testes de usabilidade, que utiliza dos usuários reais conduzindo tarefas reais na aplicação, a fim de identificar problemas de usabilidade [Cybis et al. 2015].

Das técnicas de avaliação, a inspeção ergonômica é bastante adotada entre desenvolvedores e pesquisadores devido à sua praticidade de aplicação e pelo fato de poder envolver os usuários no processo [Benyon 2011]. As inspeções visam identificar problemas ergonômicos na interface e são aplicadas por meio de *checklists* criados com base em um critério ergonômico específico. Uma ferramenta de inspeção ergonômica é o ErgoList, um *website* que apresenta uma série de questões construídas a partir dos CE, respondidas pelos participantes da avaliação, e que disponibiliza um relatório final que sumariza as respostas de acordo com os CE [Cybis et al. 2015].

Os CE, de acordo com [Scapin and Bastien 1997] e [Cybis et al. 2015], proporcionam orientações que, se observadas por equipes de design podem aumentar significativamente a usabilidade da aplicação [Scapin and Bastien 1997]. E, podem ser aplicados em diversas etapas de um projeto de interface, como suporte à inspeção ergonômica e aos testes de usabilidade e avaliação heurística [Cybis et al. 2015]. Ainda, no que tange aos CE, de acordo com [Scapin and Bastien 1997] e [Cybis et al. 2015], são organizados em oito critérios e dezoito subcritérios, descritos a seguir:

1. **Condução**: este critério se refere ao fato de a interface precisar orientar, guiar e instruir o usuário na utilização da aplicação por meio do emprego de *design* adequado, mensagens, sons, rótulos dentre outros itens. A aplicação desse critério melhora a aprendizagem e a memorização, de forma a permitir que o usuário compreenda os objetivos e os recursos disponibilizados pela aplicação. Seus subcritérios são: **a) Convite** - descreve quanto à estética, confiabilidade e organização proporcionada pela interface; **b) Agrupamento/distinção de itens** - voltado para a organização visual da interface com base na *localização* dos componentes ou

no *formato de apresentação*; o **c) *Feedback* imediato** - subcritério que leva em consideração a necessidade de respostas da interface para cada ação realizada pelo usuário, a fim de identificar o estado do sistema e analisar o resultado das ações; e a **d) Legibilidade**, que aborda características lexicais presentes na informação, que auxiliam ou prejudicam a leitura dos usuários (espaçamento, brilho, contraste são exemplos);

2. **Carga de trabalho**: busca a redução da carga de trabalho do usuário nas interações e a eliminação de informações ou ações desnecessárias para as tarefas. Esse critério abrange os seguintes subcritérios: **a) Brevidade**: busca a redução da carga de trabalho cognitiva e física dos usuários por meio da limitação do número de entradas e saídas ou pela redução ou automação de ações que podem ser antecipadas ou padronizadas pela aplicação, por exemplo, ao salvar um documento no *Microsoft Word* o mesmo já adota, por padrão, a extensão do arquivo (.doc), ou o preenchimento automático de opções *default* em caixas de seleção; e **b) Densidade informacional**: esse subcritério trata da carga de trabalho do usuário ao visualizar, analisar e utilizar grandes volumes de informações na tela, o que tendem a dificultar sua análise e interpretação. Nesse sentido, o projetista deve buscar uma interface minimalista ou, pelo menos, aplicando critérios para apresentação de recursos que sejam realmente necessários para o usuário.
3. **Controle explícito**: critério relacionado ao controle do usuário sobre as ações. Os subcritérios são: **a) Ações Explícitas** e **b) Controle do Usuário**, que orientam aspectos referentes ao controle da execução das ações pelos usuários como necessidade de comando explícito do usuário para ações críticas ou longas e capacidade de interromper, cancelar ou suspender uma determinada ação no sistema.
4. **Adaptabilidade**: refere-se à capacidade de adequação da interface às necessidades e preferências do usuário por meio da disponibilização de diferentes opções. Composto pelos subcritérios de: **a) Flexibilidade**, para a personalização da interface de acordo com os hábitos e preferência do usuário; e **b) Experiência do usuário**, que é a adequação da interface de acordo com os níveis de conhecimento do usuário.
5. **Gestão de erros**: esse critério orienta quanto aos recursos de interface para evitar ou mitigar a ocorrência de erros, bem como permitir a recuperação do sistema ao seu estado normal, quando eles ocorrerem. Seus subcritérios são: **a) Proteção contra erros** que indica ações de prevenção como validações ou formatação de campos de entrada de dados; **b) Qualidade das mensagens de erros** orientam quanto a apresentação dos erros aos usuários; e **c) Correção de erros**, relacionado à disponibilidade de recursos necessários para corrigir o erro.
6. **Consistência**: diz respeito à padronização dos elementos das interfaces de forma a manter contextos similares quando estes pertencerem ao mesmo domínio;
7. **Significado dos códigos**: orienta quanto à relação existente entre um elemento do domínio e o componente de interface ou ação relacionada. Esse critério visa estabelecer uma adequação semântica e favorecer o aprendizado, a memorização e o reconhecimento por parte do usuário.
8. **Compatibilidade**: orienta quanto à compatibilidade do sistema com as expectativas do usuário, necessidades de tarefas e do domínio.

Para inspeções ergonômicas de interface, os CE apresentam os conceitos e as diretrizes para construção e avaliação de interfaces. Já o processo de inspeção pode ser feito pelo emprego das questões do ErgoList, que instanciam os CE. Assim, pode-se afirmar que os CE, por meio das questões do ErgoList, proporcionam orientações que, se observadas por equipes de *design*, podem aumentar significativamente a usabilidade da aplicação [Scapin and Bastien 1997]. Os critérios podem ser aplicados em diversas etapas de um projeto de IHC, como suporte à inspeção ergonômica, e também, aos testes de usabilidade e à avaliação heurística [Cybis et al. 2015].

A próxima seção discute sobre padrões de *design* para aplicações móveis.

2.2. Interfaces gráficas para dispositivos móveis

A construção de interfaces para dispositivos móveis tem padrões de *design* a serem seguidos. Por padrões, entende-se representações válidas do senso comum em um determinado campo que apoiam a construção de aplicações interativas. No que tange aos aplicativos para dispositivos móveis, mais especificamente os *smartphones* e *tablets*, uma série de mudanças foram necessárias para permitir uma melhor adequação das estratégias de design e interação às características dos dispositivos móveis [Neil 2014, Wroblewski 2011].

Também se considera o fato de que aplicações *desktop* e *web* são construídas para atividades às quais o usuário está sentado, concentrado e com objetivos bem específicos para sua tarefa. Nos aplicativos móveis, o usuário desempenha tarefas que podem estar compartilhadas com outras e podem interagir com o dispositivo utilizando gestos, comandos de voz e toque com a mão, algo menos praticado nas aplicações *desktop*. Exemplo da forma de interação com dispositivos móveis é o uso de aplicativos para GPS, os quais o usuário divide a atenção entre dirigir e utilizar o aplicativo [Giovanni 2013]. O GPS e outros sensores também influenciaram a mudança dos padrões de *design*, pois os dispositivos móveis permitem experiências diferenciadas, integradas com imagens reais e/ou que permitem a imersão em informações em tempo real [Neil 2014].

Sem os padrões de design para aplicações móveis, o processo de criação das interfaces *mobile* seria mais complexo e provavelmente comprometido, implicando na produção de interfaces ruins, com baixa usabilidade, que proporcionariam uma experiência inadequada para os usuários [Cybis et al. 2015, Neil 2014]. Pode-se afirmar que existiria um risco de prevalecer uma ação de miniaturização e adaptação indevida de componentes de interface e na replicação da experiência *desktop* e *web*, o que poderia produzir interfaces complexas, com excesso de conteúdos e dificuldades de interação e, provavelmente, não permitiriam a utilização de todas as possibilidades propiciadas pelos *smartphones*[Nudelman 2013].

A utilizações dos CE e padrões de *design* tem por objetivo auxiliar na construções de interfaces de fácil interação. Como já citado, os CE foram criados para priorizar as demandas das aplicações *web* e *desktop*, enquanto os padrões de *design* têm por finalidade atender as características dos dispositivos móveis. Estudos relacionados aos CE e aos padrões de *design* não são novos na área de IHC, mas continuam sendo realizados por pesquisadores e desenvolvedores [Coleti et al. 2015, Viana et al. 2021, Filho et al. 2022] na busca por qualidade dos produtos, no entanto, ainda são pouco usados no contexto móvel. A seguir, dois exemplos dessas pesquisas, consideradas correlatas, são apresentadas.

2.3. Trabalhos Relacionados

Nascimento [Nascimento et al. 2016b], criou seu próprio método de avaliação, que envolve tanto a usabilidade quanto a experiência do usuário para aplicações móveis, avaliações que usualmente são feitas em separado, por diferentes técnicas de avaliação, salientando que a utilização de dois métodos separados, além de levar mais tempo, pode deixar de identificar questões importantes de usabilidade. Com isso, propuseram o *Userbility*, que tem por objetivo auxiliar na identificação de problemas de usabilidade e experiência de usuário em uma única avaliação. Essa técnica apresentou um grau de precisão maior do que a concorrente (UUGA), resultando em menos resultados incertos, além de permitir que os inspetores apontassem problemas específicos e sugestões de melhorias nas aplicações avaliadas.

Costa [Da Costa et al. 2019] apresentou uma revisão sistemática da literatura que teve como objetivo apontar quais heurísticas e métricas de usabilidade estão sendo mais utilizadas, tanto na literatura acadêmica quanto na indústria. Em seus resultados, foi apresentado um conjunto de heurísticas de usabilidade específicas, focadas em aplicações móveis que considera principalmente o usuário, a tarefa, o contexto e a carga cognitiva como importantes atributos de usabilidade. Sua principal motivação vem do fato dos CE não terem sido criados para avaliar a usabilidade de aplicativos móveis.

Ambos os trabalhos reconhecem o crescimento na utilização dos *smartphones* para as mais diversas finalidades, e também tem por objetivo criar métricas para avaliar a usabilidade de suas aplicações, cada qual seguindo seus próprios métodos. Embora os trabalhos relacionados tenham o mesmo objetivo em comum, analisar a usabilidade de aplicativos móveis, não analisaram a adequação dos CE, mas sim, criaram novas métricas para avaliar a usabilidade dos aplicativos móveis. A próxima seção traz os materiais e métodos para a inspeção com os CE em aplicativos de ambientes móveis.

3. Materiais e Métodos

Esta seção apresenta as etapas para a condução desta pesquisa, que compreenderam a escolha dos aplicativos, condução da inspeção, a análise dos dados e discussão dos resultados.

3.1. Escolha dos aplicativos

Para a avaliação, foram considerados aplicativos para serviços públicos, plataformas de entretenimento com vídeos e músicas, ensino de idiomas, serviços financeiros e mensagens, vislumbrando a diversidade de aplicativos conhecidamente utilizados pela população em geral e disponíveis para *download* de forma parcial ou totalmente gratuita em lojas virtuais.

Também foi considerada a variedade de componentes de interface possíveis de utilização, as diferenças nos modelos de interação e a capacidade de manipulação de mídias disponíveis nos aplicativos. Esses aspectos permitiram assumir que as interfaces já estariam bem consolidadas e de acordo com padrões de *design*, o que forneceria mais subsídios para analisar a adequação dos critérios ergonômicos. Os seguintes aplicativos foram selecionados para inspeção:

- **Carteira Digital de Trânsito**: aplicativo para acesso às versões digitais de documentos e informações de débitos e infrações do Departamento Estadual de Trânsito (DETRAN), na versão 3.3.0 tanto para IOS quanto para Android;
- **Duolingo**: aplicativo para o ensino de idiomas nas versões 6.72.0 para IOS e 4.68.5 para Android, ambas de acesso gratuito;
- **Gmail**: aplicativo de gestão de e-mails da Google, nas versões 6.0.200531 para IOS e 2020.05.17.31313047 para Android;
- **Google Drive**: aplicativo da Google para armazenamento de arquivos em nuvem, nas versões 4.2020.24202 para IOS e a 2.20.241.03.35 para Android;
- **Minha Claro Móvel**: aplicativo para autoatendimento da operadora de telefonia Claro, versão 8.2.1 para IOS e 8.4.18-2 para Android.
- **Netflix**: aplicativo de streaming de filmes e séries, na 12.36.0 para IOS e a 7.60.1 build 6334929 para Android.
- **Nubank**: aplicativo de serviços bancários digitais, na versão 7.1.58 para IOS e 5.48.81 para Android.
- **Spotify**: aplicativo de streaming de músicas, versões 8.5.60.881 para IOS e 8.5.62.904 para Android.
- **Trello**: aplicativo que tem como objetivo permitir a gestão, colaboração, organização e monitoramento de projetos, versões 2020.8.1 para IOS e 2020.7.14065-production para Android.
- **WhatsApp**: aplicativo de envio de mensagens de texto, áudio e imagens, nas versões 2.20.61 para IOS e 2.20.189 para Android.

3.2. Condução da inspeção

As inspeções seguiram protocolo definido pelos pesquisadores autores e realizadas por um conjunto de estudantes em último semestre do curso de Sistemas de Informação com conhecimentos em IHC adquiridos em disciplinas já cursadas, nas quais atividades específicas de avaliação foram conduzidas, em conjunto com um pesquisador com conhecimentos avançados em projeto e avaliação de *design*/usabilidade e experiente no uso dos CE, que responderam ao *checklist* do ErgoList para inspecionar as interfaces dos aplicativos supracitados, analisando os conceitos e a aplicabilidade de cada questão e o critério/subcritério ergonômico respectivo aos componentes da interface.

Primeiramente, foi feita a inspeção de todos os aplicativos selecionados. Posteriormente, os resultados foram apresentados para o pesquisador-responsável que os revisou e verificou eventuais inconsistências ou dúvidas nos mesmos. Após esta atividade, o resultado da avaliação foi consolidado em um relatório final, que foi analisado pelos demais pesquisadores envolvidos na pesquisa.

A inspeção se baseou na premissa de que os CE não estariam vinculados, especificamente, aos componentes de interface e, embora propostos em um período no qual interfaces *desktop* predominavam e as interfaces *web* estavam no seu início, as diretrizes baseavam-se em conceitos de interação não atrelados a um limite temporal, podendo ser aplicadas a interfaces de dispositivos móveis. Assim, foram consideradas as questões disponibilizadas pelo ErgoList, que instanciam as diretrizes propostas pelos CE e permitem, por meio da inspeção, atribuir um valor ou uma nota para um recurso de interface.

O processo de análise dos critérios foi iniciado com uma discussão sobre os resultados possíveis na inspeção. Por resultados possíveis, entende-se o resultado da análise da aplicabilidade da questão para a avaliação de interfaces para dispositivos móveis, sendo definidas quatro classes de resultados:

- AT (Apropriado Totalmente): a questão permitiu a inspeção em um aplicativo sem adequações ou alterações em seu contexto original;
- AP (Apropriado Parcialmente): a questão permitiu a inspeção em um aplicativo, mas com adequações, alterações ou ressalvas em relação ao seu contexto original;
- PA (Pouco Apropriado): a questão não permitiu a inspeção em um aplicativo;

Na sequência, foi realizada uma atividade de **Estudo/exploração do aplicativo**, na qual cada aplicativo foi utilizado de forma a serem exploradas suas funcionalidades observando os padrões de *design* utilizados e aspectos de ergonomia aplicados. Nessa primeira fase, o objetivo principal era a familiarização com os recursos dos aplicativos.

Com conhecimento sobre as funcionalidades dos aplicativos, os mesmos passaram pelo processo de **Inspeção Ergonômica com o ErgoList**. Nessa fase, os avaliadores realizaram a inspeção das interfaces gráficas como um todo, ou seja, não foram selecionadas tarefas específicas porque o objetivo era o de verificar a adequação das questões dos CE com os componentes de interface e com a interação dos aplicativos.

Os avaliadores inspecionaram a interface utilizando o texto original da questão, comparando-o com os aspectos de *design* existentes nas ferramenta. Quando o resultado foi positivo para essa análise, 1 (um) ponto foi atribuído na classe **Apropriado Totalmente (AT)**. Um exemplo de questão enquadrada nessa classe pertence ao CE Consistência e tem o texto: *Os ícones são distintos uns dos outros e possuem sempre o mesmo significado de uma tela para outra?*, nesse caso, a utilização dos ícones é ampla em aplicativos móveis e ainda requer os cuidados indicados pela questão.

Caso a questão do ErgoList não permitisse a inspeção com seu texto original, os avaliadores realizavam uma **Análise de adequações**. Nesse processo, os pesquisadores analisaram se era possível fazer ajustes ou atualizações no texto da questão de forma que a mesma pudesse ser usada sem alterar seu objeto de inspeção. Para essas questões, foi atribuído um ponto na categoria **AP (Apropriado Parcialmente)**.

Um exemplo dessa adequação foi na questão do CE Ações Explícitas, com o texto: *Para iniciar o processamento dos dados, o sistema sempre exige do usuário uma ação explícita de "ENTER"?*. A adequação deu-se na substituição do ENTER por outras ações como o clique, comando de voz, gestos e outros inerentes da interação *mobile* uma vez que o uso literal da tecla ENTER é pouco praticado nos aplicativos móveis, o que modificou o texto para *Para iniciar o processamento dos dados, o sistema sempre exige do usuário um comando explícito como um clique, um comando de voz ou um gesto?*.

Em caso de negativa para as duas possibilidades anteriores, a questão era classificada como PA (Pouco Apropriado), ou seja, sua utilização não seria viável para inspecionar um aplicativo móvel, pois tem seu conteúdo fortemente relacionado aos conceitos de aplicações *desktop* da década de 90, como é o caso da questão *Existe a possibilidade do usuário obter a lista de comandos básicos da linguagem*, do subcritério Brevidade, que considera o uso de comando de texto em aplicativos móveis.

Destaca-se que o ErgoList contém 194 questões divididas nos 18 grupos (critérios/subcritérios). Assim, para inspecionar os 10 aplicativos, um total de 1940 questões foram resolvidas. Os valores obtidos por essa inspeção, conforme atividades supracitadas, são mostrados na Tabela 1.

4. Análise dos Dados

Esta seção evidencia os resultados da inspeção e traz considerações sobre os CE e seus enquadramentos para a inspeção de aplicativos móveis (Tabela 1). Os números apresentados para cada classe representa o número de inspeções.

Tabela 1. Resultado das inspeções com os CE em aplicativos móveis

Critério	Subcritério/Subsubcritério	AT	AP	PA	Total
1 - Condução	1.1 - Presteza	51	44	75	170
	1.2 - Agrupamento e distinção - 1.2.1 - Por localização	58	20	32	110
	1.2 - Agrupamento e distinção - 1.2.1 - Por formato	86	24	60	170
	1.3 *Feedback* imediato	72	10	38	120
	1.4 Legibilidade	187	17	66	270
2 - Carga de Trabalho	2.1 - Brevidade - 2.1.1 - Concisão	67	18	55	140
	2.1 - Brevidade - 2.1.2 - Ações Mínimas	22	4	24	50
	2.2 - Densidade Informacional	69	11	10	90
3 - Controle Explícito	3.1 - Ações explícita	24	10	6	40
	3.1 - Controle do usuário	20	8	12	40
4 - Adaptabilidade	4.1 - Flexibilidade	6	14	10	30
	4.2 - Experiência do usuário	26	3	31	60
5 - Gestão de Erros	5.1 - Proteção contra erros	22	6	42	70
	5.2 - Qualidade da mensagem de erro	62	7	21	90
	5.3 - Correção de erros	10	4	36	50
6 - Consistência	Não há	78	8	24	110
7 - Significados de códigos e denominações	Não há	83	14	23	120
8 - Compatibilidade	Não há	108	25	77	210
Total	–	**1051**	**247**	**642**	**1940**
Percentuais	–	**54%**	**13%**	**33%**	**100%**

Os dados apresentados na Tabela 1 permitem concluir que não há um critério totalmente aplicável ou não, uma vez que os percentuais médios mostram a classe com maior pontuação (AT) teve 54% dos apontamentos e a análise individual dos critérios mostra o CE *Densidade Informacional* com maior percentual de AT (77%), e se consideradas as questões passíveis de adequações, o percentual de adequação sobe para 67%, sendo o CE de *Densidade Informacional* com o melhor resultado de AT + AP (89%). Esses resultados foram considerados pelos pesquisadores envolvidos como favoráveis, desde que observadas as particularidades de certas questões, uma vez que 33% foram indicadas como Não Apropriadas, percentual relativamente alto e que indica a necessidade de muita atenção ao utilizar alguns critérios e questões para inspecionar um aplicativo móvel, pois podem gerar um indicativo de problema ou de impossibilidade de inspeção para um recurso que não pode ser inspecionado pelas questões.

Na sequência, são apresentadas considerações a respeito dos CE e algumas questões a título de exemplificação das análises realizadas, e como forma de apoiar a decisão pelo uso, ou não, dos CE para avaliação de aplicativos móveis. Para as considerações dos critérios, os mesmos foram classificados nas seguintes classes:

- CE com mais de 66% de apontamentos para classe AT;
- CE com mais de 66% de apontamentos para a soma das classes AT e AP. Para essas considerações, foi considerado que os CE não atingiram 66% de indicações para classe AT ou AP de forma isolada, mas que somados permitem chegar nesse valor.
- CE com mais de 66% dos apontamentos para classe PA.

Usou-se o valor de 66%, por decisão de projeto, por não haver uma métrica clara sobre como avaliar a eficácia e eficiência desses critérios. Na próxima subseção, serão apresentadas as considerações para os CE com questões apropriadas.

4.1. Considerações sobre critérios/subcritérios com questões apropriadas

Nesta análise, considerou-se os critérios com pontuação miníma de 66 pontos no critério AT, sendo eles: Legibilidade, Densidade Informacional, Mensagem de Erro, Consistência e Significado de códigos e denominações. Os valores que levaram a esse resultado são mostrados na Tabela 2.

Tabela 2. CE com indicações de AT superior à 66%

Critério/Subcritério	AT	Questões Ergo-List	% Final
Condução/Legibilidade	187	270	69%
Carga de Trabalho/Densidade Informacional	69	90	77%
Gestão de Erros/Mensagem de erros	62	90	69%
Consistência	78	110	71%
Significado de código	83	120	69%

Assumiu-se que esses resultados ocorreram pelo fato de esses critérios orientarem quanto a requisitos primários de *design* de interface e que estão intimamente ligados com a usabilidade e à experiência que o usuário tem ao utilizar um aplicativo.

Nos aplicativos móveis, a preocupação com questões de arquitetura de informação foi evidenciada em virtude das características do dispositivos, como o tamanho da tela, orientação do uso do disposição e/ou diversidade de formas de interação. Assim, questões relacionadas aos critérios de Legibilidade e Densidade Informacional são constantes para os *designers* desses aplicativos. Portanto, questões do ErgoList voltadas a inspecionar recursos para o acesso, a visualização e a compreensão dos conteúdos na tela se mostraram aplicáveis para os aplicativos móveis.

Ainda, os aplicativos móveis levaram à grande expansão do uso de software por pessoas que não são especialistas, o que demanda dos *designers* preocupações com a forma de se comunicar, pela interface, com essas pessoas. As mensagens apresentadas devem ser claras, objetivas e compreensíveis e devem orientar o usuário quando uma tarefa ou recurso são utilizados de maneira indevida, sem apresentar mensagens técnicas e/ou exageradas. Nesse contexto, 70% das questões do subcritério de mensagem de erro foram consideradas apropriadas.

Sobre as questões dos critérios de Significado de códigos e Consistência, estas ampararam preocupações relacionadas à capacidade de a interface transmitir a informação sobre o recurso disponível e se fazer ser compreendida e lembrada pelo usuário. Em relação aos Significados de códigos, uma aplicativo de serviços bancários deve usar termos compreensíveis para o usuário dentro daquele domínio específico de uso, por exemplo. Para exemplificar o critério de Consistência, assumindo um aplicativo para ensino de idiomas, este deve manter um mesmo padrão de interface para exercícios similares, de forma que o usuário possa facilmente se recordar de como resolvê-los e não precise ter que (re)aprender as técnicas de resolução para cada interação.

Na Tabela 3 são apresentadas algumas questões consideradas Aplicáveis Totalmente para os critérios supracitados.

Tabela 3. Relação de questões do ErgoList para critérios Aplicados Totalmente

Critério	Questão
Legibilidade	O uso exclusivo de maiúsculas nos textos é evitado?
	Os rótulos de campos começam com uma letra maiúscula, e as letras restantes são minúsculas?
Densidade Informacional	As telas apresentam somente os dados e informações necessários e indispensáveis para o usuário em sua tarefa?
Mensagem de erro	As mensagens de erro ajudam a resolver o problema do usuário, fornecendo com precisão o local e a causa específica ou provável do erro, bem como as ações que o usuário poderia realizar para corrigi-lo?
	As mensagens de erro estão isentas de abreviaturas e/ou códigos gerados pelo sistema operacional?
Consistência	Os ícones são distintos uns dos outros e possuem sempre o mesmo significado de uma tela para outra?
	A localização dos dados é mantida consistente de uma tela para outra?
Significado de códigos	Os títulos das páginas de menu são distintos entre si?
	As denominações dos títulos estão de acordo com o que eles representam?

Na próxima subseção são discutidas as questões do ErgoList que também podem ser usadas para inspeção, porém, com adequações.

4.2. Considerações sobre CE com questões apropriadas com adequações

Nessa análise, como dito, discutem-se os critérios que tiveram mais de 66% dos pontos somando as categorias de Apropriado Totalmente e Apropriado Parcialmente, excluindo os critérios discutidos na subseção anterior. Essa análise é justificada pela necessidade de demonstrar que há critérios que podem ser aplicados na inspeção se o avaliador considerar que adequações são necessárias para atender características específicas do desenvolvimento de aplicativos móveis. Os percentuais e valores dos CE discutidos nessa subseção sã mostrados na Tabela 4.

Ao analisar as questões dos critérios indicados, percebeu-se que as adequações seriam bastante pontuais, uma vez cinco critérios tiveram indicativo médio de adequação das questões de 15%. Exceção a esse número foi o critério/subcritério de Adaptabilidade/Flexibilidade, que teve um percentual e ajustes de 47% das inspeções. Para questões com adequações pontuais, percebeu-se que tratavam-se de aspectos que herdavam características muito comuns para aplicativos *desktop*, mas que são empregadas em aplicativos móveis de maneira ligeiramente diferente, em casos onde a evolução da tecnologia exigiu

Tabela 4. CE com indicações de AT+AP superior à 66%

Critério/Subcritério	AT+AP	**Questões Ergo-List**	% **Final**
Condução/Agrupamento por Localização	78	110	71%
Condução/Agrupamento por Formato	110	170	66%
Condução/*Feedback* imediato	82	120	68%
Controle Explicito/Ações Explícitas	34	40	85%
Controle Explícito/Controle do Usuário	28	40	70%
Adaptabilidade / Flexibilidade	20	30	67%

tal mudança. Exemplos de questões e suas propostas de adequações são mostradas na Tabela 5.

Tabela 5. Exemplos de adequações para questões do ErgoList

CE	Questão	Possível Adequação
Agrupamento e distinção por Formato	Os cabeçalhos de uma tabela estão diferenciados pelo emprego de cores diferentes, letras maiores ou sublinhadas?	Há diferentes padrões de *design* para tabelas em aplicativos móveis, conforme mostrado por [Neil 2014] e todos tem suas características de escrita de cabeçalho, assim, a questão poderia inspecionar se o cabeçalho está de acordo com o padrão de tabela aplicado.
Feedback Imediato	Quando, durante a entrada de dados, o sistema torna-se indisponível ao usuário, devido a algum processamento longo, o usuário é avisado desse estado do sistema e do tempo dessa indisponibilidade? e O sistema fornece ao usuário informações sobre o tempo de processamentos demorados?	Questões relacionadas ao Feedback de processamento devem evitar indicativos de tempo e percentual de processamento e considerar uma provável falta dessas informações, pois os mesmos podem ser feitos de maneira assíncrona, algo não tão difundido na década de 90.
Ações Explícitas	Para iniciar o processamento dos dados, o sistema sempre exige do usuário uma ação explícita de "ENTER"?	Adequar a questão para considerar que o comando o usuário pode ser feito por comando de voz, gestos ou clique, uma vez que o uso literal da tecla ENTER é pouco praticado nos aplicativos móveis.

Em relação ao subcritérios de Flexibilidade, há somente três questões relacionadas à capacidade de personalizar recursos do aplicativo e essa característica nem sempre é adotada por aplicativos móveis, que costumam ser muito rígidos quanto às suas funcionalidades. Os aplicativos permitem a personalização de alguns recursos inerentes ao seu uso, por exemplo, selecionar as funções mais utilizadas em um painel de acesso rápido ou em uma lista de favoritos, mas o processo de execução da funcionalidade não costuma ser flexível, até mesmo por questões estruturais e arquiteturais da aplicação. Assim, houve a necessidade de adequações nas questões para contemplar o que é flexibilidade em aplicativos móveis, por exemplo, a questão: *"Ao usuário é permitido personalizar o diálogo, através da definição de macros?"* foi adaptada para: *"Ao usuário é permitido selecionar recursos para uma lista de acesso rápido?"*, o que está mais próximo dos modelos de interação praticados nos dispositivos móveis.

A próxima subseção discute os critérios considerados como pouco apropriados.

4.3. Considerações sobre CE com questões pouco apropriadas

Aqui se enquadraram os critérios para os quais as questões não atingiram os 2/3 de avaliação apropriada ou apropriada com adequações. São critérios dessa análise: Presteza; Brevidade/Concisão; Brevidade/Ações Mínimas; Adaptabilidade/Experiência do Usuário; Gestão de Erros/Proteção Contra Erros; Gestão de Erros/Correção de Erros; e Compatibilidade. Exemplos de questões Não Apropriadas ou que Não se Aplicam são apresentados, com sugestões de adequações, na Tabela 6.

Tabela 6. Exemplos de questões Não Apropriadas ou Não Aplicáveis

CE	Questão	Dificuldade em aplicar
Brevidade	Existe a possibilidade do usuário obter a lista de comandos básicos da linguagem?	Com raras exceções para aplicativos específicos, a utilização de comandos de texto não é uma prática comum em aplicativos móveis.
Ações Mínimas	Na realização das ações principais em uma caixa de diálogo, o usuário tem os movimentos de cursor minimizados através da adequada ordenação dos objetos?	Nos aplicativos móveis não há o uso de cursores, conforme era aplicável em ferramentas *desktop*. O uso de toque, gestos e fala é predominante na manipulação de informações.
Proteção contra erros	As teclas de funções perigosas encontram-se agrupadas e/ou separadas das demais no teclado?	Embora o teclado tradicional é emulado na tela do celular, com opções de teclado numérico e com símbolos, a separação está mais orientada à facilidade de uso.
Correção de erros	Os comandos para DESFAZER e REFAZER o diálogo estão diferenciados?	A utilização desses botões não foi identificada na inspeção.

As questões apontadas na Tabela 6 estão fortemente vinculadas às características específicas das aplicações *desktop* e *web* da década de 90 e do começo dos anos 2000. Tal vinculação impede o uso e/ou adequação dessas questões em aplicativos móveis. Dessa forma, algumas dessas questões devem ser evitadas ou substituídas.

Como exemplos de substituições, podem ser destacados: (a) para o critério de *Brevidade*, uma nova questão sugerida é: *O aplicativo disponibiliza um tutorial com as principais funcionalidades da ferramenta?*; (b) para o subcritério de *Ações mínimas*, pode ser criada uma questão que verifique se o aplicativo dispensa o usuário de ações redundantes ou desnecessárias; (c) para os subcritérios relacionados ao critério de *Gestão de Erros,* no subcritério *Proteção contra erros*, uma sugestão de questão seria: *As interfaces evidenciam e protegem recursos que inicializam funções perigosas?*; e (d) para o subcritério de *Correção de erros*, em aplicativos móveis, ações de *desfazer* podem se complexas devido às arquiteturas distribuídas da maioria das aplicações, mas podem ser sugeridas questões relacionadas a um histórico de ações ou funções.

5. Ameaças à validade

As limitações e ameaças para os resultados desta pesquisa estão no fato de os dados refletirem a análise dos pesquisadores que conduziram a inspeção e pelo fato da inspeção ter sido realizada em um conjunto restrito de aplicativos. Assim, considerando que uma inspeção ergonômica tem seus resultados influenciados por fatores subjetivos, relacionados à percepção do(s) inspetor(es) em relação ao problema, e que os aplicativos podem variar em função dos requisitos e padrões de *design*, os resultados desta pesquisa ficam restritos às estratégias de inspeção e análise conduzidas pelos pesquisadores, podendo variar à medida que outros aplicativos venham a ser inspecionados por outas pessoas, ou que os aplicativos-alvo de inspeção mudem. No entanto, trazem evidências importantes sobre a constatação da aplicabilidade dos CE à aplicações móveis, ainda que com necessidade de adaptações.

Ainda, todos os CE tiveram questões enquadradas nas três categorias de análise, e atribuiu-se essa distribuição de avaliações aos fatores: (a) a inspeção ergonômica tem seus resultados influenciados pela subjetividade do avaliador, que pode ter uma interpretação direcionada ou enviesada em alguma análise; (2) todos os aplicativos foram inspecionados em todas as questões e, uma vez que os aplicativos tinham objetivos diferentes, componentes de interface distintos e modelos de interação diversos, pode ter ocorrido algum viés na resposta.

6. Considerações Finais

Neste artigo discutiu-se, com base na análise das questões do ErgoList, a adequação dos Critérios Ergonômicos como guia para o desenvolvimento e avaliação de interfaces para dispositivos móveis. Os resultados mostraram que as questões do ErgoList foram, em sua maioria, apropriadas ou apropriadas com adequações pontuais, o que permitiu assumir que os CE também são, do ponto de vista conceitual, em sua maioria, adequados à finalidade estudada. Entretanto, para algumas questões, existe a necessidade de adequações no texto para refletir padrões de *design* ou estratégias de interação que emergiram com as tecnologias móveis.

Cabe destacar também que dentre as questões do ErgoList, existem algumas que receberam respostas "Pouco Aplicáveis"para dispositivos móveis. Portanto, para uma Inspeção Ergonômica mais precisa, essas questoes precisam ser revistas, redigitas, ou mesmo, excluídas da lista de inspeção, algo que não é maléfico, considerando pesquisas para a utilização de questionários personalizados como forma de melhorar a eficácia da inspeção.

Como trabalhos futuros, pretende-se: (i) revisar as questões do ErgoList a fim de adequá-las para a inspeção em aplicativos móveis; (ii) a proposição de uma ferramenta para seleção e aplicação de questões específicas para o domínio e escopo do aplicativo móvel inspecionado; (iii) replicar esse estudo para outros aplicativos adicionais procurando analisar se os resultados obtidos serão similares; e (iv) realizar avaliações similares dos mesmos aplicativos analisados, mas com pesos e considerações variados para Critérios e/ou subcritérios ergonômicos específicos, procurando apresentar graus diferentes de adequabilidade às avaliações. Em particular, pode-se pensar em pesos maiores para certos subcritérios, a exemplo de Condução ou *Feedback* Imedidato ou outros, dependendo do domínio de aplicação do ambiente a ser inspecionado.

Referências

Barreto, J. d. S., Pasqual Jr., P. A., Barbosa, F. F. M., and Frigeri, S. R. (2018). *Interface Humano-Computador*. Grupo A.

Benyon, D. (2011). *Interação Humano Computador*. Pearson Education, São Paulo.

Coleti, T. A., Morandini, M., Correa, P. L. P., da Silva, D. L., and Boscarioli, C. (2015). Using keywords to support the verbalization in usability evaluation. In *Proceedings of the 14th Brazilian Symposium on Human Factors in Computing Systems*, pages 1–10.

Cybis, W. d. A., Holts, A. B., and Faust, R. (2015). *Ergonomia e Usabilidade: Conhecimentos, Métodos e Aplicações*. Novatec Editora, São Paulo.

Da Costa, R. P., Canedo, E. D., De Sousa, R. T., Albuquerque, R. D. O., and Villalba, L. J. G. (2019). Set of usability heuristics for quality assessment of mobile applications on smartphones. *IEEE Access*, 7:116145–116161.

Filho, G. E. K., Guerino, G. C., and Valentim, N. M. C. (2022). A systematic mapping study on usability and user experience evaluation of multi-touch systems. In *Proceedings of the 21st Brazilian Symposium on Human Factors in Computing Systems*, IHC '22, New York, NY, USA. Association for Computing Machinery.

Giovanni, P. D. (2013). Integrating Mobile Design Patterns within a User Interface Development Environment. pages 1–4.

Nascimento, I., Silva, W., Lopes, A., Rivero, L., Gadelha, B., Oliveira, E., and Conte, T. (2016a). An empirical study to evaluate the feasibility of a UX and usability inspection technique for mobile applications. *Proceedings of the International Conference on Software Engineering and Knowledge Engineering, SEKE*, 2016-January:595–599.

Nascimento, I., Silva, W., Lopes, A., Rivero, L., Gadelha, B., Oliveira, E., and Conte, T. (2016b). An empirical study to evaluate the feasibility of a ux and usability inspection technique for mobile applications. In *28th International Conference on Software Engineering & Knowledge Engineering, California, USA*.

Neil, T. (2014). *Mobile Design Pattern Gallery*. OReilly, 2 edition.

Nudelman, G. (2013). *Padrões de Projeto para o Android - Soluções de projetos de Interação para desenvolvedores*. Novatec Editora, 1 edition.

Parente Da Costa, R., Canedo, E. D., De Sousa, R. T., De Oliveira Albuquerque, R., and Garcia Villalba, L. J. (2019). Set of Usability Heuristics for Quality Assessment of Mobile Applications on Smartphones. *IEEE Access*, 7:116145–116161.

Rocha, L. C., Andreade, R. M. C., and Sampaio, A. L. (2014). Heurísticas para avaliar a usabilidade de aplicações móveis : estudo de caso para aulas de campo em Geologia. *Nuevas Ideas en Informática Educativa TISE*, pages 367–378.

Scapin, D. L. and Bastien, J. M. (1997). Ergonomic criteria for evaluating the ergonomic quality of interactive systems. *Behaviour and Information Technology*, 16(4-5):220–231.

Sobral, W. S. (2019). *Design de Interfaces*. Editora Saraiva.

Viana, L., Passos, L., Oliveira, E., and Conte, T. (2021). Applying usability heuristics in the context of data labeling systems. In *Proceedings of the XX Brazilian Symposium on Human Factors in Computing Systems*, pages 1–7.

Wroblewski, L. (2011). *Mobile First*.

Uso de *Technology Probe* na Engenharia de Sistemas de Software para Saúde

Luciana Nascimento[1], Larissa Galeno[1], Clinton Hudson Pessoa[1], Patricia Furtado Silva[1], Guilherme Horta Travassos[1]

[1]Programa de Engenharia de Sistemas e Computação– Universidade Federal do Rio de Janeiro (UFJ) – Rio de Janeiro – RJ – Brasil

{lmnascimento, galeno, chmp, pfurtado, ght}@cos.ufrj.br

Abstract. *The growing demand for IoT systems in healthcare drives the creation of wearable devices for continuous patient monitoring. However, effectively building these devices requires a comprehensive engineering approach seeking quality hardware, software, and manufacturing. This study describes two Technology Probe (TP) sessions to evaluate the usability and suitability of an IoT device for collecting patient clinical condition data (oxygen saturation, temperature, and heart rate) to support hospital monitoring and share strategies and learned lessons on executing validated learning cycles to gather insight from prospective users, in terms of emotional reactions, opinions, and ideas. A set of requirements proposals was organized to support decisions on evolving the idealized proposal, and improvement possibilities to the TP strategy were identified.*

Resumo. *A crescente demanda por sistemas IoT na saúde impulsiona a criação de dispositivos vestíveis para monitoramento de pacientes continuamente. Entretanto, a construção eficaz destes dispositivos requer uma abordagem abrangente de engenharia buscando qualidade de hardware, software e manufatura. Este estudo descreve a condução de duas sessões de Technology Probe (TP) para avaliar a usabilidade e adequação de um dispositivo IoT para coletar dados de condições clínicas de pacientes (saturação de oxigênio, temperatura e frequência cardíaca) para apoiar o acompanhamento hospitalar e compartilha estratégias e lições aprendidas sobre a execução de ciclos de aprendizado validado com coleta de percepção de usuários prospectados, em termos de reações emocionais, opiniões e ideias. Um conjunto de propostas de requisitos foi organizado para apoiar as decisões de evolução da proposta ideada e foram identificadas possibilidades de melhorias para a estratégia de TP.*

1. Introdução

A Internet das Coisas (IoT) abriu portas para uma ampla gama de oportunidades e transformou a forma como interagimos com o mundo. Com a crescente interconexão de dispositivos e sensores, a IoT tem impulsionado uma revolução tecnológica, permitindo a coleta e análise de dados em tempo real, o que resulta em uma tomada de decisão mais inteligente e baseada em informações fidedignas [Motta et al. 2018].

Na área da engenharia da saúde, a IoT tem sido utilizada para integrar dispositivos inteligentes, apoiando serviços e profissionais por meio da coleta e análise contínua de dados dos pacientes, dos equipamentos, do ambiente, entre outros, proporcionando interação entre objetos, seu monitoramento e ações remotas. A aplicação dessa tecnologia proporciona ganhos na eficiência gerencial e na qualidade dos serviços prestados [Kelly et al. 2020].

A pandemia da COVID-19 influenciou a evolução do modelo de atenção à saúde, ressignificado com a introdução de tecnologias contemporâneas no monitoramento dos indivíduos doentes. A integração de dispositivos inteligentes com o uso da tecnologia IoT foi experimentada para disponibilizar um volume de dados útil, auxiliando na identificação de surtos de doenças e das variáveis envolvidas, para o monitoramento de dados clínicos dos indivíduos, auxiliando o manejo dos casos dentro e fora dos hospitais, e para a gestão estratégica dos recursos [Al-Atawi et al. 2022]. Adicionalmente, a crise pandêmica revelou a carência de tecnologia nos hospitais públicos brasileiros e estimulou o direcionamento de esforços em prol da engenharia de sistemas de software contemporâneos IoT para a área da saúde [Al-Atawi et al. 2022].

Este artigo relata observações acerca da aplicação de uma abordagem de *Technology Probe* (TP) [Hutchinson et al. 2003] na avaliação de um dispositivo IoT desenvolvido para auxiliar no monitoramento e análise de dados vitais de pacientes, como os dispositivos convencionais de oximetria, porém, a um custo mais acessível. O dispositivo IoT, parte de um sistema de software mais abrangente, está sendo construído em um contexto de inovação com alto grau de incerteza, visto que os requisitos foram conjecturados pelo time de desenvolvimento, visando sua disponibilização em complexos hospitalares. Não há antecipadamente clientes e/ou usuários responsáveis por definir, priorizar e validar os requisitos do produto. Situações como esta levam as organizações a operarem em um contexto de grandes incertezas quanto ao domínio do problema, à adequação da solução proposta e aos possíveis usuários.

Nessas circunstâncias, é viável adotar estratégias iterativas e evolutivas que permitam a equipe desenvolver o produto de software por meio de ciclos de aprendizado validado [Ries 2011] que viabilizem experimentar ideias e propostas com os potenciais usuários, aprender com isso, evoluir a proposta e basear tomadas de decisão para o ciclo de desenvolvimento subsequente. Também é conhecido como ciclo de *probe and learn* [Cole 2002], *loop* Construir-Medir-Aprender [Ries 2011] [Blanck 2013] ou experimentação contínua [Holmström Olsson e Bosch 2016] [Lindgren e Münch 2015]. Esta abordagem tem como objetivo ajudar a reduzir incertezas como sobre as características do produto de software, sua aceitação pelo possíveis usuários, adequabilidade ao contexto pretendido e sobre o modelo de negócio adequado, além de obter novas ideias para o desenvolvimento contínuo, especialmente no desenvolvimento de software para inovação [Cole 2002].

Neste sentido, descrevemos nossa experiência em utilizar uma abordagem de TP em sessões de avaliação de um dispositivo IoT de baixo custo pertencente a um projeto de sistema de software para a saúde, com o objetivo de capturar a atitude e a percepção de uma amostra de possíveis usuários, além de ideias de requisitos. Foram usados instrumentos para coleta de reações emocionais como indicador de nível de aceitação, bem como os adjetivos utilizados para qualificar o dispositivo e sugestões de evolução como indicadores da experiência do usuário e de sua avaliação das características do dispositivo. Os resultados foram organizados para apoiar o time do projeto a decidir as evoluções necessárias no dispositivo nos próximos ciclos de desenvolvimento.

Os resultados apresentados neste trabalho permitem que profissionais da prática percebam as estratégias e instrumentos envolvidos na realização de uma sessão de avaliação com TP, a qual pode contribuir na aquisição de dados qualitativos de seu produto de software inovador voltado para o mercado sob a perspectiva do usuário.

A próxima seção descreve o sistema de software e o dispositivo IoT utilizado. A Seção 3 apresenta a fundamentação teórica acerca da abordagem de TP. A Seção 4 apresenta o planejamento e a execução das sessões de avaliação. Em seguida, a Seção 5 apresenta os resultados discutindo as lições e oportunidades de melhoria para o dispositivo IoT. Por fim, a Seção 6 apresenta nossas considerações finais, incluindo uma discussão sobre as limitações dos resultados e expectativas de evolução do produto.

2. O Sistema OxímetroIoT

O propósito do sistema OxímetroIoT é oferecer uma ferramenta de baixo custo para complexos hospitalares de forma a facilitar o monitoramento de condições físicas (porcentagem de oxigenação, temperatura e frequência cardíaca) de pacientes em enfermarias, permitindo a coleta frequente destes sinais vitais com o minimo de intervenção humana e, por consequência, a diminuição do tempo para detectar necessidade de ação e executar a ação. Para tal, foi projetado um dispositivo (hardware de baixo custo encapsulado em elementos manufaturados) e utilizando software no paradigma IoT que coleta dados vitais dos pacientes por meio de sensores e os transmite por meio de um *broker* (*middleware*) para um *dashboard* de monitoramento.

O sistema de software OxímetroIoT possui três componentes que se comunicam por meio de um *Broker* (Figura 1A): (i) dispositivo IoT e sua parte vestível, (ii) dashboard para monitoramento remoto e (iii) banco de dados. A Figura 1B mostra a pulseira, onde estão localizados os sensores e ao lado o dispositivo IoT onde é realizado o cálculo das medidas com seu visor, que exibe as medidas coletadas e que são transmitidas para o Dashboard por meio do *broker*. A pulseira e a caixa do dispositivo IoT utilizaram impressão 3D para sua confecção.

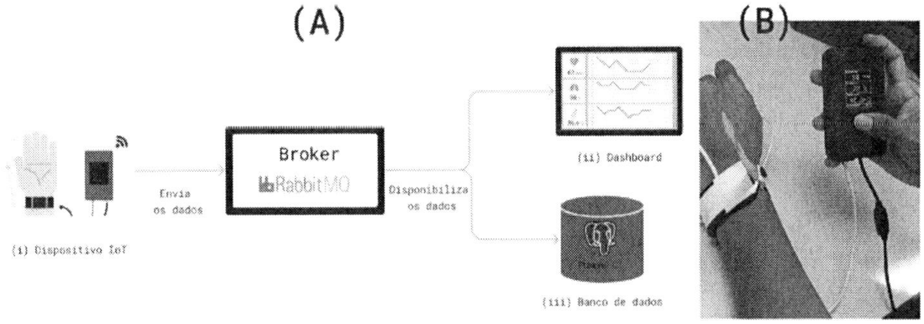

Figura 1. OxímetroIoT: A) Componentes principais e B) Exemplo de uso

A comunicação entre os componentes do sistema de software ocorre da seguinte forma: (i) a pulseira (com sensores MAX 30105 e MLX 90614) é responsável por fazer a captura dos dados de oxigenação, frequência cardíaca e temperatura dos pacientes e os envia para o dispositivo IoT (processador ESP8266), que por sua vez realiza os tratamentos necessários, exibe no visor (ST7735) integrado (ver a Figura 1) e os envia para o *broker* (*RabbitMQ*, sistema de comunicação intermediário que viabiliza a transferência de informações entre dispositivos e sistemas). O dashboard consome os dados dos dispositivos IoT por meio do *broker* e os apresenta em sua interface web (ii), permitindo o monitoramento remoto, e também armazena estes dados no banco de dados (implementado em PostgreSQL) para uso em atividades futuras de investigação de saúde (iii). A Figura 1(A) ilustra essa arquitetura de comunicação.

O desenvolvimento do sistema OxímetroIoT e seus componentes ocorreu em processo de evolução contínua. Antes do desenvolvimento do dispositivo ilustrado na Figura 1, foram criados MVPs (Minimum Viable Products - Produto Minimamente Viável) para permitir à equipe avaliar as soluções propostas, como por exemplo, para o formato e o material do vestível onde os sensores são embutidos, assim como o refinamento do algoritmo que calcula as medidas para os sinais vitais. A equipe era formada por gerentes, desenvolvedores de software, *designers* industriais e uma especialista na área da saúde. Os desenvolvedores focaram na construção do sistema web, confecção do dispositivo IoT e sua integração ao sistema. A parte de design industrial teve como objetivo a modelagem e impressão do dispositivo e da pulseira por meio de manufatura assistida com impressora 3D. Por fim, a especialista na área da saúde, devido a sua experiência como enfermeira com atuação na linha de frente da pandemia de COVID-19, teve o papel de consultora do desenvolvimento, auxiliando no processo de elicitação de requisitos iniciais para o sistema, ajudando na calibração dos sensores do dispositivo e no design da pulseira, componente vestível do OxímetroIoT.

A participação de uma especialista em saúde na equipe de desenvolvimento, composta por seis profissionais da prática de software, não foi suficiente para tratar algumas incertezas sobre a solução proposta, tais como sobre: a) Tecnologia de coleta dos dados: compreender a confiabilidade das informações coletadas pelos sensores; b) Software de tratamento de dados: definir a estratégia de tratamento de dados e sua apresentação aos profissionais de saúde. O processo de tratamento gera incertezas, como por exemplo sobre a precisão da informação dos valores exibidos e adequabilidade do tempo de execução do software; e c) Dispositivo IoT: caracterizar o conforto necessário para o uso da solução vestível e a adequação na forma de exibir os dados no display integrado (estilo do texto e estrutura de informação).

Adicionalmente, ainda era preciso garantir que as informações apresentadas fossem úteis para os profissionais de saúde no contexto hospitalar. Essas incertezas nos motivaram a buscar alguma estratégia de avaliação com possíveis usuários antes de evoluir a proposta com novos requisitos conjecturados. Devido a disponibilidade de versão operacional do sistema de software e o estágio de desenvolvimento do produto ainda ter altas incertezas sobre os requisitos, identificamos a oportunidade de executar uma abordagem de TP como base para o planejamento e a execução do primeiro ciclo de aprendizado validado envolvendo possíveis usuários. Duas sessões de TP com profissionais da saúde foram executadas e são descritas neste artigo.

3. Abordagem de *Technology Probe*

Technology Probe (TP) é uma abordagem de co-criação de tecnologias com os usuários, em que um *Probe* representa um "instrumento usado para descobrir o desconhecido e, possivelmente, coletar dados úteis e interessantes" [Hutchinson et al. 2003]. O método exige a instalação do instrumento (o *probe,* produto tecnológico) em um contexto real, para que seja possível observar os usuários utilizando-o e, assim, coletar percepções e cenários de uso para seu aprimoramento. Em comparação com outros métodos de testes e observação do usuário, TP tem como foco produtos em que as especificações e o contexto não são conhecidos ou são parcialmente conhecidos. Nestes casos, existe a necessidade de explorar o ambiente do usuário e coletar ideias para promover a evolução do produto que está sendo proposto.

Em uma sessão de avaliação com TP é necessário utilizar uma versão funcional e simples da solução tecnológica e que transmita a ideia geral do produto sendo desenvolvido. Diferente de um protótipo, os usuários devem ser capazes de interagir com o produto tecnológico de forma a explorar maneiras de utilização, gerando informações relacionadas às seguintes perspectivas [Hutchinson et al. 2003]: (1) social, que diz respeito à relação do usuário com o produto; (2) engenharia, relacionada à operação adequada do produto; e (3) design, relacionada com a identificação de oportunidades de inovação.

Uma abordagem de TP não indica procedimentos e nem instrumentos para a execução da avaliação de uma tecnologia, cabendo a quem planeja a sessão de avaliação com TP analisar os objetivos da avaliação, e assim definir os perfis dos participantes, os instrumentos, as atividades e o contexto da sessão de avaliação. Na seção a seguir serão apresentados casos em que uma abordagem de TP foi utilizada para executar sessões de avaliação do dispositivo IoT do Sistema OxímetroIoT por possíveis usuários, com descrição dos procedimentos e instrumentos utilizados.

4. Avaliando o *Probe* do OxímetroIoT

Para que um produto como o OxímetroIoT possa ser disponibilizado, é necessário executar diferentes tipos de avaliação. Um desses tipos envolve a submissão obrigatória do dispositivo aos protocolos da Anvisa [Anvisa 2024] e conformidade com a ISO 81001 (2021), objeto de outras avaliações e fora do escopo deste artigo, incluindo o registro na plataforma Brasil, necessário para qualquer produto para a saúde no Brasil.

Além da avaliação dos aspectos de qualidade em termos de seus requisitos funcionais e não-funcionais, analisar a experiência do usuário e a aceitabilidade da proposta aqui relatada é importante por se tratar de algo ideado para ser utilizado por pessoas em um ambiente de saúde. Porém, existem protocolos e etapas de experimentação que devem ser seguidos antes de se realizar avaliações envolvendo pacientes e monitoramento de seus sinais vitais. Assim, um desafio nesse contexto é a execução de avaliações em ambiente real o mais cedo possível para desenvolvê-lo com estratégia de aprendizado validado quanto às suas características e funcionalidades, até produzir uma versão considerada estável e madura o suficiente para ser avaliada seguindo os protocolos de tecnologia de saúde da Anvisa.

As subseções a seguir descrevem a abordagem aplicada para a execução da primeira avaliação com participação de possíveis usuários do OxímetroIoT.

4.1. Sessões de Avaliação de Usuário Baseadas em *Technology Probe*

No caso do OxímetroIoT, definimos dois tipos de usuários primários, os pacientes e os profissionais de saúde, que representam os usuários prospectados para usar o sistema de software diretamente e que podem avaliar aspectos como, por exemplo, a experiência de ser monitorado usando o OxímetroIoT, a manipulação do dispositivo, o impacto nas atividades dos profissionais que monitoram os sinais vitais ou que precisam obter valores de sinais vitais monitorados, a confiança nos resultados, dentre outros aspectos inerentes ao ambiente hospitalar ou de enfermaria.

Dado que havia uma versão operacional do OxímetroIoT, uma possibilidade mais próxima do contexto real que poderíamos executar sem ferir os protocolos experimentais com pacientes humanos foi entrevistar profissionais de saúde com experiência em monitoramento de sinais vitais de pacientes em ambiente hospitalar e/ou enfermaria. Definimos como abordagem preferencial a execução de sessões de avaliação com TP em grupo, para permitir a troca de ideias e questionamentos entre os participantes e assim aumentar as chances de coletar mais percepções e ideias.

As sessões de avaliação foram organizadas para serem executadas em três etapas: (1) apresentação da proposta, (2) utilização do OxímetroIoT e (3) entrevista.

Durante a etapa 1, os participantes recebem informações sobre o objetivo geral da proposta - o que é, quais suas funcionalidades, quais são os usuários prospectados, para qual contexto de uso foi elaborado, quem são os responsáveis principais, qual sua etapa atual (protótipo funcional) e qual o escopo atual de avaliação. Espera-se assim obter alinhamento sobre as metas e limitações da proposta e da sessão de avaliação.

Para ajudar o participante a focar em um contexto de uso do produto tecnológico, foram estabelecidas Jornadas do Usuário, que são as principais etapas e atividades de interação do usuário com o produto. Para a sessão de avaliação com profissionais de saúde, definimos as seguintes Jornadas de Usuário: J1) Preparação do Equipamento para Monitoramento, J2) Colocação do Equipamento no Paciente, J3) Monitoramento Presencial do Paciente, J4) Monitoramento Remoto do Paciente, J5) Retirada do Equipamento do Paciente. Foram definidas atividades necessárias para a utilização do dispositivo por jornada, como por exemplo, Conexão do cabo da Pulseira com o Dispositivo para a jornada J1.

Na etapa 2, os participantes são estimulados a manipular o produto tecnológico (*probe*). Como a sessão de avaliação com TP não envolve a participação de pacientes, os profissionais de saúde podem assumir o papel de pacientes e experimentar o dispositivo. Durante essa etapa de uso, a perspectiva de engenharia da abordagem TP é a mais observada, porém, os participantes podem tirar dúvidas sobre o produto e comentar livremente suas ideias e sugestões, tendo um espaço para troca de percepções em que aspectos das perspectivas sociais e design também podem surgir.

A etapa final da sessão de avaliação com TP é a de entrevista (3), cujo objetivo é coletar dos participantes as suas percepções sobre o produto, expressas em termos de suas reações emocionais, para indicar aceitabilidade, de seus julgamentos qualificadores sobre as características do produto, e suas ideias e sugestões para evoluções da proposta. Logo, essa etapa foca nas perspectivas social e de design da abordagem de TP. Para esta etapa foi elaborado um instrumento em formato de documento com possibilidade de uso de forma impressa ou digital, já que não tínhamos garantia de disponibilidade de computadores e de Internet nos ambientes que conseguíssemos parceria com profissionais de saúde para executar as sessões de avaliação.

O instrumento de apoio à entrevista possui três perguntas principais a serem respondidas pelos participantes individualmente. A primeira pergunta é sobre a reação do participante, com as opções de respostas exibidas na Figura 2, adaptadas de [Asiegbu et al. 2012]. Definimos que ao menos uma opção deve ser selecionada como resposta e não há restrições para o máximo de escolha de opções.

Figura 2. Reações dos Participantes. Adaptado de [Asiegbu et al. 2012]

A segunda pergunta é aberta e questiona o participante que adjetivos ele usaria para qualificar o produto e suas características. Assim como as reações emocionais, os adjetivos são utilizados para capturar algumas das percepções conforme a experiência do usuário. As reações emocionais e os adjetivos se complementam. Por exemplo, a coleta de reações emocionais positivas junto com adjetivos negativos pode indicar possível aceitação da proposta e seu potencial, porém grande expectativa pela evolução de suas características. Dentro da abordagem de ciclo de aprendizado validado, tem grande chance de indicar uma suposição a ser melhor investigada para apoiar tomada de decisão sobre a tecnologia proposta.

Por fim, o último item do instrumento também é aberto e pede ao participante que escreva observações adicionais, ideias e/ou sugestões. Apesar de ser uma etapa final, durante as entrevistas os participantes podem continuar a explorar o produto proposto, fazer perguntas e expressar suas opiniões.

A seguir, tem-se a descrição de execução das sessões de avaliação com TP em duas ocasiões, uma em um hospital universitário (HU) e outra, dois dias depois, em uma unidade de pronto atendimento (UPA) infantil. Nas duas experiências, os participantes dispuseram de tempo durante seus expedientes para colaborar nas sessões de avaliação.

4.1.1 Sessão de Avaliação com TP em um Hospital Universitário

Executamos uma sessão de avaliação baseada em TP em uma Unidade de Tratamento Intensivo (UTI) de um Hospital Universitário Federal (HU). Por motivo de segurança dos pacientes internados, realizamos a sessão em uma sala de atividades administrativas dentro da UTI, tendo a participação de quatro profissionais de saúde com mais de dez anos de atividade e com experiência em monitoramento de pacientes. Da equipe de desenvolvimento, constavam quatro pessoas, das quais duas no papel de facilitadoras da sessão e duas apoiando os participantes na manipulação dos dispositivos. Três oxímetros estavam disponíveis para avaliação, havendo apenas diferença na largura da pulseira de um deles.

A etapa de apresentação do produto ocorreu como planejado, porém no local disponibilizado não havia sinal de Internet e nem de rede celular. Dado que o uso do componente Dashboard (vide Figura 1) precisa de conexão a internet, as etapas de uso do

OxímetroIoT e de entrevistas foram ajustadas, sendo apresentadas imagens exemplificando o funcionamento do Dashboard.

A sessão de avaliação com TP durou cerca de 50 minutos e todos os participantes tiveram a oportunidade de manipular os oxímetros. Durante a etapa de uso dos dispositivos, um deles apresentou falha no funcionamento, um ficou sendo usado por um único participante durante toda a etapa e o outro foi manipulado por outros três participantes. Um dos participantes preferiu observar os outros utilizando os dispositivos alegando já conhecer bastante sobre as possibilidades de sistemas IoT. Durante a etapa de entrevista, um OxímetroIoT foi usado por um membro do time da proposta, sendo observado pelos profissionais de saúde, e o outro dispositivo continuou sendo utilizado pelo mesmo participante que o estava utilizando na etapa de uso, somando para ele mais de 30 minutos de utilização. Conforme planejado, os participantes puderam trocar ideias e tirar dúvidas livremente durante a entrevista, porém preencheram suas respostas individualmente em formulário impresso.

4.1.2 Sessão de Avaliação com TP em uma Unidade de Pronto Atendimento

A execução da sessão de avaliação com TP em uma UPA especializada no público infantil ocorreu dois dias depois da experiência anterior. Uma característica do contexto da UPA é que o número de pacientes sendo atendidos é geralmente maior, e o fluxo de pessoas chegando em busca de atendimento muda ao longo das 24 horas do dia. Com isso, a sessão de avaliação foi executada à noite, quando o risco dos participantes precisarem desistir da avaliação para atender pacientes é menor do que durante o dia. A etapa de entrevista também foi ajustada para que as respostas considerassem todas as etapas e atividades das Jornadas do Usuário em conjunto, ou seja, cada participante respondeu ao instrumento uma única vez.

A sessão de avaliação ocorreu em uma sala de reunião com participação de cinco profissionais de saúde e três membros da equipe de desenvolvimento, sendo um facilitador e dois desenvolvedores para apoiar os participantes. Dois oxímetros estavam disponíveis para a sessão na UPA, visto que o dispositivo que apresentou falha de funcionamento na sessão de avaliação no HU não pôde ser reparado a tempo.

A etapa de apresentação ocorreu como planejado, porém, assim como na experiência anterior, surpreendentemente não havia Internet disponível e a rede celular era instável. Durante a etapa de uso dos oxímetros, inicialmente sentimos resistência dos participantes em os utilizar pelo motivo das cadeiras na sala de reunião estarem localizadas distantes das tomadas de energia e o tamanho dos cabos de alimentação dos oxímetros não ser suficiente para alcançar os participantes, que naquele momento do dia estavam cansados e preferiam não se levantar.

Apesar da resistência de ir até o local dos dispositivos ligados, os participantes estavam curiosos, fazendo perguntas e discutindo ideias entre si. A etapa então foi ajustada: colocamos um dos oxímetros em um dos membros do time de desenvolvimento e o outro dispositivo foi desligado e entregue para os participantes manipularem, o que estimulou ainda mais discussões. Algumas dúvidas eram direcionadas para o membro da equipe que estava usando o OxímetroIoT, como por exemplo sobre os valores exibidos no visor, sua frequência de atualização, entre outros.

Assim como na experiência anterior, na etapa de entrevista os participantes puderam conversar sobre suas ideias, observações e dúvidas, respondendo ao questionário individualmente. No total, a sessão durou cerca de 30 minutos.

4.2 Resultados

A Figura 3 apresenta quantos participantes distintos escolheram uma dada imagem para expressar sua reação emocional (cada participante poderia escolher mais de uma figura para representar sua reação), assim como apresenta o quantitativo de respostas obtidas dos participantes nas sessões de avaliação. Para facilitar a análise, os adjetivos utilizados para qualificar a proposta foram classificados nas categorias Ponto Negativo e Ponto Positivo. Os participantes do HU reportaram suas respostas após a discussão de cada Jornada de Usuário, enquanto que os participantes da UPA reportaram em um único momento e após todas as jornadas serem discutidas. Somado ao tempo de 20 minutos a mais de duração na avaliação, isso pode ter contribuído com o maior número de respostas pelos participantes do HU, fato a ser observado em futuras avaliações.

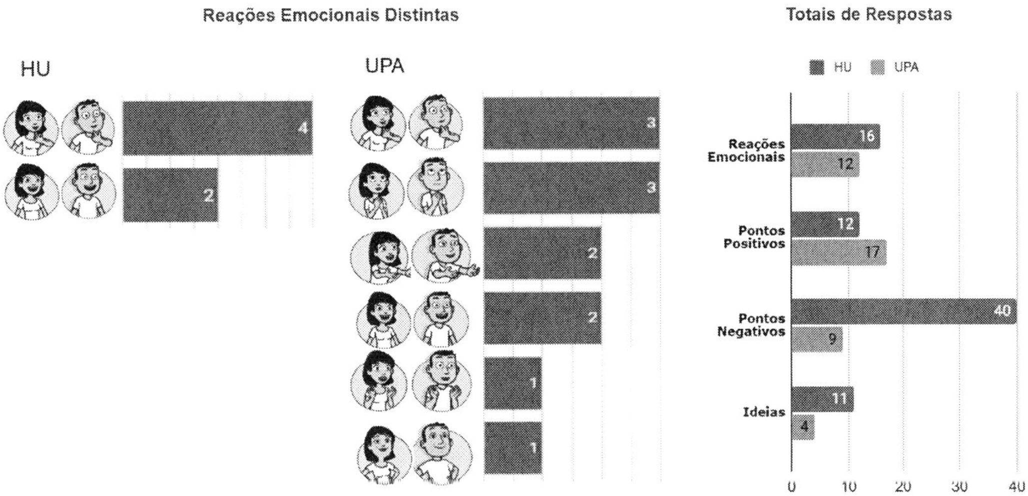

Figura 3. Resultados: Reações Emocionais distintas e Totais de Respostas

A subseções a seguir apresentam a discussão sobre os resultados, primeiro para as reações emocionais e subsequentemente os pontos positivos/negativos e as ideias.

4.2.1 Análise das Reações Emocionais

Durante as sessões de avaliação com TP não foram observadas reações de rejeição ao produto, o que foi refletido nas respostas preenchidas no questionário.

No caso do HU, apesar dos participantes terem reportado suas reações emocionais dezesseis vezes (Figura 3), na maioria das respostas os participantes usaram as mesmas expressões de curiosidade ou de recepção positiva à proposta. Uma suposição resultante da análise é que o resultado está relacionado ao que observamos durante a sessão de avaliação: os participante expressaram preocupação e dúvidas em relação ao método de aferição dos sinais vitais e aos procedimentos de manipulação e limpeza do dispositivo, porém reportaram terem expectativas de evolução desses pontos nas próximas versões do dispositivo.

Por sua vez, os participantes da UPA demonstraram empolgação com a possibilidade de uma solução como a apresentada ser implantada no contexto do Sistema Único de Saúde. Suas preocupações focaram na usabilidade e na necessidade de aumentar ou criar solução sem o cabo de alimentação de energia para que possa ser usado nas enfermarias sem atrapalhar o fluxo das pessoas no local e permitindo mobilidade ao paciente, como detalha a próxima seção.

Tanto no caso do HU quanto na UPA, as reações de curiosidade foram as mais reportadas. Um maior número de expressões positivas foi indicado pelos participantes da UPA, conforme pode ser observado na Figura 3.

4.2.2 Análise das ideias e sugestões

Com base nas respostas coletadas, foi possível elaborar uma análise acerca das ideias, demandas e problematizações relatadas pelos participantes das sessões de avaliação. O processo iniciou pela extração das respostas documentadas, com os trechos descritos nas palavras dos próprios participantes, gerando um conjunto amplo de descrições e opiniões pessoais sobre a utilização do produto avaliado. Tais trechos de opiniões foram divididos em duas modalidades, o primeiro, nomeado como "*Pain Points*", descreve as problematizações identificadas pelos participantes, o que de alguma forma lhes causou desconforto no uso do OxímetroIoT. Na segunda modalidade, foram analisados os trechos identificados como "Oportunidades", já que mencionam estratégias que podem ser adotadas como funcionalidades novas ou melhorias para o produto. Os trechos da modalidade "*Pain Points*" tiveram uma quantidade significativamente maior, e por se tratar de pontos de melhoria receberam uma atenção redobrada.

A partir dos trechos descritos foi possível abstrair e sumarizar alguns pontos importantes como por exemplo a característica, o componente do OxímetroIoT e a categoria funcional a qual se refere. As características referem-se às funções ou finalidades mencionadas pelos participantes como pontos de melhoria. Os componentes do OxímetroIoT descrevem a qual parte do produto está direcionado o argumento, seja sobre a pulseira (parte vestível), o oxímetro (com display integrado) ou os cabos de alimentação de energia e de conexão da pulseira com o dispositivo. A categoria funcional surgiu da necessidade de especificar a qual parte tecnológica o referido argumento é direcionado, seja ele para hardware, software ou manufatura, sendo a manufatura ligada aos processos de fabricação, montagem e produção dos componentes.

Com os dados sumarizados e mantendo o rastro de cada item para o trecho da resposta do participante, pudemos analisar temas e pontos em comum e assim inferir com base nas respostas quais os pontos mais críticos da proposta devem ser reavaliados, fornecendo insumos para a evolução e melhoria da qualidade dos componentes do OxímetroIoT. No total, foram coletadas 50 transcrições de respostas classificadas na modalidade *Pain Points* (vide Figura 4), sendo 56% relacionadas com a manufatura do OxímetroIoT, 24% com o software e 20% com o hardware. Destacamos inicialmente os *Pain Points* de software, pois mesmo que a porcentagem apresentada não represente o valor de maior destaque, as observações descritas pelos participantes impactam diretamente nas funcionalidades disponibilizadas pelo OxímetroIoT.

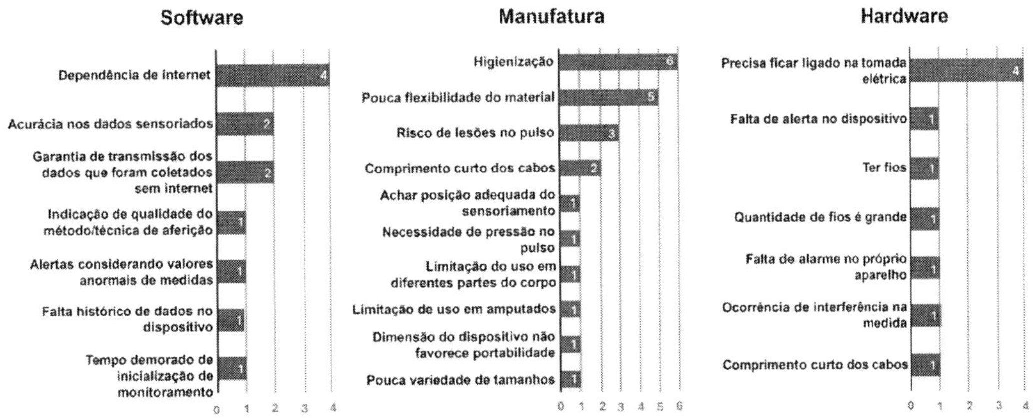

Figura 4. *Pain Points*

Nos temas de *Pain Points* relacionados ao software, o mais citado foi a necessidade de haver internet disponível para que a proposta possa funcionar por completo, com a informação podendo ser visualizada tanto no display do dispositivo quanto no Dashboard do sistema. Nos dois contextos das sessões de avaliação com TP, a falta de internet e rede celular no ambiente de trabalho é uma realidade comum segundo os profissionais de saúde participantes e inesperada pelos membros do time de desenvolvimento tendo em vista o tipo de ambiente sendo considerado.

Para as categorias de Manufatura e de Hardware, obtivemos observações que apoiam as melhorias necessárias a nível da qualidade do produto físico palpável. Para Manufatura, os dois pontos que se destacaram foram sobre a higienização e a resistência do material utilizado. Ambos derivam da complexidade identificada pelos participantes sobre o tipo de material utilizado na construção dos encapsuladores do OxímetroIoT, pois mesmo garantindo um baixo custo, certas condições se fazem necessárias acerca dos materiais utilizados, dado o contexto hospitalar em que estará inserido. Assim, grande parte das observações persistiram com esse cuidado extra na durabilidade do material e facilidade de higienização e sobre as condições de acomodação da parte vestível nos pacientes.

Para os *Pain Points* classificados na categoria de Hardware, o maior destaque foi a dependência do dispositivo em ficar ligado diretamente na tomada de energia elétrica, limitando parte da mobilidade do usuário. As observações feitas pelos usuários nesta modalidade incluíram a necessidade de inclusão de baterias no OxímetroIoT, de forma que ele possa se manter ativo ainda que distante de tomadas de alimentação de energia. Esse foi um dos grandes empecilhos de hardware observados, o que permitiu que mesmo associado aos *Pain Points* do projeto, tal característica fosse adotada como ponto de Oportunidade, que se adotadas nas futuras evoluções do produto podem agregar um enorme valor, pois trata diretamente de uma necessidade advinda dos próprios possíveis usuários no contexto de uso real.

Os *Pain Points* extraídos a partir das respostas dos usuários permitiram identificar os elementos-chave a serem melhorados no sistema, pois representam as necessidades, desejos e expectativas dos usuários, bem como as funcionalidades críticas para o sucesso do sistema. Ao usá-las para a geração, confirmação, priorização ou mesmo refinamento dos requisitos, buscamos assegurar um sistema desenvolvido como foco em atender às reais demandas do público-alvo, principalmente no que tange aos profissionais de saúde.

Parte das oportunidades identificadas nas observações dos facilitadores das sessões e nos relatos dos usuários mantiveram consistência com as limitações do projeto e, se adotados, tendem a aprimorar o uso e a qualidade do produto final a ser entregue ao usuário. Dentre essas oportunidades podemos mencionar: a utilização de bateria no dispositivo, como já destacado; a possibilidade de aferição dos dados do paciente em outras partes do corpo, o que exigiria uma reestruturação do encapsulador dos sensores da pulseira; sinais de alarme avisando sobre possíveis inconsistências nos valores das medições ou mesmo no desacoplamento do dispositivo à tomada; e também na disponibilização de um modelo de controle visual por aplicativo, facilitando o acesso ao monitoramento remoto dos pacientes.

5. Lições Aprendidas nas Sessões de Avaliação com TP

Por ser um produto idealizado, cujos requisitos foram elaborados e experimentados pelos próprios proponentes e pelo time de desenvolvimento, definir e priorizar características do sistema é um desafio, dada a gama de possibilidades, a falta de vivência nos contextos de uso da proposta e necessidade de capturar as perspectivas dos possíveis usuários. A aplicação da estratégia de TP permitiu uma maior compreensão do contexto de uso do OxímetroIoT e forneceu percepções sobre como este produto poderá ser integrado ao cotidiano dos profissionais de saúde e, eventualmente, pacientes. Essa compreensão é essencial para projetar uma experiência que retorne dados e informações relevantes para possíveis evoluções nos componentes do sistema. A imersão no contexto de uso do produto avaliado e a interação direta com os usuários pode inspirar no surgimento de novas ideias e oportunidades de inovação dentro do contexto explorado, que não seriam perceptíveis facilmente apenas por meio de pesquisas mais tradicionais.

Outro ponto positivo na utilização das sessões de avaliação com TP está na confirmação de requisitos conjecturais e não triviais, percebendo funcionalidades que não foram consideradas inicialmente mas que devem ser melhor discutidas, já que se baseiam em atribuições definidas por possíveis usuários. Podemos observar tal cenário nas modalidades definidas de *Pain Points* e oportunidades identificadas nas percepções coletadas das transcrições dos resultados coletados.

As percepções obtidas dos participantes do estudo, que são parte dos usuários prospectados do OxímetroIoT, ajudaram a ter uma percepção de quais características mais chamaram atenção e quais eles sentiram falta na versão atual da proposta. Por conta do uso das atribuições de *Pain Points* na abordagem de TP, em conjunto com a análise de suas reações emocionais, passa a ser viável atribuir uma estimativa mais aproximada de aceitação e adoção do produto pelos usuários.

Vale ressaltar a contribuição dessa abordagem para a descoberta de desafios e dificuldades que os usuários podem enfrentar ao utilizar o produto, informações que são valiosas para o aperfeiçoamento da proposta e minimização dos possíveis obstáculos à adoção do produto final. Apesar de não ter sido possível realizar testes com os pacientes, obter a percepção de profissionais de saúde permitiu adquirir conhecimento antes mesmo de chegar na etapa de realização de experimentos clínicos nos ambientes de saúde. Este conhecimento é de grande valia para a fase atual do projeto, pois apoia a evolução contínua do produto reduzindo as incertezas no ambiente em que seu desenvolvimento está inserido.

Já no tocante aos observadores e facilitadores da sessão, é vista a oportunidade de elaborar instrumentos que apoiem o registro das observações e fatos relevantes que emergem durante uma sessão de avaliação com TP. Nas sessões apresentadas as anotações realizadas não puderam seguir o direcionamento previsto tendo em vista os eventos inesperados de indisponibilidade de internet, por exemplo, dificultando o processo de análise dos dados qualitativos. Ao mesmo tempo, tal evento provocou a evolução de estrutura do sistema de software, acrescentando o requisito não funcional relacionado ao encapsulamento do componente Broker e a configuração de intranet específica para atender a comunicação dos dispositivos IoT com o Dashboard.

6. Considerações Finais, Limitações e Próximos Passos

Este trabalho teve como objetivo relatar a experiência do uso de sessões de avaliação com TP para avaliar um dispositivo componente de um sistema de software IoT tendo em vista o cenário de incerteza do desenvolvimento da solução. Para tal, foram agendadas duas sessões para avaliação do OxímetroIoT e, a partir delas, coletados dados qualitativos acerca da percepção dos participantes sobre o produto. Com essas informações foi possível compreender pontos de melhoria e captar novas funcionalidades, ambos são aspectos que impactam na qualidade da solução proposta.

Vale ressaltar as limitações e dificuldades acerca da experiência apresentada. A questão da disponibilidade dos participantes para a avaliação foi um fator que pode ter afetado as sessões de avaliação com TP, como o caso da UPA que precisou ser durante um plantão noturno dos profissionais. Ainda sobre o momento das sessões, em ambos os casos ocorreram problemas de conexão com a internet, o que não permitiu a exibição do *Dashboard* de monitoramento remoto, afetando parte do planejamento inicial. Adicionalmente, foi observada a relevância de garantir um ambiente com tomadas de alimentação de energia em locais próximos ao uso do OxímetroIoT para garantir que tenha um produto disponível para os participantes, como relatado no caso da UPA era necessário que os indivíduos se deslocassem para usar o dispositivo, novamente, podendo afetar a experiência da sessão. Estes eventos contribuíram para evolução do produto, que passou a incluir requisitos não funcionais referentes a configuração de intranet e o uso alternativo de baterias externas (*power banks*) para alimentar os dispositivos no caso de indisponibilidade de pontos de energia.

Outro ponto de limitação se dá pelo público-alvo. Como é um produto voltado para área da saúde não é possível colocar imediatamente o produto em situação de uso real e direto com os pacientes, situação ideal para uma sessão de avaliação com TP. Por conta disso, foram projetadas as Jornadas do Usuário, de forma a imergir os participantes no contexto de uso do OxímetroIoT.

Apesar da versão do OxímetroIoT estar totalmente operacional, devido às incertezas sobre requisitos não-funcionais do produto, não tivemos a ambição de aprofundar com avaliação de campo das suas funcionalidades, o que é a perspectiva de engenharia da abordagem de TP. Nenhuma falha comportamental ocorrida durante as avaliações era desconhecida pelo time de desenvolvimento. Entretanto, nos surpreendeu a falha de hardware em um dos oxímetros, provocada pelo rompimento de uma conexão interna do display provavelmente por vibração durante o transporte do dispositivo. Essa falha contribuiu para modificar o processo de encapsulamento do hardware e identificar material mais robusto para realizar as conexões internas. Mesmo assim, consideramos uma limitação do trabalho a ausência de instrumentos e/ou procedimentos focados na perspectiva de engenharia da abordagem TP, o que pode ser elaborado para os próximos ciclos de aprendizado validado do OxímetroIoT.

É importante ressaltar que, apesar da experiência ser adaptada e um contexto real de uso não ter sido totalmente possível, as sessões de avaliação com TP ocorreram em dois cenários em que percebemos terem requisitos de qualidade diferentes, o que será posteriormente avaliado como possível fator para evoluir a delimitação de contexto para a proposta do OxímetroIoT. Enquanto no cenário do HU os *Pain Points* citados foram mais sobre aspectos como a acurácia de aferição, a existência de alarmes e a garantia de persistência dos dados históricos, no cenário da UPA os *Pain Points* mais citados foram sobre o conforto e segurança do usuário e apoio à mobilidade.

Para que a proposta do OxímetroIoT evolua para um produto mais robusto os próximos passos deverão contemplar a ideação de soluções, seleção e priorização de novos requisitos para o sistema de software IoT; a priorização destes requisitos, e a construção de uma nova versão do OxímetroIoT. Com isso, será possível realizar novas avaliações com o produto, para então, preparar os protocolos para observar o uso experimental do OxímetroIoT nos complexos hospitalares com pacientes reais.

Por fim, este trabalho buscou contribuir com a comunidade de engenharia de software uma vez que apresenta uma experiência de avaliação de um sistema contemporâneo de software em um ambiente de inovação e incerteza baseado em *Technology Probe*. Por auxiliar em obter as percepções de usuários reais frente ao produto avaliado, esta abordagem pode ser escolhida, especialmente, em cenários que envolvem inovação, incerteza, requisitos conjecturados e necessidade de observação da experiência de usuário. Estes fatores implicam na elicitação de requisitos, por exemplo, e a partir do uso da TP é viável obter a percepção de possíveis usuários e ideias que podem ser analisadas, filtradas, selecionadas e aceitas como requisitos.

Agradecimentos

Agradecemos aos participantes das sessões de avaliação por sua contribuição para o aprimoramento do OxímetroIoT. Ao Complexo Hospitalar da UFRJ que proporciona um ambiente de trabalho tecnologicamente inovador. Esta pesquisa tem apoio das agências de fomento CAPES, CNPq (305701/2022-3) e Faperj (E-26/201.170/2021).

Referências

Motta, R. C., de Oliveira, K. M. e Travassos, G. H. (2018). On challenges in engineering IoT software Systems. *CBSOFT/SBES'18*, pages 42-51.

Kelly, J., Campbell, K., Gong, E., e Scuffham, P. (2020). The internet of things: Impact and implications for health care delivery. *Journal of Medical Internet Research*, 22(11):e20135.

Al-Atawi, A., Khan, F., Kim, C. (2022). Application and Challenges of IoT Healthcare System in COVID-19. *Sensors*, 22(7304).

Hutchinson, H., Mackay, W., Westerlund, B., Bederson, B., Druin, A., Plaisant, C., Beaudouin-Lafon, M., Conversy, S., Evans, H., Hansen H., Roussel, N., e Eiderbäck, B. (2003). Technology probes: inspiring design for and with families. *SIGCHI 2003.*

ISO 81001. 2021. Health software and health IT systems safety, effectiveness and security.

Ries, E. (2011). *The Lean Startup: How Today's Entrepreneurs Use Continuous Innovation to Create Radically Successful Businesses.* Crown Business. eISBN: 978-0-307-88791-7.

Cole, R. E. (2002). From continuous improvement to continuous innovation, *Total Quality Management*, 13:(8), 1051-1056.

Blanck, S. (2013). "Why the lean start-up changes everything". *Harvard Business Review*, vol. 91, no. 5, pp. 63-72.

Holmström Olsson, H. E Bosch, J. (2016). From requirements to continuous re-prioritization of hypotheses. *CSED '16.*

Lindgren, E. e Münch, J. (2015). Software Development as an Experiment System: A Qualitative Survey on the State of the Practice. *Agile Processes in Software Engineering and Extreme Programming,* volume 212. Springer, Cham.

ANVISA. Agência Nacional de Vigilância Sanitária. https://www.gov.br/anvisa/pt-br/assuntos/regulamentacao/legislacao/bibliotecas-tematicas/arquivos/produtos. Acessso em 04-01-2024.

Asiegbu, I. F., Daubry, P. e Iruka C. H. (2012). Consumer Attitude: Some Reflections on Its Concept, Trilogy, Relationship with Consumer Behavior, and Marketing Implications, *European Journal of Business and Management,* 4(13):38-50.

Tracking technical debt in agile low code developments

Renato Domingues[1,2], **Miguel Reis**[2], **Miguel Araújo**[2], **Marcelo Marinho**[1], **Mário J. Silva**[2,3]

[1]Departamento de Computação – Universidade Federal Rural de Pernambuco (UFRPE)
Recife – PE – Brazil

[2]Truewind, Axians Portugal
Recife – PE – Brazil
Lisboa – Portugal

[3]INESC-ID, IST, Universidade de Lisboa
Lisboa – Portugal

renato.domingues@ufrpe.br, miguel.reis@axians.com,

miguel.araujo@axians.com, marcelo.marinho@ufrpe.br, mjs@inesc-id.pt

Abstract. *We present a new practice for tracking technical debt in agile low code developments using new metrics obtained from the development environment. The automated collection of some of the metrics has significantly reduced the effort devoted to collecting project meta-data and makes it possible to run frequent self-assessments and internal audits with little effort. We have obtained evidence that more frequent audits during development help to identify and reduce technical debt, thus improving the quality of delivered software. In addition, we witness a general increase in the quality score of projects developed under the new practice.*

1. Introduction

Software organizations aim to deliver high-quality products and services, on time and at the lowest cost. However, in practice, design trade-offs and unplanned events frequently force developers to take shortcuts when developing their code. These time-saving shortcuts, which solve near-term problems but do not account for long-term implications, are one of the causes of what is known as technical debt [Cunningham 1992].

Low code is becoming prevalent for fast development of enterprise application software. However, higher productivity and reduced costs of low code development could be achieved at the expense of quality management practices established for software engineering. We believe that the quality of reliable complex enterprise software solutions based on agile low code platforms does not need to be sacrificed for speed. In fact, low code development methods, when supported by an appropriate methodology relying on automated metrics collection, should enable software engineers to achieve higher productivity while delivering high-quality complex enterprise solutions.

Some low code platforms help manage tech debt. AI Mentor Studio, from the OutSystems platform for enterprise software development, provides tech debt management support[1]. However, managing technical debt growth is hard to achieve, since ke-

[1]https://success.outsystems.com/documentation/11/managing_the_applications_lifecycle/manage_technical_debt/get_an_overview_of_the_overall_technical_debt/

eping it under control depends on teams behavior. Hence, establishing practices and software audits remains necessary to make the technical debt visible beyond the scope of individual project teams.

To address these challenges, we developed a lightweight, largely automated software auditing process tailored to our practice. This new process complements the data provided by the Outsystems platform with self-reported assessments and automated metrics.

The main objective of this paper is to introduce *QSP - Quality Solutions Program*, our approach for tackling technical debt in low code-based software solutions. QSP includes a tool that collects data from developers and exposes the internal audit results to end-users quickly and visually. QSP has been developed and used for the last two years at Truewind[2], an international company focused on agile transformation and agile low code development.

With QSP, we reduce the effort and time costs of carrying out project audits and allow them to be more frequent. Using the plots and charts generated in QSP, we have observed a general improvement in tech-debt scores over time, showcasing the success of our approach to managing tech debt with minimal additional effort (cost).

2. Background

2.1. Technical Debt

Cunningham introduced technical debt stating that *Shipping first-time code is like going into debt. A little debt speeds development so long as it is paid back promptly with a rewrite... The danger occurs when the debt is not repaid. Every minute spent on not quite right code counts as interest on that debt* [Cunningham 1992].

McConnell later defined technical debt as *delayed technical work that is incurred when technical shortcuts are taken, usually in pursuit of calendar-driven software schedules* [McConnell 2008].

In 2016, at the Dagstuhl Seminar 16162, academic and industrial experts proposed the most widely accepted definition of technical debt in software systems as *a collection of design or implementation constructs that are expedient in the short term, but set up a technical context that can make future changes more costly or impossible. Technical debt presents an actual or contingent liability whose impact is limited to internal system qualities, primarily maintainability and evolvability* [Avgeriou et al. 2016].

Krutchen classified the entries in a backlog according to their Visibility and value [Kruchten et al. 2012]: *Green*/Visible features are visible and have positive value; *Red*/Visible defects are visible and have negative value; *Yellow*/Architectural features are invisible and have positive value; and *Black*/Technical debt is invisible and has negative value. When determining the work of an iteration, the Product Manager wants more green items to be worked on, Customer Support wants more red items, and Architects the yellow ones, but no one wants to deal with the black items.

Li et al. carried out a systematic review to identify and classify the types of tech debt and tech debt management. Ten types of tech debt were identified: Requirements,

[2]`https://www.truewindglobal.com/`

Architectural, Design, Code, Test, Build, Documentation, Infrastructure, Versioning and Defect, as well as eight types of management: Identification, Measurement, Prioritization, Prevention, Monitoring, Repayment, Representation and Communication [Li et al. 2015].

2.2. Software Audits

Technical debt can be tackled as a quality issue. Asserting the quality of software is a complex task requiring multiple instruments, and one of the most used is audits [Helgeson 2009]. A software audit may be conducted at three levels: product, process, and system. The product audit is the lowest level and focuses on the final product. At the intermediate level, the process audit checks the methodology used in the product and its behavior. This audit yields the most visible results and is thus the most common. Lastly, the system audit (or quality audit) is the most complete, complex, and laborious. A system audit can cover the organization as a whole. Additionally, the development team (internal) can conduct these audit types or require an independent expert (external audits).

Audit processes are often only carried out at the end of a project, since they can be very expensive due to hiring third-party services and consume time. Depending on depth and complexity, an audit could take hours, days, or weeks. Excessive time (and cost) in an agile environment can be prohibitive. On the other hand, when an audit is carried out at the end stage of software development, it is often not possible to invest on substantial code refactoring, whether due to meeting delivery deadlines or lack of budget, which could remove identified technical debts.

2.3. Metrics and Audits for Agile Project Management

Metrics to define the success of an agile project include customer satisfaction, business value delivered, velocity, budget against actual cost, defects into production, cycle time, defects resolution, customer retention, estimation accuracy, test pass/fail overtime, revenue/sales impact, product utilization, and scope change in a release [Mkoba and Marnewick 2020]. Software quality can improve by automating the collection of metrics to measure agile teams' quality as it makes it possible to provide sprint-by-sprint performance feedback [Guerrero et al. 2019]. In a case study of 120 students divided into 20 teams carrying out a project in four two-week iterations, students worked without feedback in the first two iterations. In the two final iterations, they gained access to a software tool providing feedback, and their quality metrics showed a positive increase.

To identify problems earlier and facilitate their correction in agile development projects, it is important to know which metrics have to be audited, and the interaction between the auditor and the team so that the auditor understands what is being audited and the need to conduct audits at each project cycle [Truong 2020].

Joshi identifies three key components for an agile audit [Joshi 2021]: Backlog (collection of scoped work like audit plan), Sprints (scoped items divided into sprints time period), and Scrums (short and concise meetings to evaluate the work done and identify bottlenecks). He also defines five levels of maturity for an audit:

1. Minimal stakeholder engagement.
2. Improving team cooperation and planning methods.
3. Integration with agile practices and stakeholder collaboration.

4. Well-defined metrics are measured.
5. Audit optimization and agile audit tools are applied.

An agile audit has three main phases [KPM 2020]:

Planing and preliminary research: Determine what will be audited, what aspects are relevant to the audit, and define some metrics such as Definition of Ready and Definition of Done.

Audit execution: Defines how the sprint planning will be carried out, how the workload will be distributed, and based on the results of the previous sprint to schedule the next audit.

Completion and evaluation: Once the activities have provided enough information, carry out a product audit shared with all members involved; this audit contains objective, scope, conclusion, recommendations, and action plans.

2.4. Low code software development tools

For Waszkowski one of the advantages of Low code platforms is the support to visual programming tools with graphical user interfaces for application design, instead of hard-coded programming techniques [Waszkowski 2019]. Meanwhile, Sahay et al. state that by using low code platforms, developers can focus on the business logic rather than dealing with setting up computing infrastructure, managing data integrity across different environments, and ensuring non-functional aspects [Sahay et al. 2020].

The Outsystems low code development platform offers several tools that help manage software quality. Among these tools, we have the Quality Apps Program[3], which is used to monitor the quality of low code application developments made on the platform, and AI Mentor Studio[4], for static code analysis.

3. Auditing Low code developments with QSP

In our earlier practice, internal audits were established, but they were not frequent due to the effort of time and personnel needed to conduct them. Audits were normally postponed until the late stages or even after the last iteration before releasing a software project. So, it was also common that some of the problems encountered could not be properly resolved, with a negative impact on the perceived quality of Truewind's agile low code process for complex systems development. Some customers were reluctant to pay for what they perceived as expensive additional work.

Our new methodology for auditing agile low code projects relies on fast and short self-assessments, inspired by Kim et al.'s approach of increasing the frequency of internal audits in the agile development process [Kim et al. 2013]. In addition, new audit metrics are also proposed to better represent the concept of agile, including productivity, team performance, and correct selection of stories.

Our Quality Solutions Program (QSP) is our internal agile low code development process for complex enterprise solutions. QSP presently supports three practices:

[3] https://www.outsystems.com/blog/posts/launching-the-quality-apps-program/
[4] https://www.outsystems.com/product-updates/ai-mentor-studio/

Engagement Practice: monitors the use of agile methodologies and practices such as the use of Key Performance Indicators (KPIs), and the preparation and development of the sprints. The stakeholders conducting this practice are the Engagement Manager and the project's Auditor.

QA Practice: manages quality of the development process and mainly takes care of testing. The Stakeholders for this practice are the QA Lead and the Auditor.

Engineering Practice: The engineering part is responsible for the code, in this part, the issues present and the code developed are checked to verify the existence of possible problems and/or bad practices. The Stakeholders responsible for this practice are the Tech Lead and the Auditor.

3.1. Self-assessments in QSP

To guide a QSP self-assessment, we provide a checklist that teams use to evaluate their adherence to QSP best practices. The QSP self-assessment checklist provides a systematic approach to ensuring that crucial quality benchmarks are met throughout the project. Teams can effectively gauge their progress by answering key questions, such as:

- Does the project have a demo?
- Does the project have security tests planned?
- Is the team running sprint reviews?
- Is the team running sprint retrospectives?
- Is the team keeping optimal test coverage rates?

One of OutSystems AI Mentor Studio functions is to identify tech debts present in the code during development, so we can collect data from it and use it as one of the self-assessment inputs metrics to be able to monitor the amount of tech debts present throughout the process.

Most self-assessment questions in audits are framed as Boolean to keep the time required to complete an audit as short as possible. An answer score of 1/0 on a Boolean question means that the requirement was considered met/not met. For non-Boolean questions, answers with half scores (0.5) are also possible. The final score is calculated by averaging the scores of all provided answers:

$$FinalScore = \frac{\sum answer}{\sum Questions} \tag{1}$$

The Quality Apps Program of OutSystems awards a high-quality seal to those projects that obtain a minimum score of 85% in their assessment. In QSP we adopted the same threshold of 85% to award high-quality recognition to our teams' development teams.

All self-assessment scores are saved in the database and compared throughout the project, so a team's progress can be tracked throughout the entire process.

A key aspect of these self-assessments is that audit responses are visible to all company employees. Enabling this type of peer monitoring helps keep the reliability of responses high and helps promote and disseminate team practices that obtain higher QSP assessment scores.

3.2. Audits in QSP

A QSP audit lasts a maximum of two hours. If some questions remain unanswered within that time, the audit stops and only the answered questions are considered. To ensure that the most relevant questions are answered more frequently, all questions have a priority value and are asked by the order of priority. Priorities are calculated based on the time it takes to answer a question, its category, and/or internal rules.

Many development services at Truewind do not start with a clean slate. Projects may take on earlier developments by other teams or may even have been initially developed by other organizations. Such projects, in turn, may present different forms of technical debt that would influence both the team's work and the audit scores of the project. We call these debts *legacy items*. As the scores are public within the company, a project team could be unfairly perceived negatively by peers unaware of the project's starting point.

With this in mind, we give two scores to every QSP audit:

Project score: Sum of the self-assessment and the audit results considering the legacy issues.

Team score: Sum of the self-assessment and the audit results excluding the legacy issues.

All data submitted to QSP by a team and obtained self-assessment results are stored and compared against their previous submission. As a result, teams receive real-time feedback on how their tech debt is evolving. With this information in hand, teams can analyze and better understand what they did right and what needs to be reviewed and improved.

4. Metrics collection automation

With the QSP, engagement managers can run a self-assessment of a project, which provides results obtained from automatically collected data. Within a self-assessment, there are six categories of metrics: Lean, Reliability, Methodology, Delivery, Dev Ops, and Strategy – Value. Each of these metrics may or may not weigh on the final result of the self-assessment. Table 1 shows some of these metrics (those that do not weigh on the final score of the self-assessment are marked with * at the end of their title).

4.1. Information extraction

We initially established the company's Jira[5] issue tracking system as the primary data source. However, after an initial analysis of the historical data, we realized that the lack of common guidelines for filling out Jira forms was destroying the usefulness of the extracted data. Some of the problems encountered are:

- Lack of filling in relevant text fields, such as description and summary, as well as numeric fields, such as time spent and estimated time;
- Multiple interpretations for the meaning of a given field;
- Incorrect use of the issue type when creating an issue.

We then defined new practices for structuring and standardizing the meta-data in Jira projects, enabling automatic extraction of information. The newly adopted practices include, among others:

[5] `https://www.atlassian.com/software/jira`

Audit Category	Metric
Lean	Project FTE vs User Stories and Cycle time*
Reliability	Reported incidents since last assessment
Reliability	Number of non-trivial bugs in Quality*
Methodology	Definition of Ready
Methodology	Definition of Done
Methodology	Sprint planning done
Methodology	Sprint review done
Methodology	Sprint retrospective done
Delivery	Deploy & Rollback plan available
Delivery	Sprint duration according to the plan
Delivery	Backlog management (prioritized, refined for sprint n and n + 1 and high-level for the remaining)
Delivery	% of Story items done
Delivery	Estimation accuracy (Delivery - fixed price) & Velocity (AMS)
Dev-ops	Time taken from code being deployed into QA to Production
Dev-ops	Time to restore
Dev-ops	Change fail %
Strategy - Value	Identified Business and Operational Outcomes
Strategy - Value	Available Stakeholder map analysis

Table 1. EM's self-assessment metrics in QSP's Audit categories

Project creation centralization: New projects must be created through a form requesting the necessary information. Previously, we let our project leaders define their projects however they found most suited, thus creating a hard-to-manage variety of project patterns.

Boards template: Project boards must be created using a pre-defined template for each project type. Previously, leaders could also create several attributes in Jira and name them arbitrarily, making it hard to find what each one represented.

Issue types standardization: Allowed issue types have been limited to a pre-defined set. We found that the semantics of each issue type among engagement managers were very subjective, so there was no standard defining what each project metadata attribute represented.

Standardization of the project title: The name of projects in the company´s Jira repository must follow a defined pattern coding its project type. As the predefined project types in Jira do not comply with our internally defined types, we standardized project naming rules so that it is possible to identify a project's type by scanning a project's name on Jira.

Burn remaining estimate: As soon as a ticket enters the Testing phase, any remaining estimates should automatically be burned (dropped to zero) so that the total remaining effort is always up to date. One of the problems identified during the data analysis was that several issues were transferred to the "Done"state but the estimate was not correctly filled, causing the sprint remaining effort on our Jira repository to show incorrect values.

After implementing these new practices in Jira, we waited approximately six months for new data to be generated. With the new data in hand, we observed six projects to assess to what extent the new practices achieved the desired objectives. We concluded that the data of all six tested Jira projects was ready for automation.

4.2. QSP metrics collection

Many metrics of QSP self-assessments cannot be obtained from the data in Jira, just as some information that the data contains is not always clear to the Engagement Manager when performing a self-assessment. Therefore, it was necessary to select which metrics could be extracted automatically for QSP self-assessments. We arrived at three categories of metrics:

1) User Story Definition metrics:

INVEST criteria: User Stories should be focused on features – not tasks, and written in business language. Doing so will enable business people to understand and prioritize the User Stories.

User stories sizing: A User story is the smallest unit of work that needs to be done. Taking the INVEST acronym for Story definition, the S (Small) is the most important, and we should guide our teams to cut their work into less than 2 days chunks wherever possible.

User stories average size: Purely informative data that compares the average number of hours in user stories for this sprint against the company average.

Acceptance criteria: It clearly defines the scope, desired outcomes, and testing criteria for pieces of functionality that the delivery team is working on.

Definition of Ready (DoR) & Definition of Done (DoD): Reinforce transparency, assure Built-In Quality, and set the right expectations for the work items to be planned, developed, and completed.

Work item type: Purely informative data that shows the number of issues of each type created in this sprint.

2) Board Management metrics:

Reported defects: It is purely informative information that shows the quantity of each type of defect severity created in this sprint.

Backlog prioritization or MoSCoW: Backlog is prioritized in a way that helps build consensus, establish a unified direction, and gain a broader perspective.

Defects management: Verify if the defects are being handled as any other Backlog item (sized, classified).

UX/UI management: UX/UI Backlog should be handled as any other activity: Planned, developed, and reviewed / validated. As such, it is checked whether there are issues of this type in this sprint.

Sprint goal defined: While it's easy to gather a bunch of Backlog Items to work on in a Sprint, it's a little harder (but much more valuable) to have a set of Backlog Items that fit together and in this way, provide more business value.

3) Quality & Control metrics:

Sprint Definition: Compare the difference between the items that were planned at the beginning of the sprint and how many of them were completed.

Capacity Tracker: Calculates the capacity in hours of this team for this sprint, based on the number of sprint days, developers, team members' off days, and a constant to represent the sprint stabilization period, then compares it with the estimated time for the issues planned for this sprint.

Estimation Accuracy: Compares the number of worklog hours logged within the sprint period against the capacity value of that sprint. If a defined minimum threshold is not met, it is assumed that the project team did not log the correct number of hours for the sprint and will receive the maximum penalty for this metric (0%). If above the threshold the Estimation accuracy is computed by subtracting from 100% the absolute value of the observed Relative Accuracy Error of the estimation:

$$RelAccuracyError = \frac{(\sum planned - \sum logged)}{\sum planned} \quad (2)$$

$$EstimationAccuracy = 100\% - |RelAccuracyError| \quad (3)$$

Issues Estimation: Compares the number of issues that were planned for the sprint and defects with severity *Major* or *Critical* that have effort estimation with the total number of issues of these types.

# of bugs in Quality: That is a two-step metric:

1. Get the list of Stories belonging to this project and compare it with the list of issues that have test coverage. If the result of this comparison is larger than the minimum threshold defined, then this sprint has a minimum test coverage and can go to the next step, otherwise, it means that not enough tests were planned for this project and it receives the maximum penalty for this metric.
2. We compare the number of defects that are of *Critical*, *Major*, and *Minor* severity with the number of Increments (Stories and Improvements).

4.3. QSP Audit scores

We assign four score grades to each metric: *Excellent*, *Good*, *To improve*, and *Not met*, which corresponds to obtaining 100% of the metric's full score, 2/3, 1/3 and 0%, respectively. Furthermore, we have also developed the metrics so that they are always categorized into one of the four available grades or are in a range of 0 to 100%. By default, we consider *Excellent* those with 85% or above, *Good* from 84 to 75%, *To improve* 74 to 50%, and below that is *Not met*. Similar to the final self-assessment score, we can calculate the final audit score using Equation 4:

$$AuditScore = \sum_{i=1}^{f} Metric_i * weight_i \quad (4)$$

4.4. QSP Dashboards

To give a perspective on what data is provided to developer teams, we will be showing throughout this section some of the QSP dashboards of audited projects. While the data are real, all project and employee names given below, as well as some acronyms are replaced with pseudonyms to preserve confidentiality.

Figure 1 shows an example of what information is presented on a project dashboard. Figure 1a, displays the self-assessment delivery deadlines. If a deadline is being reached/has passed and the result has yet to be delivered/has already passed, the orange/red color is used to highlight it. The central part of the panel shows the Project Score and the Team Score of the project in this assessment, together with a comparison with the past score (both scores had a drop of 0.92%). As the grade is above 85%, this card is colored green, otherwise, it would be colored red. Below we can see some project indicators, prioritizing those that did not pass the tests, thus making it clearer what needs to be improved. In the displayed project, two indicators are colored red (*n*ot passed), one yellow (*T*o be improved), and one green. Figure 1b displays the complete history of scores of a project.

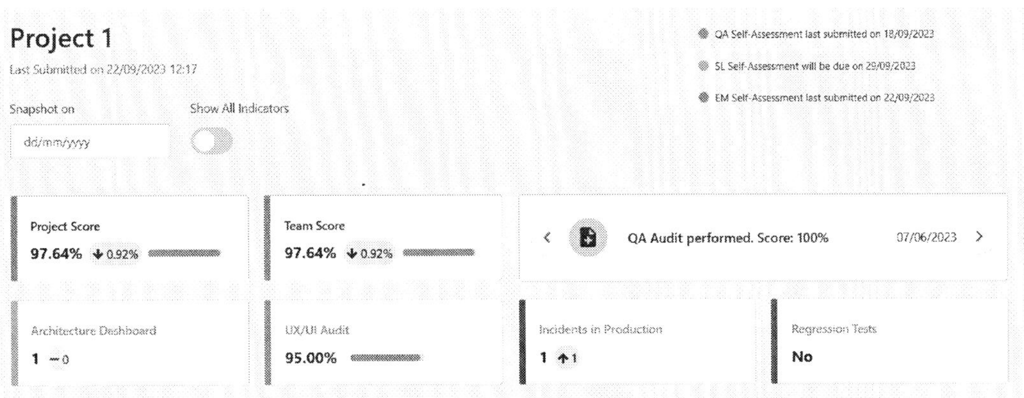

a) self-assessment delivery deadlines

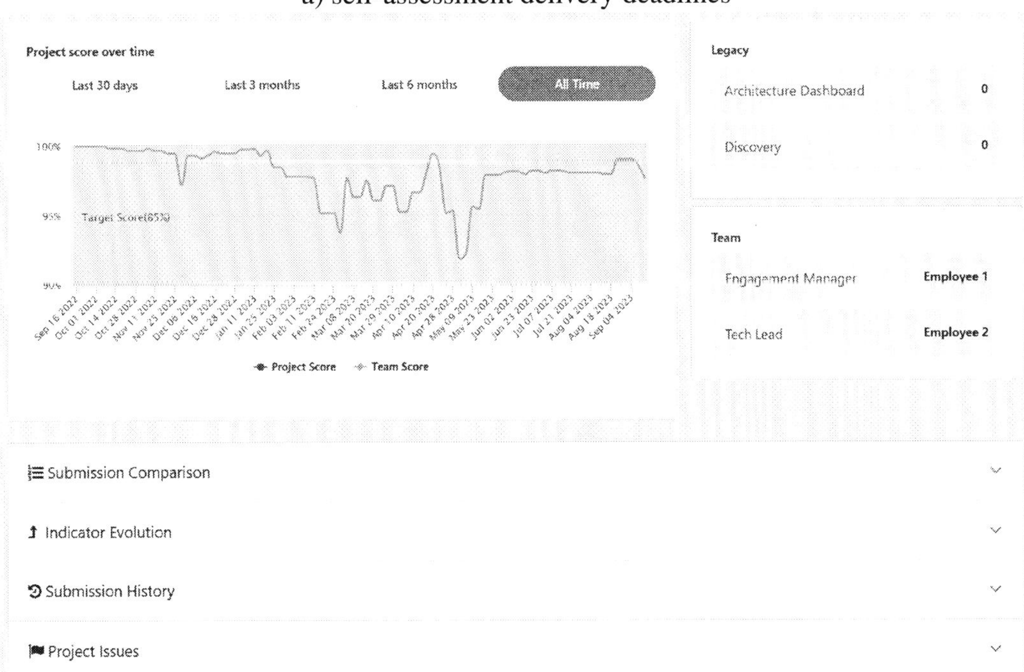

b) QSP scores timeline; as the project does not have legacy items, the Project and Team Scores are always the same

Figure 1. QSP-audited project summary.

Figure 2 shows the Methodology audit score and metrics to be improved and presented to Engagement Managers.

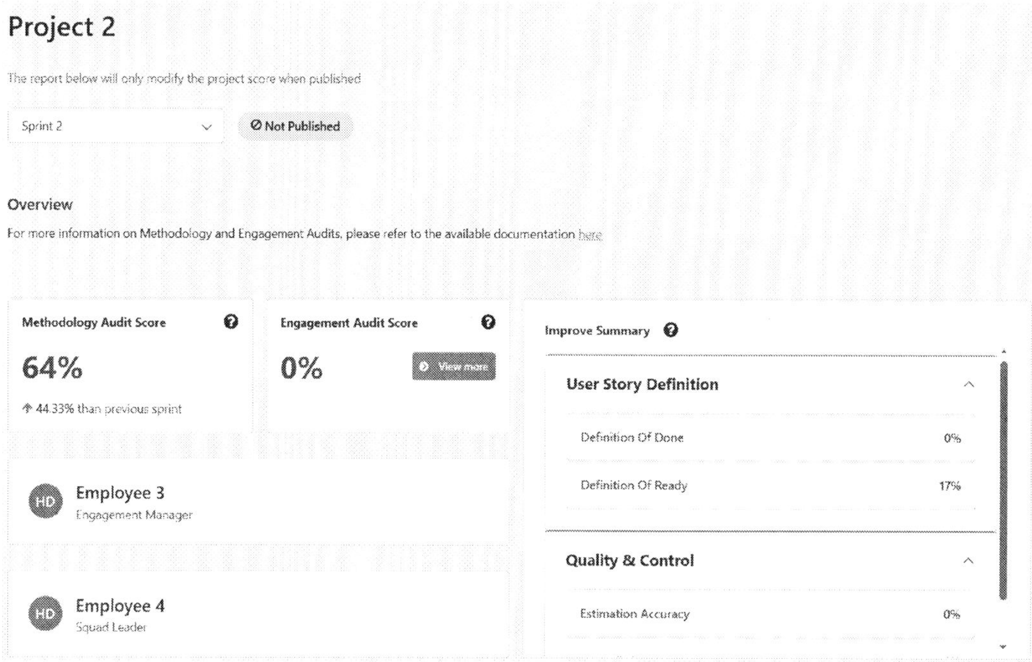

Figure 2. Engagement Manager details of a QSP audited project. The audit score is shown on the left and the metrics that need to be improved on the right.

5. Results

At the time of writing this article, the QSP has been used in more than 30 projects and currently has 8 others active, by teams from different sizes, from 3 to 10 members per team.

Figure 3a) shows the average score of the projects in the metrics most directly related to technical debts, such as the number of debts and discovery, which represent the number of simple technical debts found in the project and an analysis of the application architecture in search of debts, respectively. Initially, in the first four months, we had the lowest team scores, but since the third month, all team scores are already above the desired 85%. Meanwhile, project scores are most often below expectations, this may be because the project was started by the team at that time but is a project with many legacy items. This shows the importance of using the two scores to account for legacy items, as this could negatively impact team morale and mislead managers. Figure 3b), shows the average of the scores of all internal audits carried out by all QSP projects, such as EM Audits, Quality Audits, and UX/UI audits, when applicable. Initially, the projects were not performing so well, but since December 2022 they have reached values above the target score. The quality part took a little longer to be developed and that is why we only have data from 2023, but as shown in Figure 3c), despite having only reached the target in June, from that month onwards, all scores reached the target value.

Finally, Figure 3d) shows the mean of the final score of all the projects and teams. Although once again the first four months had the lowest results, since then, we have always achieved the target score. The Project score on the other hand, despite reaching the 85% mark in every month except the first four and December of 2023, likely because the teams inherited a new project with high technical debt, still reached the target score in all other months.

When we take the grades for the year 2022 we obtain an average score of 88.22% for tech debt, 85.80% for audits and 87.64% for the final score, in 2023 these metrics rose to 93.88 %, 91.52% and 91.96% respectively. The quality metric cannot be calculated in this way given that the 2022 sample is only one month, however if we take the first 6 months and compare them with the following 6 months we obtain 78.12% and 94.62%. With this we can see that the score of projects in year 2023 were better than those in 2022 in all aspects, where the tech debt score increased by 6.42%, audit score 6.67% and the final score in 4.93%. The sum of all these indicated results, together with other non-measurable results such as greater interest among employees in talking about how to improve, lead us to consider the QSP as a successful project in our environment.

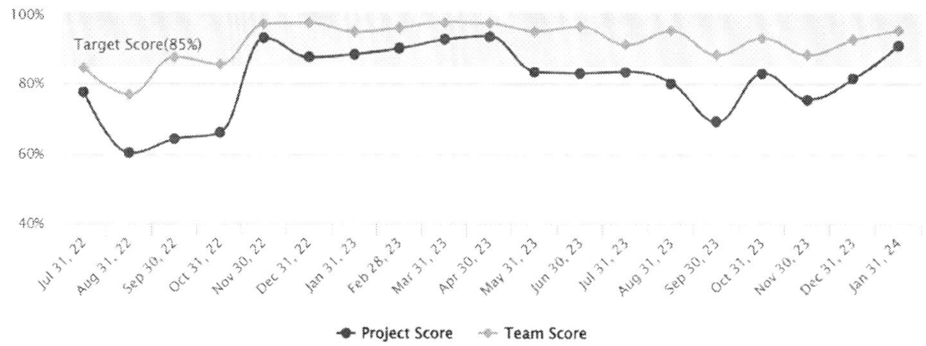

a) Technical debit metrics score

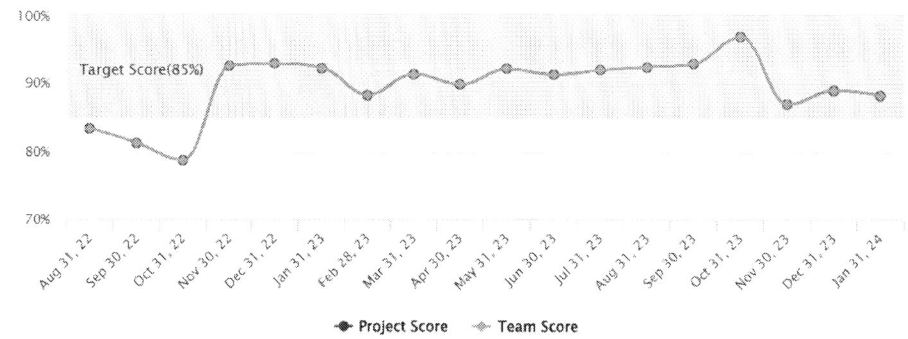

b) Project audit score

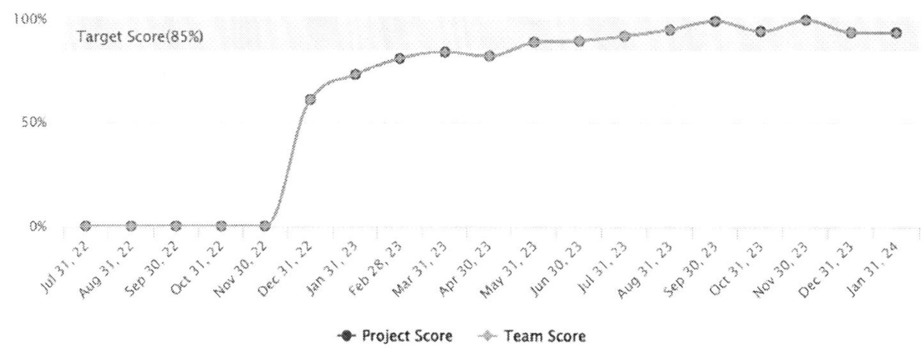

c) Quality metrics score

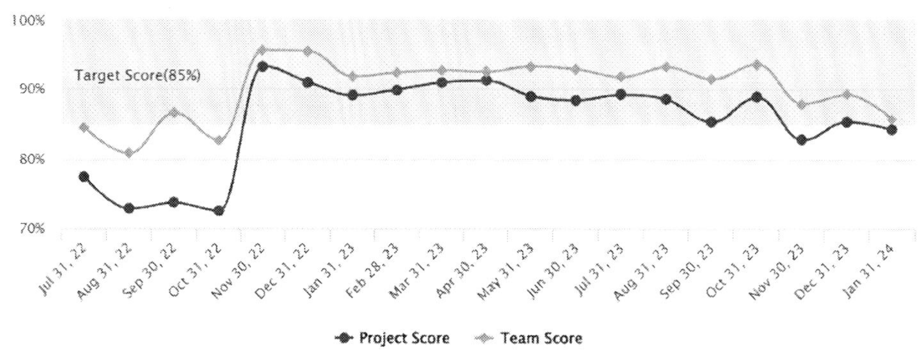

d) Final score

Figure 3. Overall performance of projects in the QSP

6. Conclusion

Our new QSP is supported by an app that easily and graphically presents the technical debts of a project. The app includes an automatic metrics collection module that enables fast and frequent self-assessments. We presented various metrics used both in internal audits and self-assessment questionnaires, along with the new practices established across software teams in our organization.

A notorious outcome of introducing QSP is that it helps trigger technical conversations among development teams. Previously it was uncommon to observe co-workers talking about their difficulties. Co-workers often did not even know they could obtain help until it was too late. Through QSP they are now able to find and contact those who had succeeded in overcoming similar hardships.

It is important to also highlight some of the limitations and points for improvement identified throughout the development of QSP. The first major current limitation is the fact that we are heavily dependent on the API provided by Jira. The second is also related to a recurring situation in projects developed for customers who required that all the project development artifacts be maintained in their Jira instance, or in some other repository that they use, and do not provide open access to the API by QSP. Therefore, we do not have direct access to project data and are unable to perform automatic extraction and auditing. This problem, however, could be mitigated by informing customers of the benefits of using QSP to track tech debt and offering them access to the collected data, in exchange for opening access to their repository for collecting project data. A third problem is somewhat more complex and does not directly involve our code. In our self-assessments, lies in the answers are not encouraged nor rewarded. However, if in our working culture lies becomes pervasive and unreported, auditors would need to constantly check the veracity of obtained answers. This would create an even greater workload on auditors than if no self-assessment had been made, leading to a reduction of our auditing capacity and consequently removing the advantage of our approach.

There are some points where data collection automation needs improvement. For example, for String fields the automation only checks if they are not empty, no content validation is performed. Presently, there is an optional manual intermediate step in the audit, where an auditor can manually look at the values of each field and change their scores if he deems it necessary.

Referências

(2020). Agile internal audit: White paper on working agile within internal audit functions (part ii: Concrete guidance for the set-up of the agile internal audit function and the execution of agile audits). KPMG, `https://assets.kpmg.com/content/dam/kpmg/nl/pdf/2020/sectoren/agile-internal-audit-2.pdf`. Accessed: 2023-09-23.

Avgeriou, P., Kruchten, P., Ozkaya, I., and Seaman, C. (2016). Managing technical debt in software engineering (dagstuhl seminar 16162). In *Dagstuhl reports*, volume 6. Schloss Dagstuhl-Leibniz-Zentrum fuer Informatik.

Cunningham, W. (1992). The wycash portfolio management system. *ACM Sigplan Oops Messenger*, 4(2):29–30.

Guerrero, A., Fresno, R., Ju, A., Fox, A., Fernandez, P., Muller, C., and Ruiz-Cortés, A. (2019). Eagle: A team practices audit framework for agile software development. In *Proceedings of the 2019 27th ACM Joint Meeting on European Software Engineering Conference and Symposium on the Foundations of Software Engineering*, pages 1139–1143.

Helgeson, J. W. (2009). *The software audit guide*. Quality Press.

Joshi, P. L. (2021). A review of agile internal auditing: Retrospective and prospective. *International Journal of Smart Business and Technology*, 9(2):13–32.

Kim, D. H., Kim, D. S., Koh, C., and Kim, H. W. (2013). An information system audit model for project quality improvement by the agile methodology. *International Journal of Information and Education Technology*, 3(3):295.

Kruchten, P., Nord, R. L., and Ozkaya, I. (2012). Technical debt: From metaphor to theory and practice. *Ieee software*, 29(6):18–21.

Li, Z., Avgeriou, P., and Liang, P. (2015). A systematic mapping study on technical debt and its management. *Journal of Systems and Software*, 101:193–220.

McConnell, S. (2008). Managing technical debt. Construx Software white paper: `https://www.construx.com/wp-content/uploads/2019/02/CxWhitePaper_TechnicalDebt.pdf`. Accessed: 2023-09-27.

Mkoba, E. and Marnewick, C. (2020). Conceptual framework for auditing agile projects. *IEEE Access*, 8:126460–126476.

Sahay, A., Indamutsa, A., Di Ruscio, D., and Pierantonio, A. (2020). Supporting the understanding and comparison of low-code development platforms. In *2020 46th Euromicro Conference on Software Engineering and Advanced Applications (SEAA)*, pages 171–178. IEEE.

Truong, L. (2020). Agile auditing: More value, less resources. *Edpacs*, 62(1):4–7.

Waszkowski, R. (2019). Low-code platform for automating business processes in manufacturing. *IFAC-PapersOnLine*, 52(10):376–381.

Um Mapeamento do MPS.Br para o Desenvolvimento de Dispositivos Médicos com Foco em Engenharia de Requisitos

Johnny Marques[1], **Everton Machado**[1]

[1]Programa de Pós-graduação em Engenharia Eletrônica e Computação
Instituto Tecnológico de Aeronáutica (ITA)

{johnny, everton}@ita.br

Abstract. *All Medical Devices must comply with regulations to ensure user and patient safety. This includes the embedded software in these products. In Brazil, the ABNT NBR 62304:2023 was recently nationalized, focusing on the software lifecycle for medical devices. Conversely, Brazil has a Brazilian Software Process Improvement Program, MPS.Br for Software, which also sets Expected Outcomes reflecting good quality in development. Also in 2023, MPS.Br for Software was updated. Therefore, the research problem addressed in this work involves "How does MPS.Br, through the 4 software development design processes, manage to meet the clauses of ABNT NBR 62304:2023?" The proposed solution involves constructing a mapping initially focused on the "Software Requirements Analysis"activity of ABNT NBR 62304:2023 to the Expected Outcomes of the Software Requirements Engineering process of MPS.Br for Software. Thus, the methodological procedures involved five stages described in this work, including a focus group of experts in this software domain for medical devices. Promoting mapping of the clauses involved in ABNT NBR 62304:2023 to the Outcomes of the Software Requirements Engineering process of MPS.Br for Software.*

Resumo. *Todos os Dispositivos Médicos precisam atender às regulamentações para garantir a segurança do usuário e do paciente. Isso inclui o software embutido nestes produtos. No Brasil, foi recentemente nacionalizada a ABNT NBR 62304:2023, que se preocupa com o ciclo de vida de software para os dispositivos médicos. Em contrapartida, o Brasil possui um programa de Melhoria do Processo de Software Brasileiro, o MPS.Br de Software, que também estipula Resultados Esperados que refletem uma boa qualidade no desenvolvimento. Também em 2023, o MPS.Br de Software foi atualizado. Assim, o problema de pesquisa abordado neste trabalho envolve "Como que o MPS.Br, por meio dos 4 processos de projeto de desenvolvimento de software é capaz de satisfazer as cláusulas da ABNT NBR 62304:2023?". A solução proposta envolve a construção de um mapeamento focado inicialmente na atividade "Análise de Requisitos de Software" a ABNT NBR 62304:2023 para os Resultados Esperados do processo de Engenharia de Requisitos do MPS.Br de Software. Assim, os procedimentos metodológicos envolveram cinco etapas descritas neste trabalho envolvendo um grupo focal de especialistas neste domínio de software para dispositivos médicos. Promovendo um mapeamento das cláusulas envolvidas da ABNT NBR 62304:2023 para os Resultados Esperados do processo de Engenharia de Requisitos do MPS.Br de Software.*

1. Introdução

Normalmente, o software crítico para a segurança é desenvolvido em ambientes regulamentados por padrões e as agências reguladoras em indústrias críticas para a segurança normalmente exigem que os fornecedores de sistemas atendam a requisitos de certificação rigorosos. O desenvolvimento de sistemas críticos para a segurança geralmente faz parte de um ambiente regulamentado. Um erro de desenvolvimento de software pode causar diretamente perdas de vidas humanas ou ter outras consequências catastróficas [Marques 2019].

Os padrões publicados por comitês, entidades técnicas internacionais ou agências reguladoras influenciam o desenvolvimento de Software em Ambientes Regulamentados por meio de diretrizes para processos e produtos de software [Munch et al. 2012], visando à mitigação de erros no desenvolvimento de software. Além disso, existem várias semelhanças entre os padrões para desenvolvimento de software nas áreas de aviação, automotiva, ferrovias e especialmente na área de medicina e saúde [Marques and Cunha 2019].

Um Sistema de Saúde (SS) é composto por várias partes físicas e lógicas. Um ou mais Dispositivos Médicos (DMs) fazem parte de um SS, sendo responsáveis pelo controle das informações necessárias [Marques et al. 2021]. Um Software de Dispositivo Médico (SDM) é carregado e operado em um Dispositivo Médico (DM). Cada SDM é composto por Unidades de Software, que são qualquer parte identificável de um software.

De acordo com Magnusson (2012) , todos os Dispositivos Médicos precisam atender às regulamentações para garantir a segurança do usuário e do paciente. Em 2006, um grupo de trabalho da *International Organization for Standardization* (ISO) e a *International Electrotechnical Commission* (IEC) definiu a ISO/IEC 62304:2006 [ISO 2006]. Posteriormente, em 2015, essa norma foi revisitada a atualizada.

A Figura 1 apresenta uma associação ilustrativa desses conceitos. A ISO/IEC 62304 opera no âmbito do SDM, ISs e Unidades de Software (USs). A ISO/IEC 62304:2015 [ISO 2015] apresenta os requisitos associados ao rigor dos processos de desenvolvimento e manutenção do SDM, conforme o risco de segurança [Marques 2019]. Esta norma foi nacionalizada no Brasil por meio da ABNT NBR 62304:2023 [ABNT 2023].

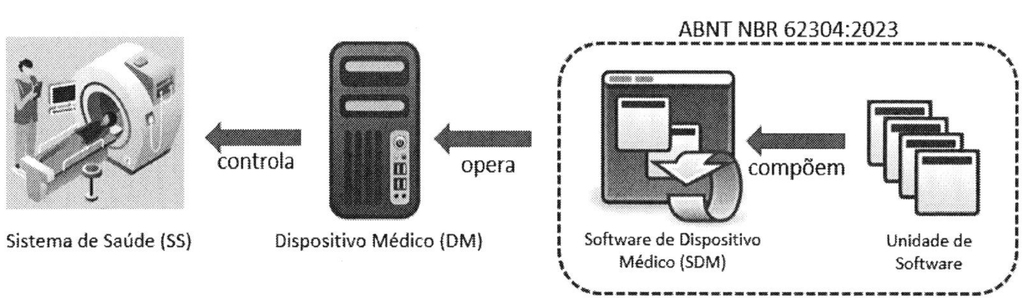

Figura 1. Escopo da ABNT NBR 62304:2023 - adaptado de [Marques et al. 2021]

O MPS.Br é um programa mobilizador, de longo prazo, criado em dezembro de 2003 e coordenado pela Associação para Promoção da Excelência do Software Brasileiro

(SOFTEX). O Guia Geral de Software do MPS [Softex 2023] apresenta 4 (quartro) processos de projeto associados diretamente ao desenvolvimento de software (Engenharia de Requisitos, Projeto e Construção de Software, Integração de Produto e Verificação e Validação).

Em virtude da recente nacionalização da norma ISO/IEC 62304:2015 no Brasil, convertida para ABNT NBR 62304:2023, e considerando a existência do consolidado programa em Engenharia de Software, o MPS.Br, com mais de duas décadas de atuação, os autores deste trabalho buscam explorar possíveis similaridades entre o MPS.Br de Software e a ABNT NBR 62304:2023. Nesse contexto, a seguinte pergunta de pesquisa é delineada: "Como que o MPS.Br, por meio dos 4 processos de projeto de desenvolvimento de software, é capaz de satisfazer as cláusulas da ABNT NBR 62304:2023?"

Com o intuito de abordar parcialmente essa indagação, o objetivo deste estudo consiste em realizar um mapeamento das cláusulas previstas na atividade "Análise de Requisitos de Software"da ABNT NBR 62304:2023 para os Resultados Esperados do Processo de Engenharia de Requisitos do MPS.Br de Software. Este trabalho representa uma pesquisa em andamento no Instituto Tecnológico de Aeronáutica e engloba a elaboração de um mapeamento abrangente, incluindo todos os Resultados Esperados do MPS.Br e as cláusulas da ABNT NBR 62304:2023.

Além desta seção introdutória, o trabalho é composto por mais 5 seções. Na seção 2, é apresentada uma fundamentação teórica. Na seção 3, são sintetizadas as etapas dos procedimentos metodológicos aplicados. Na seção 4, é detalhado um relato da execução de cada uma das etapas dos procedimentos metodológicos. A seção 5 aborda as ameaças à validade deste trabalho e, por fim, a seção 6 apresenta a conclusão.

2. Fundamentação Teórica

A engenharia de software desempenha um papel crucial na garantia da qualidade e segurança de produtos e sistemas, especialmente os de saúde. Uma das importantes neste contexto é a ABNT NBR 62304:2023, que trata dos requisitos para o ciclo de vida de software de dispositivos médicos, recentemente nacionalizada no Brasil. Essa fundamentação teórica está estruturada em 3 subseções: Uma visão geral da ABNT NBR 62304:2023; uma visão geral do MPS.Br de Software e uma síntese de trabalhos correlatos.

2.1. ABNT NBR 62304:2023

A ABNT NBR 62304:2023 define os requisitos do ciclo de vida para SDMs. A estrutura da norma segue uma hierarquia composta por processos, atividades e cláusulas, estabelecendo um quadro comum para os processos do ciclo de vida de SDMs. Um processo se divide em atividades e cada uma desta é refinada por um conjunto de cláusulas.

O cumprimento da ABNT NBR 62304:2023 é definido como a implementação de todos os processos, atividades e cláusulas identificados nesta norma, seguindo a classe de segurança de software.

A ABNT NBR 62304:2023 descreve 5 (cinco) processos: Processo de Desenvolvimento de Software, Processo de Manutenção de Software, Processo de Gerenciamento de Risco de Software, Processo de Gerenciamento de Configuração de Software e Processo de Resolução de Problemas de Software, conforme mostrado na Figura 2. O Processo de Desenvolvimento de Software contém 8 (oito) atividades que posteriormente são refinadas em cláusulas.

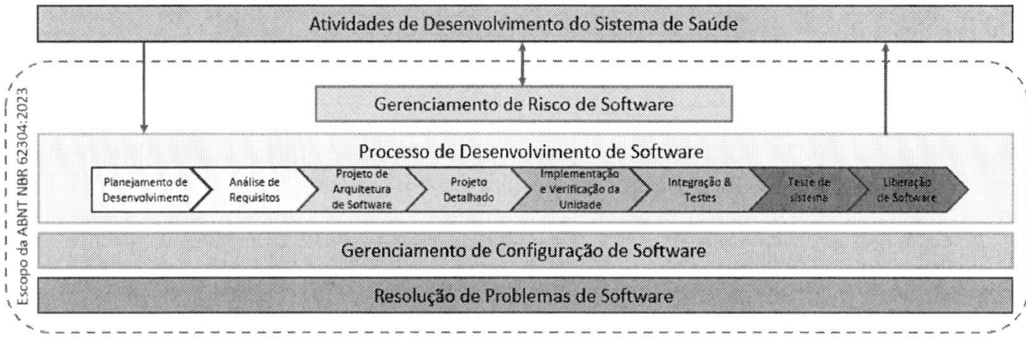

Figura 2. Visão geral dos Processos da ABNT NBR 62304:2023 - adaptado de [Marques et al. 2021]

O fabricante de Software de Dispositivo Médico deve aplicar um processo de gerenciamento de riscos usando a ISO 14971:2019 [ISO 2019], onde os riscos de segurança são identificados para os usuários (pacientes e equipe médica) em relação ao mau funcionamento do software. Essa análise definirá as classes de software (A, B e C) fornecidas pela ABNT NBR 62304:2023. As classes de segurança determinam o rigor no processo de desenvolvimento de software por meio das cláusulas. Marques et al. (2021) apresentaram a quantidade de atividades associadas a cada classe, conforme mostrado na Tabela 1. Quanto maior quantidade de cláusulas associadas, maior é o rigor que deve ser aplicado no processo de desenvolvimento de software.

Tabela 1. Classes de segurança de software, impactos e total de cláusulas requeridas

Classe	Impacto	Cláusulas Requeridas
A	Nenhuma lesão ou dano à saúde é possível.	48
B	Lesão não grave é possível.	85
C	Morte ou lesão grave é possível.	89

Uma das principais contribuições da ABNT NBR 62304:2023 é o fluxo de classificação de risco para os SDMs existentes em um Sistema de Saúde. Inicialmente, toda análise começa com a categoria mais severa (Classe C). Após seguir o fluxo fornecido na Figura 3, a classificação pode ser alterada para Classe A ou B se as condições existentes na análise de risco forem atendidas.

2.2. MPS.Br

O MPS.Br é um programa mobilizador, de longo prazo, criado em dezembro de 2003, coordenado pela Associação para Promoção da Excelência do Software Brasileiro (SOFTEX)[Softex 2023]. O MPS.Br é composto por 4 (quatro) modelos: de Software, de Serviços, de Gestão de Pessoal e de Avaliação. Esses modelos são descritos por meio de guias e, para finalidade deste estudo, a guia de interesse é a Guia Geral de Software. Esta guia detalha o Modelo de Referência do MPS.br para Software, seus componentes e as definições comuns necessárias para seu entendimento e aplicação.

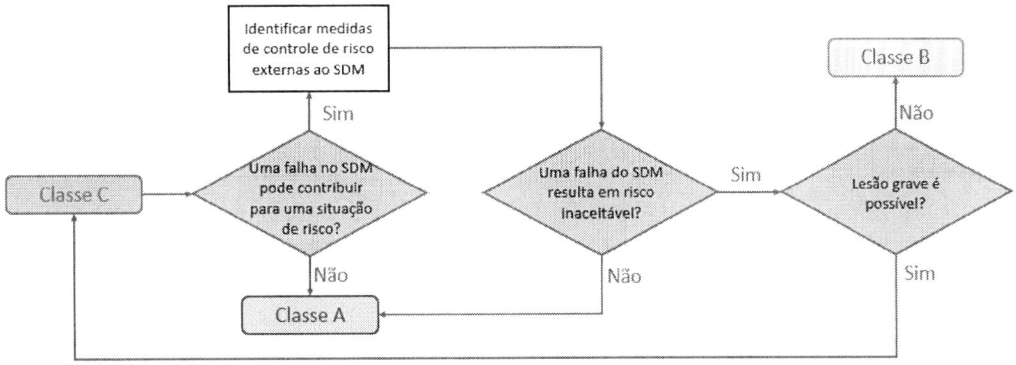

Figura 3. Atribuição da classe de software a partir da análise de risco de segurança - adaptado de [ISO 2015]

O MPS.Br de software define níveis de maturidade que são uma combinação entre processos e suas capacidades. Os processos estão divididos em dois grandes grupos: Processos de Projeto e Processos Organizacionais.

Os Processos de Projeto são aqueles executados para os projetos de software. Por outro lado, os Processos Organizacionais são os processos concebidos para fornecer os recursos necessários para que o projeto/serviço atenda às expectativas e necessidades das partes interessadas [Softex 2023]. A Tabela 2 foi adaptada da Guia Geral do MPS.br para software e mostra a organização dos processos e seus agrupamentos.

Processos de Projeto	Processos Organizacionais
Gerência de Projeto	Gerência de Recursos Humanos
Engenharia de Requisitos	Gerência de Configuração
Projeto e Construção do Produto	Gerência Organizacional
Integração do Produto	Gerência de Processos
Verificação e Validação	Medição
	Aquisição
	Gerência de Decisões

Tabela 2. Estrutura de processos do MPS.Br de Software [Softex 2023]

Os resultados esperados dos processos estão adequados a cada nível de maturidade pretendido, ou seja, nem todos os resultados estão presentes nos níveis iniciais e eles vão evoluindo à medida que evolui a maturidade da organização, conforme a Figura 4. Os resultados são acumulativos, ou seja, os resultados que aparecem no nível G deverão estar presentes, com as mesmas características ou com evoluções, no nível F e acima [Softex 2023].

2.3. Trabalhos Correlatos

Kalinowski *et al.* (2011) abordaram a importância das pesquisas desenvolvidas à cerca dos processos de software e da qualidade derivada da melhoria destes processos. Explicaram que no exterior as pesquisas estão avançadas e que o programa MPS.br é um programa estratégico do ponto de vista do Governo Brasileiro e, por fim, apresenta o papel da academia de Engenharia de Software na criação e transferência de conhecimento.

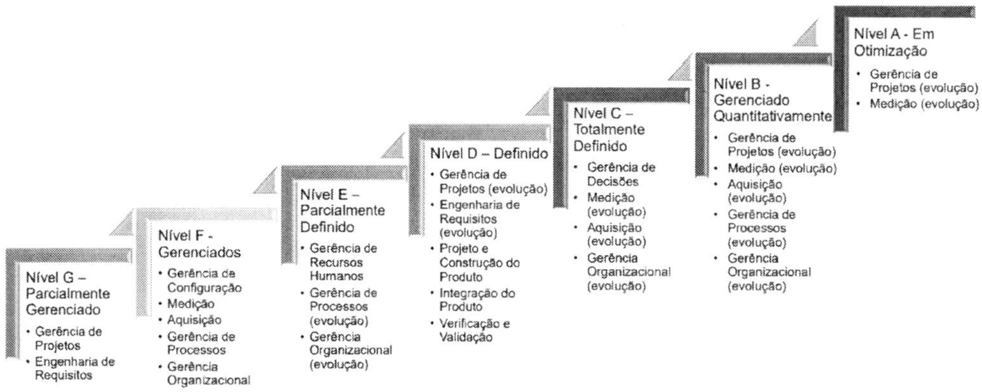

Figura 4. Evolução dos Processos nos Níveis de Maturidade [Softex 2023]

Neto *et al.* (2011) propuseram um Modelo de Referência para auxiliar pequenas empresas a instituir seus processos de software, baseado no MPS.Br de Software. Utilizando as orientações contidas na guia de referência, eles estabeleceram fases de projeto como: *Pré-Desenvolvimento*, *Desenvolvimento* e *Pós-Desenvolvimento*. Por fim, definiram áreas de concentrações que iam desde o *Planejamento Estratégico* até *Descontinuar Produto*.

Ferreiros *et al.* (2015) estudaram o nível de aderência do CMMI 1.3 [SEI 2010] em relação aos objetivos estabelecidos pela norma de segurança RTCA DO-178C [RTCA 2011], usada em Software para a Aviação. Na seção de trabalhos futuros, os autores indicam que uma metodologia para alcançar cada atividade não atendida pelo CMMI 1.3 seria um complemento ao estudo apresentado.

Kasisopha *et al.* (2019) apresentaram uma diretriz para uma pequena empresa que empregou a ISO/IEC 29110:2018 [ISO 2018] e deseja aplicar os processos da ISO/IEC 62304:2006. O trabalho relata a utilidade em se preparar a pequena empresa no planejamento da aplicação da ISO/IEC 62304:2006.

Rocha *et al.* (2020) relataram a experiência de uma avaliação remota do MPS.Br e as adaptações feitas no processo de avaliação durante o período da pandemia de COVID-19. Por fim, são discutidos os fatores críticos de sucesso na opinião da equipe de avaliação, do implementador do MPS.Br e da empresa.

Marques *et al.* (2021) apresentaram um mapeamento sistemático da literatura envolvendo os trabalhos que reportam utilizações, vantagens e dificuldades no uso da ISO/IEC 62304:2006 em seus quase 15 anos de existência.

Machado *et al.* (2023) propuseram o ME-MPS, um Modelo de Extensão ao MPS.Br de Software que agrega Processos e Resultados Esperados para orientar entidades interessadas em estudar, adaptar ou aplicar o modelo nacional em projetos críticos de software. Este trabalho também relata a aplicação em uma prova de conceito de adaptação de um dos objetivos da norma RTCA DO-178C, utilizada na certificação de software no domínio da aviação.

3. Procedimentos Metodológicos

Os procedimentos metodológicos deste trabalho envolvem 5 etapas. A Etapa 1 contém um estudo e análise do modelo MPS.Br, visando conhecer os processos que fazem parte do modelo e também os resultados esperados de cada um destes. Este estudo foi conduzido pelos autores deste trabalho.

A Etapa 2 contém um estudo e análise da ABNT NBR 62304:2023 visando conhecer todas as características existentes nesta norma para conhecê-la com profundidade. Da mesma forma da Etapa 1, este estudo também foi conduzido pelos autores deste trabalho.

A Etapa 3 descreve um grupo focal de participantes convidados com forte experiência na ISO/IEC 62304:2015. Como a ABNT NBR 62304:2023 é uma norma espelho e nacionalizada no Brasil recentemente, existe uma experiência maior nos participantes com a sua versão internacional, a ISO/IEC 62304:2015. Ainda na Etapa 3, os participantes foram expostos ao Processo de Engenharia de Requisitos do MPS.Br de Software, incluindo seus Resultados Esperados. Para facilitar o mapeamento em sua maior amplitude, foram usados os Resultados Esperados REQ 1, REQ 5, REQ 6 e REQ 7, além dos Resultados Esperados expandidos REQ 2+, REQ 3+ e REQ 4+.

Na Etapa 4, os participantes realizaram de forma independente seus mapeamentos, analisando cada uma das cláusulas da ABNT NBR 62304:2023, na atividade de *Análise de Requisitos de Software* e, havendo integração, associando para cada uma das cláusulas um possível Resultado Esperado do Processo de Engenharia de Requisitos do MPS.Br de Software.

Na Etapa 5, foi feita uma reunião de consolidação conjunta entre os participantes do grupo focal e os autores deste trabalho visando à consolidação de um mapeamento que representasse o consenso entre os participantes do grupo focal. A Figura 5 apresenta um fluxo que representa as 5 etapas deste procedimento metodológico.

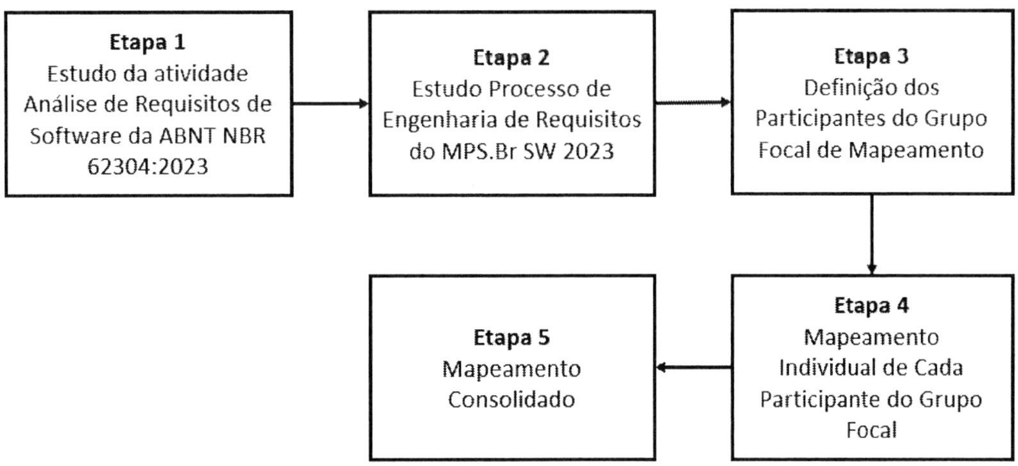

Figura 5. Etapas do Procedimento Metodológico

4. Execução das Etapas

4.1. Execução da Etapa 1

A atividade de *Análise de Requisitos de Software* da ABNT NBR 62304:2023 captura e define os requisitos de software do nível do produto que serão implementados pelo software. Ela contém 6 (seis) cláusulas. A Tabela 3 apresenta a aplicabilidade de cada cláusula dentro das classes de software.

Tabela 3. Resumo das cláusulas na atividade de *Análise de Requisitos de Software*

Cláusula	Classe A	Classe B	Classe C
5.2.1	X	X	X
5.2.2	X	X	X
5.2.3		X	X
5.2.4	X	X	X
5.2.5	X	X	X
5.2.6	X	X	X

Como parte da cláusula 5.2.1, *Definir e documentar requisitos de software a partir dos requisitos do sistema*, para cada SDM, o fabricante deve definir e documentar Requisitos de Software a partir dos Requisitos do Sistema.

Como parte da cláusula 5.2.2 *Conteúdo dos requisitos de software*, o fabricante deve definir e documentar Requisitos do Sistema de Software a partir dos requisitos de sistema. O fabricante deve incluir nos requisitos de software:

(a) Requisitos funcionais e de capacidade (cláusula 5.2.2 a);
(b) Entradas e saídas do sistema de software (cláusula 5.2.2b);
(c) Interfaces entre o sistema de software e outros sistemas (cláusula 5.2.2 c);
(d) Alarmes, avisos e mensagens ao operador por software (cláusula 5.2.2 d);
(e) Requisitos de segurança (cláusula 5.2.2 e);
(f) Requisitos de usabilidade (cláusula 5.2.2 f);
(g) Requisitos de definição de dados e requisitos de banco de dados (cláusula 5.2.2 g);
(h) Requisitos de instalação e aceitação do software entregue no local ou locais de operação e manutenção (cláusula 5.2.2 h);
(i) Requisitos relacionados a métodos de manutenção e operação (cláusula 5.2.2 i);
(j) Requisitos de documentação para o usuário (cláusula 5.2.2 j);
(k) Requisitos de manutenção do usuário (cláusula 5.2.2 k); e
(l) Requisitos regulatórios (cláusula 5.2.2 l).

Como parte da cláusula 5.2.3 *Inclusão medidas de controle de risco nos requisitos de software*, o fabricante deve incluir medidas de controle de risco implementadas no SDM para satisfazer a cláusula.

Como parte da cláusula 5.2.4 *Reavaliação da análise de risco do dispositivo médico*, o fabricante deve reavaliar a análise de risco do dispositivo médico quando os requisitos de software são estabelecidos e atualizá-la conforme apropriado.

Como parte da cláusula 5.2.5 *Atualização dos requisitos do sistema*, o fabricante deve garantir que os requisitos existentes, incluindo os Requisitos do Sistema, sejam reavaliados e atualizados conforme apropriado como resultado da atividade de *Análise de Requisitos de Software*.

Como parte da cláusula 5.2.6 *Verificação requisitos de software*, o fabricante deve verificar e documentar que os requisitos de software:

(a) Implementam os Requisitos do Sistema (cláusula 5.2.6 a);
(b) Não contradizem uns aos outros (cláusula 5.2.6 b);
(c) São expressos em termos que evitam ambiguidade (cláusula 5.2.6 c);
(d) São declarados em termos que permitem o estabelecimento de critérios de teste e realização de testes para determinar se os critérios de teste foram atendidos (cláusula 5.2.6 d);
(e) Podem ser identificados de forma única (cláusula 5.2.6 e); e
(f) São rastreáveis aos Requisitos do Sistema ou outra fonte (cláusula 5.2.6 f).

Sintetizando, os Requisitos de Software são refinados a partir dos Requisitos de Sistemas que contém um conjunto de características. Com todas as características definidas, os requisitos são revisados para garantir algumas características. A Figura 6 apresenta uma visão geral da atividade de *Análise de Requisitos de Software*.

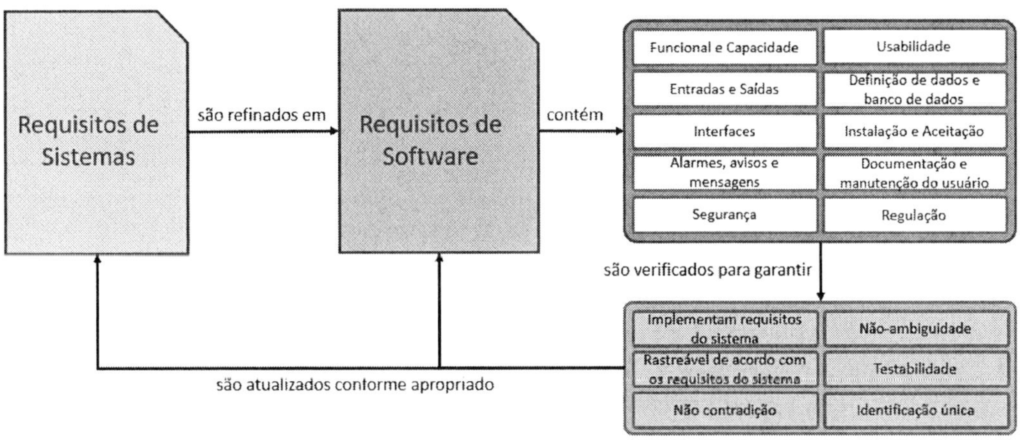

Figura 6. Visão geral da atividade de *Análise de Requisitos de Software*

4.2. Execução da Etapa 2

O propósito do processo de Engenharia de Requisitos do MPS.Br é definir, gerenciar e manter atualizados os requisitos das partes interessadas e do produto, garantindo que inconsistências entre os requisitos, os planos e os produtos de trabalho sejam identificadas e tratadas [Softex 2023]. Este processo contém 7 Resultados Esperados (REQ 1 a REQ 7), com 3 (três) destes evoluídos a partir do Nível D (REQ 2+, REQ 3+ e REQ 4+). O processo de Engenharia de Requisitos é implementado no nível G, mas evolui no nível D, com Resultados Esperados modificados. A Tabela 4 apresenta a lista dos Resultados Esperados do MPS.Br de Software.

REQ 1	(A partir do nível G) As necessidades, expectativas e restrições das partes interessadas, tanto em relação ao produto quanto a suas interfaces, são identificadas.
REQ 2+	(A partir do nível D) Os requisitos são especificados, priorizados, refinados, alocados para implementação e mantidos atualizados a partir das necessidades, expectativas e restrições identificadas, o que inclui a especificação de conceitos operacionais, cenários e interfaces internas e externas.
REQ 3+	(A partir do nível D) Os requisitos são entendidos e analisados junto aos fornecedores de requisitos para garantir que sejam claros, necessários e suficientes e para balancear as necessidades das partes interessadas com as restrições existentes.
REQ 4+	(A partir do Nível D) Os requisitos são validados.
REQ 5	(A partir do nível G) O compromisso da equipe técnica com a implementação dos requisitos é obtido.
REQ 6	(A partir do nível G) A rastreabilidade bidirecional entre requisitos, atividades e produtos de trabalho do projeto é estabelecida e mantida.
REQ 7	(a partir do Nível G) Os planos, atividades e produtos de trabalho relacionados são revisados visando identificar e tratar inconsistência em relação aos requisitos

Tabela 4. Resultados Esperados do Processo de Engenharia de Requisitos do MPS.Br [Softex 2023]

4.3. Execução da Etapa 3

Um Grupo Focal (GF) composto por 03 (três) especialistas convidados atuantes no desenvolvimento de software para dispositivos médicos. Os participantes foram convidados a partir da busca por profissionais atendessem os seguintes requisitos:

- Req 1: O convidado deve atuar em projetos de software da área médica; e
- Req 2: O convidado deve ter conhecimento e experiência mínima de 3 anos na ISO/IEC 62304:2015.

Por conta da similaridade entre a ISO/IEC 62304:2015 e a ABNT NBR 62304:2023 e a recente disponibilização da versão em Língua Portuguesa apenas em 2023, não foi possível que o Req 2 citasse 3 anos da ABNT NBR 62304:2023, pois esta nem havia completado seu primeiro ano na ocasião do convite. Por este motivo, foi utilizada a versão em Língua Inglesa que a deu origem. Os convidados foram selecionados a partir da busca de perfis de 11 profissionais na ferramenta LinkedIn©, onde 3 (três participantes aceitaram participar do grupo focal. Cada um destes participantes recebeu:

- Um extrato da ABNT NBR 62304:2023 com todas as cláusulas da atividade *Análise de Requisitos de Software*; e
- Um extrato dos Resultados Esperados do Processo de Engenharia de Requisitos do MPS.Br de Software.

4.4. Execução da Etapa 4

A partir da análise e estudo tanto do MPS.Br, quanto na ABNT NBR 62304:2023, foi possível cada participante do Grupo Focal realizar uma análise com mapeamento unidirecional. Cada participante foi orientado para realizar seu mapeamento das cláusulas da ABNT NBR 62304:2023 para os Resultados Esperados do Processo de Engenharia de Requisitos do MPS.BR com três possibilidades:

- Completo: A cláusula da ABNT NBR 62304:2023 é completamente satisfeita por um ou mais Resultados Esperados do MPS.Br;
- Parcial: A cláusula da ABNT NBR 62304:2023 é parcialmente satisfeita por um ou mais Resultados Esperados de um processo do MPS.Br, sendo necessária complementação para satisfação integral; ou
- Não satisfeito: A cláusula da ABNT NBR 62304:2023 não é satisfeita por um ou mais Resultados Esperados de um processo do MPS.Br.

A Figura 7 consolida as respostas dos avaliadores seguindo as possibilidades de mapeamento apresentadas anteriormente.

Participante 1

Cláusula	Resultado Esperado	Mapeamento do Participante 1
5.2.1	REQ 1	Completo
5.2.2	REQ 2+	Completo
5.2.3	REQ 2+	Completo
5.2.4	Nenhum	Não satisfeito
5.2.5	Nenhum	Não satisfeito
5.2.6	REQ 4+ REQ 6	Completo

Participante 2

Cláusula	Resultado Esperado	Mapeamento do Participante 2
5.2.1	REQ 1 REQ 2+	Completo
5.2.2	REQ 2+	Completo
5.2.3	REQ 2+	Parcial
5.2.4	Nenhum	Não satisfeito
5.2.5	REQ 3+	Completo
5.2.6	REQ 6	Parcial

Participante 3

Cláusula	Resultado Esperado	Mapeamento do Participante 2
5.2.1	REQ 1	Completo
5.2.2	REQ 2+	Parcial
5.2.3	REQ 2+	Parcial
5.2.4	Nenhum	Não satisfeito
5.2.5	REQ 3+	Completo
5.2.6	REQ 4+ REQ 6 REQ 7	Completo

Figura 7. Resultados Individuais do Mapeamento pelos Participantes do Grupo Focal

4.5. Execução da Etapa 5

Para cada uma das cláusulas da ABNT NBR 62304:2023, associadas com a atividade de "*Análise de Requisitos de Software*" previsto nessa norma, foram encontradas um ou mais Resultados Esperados do MPS.Br que atendem parcialmente ou completamente o conteúdo das cláusulas.

A cláusula 5.2.1 prevê que o fabricante do dispositivo médico deve definir os requisitos de software, refinando a partir dos requisitos do Sistema de Saúde. Isso é completamente satisfeito pela combinação dos Resultados Esperados do MPS.Br (REQ 1 e REQ 2+). No REQ 1, as necessidades, expectativas e restrições das partes interessadas, tanto em relação ao produto, quanto a suas interfaces, devem ser identificadas. No REQ 2+ são especificados, priorizados e refinados, também atendendo a necessidade de refinamento dos requisitos de software, a partir dos requisitos de sistemas, conforme previsto na cláusula 5.2.1.

A cláusula 5.2.2 possui 11 itens (de *a* a *l*). Estes itens versam sobre detalhes técnicos para os requisitos como: capacidade, alarmes, segurança, detalhes de bases de dados, entre outros. O MPS.Br não possui Resultados Esperados que explicitamente tratem essas características de requisitos. Então entende-se que o REQ 2+, engloba parcialmente todas as características necessárias para a especificação de um requisito, sendo estes detalhes técnicos naturalmente capturados com as necessidades do software que estará sendo desenvolvido.

A cláusula 5.2.3 prevê que medidas de controle de risco para falhas de hardware e software devem ser especificadas. Entende-se que esse requisito é parcialmente coberto pelo REQ 2+ que versa sobre a especificação de conceitos operacionais e cenários.

A cláusula 5.2.4 prevê a reavaliação dos riscos de segurança previsto na cláusula 5.2.3, sendo esta cláusula a única não satisfeita completamente pelos Resultados Esperados do MPS.Br de Software.

A cláusula 5.2.5 prevê que os requisitos existentes são reavaliados e atualizados. Isso é atendido completamente pelo Resultado Esperado REQ 3+. No REQ 3+, os requisitos são entendidos e avaliados pelos seus fornecedores visando mantê-los atualizados.

A cláusula 5.2.6 possui 6 itens (de *a* a *f*). Os itens *a* até *d* prevê que os requisitos devem ser revisados para garantir que: implementam os Requisitos do Sistema (cláusula 5.2.6 a); não contradizem uns aos outros (cláusula 5.2.6 b); são expressos em termos que evitam ambiguidade (cláusula 5.2.6 c); e são declarados em termos que permitem o estabelecimento de critérios de teste e realização de testes para determinar se os critérios de teste foram atendidos (cláusula 5.2.6 d). Entende-se que o REQ 4+ é completamente suficiente para garantir que com a validação prevista nesse Resultado Esperado, o requisito esteja considerado como correto por meio de sua revisão.

Os itens *e* e *f* são cobertos pelo REQ 6. O item *e* prevê que os requisitos precisam ser identificados de forma única. Isso não é explícito em nenhum Resultado Esperados do MPS.Br, porém é uma prática comum e, normalmente utilizada quando a rastreabilidade é algo requerido. A rastreabilidade é mencionada no REQ 6 então entende-se que esse item *e* da cláusula 5.2.6 é parcialmente atendido pelo REQ 6. Para o item *f*, a rastreabilidade dos requisitos deve ser completa para suas fontes e produtos de trabalho, estando este item este *f* satisfeito completamente pelo REQ 6.

A Tabela 5 apresenta o mapeamento unidirecional das cláusulas previstas na atividade de "Análise de Requisitos de Software" da ABNT NBR 62304:2023 para os Resultados Esperados do Processo de Engenharia de Requisitos do MPS.Br.

Percebe-se que o MPS.Br de Software, especialmente no processo de Engenharia de Requisitos, é bastante abrangente para a cobertura das cláusulas da atividade de Análise de Requisitos de Software da ABNT NBR 62304:2023.

5. Ameaças à Validade

Durante a execução do mapeamento, observou-se um distanciamento entre o MPS.Br de Software e as cláusulas da ABNT NBR 62304:2023, especialmente na cláusula 5.2.4, que foi considerada como não satisfeita pelos Resultados Esperados do MPS.Br de Software. Embora o mapeamento tenha sido feito de forma individualizada pelos 3 (três) integrantes convidados na Etapa 3, houve uma integração que promoveu um mapeamento único (na Etapa 4). Porém, o mapeamento pode ter um viés representativo apenas dos 3 (três) integrantes que, se fosse possível aumentar a quantidade de integrantes, talvez os resultados

Cláusula da ABNT NBR 62304:2023	Resultado Esperado do MPS.Br	Mapeamento
5.2.1	REQ 1 e REQ 2+	Completo
5.2.2	REQ 2+	Parcial
5.2.3	REQ 2+	Parcial
5.2.4	Nenhum	Não satisfeito
5.2.5	REQ 3+	Completo
5.2.6 (itens *a* até *d*)	REQ 4+	Completo
5.2.6 (item *e*)	REQ 6	Parcial
5.2.6 (item *f*)	REQ 6	Completo

Tabela 5. Mapeamento das Cláusulas da ABNT NBR 62304:2023 para os Resultados Esperados do MPS.Br de Software

do mapeamento pudessem ser levemente diferentes.

É importante salientar a presença de subjetividade na implementação do mapeamento, especialmente nas análises estabelecidas e nas correlações identificadas. Em uma tentativa de mitigar as incertezas científicas decorrentes desse fato, foi estabelecido um processo de harmonização conjunta na Etapa 5, que, por si só, também inclui análises subjetivas que representam a consolidação da visão dos três convidados.

É válido ressaltar que a ausência de uma RSL (Revisão Sistemática da Literatura) referente à aplicação do MPS.Br em ambientes de desenvolvimento de software médico gera alguma insegurança em relação à originalidade deste trabalho. Porém mitiga-se esse risco com a coleta *adhoc* dos trabalhos correlatos apresentados na seção 2.3, onde não foram encontrados trabalhos que investigassem a intereseção entre o MPS.Br ou a ISO/IEC 62304:2015.

6. Conclusão

O objetivo deste trabalho, enunciado na seção 1, foi apresentar um mapeamento das cláusulas previstas na atividade "Análise de Requisitos de Software" da ABNT NBR 62304:2023 para os Resultados Esperados do Processo de Engenharia de Requisitos do MPS.Br de Software. Este objetivo foi satisfeito com a execução dos procedimentos metodológicos apresentados na seção 3, constituído de 5 etapas completamente executadas e relatadas de forma sintética na seção 4.

No mapeamento apresentado na Tabela 5, consolidado na visão dos 3 (três) convidados selecionados para confecção, mostra boa aderência dos Resultados Esperados do MPS.Br de Software para as cláusulas da atividade "Análise de Requisitos de Software" da ABNT NBR 62304:2023.

Destaca-se também que apesar do mapeamento apresentado na Tabela 5 não ser suficiente para que todos os Resultados Esperados do MPS.Br de Software atendam as cláusulas da ABNT NBR 62304:2023, dois Resultados Esperados (REQ 5 e REQ 7) apresentam diretivas no MPS.Br ainda mais rigorosas que a própria ABNT NBR 62304:2023 requer.

Na seção 1, foi enunciada a seguinte pergunta de pesquisa: **"Como que o MPS.Br, por meio dos 4 processos de projeto de desenvolvimento de software, é capaz de satisfazer as cláusulas da ABNT NBR 62304:2023?"**. Essa pergunta de pesquisa não foi completamente respondida neste trabalho, pois ainda não se encontra realizado um mapeamento completo da ABNT NBR 62304:2023 para todos os Resultados Esperados de todos os processos previstos no MPS.Br. Porém, se enxerga como possível que esse mapeamento possa ser realizado, uma vez que neste trabalho foi apresentado um mapeamento da atividade "Análise de Requisitos de Software". Assim, um natural trabalho futuro envolve o mapeamento completo na ABNT NBR 62304:2023 para todos os Resultados Esperados de todos os processos previstos no MPS.Br.

Referências

ABNT (2023). Abnt nbr 62304:2023 software de dispositivo médico - processo do ciclo de vida do software. Technical report, Associação Brasileira de Normas Técnicas.

Colenci Neto, A. and Cazarini, E. W. (2011). A referencial model for small companies of development software. *IEEE Latin America Transactions*, 9(1):89–95.

Ferreirós, A. (2015). Evaluation of accomplishment of do-178c objectives by cmmi-dev 1.3. Master's thesis, Intituto Tecnológico de Aeronáutica (ITA).

ISO (2006). Iso/iec 62304:2006 medical device software - software life-cycle processes. Technical report, International Electrotechnical Commission.

ISO (2015). Iso/iec 62304:2015 medical device software - software life-cycle processes – amendment 1. Technical report, International Electrotechnical Commission.

ISO (2018). Iso/iec 29110:2018 systems and software engineering — lifecycle profiles for very small entities (vses). Technical report, International Standardization Organization.

ISO (2019). Iso 14971:2019 medical devices — application of risk management to medical devices. Technical report, International Standardization.

Kalinowski, M., Santos, G., Prikladnicki, R., Rocha, A. R., Weber, K. C., and Antonioni, J. A. (2011). From software engineering research to Brazilian software quality improvement. In *Proceedings - 25th Brazilian Symposium on Software Engineering, SBES 2011*, pages 120–125.

Kasisopha, N. and Meananeatra, P. (2019). Applying iso/iec 29110 to iso/iec 62304 for medical device software sme. In *Proceedings of the 2nd International Conference on Computing and Big Data*, ICCBD 2019, page 121–125, New York, NY, USA. Association for Computing Machinery.

Machado, E. and Marques, J. (2023). Me-mps: An mr-mps-sw extension model for critical software in regulated environments. In *Proceedings of the XXII Brazilian Symposium on Software Quality*, SBQS '23, page 52–61, New York, NY, USA. Association for Computing Machinery.

Magnuson, A. (2012). Iec/iso 62304 regulations for the development of medical software devices. Master's thesis, Chalmers University of Technology.

Marques, J. (2019). Uma análise das características de especificação de requisitos de software em normas de ambientes regulados. In *22º Workshop de Engenharia de Requisitos (WER 2019)*.

Marques, J. and Cunha, A. (2019). Ares: An agile requirements specification process for regulated environments. *International Journal of Software Engineering and Knowledge Engineering (IJSEKE)*, 29(10):1403–1438.

Marques, J., Yelisetty, S., and Barros, L. (2021). Um mapeamento sistemático da literatura no uso da iec 62304. *Journal of Health Informatics*.

Munch, J., Armbrunt, O., Kowalczyk, M., and Soto, M. (2012). *Software Process Definition and Management*. Springer-Verlag, Berlim, Germany.

Rocha, A., Oliveira, S., Souza, G., Brito, A., Santos, F., and Nunes, E. (2020). Mps appraisal online: An experience on covid-19 times. In *Anais do XIX Simpósio Brasileiro de Qualidade de Software*, pages 333–344, Porto Alegre, RS, Brasil. SBC.

RTCA (2011). Rtca do -178c software considerations in airborne systems and equipment certification. Technical report.

SEI (2010). Cmmi for development, version 1.3. Technical Report CMU/SEI-2010-TR-033, Software Engineering Institute, Carnegie Mellon University, Pittsburgh, PA.

Softex (2023). Guia geral mps de software.

Tomada de decisões arquiteturais em projetos de software: um estudo exploratório com profissionais

Lucas de O. Carvalho[1], **Tayana U. Conte**[2]

[1]Instituto de Ciências Matemáticas e de Computação – Universidade de São Paulo (USP)
São Carlos – SP – Brasil

[2]Instituto de Computação – Universidade Federal do Amazonas (UFAM)
Manaus – AM – Brasil

Abstract. *During the software development cycle, architecture is fundamental for the success of the solution and, beyond structural and behavioral aspects, architecture comprises several critical decisions made about the software. In this context, some studies in the literature have been conducted about software architecture decision-making, but they are restricted to a specific business context and conducted with professionals out of the Brazilian perspective. For this reason, this study aims to present a preliminary perspective and understand the decision-making process from the view of Brazilian software practitioners who work in the software industry. The results, collected by nine semi-structured interviews with software practitioners from different companies and with a varied range of skills, bring findings related to the decision-making process, including how decisions are taken and how architecture design is made.*

Resumo. *Durante o ciclo de desenvolvimento de software, a arquitetura é fundamental para o sucesso da solução e, além de aspectos estruturais e comportamentais, a arquitetura contempla várias decisões críticas tomadas sobre o software. Nesse contexto, alguns estudos da literatura foram conduzidos sobre o processo de tomada de decisões de arquitetura, porém eles estão restritos a um domínio de negócio específico e foram conduzidos com profissionais fora do panorama brasileiro. Por esse motivo, esse estudo tem como objetivo apresentar uma perspectiva preliminar e entender sobre o processo de tomada de decisões de arquitetura de software na visão de profissionais brasileiros atuantes na indústria de software. Os resultados, obtidos a partir de entrevistas semiestruturadas com nove profissionais atuando em empresas diferentes e com variadas habilidades, trazem achados sobre o processo de tomada de decisão, incluindo como as decisões são tomadas e a definição da arquitetura é feita.*

1. Introdução

A arquitetura de um software é tradicionalmente vista como organização de alto nível de como os componentes e subsistemas estão dispostos e interagem entre si, mas nos últimos anos, a arquitetura tem sido vista como o "porquê" da solução, como o conjunto de decisões de projeto, a motivação para as decisões e o conhecimento capturado por elas [van Vliet and Tang 2016]. Essas decisões são o cerne da arquitetura de um sistema e são vitais para que o sistema atinja seus principais objetivos [Tofan et al. 2013]. Quando comparadas a outros tipos de decisões tomadas durante o desenvolvimento, sejam elas ligadas a processos ou ferramentas, decisões arquiteturais têm um peso adicional, visto que são feitas em etapas iniciais do processo de desenvolvimento e têm uma influência significativa no sistema [Shaw 1995].

Além de sua importância no sucesso do software, a tomada de decisões em arquitetura é considerada complexa por envolver aspectos de produto, de negócio e de desenvolvimento. Algumas das dificuldades enfrentadas neste processo são: dependências em outros times, limitações técnicas impostas, requisitos dinâmicos e documentação imprópria [Dasanayake et al. 2016].

Na literatura, alguns trabalhos foram conduzidos relacionados a como as decisões de arquitetura de software são tomadas, porém estes trabalhos estão normalmente restritos ao processo adotado por profissionais de uma empresa específica e foram conduzidos fora do panorama brasileiro. Com o crescimento da indústria de software no Brasil nos últimos anos [Souza 2022], torna-se importante também avaliar como as decisões ligadas à arquitetura são tomadas nesse cenário emergente. Portanto, esse artigo tem o objetivo de apresentar uma perspectiva inicial e entender sobre o processo de tomada de decisões de arquitetura de software na visão de profissionais brasileiros atuantes na indústria. A partir disso, a Questão de Pesquisa (QP) a ser respondida a partir desse estudo é "*Como são tomadas as principais decisões de arquitetura de software?*".

Esse artigo tem como principais contribuições achados sobre como é o processo de definição da arquitetura e da tomada de decisões arquiteturais por profissionais brasileiros, aspectos sobre colaboração de outros profissionais, os fatores que influenciam o processo, as ferramentas utilizadas para apoiar a tomada de decisão, como as decisões são registradas e se as decisões são revisitadas; por fim, uma comparação com outros trabalhos da literatura é feita a respeito dos principais achados.

2. Trabalhos relacionados

Nos últimos anos, diversos trabalhos relacionados ao processo de tomada de decisão na arquitetura de software foram conduzidos devido à sua crescente importância. Razavian, Paech, and Tang (2019) realizam um mapeamento sistemático de 38 trabalhos relacionados ao processo de tomada de decisões em arquitetura e, dentre os achados, os autores descrevem que poucos trabalhos se relacionam a aspectos humanos e psicológicos ligados ao processo de tomada de decisão e que existem oportunidades de pesquisa em aspectos comportamentais, considerando fatores e impactos do comportamento na tomada de decisões. Os demais trabalhos relacionados foram identificados através deste mapeamento.

Dasanayake et al. (2015) exploram o processo de tomada de decisões em três empresas de software europeias, cada uma com cerca de 60 funcionários. A pesquisa aborda como é o processo de tomada de decisões, os motivos para sua adoção, as dificuldades enfrentadas e possíveis melhorias. Os dados foram coletados por meio de entrevistas semiestruturadas e análise de documentações usadas/criadas durante o processo. Os resultados indicam que arquitetos preferem abordagens informais, mas estruturadas, com experiência e intuição sendo fatores-chave. Além disso, os aspectos de qualidade considerados incluem manutenibilidade, confiabilidade, testabilidade, desempenho e segurança. As dificuldades mencionadas estão relacionadas à falta de uma abordagem formal e sistemática, atribuída à ausência de gestão de conhecimento.

Dasanayake et al. (2016) investigam sobre a colaboração no processo de projeto de arquitetura em uma empresa com cerca de mil funcionários distribuídos globalmente. Entrevistas foram conduzidas com 15 arquitetos de software experientes. Os resultados mostraram que a maioria dos times adota uma abordagem colaborativa para a tomada de decisão, com decisões de alto impacto sendo feitas por comitês e decisões de escopo menor sendo tomadas pelos próprios times. Os arquitetos destacaram a importância do trabalho em grupo para gerar ideias criativas, enquanto enfrentam desafios relacionados à organização, processos e aspectos humanos, incluindo problemas com a documentação do *design* e as mudanças organizacionais.

Power and Wirfs-Brock (2018) analisam as abordagens de tomada de decisão e os desafios enfrentados, além do impacto dessas decisões nas empresas. Através de uma pesquisa com 62 profissionais, os autores investigaram os aspectos do dia a dia e realizaram grupos focais com participantes de diferentes contextos. Os resultados mostram que os arquitetos tendem a utilizar abordagens informais e coletivas, e destacam que a persuasão e os relacionamentos influenciam nas decisões. Os arquitetos destacaram que normalmente precisam tomar decisões pressionados e fazer *tradeoffs* entre escolhas imediatas e uma sustentação a longo prazo.

Também com foco em profissionais, Heesch and Avgeriou (2011) buscam entender o raciocínio por trás do processo de arquitetura em um *survey* com 53 arquitetos. Os autores utilizam o modelo de projeto de arquitetura de Hofmeister et al. (2007) como referência e investigam como são feitas as etapas de arquitetura. Os arquitetos citaram que requisitos são fatores importantes para decisões, que buscam várias alternativas durante seu processo, dando prioridade para soluções conhecidas e que consideram prós e contras em cada decisão de arquitetura.

Por fim, Tofan et al. (2013) realizaram um *survey* com 43 arquitetos experientes de países diferentes para entender aspectos não explorados em outros trabalhos, como as características das decisões arquiteturais e quais fatores as tornam difíceis. Os resultados encontrados indicam que, quanto a características, decisões arquiteturais levam em média oito dias de trabalho, envolvem indiretamente três pessoas e consideram um número próximo de cinco atributos de qualidade na decisão. Já quanto aos fatores que tornam as decisões difíceis, os participantes indicaram dependências em outras decisões, impacto grande no negócio e consequências negativas.

Em síntese, a Tabela 1 apresenta os interesses de cada trabalho relacionado mencionado, bem como o método de pesquisa usado. Nota-se que esses trabalhos estão próximos a este por investigarem o processo de tomada de decisões em arquitetura, porém, nenhum dos trabalhos citados realizou a pesquisa com profissionais brasileiros e, além disso, os estudos focaram na perspectiva dos profissionais de uma mesma empresa. Apesar dos conceitos relacionados à arquitetura serem os mesmos, é necessário considerar as diferenças entre profissionais brasileiros e estrangeiros, como comportamentos culturais, experiências profissionais, formação acadêmica, e até disparidades organizacionais, que endossam a necessidade deste estudo.

3. Metodologia

A QP a ser respondida neste estudo é "*Como são tomadas as principais decisões de arquitetura de software?*", buscando identificar detalhes sobre o processo de tomada de decisões de arquitetura e, por este motivo, optou-se por realizar um estudo qualitativo.

Tabela 1. Interesses de pesquisa e métodos dos trabalhos relacionados.

Trabalho	Interesses da pesquisa	Coleta de dados
[Dasanayake et al. 2015]	Como as decisões são feitas O que leva os arquitetos a fazerem desse jeito Quais os desafios associados Como esse processo pode ser melhorado	Entrevistas semiestruradas com arquitetos de três empresas e documentações de arquitetura
[Dasanayake et al. 2016]	Como os times tomam decisões Quais os desafios de tomar decisões em grupo	Entrevistas com arquitetos de uma empresa
[Power and Wirfs-Brock 2018]	Quais abordagens são utilizadas Quais os desafios com essas abordagens Como o contexto influencia as decisões Como as decisões impactam os outros	Survey e Grupos Focais com arquitetos de uma empresa de larga escala
[Heesch and Avgeriou 2011]	Como acontece a análise da arquitetura Como acontece a síntese da arquitetura Como acontece a avaliação da arquitetura	Survey com profissionais
[Tofan et al. 2013]	Quais as características das decisões Que fatores dificultam as decisões Diferenças entre arquitetos júnior e sênior Diferenças entre decisões boas e ruins	Survey com arquitetos

Maxwell (2012) cita que pesquisas qualitativas são usadas quando se busca: entender o significado dos eventos, situações e ações em que os participantes estão envolvidos; entender um contexto específico em que os participantes agem e como o contexto influencia suas ações; e entender os processos nos quais eventos e ações acontecem. Para coleta dos dados qualitativos, entrevistas semiestruturadas foram escolhidas como método, uma vez que entrevistas são úteis quando se deseja obter as perspectivas das pessoas sobre determinado tópico, além de opiniões e pensamentos [Seaman 1999].

3.1. Guia da entrevista

Para auxiliar na condução das entrevistas, elaborou-se um guia de entrevista, disponível na Tabela 2, com algumas perguntas que norteiam a entrevista a atingir seus objetivos e que foram elaboradas pelos pesquisadores considerando a QP e algumas QPs mencionadas nos trabalhos relacionados mencionados na Seção 2. O guia possui duas seções: (i) Experiência, que tem como objetivo identificar a experiência profissional da pessoa participante com desenvolvimento e arquitetura; e (ii) Tomada de decisões de arquitetura, que é relativa a QP, e questiona sobre aspectos do processo adotado/usado pela pessoa participante para tomar decisões. Após a elaboração, o guia foi revisado por uma pessoa especialista em pesquisa qualitativa, que possui mais de 10 anos de experiência.

3.2. As pessoas participantes da pesquisa

As pessoas de interesse da pesquisa são profissionais da indústria de software, que estejam trabalhando na indústria há, pelo menos, três anos e que tenham funções relacionadas à arquitetura ou ao processo de tomada de decisões arquiteturais em suas funções atuais. Foram excluídas pessoas que: (i) não possuem o mínimo dos anos de experiência mencionado por desejar-se entender o processo de profissionais com maior senioridade; (ii) não desempenham as funções relacionadas à arquitetura, pois a contribuição ao estudo não seria a esperada.

O recrutamento dos participantes se deu, inicialmente, a partir da rede de contatos das pessoas pesquisadoras, de forma que algumas pessoas foram contatadas para saber do seu interesse em participar da pesquisa. Além disso, a rede social Linkedin, que possui propósitos profissionais e acadêmicos, serviu para descobrir pessoas que poderiam contribuir com a pesquisa.

Tabela 2. Guia de entrevista elaborado para coleta de dados.

Seção da entrevista	Sugestão de perguntas
Experiência	1. Fale um pouco da sua experiência com desenvolvimento de software 2. Fale um pouco da sua experiência com arquitetura de software
Tomada de decisões de arquitetura	1. Como vocês costumam fazer o projeto da arquitetura do software? 2. Quais são as pessoas envolvidas na etapa de projeto e quais os papéis delas? 3. Como as principais decisões são tomadas na etapa de projeto da arquitetura? 4. Quais os fatores principais que influenciam a tomada de decisão? 5. As decisões são tomadas de forma individual ou coletiva? Por que? 6. Quais são as ferramentas usadas para apoiar durante a tomada de decisão? 7. Como as decisões tomadas ficam registradas? 8. Conforme o projeto avança, as decisões iniciais são revisitadas?

3.3. Coleta dos dados

Para iniciar a coleta dos dados, uma entrevista piloto foi conduzida com uma das pessoas recrutadas para a entrevista. A entrevista piloto é importante para entender o comportamento da entrevista real, sendo usada para avaliar o entendimento das perguntas na visão do participante e também aspectos operacionais, como tempo de duração e ferramenta. Após a entrevista piloto, alguns apontamentos foram feitos na versão inicial do guia, que foi evoluído para uma segunda versão, com perguntas reescritas, ajustadas ou removidas. As versões do guia de entrevista, incluindo a versão final mostrada na Tabela 2, está disponível em um material suplementar [1].

Com as correções feitas no guia, os pesquisadores conduziram a primeira rodada de entrevistas, com seis participantes, entre Dezembro de 2022 e Janeiro de 2023. A segunda rodada de entrevistas, que incluiu mais três participantes, aconteceu entre Dezembro de 2023 e Janeiro de 2024. Antes de cada entrevista, o Termo de Consentimento Livre e Esclarecido (TCLE) foi enviado aos participantes para que eles estivessem cientes sobre sua contribuição na pesquisa. As entrevistas, a exemplo do piloto, foram conduzidas de forma remota utilizando o Google Meet e com duração aproximada de 30 minutos. Todos os participantes concordaram com a gravação dos áudios das entrevistas para que a transcrição fosse feita posteriormente.

3.4. Análise dos dados

A partir dos áudios gravados das entrevistas, as trancrições foram feitas e a análise das entrevistas foi feita seguindo os procedimentos da Teoria Fundamentada nos Dados, em inglês *Grounded Theory* - GT, que é um método de pesquisa qualitativa para descoberta de teorias a partir de dados semiestruturados, como as transcrições feitas [Stol et al. 2016]. GT é útil para descoberta de padrões comportamentais que moldam processos sociais

[1] `https://doi.org/10.6084/m9.figshare.25150940`

conforme ocorrem interações entre pessoas em grupos [Adolph et al. 2011]. Na GT, a análise é feita a partir de códigos (conceitos) e categorias identificadas durante o processo de codificação, que pode ser dividida em 3 fases: aberta, axial e seletiva [Corbin and Strauss 2008]. Por ser um estudo exploratório, do qual não se pretende gerar uma teoria, foi realizada apenas a primeira etapa de GT (codificação aberta). Os resultados da codificação com as citações de cada um dos participantes está disponível em um material suplementar[2] e podem ser consultados para mapear os principais achados do trabalho.

4. Resultados

No total, nove pessoas foram entrevistadas durante a coleta de dados. Todos os profissionais entrevistados desempenham funções relacionadas à arquitetura e/ou colaboram no processo de tomada de decisões arquiteturais, apesar de nenhum deles possuir uma função especializada de arquitetura. As principais características desses profissionais foram resumidas na Tabela 3, que identifica cada profissional com um número que será utilizado no restante deste trabalho, que está na coluna "Participante". Esta tabela ainda exibe outras informações mencionadas pelos participantes, como o número de anos de experiência do participante, o cargo em que o participante atua e em qual empresa e suas habilidades no ciclo de desenvolvimento.

Tabela 3. Dados sobre pessoas entrevistadas.

Participante	Anos de experiência	Cargo atual	Empresa	Habilidades
P1	3-5	Desenvolvedor Sênior	E1	Backend/Infraestrutura
P2	10-15	Desenvolvedor Especialista	E2	Mobile
P3	10-15	Tech Manager	E3	Backend/Cloud
P4	10-15	Tech Leader	E4	Frontend
P5	15-20	Gerente de Sistemas	E5	Frontend/Backend
P6	5-10	Analista de Testes Sênior	E6	QA
P7	5-10	Desenvolvedor Sênior	E3	Backend
P8	3-5	Desenvolvedor Sênior	E7	Frontend/Backend
P9	5-10	Desenvolvedor Sênior	E8	Backend

Na coluna "Empresa" da Tabela 3, há uma referência para a Tabela 4, que mostra detalhes a respeito da empresa atual dos participantes, como domínio do negócio e o número de funcionários. Essa informação é interessante para considerar a relevância dos profissionais entrevistados no mercado e a diversidade das entrevistas.

Tabela 4. Detalhes sobre as empresas das pessoas entrevistadas.

Empresa	Domínio do negócio	Número de funcionários
E1	Pesquisa e Desenvolvimento	500-1000
E2	Financeiro	1000-5000
E3	Financeiro	1000-5000
E4	Financeiro	+10000
E5	Público	500-1000
E6	Pesquisa e Desenvolvimento	50-200
E7	Financeiro	200-500
E8	Imobiliário	1000-5000

[2]`https://doi.org/10.6084/m9.figshare.24126684`

4.1. QP - Como são tomadas as principais decisões de arquitetura de software?

Para responder a QP, os códigos que surgiram do processo de codificação e que elucidam aspectos relacionados ao objetivo de entender o processo de tomada de decisões de arquitetura são:

- Como a definição da arquitetura é feita
- Quais as pessoas envolvidas nas definições da arquitetura e quais os papéis delas
- Como as principais decisões são tomadas na definição da arquitetura
- Os fatores que influenciam a tomada de decisão
- As ferramentas usadas para apoiar a tomada de decisão
- Como é o processo de documentação das decisões tomadas
- Como e com que frequência as decisões são revistas

4.1.1. Como a definição da arquitetura é feita

Inicialmente, a definição da arquitetura pode ser entendida como todo o processo de planejamento e definição de componentes, tecnologias e padrões que serão utilizados. De maneira resumida, os profissionais afirmaram que a definição da arquitetura é feita:

1. Focando no que o cliente deseja: P1 menciona olhar para as regras de negócio do cliente. P6 declara que o projeto da arquitetura acontece de maneira incremental, em blocos, que são os entregáveis que o cliente deseja em determinado prazo. P7 afirma que os requisitos do negócio são norteadores do que o produto deve e não deve ter.

   > "Conforme o que o cliente quer como produto final, a gente planeja em etapas, ou seja, entregas de mês tal a mês tal, a gente tem entrega Y, ou seja, a gente tem que entregar o módulo tal e o cliente avalia e gente vai pro próximo módulo." - P6

2. Fazendo Provas de Conceito (em inglês, *Proof of Concept* - PoC): P3 menciona que, muitas vezes, é necessário desenvolver o conhecimento para fazer algo e PoCs ajudam a levantar prós e contras. P4 fala sobre testar pequenas partes para verificar a viabilidade e depois integrar as partes.

   > "A gente trabalha com tecnologia que muda todo dia e muitas vezes a gente não tem o conhecimento necessário. Então, eu sempre preferi pedir tempo para eu fazer PoC e testar e levar com prós e contras." - P3

3. Utilizando o padrão da empresa como referência: P5 informa que a empresa em que trabalha possui um documento que norteia os princípios de arquitetura a serem seguidos pelos desenvolvedores e que, apenas caso algo seja necessário, essas documentações são revisadas. P8 afirma que cada time é independente quanto às decisões, mas a empresa possui algumas convenções e P9 afirma que o padrão definido inicialmente pela empresa é replicado por todos os times.

   > "A gente tem lá um documento formal, inclusive instituído por portaria. É uma portaria que saiu formalizando essa arquitetura [...] Durante as reuniões de planejamento do sistema, a gente verifica se existe a necessidade de algum componente, algum framework,

> alguma biblioteca diferente das que a gente já usa. Se tiver, aí a gente também faz o estudo, se é viável incluir nesse documento ou se é uma biblioteca que só vai ser utilizada para aquele projeto." - P5

Em resumo, as pessoas entrevistadas definem a arquitetura focando nos requisitos e limitações de cliente, através de PoCs para validar a viabilidade de uma solução e seus prós e contras e também utilizando o padrão da empresa como uma referência. Um aspecto interessante sobre a definição da arquitetura é a relevância do entendimento dos requisitos para que essa etapa tenha sucesso, sendo citada como fundamental por P2.

4.1.2. Quais as pessoas envolvidas nas definições da arquitetura e quais os papéis delas

Na etapa de definição da arquitetura, os profissionais também foram questionados sobre quais as pessoas envolvidas e quais os papéis delas. É consenso entre todos os entrevistados que a discussão é feita em grupo e que discussões são estimuladas entre o time para que todos tenham o mesmo entendimento.

> "Então quando vai definir as coisas, a gente faz testes e a gente nunca é uma pessoa isolada, a gente faz um grupo de pesquisa, grupo de trabalho, esse grupo vai avaliar alguns critérios, objetivos e definir se vale a pena ou não o que está pra utilizar." - P5

P3 cita ainda sobre ter participado de projetos em que seu time tomou decisões e precisaram propor a um grupo especializado em decisões de arquitetura, que faz questionamentos sobre a solução e propõe modificações. Isso também é citado por P4.

> "Na consultoria que eu trabalhava quando eu estava focado em um time, eu fazia as propostas de solução e aí eu tinha que levar para um comitê que normalmente era composto de outros arquitetos que estavam em time semelhantes ou no mesmo cliente." - P3

Sumarizando, as definições de arquitetura normalmente são feitas em conjunto por toda a equipe envolvida no desenvolvimento, incluindo pessoas do negócio e de qualidade. Além disso, como grupos especializados de arquitetura foram citados por profissionais de empresas com risco financeiro (P3 e P4), conclui-se que estas empresas possuem padrões mais rigorosos de aprovação de arquitetura. P1 e P2 citam que, como mais especialistas no time, buscam trazer discussões e requisitos a serem considerados. P8 menciona que, quando a mudança arquitetural afeta a empresa inteira, todos os desenvolvedores participam.

4.1.3. Como as principais decisões são tomadas na definição da arquitetura

Sobre como as principais decisões são tomadas, P1 menciona que as decisões são tomadas a partir de diversas possibilidades e uma posterior validação da melhor alternativa considerando o contexto do time. P3 afirma que muitas vezes tecnologias homologadas são utilizadas ou o padrão que o cliente deseja precisa ser seguido.

> "Depois de escolher as ferramentas que tem bastante suporte e verificar se o meu time tem domínio daquelas ferramentas, eu tenho uma base pra começar. A partir disso, conversando com o cliente, vendo as viabilidades e nessas trocas de informações vão surgindo novas ideias." - P1

P2 e P6 comentam que a escolha das melhores decisões que são tomadas vem do conhecimento que é adquirido de forma empírica pelos arquitetos, ratificando o que foi mencionado anteriormente. P8 comenta que os alinhamentos técnicos são um momento de discussão e troca de conhecimento entre o time.

> "Quando você roda o suficiente, então quando você adquire conhecimento suficiente de modelagem, de estruturação, de componentes, de bibliotecas, de linguagens, em que aquela solução pode ser feita, fica mais tranquilo de você fazer esse julgamento." - P2

P4 fala sobre a sustentação da decisão dado o futuro da empresa e do negócio e isso também é mencionado por P5 falando sobre decisões que precisam ser tomadas pensando a longo prazo. Dessa forma, a tomada de decisões mencionada pelos profissionais pode ser vista como um processo que considera aspectos do negócio, como os requisitos, o que está homologado e o padrão a ser seguido, o conhecimento do time e a viabilidade da solução. Nenhum processo sistemático ou estruturado foi mencionado pelos profissionais.

4.1.4. Os fatores que influenciam a tomada de decisão

A respeito de fatores que influenciam a tomada de decisão, os profissionais mencionaram:

1. Desempenho: P1 cita que, como as entregas são para um cliente, é importante que se encontre um balanço entre uma solução robusta em desempenho, mas que não tenha custo tão elevado para não assustar o cliente. P8 fala que desempenho é o principal fator considerado.

   > "Qual arquitetura é melhor e mais performática eu identificar, sempre levando em consideração a questão de ser performático e não gerar muito custo." - P1

2. Custo: P1 menciona que este é um fator primordial considerando que o que faz sentido para o cliente é aquilo que possui o melhor custo. O custo do desenvolvimento é mencionado também por P5 e P9.

   > "Para a gente fazer isso, a gente já sabe que vai ter que pagar mais caro para a fábrica, então são coisas que a gente nem sempre consegue tudo o que o que quer, então a gente faz o que tem recurso." - P5

3. Conhecimento do time: citado por P3, que menciona que uma alta curva de aprendizado de algo complica a situação do time.

   > "Você tem que saber o conhecimento que seu time tem. Porque às vezes, se a curva de aprendizado for muito grande ou se eles forem se deparar com muitos problemas, não vão conseguir resolver." - P3

4. Segurança: P2 afirma que segurança é um ponto inegociável, considerando a confidencialidade do cliente e a Lei Geral de Proteção de Dados (LGPD), vigente no Brasil, devendo ser levada em consideração como premissa para as decisões.

   > "Você não vai encontrar hoje um cliente em potencial que não pense primeiro em segurança. Primeiro em proteger os dados do cliente, então ela é o fator hoje. Então, o meu produto, ele tem que entregar o que ele propõe, tem que entregar aquela solução e eu preciso garantir 100% de segurança dos dados." - P2

5. Padrão da empresa: P3 reafirma que o padrão da empresa deve ser sempre respeitado para que não seja necessário gastar esforço com algo que já está homologado e nem adicionar mais dependências à empresa.

   > "Você tem que ter aquelas tecnologias homologadas. E ali dentro que você vai ter que escolher qual que é a melhor para resolver aquele problema." - P3

6. Profissionais disponíveis no mercado: P4 confirma que um dos fatores levados em consideração é a disponibilidade de profissionais com o domínio de algum aspecto específico da arquitetura. P7 também menciona os profissionais citando o ponto de contratação.

   > "Acho que é um ponto legal se considerar também como é a adoção do quanto (sic) profissionais que a gente tem que a gente pode contratar? Eu acho que leva um pouco em conta isso também. Não adianta nada eu querer usar um framework que nasceu ontem que ninguém sabe e a empresa não vai conseguir colocar nada no ar." - P4

7. Requisitos do cliente: o que é desejado pelo cliente é exposto por P6, que diz que o ponto fundamental é atender a todos os critérios definidos pelo cliente.

   > "A gente tá fazendo o que o cliente quer? Os requisitos que eles solicitaram estão sendo atendidos?" - P6

8. Velocidade da entrega: P9 menciona que entregar rápido é fundamental, considerando as necessidades do mercado.
9. Facilidade para manutenção: P7 e P9 mencionam que a manutenção no sistema deve ser simples de ser executada posteriormente e que esse é um fator primordial nas soluções escolhidas.

Em suma, os fatores citados como aqueles que possuem impacto nas decisões foram: desempenho, custo, conhecimento do time, segurança, padrão da empresa, quantidade de profissionais disponíveis no mercado, requisitos desejados pelo cliente, velocidade da entrega e facilidade para manutenção.

4.1.5. As ferramentas usadas para apoiar a tomada de decisão

Para apoiar a tomada de decisão, nenhuma ferramenta específica foi citada ou lembrada diretamente pelos profissionais. As ferramentas citadas para esta pergunta estão relacionadas a outros aspectos do processo de desenvolvimento, como a etapa de desenho da arquitetura, teste, documentação e codificação. Normalmente, os profissionais não costumam utilizar ferramentas para apoiar a tomada de decisão, o que faz com que o processo se adapte à maneira que o desenvolvedor ou a equipe decidem seguir.

4.1.6. Como é o processo de documentação das decisões tomadas

O processo de documentação das decisões arquiteturais também parece ser um consenso entre os profissionais entrevistados: todos reconhecem a importância da documentação para manutenção e evolução da arquitetura. A documentação é citada como aspecto fundamental da arquitetura por dar visibilidade a todos de todas as decisões e do *design rationale* da solução e permitir a troca de conhecimento entre os membros. P1 cita a importância de criar uma cultura de documentação para a empresa em que trabalha, P2 diz que, sem documentação, não é possível prosseguir com o desenvolvimento. P3 ainda traz o conceito de documentação de arquitetura evolutiva, que dá visibilidade às decisões e ao que está sendo mantido no ambiente de produção.

> "Eu costumo fazer documentos de arquitetura evolutiva, então, um documenta com a última versão, "Isso aqui é o que está em vigor, é o que está em produção". E aí o outro documenta com com as fases e por que que foi tomada cada decisão. Assim, por exemplo, se eu sair e você assumir aquela solução então, se você ler, você sabe o porquê de cada coisa." - P3

P5 ainda menciona sobre as documentações formais do órgão como referência. Portanto, os profissionais entendem a importância da documentação e adotam a prática de documentar o que está sendo projetado. Além disto, a prática de documentação também é citada como ponto importante para a revisão das decisões que foram tomadas.

4.1.7. Como e com que frequência as decisões são revistas

No que se trata de revisitar as decisões tomadas em momentos anteriores, também é unanimidade que as decisões tomadas na definição da arquitetura precisarão ser revistas.

> "As decisões sempre são revisitadas. Não é uma cláusula pétrea que o que eu defini no início do projeto vai ser unanimidade ao longo do projeto porque às vezes o cliente pode mudar algum serviço, algum banco de dados não atendeu o que a gente precisava. Essa pesquisa é feita, mas às vezes entra uma feature nova e vai precisar acrescentar coisas na arquitetura, então ela é sempre revisitada e ela tá sempre sendo atualizada, não tem pra onde fugir." - P1

P8 cita que, dependendo do momento da empresa, as decisões são revistas, porque o foco pode estar em novas entregas e não na revisão. Assim sendo, os profissionais costumam revisitar as decisões tomadas em fases anteriores do fluxo de desenvolvimento para fazer modificações e refatorações e relembrar o que já foi feito. Uma das razões levantadas para essa revisão constante são as mudanças que acontecem nos projetos, como novas ideias que surgem e a necessidade de visualização do que já foi feito.

5. Discussão

A seguir, é apresentada uma discussão sobre os principais achados em comparação aos trabalhos relacionados.

5.1. Discussão sobre como é feita a definição da arquitetura

Na literatura, Dasanayake et al. (2015) mencionam que os arquitetos do estudo dizem que não há um processo padrão ou *guidelines* para definir a arquitetura e isso também é mencionado em algumas entrevistas neste, que dizem não possuir um padrão de definição em sua empresa. Como diferença, uma das pessoas entrevistadas cita que existe um documento oficial de arquitetura com as principais recomendações (P5). Os autores ainda mencionam que a maioria dos times utiliza uma mistura entre o projeto da arquitetura em uma etapa inicial e um projeto contínuo, o que está de acordo principalmente com o que é citado por P5 e P6 que falam de abordagens ágeis.

Os autores ainda citam que os times raramente usam uma abordagem metodológica para definição da arquitetura e que experiência e intuição são as principais fontes de apoio, mas também usam prototipação de soluções, especialistas externos e reuso de soluções já usadas. Isso também é mencionado por Dasanayake et al. (2016), que encontraram processos informais, mas cada time tem sua prática estruturada de tomar decisões. Como concordância, P3 e P6 citam que a experiência é importante e que a partir delas se constrói o projeto da arquitetura e alguns entrevistados afirmam utilizar PoCs, que são soluções prototipadas, para apoiar o projeto da arquitetura.

5.2. Comparação sobre quem participa da definição da arquitetura

Dasanayake et al. (2016) afirmam que a maioria dos times utiliza tomada de decisão em grupo e essa abordagem também é mencionada pelos profissionais entrevistados, que utilizam da equipe para a criação da arquitetura, além de envolverem pessoas também envolvidas no negócio, como citado por P1, P3 e P6. Alguns ainda mencionam a participação de um grupo externo ao time de desenvolvimento que faz uma avaliação da arquitetura e isso é também mencionado por Dasanayake et al. (2016), que cita um grupo especializado em arquitetura.

5.3. Discussão sobre como as decisões são tomadas

Na literatura, Tofan et al. (2013) encontraram que os arquitetos costumam considerar em média 3 alternativas no início da tomada de decisão. Heesch and Avgeriou (2011) mostram que todos os participantes da pesquisa indicaram buscar por mais de uma alternativa de projeto quando tomam decisões. P1 fala sobre considerar possibilidades, mas P3 cita que as tecnologias homologadas na empresa precisam ser utilizadas. P2 e P6 mencionam sobre as decisões terem influência do conhecimento dos arquitetos. Um ponto não encontrado na literatura é mencionado por P4 e P5 que falam sobre a sustentação do negócio dada uma decisão.

Além disso, Dasanayake et al. (2015) dizem que três formas principais foram observadas para tomar decisões: uma escolha que satisfaz critério, uma escolha selecionada através de prós e contras, a primeira escolha que satisfaz o critério estabelecido. Além da seleção através de prós e contras, nenhuma das demais abordagens foi mencionada pelos profissionais entrevistados.

5.4. Discussão sobre fatores que influenciam a tomada de decisões

Heesch and Avgeriou (2011) afirmam que mais de 70% dos participantes da pesquisa afirmaram que os requisitos são considerados fundamentais para decisões quando comparados a outros fatores e que atributos de qualidade foram considerados importantes por

81% dos participantes. Isto está em concordância com o que é mencionado pelas pessoas entrevistadas, que consideram os requisitos como a maior parte do projeto da arquitetura (P2, P4) e tomam como referência as necessidades e limitações do cliente para desenvolver a solucão (P1 e P6). Dentre outros fatores mencionados neste estudo, apenas o conhecimento do time, a quantidade de profissionais disponíveis no mercado, a velocidade da entrega e a facilidade para manutenção não foram encontrados referenciados na literatura.

5.5. Discussão sobre uso de ferramentas na tomada de decisão

Não foram feitas menções a ferramentas ou técnicas utilizadas para apoiar a tomada de decisões. As ferramentas mencionadas têm relação ou apoiam o desenho da arquitetura, a documentação, os testes ou o desenvolvimento. Isso é também percebido por todos os trabalhos que avaliam esse aspecto, como Dasanayake et al. (2016) e Dasanayake et al. (2015).

5.6. Discussão sobre processo de documentação das decisões

As pessoas entrevistadas citam que valorizam a documentação e costumam atualizá-la com frequência de forma detalhada sobre o processo, sobre as decisões e com exemplos de como aplicar na prática. Isto é visto e mencionado como ponto importante para revisão das decisões, o que leva a conclusão de que documentar as decisões e o projeto da arquitetura contribuem para que as decisões sejam compreendidas e atualizadas. Esse é um dos pontos que mais difere quando se compara com a literatura. Dasanayake et al. (2016) explicam que as documentações são mínimas ou não existentes e a maioria dos arquitetos tem dificuldades com qualidade e manutenção dos documentos. Dasanayake et al. (2015) citam que as documentações tem problemas de qualidade e manutenção. Por fim, Power and Wirfs-Brock (2018) discorrem que a falta de informação sobre decisões passadas tem impacto significativo no projeto que os arquitetos estão trabalhando.

5.7. Discussão sobre revisitar as decisões

Assim como mencionado no tópico anterior, esta é uma diferença grande quando comparado com a literatura, pois as pessoas entrevistadas citam que revisitar as decisões são parte do fluxo normal, explicando que o processo de revisão serve para refatorar e relembrar o que foi feito e os principais motivos para isto são as mudanças que acontecem com a evolução do projeto. Heesch and Avgeriou (2011) mostram que 76% dos arquitetos da pesquisa responderam que não refazem as decisões que tomam no início do projeto com indicações de que decisões feitas previamente são dificilmente revisitadas. Os autores mencionam que não há tempo e recursos para refletir em decisões passadas, os arquitetos finalizam e vão para a próxima decisão. Dasanayake et al. (2016) também expõem que revisitar o *design rationale* foi um dos problemas mais mencionados.

6. Limitações e ameaças à validade

De acordo com o ACM Empirical Standards [Ralph et al. 2020], esse estudo pode ser classificado como um *"Interview Study"*, que é um estudo composto de entrevistas semi-estruturadas ou de perguntas abertas, então critérios quantitativos como validação interna, validação à construção, generalização e confiabilidade tipicamente não se aplicam. Se esse estudo fosse quantitativo, uma ameaça à validade seria o baixo número de entrevistados, porém, como é qualitativo, não se pretende alcançar a generalização de resultados. Uma possível ameaça seria entrevistar apenas pessoas semelhantes, criando a ilusão de convergência e saturação (R2Q4 de [Ralph et al. 2020]), que foi mitigada realizando entrevistas com pessoas atuantes em empresas de diferentes segmentos e com diferentes experiências. Em termos de Validade Interpretativa (em inglês, *"Interpretive Validity"*), a validade da pesquisa foi analisada em termos do quanto as conclusões são baseadas nos dados adquiridos nas entrevistas, visto que todos os conceitos apresentados podem ser mapeados para citações de entrevistas.

7. Conclusão e Trabalhos Futuros

Esse artigo apresentou um estudo qualitativo com o objetivo de entender e avaliar o processo de tomada de decisões de arquitetura de software por profissionais brasileiros. Para isso, nove entrevistas semiestruturadas foram conduzidas com pessoas que possuem atribuições de arquitetura e que atuam em diferentes empresas e as transcrições das entrevistas foram analisadas utilizando os procedimentos da GT.

A respeito de como é o processo de tomada de decisões (QP), os principais achados indicam que os desenvolvedores entrevistados costumam utilizar PoCs, o padrão da empresa ou os requisitos para definir a arquitetura. As principais decisões são tomadas em grupo e não seguem um processo sistemático, sendo os principais fatores levados em consideração desempenho, custo, conhecimento do time, segurança, padrão da empresa, quantidade de profissionais disponíveis no mercado e requisitos do cliente, velocidade da entrega e facilidade de manutenção. Normalmente, não se usam ferramentas para apoiar a tomada de decisões, que são documentadas e revisitadas de forma constante.

Como oportunidades futuras de trabalho, aponta-se a continuação no processo de codificação da GT para identificar relacionamentos entre os códigos. Além disso, a condução de entrevistas com profissionais para avaliação da influência do processo de tomada de decisão de arquitetura sobre outros aspectos do processo de desenvolvimento. Por fim, a condução de entrevistas com profissionais de menor experiência para entendimento do processo de tomada de decisões adotado por estes.

Agradecimentos

Agradecemos a todos participantes do estudo pela colaboração e ao grupo de pesquisa USES/UFAM. Também agradecemos o suporte financeiro do CNPq 314797/2023-8 e CAPES - Código de Financiamento 001.

Referências

Adolph, S., Hall, W., and Kruchten, P. (2011). Using grounded theory to study the experience of software development. *Empirical Software Engineering*, 16:487–513.

Corbin, J. and Strauss, A. (2008). *Basics of qualitative research: Techniques and procedures for developing grounded theory (3rd ed.)*. Sage.

Dasanayake, S., Markkula, J., Aaramaa, S., and Oivo, M. (2015). Software architecture decision-making practices and challenges: An industrial case study. In *2015 24th Australasian Software Engineering Conference*, pages 88–97.

Dasanayake, S., Markkula, J., Aaramaa, S., and Oivo, M. (2016). An empirical study on collaborative architecture decision making in software teams. In Tekinerdogan, B., Zdun, U., and Babar, A., editors, *Software Architecture*, pages 238–246, Cham. Springer International Publishing.

Heesch, U. v. and Avgeriou, P. (2011). Mature architecting - a survey about the reasoning process of professional architects. In *2011 Ninth Working IEEE/IFIP Conference on Software Architecture*, pages 260–269.

Hofmeister, C., Kruchten, P., Nord, R. L., Obbink, H., Ran, A., and America, P. (2007). A general model of software architecture design derived from five industrial approaches. *Journal of Systems and Software*, 80(1):106–126.

Maxwell, J. (2012). Qualitative research design : An interactive approach / j.a. maxwell.

Power, K. and Wirfs-Brock, R. (2018). Understanding architecture decisions in context - an industry case study of architects' decision-making context. In *ECSA*, volume 11048 of *Lecture Notes in Computer Science*, pages 284–299. Springer.

Ralph, P., Baltes, S., Bianculli, D., Dittrich, Y., Felderer, M., Feldt, R., Filieri, A., Furia, C. A., Graziotin, D., He, P., Hoda, R., Juristo, N., Kitchenham, B. A., Robbes, R., Méndez, D., Molléri, J. S., Spinellis, D., Staron, M., Stol, K., Tamburri, D. A., Torchiano, M., Treude, C., Turhan, B., and Vegas, S. (2020). ACM SIGSOFT empirical standards. *CoRR*, abs/2010.03525.

Razavian, M., Paech, B., and Tang, A. (2019). Empirical research for software architecture decision making: An analysis. *Journal of Systems and Software*, 149:360–381.

Seaman, C. B. (1999). Qualitative methods in empirical studies of software engineering. *IEEE Trans. Software Eng.*, 25:557–572.

Shaw, M. (1995). Making choices: A comparison of styles for software architecture. *IEEE Software*, 12(06):27–41.

Souza, L. (2022). Indústria de software e serviços de tic cresceu 6,5% em 2021. Disponível em `https://agenciabrasil.ebc.com.br/economia/noticia/2022-07/industria-de-software-e-servicos-de-tic-cresceram-65-em-2021`. Acesso em 15 de novembro 2022.

Stol, K.-J., Ralph, P., and Fitzgerald, B. (2016). Grounded theory in software engineering research: A critical review and guidelines. In *2016 IEEE/ACM 38th International Conference on Software Engineering (ICSE)*, pages 120–131.

Tofan, D., Galster, M., and Avgeriou, P. (2013). Difficulty of architectural decisions – a survey with professional architects. In Drira, K., editor, *Software Architecture*, pages 192–199, Berlin, Heidelberg. Springer Berlin Heidelberg.

van Vliet, H. and Tang, A. (2016). Decision making in software architecture. *Journal of Systems and Software*, 117:638–644.

Privacy in Practice: Exploring Concrete Relationships Between Privacy Patterns and Privacy by Design Principles in Software Engineering

Vinícius C. Andrade[1], Richard D. Ribeiro[1], Rafael dos P. Canteri[2], Sheila Reinehr[3], Cinthia O. de A. Freitas[3], Andreia Malucelli[3]

[1]Federal Technology University – Paraná (UTFPR)
CEP 84017-220 – Ponta Grossa – PR – Brazil

[2]Federal University of Mato Grosso do Sul (UFMS)
CEP 79304-902 – Corumbá – MS – Brazil

[3]Pontifícia Universidade Católica do Paraná (PUCPR)
CEP 80215-901 – Curitiba – PR – Brazil

{vcandrade, richardribeiro}@utfpr.edu.br, rafael.canteri@ufms.br,
{sheila.reinehr, cinthia.freitas, andreia.malucelli}@pucpr.br

Abstract. *Ensuring the fulfillment of customer preferences and requirements and adherence to legal compliance have emerged as critical considerations for software development organizations. Legislation such as the Brazillian LGPD and the European Union's GDPR highlight the importance of integrating personal data privacy rights from the beginning of system development and throughout the data lifecycle, as mentioned in the fundamental principles of Privacy by Design. However, recent studies still emphasize the need for processes, methods, guides, and tools that help translate Privacy by Design principles into practical software engineering activities. In this context, this article aims to explore the integration of abstract Privacy by Design principles into tangible Software Engineering practices. To this end, a mapping was carried out between Privacy Patterns and the principles of Privacy by Design. This process translated abstract concepts into practical activities. The reliability of the mapping process among the researchers was assessed by calculating the Intraclass Correction Coefficient (ICC). The findings underscore that when software engineers apply one or more Privacy Patterns to address personal data privacy requirements, as revealed through the correlations conducted in this study, they also tend to adhere to one or more Privacy by Design principles.*

Keywords. *Privacy, Privacy by Design, Privacy Patterns, Software Engineering.*

1. Introduction

Concerns among data subjects regarding the collection, usage, storage, and sharing of personal information are growing [Ferrão et al. 2021]. Despite the crucial importance of safeguarding personal data privacy, companies misusing this information persist. Notable examples include the scandal involving Facebook and Cambridge Analytica, where personal data of 87 million users was collected and misused in 2018 [Rosenberg 2018; Team 2018]. In 2021, Twitch, Amazon's streaming platform, experienced a data leak of 128 gigabytes of personal information from streamers [Browning 2021; Tidy and Molloy 2021]. In 2024, the most significant data leak in history, known as "Mother of All Breaches" (MOAB), with 26 billion user records from various services, such as Tencent, Weibo, MySpace, X (formerly Twitter), among others [Petkauskas 2024].

In the Brazilian context, an incident of data leakage occurred at Inter Bank in 2018, resulting in the loss of personal information from 19,961 account holders [Redação Veja 2018]. Subsequently, in 2021, Brazil witnessed the most extensive data leak in its history, exposing the unique identification numbers of 223 million individuals [Rohr 2021]. In 2022, 137,285 instant payment keys, known as "PIX," containing holders' data, were disclosed [Malar 2022].

Data privacy may encounter challenges across the software life cycle, potentially compromising its ultimate quality [Andrade et al. 2022; Brito et al. 2020]. Consequently, laws and regulations, including the General Data Protection Law (Lei Geral de Proteção de Dados - LGPD) [BRASIL 2018] and the European General Data Protection Regulation (GDPR) [EU 2016], emphasize the significance of incorporating Privacy by Design (PbD) principles [Cavoukian 2009]. PbD not only addresses the privacy of personal data but also clarifies the procedures for collecting and processing personal data while upholding the data life cycle from an information security perspective [Cavoukian 2009, 2012].

While implementing PbD principles in software projects is feasible, a significant level of abstraction remains [Andrade et al. 2022; Baldassarre et al. 2020; Morales-Trujillo et al. 2018; Peixoto et al. 2023]. PbD lacks the detailed guidance necessary for software engineers to seamlessly adopt regulations during the design and development of applications, thereby posing challenges to its effective implementation. As suggested by Cavoukian [2012], the next step in PbD's evolution involves "translating PbD's 7 Foundational Principles into concrete, prescriptive requirements, specifications, standards, best practices, and operational performance criteria" to provide more practical guidance for implementation.

From this scenario, which strongly impacts the entire software development cycle, the following research question arose: How can the fundamental principles of PbD be related to the best software engineering practices? To answer the research question, the PbD principles were mapped to the 72 Privacy Patterns cataloged by the University of California [UC Berkeley School of Information 2024]. In total, three privacy and personal data protection experts carried out the mapping in cycles. At the end of each cycle, they had meetings in which conflicting points were discussed to reach a consensus on the final mapping.

Integrating Privacy Patterns and Privacy by Design principles brings substantial benefits to both organizations and end users, strengthening the relationship of trust between them, as it facilitates the understanding of how abstract Privacy by Design concepts can be implemented practically in software development. This allows software engineering teams to have clear, tangible guidelines to ensure regulatory compliance, mitigate privacy risks, and meet customer expectations for personal data protection.

Furthermore, effectively enforcing Privacy Patterns increases transparency and user trust in products and services, promoting a culture of Privacy by Design.

This work is organized as follows: Section 2 presents a background on related concepts. Section 3 describes the research method. Section 4 presents the results. Section 5 discusses the relevance of the results. Section 6 presents the threats to validity, and Section 7 concludes the paper with final considerations.

2. Background

2.1. Privacy by Design

According to Cavoukian [2014], PbD is recommended for seamlessly incorporating privacy and data protection throughout the entire system development lifecycle. This integration spans from the early stages of development, extending to design, organizational processes, network architectures, and enhancements in governance systems. Additionally, PbD operates under the premise that achieving satisfactory levels of privacy protection goes beyond mere compliance with legal standards. Instead, it advocates for privacy assurance to be ingrained as a standard mode of operation [Cavoukian 2009].

PbD comprises seven foundational principles for the proactive integration of privacy considerations in the early phases of the design process [Cavoukian 2009]: (i) proactive not reactive; preventative not remedial: emphasizes a proactive stance in preventing privacy issues rather than addressing them reactively; (ii) privacy as the default: advocates for privacy protection as the automatic default, requiring explicit user choices to deviate from this setting; (iii) privacy embedded into design: calls for the seamless incorporation of privacy features directly into the design and architecture of systems; (iv) full functionality – positive-sum, not zero-sum: promotes solutions where privacy protection does not compromise system functionality, seeking positive-sum outcomes; (v) end-to-end security – lifecycle protection: advocates for security measures across the entire data lifecycle, from collection to disposal; (vi) visibility and transparency: encourages openness regarding privacy policies, practices, and procedures, ensuring transparent communication with users; and (vii) respect for user privacy: fosters a user-centric environment by empowering individuals to control their personal information and make informed decisions about its usage.

2.2. Privacy Patterns

According to Colesky et al. [2016], Privacy Patterns provide knowledge collected from experts in a structured, documented, and reusable way and contribute to constructing a secure information system.

The solutions offered for using these Privacy Patterns involve detailing the information assets and the level of criticality of these assets, including implementation details in a real environment, and also taking into account the architecture and technologies that must be used [Moral-García et al. 2010].

Therefore, Privacy Patterns support the documentation of standard solutions to privacy problems. They can improve systems' development by describing classes, collaborations between objects, and their purposes and help designers identify and resolve privacy-related issues [Colesky et al. 2016, 2018].

To gather proposed Privacy Patterns, researchers at the University of California maintain a catalog currently containing 72 (seventy-two) Privacy Patterns organized into categories. Each pattern is structured according to the following characteristics [Moral-García et al. 2010; UC Berkeley School of Information 2024]: (i) name: represents the problem addressed; (ii) context: contains a generic description of the configuration and specifies the conditions under which the privacy pattern should be applied; (iii) problem: presents the situation that led to the need to apply privacy mechanisms and obtain a solution; and (iv) solution: describes the solution based on the scenario and problem considered.

2.3. Privacy Design Strategies

Hoepman [2014] proposed a set of eight strategies that describe fundamental approaches to achieving a given objective and, consequently, satisfactory levels of privacy protection.

Hoepman's [2014] privacy strategies were constructed from existing privacy principles and personal data protection laws and are divided into two categories: Data-Driven Strategies and Driven Strategies to Processes. The first refers to privacy-friendly data processing and has the following strategies: (i) Minimise: limit the collection and processing of personal data to only what is strictly necessary for the intended purpose; (ii) Hide: protect sensitive information by implementing mechanisms to conceal or encrypt it; (iii) Separate: segregate different types of data to ensure that sensitive and non-sensitive information is stored separately; and (iv) Aggregate/Abstract: combine and analyze data in an aggregated, de-identified manner to extract insights without compromising individual privacy.

The second category highlights the processes that involve the responsible processing of personal data. It contains the following strategies: (v) Inform: keep individuals informed about the collection, use, and processing of their data through clear and transparent communication; (vi) Control: empower individuals with control over their personal information, enabling them to manage access and permissions; (vii) Enforce: implement mechanisms and policies to enforce privacy measures and ensure compliance; and (viii) Demonstrate: showcase and provide evidence of compliance with privacy principles and regulations [Hoepman 2014].

3. Research Method

To carry out the mapping, three privacy and personal data protection experts independently mapped the 7 (seven) fundamental principles of PbD to 72 (seventy-two) Privacy Patterns cataloged by the University of California. Figure 1 illustrates the steps of the research method.

The first stage, Planning and Preparation, has two activities: (i) Design the Mapping Protocol and (ii) Conduct Training. At this stage, each participant received a guide containing an introduction to the concept and principles of PbD [Cavoukian 2009] and a description of the introduction to Privacy Patterns containing context, problem addressed, and proposed solution [UC Berkeley School of Information 2024]. As training, 7 (seven) Privacy Patterns were chosen randomly (approximately 10% of the total). Three experts jointly mapped out the Location Granularity privacy pattern, discussing why the pattern does or does not include a specific Privacy by Design principle. Subsequently, each researcher individually and independently mapped the remaining 6 (six) patterns: Ambient Notice, Enable/Disable Functions, Informed Consent for Web-based Transactions, Negotiation of Privacy Policy, Privacy Icons, and Protection Against Tracking.

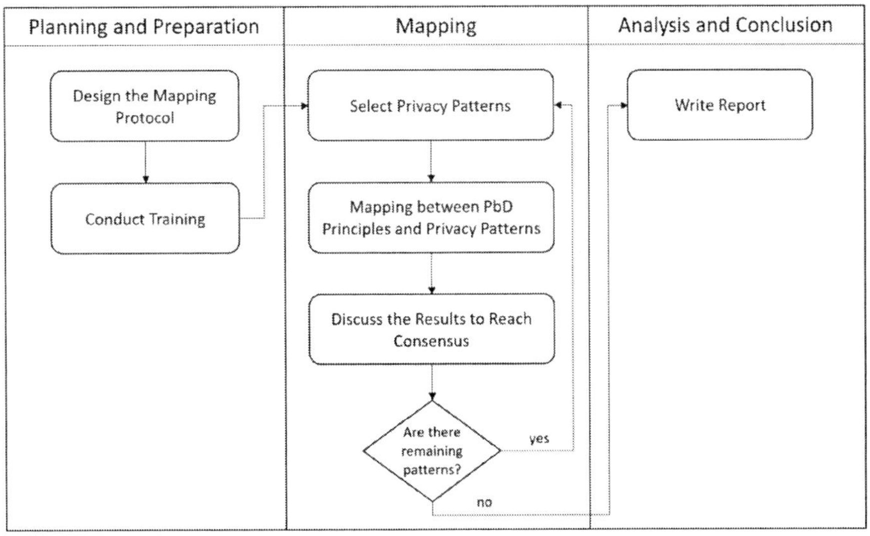

Figure 1. Research Method

To assess the agreement among researchers during the mapping process, we calculated the Intraclass Correlation Coefficient (ICC) [Fleiss et al. 2013]. An ICC value below 40% indicates weak agreement, while a range of 40% to 75% is considered satisfactory to good, and an ICC value of 75% or higher is deemed excellent. The ICC between researchers A and B was 77.55%, an excellent agreement rate; between researchers A and C, 79.59%, also an excellent agreement rate; and between researchers B and C, 65.31%, a satisfactory agreement rate. Following the calculation of ICC values, a meeting was convened to compare the results of each mapping. Discussions were held to reconcile any divergent findings and achieve consensus among all researchers.

The next step, Mapping, has the following activities: (i) Select Privacy Patterns, (ii) Mapping between PbD Principles and Privacy Patterns, and (iii) Discuss the Results to Reach Consensus. As this is a cyclical stage, the remaining 65 (sixty-five) Privacy Patterns were divided into 5 (five) sessions, with 13 (thirteen) patterns being chosen and mapped per session. At the end of each session, new meetings were held to discuss differences and reach a consensus among participants.

Finally, the Analysis and Conclusion stage aims to write a report containing the results obtained from the mapping carried out by the participants. At this stage, the ICC calculation was performed again. However, this time, the 72 Privacy Patterns were considered. The ICC between all researchers was considered excellent: A and B (81.55%), A and C (86.31%), and B and C (79.37%).

4. Results

The final mapping result between the Privacy Patterns and the Privacy by Design Principles is presented in Table 1, organized according to the corresponding Hoepman Strategies [Hoepman 2014]. The lines that display the character (●) indicate that the Privacy Pattern contemplates the Privacy by Design Principle corresponding to the column. On the other hand, its absence indicates a non-relationship.

Table 1. Final Result of the Mapping between Privacy Patterns and PbD Principles.

Hoepman Design Strategies [2014]	Privacy Patterns	Privacy by Design Principles						
		1. proactive not reactive	2. privacy as the default	3. privacy embedded into design	4. full functionality	5. end-to-end security	6. visibility and transparency	7. respect for user privacy
Abstract	Location Granularity	●	●	●				●
Control	Decoupling [content] and location information visibility	●	●	●				●
Control	Active broadcast of presence		●				●	●
Control	Buddy List				●			●
Control	Discouraging blanket strategies	●		●				●
Control	Enable/Disable Functions			●			●	●
Hide Control	Encryption with user-managed keys	●	●	●		●		
Control	Incentivized Participation		●					●
Inform Control	Informed Consent for Web-based Transactions						●	●
Control	Lawful Consent	●		●			●	●
Control	Masquerade			●		●		●
Control	Negotiation of Privacy Policy	●	●					●
Control	Outsourcing [with consent]	●					●	
Control	Pay Back			●				●
Control	Obtaining Explicit Consent						●	●
Separate Control	Personal Data Store			●		●	●	●
Control	Private link		●	●				
Control	Reasonable Level of Control	●		●				●
Control	Reciprocity			●			●	●
Control	Selective access control		●	●				●
Control	Selective Disclosure	●	●	●				●
Control	Sign an Agreement to Solve Lack of Trust on the Use of Private Data Context						●	●
Control	Single Point of Contact	●		●		●		●
Separate	User data confinement pattern	●	●	●				
Minimise Hide	Added-noise measurement obfuscation	●	●	●				
Hide	Aggregation Gateway	●	●	●		●		
Hide	Trustworthy Privacy Plug-in	●	●	●		●		
Hide	Anonymity Set	●	●					
Hide Separate	Anonymous Reputation-based Blacklisting	●	●	●	●			

Hide	Onion Routing	●	●	●		●		
Hide	Pseudonymous Identity	●	●	●	●			
Hide	Pseudonymous Messaging	●	●	●		●		
Hide	Use of dummies		●	●				
Hide	Attribute Based Credentials	●	●					●
Minimise	Protection against Tracking	●		●				●
Minimise	Strip Invisible Metadata	●	●	●	●			
Enforce	Federated Privacy Impact Assessment	●		●				
Enforce	Obligation Management	●		●			●	
Enforce	Sticky Policies	●		●			●	
Enforce	Identity Federation Do Not Track Pattern	●		●				
Inform	Abridged Terms and Conditions						●	
Inform	Appropriate Privacy Icons						●	
Inform	Ambient Notice	●		●			●	●
Inform	Appropriate Privacy Feedback						●	●
Inform	Asynchronous notice						●	●
Inform	Awareness Feed						●	●
Inform	Data Breach Notification Pattern						●	●
Inform	Privacy Aware Wording						●	
Inform	Dynamic Privacy Policy Display						●	
Inform	Privacy icons						●	
Inform	Icons for Privacy Policies						●	
Inform	Layered Policy Design						●	
Inform	Privacy Labels						●	
Inform	Privacy Policy Display						●	
Inform	Impactful Information and Feedback						●	●
Inform	Platform for Privacy Preferences			●				●
Inform	Policy Matching Display			●				●
Inform	Privacy-Aware Network Client						●	
Inform	Increasing awareness of information aggregation						●	●
Inform	Informed Credential Selection						●	●
Inform	Informed Secure Passwords	●				●		●
Inform	Unusual Activities			●				●
Inform	Informed Implicit Consent						●	●
Inform	Minimal Information Asymmetry	●	●				●	●
Inform	Personal Data Table						●	●
Inform	Preventing mistakes or reducing their impact						●	●
Inform	Privacy Awareness Panel						●	●
Inform	Privacy Dashboard						●	●
Inform	Privacy Color Coding						●	
Inform	Privacy Mirrors						●	●
Inform	Trust Evaluation of Services Sides						●	
Inform	Who's Listening						●	●

The Location Granularity pattern aims to proactively prevent the holder's location data from sharing without their consent. To achieve this, the patterns objective is to minimize the collection of information by offering different levels of granularity and offering the data subject the option of how precisely they would like to share their location. Therefore, the Location Granularity pattern favors the principles of Proactive not Reactive, Privacy as the Default, Privacy Embedded into Design, and Respect for User Privacy.

Related to the Location Granularity pattern, the Decoupling [Content] and Location Information Visibility pattern allow users to decide on the sharing, disclosure, and granularity of their location-related information to use a particular service. If the user performs no configuration, the system must, by default, proactively preserve the privacy of the user's personal data. This way, the Decoupling [Content] and Location Information Visibility pattern implements the principles of Proactive not Reactive, Privacy as the Default, Privacy Embedded into Design, and Respect for User Privacy.

The Active Broadcast of Presence pattern allows the user to choose when to share their information, preventing data from being transmitted holistically in any situation, and, in case of doubts, clarifications must be provided to them. The user can choose not to be questioned again, but this decision must be made explicitly. In this context, the Active Broadcast of Presence pattern contemplates the principles of Privacy as the Default, Visibility and Transparency, and Respect for User Privacy.

Regarding social networks, users often interact with people close to them and strangers. The Buddy List pattern allows the user to maintain lists of more relevant contacts with whom they are more likely to interact. Therefore, the Buddy List pattern directly relates to the principles of Full Functionality and Respect for User Privacy.

Still, in the context of information sharing and social networks, the Discouraging Blanket Strategies pattern gives users complete control over the privacy of the shared content, enabling them to define a level of privacy that best suits their needs. As a result, the Discouraging Blanket Strategies pattern supports the principles of Proactive not Reactive, Privacy Embedded into Design and Respect for User Privacy.

For the Enable/Disable Functions pattern to be successful in its application, one must, in advance, have knowledge of which functionalities the system has and what personal information is collected in each of these functions, allowing the holder to agree or not with the collection of certain information. Therefore, the principles of Privacy Embedded in Design, Visibility and Transparency, and Respect for User Privacy are covered by the Enable/Disable Functions pattern.

To guarantee the security and privacy of holders' personal data, the Encryption With User-Managed Keys pattern aims to encrypt holders' personal information before storing it or transferring it through online services. The principles Proactive not Reactive, Privacy as the Default, Privacy Embedded into Design, and End-to-End Security are considered in the Encryption With User-Managed Keys pattern.

Users' participation in a given system by providing personal data to improve the identification of their preferences is necessary for data controllers. In this context, the Incentivized Participation pattern encourages user participation without harming or invading the privacy of data subjects. Any activity that requires collecting user data requires prior consent. Therefore, the Incentivized Participation pattern is related to Privacy as the Default and Respect for User Privacy principles.

To maintain a profitable service and provide a better user experience, controllers need to collect personal data from data subjects. However, collection is only permitted with the data subject's informed consent. Therefore, the Informed Consent for Web-based Transactions privacy pattern aims to protect the interests of data subjects and establishes that the collection of personal information can only occur with their consent, and this can only happen after the presentation of clear and concise information about how data will be collected, stored, processed and deleted. Therefore, the Informed Consent for Web-based Transactions pattern favors the principles of Visibility and Transparency and Respect for User Privacy.

In this same context of obtaining consent from data subjects, the Lawful Consent pattern establishes that services must be separate and, for each specific service, explicit consent must be acquired, preventing the user from sharing their personal data without prior knowledge of a particular functionality. In this way, the Lawful Consent pattern covers the principles of Proactive not Reactive, Privacy Embedded into Design, Visibility and Transparency, and Respect for User Privacy.

The Mascarade pattern aims to allow the user to select the level of sharing of personal information for a given context. It is accomplished by organizing personal information into privacy scales. When the user selects a level on the scale, all information from that and lower levels is shared. In this context, the Mascarade pattern includes Privacy Embedded into Design, End-to-End Security, and Respect for User Privacy principles.

The Negotiation of Privacy Policy pattern proposes that users' privacy preferences, when not recognized, are permanently configured to preserve their privacy as much as possible. This care must be taken by incorporating techniques that protect the user's privacy from the beginning of using the service. It is done by implementing a data leakage restriction until the user allows which information can be shared, thus respecting their privacy. In this context, the Negotiation of Privacy Policy pattern involves the principles of Proactive not Reactive, Privacy as the Default, and Respect for User Privacy.

In some cases, controllers need to share data with third parties to process the holder's data. The Outsourcing [with consent] pattern establishes that, in these cases, controllers must transparently present to data subjects what the data is and how third parties will process it. Third-party data processing will only be permitted after obtaining the data subject's free, specific, and explicit consent. This way, the Outsourcing [with consent] pattern implements the Proactive not Reactive, and Visibility and Transparency.

The Pay Back pattern benefits users when they contribute or maintain content for the service, such as on a social network. However, the individual choices of users must be respected, and for those who choose to provide more information, the legal consent of the holder must be obtained. Therefore, the Pay Back pattern is related to the principles of Privacy Embedded in Design and Respect for User Privacy.

The Obtaining Explicit Consent pattern aims to provide the data subject with clear and objective notifications about how a particular service will collect, process, and store its data. The controller must ensure the holder understands the information and consequences of accepting the presented terms. Consent must be given freely by the holder. Therefore, the Obtaining Explicit Consent pattern supports the principles of Visibility and Transparency, and Respect for User Privacy.

The Personal Data Store pattern discusses combining a central server and personal tokens. In this pattern, tokens can take on USB keys and incorporate a database system and an authentication certificate for the holder. As a result, holders have greater control over their personal data, which remains secure and stored locally and can be maintained by the holder. Therefore, the Personal Data Store pattern contemplates the principles of Privacy Embedded into Design, End-to-End Security, Visibility and Transparency, and Respect for User Privacy.

The Private Link pattern aims to provide the holder with a private link to a specific resource, such as personal information about the user. If deemed necessary, the holder may share the link with others, giving them access to that personal information. Therefore, the Private Link pattern favors the principles of Privacy as the Default and Privacy Embedded into Design.

To allow users to provide information in a selective and granular manner, the Reasonable Level of Control pattern aims, in advance, to design ways to enable the holder to choose their data's privacy level, granting third parties access to the data. In this context, the Reasonable Level of Control pattern is related to the Proactive not Reactive, Privacy Embedded into Design, and Respect for User Privacy.

In systems where users must collaborate among themselves in favor of the group, the quality of the final result is given through the contribution of all members. The Reciprocity pattern mentions that each member must be rewarded in proportion to their participation in the group's earnings. Any collection and use of user data must be consented to by the user and informed of how this personal data will be used, respecting their privacy. Therefore, the Reciprocity pattern includes the principles of Privacy Embedded into Design, Visibility and Transparency, and Respect for User Privacy.

The Selective Access Control pattern gives users control over the visibility of content shared in social environments. Users can specify rules based on other users or groups of people to define who to target the post. Therefore, the Selective Access Control pattern implements the principles of Privacy as the Default, Privacy Embedded into Design, and Respect for User Privacy.

Occasionally, users wish to use a service anonymously, thus minimizing the chances of providing their personal data. On the other hand, controllers need some information, as this way, users cannot carry out malicious activities without being identified. For these cases, the Selective Disclosure pattern identifies which information is essential for the system to function, thus promoting data minimization. Furthermore, anonymous functionality must be provided to the user as long as it does not compromise the service. Therefore, the Selective Disclosure pattern considers the principles of Proactive not Reactive, Privacy as the Default, Privacy Embedded into Design, and Respect for User Privacy.

For users' personal data to be processed, the controller needs the consent of the data subjects. In this context, the Sign an Agreement to Solve Lack of Trust on the Use of Private Data Context pattern establishes that the service must present to the user mechanisms through which data will be collected and how it will be processed, in addition to binding to the controller or its representatives. This information must be presented clearly and objectively, and data collection can only be carried out after obtaining the user's consent. In this way, the Sign an Agreement to Solve Lack of Trust on the Use of Private Data Context pattern encompasses the principles of Visibility and Transparency, and Respect for User Privacy.

Distributed storage services require specialized privacy management. The Single Point of Contact pattern adopts an approach by providing security tokens to authenticate and authorize the presentation of confidential information to a given user and storing pseudonyms to preserve the data subject's identity. Therefore, the Single Point of Contact pattern supports the principles of Proactive not Reactive, Privacy Embedded into Design, End-to-End Security, and Respect for User Privacy.

When the collection of personal data represents a threat to the privacy of data subjects, the system architecture can be rethought. The User Data Confinement Pattern establishes a change in the trust relationship between data subjects and service providers. Instead of the holders' personal data being collected and processed by the service provider, the processing occurs locally in the user's trusted environment. It allows for greater control of personal data by the holders. In this context, the User Data Confinement Pattern contemplates the Proactive not Reactive, Privacy as the Default, and Privacy Embedded into Design principles.

The Added-Noise Measurement Obfuscation pattern aims to add a noise value to the actual value of an attribute collected from the data subject before transmitting it. Thus, when obtaining the data, a third party would not be able to infer the correct value of it, preserving the data subject's privacy. In this way, the Added-Noise Measurement Obfuscation pattern is related to the Proactive not Reactive, Privacy as the Default, and Privacy Embedded into Design principles.

5. Discussion

The mapping of Privacy by Design principles with Privacy Patterns resulted in a varied distribution of relationships, highlighting nuances in applying these principles in software engineering. Analysis of relationship numbers reveals significant differences between principles, raising intriguing questions about the underlying reasons for these disparities.

Respect for User Privacy, with 42 relationships, was the principle with the most relationships. Linking this principle to many patterns highlights its pervasive relevance and the centrality of respect for user privacy in software development practices. Furthermore, this principle is related mainly to Privacy Patterns categorized as Control and Inform, which suggests that promoting user autonomy and transparency are central approaches to manifesting this principle in software engineering.

The second Privacy by Design principle with the most relationships was Visibility and Transparency, related to 39 Privacy Patterns. The high number of patterns associated with this principle suggests that the emphasis on providing visibility and transparency has broad applications and is considered essential in various privacy circumstances. We note that the principle of Visibility and Transparency is predominantly associated with Privacy Patterns identified as Inform. It reflects the importance of transparent communication to ensure users' understanding, trust, and active participation in privacy practices.

Next, with 34 relationships, the Privacy Embedded into the Design principle is due to several Privacy Patterns focus on the proactive integration of privacy in the early stages of design and reflect a commitment to controlling and ensuring compliance with privacy practices throughout the software lifecycle. For this reason, this principle is mainly related to Privacy Patterns grouped into the Control, Hide, and Enforce categories.

The Proactive not Reactive principle was related to 29 Privacy Patterns as it emphasizes, from the beginning of development, anticipating threats, minimizing risks, hiding sensitive data, preventing privacy violations, and ensuring legal compliance with privacy issues. It explains the tendency to associate the principle with privacy patterns grouped under the Minimise, Hide, and Enforce categories.

Subsequently, the Privacy as the Default principle was associated with 22 Privacy Patterns. Linking this principle to fewer patterns suggests that although privacy is considered from the outset, the range of practical implementations is restricted. The limited collection of personal data combined with the concealment of information and a cautious and preventive approach in managing the data subject's privacy means that the Privacy as the Default principle has a relationship with privacy patterns mainly classified as Hide and Minimise.

Finally, the principles with the lowest number of associations are End-to-End Security (9 associations) and Full Functionality (4 associations). Despite being a fundamental pillar, End-to-End Security is not directly associated with various privacy scenarios. In turn, implementing the Full Functionality is challenging due to the complexity inherent in balancing full functionality delivery with the need to protect users' privacy in compliance with various regulations and individual expectations.

With the mapping between the Privacy Patterns and the Privacy by Design Principles, there is a complexity in correlating them, as, sometimes, the abstract nature of the Privacy by Design principles generates doubts when relating them to the Privacy Patterns. Subsequently, these doubts were resolved in meetings with the other participants, in which there was an explanation to reach a consensus on the correlation between certain Privacy Patterns and a specific Privacy by Design principle.

Furthermore, we observed a conceptual similarity between Privacy Patterns and Privacy by Design principles, thus linking practice with theory. As a result of the mapping, we obtained an instrument that can assist software engineers in making decisions and implementing specific privacy problems considering the Privacy by Design principles required by legislation and regulations.

6. Threats to Validity

In this work, a threat to the validity of the construct lies in the interpretation and definition of Privacy Patterns. Differences in understanding among researchers in the relationship between Privacy by Design principles and Privacy Patterns may impact the consistency of the mapping. Another threat relates to the interpretation of the Privacy by Design principles, as they can be interpreted differently. Divergences in researchers' understanding of these principles may influence the attribution of Privacy Patterns to specific principles. Discussions between researchers were held before and throughout the mapping to minimize this threat, aiming at reaching a consensus.

The threat to external validity can be cited as the generalization of the results. The research focused on Privacy Patterns cataloged by the University of California, which may limit the generalization of results to other sets of patterns used in different contexts or countries. This threat can be considered minimal once the used catalog is quite comprehensive.

Finally, reliability between researchers can be mentioned as a threat to internal validity. This threat was mitigated by calculating the Intraclass Correlation Coefficient (ICC), demonstrating satisfactory and excellent agreement between researchers.

7. Conclusions

The present study sought to investigate how the fundamental principles of Privacy by Design [Cavoukian 2009] can be related to better software engineering practices, recognizing the challenges highlighted by several authors regarding the difficulty of translating these highly abstract principles into practical software development activities [Andrade et al. 2022; Baldassarre et al. 2020; Morales-Trujillo et al. 2018; Peixoto et al. 2023]. Faced with this complexity, our approach aimed to create a bridge between principles and tangible actions for developers using the 72 Privacy Patterns cataloged by the University of California [UC Berkeley School of Information 2024].

This initiative aims to bridge the gap between theory and practice and provide software development teams with a solid and applicable framework for integrating privacy considerations from the earliest stages of the software development process, such as in writing user stories by identifying the personal data that will be collected or requesting the holder's consent to carry out a specific action. At this point, it is possible to use mapping to define which privacy patterns will be used and, consequently, which PbD principles will be related.

The detailed mapping of these Privacy Patterns was conducted by three privacy and personal data protection experts, who established relationships between each pattern and one or more Privacy by Design principles. We calculated the Intraclass Correction Coefficient (ICC) [Fleiss et al. 2013] to ensure reliability and consistency in the results. The agreement rates between all the researchers were considered excellent [Fleiss et al. 2013].

When faced with issues related to personal data privacy, software engineers can use one or more Privacy Patterns related to one or more Privacy by Design principles to ensure a systematic and practical approach to resolving these issues. By applying Privacy Patterns in accordance with Privacy by Design principles, software engineers ensure adherence to privacy regulations and promote user trust, transparency, and accountability in handling personal data. This proactive approach from the early phases of software development helps avoid compliance issues and potential legal sanctions. It contributes to building products and services that respect privacy and meet users' expectations. In this way, the mapping between Privacy Patterns and Privacy by Design principles is instrumental in guiding software engineering practices toward a safer, more ethical, and trustworthy digital environment, benefiting both organizations and individuals.

As future work, we are currently developing a software process focused on protecting the privacy of personal data. This process is designed to systematically integrate Privacy by Design principles from the early stages of development. Our goal is to offer clear and practical guidelines for software engineers, enabling them to seamlessly integrate privacy considerations at every stage of the software lifecycle. We are additionally in the process of creating a tool designed to aid software engineers in accessing pertinent information regarding Privacy by Design and Privacy Patterns. This tool will consist of an interactive platform equipped with educational materials, real-world examples, and customized guidelines tailored to selected patterns. By simplifying the implementation process and fostering a culture of privacy-conscious development, this tool aims to facilitate the integration of privacy considerations into software engineering practices.

References

Andrade, V. C., Gomes, R. D., Reinehr, S., Freitas, C. O. D. A. and Malucelli, A. (2022). Privacy by Design and Software Engineering: a Systematic Literature Review. In *Proceedings of the XXI Brazilian Symposium on Software Quality*.

Baldassarre, M. T., Santa Barletta, V., Caivano, D. and Scalera, M. (2020). Integrating security and privacy in software development. *Software Quality Journal*, p. 1–32.

BRASIL (2018). Lei Geral de Proteção de Dados Pessoais (LGPD). http://www.planalto.gov.br/ccivil_03/_ato2015-2018/2018/lei/l13709.htm, [accessed on Oct 9].

Brito, I. S., Moreira, A. and Araújo, J. (2020). Handling Nonfunctional Requirements for Smart Cities. In *23rd Iberoamerican Conference on Software Engineering, CIbSE 2020*.

Browning, K. (2021). A "potentially disastrous" data breach hits Twitch, the livestreaming site. https://www.nytimes.com/2021/10/06/technology/twitch-data-breach.html, [accessed on Jun 7].

Cavoukian, A. (2009). Privacy by Design - The 7 foundational principles - Implementation and mapping of fair information practices. *Information and Privacy Commissioner of Ontario, Canada*, p. 5.

Cavoukian, A. (2012). Operationalizing Privacy by Design: A Guide to Implementing.

Cavoukian, A., Shapiro, S. and Cronk, R. J. (2014). *Privacy engineering: Proactively embedding privacy, by design*. Office of the Information and Privacy Commissioner.

Colesky, M., Caiza, J. C., Del Lamo, J. M., Hoepman, J. H. and Martín, Y. S. (2018). A system of privacy patterns for user control. *Proceedings of the ACM Symposium on Applied Computing*, p. 1150–1156.

Colesky, M., Hoepman, J. and Hillen, C. (2016). A Critical Analysis of Privacy Design Strategies. In *2016 IEEE Security and Privacy Workshops (SPW)*.

EU (2016). Regulation (EU) 2016/679 of the European Parliament and of the Council of 27 April 2016 on the protection of natural persons with regard to the processing of personal data and on the free movement of such data, and repealing Directive 95/46. *Official Journal of the European Union (OJ)*, v. 59, n. 1–88, p. 294.

Ferrão, S. É. R., Carvalho, A. P., Canedo, E. D., et al. (2021). Diagnostic of Data Processing by Brazilian Organizations - A Low Compliance Issue. *Information*, v. 12, n. 4, p. 1–30.

Fleiss, J. L., Levin, B. and Paik, M. C. (2013). *Statistical methods for rates and proportions*. John Wiley & Sons.

Hoepman, J. H. J.-H. (2014). Privacy design strategies. *IFIP Advances in Information and Communication Technology*, v. 428, p. 446–459.

Malar, J. P. (2022). Banco Central anuncia vazamento de dados ligados a mais de 130 mil chaves Pix. https://www.cnnbrasil.com.br/economia/banco-central-anuncia-vazamento-de-dados-ligados-a-mais-de-130-mil-chaves-pix/, [accessed on Jan 25].

Moral-García, S., Ortiz, R., Moral-Rubio, S., Vela, B., Garzás, J. and Fernández-Medina, E. (2010). A new pattern template to support the design of security architectures. In *The Second International Conferences of Pervasive Patterns and Applications*.

Morales-trujillo, M. E., Matla-cruz, E. O., García-Mireles, G. A. and Piattini, M. (2018). Privacy by Design in Software Engineering: a Systematic Mapping Study. In *Ibero-American Conference on Software Engineering (CIbSE)*.

Peixoto, M., Ferreira, D., Cavalcanti, M., et al. (2023). The Perspective of Brazilian Software Developers on Data Privacy. *Journal of Systems and Software*, v. 195, p. 111523.

Petkauskas, V. (2024). Mother of all breaches reveals 26 billion records: what we know so far. https://cybernews.com/security/billions-passwords-credentials-leaked-mother-of-all-breaches/#:~:text=Mother of all breaches reveals,what we know so far&text=Image by Cybernews.,mind-boggling 26 billion records., [accessed on Feb 6].

Redação Veja (2018). Banco Inter vai pagar R$ 1,5 milhão por vazamento de dados de clientes. https://veja.abril.com.br/economia/banco-inter-vai-pagar-r-15-milhao-por-vazamento-de-dados-de-clientes/, [accessed on May 24].

Rohr, A. (2021). Megavazamentos de dados expõem informações de 223 milhões de números de CPF. https://g1.globo.com/economia/tecnologia/blog/altieres-rohr/post/2021/01/25/vazamentos-de-dados-expoem-informacoes-de-223-milhoes-de-numeros-de-cpf.ghtml, [accessed on May 24].

Rosenberg, M. (2018). Cambridge Analytica and Facebook: The Scandal and the Fallout So Far. https://www.nytimes.com/2018/04/04/us/politics/cambridge-analytica-scandal-fallout.html, [accessed on Mar 10].

Team, C. 4 N. I. (2018). Revealed: Cambridge Analytica data on thousands of Facebook users still not deleted. https://www.channel4.com/news/revealed-cambridge-analytica-data-on-thousands-of-facebook-users-still-not-deleted, [accessed on Mar 10].

Tidy, J. and Molloy, D. (2021). Twitch confirms massive data breach. https://www.bbc.com/news/technology-58817658, [accessed on Jun 7].

UC Berkeley School of Information (2024). Privacy Patterns. https://privacypatterns.org/, [accessed on Feb 6].

On the Challenges to Documenting Requirements in Agile Software Development: A Practitioners' Perspective

Edna Dias Canedo[1], Angelica Toffano S. Calazans[2], Geovana Ramos Sousa Silva[1], Eloisa Toffano Seidel Masson[2], Isabel Sofia Brito[3]

[1]University of Brasília (UnB) –Brasília – DF –Brazil

[2]University center – UniCEUB – Brasília – DF –Brazil

[3]Polytechnic Institute of Beja – Beja – Portugal
ednacanedo@unb.br, angelica.toffano@gmail.com, geovannna.1998@gmail.com, eloisa.masson@ceub.edu.br, isabel.sofia@ipbeja.pt

Abstract. *Agile Software Development (ASD) is an iterative and incremental methodology designed to accelerate project deliveries. In this dynamic environment characterized by constant changes, the task of documenting requirements becomes increasingly challenging, leading to the emergence of the technical debt issue. This research involved a survey of 84 practitioners to identify the techniques and practices employed in documenting software requirements within ASD teams, as well as their perceptions of the documentation process and the challenges, regarding what factors influence it and its consequences. Our key findings indicate that user stories are the most commonly utilized technique by practitioners for documenting requirements. Furthermore, a deficient documentation process results in two primary consequences: rework and a knowledge deficit. To address these challenges, various techniques are implemented across different development phases, including requirement refactoring, documentation refinement meetings, and template reviews. Participants also emphasized the significance of having a requirements expert to enhance the documentation process and expressed uncertainty regarding the adequacy of their existing requirements documentation.*

1. Introduction

Over the past two decades, the adoption of agile methodologies has increased. However, numerous studies have highlighted deficiencies in both functional and non-functional requirements (NFR) documentation within Agile Software Development (ASD) context [Theunissen et al. 2022, Behutiye et al. 2020, Behutiye et al. 2022]. ASD promotes continuous software delivery with a focus on value addition and minimal documentation while accommodating late changes to meet dynamic business demands. However, the rapid pace of change in this methodology creates challenges in requirements documentation, leading to the emergence of technical debt within ASD contexts[Behutiye et al. 2017, Mendes et al. 2019]. Technical debt serves as a metaphor to convey the repercussions of poor software development practices to non-technical stakeholders [Behutiye et al. 2017]. According to Lenarduzzi and Fucci [Lenarduzzi and Fucci 2019], there are 10 types of Technical Debt (TD): Requirements, Architectural, Design, Code, Test, Build, Documentation, Infrastructure, and Versioning.

Technical debt associated with requirements, often referred to as requirements debt, manifests itself when there is underspecification of requirements, meaning that they are outdated, incomplete, or inadequately documented [Behutiye et al. 2017, Mendes et al. 2019]. More broadly, when we refer to requirements debt, it means "the distance between the optimal requirements specification and the actual system implementation, under domain assumptions and constraints" [Ernst 2012]. There are three types of requirements debt [Lenarduzzi and Fucci 2019]: 1) incomplete user needs, when user needs are neglected; 2) requirement smells, when the user needs expressed through feedback channels (i.e., app stores, social media, interviews) are neglected; and 3) mismatch implementation. These categories directly relate to software requirements.

Documentation technical debt encompasses issues related to nonexistent, inadequate, or incomplete project documentation [Mendes et al. 2019]. Agile teams commonly employ documentation techniques like user stories and story cards, which can introduce limitations in software requirements and their documentation, often oversimplifying them [Marek et al. 2021, Jarzebowicz and Weichbroth 2021]. The lack of documentation is considered one of the most significant weaknesses of Requirements Engineering. The inadequacy of user story formats and the challenge of validating their consistency and verifiability reinforce the deficiency in documentation in ASD contexts [Curcio et al. 2018].

The consequences of technical debt in the context of ASD are far-reaching, including [Mendes et al. 2019]: inefficient testing, user dissatisfaction due to inconsistent documentation, difficulties in knowledge transfer to new team members, software maintenance and evolution problems, rework during implementation and testing, limited understanding of the system among team members, ineffective artifact utilization due to disorganized information, duplicated efforts to compensate for documentation gaps, communication problems due to poor-quality or missing documentation, schedule delays, and increased project costs due to documentation issues. Additionally, difficulties in understanding documentation and a lack of synchronization between software and its documentation compound these challenges within ASD teams [Theunissen et al. 2022].

Several authors have investigated the importance of increasing the quantity and quality of documentation in ASD teams, identifying it as a persistent challenge [Theunissen et al. 2022, Curcio et al. 2018, Behutiye et al. 2022]. According to Curcio et al. [Curcio et al. 2018], requirements engineering in the context of ASD is still immature and needs more research, particularly studies that present empirical evaluation. In this context, this work aims to identify practices and techniques utilized in literature and industry for software requirements documentation within ASD teams and assess how the artifacts support this documentation. The study also investigates ASD teams' perceptions, in terms of what factors influence it and its consequences, regarding their current documentation practices and the proposed solutions for addressing identified challenges, especially concerning the impact of technical debt on requirements and documentation.

Our main findings highlight that user stories are the predominant technique for documenting software requirements in ASD teams, and the development team's knowledge of the software solution plays a significant role in requirements documentation. Moreover, the primary consequence of absent or outdated requirements documentation is the need for rework in delivered software and a resultant decline in quality. Our findings further underscore that: i) requirements documentation is typically not carried out by practitioners with specific requirements engineering expertise; ii) maintaining updated and high-quality requirements documentation poses a challenge; iii) there is a lack of a cultural emphasis on continuous requirements documentation within the agile process.

2. Research Design

This study investigates how software requirements are documented by Agile Software Development (ASD) teams, what factors influence it, as well as the consequences of missing or outdated requirements documentation. To reach this goal, we defined the following research questions (RQs): RQ.1. How do ASD teams document software requirements? RQ.2. What factors influence requirements documentation and lack of documentation in ASD? RQ.3. What techniques do practitioners use in requirements documentation to make it easier to understand and communicate with stakeholders? RQ.4. What issues or challenges do ASD teams face in requirements documentation?

We opted for an online survey to elicit data and apply qualitative and qualitative analysis. We followed the guideline of Linaker et al. [Linaker et al. 2015]. The survey was chosen as the primary research method to capture practitioners' perceptions of how ASD teams document software requirements, what factors influence documentation, what techniques teams use, and the challenges they face in their daily activities. Therefore, the survey was performed based on two criteria: (1) obtain practitioners' profiles; (2) collect practitioners' perceptions. The survey presented open-ended and close-ended questions for both criteria.

The survey population consisted of practitioners working with agile software development from several organizations in Brazil and Portugal. A control question was included at the beginning of the survey to filter the participants and ensure that responses were only from the target audience. The participants were recruited through our personal contacts, and we also advertised the questionnaire on our social networks for self-recruitment of participants. All of this paper's authors were involved in designing and validating the survey questions. Two authors, with more than 23 years of experience in software development and requirements elicitation, described the survey questions, and the other authors (two) validated them. The survey consists of 21 questions, nine closed-ended and twelve open-ended questions. All survey questions and answer options are available in Zenodo at https://zenodo.org/records/10157806.

We used the Google Forms platform [1] to create the survey. At the beginning of the research, we presented the consent form, including the conditions and stipulations. We also presented our contact information (email). The survey was anonymous and respondents were not asked to provide any contact information. However, we asked them to provide their e-mail address if they wished. The survey was available from October 16th to November 15th, 2023 (30 days). The average response time of each participant to answer the survey was 33 minutes and 2 seconds. In total, 84 practitioners responded to the survey. After preparing the survey questions, we conducted a pilot. We validated the survey pilot with three researchers from the study and 5 representatives from agile software development teams. Grounded Theory (GT) was used for qualitative analysis to perform open and axial coding [Corbin and Strauss 2014] on the open questions.

[1] https://www.google.com/forms

3. Results and Discussions

We collected the responses of 84 practitioners, which are available in Zenodo at https://zenodo.org/records/10157806. Most participants have considerable experience in software development and agile software development and work in the requirements elicitation, development/programming, or maintenance/evolution phases of the agile software development project lifecycle in which they participate.

3.1. RQ.1. How do ASD teams document software requirements?

To answer RQ.1, we asked practitioners how requirements are documented in their ASD projects. The answers were analyzed with Grounded Theory [Corbin and Strauss 2014]. To enable traceability, we include a direct quote from one respondent along with the answer identified in open-ended questions and we present the discovered codes slanted: "The documentation of requirements by the ASD team is performed using user stories, and they are sent to the development team to implement sprints based on the importance and priority of the requirement." **Main code:** *Requirements documentation is performed using user stories.* – **Category:** *Technique* – **Subcategory:** *User Stories.* The most used technique by ASD teams to document software requirements are `User Stories and Business Rules`.

One of the participants mentioned that "Stakeholder involvement is imperative and the documentation must evolve iteratively, and all documentation must be created responsibly and reflect all the system's needs. In addition, the analysis of what needs to be included in the requirements documentation must reflect the needs of the organization, the project's specific needs, the team's, and the business rules". Another participant mentioned that "the software requirements documentation must be elaborated by the requirements engineer with the participation of the stakeholders. In addition, it is important to use prototypes and user stories to facilitate communication between team members and stakeholders, to resolve all doubts and/or inconsistencies".

It is interesting to point out that Marek et al. [Marek et al. 2021] and Jarzebowicz et al. [Jarzebowicz and Weichbroth 2021] also identify user stories as the techniques commonly used by ASD teams, although the authors also identified a common problem with the use of this technique: limitation and simplification of requirements. According to Curcio et al. [Curcio et al. 2018], the lack of data in the user stories templates and the difficulty in validating their consistency and verifiability are factors that contribute to the fragility of Requirements Engineering in the context of ASD. Heikkila et al. [Heikkilä et al. 2015] mentioned the insufficiency of the user story format, stating that properties such as consistency and verifiability of user stories are challenging to validate and user stories do not convey enough information for software design, and separate system and subsystem requirements are required, among other issues. In the answers to this question in the survey, some terms were mentioned by practitioners, such as: "insufficient", "negligent", "without due rigor", and "quickly". Thus, our findings allow us to infer that despite being the technique most used by ASD teams, this technique has some challenges that have not yet been resolved.

According to Perera et al. [Perera et al. 2023], requirements documentation debt is the insufficient or incomplete requirements specifications found in use cases and user stories. Furthermore, they are low-quality specifications or do not describe the software under development. The authors also mention outdated requirements, which are cases where specifications were developed to an appropriate level of quality in early versions of the software but are subsequently not updated with new requirements or changes to existing requirements. In our findings, user stories are the most used techniques in the literature for requirements documentation in ASD. This allows us to conclude that even though it is a technique that presents several problems, it is the one most used by software development teams.

RQ.1 Summary: Most practitioners are experienced in software development (more than ten years – 58.2%) and ASD (more than four years) and work in the requirements elicitation phase and development/programming. The ASD teams consider the requirements documentation important and should be performed by a RE practitioner, and the technique they use most is the user stories.

3.2. RQ.2. What factors influence requirements documentation and lack of documentation in ASD?

To answer RQ.2, we asked practitioners what factors might influence requirements documentation in ASD. Most participants (84%) stated the team's knowledge of the software solution; for 62%, the team members turnover; for 62%, having requirements specialists on the team; for 57%, the involvement of business representatives during software development; for 55%, the organization's requirements, such as processes and auditing; for 44%, the deadline for each iteration; for 41%, the contractual or other agency requirements; and for 35%, the criticality/risk of the solution.

Our results partially confirm the findings of Mendes et al. [Mendes et al. 2019], who identified as possible causes of documentation technical debt the lack of technical capacity of the practitioner responsible for documenting the requirements, high staff turnover, poor time management, political influences and hierarchies of the organization. Our findings are also similar to those of Behutiye et al.[Behutiye et al. 2017], who identified a lack of understanding of the system being built. In another work, Behutiye et al. [Behutiye et al. 2020] identified that the experience of developers might affect the documentation of quality requirements. Our findings ratify the findings in the literature and indicate the possibility of adding two more causes of documentation technical debt: 1) contractual or other agency requirements and 2) the criticality/risk of the solution. We also ask about the consequences of missing documentation or outdated documentation in ASD. Below is one of the statements made by a participant:"The main consequence of the absence of requirements documentation is communication problems, both between the requirements teams and the development team and between the contracting organization and the stakeholders. In addition, there may be requirement prioritization and rework issues."

Table 1 presents the coding performed to identify in survey responses what are the consequences of missing or outdated documentation. Among the categories of consequences, although rework has only one subcategory, it was mentioned by 47 participants, whereas *Communication* has the most subcategories but totaled 32 mentions. Among the subcategories, the most significant consequence was `Rework over requirements implementation`, followed by `Lack of quality in deliveries` with 28 mentions and `Project planning issues` with 17 mentions.

Table 1. Consequences of the lack or non-update documentation

Category	Subcategory	#Cited
Rework	Rework over requirements implementation	32
Communication	Communication difficulties among team members and stakeholders	11
	Difficulties to execute the products' maintenance or evolution	8
	Difficulties in requirements implementation	6
	Difficulties in understanding the software	3
	Lack of reference for team members	2
Prioritization	Difficulty in prioritizing requirements	5
Planning	Project planning issues	15
	Project schedule issues	11
	Project cost issues	9
Software Quality	Lack of quality in deliveries	17
	Dissatisfaction of end users and stakeholders	5
Risks	Non-compliance risks	7
	Financial risks	5
	Information security risks	3

These results partially ratify the findings by Mendes et al. [Mendes et al. 2019], who identified as consequences of faulty documentation: the rework over implementation and tests; communication problems due to the poor quality or absence of documentation; problems in the maintenance of the software; the difficulty of the team members having complete knowledge of the system that was being developed; lack of perception of the existing risks due to the lack of documentation. Behutiye et al. [Behutiye et al. 2017] also identified system quality degradation, increased cost of maintenance, and complete redesign or rework of the system as a consequence. Our findings also confirm these results found by the authors.

We asked which documentation issues are most relevant in ASD, and practitioners mentioned the lack of documentation for functional and non-functional requirements and system architecture, as seen in other works [Behutiye et al. 2020, Behutiye et al. 2022, Robiolo et al. 2019]. In addition, we also identified that the documentation needs to be updated at each change of the software, also reported by Theunissen et al. [Theunissen et al. 2022] for the smooth running of projects. One of the participants mentioned that "the lack of specification of business requirements that impact legal requirements, such as the Brazilian General Data Protection Law (LGPD)[Canedo et al. 2022, Canedo et al. 2021] or General Data Protection Regulation (GDPR) [Aberkane et al. 2021] may cause legal sanctions, such as changing legislation changing tax calculations or changing input/output layouts". Theunissen et al. [Theunissen et al. 2022] classified the information necessary for documenting the requirements in context and environment, which encompasses anything that affects the system but is not included in the primary goals, such as legal and environmental issues. The authors stated that the absence of this information could lead to documentation that is often lacking, incomplete, out-of-date, or of low quality.

Another participant mentioned that "The most relevant documentation problems in ASD are the difficulty developers find in implementing the functional and non-functional requirements, the dissatisfaction of the stakeholders and the team's lack of responsibility in the project's initial phases in carrying out a good requirements documentation". This statement confirms the previous findings of Behutiye et al. [Behutiye et al. 2017, Behutiye et al. 2020] and Mendes et al. [Mendes et al. 2019]. Perera et al. [Perera et al. 2023] also stated that although requirements technical debt is similar in many ways to technical debt in software code, it also has its own components, such as requirements artifacts, which have a cycle feedback that involves the user to accurately collect their needs. This involves additional costs due to sub-optimal decisions concerning requirements, which may occur during Requirements Engineering and Software Implementation activities. Our results presented in Table 1 corroborate the authors, where the rework category is the most mentioned by survey participants, followed by software quality and planning.

We also investigated what solutions are applied by the ASD teams when these documentation issues happen. The participants mentioned the following measures: requirements refactoring; recurrent meetings with the team to refine the documentation (layout, business rules, technical validation, and business validation) since the beginning of the process; review of the documentation template, workflow, or specification; correction of the requirements documentation; and improvement of the requirements detailing to depict precisely the functionalities and their respective restrictions. Regarding who has the responsibility of documenting the software requirements in the organization in which the ASD teams work, they informed that they are carried out by 1) senior software engineers together with the lead UX designer; 2) product owner; 3) scrum master; 4) all team members; 5) requirements analyst; 6) business analyst; 7) developers; 8) project managers; and 9) architects. According to the perception of most survey participants, this attribution by the ASD team of the practitioner responsible for documenting the software requirements in the organizations they work with is incorrect. Some participants mentioned: "This assignment is not correct. The organization should hire a requirements specialist to carry out the entire Requirements Engineering phase of the software to be developed by the ASD team."; and "No. The elicitation, documentation, and validation of software requirements should be carried out by a requirements practitioner who knows the creative techniques for eliciting requirements."

RQ.2 Summary 2: The main consequence of the lack of requirements documentation is rework and lack of quality in product deliveries. The factors that influence requirements documentation are the team's lack of knowledge of the software solution, staff turnover, and lack of requirements experts on the team.

3.3. RQ.3. What techniques do practitioners use in requirements documentation to make it easier to understand and communicate with stakeholders?

It is important to highlight that to answer this RQ, it was decided to research the techniques used to document requirements in three contexts: 1) the techniques used in organizations by participants; 2) the techniques used, in the participants' perception, to facilitate understanding and communication with customers; and 3) the techniques used, in the participants' perception, to facilitate understanding and cooperation between analysts and developers. According to Bomström et al. [Bomström et al. 2023], practitioners with different perspectives require information in different ways to complete their daily tasks and it is essential to identify the techniques used to understand this information.

Regarding the techniques used by requirements analysts/engineers to document software requirements in order to understand them or facilitate understanding and communication with interested parties, the most used techniques used by ASD teams are user stories (69%), business rules (60%), meetings (60%), prototyping (51%), functional description (43%), epics (33%), requirements list (27%), organization's own templates and scenarios (21%). Regarding which techniques analysts use to document the requirements for cooperation purposes between analysts and development teams to facilitate the maintenance/evolution of the product, the most used techniques are user stories (70%), meetings (49%), prototyping (46%), rule of business (46%), functional description (41%), list of requirements (31%), use cases (31%), epics (26%), organization-specific templates (20%), UML models (14%), and change decisions recording made by stakeholders (13%).

Concerning requirements specification techniques practitioners use to document requirements in ASD teams, user stories (69%) are the most commonly used technique, followed by meetings, business rules, prototyping, functional descriptions, use cases, epics, requirements lists, and the organization's own templates. These results support the findings by [Jarzebowicz and Sitko 2019], who identified user stories as the most commonly used technique by practitioners for requirements elicitation with stakeholders and for carrying out software maintenance or evolution. The authors also identified the use of epics, use cases, and prototyping techniques. As well as Jarzebowicz et al. [Jarzebowicz and Sitko 2019], we have identified a small variation in the use of these techniques by ASD teams.

We identified little variation in the use of requirements specification techniques by ASD teams, considering the two contexts analyzed in this research, customers and development teams. However, we identified a greater use of user stories by software development teams and a lesser use of this technique by customers. These findings allow us to infer that the technique most used by ASD teams is user stories. This finding corroborates the findings of Mendes et al. [Mendes et al. 2019]. However, Heikkila et al. [Heikkilä et al. 2015] stated that user stories might not be sufficient when used as the sole source of requirements documentation, leading to difficult prioritization of requirements. This also allows us to infer that part of the problems related to requirements documentation can be derived from problems already identified in previous studies due to the use of user stories. Considering that the agile process follows the software development life cycle that includes requirements specification, analysis, design, coding, testing, and delivery of partially implemented software [d Darothi Sarkar and Gupta 2012], [Sajjade 2020], we chose to rename these phases to facilitate understanding, and inserted the Modeling, Maintenance/Evolution and Management phases, as per the Swebok version 3 [Bourque 2023] and considering that other authors also identify these other phases in the software development cycle [Saravanan et al. 2020], [Gurung et al. 2020].

A significant number of practitioners (71%) reported that the techniques are used to document software requirements in the Requirements Specification phase of the software development cycle; 57% of them reported that the documentation is carried out in the Analysis and Design phase; 54% respondents said they are in the Development/Programming phase; 35% practitioners stated that it is in the Modeling phase; 31% that documentation is carried out in the Maintenance/Evolution phase; 20% practitioners claimed to be in the Testing phase; and 20% of them are in the Project Management phase. This result is not a surprise to us, since some of the techniques mentioned by the participants (meetings, scenarios, and personas) were also mentioned by Chang et al. and Dev et al. [Chang et al. 2008, Dev et al. 2023] as techniques that are used in other phases of agile software development process. This finding allows us to infer that part of the techniques used by ADS teams can and are used, even in smaller quantities, at different stages of the development process.

Most practitioners (86%) stated that the requirements artifacts derived from using the techniques to document software requirements are used later in the Development/Programming phase of the software development lifecycle. Some participants (62%) stated that artifacts are used in the Testing phase, 58% stated that they are used in the Maintenance/Evolution phase, 35% stated that they are used in the Management phase, and 35% stated that it is in the modeling, respectively. 29% of the practitioners stated that they are used in the Analysis and design phase. Finally, 23% of them stated they are used in the Elicitation phase. Our findings differ from those of Alsaqqa et al. [Alsaqqa et al. 2020]. According to the authors, documents are rarely used after the requirements identification and documentation phases, and project progress is measured through software testing rather than documentation. Our findings allow us to infer that, in practice, the use of documentation by ASD teams is more constant and frequent, especially in the requirements elicitation and development/programming phase. Heimicke et al. [Heimicke et al. 2020] presented several proposals for hybrid agile models, recognizing the need to adapt the agile manifesto [Fowler et al. 2001] in the software industry. Thus, this recognition of the use of documentation in all stages of the software development process confirms the need to make some adaptations to the principles of the manifest.

Some practitioners mentioned that the artifacts generated to document the requirements are sufficient to ensure an adequate software evolution. Below are some statements: "The generated artifacts clearly describe what should be done by the development team and help the testing team on how they should proceed."; and "By registering the business needs and the needs identified in the execution of the sprints, applying the proper prioritization, the need for two teams (one for development and one for support) is avoided, the team specializes in the product, avoiding rework and promoting a constant delivery of value to the business." Other practitioners stated that the artifacts generated in the documentation of software requirements are not sufficient to ensure proper software maintenance and evolution: "It is not enough, other documents are necessary to guarantee the maintenance of the product, for example, diagrams of behavior and structure of the system, modeled from the requirements."; and "It is not enough, the evolution of the product also depends on the management of the knowledge base of the artifacts produced by the requirements documentation. Thus, the access, organization, and understanding of the artifacts produced need to be simple and of good quality."

Regarding practices and techniques used to document requirements being consistent with Agile guidelines, practitioners mentioned that: "Are perfectly adherent to Agile. The model is for identifying and building the product backlog that will be maintained and evolved throughout the project, both by the needs identified by the business and by the needs identified by the development team. The requirements prioritization determines what goes into each sprint according to the business need and the team's ability to deliver, constantly adding value. The other characteristics of agile are preserved and can be adjusted according to the maturity and capacity of each organization."; and "It is adherent because it favors face-to-face communication and reduces waste on volatile or non-reusable artifacts. "

In the perception of a few practitioners, the practices and techniques currently adopted by ASD teams are not adherent to Agile: " I understand not. Agile privileges software over comprehensive documentation. Furthermore, it is not clear what an ideal documentation should be. In financial systems with risk of damage to the organization, internal audits and controlling bodies that require documentation, and high turnover of teams, documentation is essential and necessary, contradicting the Agile principles."; " The practices and techniques we adopt are not Agile compliant. We use cases to document the requirements because we believe that for the proper maintenance of the systems, it is necessary to have good documentation." Summarizing some answers about the adherence of documentation practices to agile, practitioners mentioned that "when complete"; "if updated"; "if they follow the evolution of the product"; "yes, but the implicit knowledge of the participants is essential"; "lack of sufficient artifacts". This allows us to infer that several factors may interfere with whether or not the artifacts generated to document the software requirements are sufficient to perform maintenance. It is noteworthy that this finding is different from other studies [Behutiye et al. 2017, Mendes et al. 2019] which identified that the documentation performed by ASD teams could be considered a technical debt, as they have several problems that result in problems such as rework, low productivity, and communication failures.

RQ.3 Summary: The techniques most used by ASD teams to document software requirements are user stories, business rules, and meetings. Furthermore, practitioners stated that these techniques are used mainly in the requirements elicitation and development phases. Small differences in usage were identified between the techniques used with customers and the techniques used by the development team.

3.4. RQ.4: What issues or challenges do ASD teams face in requirements documentation?

To answer RQ.4, we asked practitioners what challenges related to specific ASD documentation and practices they face daily in their projects. In total, 71 participants reported the challenges their teams faced in documenting software requirements, which were coded into categories. Table 2 presents all categories and subcategories identified in the process of coding the challenges faced by ASD teams in requirements documentation. We have identified 4 categories: 1) Training; 2) Knowledge; 3) ASD team culture; and 4) Documentation. The category most mentioned by participants was Training – participants mentioned that the lack of trained professionals makes it difficult to correctly understand systems requirements, leading to a very high occurrence of turnover in ASD teams. They believe that this phenomenon occurs because professionals working in Agile Software Development (ASD) need to stay consistently updated, undergoing improvement courses to enhance their job performance.

Some participants mentioned that the lack of training means that others do not know the techniques and tools available in the literature and on the market to carry out requirements documentation. The second most mentioned category was Knowledge –

participants believe that the lack of requirements specialists in ASD teams generates several problems, such as difficulty in keeping functional requirements documentation updated and accessible to all team members and in selecting existing techniques and tools in the literature to document requirements. Some of these challenges presented in Table 2 were also identified by Theunissen et al. [Theunissen et al. 2022], Behutiye et al. [Behutiye et al. 2017], and Mendes et al. [Mendes et al. 2019]. The practitioners' perceptions presented in Table 2 allow us to infer that the requirements documentation in the ASD may suffer from a problem inherent to the agile process itself due to the culture/idea that the product coding stage should start as early as possible fast as possible. Theunissen et al. [Theunissen et al. 2022] identified that documentation is hard to understand, considered a waste when it does not appear to contribute directly to the end product, and is easily out-of-sync with implementation. These concepts inherent to agile models can hinder or compromise the identification, specification, documentation, validation, updating, and tracking of software requirements.

Table 2. Challenges faced by ASD teams in requirements documentation

Category	Subcategory	#Cited
Training	Lack of trained professionals	56
Knowledge	Lack of a qualified professional	54
	Lack of requirements specialist to carry out the specification activity	44
	Lack of requirements professionals on teams	38
	Lack of a practitioner on the team with knowledge of existing techniques and practices for documenting requirements	37
	Difficulty in registering the relevant facts of the sprint and the lessons learned	33
ASD team culture	Requirements documentation is not necessary	51
	Turnover on ASD teams	47
	Lack of commitment from team members to document requirements decisions	11
Documentation	Lack of documentation	39
	Keeping the documentation up to date	38
	Lack of documentation of business rules	33
	Misconception that the agile methodology does not require documentation	32
	Lack of understanding of the importance of documentation	27
	Poorly specified and incomplete requirements	19

Our findings collaborate with the findings of Perera et al. [Perera et al. 2023] who stated that the causes of requirements technical debt are: a) neglecting user needs; b) missing to capture user feedback from one or more user feedback channels and ambiguities introduced during formalization of requirements smells; c) implementing a suboptimal solution to a requirements problem and insufficient and incomplete requirements missed due to the lack of requirements traceability or documentation inefficiencies occurred intentionally or unintentionally; d) inconsistent management of requirements from different stakeholders; e) requirements that are only partly implemented; and e) inadequate or poorly conducted requirements elicitation and analysis.

RQ.4 Summary: In the practitioners' perception, the challenges related to documentation and practices in ASD are the lack of trained practitioners in the requirements area to carry out the RE phase, lack of knowledge, and the culture of the ASD teams and organizations that documentation is not an important artifact.

4. Threats to Validity

External validity: first, given the delicacy and complexity of the subject, we cannot guarantee that participants expressed their thoughts without considering them professionally or socially desirable. To mitigate this threat, we informed participants that the information would not be made available to the organizations they work for. They were only used within the scope of this research. Secondly, the sample of participants can be considered small and only represents the perception of Brazilian and Portugal agile practitioners. To mitigate this threat, we collected the perceptions of different practitioners from different organizations and states in Brazil. Capturing the perceptions of practitioners working on ASD teams in other countries may require more effort and the use of multiple techniques. Thus, we cannot generalize the results obtained. Furthermore, participants' answers are not necessarily coherent and consistent and may contradict their words and activities in the labor market. Despite this, practitioners' perception demonstrates the complexity of Requirements Engineering activities, which emphasizes the importance of research concerning the lack of recognition of the importance of requirements documentation in ASD.

Construct validity: despite our confidence in the scientific rigor employed in conducting the study, we acknowledge the inevitability of participants' subjective interpretation of the questions. To mitigate this threat, we validated the survey with three researchers from the study and five representatives from agile software development teams. Conclusion validity: although we are confident in the scientific rigor of conducting the study, it is inevitable the subjectivity in the researchers' interpretation of the data [Seaman 1999]. To mitigate this threat the analysis of the survey's open questions was first carried out by two researchers, and a third researcher carried out the validation. In addition, any inconsistencies were discussed with the fourth researcher. These measures also allowed to avoid bias and validate the closed questions, ensuring that the list of options is sufficiently complete. Despite this, open-ended questions allow respondents to report factors beyond the list of options in closed-ended questions. Internal validity: collecting survey data allowed us to minimize threats to internal validity because the participants were selected randomly through email contacts, and the researcher did not interact with the participants. We also advertised the questionnaire on our social networks for self-recruitment, so there was no influence from the researcher on the results. Moreover, the survey has a description and questions designed to identify practitioners who meet the desired criteria, i.e. practitioners working with agile software development.

5. Conclusions and Future Work

The techniques most used by ASD teams are user stories and business rules. User stories have several problems when documenting requirements, although they are the most used by ASD teams. In the perception of the ASD teams, the main factors that influence the documentation of the requirements in the ASD are the knowledge of the software solution by the team members, team member turnover, having a requirements specialist in the team, the involvement of the business representatives during the development of the software, and the business and audit processes of their organizations.

Most practitioners mentioned that the lack or non-update of requirements documentation in ASD generates rework in the implementation of software requirements and various difficulties related to communication, mainly between agile teams and stakeholders. Furthermore, the lack of documentation significantly impacts project planning and software quality. We identified some actions that ASD teams use to solve problems related to failures in requirements documentation, such as refactoring the requirement, holding meetings with the ASD team to refine documentation, reviewing the template/flowchart used to carry out requirement documentation, and updating/correcting requirements documentation. As future work, we intend to replicate this research with practitioners from other countries to understand the challenges of the lack of documentation and what are the agile principles that led to the incorporation of the culture that agility values only the quick delivery of the product without taking into account the quality of the artifacts generated during the software development lifecycle, mainly from the software requirements documentation.

References

Aberkane, A., Poels, G., and vanden Broucke, S. (2021). Exploring automated gdpr-compliance in requirements engineering: A systematic mapping study. *IEEE Access*, 9:66542–66559.

Alsaqqa, S., Sawalha, S., and Abdel-Nabi, H. (2020). Agile software development: Methodologies and trends. *Int. J. Interact. Mob. Technol.*, 14(11):246–270.

Behutiye, W., Rodríguez, P., and Oivo, M. (2022). Quality requirement documentation guidelines for agile software development. *IEEE Access*, 10:70154–70173.

Behutiye, W., Seppänen, P., Rodríguez, P., and Oivo, M. (2020). Documentation of quality requirements in agile software development. In Li, J., Jaccheri, L., Dingsøyr, T., and Chitchyan, R., editors, *EASE '20: Evaluation and Assessment in Software Engineering, Trondheim, Norway, April 15-17, 2020*, pages 250–259. ACM.

Behutiye, W. N., Rodríguez, P., Oivo, M., and Tosun, A. (2017). Analyzing the concept of technical debt in the context of agile software development: A systematic literature review. *Inf. Softw. Technol.*, 82:139–158.

Bomström, H., Kelanti, M., Annanperä, E., Liukkunen, K., Kilamo, T., Sievi-Korte, O., and Systä, K. (2023). Information needs and presentation in agile software development. *Inf. Softw. Technol.*, 162:107265.

Bourque, P. (2023). Software Engineering Body of Knowledge (SWEBOK). [Online; accessed 18. Nov. 2023].

Canedo, E. D., Calazans, A. T. S., Bandeira, I. N., Costa, P. H. T., and Masson, E. T. S. (2022). Guidelines adopted by agile teams in privacy requirements elicitation after the brazilian general data protection law (LGPD) implementation. *Requir. Eng.*, 27(4):545–567.

Canedo, E. D., Calazans, A. T. S., Cerqueira, A. J., Costa, P. H. T., and Masson, E. T. S. (2021). Agile teams' perception in privacy requirements elicitation: Lgpd's compliance in brazil. In *29th IEEE International Requirements Engineering Conference, RE 2021, Notre Dame, IN, USA, September 20-24, 2021*, pages 58–69. IEEE.

Chang, Y., Lim, Y., and Stolterman, E. (2008). Personas: from theory to practices. In Gulz, A., Magnusson, C., Malmborg, L., Eftring, H., Jönsson, B., and Tollmar, K., editors, *Proceedings of the 5th Nordic Conference on Human-Computer Interaction 2008, Lund, Sweden, October 20-22, 2008*, volume 358 of *ACM International Conference Proceeding Series*, pages 439–442. ACM.

Corbin, J. and Strauss, A. (2014). *Basics of qualitative research: Techniques and procedures for developing grounded theory*. Sage publications.

Curcio, K., Navarro, T., Malucelli, A., and Reinehr, S. S. (2018). Requirements engineering: A systematic mapping study in agile software development. *J. Syst. Softw.*, 139:32–50.

d Darothi Sarkar, S. S. and Gupta, D. (2012). Agile processes and methodologies: A conceptual study. *International Journal on Computer Science and Engineering (IJCSE)*, 4 (05).

Dev, J., Rashidi, B., and Garg, V. (2023). Models of applied privacy (MAP): A persona based approach to threat modeling. In Schmidt, A., Väänänen, K., Goyal, T., Kristensson, P. O., Peters, A., Mueller, S., Williamson, J. R., and Wilson, M. L., editors, *Proceedings of the 2023 CHI Conference on Human Factors in Computing Systems, CHI 2023, Hamburg, Germany, April 23-28, 2023*, pages 189:1–189:15. ACM.

Ernst, N. A. (2012). On the role of requirements in understanding and managing technical debt. In Kruchten, P., Nord, R. L., Ozkaya, I., and Visser, J., editors, *Proceedings of the Third International Workshop on Managing Technical Debt, MTD 2012, Zurich, Switzerland, June 5, 2012*, pages 61–64. IEEE/ACM.

Fowler, M., Highsmith, J., et al. (2001). The agile manifesto. *Software development*, 9(8):28–35.

Gurung, G., Shah, R., and Jaiswal, D. P. (2020). Software development life cycle models-a comparative study. In *International Journal of Scientific Research in Computer Science, Engineering and Information Technology*.

Heikkilä, V. T., Damian, D. E., Lassenius, C., and Paasivaara, M. (2015). A mapping study on requirements engineering in agile software development. In *41st Euromicro Conference on Software Engineering and Advanced Applications, EUROMICRO-SEAA 2015, Madeira, Portugal, August 26-28, 2015*, pages 199–207. IEEE Computer Society.

Heimicke, J., Chen, R., and Albers, A. (2020). Agile meets plan-driven – hybrid approaches in product development: A systematic literature review. *Proceedings of the Design Society: DESIGN Conference*, pages 577–586.

Jarzebowicz, A. and Sitko, N. (2019). Communication and documentation practices in agile requirements engineering: A survey in polish software industry. In Wrycza, S. and Maslankowski, J., editors, *Information Systems: Research, Development, Applications, Education - 12th SIGSAND/PLAIS EuroSymposium 2019, Gdansk, Poland, September 19, 2019, Proceedings*, volume 359 of *Lecture Notes in Business Information Processing*, pages 147–158. Springer.

Jarzebowicz, A. and Weichbroth, P. (2021). A systematic literature review on implementing non-functional requirements in agile software development: Issues and facilitating practices. In Przybylek, A., Miler, J., Poth, A., and Riel, A., editors, *Lean and Agile Software Development - 5th International Conference, LASD 2021, Virtual Event, January 23, 2021, Proceedings*, volume 408 of *Lecture Notes in Business Information Processing*, pages 91–110. Springer.

Lenarduzzi, V. and Fucci, D. (2019). Towards a holistic definition of requirements debt. In *2019 ACM/IEEE International Symposium on Empirical Software Engineering and Measurement, ESEM 2019, Porto de Galinhas, Recife, Brazil, September 19-20, 2019*, pages 1–5. IEEE.

Linaker, J., Sulaman, S. M., Höst, M., and de Mello, R. M. (2015). Guidelines for conducting surveys in software engineering v. 1.1. *Lund University*, 50.

Marek, K., Winska, E., and Dabrowski, W. (2021). The state of agile software development teams during the covid-19 pandemic. In *Lean and Agile Software Development - 5th International Conference, LASD 2021, Virtual Event, January 23, 2021, Proceedings*, volume 408 of *Lecture Notes in Business Information Processing*, pages 24–39, https://doi.org/10.1007/978-3-030-67084-9_2. Springer.

Mendes, L., Cerdeiral, C., and Santos, G. (2019). Documentation technical debt: A qualitative study in a software development organization. In do Carmo Machado, I., Souza, R., Maciel, R. S. P., and Sant'Anna, C., editors, *Proceedings of the XXXIII Brazilian Symposium on Software Engineering, SBES 2019, Salvador, Brazil, September 23-27, 2019*, pages 447–451. ACM.

Perera, J., Tempero, E. D., Tu, Y., and Blincoe, K. (2023). Quantifying requirements technical debt: A systematic mapping study and a conceptual model. In Schneider, K., Dalpiaz, F., and Horkoff, J., editors, *31st IEEE International Requirements Engineering Conference, RE 2023, Hannover, Germany, September 4-8, 2023*, pages 123–133. IEEE.

Robiolo, G., Scott, E., Matalonga, S., and Felderer, M. (2019). Technical debt and waste in non-functional requirements documentation: An exploratory study. In Franch, X., Männistö, T., and Martínez-Fernández, S., editors, *Product-Focused Software Process Improvement - 20th International Conference, PROFES 2019, Barcelona, Spain, November 27-29, 2019, Proceedings*, volume 11915 of *Lecture Notes in Computer Science*, pages 220–235. Springer.

Sajjade, Z.-S. Z. (2020). Agile process model for software development. *Journal of Advancement in Software Engineering and Testing*, 3 (03).

Saravanan, T., Jha, S., Sabharwal, G., and Narayan, S. (2020). Comparative analysis of software life cycle models. In *2020 2nd International Conference on Advances in Computing, Communication Control and Networking (ICACCCN)*, volume 2, pages 906–909.

Seaman, C. B. (1999). Qualitative methods in empirical studies of software engineering. *IEEE Trans. Software Eng.*, 25(4):557–572.

Theunissen, T., van Heesch, U., and Avgeriou, P. (2022). A mapping study on documentation in continuous software development. *Inf. Softw. Technol.*, 142:106733.

Estudo empírico: detecção de *Code Smells* com aprendizado de máquinas

Raimundo Alan Freire Moreira[1], Lucas José Lemos Braz[1], Fischer Jônatas Ferreira[2], Márcio André Baima Amora[1]

[1] Universidade Federal do Ceará (UFC) – Sobral – CE – Brasil

[2]Universidade Federal de Itajubá – Itabira – MG – Brasil

alan.freire@alu.ufc.br, lucas.jlb19@alu.ufc.br

fischer.ferreira@sobral.ufc.br, marcio@sobral.ufc.br

Abstract. *Detecting code smells during the software development process is important for enhancing software quality, and refactoring is essential for eliminating these indicators of problems. This study evaluates an empirical approach based on training five machine learning algorithms to detect code smells in software systems, using software metrics as parameters. The results demonstrate that the machine learning approach performed exceptionally well in detecting code smells, achieving an accuracy ranging from 93.7% to 99.2%.*

Resumo. *A detecção de code smells durante o processo de desenvolvimento de software é importante para melhorar a qualidade do software e a refatoração é fundamental para eliminar esses indícios de problema. Este estudo avalia uma abordagem empírica que se baseia no treinamento de cinco algoritmos de aprendizado de máquina para detectar code smells em sistemas de software, utilizando métricas de software como parâmetros. Os resultados mostram que a abordagem de aprendizado de máquina tive um excelente desempenho para a detecção de code smells, alcançando uma acurácia entre 93,7% a 99,2%.*

1. Introdução

Code smell é uma característica estrutural do software que indica um aspecto no código ou no design que pode causar problemas na manutenção do software. *Code smell* não é um erro no sistema, pois não impede o funcionamento do programa, mas pode aumentar o risco de falha do software ou desacelerar o desempenho. Notavelmente, a predição precoce do *code smell* durante a fase de desenvolvimento é muito importante, especialmente em projetos de código-fonte em grande escala [Abdou and Ramadan, 2022]. O processo de refatoração é fundamental para eliminar os *code smells* e melhorar a manutenção e a qualidade do software. Fowler [2018] apresenta uma definição de 22 tipos de *code smells* no código-fonte e oferecem algumas operações de refatoração para corrigi-los.

O impacto dos *code smells* no software foram examinados por vários estudos e revelaram seu efeito indesejável na qualidade do software [Yamashita and Moonen, 2012, 2013; Yamashita and Counsell, 2013; Sahin et al., 2014]. Eles também investigaram os resultados da remoção dos *code smells* na redução da probabilidade de falhas e erros no sistema de software. Analisaram os desafios decorrentes dos *code smells*, os quais têm efeitos adversos no processo de desenvolvimento de software, e recomendaram a aplicação de refatoração no software para eliminá-los.

Dewangan et al. [2021] falam que na detecção de *code smells*, as métricas desempenham um papel fundamental ao medir tanto as qualidades funcionais quanto não funcionais do software, além de contribuir para a compreensão dos recursos do código-fonte. As informações estáticas do software são obtidas por meio de métricas como o número de métodos, classes e parâmetros, além da avaliação do acoplamento e coesão entre os objetos do sistema.

Trabalhos anteriores investigam a detecção de *Code Smell* por meio de detecção manual [Travassos et al., 1999; Ciupke, 1999], Moha et al. [2009] e Tsantalis and Chatzigeorgiou [2009] introduziram abordagens baseados em métricas, Yamashita and Moonen [2013] e Tarwani and Chug [2016] avaliam problemas de manutenabilidade causado por *Code Smell* e Fontana et al. [2016] e Dewangan et al. [2021] abordaram a detecção por aprendizado de máquina. Porém, o tema ainda está em aberto quando a redução de custo para a atividade de detecção de *Code smell* poder ser incorporado no processo de desenvolvimento de software. Assim, com o uso de detecção automatizada por meio de ML pode ser uma alternativa viável para que a detecção de *Smell* ocorra em todas as etapas do desenvolvimento.

Neste artigo é buscado responder sobre a eficácia dos algoritmos de aprendizado de máquina na detecção de *code smells* e se a técnica de validação cruzada melhora os resultados e ameniza as ameaças a validade dos resultados dos algoritmos de aprendizado de máquina neste caso de uso. Para isso foi adotado o conjunto de dados de *code smells* contendo quatro tipos: *God Class*, *Data Class*, *Feature Envy* e *Long Method*. Cinco algoritmos de aprendizado de máquina (*Multilayer Perceptron* - MLP, Árvore de Decisão, Floresta Aleatória, Gradiente Boost e Máquina de Vetores de Suporte - SVM) são aplicados nos conjuntos de dados e alcançaram o melhor desempenho(acurácia) no algoritmo de Floresta Aleatória (99,2%).

A contribuição buscada neste trabalho é avaliar os cinco métodos de aprendizado de máquina para a detecção de *code smells*. Em seguida, são apresentadas as métricas de desempenho (acurácia, precisão, sensibilidade e F1 score) obtidas pelo treinamento dos métodos de aprendizado de máquina para comparação dos mesmos, fazendo também a comparação dos resultados usando a técnica de validação cruzada e sem a técnica de validação cruzada.

Este trabalho está organizada da seguinte forma: Na Seção 2 faz um descritivo sobre *Code Smells*, Métricas de Software e Aprendizado de Máquinas com uma breve descrição de cada modelo usado. Também é feito um descritivo sobre Normalização de Dados e Validação Cruzada. Já a metodologia usada para o desenvolvimento deste trabalho está localizada na Seção 3. Os resultados e analise dos dados na Seção 4, a Seção 5 cita alguns trabalhos relacionados, na Seção 6 é discutido as ameaças a pesquisa e a conclusão é discutida na Seção 7.

2. Fundamentação teórica

2.1. *Code Smells e Métricas de Software*

A presença de *code smells* resulta em desafios significativos, incluindo complicações na manutenção, aumento da complexidade e redução da legibilidade do código. A manutenção de software em grande escala é particularmente problemática devido ao tamanho e à complexidade envolvidos, sendo mais de 80% do custo total do software dedicado à manutenção. Cerca de 60% do tempo durante a manutenção é gasto na compreensão do código. Portanto, a existência dos *code smells* no código agrava essas dificuldades, tornando a manutenção do software ainda mais complexa [Abdou and Ramadan, 2022].

Para este artigo, foi feito as comparações de resultados dos algoritmos de aprendizado de máquina com os seguintes *code smells* conjunto de dados de Abdou and Ramadan [2022]: ***God Class*** descreve uma classe extensa que possui muitas linhas de código, funções ou campos [Riel, 1996; Brown et al., 1998; Fontana et al., 2016; Dewangan et al., 2021]; ***Data Class*** aponta para a classe usada para armazenar os dados utilizados por outras classes. *Data Class* abrange apenas campos e métodos de acesso (*getters/setters*) [Riel, 1996; Fontana et al., 2016; Dewangan et al., 2021]; ***Feature Envy*** é um *code smell* ao nível de método que acessa dados ou utiliza operações pertencentes a classes diferentes da sua própria classe, ou seja, ele utiliza dados estrangeiros adicionais em comparação com os dados locais [Fontana et al., 2016; Dewangan et al., 2021]; ***Long Method*** é um *code smell* ao nível de método que se refere a um método de grande tamanho, devido ao número de linhas de código e funcionalidades presentes no método [McConnell, 2004; Fontana et al., 2016; Dewangan et al., 2021].

Para avaliar a qualidade do código, as métricas de software desempenham um papel crucial na engenharia de software. As métricas cobrem aspectos como coesão, acoplamento, complexidade e tamanho nos níveis de método, classe, projeto e pacote. As métricas ao nível de método incluem complexidade ciclomática, tamanho do método e contagem de parâmetros. No nível de classe abrangem coesão, acoplamento, tamanho da classe e contagem de métodos. Em nivel de projeto incluem complexidade, tamanho e contagem de classes, enquanto as métricas ao nível de pacote envolvem coesão, acoplamento, complexidade e tamanho [Ashraf Abdou, 2022].

2.2. Aprendizado de máquina

No Aprendizado de Máquina, segundo Ray [2019], um programa de computador é designado para realizar algumas tarefas e diz-se que a máquina aprendeu com sua experiência se seu desempenho mensurável nessas tarefas melhora à medida que adquire cada vez mais experiência na execução delas. Portanto, a máquina toma decisões e faz previsões/-baseadas em dados.

Neste trabalho foi escolhido cinco algoritmos de aprendizado de máquinas para fazermos a comparação no desempenho de cada um quanto a detecção de *code smells*, são eles: ***Multilayer Perceptron*** ou **MLP** [Ruck et al., 1990], **Árvore de Decisão** [Quinlan, 1990], **Floresta Aleatória** [Breiman, 2001], **Gradiente Boost** [Friedman, 2001] e ***Support Vector Machines*** ou **SVM** [Noble, 2006].

2.3. Normalização e validação dos dados

A normalização é uma técnica crucial para harmonizar escalas de conjuntos de dados numéricos [Al Shalabi et al., 2006]. Essa etapa é essencial para garantir o equilíbrio em modelos, especialmente aqueles baseados em diferentes métricas ou otimizações baseadas em gradiente.

Ao aplicar esta técnica, um vetor de atributos x em x' usando um escalonamento (E') e fatores de tradução (T): $x' = Ex + T$. Métodos como escalonamento para um intervalo, dimensionamento logaritmo, Z-score e Min-Max atendem a diversas distribuições de dados e requisitos de modelo [Han et al., 2022]. Neste trabalho, utilizamos a normalização Min-Max, que dimensiona os valores para $[0, 1]$, dada por: $x' = \frac{(x - min(x))}{(max(x) - min(x))}$ [Han et al., 2022].

Por outro lado, a validação é crucial para evitar *overfitting*, garantindo que o modelo generaliza bem para dados inéditos [Arlot and Celisse, 2010]. Matematicamente, dado o conjunto de dados D com N amostras (X, y), onde X representa a matriz de atributos de entrada e y o vetor alvo, treinamos o modelo M em um subconjunto D_{train} e avaliar seu desempenho em um subconjunto de validação D_{val}, onde $D = D_{train} \cup D_{val}$.

3. Metodologia

Questões problemas abordados no artigo:

1. Qual a eficácia das técnicas de *machine learning* MLP, Árvore de Decisão, Floresta Aleatória, Gradiente Boost e SVM para detecção de *code smell*?
2. Qual o impacto da validação cruzada no conjunto de dados utilizado?

Neste estudo foi definido como objetivo principal a avaliação das técnicas de aprendizado de máquina para a detecção de *code smells* e como objetivo específico avaliar o impacto da validação cruzada na precisão dos algoritmos de aprendizado de máquina.

As etapas seguidas por esse trabalho são mostradas na Figura 1. Inicialmente o conjunto de dados é coletado, em seguida é feito a etapa de pré-processamento (Normalização) é aplicada ao conjunto de dados para cobrir as diferentes faixas dos conjuntos de dados e obter os melhores parâmetros dos algoritmos. Em seguida, os algoritmos de aprendizado de máquina no conjunto de dados são treinados e seu desempenho é calculado. A técnica de validação cruzada em 10 partes é aplicada para avaliar e comparar o desempenho de cada experimento durante o processo de treinamento.

3.1. Conjunto de dados

Os conjuntos de dados usados neste estudo são fornecidos por Abdou and Ramadan [2022] que se basearam no trabalho de Fontana et al. [2016], definidos como dados de referência. Este conjunto de dados pertence a diferentes domínios, sendo compostos por 76 sistemas de diferentes tamanhos escritos em Java. Em Fontana et al. [2016] é descrito o conjunto de métricas orientadas a objetos aplicados em 76 sistemas do Qualitas Corpus (QC) de Tempero et al. [2010], abrangendo os níveis de método, classe, pacote e projeto. Algumas dessas métricas foram definidas conforme o aspecto da qualidade de software, como complexidade, tamanho e acoplamento. Outras métricas dependem da contagem da composição em pacotes ou classes. Os *code smells* foram definidos no nível de método

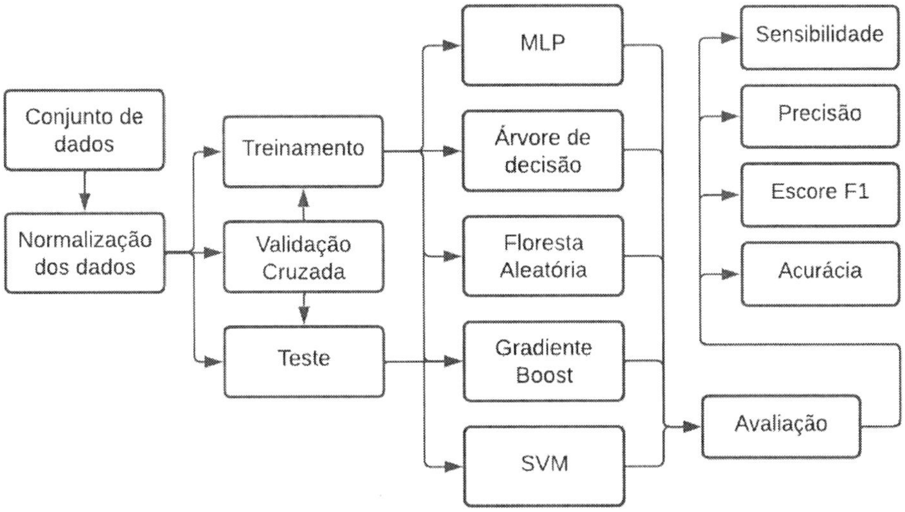

Figura 1. Fluxo de trabalho proposto.

ou classe. No nível de método, foi escolhido para detectar *Feature Envy* e *Long Method*, enquanto no nível de classe, detectamos *Data Class* e *God Class*. Os autores do conjunto de dados escolheram estes quatro *code smells* devido sua alta incidência e por ter grande impacto negativo na qualidade dos softwares.

A Tabela 1(a) mostra o tamanho geral dos sistemas selecionados. Abdou and Ramadan [2022] diz que o grande número de sistemas heterogêneos usados neste estudo é fundamental para garantir que os resultados do processo de aprendizado de máquina não dependam de um conjunto de dados específico e para permitir a generalização dos resultados obtidos.

As ferramentas empregadas para identificar os *code smell* são apresentadas na Tabela 1(b). Essas ferramentas foram selecionadas baseadas nas seguintes regras: serem gratuitas, de fácil configuração e generalização e terem regras de detecção diferentes das demais.

(a) **Características dos sistemas. Fonte: [Fontana et al., 2016]**

Característica	Valores
Quantidade de Sistemas	74
Quantidade de Pacotes	3.420
Quantidade de Classes	51.826
Quantidade de Métodos	404.316
Linhas de Código	6.785.568

(b) **Detectores de *code smells*. Fonte: [Abdou and Ramadan, 2022]**

Code Smell	Ferramenta: regras de detecção
Long method	iPlasma, PMD
Data class	iPlasma, Fluid Tool, Anti-Pattern Scanner
God class	iPlasma, PMD
Feature Envy	iPlasma, Fluid Tool

Tabela 1. Características e ferramentas

O conjunto de dados está dividido como mostrado na Tabela 2, onde os mesmos são classificados como falsos positivos e verdadeiros positivos. Essa classificação se da através da análise feita por [Abdou and Ramadan, 2022], onde o mesmo cria uma tabela de severidade dos *code smells* fazendo uma divisão em quatro níveis, onde o nível 1 indica não haver presença de *code smell*, assim classificamos como falsos positivos. Os demais níveis classificamos verdadeiros positivos, por haver presença de *code smells* no projeto.

Tabela 2. Composição do conjunto de dados.

Code Smell	Falsos Positivos	Verdadeiros Positivos	Total
Long method	280	140	420
Data class	151	269	420
God class	154	266	420
Feature Envy	280	140	420

As métricas de software usadas estão descritas no trabalho de [Abdou and Ramadan, 2022], essas foram selecionadas e classificadas para abranger diversos aspectos do controle de qualidade de software, como Acoplamento, Complexidade, Coesão, Tamanho, Herança e Encapsulamento.

3.2. Avaliação de desempenho

Para medir o desempenho dos algoritmos de aprendizado de máquina neste trabalho, foram considerados quatro parâmetros de desempenho: precisão, sensibilidade, pontuação F1 e Acurácia. Para calculá-los, são utilizados verdadeiro positivo (TP), verdadeiro negativo (TN), falso positivo (FP) e falso negativo (FN).

Esses parâmetros são calculados usando uma matriz de confusão que contém as informações reais e previstas reconhecidas pelos classificadores de detecção de padrões de projeto [Catal, 2012]. As equações para o cálculo das avaliações de desempenho são mostradas na Tabela 3.

Tabela 3. Fórmulas das Métricas de Avaliação. Fonte: [Hossin and Sulaiman, 2015]

Métricas	Formula
Acurácia (Accuracy)	$\frac{VP+VN}{VP+FP+VN+FN}$
Precisão (Precision)	$\frac{VP}{VP+FP}$
Sensibilidade (Recall)	$\frac{VP}{VP+FN}$
F1-Score	$2 \times \frac{\text{Precisao} \times \text{Recall}}{\text{Precisao} + \text{Recall}}$

4. Resultados

Neste artigo, como mencionado anteriormente, foi adotado cinco técnicas de aprendizado de máquina para predição de *code smells* em projetos de software. Foram analisados quatro tipos de *code smells* divididos em dois níveis: *smells* de classe e *smells* de métodos.

Na Tabela 4 é mostrado uma comparação entre os resultados das métricas com todos os *code smells* usando a técnica *holdout* dividindo o conjunto de dados em 70% para treino e 30% para validação. Como é possível observar os algoritmos tem um ótimo desempenho. Com resultados variando entre 89,7% para o algoritmo Árvore de Decisão no *code smell Data class* em seu pior desempenho e 99,2% para os algoritmos Gradiente *Boost*, Floresta Aleatória e Árvore de Decisão treinados para o *code smell Long Method* no melhor desempenho.

Tabela 4. Comparação das métricas

Code Smells	Algoritmo	Precisão	Sensibilidade	Pontuação F1	Acurácia
Data Class	MLP	93,1%	93,7%	93,4%	93,7%
	Árvore de Decisão	88,9%	90,0%	89,3%	89,7%
	Floresta Aleatória	96,7%	**96,7%**	**96,7%**	**96,8%**
	Gradiente Boost	**97,0%**	96,3%	96,6%	**96,8%**
	SVM	91,3%	91,2%	91,3%	92,3%
God Class	MLP	**92,9%**	91,7%	92,3%	92,9%
	Árvore de Decisão	88,9%	89,2%	89,0%	89,7%
	Floresta Aleatória	84,1%	**92,4%**	**93,1%**	**93,7%**
	Gradiente Boost	**92,9%**	91,7%	92,3%	92,9%
	SVM	91,1%	87,0%	88,5%	89,7%
Feature Envy	MLP	93,2%	93,8%	93,5%	94,4%
	Árvore de Decisão	95,7%	96,6%	96,3%	96,8%
	Floresta Aleatória	**98,1%**	**98,1%**	**98,1%**	**98,4%**
	Gradiente Boost	97,5%	96,8%	97,2%	97,6%
	SVM	91,2%	89,8%	89,2%	91,3%
Long Method	MLP	95,2%	95,8%	95,5%	96,0%
	Árvore de Decisão	**99,4%**	98,8%	**99,1%**	**99,2%**
	Floresta Aleatória	98,8%	**99,4%**	**99,1%**	**99,2%**
	Gradiente Boost	**99,4%**	98,8%	**99,1%**	**99,2%**
	SVM	92,8%	92,8%	92,8%	93,7%

Analisando os dados gerado pelo algoritmo MLP, é visto que seu melhor desempenho foi para o *code smell Data Class*, porém o mesmo ainda se mostra muito eficiente na detecção dos demais *code smells*. Para o algoritmo da Árvore de decisão, o seu melhor resultado foi para o *code smell Long Method*, alcançou um excelente valor para a acurácia de 99,2%, mas também teve o pior desempenho entre os algoritmos analisados para os *code smells Data Class* e *God Class*. O SVM se mostrou muito promissor, como sua melhor pontuação para *Long Method* (93,7%) e para *Data Class* e *Feature Envy* alcançou valores de acurácia acima de 91%. Os dados para Floresta Aleatória são os mais promissores, pois a mesma atingiu as melhores pontuações nos quatro code smells, com destaque para Long Method que o valor ficou acima de 99%. Já o Gradiente *Boost* ficou logo atrás da Floresta Aleatória com pontuação igual nos *code smells Data Class* e *Long Method*, mas um pouco menos eficiente para *God Class* e *Feature Envy*.

Tabela 5. Desempenho dos algoritmos com validação cruzada em 10 partes (Acurácia)

	Data Class	God Class	Featury Envy	Long Method
MLP	91,9%	91,6%	90,5%	98,3%
Árvore de Decisão	90,8%	91,2%	93,6%	98,6%
Floresta Aleatória	**94,2%**	**96,3%**	**94,5%**	**99,0%**
Gradiente Boost	93,2%	94,6%	93,9%	98,6%
SVM	91,2%	91,2%	88,5%	97,3%

Na Tabela 5 são apresentados os dados referentes ao desempenho dos algoritmos empregando a técnica de validação cruzada de 10 partes. E a seguir fazemos uma comparação de desempenho entre as técnicas *holdout* e validação cruzada, porém essa comparação é apenas para efeito didático, já que a finalidade da validação cruzada é a mitigação de possíveis falhas no processo de treinamento do da técnica *holdout*.

Ao analisar os resultados dos algoritmos, é notório que, para os *code smells Data Class* e *God Class*, tanto os algoritmos MLP quanto Árvore de Decisão não demonstram melhora de desempenho. Por outro lado, os algoritmos Floresta Aleatória, Gradiente *Boost* e SVM mostraram melhorias no reconhecimento de *God Class*. No caso do *code smell Feature Envy*, os resultados foram contrários às expectativas, resultando em uma redução média de eficiência de 3,5%. Finalmente, em relação ao *code smell Long Method*, somente os algoritmos MLP e SVM foram beneficiados positivamente pela validação cruzada.

Podemos ver que os resultados da técnica de validação cruzada (Tabela 5) está bem parecida com a técnica *holdout* (Tabela 4), evidenciando que possíveis vícios, *overfit* ou outros problemas relacionados ao treinamento com o conjunto de dados adotado estão mitigados.

4.1. Análise dos resultados

Para responder a primeira questão levantada neste trabalho, na qual é indagado sobre a eficiência das cinco técnicas de aprendizado de máquina na detecção de *code smells*, é exposto na Tabela 4 que as mesmas alcançam valores superiores a 93% para o algoritmo Floresta Aleatória, demonstrando ser um caminho promissor para desenvolvimento de ferramentas para auxiliar programadores a escrever códigos de melhor qualidade, redução da complexidade, facilidade na manutenção e aumento da produtividade.

Quanto a resposta da segunda questão, que levanta uma interrogação sobre o impacto da validação cruzada em 10 partes, é possível ver os valores da Tabela 5 que mostra o desempenho dos algoritmos usando a técnica e fazer uma comparação com os números para acurácia da Tabela 4 que usa *holdout*, fica evidenciado que a validação cruzada mostra ganhos para os *code smells Feature Envy* e *Long Method*. Sendo que para o *Feature Envy* o algoritmo MLP não apresentou melhora no desempenho. E para *Long Method* a validação cruzada mostrou melhora no desempenho apenas em dois algoritmos: MLP e SVM.

5. Trabalhos Relacionados

Foram propostas diversas ferramentas para detecção de *code smells*, abrangendo tanto ferramentas comerciais quanto protótipos de pesquisa. Fontana and Zanoni [2017] falam que essas ferramentas utilizam uma variedade de técnicas para identificar *code smells*: algumas se baseiam em métricas [Lanza and Marinescu, 2007; Fontana et al., 2015], outras empregam uma linguagem de especificação própria [Moha et al., 2009], realizam análise de programas para encontrar oportunidades de refatoração [Tsantalis and Chatzigeorgiou, 2009, 2011], exploram a análise de repositórios de software [Palomba et al., 2015] ou ainda recorrem a técnicas de aprendizado de máquina. Focalizamos em abordagens que empregam técnicas de aprendizado de máquina.

Pushpalatha and Mrunalini [2021] propuseram uma abordagem de aprendizado de máquina para detectar *code smells* de software e observaram as métricas que desempenham papéis críticos no processo de detecção. Eles aplicaram algoritmo genético baseado em duas técnicas de seleção de recursos e técnica de otimização de parâmetros baseada em uma pesquisa em grade. Eles obtiveram melhor precisão na previsão dos *code smells* de *Data Class*, *God Class* e *Long Method* em 98,05%, 97,56% e 94,31%, respectivamente, usando o método GA_CFS, e no *Long Method* obtiveram a melhor precisão de 98,38% usando o recurso GA-Naïve Bayes método de seleção.

Abdou and Ramadan [2022] apresentam um estudo comparativo de técnicas de aprendizado de máquina para classificar a gravidade de *code smells* em software. Os pesquisadores propuseram um modelo baseado em métricas de software e aprendizado de máquina para detectar esses problemas de design. Eles utilizaram diferentes abordagens, incluindo classificação multinomial, ordinal e regressão, e avaliaram a precisão na ordenação e classificação da gravidade dos *code smells*. Além disso, identificaram limitações e propuseram direções para pesquisas futuras, como a inclusão de mais tipos de *code smells* e a avaliação de técnicas de balanceamento de dados e aprendizado em conjunto.

Kaur and Kaur [2021] apresentaram a técnica de aprendizado de conjunto (*Ensemble Learning*) e a técnica de seleção de características de correlação em três conjuntos de dados Java de código aberto para detecção de *code smells*. Eles aplicaram o classificador *Bagging* e Floresta Aleatória para analisar cada abordagem com quatro medidas de desempenho: acurácia (P1), G-*mean* 1 (P2), G-*mean* 2 (P3) e F-*measure* (P4).

A Tabela 6 representa uma breve comparação dos resultados obtidos por nós com outros trabalhos relacionados. Esses métodos aplicaram técnicas de aprendizado de máquina em conjunto de dados de *code smells* fornecido por [Fontana et al., 2016].

Tabela 6. Comparação dos resultados (Acurácia).

Autor	Conjunto de Dados			
	Data Class	**God Class**	**Feature Envy**	**Long Method**
[Fontana and Zanoni, 2017]	77,0%	74,0%	93,0%	92,0%
[Di Nucci et al., 2018]	83,0%	83,0%	84,0%	82,0%
[Mhawish and Gupta, 2020]	99,7%	98,5%	98,0%	96,0%
[Abdou and Ramadan, 2022]	93,0%	92,0%	97,0%	97,0%
Presente trabalho	96,8%	96,3%	98,4%	99,2%

6. Ameaças a pesquisa

Neste estudo podemos considerar algumas ameaças à validade da pesquisa, primeiramente a validade interna, têm efeito na correção dos resultados do experimento, e o segundo tipo de validade é a validade externa, que está relacionada à capacidade de generalização desse estudo em outros contextos.

A validade interna está relacionada ao grau de erro nos resultados devido à avaliação manual dos *code smells*, juntamente com a capacidade dos desenvolvedores de compreenderem os problemas de definição dos *code smells* e o nível de experiência e conhecimento dos desenvolvedores em programação orientada a objetos. Esses fatores afetam a faixa de valores apropriados que devem ser atribuídos à variável de classe pelo avaliador de *code smells*, podendo causar distorção no conjunto de dados.

Em segundo lugar, a validade externa está relacionada à generalização dos resultados deste estudo, limitada por alguns fatores, como as fontes de dados, construídas a partir de 76 sistemas pertencentes a diferentes domínios escritos em Java, o que não pode ser generalizado para software não-Java. Além disso, o grau de equilíbrio entre a ausência e a presença de *code smells* em conjuntos de dados para diferentes níveis de gravidade é um dos fatores que afetam a validade externa. Neste estudo, o grau de equilíbrio dos *code smells* é mantido na faixa de 33% a 66% e não é homogêneo nos conjuntos de dados.

7. Conclusão

Neste estudo propusemos uma abordagem baseada em aprendizado de máquina usando cinco algoritmos: MLP, Árvore de Decisão, Floresta Aleatória, Gradiente Boost e SVM e métricas de software para detectar *code smells* em sistemas de software. O conjunto de dados usado neste estudo foi retirado de [Fontana et al., 2016] para quatro tipos de *code smells*, conforme descrito na Subseção 3.1.

Duas são as principais contribuições desta pesquisa: na primeira, algoritmos de aprendizado de máquina são usados para identificar os quatro *code smells*. Na segunda etapa, as medidas de desempenho (Acurácia, Precisão, Sensibilidade e F1-score) são calculadas e usadas para avaliação do desempenho dos algoritmos. Também foi usada a validação em 10 partes para buscar a melhoria do desempenho das algoritmos usadas.

Observamos que as abordagens de aprendizado de máquina, Árvore de Decisão, Floresta Aleatória e Gradiente Boost tiveram um excelente desempenho para a detecção de *code smell Long Method* alcançando uma acurácia de mais de 99%, para *Feature Envy* valores superiores a 96% de acurácia. Já para *Data Class* o desempenho caiu um pouco para o algoritmo Árvore de Decisão ficando em 89,7%, os demais ficam em 96,8% de acurácia. E para *code smell God Class* a abordagem com Árvore de Decisão ganhou desempenho com a técnica de validação cruzada em 10 partes atingindo percentual de 91,2%, Floresta Aleatória conseguiu 96,3% e Gradiente Boost 94,6%. As técnicas de aprendizado de máquina MLP e SVM também tiveram um ótimo desempenho, mas abaixo das demais. Conseguindo valores de acurácia de 98,3% e 97,3% para *Long Method*, 94,4% e 91,3% para *Feature Envy*, 93,7% e 92,3% para *Data Class* e 92,9% e 91,2% para *God Class*.

Nos trabalhos futuros, pretende-se estender os experimentos para novos conjuntos de dados, incluindo mais tipos de *code smells*, buscar também formas de definições mais sólidas, ou melhor, generalizadas, para identificação dos *code smells*. Além disso, podemos testar a capacidade de generalizar os resultados dos experimentos para estudos com linguagens de programação orientadas a objetos diferentes de Java. E também desenvolver uma ferramenta para editores de código e/ou IDEs com intuito de identificação de *code smells* durante o processo de desenvolvimento do software.

Referências

Abdou, A. and Ramadan, N. (2022). Selected code-quality characteristics and metrics for internet of things systems. *Journal of Software: Evolution and Process*, 34:18.

Al Shalabi, L., Shaaban, Z., and Kasasbeh, B. (2006). Data mining: A preprocessing engine. *Journal of Computer Science*, 2(9):735–739.

Arlot, S. and Celisse, A. (2010). A survey of cross-validation procedures for model selection.

Ashraf Abdou, N. R. (2022). Severity classification of software code smells using machine learning techniques: A comparative study. *Journal of Software: Evolution and Process*, page 37.

Breiman, L. (2001). Random forests. *Machine learning*, 45:5–32.

Brown, W. H., Malveau, R. C., McCormick, H. W. S., and Mowbray, T. J. (1998). *AntiPatterns: Refactoring Software, Architectures, and Projects in Crisis*. John Wiley & Sons, Inc., USA, 1st edition.

Catal, C. (2012). Performance evaluation metrics for software fault prediction studies. *Acta Polytechnica Hungarica*, 9(4):193–206.

Ciupke, O. (1999). Automatic detection of design problems in object-oriented reengineering. In *Proceedings of technology of object-oriented languages and systems-TOOLS 30 (Cat. No. PR00278)*, pages 18–32. IEEE.

Dewangan, S., Rao, R. S., Mishra, A., and Gupta, M. (2021). A novel approach for code smell detection: An empirical study. *IEEE Access*, 9:162869–162883.

Di Nucci, D., Palomba, F., Tamburri, D. A., Serebrenik, A., and De Lucia, A. (2018). Detecting code smells using machine learning techniques: are we there yet? In *2018 ieee 25th international conference on software analysis, evolution and reengineering (saner)*, pages 612–621. IEEE.

Fontana, F. A., Ferme, V., Zanoni, M., and Roveda, R. (2015). Towards a prioritization of code debt: A code smell intensity index. In *2015 IEEE 7th International Workshop on Managing Technical Debt (MTD)*, pages 16–24. IEEE.

Fontana, F. A., Mäntylä, M., Zanoni, M., and Marino, A. (2016). Comparing and experimenting machine learning techniques for code smell detection. *Empirical Software Engineering*, 21:1143–1191.

Fontana, F. A. and Zanoni, M. (2017). Code smell severity classification using machine learning techniques. *Knowledge-Based Systems*, 128:43–58.

Fowler, M. (2018). *Refactoring: Improving the Design of Existing Code*. Addison-Wesley, 2nd edition.

Friedman, J. H. (2001). Greedy function approximation: A gradient boosting machine. *The Annals of Statistics*, 29(5):1189–1232.

Han, J., Pei, J., and Tong, H. (2022). *Data mining: concepts and techniques*. Morgan kaufmann.

Hossin, M. and Sulaiman, M. N. (2015). A review on evaluation metrics for data classification evaluations. *International journal of data mining & knowledge management process*, 5(2):1.

Kaur, I. and Kaur, A. (2021). A novel four-way approach designed with ensemble feature selection for code smell detection. *IEEE Access*, 9:8695–8707.

Lanza, M. and Marinescu, R. (2007). *Object-oriented metrics in practice: using software metrics to characterize, evaluate, and improve the design of object-oriented systems*. Springer Science & Business Media.

McConnell, S. (2004). *Code complete : a practical handbook of sofware construction*. Microsoft Press.

Mhawish, M. Y. and Gupta, M. (2020). Predicting code smells and analysis of predictions: Using machine learning techniques and software metrics. *Journal of Computer Science and Technology*, 35:1428–1445.

Moha, N., Guéhéneuc, Y.-G., Duchien, L., and Le Meur, A.-F. (2009). Decor: A method for the specification and detection of code and design smells. *IEEE Transactions on Software Engineering*, 36(1):20–36.

Noble, W. S. (2006). What is a support vector machine? *Nature biotechnology*, 24(12):1565–1567.

Palomba, F., Di Nucci, D., Tufano, M., Bavota, G., Oliveto, R., Poshyvanyk, D., and De Lucia, A. (2015). Landfill: An open dataset of code smells with public evaluation. In *2015 IEEE/ACM 12th Working Conference on Mining Software Repositories*, pages 482–485. IEEE.

Pushpalatha, M. and Mrunalini, M. (2021). Predicting the severity of open source bug reports using unsupervised and supervised techniques. In *Research Anthology on Usage and Development of Open Source Software*, pages 676–692. IGI Global.

Quinlan, J. R. (1990). Decision trees and decision-making. *IEEE Transactions on Systems, Man, and Cybernetics*, 20(2):339–346.

Ray, S. (2019). A quick review of machine learning algorithms. In *2019 International conference on machine learning, big data, cloud and parallel computing (COMITCon)*, pages 35–39. IEEE.

Riel, A. J. (1996). *Object-Oriented Design Heuristics*. Addison-Wesley Longman Publishing Co., Inc., USA, 1st edition.

Ruck, D. W., Rogers, S. K., and Kabrisky, M. (1990). Feature selection using a multilayer perceptron. *Journal of neural network computing*, 2(2):40–48.

Sahin, D., Kessentini, M., Bechikh, S., and Deb, K. (2014). Code-smell detection as a bilevel problem. *ACM Transactions on Software Engineering and Methodology (TOSEM)*, 24(1):1–44.

Tarwani, S. and Chug, A. (2016). Predicting maintainability of open source software using gene expression programming and bad smells. In *2016 5th international conference on reliability, Infocom technologies and optimization (trends and future directions)(ICRITO)*, pages 452–459. IEEE.

Tempero, E., Anslow, C., Dietrich, J., Han, T., Li, J., Lumpe, M., Melton, H., and Noble, J. (2010). The qualitas corpus: A curated collection of java code for empirical studies. In *2010 Asia Pacific Software Engineering Conference*, pages 336–345.

Travassos, G., Shull, F., Fredericks, M., and Basili, V. R. (1999). Detecting defects in object-oriented designs: using reading techniques to increase software quality. *ACM sigplan notices*, 34(10):47–56.

Tsantalis, N. and Chatzigeorgiou, A. (2009). Identification of move method refactoring opportunities. *IEEE Transactions on Software Engineering*, 35(3):347–367.

Tsantalis, N. and Chatzigeorgiou, A. (2011). Ranking refactoring suggestions based on historical volatility. In *2011 15th European conference on software maintenance and reengineering*, pages 25–34. IEEE.

Yamashita, A. and Counsell, S. (2013). Code smells as system-level indicators of maintainability: An empirical study. *Journal of Systems and Software*, 86(10):2639–2653.

Yamashita, A. and Moonen, L. (2012). Do code smells reflect important maintainability aspects? In *2012 28th IEEE international conference on software maintenance (ICSM)*, pages 306–315. IEEE.

Yamashita, A. and Moonen, L. (2013). Exploring the impact of inter-smell relations on software maintainability: An empirical study. In *2013 35th International Conference on Software Engineering (ICSE)*, pages 682–691. IEEE.

Technical Debt in Continuous Software Engineering: An Overview of the State of the Art and Future Trends

Lucas de Oliveira Carvalho[1], **João Paulo Biazotto**[1,2], **Daniel Feitosa**[2], **Elisa Yumi Nakagawa**[1]

[1]University of São Paulo (USP), São Carlos, Brazil

[2]University of Groningen, Groningen, The Netherlands

Abstract. *Large software companies strive to make their engineering processes fast, and agile development has been a key enabler for flexible delivery of solutions following the market needs. In this context, continuous software engineering (CSE) has emerged as a way to iteratively develop software using practices that encompass business strategy, development, and operations that are aligned with the agile methodology. However, these practices can also lead to the accumulation of technical debt (TD), which has shown to be harmful to the software in the long-term. Due to its impact, TD should be managed in the context of CSE. However, to the best of our knowledge, there is a lack of an overview of how TD has been addressed in this context. In this study, we present the state of the art of TD in CSE; for this, we scrutinized the literature and found 41 studies. Our main findings show that this field of study is relatively new, with active participation of the industry, and that most CSE activities are not addressing TD yet; therefore, presenting a number of opportunities for future research.*

1. Introduction

Large software companies have attempted to make their development processes responsive and with minimal time between the identification of the market needs and the delivery to end users, and these attempts have found an ally with agile development [Dingsøyr et al. 2012]. In the last years, the software industry has widely adopted agile software development as a suitable way of engineering software systems. Agility has proved to be beneficial to the industry in various aspects, like software environments, technologies, requirements, user needs, and market changes [Papatheocharous and Andreou 2013, Vijayasarathy and Turk 2012].

In this context, Continuous Software Engineering (CSE) has emerged as a way to iteratively develop software using practices, such as continuous planning, continuous integration (CI), continuous deployment (CD), and continuous monitoring [Fitzgerald and Stol 2017]. As an instance, DevOps is a broadly used and well-recognized concept that has attracted much interest from both academia and industry because of its focus on leveraging the continuous delivery of software products to end users, matching then the current industry needs [Chen 2015]. CSE handles software engineering as a continuous flow and comprises three phases [Fitzgerald and Stol 2017]:

- Business Strategy: The operations feedback (e.g., end user needs, market changes, production metrics) is used to replan the software evolution aiming at aligning the development of new features with the business needs;

- Development: It covers the main activities of the software development process from analysis to maintenance. These activities also handle a stream of new features to be developed by applying techniques associated with continuous architecting, integration, deployment, verification, and others; and
- Operations: This phase focuses on the continuity of the software in terms of usage and runtime management. The companies need to ensure that the software systems deliver the values that fulfill the users' needs and also assure the reliability of these systems through runtime monitoring and dynamic adaptation over time.

Although agile software development is usually seen as beneficial, the short deadlines that are imposed by this process can lead to bad decisions. Such sub-optimal decisions tend to meet short-term goals (e.g., speeding up the development), but may lead negative impacts in the long-term (such as quality issues or development gaps), which is called technical debt (TD) [Kruchten et al. 2012]. Alves et al. [2016] highlight that TD can refer to various artifacts (e.g., code, test, documentation) or processes (e.g., build, requirements) in the software and its development. And, on this note, Seaman et al. [2012] illustrate several consequences if TD is not solved, such as large cost overruns, quality issues, inability to add new features without disrupting new ones, and the premature loss of the system. In summary, although TD is being increasingly discussed in the software community and being investigated as a phenomenon that can occur in any phase of the software life cycle, several aspects of it need to be still investigated, and some issues are still open for research.

While the concept of TD has existed for some time, the agile development adoption has given to it the known visibility [Codabux and Williams 2013]. Due to the impact of TD and the necessity of TD management, it should be evaluated in the context of CSE, specially with the companies and software projects adopting CSE activities in a daily basis [Klotins and Gorschek 2022]. However, to the best of our knowledge, there is a lack of an overview of how TD has been addressed in the CSE context.

In this scenario, the main contribution of this study is to present a rundown of the state of the art of how TD has been addressed in CSE. For this, we conducted a systematic mapping study (SMS) and selected 41 studies. The results of our SMS show that researching TD in CSE is relatively new, with studies distributed in the last 10 years; besides, some activities of CSE, specially continuous architecting, have addressed TD, while other fundamental activities (e.g., CI) have not yet and no study has addressed TD in the whole CSE cycle. Another important finding is that the industry has been considerably involved with the field, showing its interest in investigating the problem. For the future, further research is essential to progress and consolidate the TD management within the CSE activities and future perspectives are also presented.

This paper is organized as follows: Section 2 presents the research method and how it was planned and conducted; Section 3 presents the established state of the art; Section 4 discusses the findings, perspectives of future research, and threats to validity; and Section 5 concludes this work.

2. Research method

To conduct this SMS, we followed the guidelines proposed by [Petersen et al. 2008] and [Kitchenham et al. 2015]. Three main phases were followed to conduct this study: (i)

Planning: creation of the protocol, which addresses objective, research questions, search criteria and selection criteria of the studies; (ii) Conduction: selection of the studies based on the protocol; and (iii) Results: synthesis and description of the results. These phases (illustrated in Figure 1) are detailed in Sections 2.1, 2.2, and 2.3.

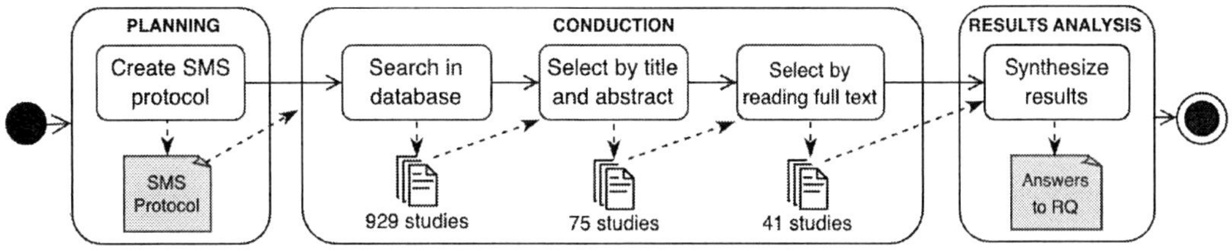

Figure 1. Phases for the conduction of this SMS.

2.1. SMS Planning

With the objective of uncovering the main characteristics of TD in CSE, this SMS addresses the following research question (RQ): *Which of the CSE activities address TD?*

The search strategy started by creating a search string that could collect the maximum amount of relevant studies.The main related terms were discussed by experts and were used in a pilot search to build a search string composed of the main terms related to TD and CSE. The final search string was:

("debt" AND ("continuous" OR "devops" OR "bizdev" OR "agile" OR "lean"))

Considering that Scopus[1] indexes more than 7,000 publishers[2], including the most relevant journals and conferences for the field of Software Engineering besides being widely adopted in SMS and SLR (systematic literature review) in this field, we decided to adopt only it to reveal the overview of the state of the art intended in this study. For this preliminary study that offers such an overview, we decided not to perform a snowballing-based review [Wohlin 2014].

In order to systematically filter the studies and select only the relevant ones to answer the RQ, one inclusion criterion (IC) and five exclusion criteria (EC) were established, as follows:

- IC1: Study addresses TD in CSE activities/environments (e.g., agile development, continuous integration, continuous delivery, etc);
- EC1: Study is not written in English;
- EC2: Study is a shorter version of another study already included;
- EC3: Study's full text is not available;
- EC4: Study is a conference proceedings, tutorial, interview, editorial, workshop, keynotes or summary of keynotes, preview or a preliminary study;
- EC5: Study is not a primary study;

[1]https://www.scopus.com/
[2]https://www.elsevier.com/solutions/scopus/how-scopus-works

2.2. SMS Conduction

Figure 1 summarizes the SMS conduction steps, also showing the number of selected studies at the end of each step. The SMS was conducted between August 2023 and November 2023 and split into three main steps:

- Search in database: The final search string created in the Planning phase was configured for the Scopus database to retrieve studies. The string was used to search studies through titles, keywords, and abstracts. At the end of this step, the total amount of primary studies returned was 929;
- Selection by title and abstract: The selection criteria settled at the Planning phase were applied by reading the title and abstract of each study. At the end of this step, 75 studies were selected;
- Selection by full-text reading: The selection criteria were applied once again after reading the full text of each study, and 41 studies were selected and are listed in Table 1.

2.3. SMS Synthesis

To synthesize the data collected from the studies, we extracted the information related to the RQ. Along with the authors, publication date, and publication venue, we also extracted: study type, relationship between academia and industry, application domain, types and/or sources of TD. The results uncovered in this study are presented in Section 3.

3. Results

Table 1 summarizes the selected studies after executing the steps discussed in Section 2. This table shows an identification and the reference for each study. We show them here instead of among the bibliographic references to facilitate the reading of the paper. Furthermore, supplementary material[3] presents the data synthesized in this section and discussed further in this work.

Table 1. Selected studies for the SMS.

ID	Reference
S1	Dos Santos, P. S., Varella, A., Dantas, C., and Borges, D. (2013). **Visualizing and managing technical debt in agile development: An experience report** page 14.
S2	Codabux, Z. and Williams, B. (2013a). **Managing technical debt: An industrial case study**. In 4th International Workshop on Managing Technical Debt (MTD), page 8 – 15
S3	Martini, A., Bosch, J., and Chaudron, M. (2014). **Architecture technical debt: Understanding causes and a qualitative model**. In 2014 40th EUROMICRO Conference on Software Engineering and Advanced Applications, pages 85–92
S4	Holvitie, J., Lepp anen, V., and Hyrynsalmi, S. (2014). **Technical debt and the effect of agile software development practices on it - an industry practitioner survey**. In 2014 Sixth International Workshop on Managing Technical Debt, pages 35–42.
S5	Sandberg, A. B., Staron, M., and Antinyan, V. (2015). **Towards proactive management of technical debt by software metrics**. In Symposium on Programming Languages and Software Tools

Continued on next page

[3]https://doi.org/10.6084/m9.figshare.25481542

Table 1 – *Continued from previous page*

Id	Reference
S6	Martini, A. and Bosch, J. (2015b). **Towards prioritizing architecture technical debt: Information needs of architects and product owners**. In 2015 41st Euromicro Conference on Software Engineering and Advanced Applications, pages 422–429.
S7	Soares, H., Rios, N., Mendes, T., Mendonc a, M., and Sp ınola, R. (2015). **Investigating the link between user stories and documentation debt on software projects**. Proceedings - 12th International Conference on Information Technology: New Generations, ITNG 2015, pages 385–390.
S8	Martini, A. and Bosch, J. (2015a). **The danger of architectural technical debt: Contagious debt and vicious circles**. In 2015 12th Working IEEE/IFIP Conference on Software Architecture, pages 1–10
S9	Martini, A., Bosch, J., and Chaudron, M. (2015). **Investigating architectural technical debt accumulation and refactoring over time: A multiple-case study**. Information and Software Technology, 67:237–253.
S10	Griffith, I., Taffahi, H., Izurieta, C., and Claudio, D. (2014). **A simulation study of practical methods for technical debt management in agile software development**. In Proceedings of the Winter Simulation Conference 2014, pages 1014–1025
S11	Mendes, T., Soares, H., Farias, M., Kalinowski, M., Mendonça, M., and Spínola, R. (2016). **Impacts of agile requirements documentation debt on software projects: A retrospective study/**
S12	Vathsavayi, S. H. and Syst a, K. (2016). **Technical debt management with genetic algorithms**. In 2016 42th Euromicro Conference on Software Engineering and Advanced Applications (SEAA), pages 50–53.
S13	Vassallo, C., Zampetti, F., Romano, D., Beller, M., Panichella, A., Di Penta, M., and Zaidman, A. (2016). **Continuous delivery practices in a large financial organization**. In 2016 IEEE International Conference on Software Maintenance and Evolution (ICSME), pages 519–528.
S14	Gupta, R. K., Manikreddy, P., Naik, S., and Arya, K. (2016). **Pragmatic approach for managing technical debt in legacy software project**. In Proceedings of the 9th India Software Engineering Conference, ISEC '16, page 170–176, New York, NY, USA. Association for Computing Machinery
S15	Martini, A. and Bosch, J. (2017a). **The magnificent seven: towards a systematic estimation of technical debt interest**. In Proceedings of the XP2017 Scientific Workshops, XP '17, New York, NY, USA. Association for Computing Machinery.
S16	Ciolkowski, M., Guzmán, L., Trendowicz, A., and Salfner, F. (2017). **Lessons learned from the prodebt research project on planning technical debt strategically**. pages 523– 534.
S17	Bomfim, M. and Santos, V. (2017). **Strategies for reducing technical debt in agile teams**. pages 60–71
S18	Martini, A. and Bosch, J. (2017b). **On the interest of architectural technical debt: Uncovering the contagious debt phenomenon**. Journal of Software: Evolution and Process, 29:e1877.
S19	de Assunçãao, T. R., Rodrigues, I., Venson, E., Figueredo, R. M. d. C., and De Sousa, T. L. (2015). **Technical debt management in the brazilian federal administration**. In 2015 6th Brazilian Workshop on Agile Methods (WBMA), pages 6–9.
S20	Caires, V., Rios, N., Holvitie, J., Lepp anen, V., Mendonc a, M., and Spínola, R. (2018). **Investigating the effects of agile practices and processes on technical debt - The viewpoint of the brazilian software industry**. pages 506–559.
S21	Rios, N., Spínola, R. O., Mendonça, M., and Seaman, C. (2018). **The most common causes and effects of technical debt: First results from a global family of industrial surveys**. In Proceedings of the 12th ACM/IEEE International Symposium on Empirical Software Engineering and Measurement, ESEM '18, New York, NY, USA. Association for Computing Machinery
S22	Holvitie, J., Licorish, S., Spínola, R., Hyrynsalmi, S., MacDonell, S., Mendes, T., Buchan, J., and Leppanen, V. (2017). **Technical debt and agile software development practices and processes: An industry practitioner survey**. Information and Software Technology, in press

Continued on next page

Table 1 – *Continued from previous page*

Id	Reference
S23	Martini, A., Besker, T., and Bosch, J. (2018). **Technical debt tracking: Current state of practice: A survey and multiple case study in 15 large organizations**. Science of Computer Programming, 163:42–61
S24	Martini, A., Sikander, E., and Madlani, N. (2017). **A semi-automated framework for the identification and estimation of architectural technical debt: A comparative case-study on the modularization of a software component**. Information and Software Technology, 93.
S25	Toledo, S., Martini, A., Przybyszewska, A., and Sjøberg, D. (2019). **Architectural technical debt in microservices: A case study in a large company**.
S26	Rios, N., Mendonça, M., Seaman, C., and Spínola, R. (2019). **Causes and effects of the presence of technical debt in agile software projects**
S27	Martini, A., Stray, V., and Moe, N. (2019). **Technical-, social- and process debt in large-scale agile: An exploratory case-study**, pages 112–119.
S28	Martini, A. and Bosch, J. (2020). **Architectural technical debt in embedded systems**, pages 77–103.
S29	Rios, N., Spínola, R., Mendonça, M., and Seaman, C. (2020). **The practitioners' point of view on the concept of technical debt and its causes and consequences: A design for a global family of industrial surveys and its first results from brazil**. Empirical Software Engineering, 25
S30	Freire, S., Rios, N., Pérez, B., Castellanos, C., Correal, D., Ramac, R., Mandic, V., Tausan, N., Pacheco, A., López, G., Mendonça, M., Izurieta, C., Falessi, D., Seaman, C., and Spínola, R. (2021). **Pitfalls and solutions for technical debt management in agile software projects**. IEEE Software, 38(6):42–49.
S31	Malakuti, S. and Heuschkel, J. (2021). **The need for holistic technical debt management across the value stream: Lessons learnt and open challenges**. In 2021 IEEE/ACM International Conference on Technical Debt (TechDebt), pages 109–113.
S32	Bonfim, V. D., Benitti, F. B. V. (2022). **Requirements debt: Causes, consequences, and mitigating practices**. In Seke (pp. 13–18).
S33	Soares, G., Freire, S., Rios, N., Pérez, B., Castellanos, C., Correal, D., Mendonçaa, M., Izurieta, C., Seaman, C., and Spínola, R. (2022). **Investigating how agile software practitioners repay technical debt in software projects**. In Anais do XXI Simpósio Brasileiro de Qualidade de Software, pages 120–129, Porto Alegre, RS, Brasil. SBC.
S34	Wiese, M., Rachow, P., Riebisch, M., and Schwarze, J. (2022). **Preventing technical debt with the tap framework for technical debt aware management**. Information and Software Technology, 148:106926.
S35	Stochel, M. G., Wawrowski, M. R., and Chołda, P. (2022b). **Technical debt prioritization in telecommunication applications: Why the actual refactoring deviates from the plan and how to remediate it? Case study in the covid era**. Applied Sciences, 12(22).
S36	Eldh, S. (2022). **On technical debt in software testing - Observations from the industry**. Berlin, Heidelberg. Springer-Verlag.
S37	Stochel, M. G., Chołda, P., and Wawrowski, M. R. (2022a). **Adopting devops paradigm in technical debt prioritization and mitigation**. In 2022 48th Euromicro Conference on Software Engineering and Advanced Applications (SEAA), pages 306–313
S38	Jamil, M. and Nour, M. (2022). **Managing software testing technical debt using evolutionary algorithms**. Computers, Materials and Continua, 73:735–747.
S39	Bonet Faus, J., Le Masson, P., Pelissier, U., Jibet, N., Bordas, A., and Pajot, S. (2023). **Design methods for diagnosing and locating entangled technical debt in devops frameworks**. Proceedings of the Design Society, 3:1267–1276.
S40	Aldaeej, A., Nguyen Duc, A., and Gupta, V. (2023). **A lean approach of managing technical debt in agile software projects – A proposal and empirical evaluation**, pages 67–76.
S41	Doshi, M. and Virparia, P. (2023). **Agile development methodology for software re- engineering**. In Goar, V., Kuri, M., Kumar, R., and Senjyu, T., editors, Advances in Information Communication Technology and Computing, pages 401–409, Singapore. Springer Nature Singapore.

3.1. Overview of selected studies

Figure 2 shows the distribution of studies according to publication year, application domain, venue type and study type. The first selected study was published in 2013, indicating a more recent interest in this field. This could be evidence that TD in CSE is a relatively new research topic. Also, analyzing the distribution per year, there is no concentration of publications in a specific year.

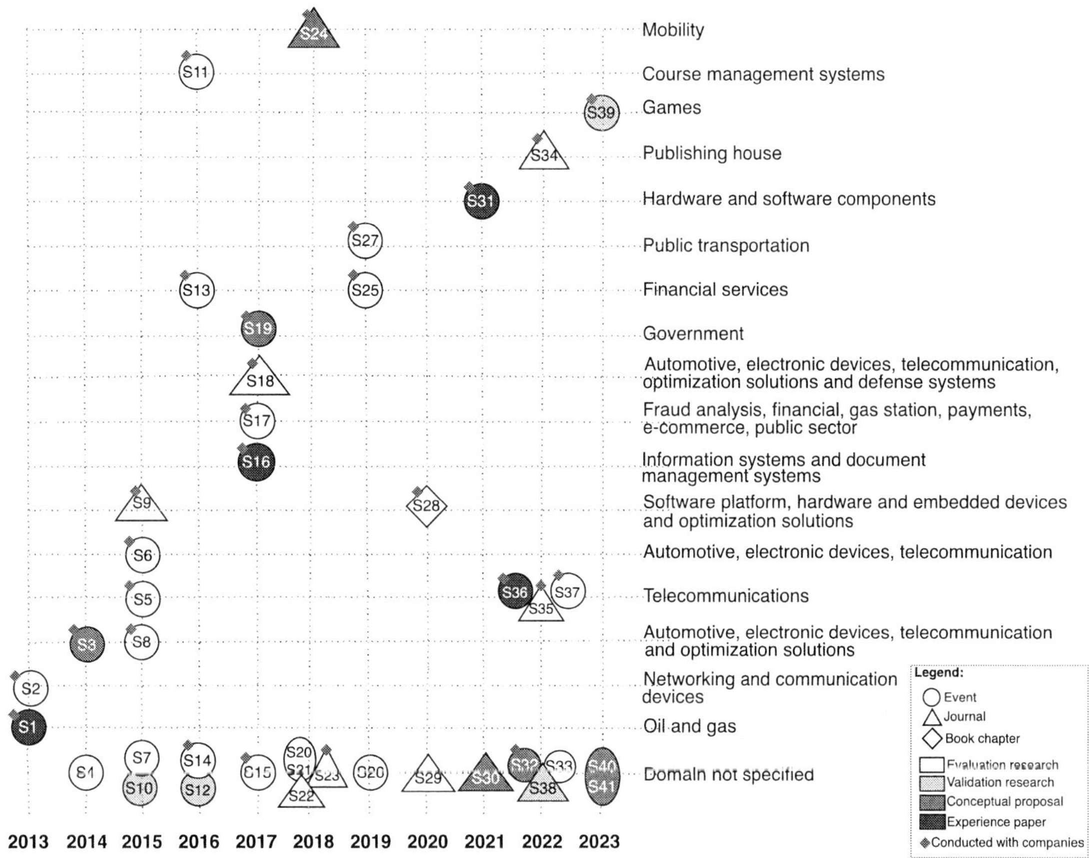

Figure 2. Overview of studies.

The majority of the studies (30) are published in events, while 10 were published in journals and only one as a book chapter. All publications are peer-reviewed, while in general, journal articles report more robust and complex studies. The only study published as a book chapter discusses about TD in CSE applied in the context of embedded systems, which is not discussed in other studies. Altogether, the combined observations may indicate that the research on TD in CSE is still maturing, with several open topics for investigation.

To analyze the study type, we used the classification proposed by [Wieringa et al. 2006]. In summary, studies classified as *evaluation research* are the most mature since they are based on empirical data and seek objective evidence about the results of an intervention, followed by studies classified as *validation research*. Studies classified as *solution proposal*, *conceptual proposal*, *experience paper*, or *opinion paper* correspond to those with less maturity; however, they contribute to introducing new ideas and emerging results. In the selected studies, 30/41 were classified as evaluation or validation research, which shows that this topic have been investigated mostly using empirical data and practical evidence (e.g., S8). The other 11/41 were classified as conceptual proposal or experience paper and are studies conducted generally in partnership with the industry to report a specific situation or phenomena (e.g., S24). Thus, these findings suggest that this topic has high relevance on the industry and is aligned with the interest of different companies that use one or more of CSE practices.

Regarding the application domains or types of systems, this information is directly extracted from the studies, which are mostly not specific about the application domain. This is mainly because these studies were conducted with practitioners but were not validated in a specific company, bringing a wider vision to the objective of the study instead of being limited to a specific context. The studies that specify a domain are conducted in a diverse set of areas, but many can be seen as critical, such as telecommunication (e.g., S5), government (e.g., S19) and finance (e.g., S25). Hence, this could show that this topic is being investigated with these kind of domains for having high relevance and impact in the industry. It also shows that this topic can be evaluated in different kinds of domains while maintaining its value.

Evaluating the studies that were conducted with the industry, it was mentioned that most studies are evaluation or validation research and this is endorsed by the fact that 27 studies were guided using data directly from different companies. There are different kinds of validation from these companies: some studies use the company as a case study to apply the research and collect the results (e.g., 35), while others gather results from a settled process in a company (e.g., S1), some others apply surveys or conduct interviews with practitioners to get answers and insights (e.g., S22). Case studies are the most used research method in studies that are conducted with companies and most of them are conducted in European companies. As a consequence, these findings validate that this topic has been mainly conducted in the industry. They also suggest that industry is also open to sharing their experiences to improve the state of the art and the state of the practice. Furthermore, there are two types of studies conducted in industrial contexts: the ones that are conducted by researchers who have some position in the company where the study is placed and the ones that are conducted by researchers with no relation to the context where the study takes place.

Finally, it is worth mentioning that all selected studies apply one or more of the known CSE practices, like agile development, CI, and continuous delivery, and analyze the TD that might be incurred in these practices. However, none of the selected studies discuss approaches to managing TD as a whole or how to characterize TD in CSE environments. Thus, a holistic approach to TD management in these environments is missing.

3.2. RQ - Which of the CSE activities address TD?

Figure 3, adapted from [Fitzgerald and Stol 2017], synthesizes the types of TD that are addressed or uncovered by the selected studies. The types are mapped to the flow of CSE as proposed by [Fitzgerald and Stol 2017].

The types of debt that we use are based on the classification of [Li et al. 2015]. Out of the studies, 19/41 do not mention any specific debt type related to the study,

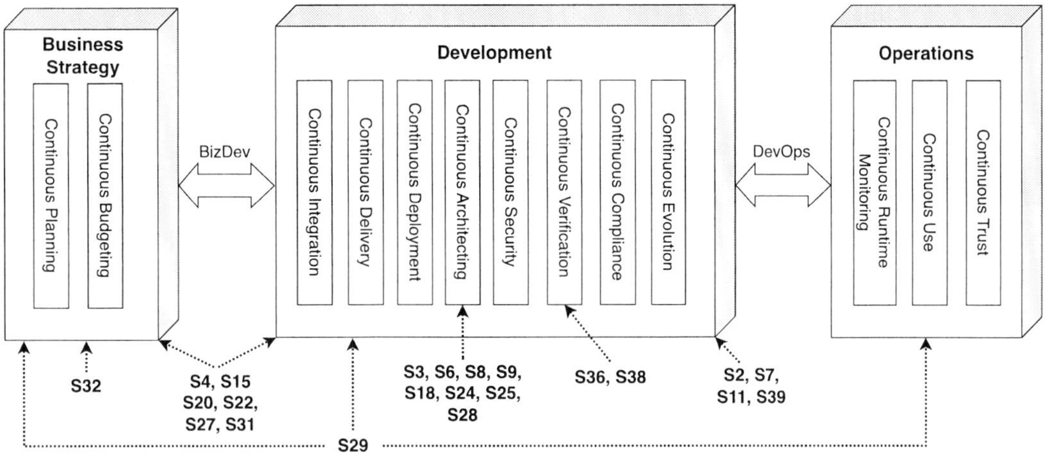

Figure 3. CSE activities in which TD was addressed (Based on [Fitzgerald and Stol 2017]).

focusing on other aspects of TD, like debt management, methods and approaches for TD. The rest of the studies (22/41) are specific about the debt type that is addressed or uncovered by the study; some of them mention more than one type and one of the studies mentions all of them and points out others not specified by [Li et al. 2015].

The studies mention these types of debt: architecture debt, build debt, code debt, defect debt, design debt, documentation debt, infrastructure debt, process debt, requirement debt, service debt, test debt, usability debt, versioning debt, but the CSE cycle is more generic and each step might encompass multiple activities of software engineering, so the studies in Figure 3 are connected to the step where the type of debt mentioned by the study might occur:

- S3, S6, S8, S9, S18, S24, S25, S28 explicitly handle architecture debt and the great number of studies specifically dealing with this type of debt show its importance;
- S36 and S38 deal with test debt and these studies discuss contemporary topics in continuous testing, like automation, TDD and test scenarios management;
- S32 is related to business strategy, but addresses requirements debt and this study mentions which facts and causes might happen in projects related to requirements engineering;
- S2, S7, S11 and S39 are associated to Development activities. S2 mention architecture, automation and infrastructure debt. S7 and S11 refers to documentation debt. S39 comments on design debt;
- S29 is connected to Business Strategy, Development and Operations because this study is related to different kinds of debt in the whole cycle: architecture debt, build debt, code debt, defect debt, design debt, documentation debt, infrastructure debt, process debt, requirement debt, service debt, test debt, usability debt and versioning debt; and
- S4, S15, S20, S22, S27, S31 are linked with both Business Strategy and Development because these studies mention types of debt that happen in both.

S4, S20 and S22 debates requirements, design, implementation and test debt. S15 touches upon architecture, design, documentation and test debt. S27 brings up architecture, infrastructure, documentation and test debt. S31 brings up architecture, requirements, build, code and test debt.

The most cited type of debt is architecture, followed by requirements, documentation and test debt, in no specific order. With regard to the CSE cycle, Business Strategy and Development activities are the ones with the most citation from the studies, while only one study addresses debt in Operations. The steps with the most citations are known for having high impact in the cycle of engineering a software [Singh and Gautam 2016] and all of them relate to quality. Therefore, there is an indication that TD has been more broadly studied in some steps of the CSE cycle because they usually interfere in main aspects of the quality of the software than in the rest of the CSE cycle, but more on this should be studied.

There are some activities in the CSE cycle that are not related to any kind of debt mentioned in the studies. Continuous budgeting, continuous compliance, and continuous trust are regular activities in some companies, but not directly related to the development cycle, so this might be the reason why there is no mention for a debt related to these activities. CI, continuous delivery, CD, and continuous security are widely adopted practices in the industry, but no study directly addresses TD in these activities. Continuous evolution activities might encompass TD management because it is usually the phase where the software is maturing and the issues related to it are found, so this might be the reason why the studies do not mention this activity. Continuous monitoring is another activity usually adopted in modern software development, specially in microservices, but no study mention any kind of debt related to it.

The studies that do not specify any kind of debt usually use some of the CSE practices, and apply some method for TD management, bringing light to a more generic approach. For instance, S19 proposes a strategy to check the quality of the code based on the TD volume, making TD identification and measurement in four stages: definition of violations, attribution of value to the pointers, measurement of non-conformances, and obtention of the results. Although studies like S19 are the minority of the selected studies, they indicate that TD might or might not be analyzed being related to a specific activity in the CSE cycle.

4. Discussion

The first study that was selected in this SMS was published in 2013, and this fact indicates that the interest on the intersection between TD and CSE practices is relatively new. Besides this, in the decade of 2010, the adoption of and the interest in CSE practices applied to software projects grew when compared to the previous decade in several places, like Fontana et al. [2022] exemplifies in Brazil, which might be one of the factors that drew attention to the discussion of TD in projects that use these practices. Thus, the combination of the growth in the adoption of CSE practices and the concerns related to software quality could have been the origin of this field of study.

While CSE activities have proved to be beneficial to software projects and business, the relationship between TD and CSE activities have not been fully addressed in previous studies. Our study shows, for instance in Figure 3, that some CSE activities have no TD study associated, which indicates the need for more research. As mentioned before, some of these uninvestigated activities (such as CI, continuous delivery, and continuous monitoring) have great impact in modern software development, and some of the studies address types of debt that are not in the original figure proposed by [Fitzgerald and Stol 2017].

Another finding is that industry is highly involved in studies addressing TD and CSE, as shown in Figure 2. Specifically, most of the selected studies (27/41) were either conducted by practitioners or used data collected from industrial settings (e.g.,companies or practitioners). To some extent, the growing interest on TD in CSE can indicate that bad practices (from which TD is derived) in CSE can have a high negative impact in the companies.

Finally, some application domains that normally adopt CSE activities, e.g., Industry 4.0 and Information Systems, have few or no studies addressing TD. This indicates that this topic has been researched in a varied range of domains, showing the industry is not focused on a single domain when addressing TD in CSE. It also shows that there are still open issues to be discussed in widely used types of systems. As an instance, S16 explores a prediction model in TD management in information systems and document management solutions and highlight that the main lessons learned were regarding data quality and evaluation, identification of key drivers of TD and credibility of prediction model for TD. Just as S16, when addressing TD in CSE in these types of systems or domains, some particularities could be found and used as a foundation for the evolution of the field.

4.1. Future perspectives

Considering the studies found in this SMS, it can be observed there are still diverse open issues to be addressed by future research and advance the state of the art in TD in CSE activities. Some of the main open issues are:

- Focus on CSE activities: Although several studies have addressed TD in CSE activities, some activities are still open for discovery and discussion of how TD is characterized and managed. These activities are CI, continuous delivery, CD, continuous security, and continuous monitoring. For future work, studies could specifically focus on these activities and verify which approaches or techniques are feasible for managing TD;
- TD management in the CSE as a whole: There is no study analyzing or evaluating TD management approaches or techniques destined for CSE as a whole or investigating its particularities. Hence, future works could present unified approaches, models, or techniques to manage TD considering all CSE activities, as well as applying them in practice. Besides this, we foresee that machine learning algorithms and supporting tools could be proposed to help uncover and manage TD in CSE activities; and
- TD in domains that adopt CSE: Some domains have usually applied CSE activities, e.g., Industry 4.0 and information systems, but few studies have addressed TD in systems of these domains. Hence, it is relevant to investigate

how TD could occur in these systems and how they could be managed in these domains' projects.

4.2. Threats to validity

In this section, we present and discuss the threats that could have potentially affected the validity of our SMS. There is also a discussion of the measures we took to mitigate these threats, considering the guidelines proposed by [Ampatzoglou et al. 2019], that are classified as study selection validity, data validity, and research validity, as presented below.

- **Study selection.** One of the most relevant threats to study selection is the selection of non-optimal digital libraries. In this study, we decided to use Scopus as a single database because it is highly relevant for Software Engineering research and includes a great number of publishers. Another threat is the ineffective search string and, to mitigate this threat, the search string was crafted and evaluated with experts in secondary studies and software engineering, and it was also piloted in the Scopus database. Another threat is the possibility that some relevant studies were omitted or some irrelevant ones were included and this threat was mitigated by having an SMS protocol with well-defined inclusion and exclusion criteria.
- **Data validity** Unverified data extraction and author bias are some of the most critical threats to the validity of the data, as they could lead to unreliable results and study conclusions. To mitigate these threats, we discussed all data items that could be extracted from the studies considering their meaning and relevance. Also, in the extraction phase, the data that the the first author extracted was revised by the second author.
- **Research validity** Replicability is one of the main concerns regarding our study, since analysing and synthesizing qualitative data was required to answer the proposed research question. To address this, we defined a detailed protocol based on the literature guidelines for SMS [Kitchenham et al. 2015, Petersen et al. 2008].

5. Conclusions

When using Agile processes, large software companies are making constant attempts to deliver software to the customer considering its value and its impact to the market. Agile and CSE have proved to be profitable to the industry, but these initiatives should not lead to the occurrence of bad decisions in development that have negative consequences in a long-term, named TD.

This study presents the state-of-the-art of how TD has been addressed in CSE activities. For this, we conducted an SMS and evaluated 41 studies. The findings indicate that this field of study is considerably new and has emerged in 2013, that TD has been addressed in CSE mainly with an industry interest or involvement and that, although some CSE activities have studies addressing TD, critical ones (e.g., CI, CD, continuous monitoring) are not addressed and, surprinsingly, no study address TD in CSE a holistic way. The future perspectives for the field are exciting, so studies could be conducted analyzing TD on not yet addressed CSE activities, evaluating approaches or techniques for TD management and using automation and algorithms to help manage TD.

Acknowledgment

This study was financed in part by National Council for Scientific and Technological (CNPq) (Grant No.: 313245/2021-5), São Paulo Research Foundation (FAPESP) (Grant No.: 2023/00488-5), and Coordination for the Improvement of Higher Education Personnel (Capes).

References

Alves, N. S., Mendes, T. S., de Mendonça, M. G., Spínola, R. O., Shull, F., and Seaman, C. (2016). Identification and management of technical debt: A systematic mapping study. *Information and Software Technology*, 70:100–121.

Ampatzoglou, A., Bibi, S., Avgeriou, P., Verbeek, M., and Chatzigeorgiou, A. (2019). Identifying, categorizing and mitigating threats to validity in software engineering secondary studies. *Information and Software Technology*, 106:201–230.

Chen, L. (2015). Continuous delivery: Huge benefits, but challenges too. *IEEE Software*, 32(2):50–54.

Codabux, Z. and Williams, B. (2013). Managing technical debt: An industrial case study. In *4th International Workshop on Managing Technical Debt (MTD)*, page 8 – 15.

Dingsøyr, T., Nerur, S., Balijepally, V., and Moe, N. B. (2012). A decade of agile methodologies: Towards explaining agile software development. *Journal of Systems and Software*, 85(6):1213–1221.

Fitzgerald, B. and Stol, K.-J. (2017). Continuous software engineering: A roadmap and agenda. *Journal of Systems and Software*, 123:176–189.

Fontana, R. M., Wojciechowski, J., Montaño, R. R., Marczak, S., Reinehr, S., and Malucelli, A. (2022). A countrywide descriptive survey of agile software development in brazil. In Stray, V., Stol, K.-J., Paasivaara, M., and Kruchten, P., editors, *Agile Processes in Software Engineering and Extreme Programming*, pages 185–202, Cham. Springer International Publishing.

Kitchenham, B. A., Budgen, D., and Brereton, P. (2015). *Evidence-Based Software Engineering and Systematic Reviews*. Chapman & Hall/CRC.

Klotins, E. and Gorschek, T. (2022). Continuous software engineering in the wild. In Mendez, D., Wimmer, M., Winkler, D., Biffl, S., and Bergsmann, J., editors, *Software Quality: The Next Big Thing in Software Engineering and Quality*, pages 3–12, Cham. Springer International Publishing.

Kruchten, P., Nord, R. L., and Ozkaya, I. (2012). Technical debt: From metaphor to theory and practice. *IEEE Software*, 29(6):18–21.

Li, Z., Avgeriou, P., and Liang, P. (2015). A systematic mapping study on technical debt and its management. *Journal of Systems and Software*, 101:193–220.

Papatheocharous, E. and Andreou, A. (2013). Evidence of agile adoption in software organizations: An empirical survey. In *European Conference on Software Process Improvement (EuroSPI)*, volume 364, pages 237–246.

Petersen, K., Feldt, R., Mujtaba, S., and Mattsson, M. (2008). Systematic mapping studies in software engineering. In *12th International Conference on Evaluation and Assessment in Software Engineering (EASE)*, page 68–77.

Seaman, C., Guo, Y., Zazworka, N., Shull, F., Izurieta, C., Cai, Y., and Vetro, A. (2012). Using technical debt data in decision making: Potential decision approaches. In *3rd International Workshop on Managing Technical Debt (MTD)*, pages 45–48.

Singh, B. and Gautam, S. (2016). The impact of software development process on software quality: A review. In *8th International Conference on Computational Intelligence and Communication Networks (CICN)*, pages 666–672.

Vijayasarathy, L. and Turk, D. (2012). Drivers of agile software development use: Dialectic interplay between benefits and hindrances. *Information and Software Technology*, 54(2):137–148.

Wieringa, R., Maiden, N., Mead, N., and Rolland, C. (2006). Requirements engineering paper classification and evaluation criteria: a proposal and a discussion. *Requirements Engineering*, 11(1):102–107.

Wohlin, C. (2014). Guidelines for snowballing in systematic literature studies and a replication in software engineering. In *Proceedings of the 18th International Conference on Evaluation and Assessment in Software Engineering*, EASE '14, New York, NY, USA. Association for Computing Machinery.

Construindo Jogos Educacionais Através de Linha de Produto

Diego Castro[1,2]

[1] Programa de Engenharia de Sistemas e Computação
COPPE (Universidade Federal do Rio de Janeiro)
Rio de Janeiro – RJ – Brazil

[2]Centro Federal de Educação Tecnológica Celso Suckow da Fonseca (CEFET)
Campus Maria da Graça
Rio de Janeiro – RJ – Brazil

{diegocbcastro}@cos.ufrj.br

Resumo. *Numerosos estudos demonstram que os jogos possuem a capacidade de atrair a atenção dos alunos e são, portanto, utilizados para ensinar diversas disciplinas, sendo uma delas à Engenharia de Software (ES). O desenvolvimento de jogos é uma tarefa demorada que envolve vários colaboradores e estágios. Como resultado, um grande número de jogos educacionais são desenvolvidos a partir de jogos pré-existentes, o que é semelhante à abordagem oportunista de Reutilização de Software (RS). Além disso, existem diferentes tipos / versões de jogos, que em grande parte das vezes podem apresentar características semelhantes. A Linha de Produtos de Software (LPS) é uma área de pesquisa dentro da RS, que envolve uma metodologia projetada para consolidar sistemas que compartilham um conjunto comum de recursos para desenvolver softwares semelhantes. Portanto, o objetivo desta pesquisa é desenvolver uma LPS de jogos educacionais para agilizar o processo de desenvolvimento e expansão de jogos com foco em ES, disponibilizando a mesma para os docentes para que eles consigam gerar seus próprios jogos em um curto período de tempo e com mínimo esforço, podendo ainda expandir e reaproveitar jogos previamente criados por meio da LPS.*

1. Introdução

Vários estudos demonstraram que os jogos oferecem uma oportunidade significativa para melhorar o método de ensino passivo, que normalmente depende de apresentações de slides e aulas ministradas pelo professor, resultando na diminuição do envolvimento dos alunos na sala de aula [Steinkuehler e Squire 2024]. A maioria dos jogos possuem características visuais, interativas e práticas, que despertam o interesse do usuário e servem como fontes primárias de entretenimento e distração. Consequentemente, estes jogos apresentam uma oportunidade original e inovadora para reforçar o conhecimento dos alunos [Batista et al. 2022]. Devido a essas vantagens, é possível encontrar diversos jogos na literatura sendo utilizados para o ensino de diversas disciplinas, sendo a Engenharia de Software (ES) uma delas [Kosa et al. 2016].

Embora os jogos tenham o potencial de melhorar as práticas educacionais, o desenvolvimento de tais jogos é muitas vezes uma tarefa demorada e complicada, necessitando do envolvimento de numerosos especialistas e custando uma quantidade significativa de tempo e dinheiro [Bilińska-Reformat et al. 2020]. Como resultado da natureza demorada e financeiramente custosa deste procedimento, os desenvolvedores de jogos educativos frequentemente priorizam a adaptação de jogos pré-existentes ao invés do desenvolvimento de novos jogos [Abbott 2019]. Essa prática de criar um produto a partir de outro pré-existente é muito semelhante à abordagem de Reutilização de Software (RS) oportunista [Ncube et al. 2008], onde o objetivo é modificar um produto existente para gerar um novo, sem seguir necessariamente um processo claramente definido. Esta abordagem minimiza principalmente o período de desenvolvimento de software, pois utiliza o processo de modificação de soluções existentes ao invés de construir novas. Além disso, vários jogos embora sejam de tipos diferentes possuem diversas características semelhantes, o que reforça ainda mais o conceito de RS.

A Linha de Produtos de Software (LPS) é uma área de pesquisa proeminente dentro da RS, que consiste em um conjunto de sistemas de software que apresentam características comuns que podem ser customizadas. Essa customização ocorre por meio da manipulação de pontos de variação, que são pedaços do software que podem ser modificados. O principal objetivo da LPS é melhorar a produtividade, minimizar o tempo de desenvolvimento e possibilitar a expansão de softwares pré-produzidos [Krueger 1992].

Desde a concepção à implementação, desenvolver jogos educativos pode ser complicado, portanto um professor com tempo limitado não conseguiria criá-los para seus alunos. Scratch, eAdventure, Alice e Roblox Studio, são vários motores de jogos que estão disponíveis e já foram utilizados com sucesso para simplificar este processo. No entanto, mesmo com estas ferramentas e conceitos, desenvolver jogos educativos envolve bastante esforço e pode sobrecarregar um professor [González García et al. 2019].

Esta pesquisa de doutorado pretende, portanto, desenvolver uma solução que permita explorar os conceitos de LPS no desenvolvimento de videogames educativos. Ao contrário do método convencional, que pode levar dias ou até meses e requer um investimento financeiro significativo, esta proposta visa disponibilizar uma LPS para docentes que permitirá criar jogos num curto espaço de tempo e com custos reduzidos, possibilitando professores sem conhecimento nenhuma em programação consiga criar seus jogos por meio de modificações direto em pontos de variação da LPS. Embora o foco da linha seja o desenvolvimento de jogos para ES, a plataforma está sendo construída de forma genérica, podendo ser utilizada por professores de qualquer disciplina.

O restante deste artigo é apresentado da seguinte forma: a Seção 2 apresenta os objetivos que o trabalho pretende alcançar, a Seção 3 demonstra a metodologia de pesquisa que está sendo usada no trabalho, a Seção 4 detalha a proposta em construção e, por fim, a Seção 5 conclui com as considerações finais e limitações

2. Objetivos de pesquisa

Os educadores estão constantemente explorando novas abordagens pedagógicas que integrem o entretenimento à educação, a fim de melhorar o envolvimento e a motivação dos alunos [Børte et al. 2023, Munna e Kalam 2021]. Um dos principais métodos que vem sendo utilizado com esse propósito é o ensino ativo, que tem como objetivo incentivar os estudantes a aprenderem de forma autônoma, participativa e prática. Existem diversas abordagens para utilizar esse método, como, por exemplo, simulação, experimentação, aprendizagem baseada em problemas, projetos e jogos, sendo a criação deste último o foco desse trabalho, tendo como objetivo disponibilizar em um curto espaço de tempo e com custos reduzidos jogos em sala de aula, visando aumentar a motivação, engajamento e melhorar reforço do ensino [Børte et al. 2023, Diesel et al. 2017].

Como afirmado anteriormente, os jogos têm o potencial de proporcionar inúmeros benefícios para a educação. No entanto, o seu demorado processo de desenvolvimento representa um desafio à sua implementação generalizada nas salas de aula [Bellotti et al. 2013, González García et al. 2019]. Num esforço para mitigar este problema, numerosos educadores acabam por desenvolver os seus próprios jogos educativos inspirados em outros previamente construídos [Abbott 2019], se assemelhando ao processo de RS oportunista.

Nas revisões da literatura já realizadas [Castro e Werner 2021b, Castro e Werner 2023b], não foram encontradas ferramentas dedicadas à criação / expansão de jogos educacionais, ou seja, ferramentas que possibilitem a criação facilitada de jogos educacionais a partir de um previamente criado. Assim, esses jogos atualmente são criados de três formas [Hofman-Kohlmeyer 2019, Lee et al. 2020]: **(1)** Desenvolvendo o jogo do zero; **(2)** Usar kits de desenvolvimento de software (SDK) ou interfaces de usuário (UIs) fornecidos pelo desenvolvedor do jogo, o que só ocorre para grandes empresas e em pequena escala, ou; **(3)** Compreender o código-fonte e fazer as modificações necessárias, desde que o código fonte tenha sido disponibilizado, o que gera ainda um grande trabalho para o professor que precisa entender o código original para depois modificá-lo. Lembrando que esse trabalho se limita apenas a jogos digitais, ou seja, video games. Portanto, sempre que a palavra jogo for mencionada, ela está se referindo apenas a video games.

Tendo isso em mente, podemos concluir que o processo de desenvolvimento de jogos é caro e demorado, limitando muitos educadores a criar jogos para uso em suas aulas. Sendo este o problema que esta pesquisa visa explorar. Portanto, este trabalho tem como objetivo proporcionar economia de tempo e custos para o desenvolvimento de jogos educativos para ES, resultando em uma maior utilização de jogos em sala de aula adotando o conceito de LPS para conseguirmos criar os jogos em larga escala. Este objetivo geral pode ser decomposto em objetivos específicos: **[1]** Caracterizar o estado da arte sobre o uso de LPS para o desenvolvimento de jogos; **[2]** Desenhar o design da aplicação; **[3]** Implementar uma plataforma para desenvolvimento de jogos educativos por meio dos conceitos de LPS; **[4]** Realizar um estudo de avaliação da plataforma implementada.

3. Metodologia e Atividades

Esta pesquisa segue uma metodologia inspirada no modelo *Design Science Research* (DSR) [Peffers et al. 2007], seguindo três etapas básicas, sendo elas: conscientização, sugestão e solução. A Figura 1, apresenta um modelo em BPMN (*Business Process Model and Notation*) da metodologia utilizada. As cores verde, amarelo e branco demonstram respectivamente as atividades que já foram executadas, estão em andamento e que ainda não iniciaram. A seguir, cada uma das atividades são descritas com mais detalhes.

[1] Revisão da literatura preliminar: Etapa que realizou duas revisões. Ela procurou entender como estava o desenvolvimento de jogos pela comunidade e quais práticas de RS eram mais utilizadas para desenvolver jogos. Vale destacar

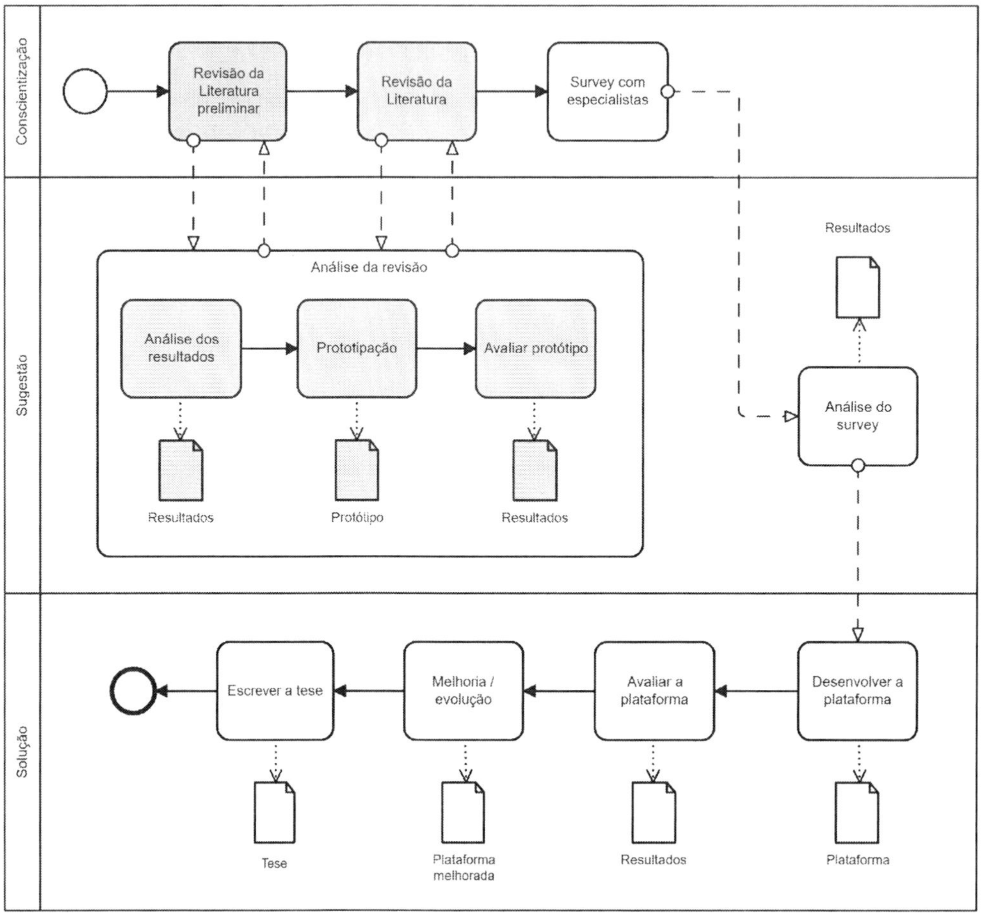

Figura 1. Metodologia desenhada em BPMN inspirada no modela de DSR [Peffers et al. 2007].

que todo o processo de revisão segui o protocolo definido por Kitchenham et al. [Kitchenham et al. 2009]. **[1.1] Multivocal sobre mods e jogos**: Essa revisão buscou demonstrar como a comunidade de jogos costumam desenvolver seus jogos [Castro e Werner 2023b]. Lembrando que mods é um termo utilizado para se referenciar a jogos que sofreram uma alteração de forma a fazê-lo operar de forma diferente da original [Bilińska-Reformat et al. 2020], ou seja, é uma forma de RS oportunista sendo realizada pela comunidade de jogos.**[1.2] Mapeamento sistemático sobre o desenvolvimento de jogos por meio de RS**: Essa revisão buscou demonstrar como a RS pode ajudar no desenvolvimento de jogos [Castro e Werner 2020]; Ajudou a buscar a forma de reuso mais adequada para criação de jogos educacionais em larga escala. **[2] Revisão da Literatura**: Como mencionado, a segunda revisão demonstrou que LPS seria a melhor abordagem para expandir / criar variantes a partir de jogos já existentes e, por isso uma terceira revisão está sendo realizada focando em desenvolvimento de jogos educacionais por meio de LPS; **[3] Análise da revisão**: Subprocesso que busca analisar as revisões executadas e propor ideias a partir dos insumos encontrados. **[3.1] Análise dos resultados**: Após o término das revisões, cada um dos insumos encontrados são analisados. **[3.2]Prototipação**: A partir dos insumos encontrados nas duas primeiras revisões, dois protótipos foram construídos para validar as informações encontradas [Castro e Werner 2021a]. **[3.2] Avaliar protótipos**: Após o desenvolvimento dos dois protótipos, eles foram validados por meio de estudos de usabilidade e experiência, por meio de modificações no questionário MEEGA [Petri et al. 2016]; **[4] Survey com especialistas**: Após a finalização da revisão mencionada no item 2, espera-se que seja executado um survey com especialistas para confirmar os insumos encontrados nas revisões e prototipações; **[5] Desenvolvimento da plataforma**: Após o término das etapas de conscientização e sugestão, espera-se ter insumos suficientes para a construção de uma plataforma para desenvolvimento de jogos por meio de LPS; **[6] Avaliar a plataforma**: Após o desenvolvimento da plataforma a mesma será avaliada em relação a usa usabilidade e experiência no desenvolvimento de jogos, comparando o tempo e o custo de desenvolvimento em relação as engines atuais [Castro e Werner 2023a]; **[7] Melhoria / evolução**: Após a avaliação da plataforma, será dedicado um tempo para o desenvolvimento das melhorias encontradas na avaliação; **[8] Escrita da tese**: Após todas as etapas anteriores será feita a escrita da tese e finalização desse trabalho.

4. Proposta

Existem uma grande variedade de tipos de jogos com diferentes características, sendo eles, jogos do tipo, *quiz*, *match*, *puzzle*, jogos de aventura, *storytelling*, entre outros. No entanto, ao pensarmos mais profundamente nas mecânicas de alguns jogos, é possível perceber semelhanças entre algumas delas, como, pontuação, barra de progresso, *feedback*, andar, pular, selecionar, entre outras. Com isso, é possível pensar em uma forma de agrupar algumas dessas características semelhantes e montar uma árvore de características com esses jogos, onde os mesmos vão se diferenciando por meio dos pontos de variação. No contexto de LPS, essa árvore de características pode ser ilustrada pelo modelo *Feature-Oriented Domain Analysis* (FODA) [Kang 2009], que é uma principais formas de ilustração de árvores de reutilização e visa agrupar as características de produtos semelhantes, demonstrar as características obrigatórias, excludentes e seus pontos de variação.

Para exemplificar a proposta iremos apresentar 3 tipos de jogos que são muito utilizados em contextos educacionais para demonstrar uma árvore de características criada com eles, sendo eles, jogos do tipo: *quiz*, *match* e *puzzle*. A seguir cada uma das características mais comuns desses jogos são brevemente descritas, lembrando que esses jogos podem possuir mais características, não limitando-se apenas às demonstradas nesse exemplo.

1. **Quiz**: Pontuação, barra de progresso, tempo, selecionar a resposta, turnos, feedback e progressão de informações;
2. **Match**: Arrastar e soltar, correlacionar, tempo, pontuação, turno, procurar a resposta certa, feedback e progressão de informações;
3. **Puzzle**: Arrastar e soltar, pontuação, tempo, turno, procurar a resposta certa, feedback e progressão de informações;

Como é possível notar, embora sejam jogos de tipos diferentes, muitas das características entre eles são semelhantes, podendo assim agrupar essas características e montar uma árvore com elas. A Figura 2 ilustra essa árvore do tipo FODA com algumas dessas características.

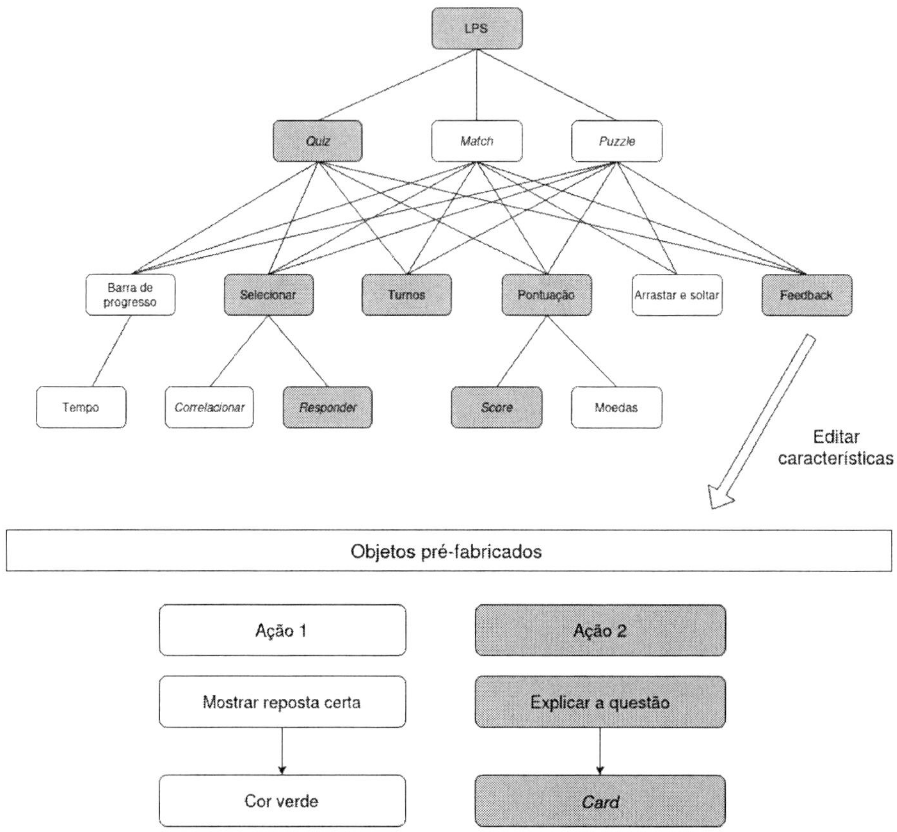

Figura 2. Árvore de características.

Na figura cada uma das características é representada por um nó (quadrado) e os pontos de variação sendo representados pelas arestas, ou seja, por exemplo, ao selecionar a característica de pontuação é possível escolher entre duas opções: *score* ou moedas, sendo este um ponto de variação. Também é possível perceber alguns nós em tons de cinza mais escuro, sendo esse um exemplo de um jogo do tipo *quiz* que poderia ser criado a partir da LPS, possuindo as características de responder as perguntas, feedback, turnos e ganhar pontuação ao longo do jogo.

Através da figura é evidente que vários jogos acabam compartilhando muitas mecânicas, com isso, o objetivo é desenvolver uma plataforma que disponibilize essa LPS para o professor, permitindo ao mesmo selecionar as características que deseja em seu jogo e então ter um jogo criado para sua turma, possibilitando ainda opções de evolução e edição da linha.

É possível ainda observar diversas características dos jogos que podem ser selecionadas, no entanto, para que seja possível criar diferentes jogos para o ensino de ES e deixar a plataforma mais genérica seria necessário permitir a edição e evolução dessas características. Uma linha de produto convencional é composta por componentes pré-fabricados que possam ser editados, com isso, existe a necessidade de permitir essa edição para o professor que esteja criando seu jogo a partir da plataforma. Portanto, todos os componentes da linha poderão ser editados diretamente pelo usuário permitindo que ele customize o que deseja.

Para ilustrar melhor, considere o exemplo do *quiz* já mencionado, no recurso de feedback, por exemplo, haverá uma ação indicando que o jogo deve exibir a resposta correta para o jogador que pode ser editada; no entanto, esse recurso de feedback foi modificado, adicionando uma nova ação para exibir uma explicação ao jogador caso ele erre a pergunta. A Figura 2, na parte de baixo, demonstra um exemplo da ideia de objetos pré-fabricados dentro da LPS. Nela, uma nova ação de explicar a questão está sendo adicionada.

5. Considerações Finais e Trabalhos Futuros

O objetivo deste artigo foi apresentar o andamento da proposta de uma tese sobre jogos educacionais e RS. Ao longo do trabalho foram descritas todas as etapas da metodologia utilizada para realização da pesquisa, como, revisões da literatura, prototipação, avaliação, desenvolvimento, melhorias, entre outras atividades. Algumas delas já foram totalmente ou parcialmente finalizadas e outras ainda precisam ser iniciadas.

Espera-se que ao final deste trabalho de pesquisa seja possível disponibilizar para os docentes uma LPS para o desenvolvimento, expansão e evolução de jogos educativos, possibilitando a criação de N jogos e N versões de jogos previamente criados em um curto espaço de tempo e com custos reduzidos. Espera-se que a ferramenta esteja pronto e avaliada até o final de dezembro, com previsão de defesa da tese de doutorado para março de 2025.

Referências

Abbott, D. (2019). Modding tabletop games for education. In *Games and Learning Alliance: 7th International Conference, GALA 2018, Palermo, Italy, December 5–7, 2018, Proceedings 7*, pages 318–329. Springer.

Batista, K., Costa, L. E. O., Oliveira, S. d., Bastos, L., Marins, P., Lima, L., Spiegel, C., Butcher, I., Vitiello, P., Palheiros, R., Quast, K., Jr., O. d. P., Xexéo, G., e Neri, F. (2022). *Jogos de Tabuleiro na Educação*. DEVIR, Brasil.

Bellotti, F., Kapralos, B., Lee, K., Moreno-Ger, P., e Berta, R. (2013). Assessment in and of serious games: An overview. *Advances in human-computer interaction*, 2013:1–1.

Bilińska-Reformat, K., Dewalska-Opitek, A., e Hofman-Kohlmeyer, M. (2020). To mod or not to mod—an empirical study on game modding as customer value co-creation. *Sustainability*, 12(21):9014.

Børte, K., Nesje, K., e Lillejord, S. (2023). Barriers to student active learning in higher education. *Teaching in Higher Education*, 28(3):597–615.

Castro, D. e Werner, C. (2020). Reusing and deriving games for teaching software reuse. *International Journal on Advances in Software*, pages 207–216.

Castro, D. e Werner, C. (2021a). Rebuilding games at runtime. In *2021 36th IEEE/ACM International Conference on Automated Software Engineering Workshops (ASEW)*, pages 73–77. IEEE.

Castro, D. e Werner, C. M. L. (2021b). A structured review of game coding through modeling. *Anais Estendidos do XX Simpósio Brasileiro de Jogos e Entretenimento Digital*, pages 309–313.

Castro, D. e Werner, C. M. L. (2023a). Exploring product line concepts in game building. *2023 IARIA Annual Congress on Frontiers in Science, Technology, Services, and Applications*, pages 150–152.

Castro, D. e Werner, C. M. L. (2023b). A multivocal review on derivation games. *2023 IARIA Annual Congress on Frontiers in Science, Technology, Services, and Applications*, pages 144–149.

Diesel, A., Santos Baldez, A. L., e Neumann Martins, S. (2017). Os princípios das metodologias ativas de ensino: uma abordagem teórica. *Revista Thema*, 14(1):268–288.

González García, C., Núñez-Valdez, E. R., Moreno-Ger, P., González Crespo, R., Pelayo G-Bustelo, B. C., e Cueva Lovelle, J. M. (2019). Agile development of multiplatform educational video games using a domain-specific language. *Universal Access in the Information Society*, 18(3):599–614.

Hofman-Kohlmeyer, M. M. (2019). Players as content creators. the benefits of game modding according to polish users. *International Scientific Journal News*, 2:8–26.

Kang, K. C. (2009). Foda: Twenty years of perspective on feature models. *the keynote of SPLC*.

Kitchenham, B., Brereton, O. P., Budgen, D., Turner, M., Bailey, J., e Linkman, S. (2009). Systematic literature reviews in software engineering–a systematic literature review. *Information and software technology*, 51(1):7–15.

Kosa, M., Yilmaz, M., O'Connor, R., e Clarke, P. (2016). Software engineering education and games: a systematic literature review. *Journal of Universal Computer Science*, 22(12):1558–1574.

Krueger, C. W. (1992). Software reuse. *ACM Computing Surveys (CSUR)*, 24(2):131–183.

Lee, D., Lin, D., Bezemer, C.-P., e Hassan, A. E. (2020). Building the perfect game–an empirical study of game modifications. *Empirical Software Engineering*, pages 1–34.

Munna, A. S. e Kalam, M. A. (2021). Teaching and learning process to enhance teaching effectiveness: a literature review. *International Journal of Humanities and Innovation (IJHI)*, 4(1):1–4.

Ncube, C., Oberndorf, P., e Kark, A. W. (2008). Opportunistic software systems development: making systems from what's available. *IEEE Software*, 25(6):38–41.

Peffers, K., Tuunanen, T., Rothenberger, M., e Chatterjee, S. (2007). A design science research methodology for information systems research. *Journal of Management Information Systems*, 24:45–77.

Petri, G., von Wangenheim, C. G., e Borgatto, A. F. (2016). Meega+: an evolution of a model for the evaluation of educational games. *INCoD/GQS*, 3:1–40.

Steinkuehler, C. e Squire, K. (2024). Gaming in educational contexts. In *Handbook of educational psychology*, pages 674–695. Routledge.

Creación de un Framework que nos Ayude a Seleccionar el Equipo Adecuado para Proyectos Remotos

Julio Suárez Albanchez [0000-0003-2360-0220],

Grupo Alarcos, Universidad de Castilla-La Mancha, Paseo de la Universidad 4, Ciudad Real{Julio.suarez@alu.uclm.es}

Abstract. El objetivo principal de este trabajo es crear un Framework que ayude a especificar las características de un proyecto remoto y ayude en la selección de los equipos de trabajo más apropiados teniendo en cuenta las características de los miembros del equipo. Este Framework, además, será capaz de predecir cuáles serán los principales desafíos que va a experimentar el equipo de trabajo en función de las características del proyecto.

Keywords: Trabajo remoto, GSD, Motivación, Estrés, Rendimiento.

1 Introducción

El factor humano tiene una gran influencia en los proyectos de desarrollo de software. En este sentido buena parte de la investigación ha sido orientada a los aspectos metodológicos y tecnológicos que pueden dar soporte a las personas que trabajan en estos proyectos, siendo también clave abordar otros factores personales y de bienestar que también pueden ser fundamentales, dentro de los cuales el estrés y la motivación son dos factores de especial interés. El estrés es un fenómeno que varía mucho entre diferentes personas y depende de diferentes aspectos como la vulnerabilidad individual, la resiliencia o el trabajo a realizar (Fink, 2016). Por su parte, la motivación se considera cada vez más uno de los principales problemas de la Ingeniería del Software, por lo que diferentes autores han analizado su impacto en un entorno de trabajo global, como (Noll et at., 2017). Después de la pandemia existe una clara tendencia hacia el desarrollo de software de forma remota (Manjavacas et al., 2020; Akbar et al.,2020), de hecho, han aparecido los términos WFH (de las siglas en inglés Work From Home), o WFA de ("Work From Anywhere"), teletrabajo e incluso de trabajo híbrido (Šmite et al. 2023a).

Los retos planteados en el desarrollo global y remoto del software, y la creciente tendencia al teletrabajo, implican la necesidad de analizar de forma completa y profunda los factores que afectan al estrés, motivación y rendimiento con el fin de mejorar la sostenibilidad humana en las empresas de software. Además, mejorando la calidad del proceso se suele mejorar la calidad del producto, en este caso el software.

2 Preguntas y objetivos de la investigación

Con el fin de conocer el estado del arte se realizó un mapeo de la literatura con estas 6 preguntas de investigación:

- RQ1: ¿Qué factores provocan estrés en los miembros de equipos de desarrollo de software distribuidos o globales?
- RQ2: ¿Qué factores afectan la motivación de los miembros de equipos de desarrollo de software distribuidos o globales?
- RQ3: ¿Qué factores afectan la productividad y el desempeño de los miembros de equipos de desarrollo de software distribuidos o globales?
- RQ4: ¿La literatura propone algún medio para reducir el estrés?
- RQ5: ¿La literatura propone algún medio para aumentar la motivación en el desarrollo de software distribuido o global?
- RQ6: ¿La literatura propone algún medio para aumentar la productividad y el rendimiento en el desarrollo de software distribuido o global?

Los resultados de este mapeo han sido publicados en Suárez y Vizcaíno (2023).

En base a este trabajo previo se han podido identificar los principales aspectos que afectan al rendimiento de los desarrolladores en entornos de trabajo remoto, así como los aspectos que influyen en sus niveles de estrés y motivación, dada la importancia que estas variables tienen en el rendimiento de los profesionales de desarrollo del software.

El objetivo de esta tesis trabajo es, teniendo en cuenta estos aspectos, definir e implementar un Framework que nos ayude a, especificar las características de un proyecto remoto indicando por ejemplo los nodos que tiene, en qué países, si hay diferencia horaria, etc. Una vez caracterizado el tipo de proyecto. Se indicarán qué desafíos puede plantear ese tipo de proyecto y qué perfil de empleado sería el más adecuado para el mismo. Como parte del trabajo de tesis se pretende indicar un algoritmo para seleccionar a los mejores candidatos de entre las persones disponibles.

3 Metodología de la investigación

La metodología utilizada en este trabajo es la de Design Science (ciencia del diseño), la cual plantea un enfoque de investigación que se utiliza principalmente en campos como la informática y la ingeniería para abordar problemas complejos y desarrollar soluciones innovadoras. Esta metodología se centra en la creación de artefactos o sistemas que resuelvan problemas prácticos y que puedan ser evaluados y mejorados a lo largo del tiempo.

Esta metodología se compone de las siguientes partes:

- Identificación del problema: El primer paso en la metodología de Design Science es identificar y definir claramente el problema que se desea abordar. En nuestro caso el problema es que las personas ya no se sentían contentas trabajando de forma remota y que la productividad decrecía. Šmite et al. (2023a) consideran el trabajo desde casa como un caso particular de trabajo distribuido, indicando además que aumenta la sensación de aislamiento, deteriora los lazos sociales y la cohesión del equipo y disminuye el interés por el trabajo colaborativo (Šmite et al.,2023b). Los factores que afectaron al bienestar y la productividad de los ingenieros del software durante la pandemia también fueron analizados por Russo et al., (2021), que explicaron, por ejemplo, cómo la ansiedad, las distracciones o la motivación laboral empezaron a cambiar en ese periodo de tiempo.

- Definición de objetivos: Una vez que se ha identificado el problema, se establecen objetivos específicos para la solución que se va a diseñar. En nuestro caso el objetivo es diseñar un Framework que ayude a crear equipos más productivos para trabajar de forma remota.
- Diseño y creación de artefactos: En nuestro caso el artefacto será el Framework que se pretende desarrollar en esta tesis.
- Evaluación y validación: Una vez que se haya creado el artefacto, se someterá a evaluación y validación. Nuestro artefacto será evaluado en un primer lugar con encuestas a profesionales para que nos den su opinión y propuestas de mejora. Una vez lograda una calidad aceptable por los expertos, se utilizará el framework en varios proyectos en la empresa donde el doctorando trabaja para comprobar si los equipos de trabajo se sentían cómodos y se comparará el rendimiento de los creados con la ayuda de este framework con el rendimiento medio del resto de equipos de trabajo.
- Iteración y mejora: Si la solución no cumple completamente con los objetivos o se identifican áreas de mejora, se realiza una iteración en el proceso de diseño para realizar ajustes y mejoras en el artefacto. Este ciclo de iteración puede repetirse varias veces hasta que se alcance una solución satisfactoria.
- Utilización práctica: Finalmente, la solución diseñada se pone en práctica en un entorno relevante para abordar el problema real para el cual fue creada. Se monitoriza su desempeño y se realiza un seguimiento para garantizar que continúe siendo efectiva a lo largo del tiempo.

Me gustaría aclarar que como método para estudiar el estado del arte se utilizó un mapeo sistemático de la literatura. Además, se realizó una encuesta entre profesionales en la que se preguntaba su opinión sobre cómo influyen distintos factores detectados en la revisión sistemática en el trabajo remoto, con el fin de comparar si los encuestados estaban de acuerdo con los resultados encontrados en la literatura y además se utilizó el modelo PLS-SEM para analizar el grado de influencia de cada factor.

4 Resultados obtenidos y próximos pasos

Hasta el momento hemos publicado un artículo JCR con los resultados del mapeo sistemático de la literatura (Suárez y Vizcaíno, 2023) y queremos preparar otro artículo donde se describan y analicen estadísticamente como diferentes aspectos (las habilidades y experiencias previas de los miembros del equipo de trabajo, la confianza y comunicación entre ellos y los problemas en la transferencia del conocimiento) afectan al estrés, motivación y rendimiento de los mismos, así como el impacto que la comunicación tiene sobre la confianza entre los miembros del equipo de trabajo y los problemas en la transferencia del conocimiento.

Con el fin de comprobar si los resultados encontrados en la literatura coinciden con la opinión de los ingenieros del software de las empresas se decidió realizar una encuesta de 74 preguntas, la cual fue distribuida entre profesionales del desarrollo del software de diferentes países durante marzo del 2023, recibiendo un total de 191 respuestas de desarrolladores en remoto y 101 que trabajaban en proyectos GSD. Las preguntas fueron obtenidas de trabajos previos y se adaptaron a las necesidades de nuestro trabajo. Con las primeras 7 preguntas extrajimos la información demográfica, así como si trabajaban o no en remoto o GSD. El resto de las preguntas fueron divididas en 10 constructos (Productividad, Estrés, Motivación, Autonomía del equipo, Confianza, Interacción social, Distancia lingüística, Geográfica, Temporal y Diferencias Culturales).

En base a esta información se han generado dos modelos estadísticos utilizando el método PLS-SEM con ayuda de la herramienta SmartPLS 4, el cual hace uso del modelado de ecuaciones estructurales. PLS-SEM ha experimentado un gran aumento en los últimos años, consolidándose en la investigación de la Ingeniería del Software (Roldan and Sanchez-Franco, 2012).

Uno de los modelos generados analiza el impacto que las habilidades y experiencias previas de los desarrolladores, la confianza en el equipo de trabajo, la comunicación y los problemas en la transferencia de conocimiento tienen sobre la motivación, estrés y productividad de los trabajadores en remoto. Este modelo adicionalmente evalúa el impacto que la comunicación tiene sobre la confianza de los desarrolladores y sobre los problemas en la transferencia del conocimiento.

El otro modelo analiza el impacto que la distancia lingüística, temporal y cultural tiene sobre el estrés, motivación y rendimiento de los trabajadores GSD.

Parte de este estudio se ha publicado en (Ebert et al., 2023) en el cual se analizan las causas de los problemas de rendimiento en los desarrolladores de software.

Los próximos pasos a seguir serán definir e implementar el Framework, la idea es que el jefe de proyecto pueda configurar las características del proyecto, por ejemplo, indicando el número de "sites" involucrados, de países, idiomas, distacias culturales, diferencias horarias etcs. Una vez definidas las características del proyecto el framework recomendará cómo proceder en dicho proyecto, qué desafíos se pueden plantear y cómo resolverlo. El framework también debería indicar qué pefil de empleados serían los más adecuados para ese proyecto. En el futuro se podría implementar un sistema recomendador que utilizando el framework ayude a los ingenieros a formar equipos de trabajos productivos para un determinado proyecto.

La primera etapa para la implementación del Framework será la configuración del proyecto, definiendo las características particulares del proyecto. Una vez definido el proyecto y en base a sus características se podrán predecir los problemas que podrían aparecer y las características personales deseables para los miembros del equipo.

En la segunda etapa determinaremos qué personas de entre las disponibles se adecuan más a las características del proyecto, para lo cual se hará uso de una serie de cuestionarios que nos ayuden a conocer las características de los desarrolladores. Una vez que tenemos los perfiles de las personas analizaríamos el grado de adecuación de las mismas al proyecto.

En una tercera etapa analizaríamos el grado de compatibilidad entre los integrantes del equipo, para lo cual tendremos también en cuenta las características personales de los mismos y su grado de afinidad.

5 Conclusiones

Conocer y entender los diferentes factores que pueden afectar el nivel de estrés, motivación y rendimiento de los desarrolladores de software es crucial, más aún en la actualidad que se trabaja de forma remota y/o global. En este artículo se ha presentado el trabajo en curso para caracterizar estos factores con el fin de diseñar un framework que ayude a los jefes de proyecto a conocer de antemano los principales desafíos a los que se pueden enfrentar según las características del proyecto, qué características deberían tener los empleados que vayan a trabajar en el mismo de forma remota y ayudarle a elegir a los más adecuados con el fin de que tengan el mínimo estrés pero sí la máxima motivación y rendimiento.

Referencias

1. Akbar, M. A., Khan, A. A., Khan, A. W., & Mahmood, S. (2020). Requirement change management challenges in GSD: An analytical hierarchy process approach. Journal of Software: Evolution and Process, 32(7), e2246.
2. Ebert, C., Vizcaíno, A., García, F. O., & Albanchez, J. S. (2023). Measure and Improve Software Productivity. IEEE Software, 41(1), 35-44.
3. Fink, G. (2016). Stress, definitions, mechanisms, and effects outlined: Lessons from anxiety. In Stress: Concepts, cognition, emotion, and behavior (pp. 3-11). Academic Press.
4. Manjavacas, A., Vizcaíno, A., Ruiz, F., & Piattini, M. (2020). Global software development governance: Challenges and solutions. Journal of Software: Evolution and Process, 32(10), e2266.
5. Moe, N. B. & Šmite, D. (2007), Understanding Lacking Trust in Global Software Teams: A Multi-case Study, in Product-Focused Software Process Improvement, Berlin, Heidelberg, pp. 20–34.
6. Noll, J., Razzak, M. A., & Beecham, S. (2017, June). Motivation and autonomy in global software development: an empirical study. In Proceedings of the 21st International Conference on Evaluation and Assessment in Software Engineering (pp. 394-399).
7. Roldán, J. L., & Sánchez-Franco, M. J. (2012). Variance-based structural equation modeling: Guidelines for using partial least squares in information systems research. In Research methodologies, innovations and philosophies in software systems engineering and information systems (pp. 193-221). IGI global.
8. Russo, D., Hanel, P. H., Altnickel, S., & van Berkel, N. (2021). Predictors of well-being and productivity among software professionals during the COVID-19 pandemic–a longitudinal study. Empirical Software Engineering, 26(4), 62.
9. Šmite, D., Moe, N. B., Klotins, E., &Gonzalez-Huerta, J. (2023a). From forced working-from-home to voluntary working-from-anywhere: two revolutions in telework. Journal of Systems and Software, 195, 111509.
10. Šmite, D., Moe, N. B., Hildrum, J., & Gonzalez-Huerta, J. (2023b). Work-from-home is here to stay: Call for flexibility in post-pandemic work policies.. Journal of Systems and Software, 195, 111552.
11. Suárez, J., & Vizcaíno, A. (2023). Stress, motivation, and performance in global software engineering. Journal of Software: Evolution and Process, e2600.

Método de gestión de requisitos para promover la sostenibilidad en DevOps: CRETS4DevOps

Rogelio Fernando Hernández Alarcón[1], Begoña Moros Valle[2], Joaquín Nicolás Ros[2]

[1]Facultad de Ingeniería – Universidad Autónoma de Guerrero – Chilpancingo, México

[2]Departamento de Informática y Sistemas – Universidad de Murcia – España

rogeliofh@uagro.mx[1], bmoros@um.es[2], jnr@um.es[2]

Resumen. *La adopción de prácticas ágiles en contextos DevOps impacta positivamente en el desarrollo de software, aunque existen preocupaciones respecto a la gestión de los requisitos y la durabilidad de los desarrollos en estos contextos. Las organizaciones software enfrentan el desafío de entregas rápidas, continuas, junto con necesidades de sostenibilidad a largo plazo. El Manifiesto de Karlskrona ha subrayado la necesidad de integrar la sostenibilidad en todas las etapas del desarrollo de software, pero se carece de una comprensión compartida de la sostenibilidad entre todos los actores involucrados en el desarrollo, y además no existen metodologías de Ingeniería de Requisitos (IR) que consideren los factores de sostenibilidad en un contexto de prácticas continuas. Por todo ello presentamos CRETS4DevOps (Continuous Requirements Engineering and Technical Sustainability for DevOps), un método que integra la gestión de la sostenibilidad técnica en la IR en el marco de DevOps. CRETS4DevOps combina prácticas tradicionales de IR con prácticas ágiles en el marco de la IR continua, apoyándose en la reutilización de requisitos para fomentar la sostenibilidad técnica.*

1. Introducción

La Ingeniería de Requisitos (IR) está en constante evolución y se enfrenta a desafíos entre los que destaca la sostenibilidad del software. Los ingenieros de requisitos tienen la tarea de analizar los impactos del software en todas las dimensiones de la sostenibilidad (social, medioambiental, económica, técnica y humana), incluyendo el diseño y las posibles consecuencias (Becker et al., 2015; Silveira et al., 2022). Surge así el concepto de requisitos de sostenibilidad, "requisitos que pueden utilizarse para especificar el comportamiento del sistema (por ejemplo, requisitos que reduzcan el consumo de energía de un sistema), así como para influir en el comportamiento de los usuarios" (Venters et al., 2017).

Mireles et al. (2017) muestran propuestas para considerar la sostenibilidad en el campo de la IR, pero los ingenieros de requisitos suelen carecer de los conocimientos, la experiencia y el apoyo metodológico necesarios para actuar como facilitadores de un debate sobre los efectos de la sostenibilidad, especialmente si tenemos en cuenta contextos DevOps: *¿Qué aspectos de la sostenibilidad puede soportar el software? ¿Cómo podemos priorizar los requisitos de sostenibilidad?* (Duboc et al., 2020).

Un desafío presente en la mayoría de los equipos de ingeniería de software es que carecen de expertos en sostenibilidad medioambiental, lo que hace difícil abordar la complejidad de los problemas de sostenibilidad en los sistemas software. En ocasiones se propone el uso de patrones de requisitos de sostenibilidad, que explican cuándo y cómo aplicar prácticas sostenibles en el desarrollo de software. Estos patrones recogen su relevancia, objetivos, ejemplos de implementación, debates y conexiones con otros patrones de requisitos de sostenibilidad (Roher & Richardson, 2013).

Bambazek et al. (2023) analizan las propuestas de integración de la sostenibilidad en la IR y determinan que una de las principales carencias es la ausencia de evaluación de cómo estas propuestas se pueden aplicar a los procesos de desarrollo ágiles. La carencia de prácticas sostenibles en proyectos ágiles motiva la necesidad de definir un framework de Scrum consciente de la sostenibilidad, que integre los aspectos de la sostenibilidad en las tareas de IR para favorecer la sostenibilidad del software desarrollado. La elección de Scrum está justificada al ser el framework de desarrollo ágil predominante en la actualidad (Garscha, 2021).

Dado que las prácticas ágiles son la base sobre la que se construye DevOps (Ebert et al., 2016) podríamos inferir que las carencias detectadas para las metodologías ágiles son trasladables al contexto de DevOps. Así, un estudio previo (Hernández et al., 2023) reveló que en DevOps no existe una metodología específica que permita llevar el seguimiento de todos los aspectos relacionados con los requisitos. Además, en este estudio también se concluye que es necesario un método específico de IR para DevOps que apoye la entrega continua y sostenible de requisitos, la reutilización de requisitos, la gestión adecuada de requisitos de calidad y la provisión de documentación de requisitos clara y actualizada en el marco de un proceso de IR continuo integrado en la cadena de herramientas DevOps. La trazabilidad de los requisitos es necesaria para mejorar la comunicación de los requisitos e implicar no sólo a los equipos de desarrollo, sino también a los equipos de operaciones y negocio, lo cual permitiría mejorar la obtención de requisitos de las áreas de negocio y operaciones.

En este estudio se propone CRETS4DevOps (*Continuous Requirements Engineering and Technical Sustainability for DevOps*), un método diseñado para gestionar los requisitos que promuevan la dimensión técnica de la sostenibilidad en entornos DevOps. CRETS4DevOps propone combinar las prácticas de IR tradicionales y las ágiles para paliar: (1) el problema de requisitos no explícitos en las especificaciones, al confiar las compañías en la comunicación directa entre los interesados (*stakeholders*) en lugar de apoyarse en la documentación (Moreira & Schneider, 2022); y (2) las limitaciones de las historias de usuario para la especificación de requisitos (Kasauli et al., 2021). CRETS4DevOps promueve la retroalimentación e integración continua de requisitos, otorgando a los interesados la capacidad de analizar y evaluar el progreso del proyecto en las diferentes etapas de su desarrollo, alineado a los requisitos.

2. Contexto de CRETS4DevOps

2.1 Ingeniería de requisitos continua y DevOps

Es importante que los métodos de IR consideren los procesos del negocio, faciliten la comunicación entre diferentes roles y promuevan la reutilización de requisitos en procesos continuos (Hernández et al., 2023). Son necesarios procesos continuos de planificación, construcción, operación, despliegue y evaluación para desarrollar productos que cumplan con las necesidades y expectativas de los clientes, faciliten la toma de decisiones y permitan identificar oportunidades de negocio (Barcellos, 2020; Silveira et al., 2022).

La entrega continua es vital en ingeniería de software, y un factor a tener en cuenta al adoptar la entrega continua es que exista un canal de comunicación entre los equipos, de modo que no exista desalineación entre departamentos e inflexibilidad en la comunicación, que puede afectar al éxito de las prácticas DevOps (Azad, 2022).

En el proceso de planificación continua se deben integrar múltiples fuentes de información, como los comentarios de los clientes y datos del mercado. Una parte crucial de este proceso es la retroalimentación continua, que incorpora las opiniones de los clientes en la planificación futura del producto. Para monitorear este proceso, se sugiere utilizar: (1) métricas como el tiempo de desarrollo; (2) tamaño del producto en desarrollo; (3) tiempo medio de recuperación en caso de fallo; y (4) rendimiento del producto desarrollado (Klotins et al., 2022). La implementación de *Quality FeedBack Loop* (QFL) ayuda a que los equipos combinen herramientas de análisis de datos con la planificación del proyecto, para permitir a los gerentes supervisar el proceso completo y tomar decisiones informadas (Lopez et al., 2021).

La integración continua es el proceso que busca eliminar brechas entre el desarrollo y la entrega continua. Además, es necesario ampliar la visión de los requisitos a otros niveles, como el negocio. En esta línea BizDevOps indica que la continuidad debe existir no sólo en el proceso de software, sino también entre el software y los procesos estratégicos de la organización (Barcellos, 2020; Klotins et al., 2022). El analista de negocio incluye entre sus responsabilidades la comunicación continua (Forbrig, 2018).

Ya existen propuestas de flujo constante de gestión de requisitos, como la de Michailidis et al. (2021), que utilizan herramientas específicas para fomentar la colaboración y la creación de documentación de requisitos que permiten su reutilización, mejora y la comunicación continua dentro de la organización. Este método de gestión de requisitos permite la priorización, seguimiento y renegociación de requisitos, siendo crucial para adaptarse a los rápidos cambios en los entornos del proyecto. El resultado de esta propuesta es ayudar a las organizaciones a conocer la estructura del proceso de transformación digital desde el principio y tener una visión global de los pasos que hay que dar. Además, el enfoque adopta una perspectiva de continuidad y apertura al cambio.

2.2 Ingeniería de Requisitos y sostenibilidad

La sostenibilidad es la capacidad de perdurar, por lo que la sostenibilidad de un sistema describe qué continuará existiendo y funcionando, incluso cuando cambian las circunstancias. La sostenibilidad normalmente se compara con aspectos ambientales, pero cada vez es más claro que requiere la consideración simultánea de los recursos ambientales, el bienestar social e individual, la estabilidad económica y la durabilidad a largo plazo de la infraestructura técnica (Becker et al., 2016). Al considerar la sostenibilidad se tiene que pensar en las siguientes preguntas: *¿Qué se debe sostener? ¿Para quién? ¿Por cuánto tiempo? ¿A qué costo?* (Venters et al., 2017).

La IR debe tener un papel importante para promover la sostenibilidad. Sin embargo, existe una falta de directrices concretas que ofrezcan una descomposición tangible de la sostenibilidad. Actualmente no existe un soporte específico para analizar, diseñar, medir, manejar y respaldar de manera efectiva los requisitos de sostenibilidad (Saputri & Lee, 2020). Para fomentar un cambio en las prácticas de diseño sostenible en IR es importante transmitir a los interesados la importancia de la sostenibilidad y su influencia en el sistema en desarrollo, así como identificar y evaluar los desafíos actuales en el software, con el objetivo de definir estrategias que permitan abordar la sostenibilidad a medio y largo plazo (Chitchyan et al., 2016; Karita et al., 2022; Silveira et al., 2022).

Existen estudios que muestran desafíos en la sostenibilidad (Mireles et al., 2017) que se centran en cómo el software puede impulsar el desarrollo sostenible (efectos de segundo orden) y en definir requisitos al inicio del desarrollo del software. Sin embargo, hay una falta de investigación en la validación de estos requisitos. En consecuencia, se tiene la necesidad de que los métodos de IR contemplen la sostenibilidad y proporcionen una estructura metodológica para formular requisitos de software basados en metas sostenibles. Se debe considerar la sostenibilidad desde múltiples perspectivas, asegurando que los sistemas no solo sean eficientes y amables con el medio ambiente, sino también duraderos para evolucionar de acuerdo con las necesidades futuras (Christoph, 2014).

Dentro de la sostenibilidad técnica, uno de los desafíos es la elicitación continua de requisitos, para mantener alineados los requisitos cambiantes de los usuarios. Así mismo, existe la preocupación de que los enfoques de IR actuales no abordan explícitamente la sostenibilidad en la evolución de los sistemas (Seyff et al., 2018). Requisitos de calidad que influyen en la sostenibilidad técnica son la continuidad, durabilidad, seguridad, usabilidad, eficiencia energética, escalabilidad, mantenibilidad, buenas prácticas en la evolución del sistema, optimización y uso de código abierto (Karita et al., 2022). En esta línea, Moreira et al. (2023) definen un catálogo de requisitos reutilizables de sostenibilidad técnica y social, que se ha representado utilizando modelos iStar; los aspectos relacionados con la sostenibilidad técnica que se proponen están alineados con el modelo de calidad del estándar ISO/IEC 25010:2011.

3. CREST4DevOps

De acuerdo con Karita et al. (2022), para alcanzar los objetivos de desarrollo sostenible, en la IR se deben incorporar actividades que permitan: (1) analizar el contexto de sostenibilidad en proyectos de software; (2) identificar a los interesados relacionados con la sostenibilidad, que se consideran "expertos en sostenibilidad" y se encargan de documentar los efectos del desarrollo del producto en las dimensiones de la sostenibilidad; y (3) conseguir los objetivos de sostenibilidad. Por un lado, modelar los objetivos de sostenibilidad proporciona una visión clara del sistema y permite verificar si se implementa según lo planeado; por otro lado, se puede incluir una sección dedicada a la sostenibilidad dentro del documento de especificación de requisitos del software. Todo esto permitirá que los requisitos contribuyan a los objetivos de sostenibilidad, ofreciendo un marco de referencia durante todo el proyecto y asegurando que la sostenibilidad permanezca como una prioridad central en todo el ciclo de vida del software.

CRETS4DevOps es un método que se propone para una gestión de requisitos continua en DevOps que fomente la sostenibilidad. Las actividades de CRETS4DevOps se representan en un infinito, como se muestra en la Figura 1, siguiendo la analogía de la filosofía de DevOps, poniendo de relieve el enfoque de continuidad. En esta propuesta juega un papel importante la reutilización de requisitos, en concreto los requisitos de sostenibilidad de la dimensión técnica. El soporte a la reutilización se propone mediante el uso de catálogos de requisitos reutilizables de sostenibilidad que preserven el conocimiento de los expertos en este campo.

Para identificar los requisitos de sostenibilidad son necesarios artefactos que ayuden a determinar el impacto de la sostenibilidad (Penzenstadler & Femmer, 2013).

Dado que los requisitos se suelen documentar en lenguaje natural en la industria (Franch et al., 2023), en esta propuesta preferimos esta aproximación en lugar de otras basadas en un lenguaje de dominio, ontologías o modelos iStar. En particular, en los catálogos se usará una especificación basada en el formato habitual de las historias de usuario.

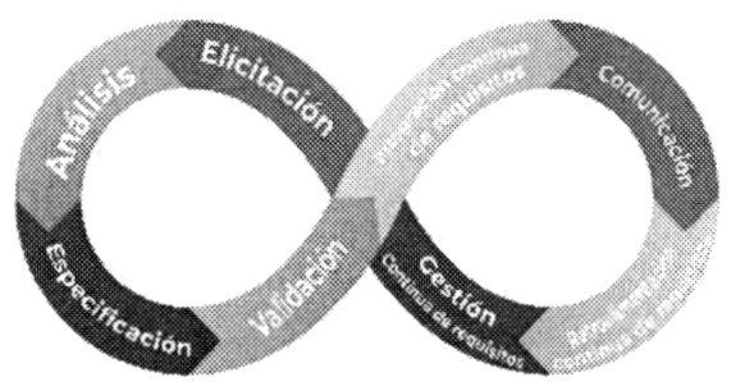

Figura 1 Actividades CREST4DevOps

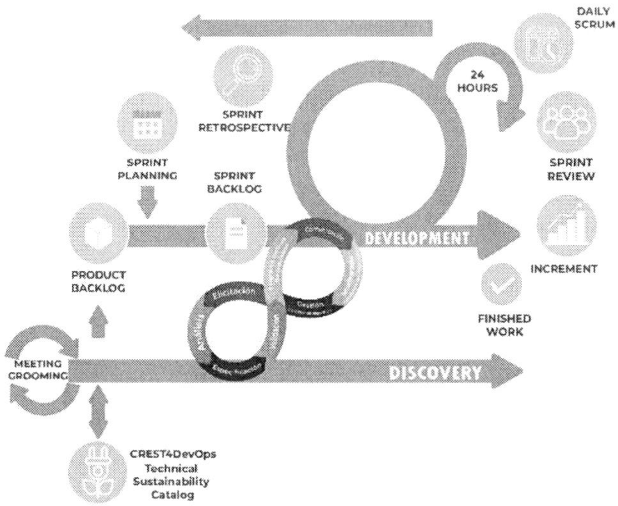

Figura 2 Integración de CREST4DevOps en Scrum

Siguiendo las recomendaciones de Karita et al. (2022), en CRETS4DevOps se incorpora el rol de *experto en sostenibilidad,* que será responsable de: (1) gestionar y mantener un catálogo de requisitos reutilizables de sostenibilidad; (2) ayudar a la definición de los objetivos de sostenibilidad del proyecto actual; y (3) alinear los requisitos de sostenibilidad con la legislación o estándares aplicables. Por otro lado, también se propone el rol de *analista del negocio*, integrando de este modo el enfoque BizDevOps (Forbrig, 2018) en la propuesta. Este rol será el responsable de mantener la visión global del proyecto y armonizar las necesidades de todos los interesados. Por último, el rol del *ingeniero de requisitos* será el responsable de la integración y entrega continua de requisitos a lo largo del proceso de desarrollo.

CRETS4DevOps incorpora las actividades típicas de la IR (SWEBOK 2022): *elicitación*, *análisis*, *especificación*, y *validación* de requisitos, considerando la sostenibilidad desde el principio, bien reutilizando los requisitos de sostenibilidad incluidos en el catálogo o bien definiendo requisitos nuevos con la ayuda del experto en sostenibilidad. Además, en la actividad de *integración continua de requisitos*, el experto en sostenibilidad, el analista del negocio y el ingeniero de requisitos colaboran conjuntamente para actualizar y validar de forma continua los requisitos del proyecto, incluyendo los requisitos de sostenibilidad, asegurando su integración continua en el desarrollo. La actividad de *comunicación continua* con los interesados del proyecto garantiza una comprensión común de los requisitos, lo cual permite un trabajo colaborativo entre los diferentes roles. La actividad de *retroalimentación continua* de requisitos implica recopilar comentarios, opiniones y sugerencias de los interesados, con el objeto de mejorar y refinar tanto los requisitos del proyecto como los requisitos reutilizables contenidos en el catálogo. Estas propuestas de cambio serán integradas durante la actividad de *gestión continua de requisitos*, encargada de controlar y administrar los cambios en los requisitos garantizando su alineación con los objetivos del proyecto incluyendo los objetivos de sostenibilidad establecidos.

En la Figura 2 se representa la integración de CRETS4DevOps en Scrum. Se puede observar cómo el catálogo de requisitos reutilizables interviene en la línea de Descubrimiento (*Discovery track*) tanto para extraer requisitos de sostenibilidad que sean aplicables en el proyecto actual como para modificar y actualizar el contenido del catálogo. El infinito se representa abarcando las líneas de Descubrimiento y Desarrollo para significar que habrá una etapa durante el Descubrimiento, en la que se llevará a cabo la elicitación de requisitos que poblará el *Product Backlog*, pero que, durante el Desarrollo, de forma continua, se podrán definir nuevos requisitos o modificar los existentes, que se tendrán que integrar de forma continua en la especificación de requisitos actual. El ingeniero de requisitos será el encargado de supervisar y garantizar la integración continua de los requisitos a lo largo del proceso de desarrollo.

4. Conclusiones y trabajo a futuro

La integración de la sostenibilidad en IR con procesos de desarrollo ágil, en concreto en DevOps, es un problema que está todavía abierto. Para contribuir a cubrir este vacío, en este trabajo se propone CRETS4DevOps, un método para la gestión de requisitos continua enfocado a promover la dimensión técnica de la sostenibilidad en entornos DevOps. Los elementos que constituyen CRETS4DevOps se pueden integrar en diferentes métodos de desarrollo ágil, como por ejemplo Scrum. El uso de catálogos de requisitos reutilizables de sostenibilidad permite cubrir la ausencia de expertos en sostenibilidad en los equipos de desarrollo. La integración continua de requisitos a lo largo del proceso, asistida por el ingeniero de requisitos, permite mantener en todo momento la visión global del sistema que se está desarrollando, manteniendo la documentación clara y actualizada. No obstante, es necesaria la validación de la propuesta en un entorno real para potenciar su aplicación. Para ello, estamos trabajando en el desarrollo de una herramienta de soporte integrada en Azure DevOps que favorezca la integración continua de requisitos y la comunicación entre los interesados. Una vez desarrollada se intentaría implantar en un proyecto en la industria o, en su defecto, se evaluaría mediante una encuesta a expertos en DevOps.

Agradecimientos

Esta investigación es parte del proyecto OASSIS-UMU (PID2021-122554OB-C32) y la Red de Excelencia en Calidad del Software y Sostenibilidad (RED2022-134656-T), financiados por el Ministerio de Ciencia e Innovación y el Fondo de Desarrollo Regional Europeo.

Referencias

Azad, N. (2022). Understanding DevOps critical success factors and organizational practices. *Proc. 5th Int. Workshop Softw.-Intens. Bus.: Sustain. Softw. Bus., IWSiB 2022*, 83–90. https://doi.org/10.1145/3524614.3528627

Bambazek, P., Groher, I., & Seyff, N. (2023). Requirements engineering for sustainable software systems: a systematic mapping study. *Requirements Engineering*, *28*(3), 481–505. https://doi.org/10.1007/S00766-023-00402-1/

Barcellos, M. P. (2020). Towards a Framework for Continuous Software Engineering. *ACM Int. Conf. Proc. Ser.*, 626–631. https://doi.org/10.1145/3422392.3422469

Becker, C., Betz, S., Chitchyan, R., & Duboc, L. (2016). Requirements: The key to sustainability. *IEEE Softw.*, *33*(1), 56–65. https://doi.org/10.1109/MS.2015.158

Becker, C., Chitchyan, R., Duboc, L., & Penzenstadler, B. (2015). Sustainability Design and Software: The Karlskrona Manifesto. *Proc. Int. Conf. Softw. Eng.*, *2*, 467–476. https://doi.org/10.1109/ICSE.2015.179

Chitchyan, R., Becker, C., Betz, S., & Duboc, L. (2016). Sustainability design in requirements engineering: State of practice. *Proc. Int. Conf. Softw. Eng.*, 533–542. https://doi.org/10.1145/2889160.2889217

Christoph, B. (2014). Sustainability and longevity: Two sides of the same quality? *CEUR Workshop Proc.*, *1216*, 1–6.

Duboc, L., Penzenstadler, B., Porras, J., & Akinli Kocak, S. (2020). Requirements engineering for sustainability: an awareness framework for designing software systems for a better tomorrow. *Req. Eng.*, *25*(4), 469–492. https://doi.org/10.1007/s00766-020-00336-y

Ebert, C., Gallardo, G., Hernantes, J., & Serrano, N. (2016). DevOps. *IEEE Software*, *33*(3), 94–100. https://doi.org/10.1109/MS.2016.68

Forbrig, P. (2018). BizDevOps and the role of S-BPM. *ACM Int. Conf. Proc. Ser.*, 1–8. https://doi.org/10.1145/3178248.3178250

Franch, X., Palomares, C., Quer, C., Chatzipetrou, P., & Gorschek, T. (2023). The state-of-practice in requirements specification: an extended interview study at 12 companies. *Requirements Engineering*, *28*(3), 377–409. https://doi.org/10.1007/s00766-023-00399-7

Garscha, P. (2021). From Sustainability in Requirements Engineering to a Sustainability-Aware Scrum Framework. *Proc. IEEE Int. Conf. Req. Eng.*, 462–467. https://doi.org/10.1109/RE51729.2021.00069

Hernández, R., Moros, B., & Nicolás, J. (2023). Requirements management in DevOps environments: a multivocal mapping study. *Requirements Engineering*. https://doi.org/10.1007/s00766-023-00396-w

IEEE_Computer_Society. (2022). *SWEBOK Guide Version 4.0*. https://sebokwiki.org/wiki/SWEBOK_Guide_Version_4.0

Karita, L., Mourão, B. C., & MacHado, I. (2022). Towards a common understanding of sustainable software development. *ACM Int. Conf. Proc. Ser.*, 269–278. https://doi.org/10.1145/3555228.3555236

Kasauli, R., Knauss, E., Horkoff, J., Liebel, G., & de Oliveira Neto, F. G. (2021). Requirements engineering challenges and practices in large-scale agile system development. *Journal of Systems and Software*, *172*. https://doi.org/10.1016/j.jss.2020.110851

Klotins, E., Gorschek, T., Sundelin, K., & Falk, E. (2022). Towards cost-benefit evaluation for continuous software engineering activities. *Empir. Softw. Eng.*, *27*(6). https://doi.org/10.1007/s10664-022-10191-w

Lopez, L., Bagnato, A., Ahberve, A., & Franch, X. (2021). QFL: Data-Driven Feedback Loop to Manage Quality in Agile Development. *Proc. Int. Conf. Softw. Eng.*, *2021-May*, 58–66. https://doi.org/10.1109/ICSE-SEIS52602.2021.00015

Michailidis, K., Strazdina, R., & Kirikova, M. (2021). Continuous requirements engineering for digital transformation. *CEUR Workshop Proc., 2991*, 26–40.

Mireles, G. A. G., Moraga, M. A., Garcia, F., & Piattini, M. (2017). A classification approach of sustainability aware requirements methods. *Iber. Conf. Inf. Syst. Technol., CISTI*. https://doi.org/10.23919/CISTI.2017.7975813

Moreira, A., & Schneider, K. (2022). Editorial. *Requirements Engineering, 27*(4), 403–404. https://doi.org/10.1007/s00766-022-00392-6

Penzenstadler, B., & Femmer, H. (2013). A Generic Model for Sustainability with Process- and Product-specific Instances. *First Intl. Workshop on Green In Software Engineering and Green By Software Engineering*. https://doi.org/https://doi.org/10.1145/2451605.2451609

Roher, K., & Richardson, D. (2013). Sustainability Requirement Patterns. *IEEE Third International Workshop on Requirements Patterns (RePa)*. https://doi.org/10.1109/RePa.2013.6602665

Saputri, T. R. D., & Lee, S. W. (2020). Addressing sustainability in the requirements engineering process: From elicitation to functional decomposition. *J. Softw.: Evol. Process, 32*(8), 1–25. https://doi.org/10.1002/smr.2254

Seyff, N., Betz, S., Groher, I., & Stade, M. (2018). Crowd-focused semi-automated requirements engineering for evolution towards sustainability. *Proc. 2018 IEEE 26th Int. Reqs. Eng. Conf., RE 2018*, 370–375. https://doi.org/10.1109/RE.2018.00-23

Silveira, C., Santos, V., Reis, L., & Mamede, H. (2022). CRESustain: Approach to Include Sustainability and Creativity in Requirements Engineering. *J. Eng. Res. Sci., 1*(8), 27–34. https://doi.org/10.55708/js0108004

Venters, C. C., Becker, C., Duboc, L., & Penzenstadler, B. (2017). Characterising sustainability requirements: A new species red herring or just an odd fish? *Proc. 2017 IEEE/ACM 39th Int. Conf. Softw. Eng.: SEIS Track, ICSE-SEIS 2017*, 3–12. https://doi.org/10.1109/ICSE-SEIS.2017.2

Um método para transformação de requisitos legais em padrões de requisitos de software: Um estudo com a LGPD

Cinara Gomes de Melo Carneiro[1], Taciana N. Kudo[1], Renato F. Bulcão Neto[1]

[1]Instituto de Informática – Universidade Federal de Goiás (UFG)
Goiânia – GO – Brazil

cinara_melo@hotmail.com, {taciana,rbulcao}@ufg.br

Abstract. *Recent studies show that requirements analysts struggle with interpreting the LGPD to obtain privacy requirements. In this paper, we propose a method to transform LGPD's legal requirements into a software requirement patterns catalogue. Reusing requirements as patterns can be a viable alternative to assist professionals since the LGPD's legal determinations are recurrent in different software projects. A preliminary evaluation of our patterns catalogue suggests the method's effectiveness.*

Resumo. *Estudos recentes mostram que analistas de requisitos têm dificuldade em interpretar a LGPD para obter requisitos de software de privacidade. Neste artigo, nós propomos um método para auxiliar na transformação de requisitos legais da LGPD em um catálogo de padrões de requisitos de software. Reusar requisitos na forma de padrões pode ser uma alternativa viável para auxiliar profissionais, uma vez que as determinações legais da LGPD são recorrentes em diferentes projetos de software. Uma avaliação preliminar do nosso catálogo de padrões aponta indícios da eficácia do método.*

1. Introdução

A Lei Geral de Proteção de Dados Pessoais (LGPD) estabelece regras para coleta, armazenamento, uso e compartilhamento de dados pessoais, e protege o direito dos titulares desses dados de acessá-los, corrigi-los e excluí-los [BRASIL 2018]. Uma das exigências dessa legislação é considerar a privacidade desde o início do desenvolvimento do produto, seguindo os princípios de *Privacy by Design* [Gürses et al. 2011]. Ou seja, é fundamental que a privacidade dos dados pessoais seja considerada desde a Engenharia de Requisitos.

Pesquisas como as de [Alves and Neves 2021] e [Canedo et al. 2021] mostram que a maioria dos profissionais da área de desenvolvimento de software não possui conhecimento sobre requisitos de privacidade, nem sobre a LGPD. Dessa forma, identifica-se a necessidade de apoiar esses profissionais na identificação dos requisitos de privacidade em conformidade com a LGPD e na adequação dos sistemas de informação.

Dada essa necessidade e a ubiquidade de privacidade em sistemas de software, um Padrão de Requisito de Software (PRS) torna-se uma opção viável. Um PRS é uma abstração que serve como modelo de reúso de requisitos para a elicitação, especificação e validação de requisitos em projetos futuros de aplicações com comportamentos semelhantes [Withall 2007]. O uso de PRS ajuda a mitigar problemas, como requisitos incorretos, omitidos, mal interpretados ou conflitantes, gerando economia de tempo e esforço e consistência ao longo do processo.

Apresentamos neste artigo um método de geração de um catálogo de padrões de requisitos de privacidade (CPRP). Na primeira etapa do método, fez-se uma análise sintática do conteúdo dos 65 artigos da LGPD, resultando em 90 requisitos funcionais e 10 não funcionais de privacidade. Em seguida, realizou-se uma análise semântica de cada RF e RNF [Kudo et al. 2023], conforme a gramática de um metamodelo chamado SoPaMM (*Software Pattern MetaModel*) [Kudo et al. 2019], transformando-os em padrões agrupados conforme os capítulos da LGPD.

Uma avaliação preliminar com um profissional com conhecimento de LGPD e Engenharia de Software considerou a completude e corretude do CPRP em relação aos requisitos legais da LGPD. Embora ainda não conclusivos, os resultados obtidos sugerem a eficácia do método. A partir da produção de um CPRP com o método proposto, espera-se auxiliar analistas na elicitação, especificação e validação de requisitos de privacidade por meio do reúso e instanciação dos padrões em projetos de software com características similares no tratamento de dados pessoais.

O artigo está assim organizado: a Seção 2 descreve fundamentação teórica; a Seção 3 analisa trabalhos relacionados; a Seção 4 apresenta o método proposto e a sua aplicação para geração do CPRP; e a Seção 5 discute considerações finais.

2. Fundamentação Teórica

Esta seção descreve o metamodelo SoPaMM como importante fundamento para compreensão desta pesquisa.

O metamodelo SoPaMM descreve como padrões de software devem ser criados, relacionados e classificados [Kudo et al. 2019]. O SoPaMM serve de referência para a construção de modelos terminais (ou padrões de software), e estes podem ser usados para gerar modelos de aplicação (ou especificações do mundo real). Os principais elementos que compõem a gramática do metamodelo SoPaMM são apresentados a seguir. Detalhes podem ser encontrados em [Kudo et al. 2023].

***Catalogue*:** permite reunir padrões de software de um domínio específico;

***SoftwarePatternBag* (SPB):** é utilizado para agrupar padrões de software por categoria;

***SoftwarePattern* (SP):** metaclasse para gerar classes de padrões de software, p.ex., *Functional Requirement Pattern* (FRP), *Non-Functional Requirement Pattern* (NFRP) e *Acceptance Test Pattern* (ATP). Todo padrão de software possui os seguintes atributos: autor, contexto, forças, problema, solução, fonte e versão.

***Functional Requirement Pattern* (FRP):** é uma composição de elementos *Feature*, descritos como histórias de usuário. Cada *Feature* é composta por elementos **Scenario**, descritos como cenários de teste de aceitação que, por sua vez, contêm elementos *Example*, com dados de exemplo para testes.

***Non-Functional Requirement Pattern* (NFRP):** é uma composição de propriedades do sistema de software (restrições comportamentais ou atributos de qualidade) descritas por atributos textuais (p.ex., nome e descrição).

***Acceptance Test Pattern* (ATP):** reúne soluções de teste para comportamentos recorrentes de diferentes cenários. No metamodelo SoPaMM, cada ATP deve ser associado a um FRP e contém um ou mais casos de teste, os quais usam dados de entrada e saída da classe *Example*, vinculada a um *Scenario* de um FRP em particular.

***CatalogueRelationship*, *SPBRelationship* e *SPRelationship*:** permitem, respectivamente, relacionar catálogos de padrões, agrupamentos e padrões de software.

3. Trabalhos Relacionados

Enquanto há pesquisas que dão suporte à elicitação, modelagem e especificação de requisitos de privacidade [Ferrão and Canedo 2022, Saraiva and Soares 2023, Mai et al. 2018, Neves Camêlo and Alves 2023, Peixoto et al. 2023], este trabalho propõe uma abordagem de reúso de requisitos de privacidade baseada nos preceitos legais da LGPD. Essa abordagem, materializada como um catálogo de padrões de requisitos, apoia não apenas a atividade de especificação, mas também de elicitação e validação de requisitos de privacidade.

A elicitação é beneficiada porque os analistas podem reusar as definições dos padrões de requisitos de privacidade do catálogo para seus projetos de software. A especificação também é apoiada porque o catálogo permite a instanciação dos padrões de requisitos sob uma notação de histórias de usuário. Por fim, a validação de requisitos de privacidade também é considerada nesta pesquisa, uma vez que cada padrão de requisito de privacidade constante no catálogo possui comportamento associado na forma de padrões de teste de aceitação, podendo assim beneficiar, não apenas analistas de requisitos, mas também analistas de testes.

Um destaque ao inventário de dados pessoais (IDP) do trabalho de Saraiva e Soares[Saraiva and Soares 2023], que foi elaborado conforme previsto no Art. 37 da LGPD, embora não seja explicitamente declarado nesse artigo. O Art. 37 foi também incluído no catálogo de padrões proposto como um padrão, chamado FRP_MANTER_REGISTRO_OPERAÇÕES. Portanto, a abordagem de Saraiva e Soares [Saraiva and Soares 2023] serve de complemento para esse padrão.

4. Método Proposto

Este trabalho propõe um método para a extração de padrões de requisitos de privacidade por meio da análise sintática e semântica dos artigos da LGPD.

4.1. Sobre a Análise Sintática

Entende-se por análise sintática o estudo da estrutura gramatical das frases e orações, envolvendo a identificação e análise das funções das palavras, a ordem das palavras na frase e as relações sintáticas entre elas. Nesta pesquisa, a análise sintática foi empregada para estruturar os requisitos extraídos da LGPD, de modo a garantir que os requisitos sejam compostos por sujeito, verbo de ação e objeto.

Com o objetivo de identificar direitos e deveres, a fim de extrair os requisitos legais, foram elaborados os seguintes procedimentos:

1. Localizar os atores em cada trecho da LGPD (artigo, artigo e inciso ou artigo e parágrafo). Um ator pode ser o **Titular dos Dados** (pessoa física a quem se referem os dados pessoais); o **Controlador** (pessoa física ou jurídica a quem competem as decisões referentes ao tratamento de dados pessoais); o **Operador** (pessoa física ou jurídica que realiza o tratamento de dados em nome do controlador); e o **Encarregado** (pessoa indicada pelo controlador e operador para intermediar comunicações entre controlador, titulares dos dados e a Autoridade Nacional de Proteção de Dados - ANPD). Esses atores desempenham papéis distintos na proteção de dados pessoais, conforme estabelecido pela LGPD. O ator que representa o sujeito da frase é utilizado inicialmente para construir o requisito.

2. Identificar o verbo de ação, que representa uma ação realizada por um ator.
3. Descobrir qual termo recebe a ação do verbo, ou seja, o objeto.
4. Classificar o requisito como funcional (RF) ou não-funcional (RNF).
5. As posições dos atores são invertidas e os passos anteriores são seguidos.

Segue um exemplo de aplicação da análise sintática do artigo 9º, inciso I da LGPD:

"Art. 9º - O titular tem direito ao acesso facilitado às informações sobre o tratamento de seus dados, que deverão ser disponibilizadas de forma clara, adequada e ostensiva acerca de, entre outras características previstas em regulamentação para o atendimento do princípio do livre acesso:

I - finalidade específica do tratamento;"

1. O ator do trecho tratado é o **Titular dos Dados**. Mas, ressalta-se que, implicitamente, o **Controlador** também é ator.
2. No trecho "o titular tem direito de acessar informações", o verbo de ação por parte do titular considerado foi **acessar**.
3. No trecho analisado, pode-se formular a seguinte pergunta: "O titular tem direito de acessar o quê?". Com base na análise do art. 9º inciso I, o objeto vinculado ao verbo de ação em questão é **a finalidade específica do tratamento**.
4. Após seguir os três passos anteriores, obteve-se o requisito de software: "**O titular acessa a finalidade específica do tratamento**". Neste passo, o requisito é classificado como RF.
5. Com a inversão da posição dos atores no RF em questão, o **Controlador** passou a ser o sujeito. Ou seja, além de "O titular acessa a finalidade específica do tratamento", foi também criado o requisito "O controlador disponibiliza a finalidade específica do tratamento", também classificado como RF.
   Além disso, há uma informação adicional no art. 9º, que exige a forma pela qual a finalidade deve ser disponibilizada — "*deverão ser disponibilizadas de forma clara, adequada e ostensiva*"— ou seja, esse texto representa uma locução adverbial. Assim sendo, uma locução adverbial pode sugerir a criação de um RNF, já que indica a maneira pela qual a ação deve ser realizada. Dessa maneira, foi possível identificar mais um requisito de software: "**O controlador deve disponibilizar a finalidade de forma clara, adequada e ostensiva**".
   Ao realizar essa inversão, foram executados os 4 primeiros passos (identificar ator, identificar verbo de ação, identificar objeto e classificar os requisitos).

Após seguir os cinco passos do método de análise sintática do artigo 9º, inciso I da LGPD, resultaram em três requisitos de software, a saber:

RF 01. O titular acessa a finalidade específica do tratamento;
RF 02. O controlador disponibiliza a finalidade específica do tratamento;
RNF 01. O controlador disponibiliza a finalidade de forma clara, adequada e ostensiva.

Ressalta-se que há requisitos que podem ser identificados como pré-requisitos de outros. Por exemplo, ao extrair o requisito "**O Controlador disponibiliza os direitos do titular**" referente ao art. 18, inciso VII da LGPD, é possível inferir o requisito "**O Controlador gerencia os direitos do titular**". Isto ocorre porque, para disponibilizar esses direitos, o referido ator necessita realizar atividades como cadastro, consulta, alteração e exclusão, a fim de garantir a integridade dos dados pessoais.

A seção do método que realiza a análise sintática dos 65 artigos da LGPD produziu 100 requisitos de software de privacidade, sendo destes 90 RF e 10 RNF. Estes requisitos foram analisados, como se descreve em seguida, para convertê-los em padrões de requisitos de privacidade conforme a gramática do metamodelo SoPaMM.

4.2. Sobre a Análise Semântica

A etapa de análise semântica do método considera o significado e o contexto dos termos dos requisitos de privacidade elicitados de modo a estruturá-los segundo a gramática do metamodelo SoPaMM. Para isso, aplica-se o método descrito por [Kudo et al. 2023] para construção de catálogos de padrões de software baseados no SoPaMM, assim como o CPRP mencionado neste trabalho. O método consiste em sete passos, a saber:

1. Se possível, reunir especificações de requisitos e de casos de teste e catálogos de padrões.
2. Estudar cada requisito e caso de teste e classificá-lo.
3. Se um padrão existente puder ser aplicado ao requisito ou caso de teste, registre esse fato e prossiga.
4. Se um padrão existente não se adequar perfeitamente, analisar se o requisito ou o caso de teste pode produzir um novo padrão novo e mais especializado. Caso afirmativo, classificá-lo como padrão de requisito funcional (FRP) ou não funcional (NFRP) ou padrão de teste de aceitação (ATP). Sugerir um nome a esse padrão e adicione-o à lista de padrões candidatos.
5. Depois de passar por todas as especificações, revise os padrões candidatos em busca de duplicatas ou sobreposições e resolva essas inconsistências.
6. Agrupar os padrões de software resultantes (SP) em *bags* de padrões de software (SPB). Observe que um SPB permite a composição de vários e diferentes tipos de SP, como FRP, NFRP e ATP.
7. Escrever cada padrão de software definido.

Considerando os passos supracitados, descreve-se, de uma forma geral, como cada passo desse método foi realizado. Em relação aos passos 1 a 4 do método de [Kudo et al. 2023], foram reunidos e analisados os 90 RF e 10 RNF resultantes da análise sintática dos trechos da LGPD. Dado que não foram encontrados padrões de requisitos de privacidade que pudessem ser reaproveitados para cada RF e RNF, todos os requisitos de privacidade extraídos da LGPD foram transformados em seus respectivos padrões (FRP e NFRP), uma vez que essa lei abrange um domínio transversal, no qual qualquer domínio de software que precise se adequar à legislação deve adotar esses requisitos. Observou-se também que para cada FRP poderia ser desenvolvido, no mínimo, um ATP, pois toda funcionalidade do software pode ser testada.

Cada padrão candidato foi nomeado e adicionado à lista de padrões candidatos. Após revisá-los, identificou-se não haver sobreposição ou duplicidade entre esses padrões (passo 5), de acordo com o conhecimento da pesquisadora sobre a legislação. Pelo passo 6, os padrões FRP, NFRP e ATP foram agrupados em *bags* que, neste caso, os padrões foram agrupados conforme o capítulo da LGPD a que se referem, p.ex. "**DO TRATAMENTO DE DADOS PESSOAIS**". Por fim, no passo 7, o catálogo contendo seus agrupamentos de padrões e a descrição de cada padrão foram especificados conforme a gramática do metamodelo SoPaMM descrita na Seção 2.

A partir dos requisitos **RF 01**, **RF 02** e **RNF 01** resultantes na análise do artigo 9º, inciso I, foram elaborados os seguintes padrões:

- **FRP_Acessar_Finalidade** e **ATP_Acessar_Finalidade**, para o **RF 01**, conforme ilustram as Figuras 1 e 2.
- **FRP_Disponibilizar_Finalidade** e **ATP_Disponibilizar_Finalidade**, relativo ao **RF 02**.
- **NFRP_Disponibilizar_Finalidade_De_Forma_Clara_Adequada_Ostensiva**, referente ao **RNF 01**, como mostra a Figura 3.

Dado que esses padrões foram extraídos de requisitos relativos ao art. 9°, que se encontra no capítulo II - DO TRATAMENTO DOS DADOS PESSOAIS, seção I - Dos Requisitos para o Tratamento dos Dados Pessoais, da LGPD, criou-se uma *bag* nomeada **SPB_Tratamento_de_Dados_Pessoais_REQUISITOS**, em que o nome da *bag* é a junção do nome do capítulo (Tratamento de dados Pessoais) com a sessão (Requisitos), em seguida os padrões foram agrupados nessa *bag*.

A Figura 1 mostra a estrutura de um FRP, utilizando como exemplo o padrão **FRP_Acessar Finalidade**. Para todo FRP identificado, são definidos os seus atributos (autor, contexto, forças, nome, problema, solução, fonte e versão – 1A), pelo menos um elemento *Feature* (1B), utilizando a sintaxe da história do usuário (AS, I CAN, SO THAT) e, para cada elemento *Feature*, um ou mais cenários (1C) na linguagem *Gherkin* (GIVEN, WHEN, THEN), com seus respectivos *Examples* (1D).

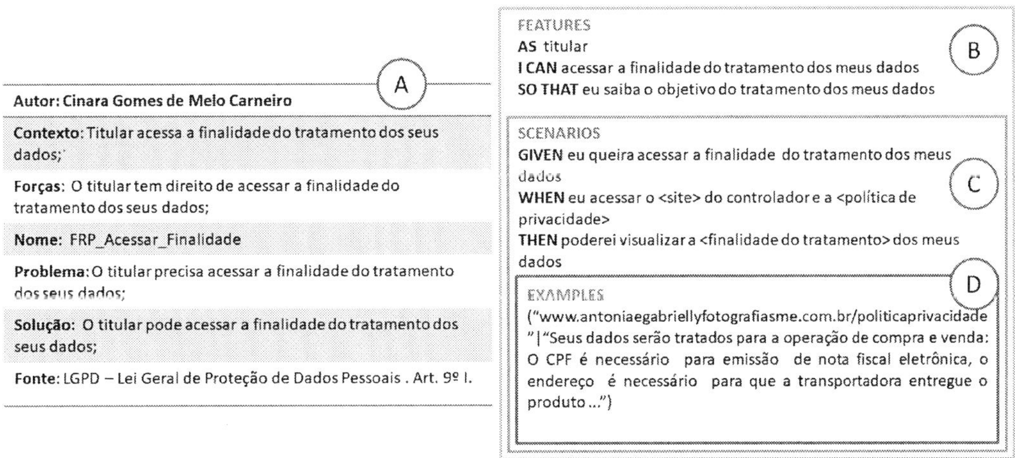

Figura 1. Descrição do Padrão FRP_Acessar Finalidade.

Para a construção de um ATP, deve-se definir os mesmos atributos de um FRP, i.e., autor, contexto, forças, nome, problema, solução, fonte e versão (vide Figura 2A). Depois, elaborar casos de teste que utilizem os cenários específicos de um FRP ao qual o ATP está vinculado. Por exemplo, o cenário **FRP_Acessar_Finalidade** da Figura 1C foi relacionado ao **ATP_Acessar_Finalidade**, conforme ilustra a Figura 2B. Os exemplos ligados a este cenário no FRP, item D da Figura 1, são empregados como entrada e saída para o caso de teste, item C da Figura 2.

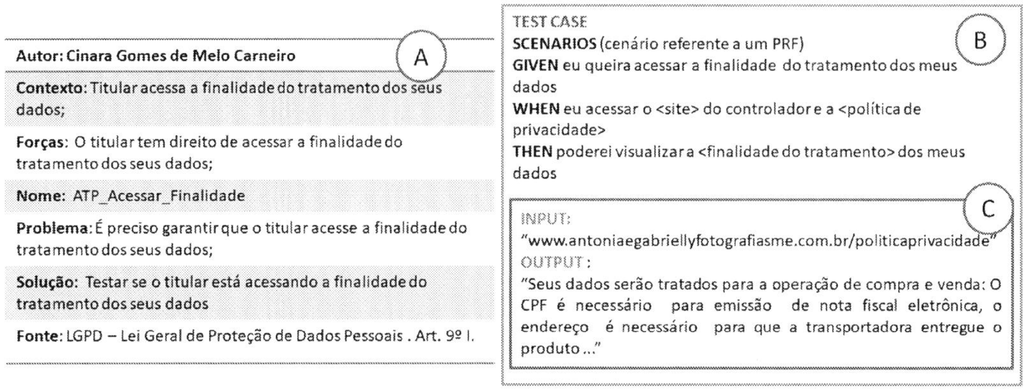

Figura 2. Descrição do Padrão ATP_Acessar Finalidade.

Por fim, para cada NFRP foram criados os seus respectivos atributos, i.e., autor, nome, problema, solução, fonte e versão (Figura 2A) e elementos do tipo *Propriedade do Sistema*, para cada restrição comportamental ou atributo de qualidade (Figura 2B).

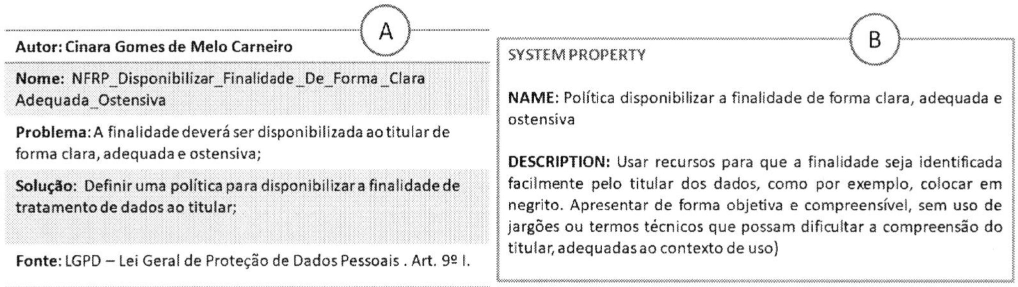

Figura 3. Descrição do Padrão NFRP_Disponibilizar_Finalidade_De_Forma_Clara_Adequada_Ostensiva

O CPRP produzido conta com 90 PRF, 10 PRNF e 91 PTA. Devido a sua extensão, disponibilizamos o catálogo completo no endereço `https://zenodo.org/records/10782808`. A construção do catálogo foi realizada por meio da ferramenta TMEd (*Terminal Model Editor*), desenvolvida pelo grupo de pesquisa [Kudo et al. 2023].

Em seu estágio atual, a qualidade do CPRP foi avaliada por um profissional com conhecimentos de LGPD e Engenharia de Software. A avaliação envolveu dois aspectos do CPRP: o quanto abrange os requisitos legais da LGPD (completude) e o quanto fornece os resultados corretos em relação à LGPD (corretude). Para cada padrão constante no catálogo, foi atribuída uma pontuação de 1 a 5, segundo a escala *Likert*.

A maioria dos padrões avaliados examinados apresentou alta corretude (valor 5), com cerca de 84,5% (160 de 189). Em relação à completude, 80% (24 de 30) dos artigos contemplados no CPRP foram avaliados com a pontuação máxima também. Além disso, a ausência de pontuações inferiores a 4 para corretude e completude indica um alto nível de qualidade nessas dimensões. A descrição completa da avaliação do CPRP desenvolvido será publicada oportunamente.

5. Considerações Finais

Este trabalho apresentou um método que analisa artigos da LGPD e os traduz em um catálogo de padrões de requisitos de privacidade (CPRP). Esses padrões podem ser reusados e instanciados em diferentes projetos onde a proteção de dados pessoais é transversal.

Como ameaças à validade, a análise semântica do método baseia-se no conhecimento da autora sobre a LGPD, apesar de possuir formação complementar compatível. Também não houve um estudo da literatura sobre métodos de análise sintática, o que poderia ter efeito sobre a qualidade do CPRP. Por fim, não foi realizada uma avaliação em uso do CPRP, algo que se planeja realizar como trabalho futuro.

Referências

Alves, C. and Neves, M. (2021). Especificação de requisitos de privacidade em conformidade com a LGPD: resultados de um estudo de caso. In *Anais do WER21 - Workshop em Engenharia de Requisitos, Brasilia, BSB, Brasil, August 23-27, 2021.*

BRASIL (2018). Lei no 13.709, de 14 de agosto de 2018. Lei Geral de Proteção de Dados Pessoais (LGPD). seção 1, Brasília, ano 155, n. 157, p. 59, 15 ago. 2018.

Canedo, E. D. et al. (2021). Agile teams' perception in privacy requirements elicitation: LGPD's compliance in Brazil. In *2021 IEEE 29th International Requirements Engineering Conference (RE)*, pages 58–69. IEEE.

Ferrão, S. É. R. and Canedo, E. D. (2022). Uma taxonomia para requisitos de privacidade e sua aplicação no Open Banking Brasil. In *Anais do WER22 - Workshop em Engenharia de Requisitos, Natal - RN, Brazil, August 23-26, 2022.*

Gürses, S., Troncoso, C., and Diaz, C. (2011). Engineering privacy by design. *Computers, Privacy & Data Protection*, 14(3):25.

Kudo, T. N., Bulcão-Neto, R. F., and Vincenzi, A. M. (2019). A conceptual metamodel to bridging requirement patterns to test patterns. In *Proceedings of the XXXIII Brazilian Symposium on Software Engineering*, pages 155–160.

Kudo, T. N., Bulcão-Neto, R. F., Neto, V. V. G., and Vincenzi, A. M. R. (2023). Aligning requirements and testing through metamodeling and patterns: Design and evaluation. *Requirements Engineering*, 28(1):97–115.

Mai, P. X. et al. (2018). Modeling security and privacy requirements: a use case-driven approach. *Information and Software Technology*, 100:165–182.

Neves Camêlo, M. and Alves, C. (2023). G-Priv: A guide to support LGPD compliant specification of privacy requirements. *iSys - Brazilian Journal of Information Systems*, 16(1):2:1 – 2.

Peixoto, M. et al. (2023). Evaluating a privacy requirements specification method by using a mixed-method approach: results and lessons learned. *Requirements Engineering*, 28(2):229–255.

Saraiva, J. and Soares, S. (2023). Adoption of the LGPD inventory in the user stories and BDD scenarios creation. In *Proceedings of the XXXVII Brazilian Symposium on Software Engineering, SBES 2023*, pages 416–421. ACM.

Withall, S. (2007). *Software requirement patterns*. Pearson Education.

Evaluación de la mantenibilidad de los sistemas híbridos (clásico-cuánticos)

Ana Díaz Muñoz[1,2], **Moisés Rodríguez Monje**[1,2], **José A. Cruz-Lemus**[2], **Mario Piattini Velthuis**[2]

[1] AQCLab Software Quality 13500 Puertollano (Ciudad Real), España

[2]Instituto de Tecnologías y Sistemas de Información y Escuela Superior de Informática, Universidad de Castilla-La Mancha 13071 Ciudad Real, España

{adiaz, mrodriguez}@aqclab.es,
{joseantonio.cruz, mario.piattini}@uclm.es

Abstract. *The remarkable development of quantum computing arose in response to the need to address problems intractable for conventional computers. However, it is essential to emphasize that quantum computing will not replace traditional computing but will coexist in hybrid systems. Similar to the scenario observed in the conventional software domain, evaluating the quality of these emerging hybrid systems becomes mandatory, with a particular focus on their maintainability to ensure their scalability. In this paper, we introduce a pioneering methodological and technological framework comprising a set of properties and metrics and a set of automated tools designed for hybrid software maintainability.*

Resumen. *El notable desarrollo de la computación cuántica surge en respuesta a la necesidad de abordar problemas que resultan intratables para las computadoras convencionales. No obstante, es fundamental destacar que la computación cuántica no reemplazará a la computación tradicional, sino que ambas coexistirán en sistemas híbridos. Similar al escenario observado en el ámbito del software convencional, se vuelve obligatorio evaluar la calidad de estos sistemas híbridos emergentes, con un enfoque particular en su mantenibilidad para asegurar su escalabilidad. En el presente trabajo, introducimos un marco metodológico y tecnológico pionero que comprende un conjunto de propiedades y métricas, así como una serie de herramientas automatizadas diseñadas para la mantenibilidad del software híbrido.*

1. Introducción

La computación cuántica ha emergido como un área clave de investigación y desarrollo, prometiendo revolucionar diversas disciplinas al ofrecer velocidades de cálculo notablemente superiores a las de las computadoras convencionales, gracias a la explotación de los principios de la mecánica cuántica [Bernhard 2019]. No obstante, este avance plantea importantes desafíos, especialmente en el desarrollo de software capaz de aprovechar eficientemente estas capacidades cuánticas. Una solución a esto ha sido la creación de software híbrido, que integra componentes tradicionales y cuánticos para potenciar las soluciones ofrecidas.

Con la expansión de la computación cuántica en áreas como la inteligencia artificial y la medicina, se ha vuelto crucial asegurar la calidad de estos desarrollos [Piattini et al. 2020]. La calidad del software se evalúa mediante estándares internacionales como el ISO/IEC 25010 [ISO 2011], que forma parte de la familia de ISO/IEC 25000 [ISO 2014] y se enfoca en distintos aspectos de la calidad del producto software, incluida la mantenibilidad, que es esencial para garantizar la capacidad de un software de ser modificado y mejorado de manera eficiente [Rodríguez and Piattini 2014]. La mantenibilidad incluye subcaracterísticas como la analizabilidad, que se refiere a la facilidad con la que el software puede ser entendido.

Aunque se están desarrollando prácticas para el mantenimiento del software cuántico, persisten desafíos significativos debido al soporte inmaduro de herramientas y la falta de infraestructura adecuada para adaptar prácticas ágiles al desarrollo de este tipo de software [Moll et al. 2021, Khan et al. 2023]. Además, en el desarrollo ágil de software, los análisis estáticos de código son esenciales para identificar mejoras potenciales de forma continua [Gheorghe-Pop et al. 2020].

Debido a esta importante necesidad, este artículo presenta una solución innovadora que aborda el desafío de evaluar el software híbrido (clásico-cuántico). La investigación se centra en el desarrollo de un modelo y un entorno, formado por distintas herramientas, para medir y evaluar la analizabilidad del software híbrido, lo que representa un paso crucial para lograr una calidad integral en los productos software híbridos.

En respuesta a estos retos, este artículo propone una solución novedosa centrada en evaluar la calidad del software híbrido. Presenta un modelo y un conjunto de herramientas diseñadas para medir y evaluar la analizabilidad del software híbrido, lo que constituye un avance clave hacia la mejora de la calidad integral de estos productos software. El trabajo concluye resaltando las contribuciones de esta investigación y esbozando direcciones futuras para continuar avanzando en este campo.

2. Mantenibilidad del software híbrido

Los modelos de calidad del software, como los definidos por el estándar ISO/IEC 25010, son esenciales para evaluar la calidad de los productos software, adaptándose a sus necesidades y requisitos específicos. Este estándar identifica ocho características clave de la calidad, siendo una de ellas la mantenibilidad, que engloba la capacidad del software para ser modificado de manera fácil y eficiente, ya sea para corregir fallos o adaptarlo a nuevos requerimientos [Rodríguez et al. 2015]. Dentro de la mantenibilidad, la analizabilidad juega un papel crucial, ya que un software bien estructurado y documentado facilita significativamente su comprensión y modificación a lo largo de su ciclo de vida.

Las propiedades para la evaluación de la analizabilidad del software híbrido se han diseñado considerando todos los aspectos distintivos que caracterizan este tipo de sistemas. El enfoque se centra en la representación de los componentes clásicos y cuánticos, así como en la capacidad de realizar análisis estáticos en el entorno de evaluación.

2.1. Propiedades de analizabilidad para el software cuántico

Las propiedades de calidad que influyen en la capacidad de análisis del software cuántico se han centrado principalmente en el kit de desarrollo Qiskit, ya que es el utilizado por un mayor número de usuarios de la comunidad cuántica. Éstas son las siguientes:

- Incumplimiento de reglas de codificación Qiskit (QiCR) - La existencia de código que no cumple con las convenciones y normas establecidas para la programación cuántica. En este contexto, aún no se ha establecido una guía que defina las reglas de codificación específicas para Qiskit, aunque existen contribuciones recientes en este ámbito [Chen et al. 2023].
- Anchura del circuito (CW) - La cantidad de cúbits necesarios para representar y manipular la información en un circuito cuántico. Un circuito más ancho puede exigir más recursos y ser más complicado de analizar.
- Profundidad del circuito (CD) - Número de capas que componen un circuito cuántico. Una mayor profundidad puede incrementar la complejidad del circuito y, por ende, dificultar su comprensión.
- Complejidad de las puertas del circuito (CCG) - Evalúa el número y tipo de puertas cuánticas utilizadas en un circuito, según las contribuciones de Qiskit [Qiskit-Contributors 2024]. La dificultad de entender y modificar el circuito aumenta con puertas más complejas aplicadas sobre un mayor número de cúbits.
- Instrucciones condicionales (CI) - Las operaciones realizadas en un circuito cuántico basándose en los resultados de mediciones previas sobre los cúbits. Esto agrega complejidad y puede requerir un análisis más meticuloso y detallado para comprender el circuito.
- Complejidad ciclomática cuántica (QCC) - La complejidad de un programa cuántico en términos del número de posibles caminos lógicos a través del código cuántico [Kumar 2023]. Una mayor complejidad ciclomática puede indicar un circuito más difícil de analizar.
- Operaciones de medición (MO) - Las instrucciones que permiten extraer información sobre el estado de uno o más cúbits. Son críticas en puntos específicos porque representan la interacción entre el software clásico y el cuántico; una elección inadecuada de los puntos de medida puede afectar la analizabilidad del algoritmo.
- Operaciones de inicialización y reinicio (IRO) - Las operaciones que preparan el estado inicial de los cúbits antes de la ejecución del circuito y las que los restablecen a un estado conocido después de la ejecución. Comprender cómo se establecen y restablecen los cúbits puede complicar la comprensión del circuito.
- Cúbits auxiliares (AQ) - Los cúbits adicionales para realizar determinadas operaciones en un circuito. Estos cúbits auxiliares influyen directamente en la complejidad del algoritmo y requieren un análisis adicional para comprender cómo afectan al comportamiento del circuito.

De forma análoga a la evaluación realizada sobre el software clásico y sus propiedades, se evalúan las propiedades cuánticas de Qiskit utilizando la función por perfiles. Este procedimiento se basan en la experiencia de evaluación de la mantenibilidad por parte de AQCLab a lo largo de los últimos 25 años, tal y como se puede consultar en [Verdugo et al. 2024].

2.2. Métricas de analizabilidad para el software híbrido

Los métodos de cálculo, las métricas y las propiedades de análisis mencionadas están vinculados en el proceso de evaluar la calidad del software híbrido. Los métodos de cálculo constituyen los procedimientos y algoritmos empleados para medir cuantitativamente los diversos aspectos de la capacidad de análisis; ofrecen una base cuantitativa para evaluar y comparar la aptitud del software para ser analizado y comprendido de manera efectiva. Las métricas, por su parte, son indicadores numéricos derivados de estos métodos, proporcionando medidas específicas de las propiedades de análisis. Con estas métricas en su lugar, es posible obtener una comprensión objetiva y cuantificable de la capacidad de análisis del software híbrido, identificando áreas que puedan requerir ajustes o mejoras.

En el estudio de [Díaz et al. 2024], se presentó una versión inicial de las métricas para evaluar la capacidad de análisis de los sistemas híbridos, las cuales han sido refinadas mediante diversas validaciones realizadas sobre productos reales durante este trabajo.

A continuación, se detalla un ejemplo de procedimiento de cálculo.

2.2.1. Calcular la profundidad del circuito

La propiedad de la profundidad del circuito se relaciona directamente con la cantidad máxima de operaciones aplicadas sobre un mismo cúbit en el circuito cuántico. Se muestra un ejemplo de cálculo de la profundidad de un circuito cuántico en la Figura 1, donde se obtiene un resultado de 9 para el valor de su profundidad.

Figura 1. Representación de la profundidad del circuito

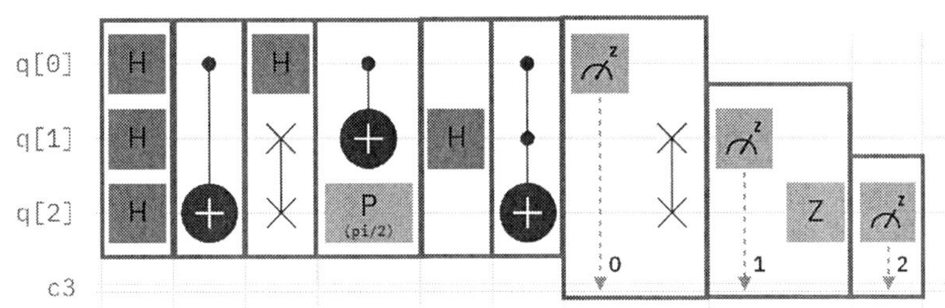

Para evaluar esta propiedad sobre el circuito cuántico se definen niveles y se utiliza una función por perfiles que indica la cantidad máxima aceptada de circuitos para cada nivel de calidad.

Una vez que los diversos circuitos han sido clasificados según sus profundidades, se procede a evaluar su distribución mediante métricas base. Estas métricas se dividen en tres niveles, siendo el nivel 3 el menos crítico y el nivel 1 el más significativo:

- NC_CD1: Número de circuitos con una profundidad del circuito de nivel 1.
- NC_CD2: Número de circuitos con una profundidad del circuito de nivel 2.
- NC_CD3: Número de circuitos con una profundidad del circuito de nivel 3.
- NCIR: Número total de circuitos.

El cálculo de estas métricas base, definidas para la propiedad de profundidad del circuito, se realiza en función de los umbrales especificados en la Tabla 1.

A partir de estas métricas base, se calculan las siguientes métricas derivadas:

- DC_CD1: Densidad de circuitos con profundidad del circuito de nivel 1.
- DC_CD2: Densidad de circuitos con profundidad del circuito de nivel 2.

Tabla 1. Niveles para la evaluación de la profundidad del circuito

Niveles	Rangos	Niveles de calidad
1	>17	Profundidad del circuito mala
2	11-17	Profundidad del circuito regular
3	1-10	Profundidad del circuito buena

- DC_CD3: Densidad de circuitos con profundidad del circuito de nivel 3.

Estas métricas derivadas se obtienen dividiendo el número de circuitos de cada nivel por el número total de circuitos evaluados, de forma similar al cálculo de las densidades para la propiedad de la anchura del circuito.

Una vez obtenidas estas tres densidades, se determina un valor de calidad normalizado para la propiedad mediante la función por perfiles. En la función por perfiles para la profundidad del circuito se definen los rangos mostrados en la Tabla 2 (consultar [Verdugo et al. 2024]). Para cada nivel de calidad, se establece el umbral máximo aceptado de densidad de circuitos. Cabe destacar que la tabla no incluye el nivel de anchura más deseable, que corresponde a una buena anchura de los circuitos.

Tabla 2. Niveles y rangos para la evaluación de la profundidad del circuito

Rangos	Niveles 1	Niveles 2	Niveles de calidad
0	-	-	0
1	20	40	(0-33)
2	15	30	[33-66)
3	10	20	[66-100)
4	5	15	100

3. Entorno para la evaluación de la analizabilidad del software híbrido

En este apartado presentamos el entorno tecnológico desarrollado y diseñado para medir, evaluar y visualizar los resultados de la analizabilidad del software híbrido.

Sobre la Figura 2 se proporciona una representación de la arquitectura de las distintas tecnologías. Este entorno se encuentra compuesto de tres herramientas: la herramienta de medición, la herramienta de evaluación y la herramienta de consulta y análisis de datos. La arquitectura modular y bien definida del entorno facilita una interacción fluida entre estas herramientas, lo que permite llevar a cabo una evaluación eficiente de la capacidad de análisis del software híbrido. Además, la elección de PostgreSQL como punto central de almacenamiento y comunicación entre las herramientas asegura la integridad y disponibilidad de los datos a lo largo de todo el proceso de evaluación.

Principalmente, hemos optado por utilizar SonarQube[1] en el entorno de desarrollo para el componente de medición, basándonos en dos ventajas clave. En primer lugar,

[1] https://www.sonarsource.com/products/sonarqube/

Figura 2. Arquitectura del entorno tecnológico para la evaluación de la analizabilidad

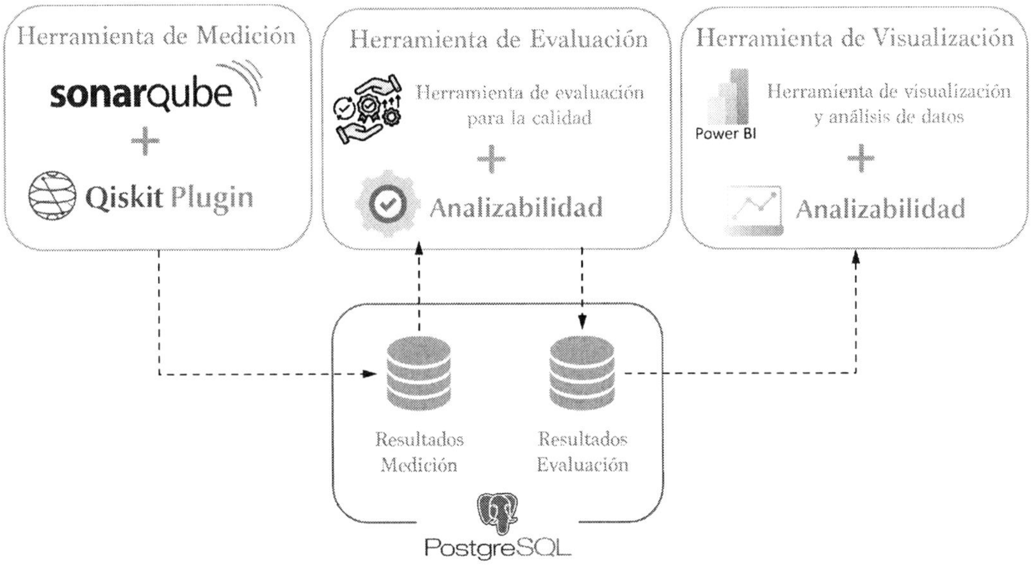

destaca su capacidad para ser compatible con una amplia gama de lenguajes de programación, lo que lo convierte en una solución idónea para entornos híbridos que emplean diversas tecnologías.

En segundo lugar, la flexibilidad que ofrece SonarQube al incorporar extensiones o *plugins* personalizados resulta fundamental. Esta característica nos brinda la capacidad de ajustar la herramienta según las necesidades específicas de los sistemas híbridos desarrollados con Qiskit. Hemos creado un 'Qiskit Plugin' que integra las métricas propuestas para evaluar la analizabilidad del software híbrido. Gracias a esta funcionalidad, podemos adaptar las mediciones de la plataforma de manera personalizada para satisfacer los requisitos específicos de nuestro proyecto.

La evaluación del software híbrido se basa en una herramienta compuesta por un archivo XML, que detalla propiedades, métricas, métodos de cálculo y niveles de calidad, y un programa en Python. Este último automatiza la aplicación de los criterios definidos en el XML a los resultados de medición del código, calculando el nivel de analizabilidad del software, tanto en sus componentes clásicos como cuánticos, y del sistema híbrido en su conjunto.

Finalmente, la utilidad destinada al examen y exploración de datos juega un papel fundamental en la extracción de los resultados de la evaluación desde la base de datos PostgreSQL. Este instrumento posibilita la ejecución de consultas y análisis de datos de manera eficaz, suministrando datos significativos sobre la analizabilidad del software híbrido al encargado de la evaluación o auditor de software.

4. Conclusiones

La búsqueda de excelencia en el desarrollo de software cuántico se enfrenta a desafíos significativos debido a las características únicas de este tipo de software, que pueden hacerlo propenso a errores y difícil de mantener sin las prácticas de ingeniería de software cuántico adecuadas. Esto podría impedir que el software alcance su máximo potencial [Akbar et al. 2023].

Este artículo presenta un entorno tecnológico diseñado para medir y evaluar la analizabilidad del software híbrido (clásico-cuántico), proporcionando valores cuantitativos de analizabilidad siguiendo pautas específicas. Se están realizando pruebas adicionales por auditores de software para verificar la funcionalidad y aplicabilidad del entorno.

La herramienta de medición desarrollada ha sido aplicada en investigaciones anteriores, como la realizada en [Alvarado-Valiente et al. 2023], donde se empleó para evaluar métricas en 16 algoritmos cuánticos, incluidos los algoritmos de Shor [Shor 1994] y Grover [Gover 1994], contribuyendo a la identificación de mejoras en la producción e implementación de servicios cuánticos específicos.

La integración de la medición en un entorno DevOps para realizar evaluaciones automáticas es un objetivo futuro, que eventualmente incluirá la incorporación de más herramientas a este pipeline. Este trabajo no solo sienta las bases para evaluaciones de calidad más exhaustivas y precisas en el futuro, sino que también abre la puerta a la incorporación de nuevas ideas de desarrollo, incluida la expansión del entorno de evaluación para cubrir otras características de calidad del software y para abarcar otras plataformas de desarrollo híbridas como Q#.

Agradecimientos

Esta investigación ha contado con el apoyo de Q-SERV (Quantum Service Engineering: Development Quality, Testing and Security of Quantum Microservices) financiado por el Ministerio de Ciencia e Innovación y los Fondos FEDER (PID2021-124054OB-C32); QU-ASAP (Prototipo de modernización del software quantum) financiado por el Ministerio de Ciencia e Innovación y los Fondos NextGenerationEU (PDC2022-133051-I00); y ayudas para la realización de proyectos de investigación aplicada, en el marco del Plan Propio de Investigación, cofinanciadas por el Fondo Europeo de Desarrollo Regional (Feder): UNION (2022-GRIN-34110) y MESIAS (2022-GRIN-34202)

Referencias

Akbar, M., Khan, A., and Rafi, S. (2023). A systematic decision-making framework for tackling quantum software engineering challenges. *Automated Software Engineering*, 30(22).

Alvarado-Valiente, J., Romero-Álvarez, J., Díaz, A., Rodríguez, M., García-Rodríguez, I., Moguel, E., Garcia-Alonso, J., and Murillo, J. M. (2023). Quantum services generation and deployment process: A quality-oriented approach. *QUATIC: The International Conference on the Quality of Information and Communications Technology*, 1871.

Bernhard, C. (2019). *Quantum Computing for Everyone*. The MIT Press.

Chen, Q., Câmara, R., Campos, J., Souto, A., and Ahmed, I. (2023). The smelly eight: An empirical study on the prevalence of code smells in quantum computing. pages 358–370, Melbourne, Australia: IEEE.

Díaz, A., Rodríguez, M., and Piattini, M. (2024). Towards a set of metrics for hybrid (quantum/classical) systems maintainability. *Journal of Universal Computer Science (J.UCS)*, 30(1):25–48.

Gheorghe-Pop, I.-D., Tcholtchev, N., Ritter, T., and Hauswirth, M. (2020). Quantum devops: Towards reliable and applicable nisq quantum computing. *IEEE Globecom Workshops*, pages 1–6.

Gover, L. K. (1994). A fast quantum mechanical algorithm for database search. *Proceedings of the Twenty-Eighth Annual ACM Symposium on Theory of Computing*, page 212–219.

ISO (2011). Iso/iec 25010. *Systems and software engineering - Systems and software Quality Requirements and Evaluation (SQuaRE) - Guide to SQuaRE. Retrieved from Systems and software engineering - Systems and software Quality Requirements and Evaluation (SQuaRE) - System and software quality models.*

ISO (2014). Iso/iec 25000. *Systems and software engineering – Systems and software Quality Requirements and Evaluation (SQuaRE) – Guide to SQuaRE.*

Khan, A., Akbar, M., Ahmad, A., Fahmideh, M., Shameem, M., Lahtinen, V., Waseem, M., and Mikkonen, T. (2023). *2023 IEEE International Conference on Quantum Software (QSW)*, chapter Agile Practices for Quantum Software Development: Practitioners' Perspectives, pages 9–20. IEEE.

Kumar, A. (2023). Formalization of structural test cases coverage criteria for quantum software testing. *International Journal of Theoretical Physics*, 62:1–16.

Moll, N., Barkoutsos, P., and Benjamin, S. (2021). Quantum development beyond qiskit. *npj Quantum Information*, 7(1):1–7.

Piattini, M., Peterssen, G., Pérez-Castillo, R., Hevia, J., Serrano, M., González, G. H., Guzmán, I., Andrés, C., Polo, M., Murina, E., Jiménez, L., Marqueño, J., Gallego, R., Tura, J., Phillipson, F., Murillo, J., Niño, A., and Rodríguez, M. (2020). The talavera manifesto for quantum software ingenieering and programming. Talavera de la Reina.

Qiskit-Contributors (2024). Qiskit: Circuit library.

Rodríguez, M. and Piattini, M. (2014). Software product quality evaluation using iso/iec 25000. *ERCIM News*, 99.

Rodríguez, M., Piattini, M., and Fernández, C. (2015). A hard look at software quality: Pilot program uses iso/iec 25000 family to evaluate, improve and certify software products. *Quality Progress*, 48(9):30–36.

Shor, P. (1994). Algorithms for quantum computation: discrete logarithms and factoring. *Proceedings 35th Annual Symposium on Foundations of Computer Science*, pages 124–134.

Verdugo, J., Oviedo, J., Rodríguez, M., and Piattini, M. (2024). Connecting research and practice for software product quality certification: a 25-year journey. *Accepted to IEEE Software.*

Entorno para la Evaluación de la Adecuación Funcional en Sistemas IA

Jesús Oviedo Lama[1,2], Moisés Rodríguez Monje[1,2], Mario Piattini Velthuis[2]

[1]AQCLab Software Quality, Puertollano, España

[2]Instituto de Tecnologías y Sistemas de Información y Escuela Superior de Informática, Universidad de Castilla-La Mancha Ciudad Real, España

Abstract. *Artificial Intelligence is currently a fundamental part of the digital transformation of organizations and the appearance of applications with AI algorithms means that their impact on everyday activities is increasing every day. In this situation, there is a growing need for these AI systems, as software systems, to have the necessary quality parameters to guarantee their use. This article presents a methodological and technological environment for the measurement and evaluation of Functional Suitability in AI Systems. The environment proposes a set of metrics and quality properties aligned with the new ISO/IEC 25059 standard. It also has an assessment methodology aligned with ISO/IEC 25040. On the other hand, a set of automatic tools to facilitate the evaluation of the quality of Functional in IA Systems.*

Resumen. *En la actualidad la Inteligencia Artificial es una parte fundamental de la transformación digital de las organizaciones y la aparición de aplicaciones con algoritmos de IA hace que su incidencia en las actividades cotidianas sea cada día mayor. Ante esta situación, existe una necesidad de que estos Sistemas IA, como sistemas software que son, cuenten con los parámetros de calidad necesarios para garantizar su uso. En este artículo se presenta un entorno metodológico y tecnológico para la medición y la evaluación de la Adecuación Funcional en Sistemas IA. El entorno propone un conjunto de métricas y propiedades de calidad alineadas con el nuevo estándar ISO/IEC 25059. También cuenta con una metodología de evaluación alineada con la norma ISO/IEC 25040. Por otro lado, se ha desarrollado un conjunto de herramientas automáticas para facilitar la evaluación de la Adecuación Funcional en Sistemas IA.*

1. Introducción

Históricamente las comunidades de Ingeniería del Software y de Inteligencia Artificial han permanecido poco comunicadas, teniendo sus propias terminologías, métodos y desafíos. A nivel de I+D, es más habitual que los investigadores se centren en la **"IA para la IS"** es decir cómo utilizar la Inteligencia Artificial para mejorar algunos aspectos de las Ingeniería del Software, como pueden ser los requisitos, la estimación, pruebas, etc. [Romero et al. 2023], que en usar la Ingeniería del Software para mejorar la IA, lo que se ha llamado la **"IS para la IA"**. Sin embargo, en los últimos tres años ha aumentado las investigaciones sobre técnicas de Ingeniería del Software para construir sistemas inteligentes con una calidad y productividad adecuadas, esta nueva área de investigación como indica el SEI se podría denominar "Ingeniería de la Inteligencia Artificial [1]", que se

[1]https://www.sei.cmu.edu/our-work/artificial-intelligence-engineering/

fundamenta en los principios establecidos por Horneman[Horneman et al. 2019], al que podemos denominar el padre de esta nueva área, al considerar que los sistemas de IA son sistemas intensivos, y que, por lo tanto:

- "Los principios establecidos para diseñar y desplegar sistemas de software de calidad que cumplan los objetivos de su misión a tiempo se deben aplicar a los sistemas de ingeniería de IA".
- "Los equipos deben esforzarse por entregar la funcionalidad a tiempo y con calidad, diseñar para los requisitos arquitectónicos importantes (como la seguridad, la usabilidad, la fiabilidad, el rendimiento y la escalabilidad) y planificar el mantenimiento del sistema durante toda su vida útil".

Si bien, a pesar de que "La inteligencia artificial (IA) y el aprendizaje automático (ML) son omnipresentes en el panorama actual de la informática, todavía existe una falta de experiencia en ingeniería de software y mejores prácticas en este campo" [Van Oort et al. 2021]. Los desarrolladores de sistemas intensivos en IA son conscientes de la necesidad de organizar el desarrollo de una forma sistemática aplicando métodos y herramientas de ingeniería, pero también reconocen que los métodos y herramientas tradicionales de ingeniería del software no son adecuados ni suficientes por sí mismos y deben adaptarse y ampliarse [Lavazza and Morasca 2021].

Por todo ello, en la nueva área de la Ingeniería de la Inteligencia Artificial, han surgido retos relacionados con la definición y la garantía de los atributos de comportamiento y calidad de estos sistemas y aplicaciones, que nos han impulsado a trabajar en el desarrollo de un entorno que permita la Evaluación de la Adecuación Funcional en los Sistemas IA. Por tanto, el objetivo principal del presente artículo es presentar los componentes de una primera versión de dicho entorno de evaluación, que serán utilizados próximamente de manera práctica para su validación y mejora. Para ello, el resto del artículo se estructura de la siguiente manera: en el apartado 2 se presenta el nuevo estándar para la evaluación de la calidad en los Sistemas IA como producto. En el apartado 3 se describe el modelo de calidad que se ha definido para la evaluación de la Adecuación Funcional en los Sistemas IA. En el apartado 4 se presenta cómo se lleva a cabo el proceso de evaluación del producto. En el apartado 5 se expone el conjunto de herramientas empleadas para llevar a cabo la evaluación y presentación de los resultados. Y finalmente, el apartado 6 presenta las conclusiones obtenidas con este trabajo y las líneas futuras de trabajo e investigación.

2. Nuevo estándar ISO/IEC 25059 para la Evaluación de la Calidad en los Sistemas IA

El aseguramiento de la calidad de los sistemas basados en la IA es un área emergente que no ha sido bien explorada aún y que requiere la colaboración entre las comunidades de investigación de la Ingeniería del Software (SE) y de la Inteligencia Artificial (IA). Recientemente, como ha sucedido en otros casos (sostenibilidad de productos software [Calero et al. 2021], servicios cloud [Navas 2016], sistemas de e-learning [Rahman 2019], etc.), ha sido necesario adaptar el modelo de calidad definido en la ISO/IEC 25010 para el producto software a las características especiales de la Inteligencia Artificial, surgiendo así la nueva norma ISO/IEC 25059 [ISO/IEC 2023b] conforme al marco de las normas ISO/IEC 25000. Este nuevo estándar para la "calidad para sistemas basados en IA" propone un nuevo modelo de calidad donde se recogen las características de calidad de producto que debe cumplir cualquier Sistema de IA, basándose en las

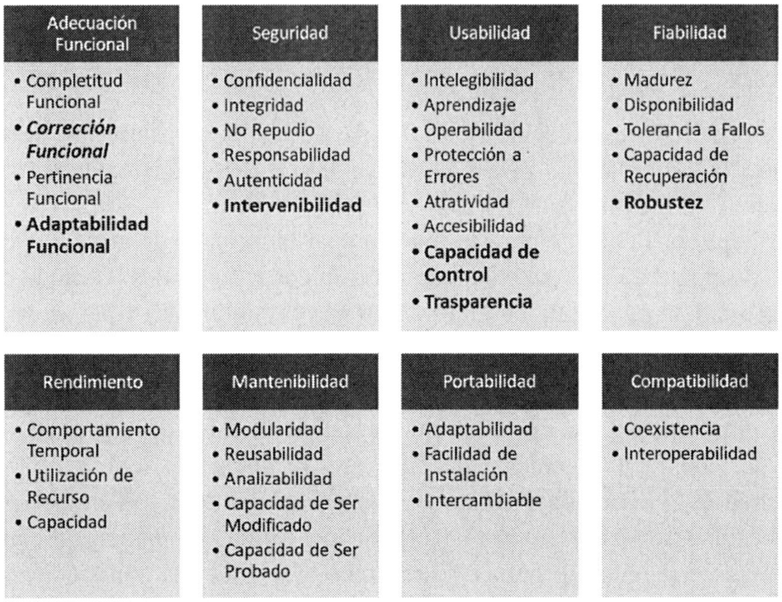

Figura 1. Modelo de calidad para sistemas IA ISO/IEC 25059 (en negrita la subcaracterísticas añadidas o modificada)

propuestas por la ISO/IEC 25010, pero presentando ciertos cambios y adaptaciones, en algunas de las características y subcaracterísticas [Oviedo et al. 2023]. En la Figura 1 se pueden ver las características y subcaracterísticas propuestas para el modelo de calidad de producto de sistema de inteligencia artificial, donde se ha resaltado en negrita las Subcaracterísticas que han sido añadidas o modificadas.

Si bien, este nuevo estándar supone un punto de partida importante, la propuesta realizada por ISO/IEC 25059 es alto nivel y está incompleta, siendo necesario para poder ser aplicable en la industria, definir un conjunto de métricas y umbrales que nos permitan determinar los valores de calidad de cada una de las subcaracterísticas y características definidas. En los siguientes apartados se describe el trabajo realizado para disponer de cada uno de los elementos necesarios para llevar a cabo la evaluación de la Adecuación Funcional para los Sistemas IA.

3. Modelo de Calidad de Adecuación Funcional para Sistemas IA

El modelo de adecuación funcional definido para los sistemas de IA está basado en el estándar ISO/IEC 25059, siendo la adecuación funcional una de las características que se han visto modificadas en este nuevo estándar. Estos cambios han motivado la necesidad de definir un nuevo modelo para abordar la calidad de los Sistemas IA, no pudiendo emplear el modelo de calidad definido por AQCLab [Verdugo et al. 2024] para la evaluación de la adecuación funcional en los productos software [Rodríguez et al. 2016], basado en la ISO/IEC 25010, siendo necesario abordar el desarrollo de un nuevo modelo que pueda evaluar la adecuación funcional para los sistemas de IA.

Este nuevo modelo propuesto en el estándar ISO/IEC 25059 está basado en el estándar ISO/IEC 25010 y presenta el mismo enfoque jerárquico donde existen diferentes niveles. En los niveles superiores del modelo se encuentran la **Característica** y **Subcaracterísticas de Calidad** que son definidas por el estándar. Sin embargo, el modelo está incompleto y ha sido necesario concretar los atributos de calidad para los niveles inferiores para hacer operativo el modelo. Así se ha definido un conjunto de Medidas de Calidad y Elementos de Medida que se han denominado en este modelo como **Propiedades de Calidad** y **Métricas Base y Derivadas**, las cuales son los elementos más concretos del modelo.

En el nivel inferior del modelo está formado por el conjunto de Métricas Base y Métricas Derivadas, las cuales son los elementos más concretos al obtenerse como resultado de las mediciones realizadas sobre el Sistema de IA y las métricas derivadas se obtienen a partir de las métricas base mediante la aplicación de alguna operación (suma, multiplicación, etc.) entre ellas.

A partir de estas métricas derivadas se calcula el siguiente nivel superior, las Propiedades de Calidad, tomando valor entre 0 y 100, las cuales nos permiten determinar el valor de las Subcaracterísticas de calidad, que también toman un valor entre 0 y 100. Por último, siguiendo el modelo jerárquico, se obtendría el valor de la Adecuación Funcional, Característica de calidad, tomando un valor discreto entre 1 y 5.

La Adecuación Funcional en el estándar ISO/IEC 25059 se define como el grado con el que un Sistema de IA proporciona funciones que satisfacen necesidades declaradas e implícitas cuando se usa con las condiciones especificadas y es evaluada tomando como base la evaluación de sus Subcaracterísticas (Figura 1) empleando una función por perfiles como la presentada en [Rodríguez et al. 2016].

3.1. Evaluación de las Subcaracterísticas de Adecuación Funcional

El modelo calidad que se ha definido ha tomado como base las subcaracterísticas definida en el estándar ISO/IEC 25059, que son las siguientes:

- **Completitud Funcional:** Esta subcaracterística no ha sido modificada respecto al modelo de calidad ISO/IEC 25010, y por tanto la definición realizada en el modelo de la evaluación de la calidad del producto software por AQCLAB [Rodríguez et al. 2016] es válida para la evaluación de la Completitud Funcional de los Sistemas IA. Si bien, esta subcaracterística se define como el grado en el que el conjunto de funciones implementadas en el producto o sistema cubren todos los requisitos funcionales y objetivos de los usuarios.
- **Corrección Funcional:** Esta Subcaracterística ha sido modificada en el estándar ISO/IEC 25059, esta modificación viene justificada porque en los Sistemas IA la corrección es un concepto más amplio que en el software tradicional [Lavazza and Morasca 2021], debido a que en los sistemas de IA los resultados correctos no se producen en la totalidad de los casos, por lo que también se espera un porcentaje de resultados incorrectos. Por ello, en la evaluación de la corrección funcional se debe tener en cuenta los resultados correctos e incorrectos.
- **Pertinencia Funcional:** Esta subcaracterística no ha sido modificada en el nuevo estándar ISO/IEC 25059. Por ello, la definición realizada en el modelo de la evaluación de la calidad del producto software por AQCLAB [Rodríguez et al. 2016] es válida para evaluar la Pertinencia Funcional de los Sistemas de IA. Así, esta subcaracterística se define cómo el grado en el que las funciones del producto o sistema facilitan el cumplimiento de las tareas y objetivos especificados.
- **Adaptabilidad Funcional:** Es la nueva subcaracterística definida en el estándar ISO/IEC 25059 para la Adecuación Funcional. Esta subcaracterística se define

como el grado en que un sistema de IA puede realizar nuevas predicciones en base a nuevo conocimiento adquirido. Esta subcaracterística presenta una diferencia significativa respecto a otras subcaracterísticas, ya que un aumento de su valor no implica una mejora de la calidad del sistema, es decir, no se puede interpretar utilizando una escala lineal. Por ello, en este modelo, se ha realizado una interpretación de la Adaptabilidad Funcional para permitir la linealidad, como en el resto de subcaracterísticas, y sólo se tiene en cuenta si la Adaptabilidad Funcional del sistema de IA mejora los resultados de éste. Así, se define la adaptabilidad funcional como la capacidad que tiene el sistema IA para mejorar sus resultados en base de su experiencia, es decir en base de nuevas entradas y/o resultados previos.

La evaluación de cada una de las subcaracterísticas se realiza a partir de un conjunto de Propiedades de Calidad. Si bien, en este artículo sólo se van a presentar las Propiedades de Calidad de las Subcaracterísticas nuevas o modificadas, ya que el resto de propiedades no presentan cambios respecto el modelo de evaluación de la adecuación funcional para el producto software de AQCLAB [Rodríguez et al. 2016].

3.2. Propiedad para evaluar la Subcaracterística Corrección Funcional

La Propiedad **Exactitud Funcional** evalúa si los requisitos que han sido implementados son exactos, es decir si su tasa de éxito es igual o superior a la tasa de éxito establecida para dicho requisito. Para conocer si un requisito es exacto es necesario conocer el porcentaje de ejecuciones correctas e incorrectas, teniendo en cuenta los falsos positivos y los falsos negativos [ISO/IEC 2023b] y que la proporción de ejecuciones correctas sea superior al umbral establecido para dicho requisito para considerar que sus resultados son exactos. Para calcular el valor de esta Propiedad es necesario conocer el número de requisitos implementados y el número de requisitos exactos.

Para determinar si un requisito es exacto se debe ejecutar varias veces cada uno de los casos de prueba asociados al requisito. El número de ejecuciones se determina mediante la formula que se muestra en la Figura 2, donde los valores asignados son:

- Los valores de p y q es 0,5 al desconocer la probabilidad del hecho (ejecución correcta o ejecución incorrecta).
- El valor de e se corresponde con el error que se quiera aceptar: 1 %, 5 %, 10 %, etc.
- El valor de Z ha sido obtenido a partir de las tablas de distribución normal, en función de los errores seleccionados. Se ha tomado una distribución normal, porque el número de veces que se puede ejecutar una funcionalidad no está limitado. Además, el resultado de la ejecución puede tratarse como una distribución nominal, el resultado de la funcionalidad puede ser correcto o incorrecto.

$$n = \frac{Z_{\sigma/2}^{2} * p * q}{e^{2}}$$

Figura 2. Ecuación para determinar el tamaño de la muestra

Tras ejecutar el caso de prueba el número de veces determinado se obtendrá el número de ejecuciones que han sido correctas, considerando los verdaderos positivos y los verdaderos negativos. Si el porcentaje de resultados correctos en todos los casos de prueba trazados con el requisito es igual o superior a la tasa de éxito establecida en la especificación del requisito entonces se podrá considerar que el requisito es exacto.

3.3. Propiedad para evaluar la Subcaracterística Adaptabilidad Funcional

La Propiedad **Aprendizaje Adecuado** examina si la utilización de nuevas entradas de datos genera mejores resultados por parte del modelo de IA, es decir si se reduce la probabilidad de resultados incorrectos. Para el análisis de esta propiedad es necesario conocer el número de requisitos que han mejorado su tasa de resultados correctos y el número de requisitos implementados. Para determinar si un requisito ha mejorado sus resultados correctos, se debe comprobar, tras la evaluación de la corrección funcional, si el porcentaje de resultados correctos del requisito es superior al umbral de corrección definido en la especificación del requisito entonces se podrá considerar que la tasa de resultados correctos del requisito ha mejorado.

4. Proceso de Evaluación

Para abordar la evaluación de la adecuación funcional de los sistemas IA se ha definido un proceso basado en el estándar ISO/IEC 25040 [ISO/IEC 2023a]. Sin embargo, existen ciertas matizaciones en el procedimiento definido con respecto al estándar. Concretamente, en el caso del proceso de la evaluación de la adecuación funcional de los sistemas de inteligencia artificial el objetivo es siempre el mismo y por ello se utiliza un módulo predefinido, lo que supone que las actividades iniciales del proceso, donde se establece el propósito de la evaluación y se define el módulo de evaluación a emplear requieran menos profundidad que la establecida en la norma ISO/IEC 25040. Lo mismo sucede en la actividad de planificación de la evaluación, ya que no es necesario identificar las tareas a realizar dado que la evaluación de la adecuación funcional se compone siempre de las mismas tareas. El resto de las actividades (ejecución y conclusión de la evaluación) se realizan en base a lo establecido en dicha norma. En la Figura 3 se muestran las actividades y tareas que componen este proceso de evaluación.

5. Herramientas de Evaluación

El entorno software para la medición y evaluación de la adecuación funcional en sistemas de IA implementado (en adelante entorno AQCLab) se encuentra compuesto fundamentalmente por cuatro componentes:

- **Herramienta de Medición** se trata de una herramienta desarrollada en JAVA para obtener métricas relacionadas con la evaluación de la adecuación funcional de los Sistemas de IA. Permite registrar información relacionada con los requisitos y casos de prueba del sistema genera un fichero XML con los resultados de las métricas, que es utilizado como entrada por la herramienta de evaluación.
- **Herramienta de Evaluación** se encarga de medir y evaluar la adecuación funcional de los sistemas IA, se compone de dos componentes, un componente estándar de evaluación y un componente específico para evaluar la adecuación funcional de los sistemas IA. Este componente específico incluye el modelo para evaluar la adecuación funcional implementado en XML y un programa implementado en Python que realiza los cálculos necesarios para llevar a cabo la evaluación a partir de los resultados de la herramienta de medición.

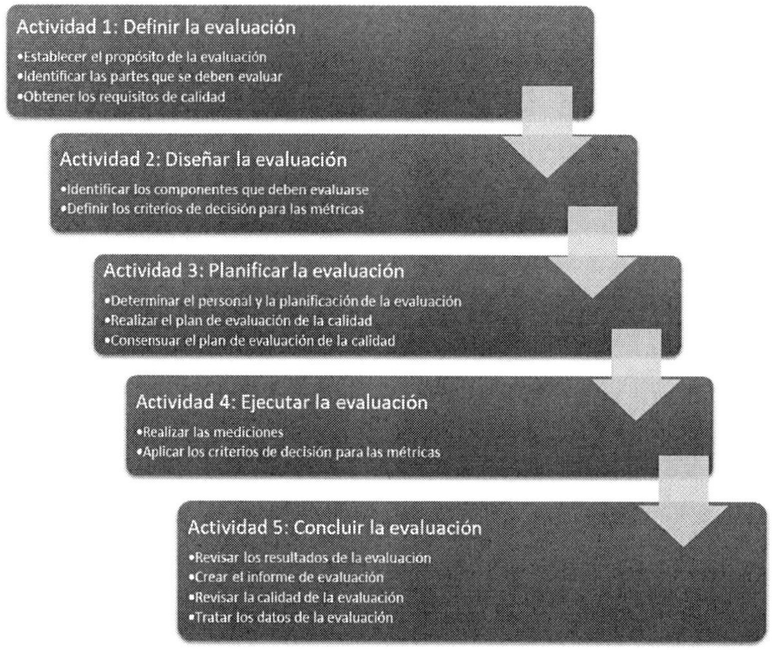

Figura 3. Proceso de evaluación de la adecuación funcional en sistemas IA

- **Herramienta de Visualización.** se trata de una herramienta formada por: un entorno de visualización proporcionado por AQCLab en PowerBI, para la creación de diferentes informes interactivos y una ampliación específica dedicada la visualización y análisis de datos de la adecuación funciona en Sistemas IA.
- **Base de Datos** el entorno se compone de una base de datos gestionada mediante PostgreSQL, donde se almacenan los resultados obtenidos tras la evaluación de la adecuación funcional de los sistemas de IA.

6. Conclusiones y Trabajo Futuro

El auge de la Inteligencia Artificial en todas las facetas de la vida cotidiana hace necesario, al igual que en el software, el empleo de técnicas de ingeniería del software, como es la Calidad, para el desarrollo de estos sistemas. Si bien, los métodos y herramientas tradicionales de la ingeniería del software deben ser adaptados a las particularidades de los sistemas de IA. Por ello, en este artículo se ha presentado un nuevo entorno para la evaluación de la adecuación funcional en sistemas IA, adaptado a las particularidades de esta nueva tecnología.

En este nuevo entorno de evaluación se ha definido un nuevo modelo de calidad alineado al nuevo estándar ISO/IEC 25059 donde se han analizado nuevas métricas con las que abordar la evaluación de los sistemas IA. También ha sido necesario adaptar el proceso de evaluación definido en la ISO/IEC 25040 a las particularidades de las actividades que se deben realizar en la evaluación de la adecuación funcional de un sistema de IA. Por último, se ha desarrollado una nueva herramienta de medición para obtener las nuevas métricas y se han realizado adaptaciones en las herramientas de evaluación y visualización de AQCLab para realizar la evaluación y la presentación de los resultados

Por tanto, una vez desarrollado este entorno de evaluación se nos plantea como línea principal de trabajo futuro el estudio de la aplicación práctica de dicho entorno, a través de evaluaciones de sistemas de IA. Además, esta aplicación práctica permitirá realizar la validación del entorno asegurando que los valores obtenidos en las evaluaciones presentan una correlación con la Adecuación Funcional de los Sistemas de IA.

7. Agradecimientos

Esta investigación ha contado con el apoyo de ADAGIO (SBPLY/21/180501/000061), financiado por la Junta de Comunidades de Castilla La Mancha, Unión Europea, Ministerio de Hacienda y Función Pública y FEDER (Programa Operativo de Castilla-La Mancha 2021-2027), UNION (2022-GRIN-34110), Ayudas para la realización de proyectos de investigación aplicada, en el marco del Plan Propio de Investigación, cofinanciadas en un 85 % por FEDER y CASIA financiado por la Junta de Comunidades de Castilla La Mancha.

Referencias

Calero, C., Moraga, M. Á., and Piattini, M. (2021). *Software Sustainability*. Springer.

Horneman, A., Mellinger, A., and Ozkaya, I. (2019). Ai engineering: 11 foundational practices-recommendations for decision makers from experts in software engineering, cybersecurity, and applied artificial intelligence white paper dm19-0624, 06.06.

ISO/IEC (2023a). Iso/iec 25040:2023. In *Systems and software engineering — Systems and software Quality Requirements and Evaluation (SQuaRE) — Evaluation process.*

ISO/IEC (2023b). Iso/iec 25059:2023. In *Software engineering - Systems and software Quality Requirements and Evaluations (Square) - Quality model for AI systems.*

Lavazza, L. and Morasca, S. (2021). Understanding and modeling ai-intensive system development. In *2021 IEEE/ACM 1st Workshop on AI Engineering-Software Engineering for AI (WAIN)*, pages 55–61. IEEE.

Navas, R. (2016). Modelo de calidad para servicios cloud.

Oviedo, J., Márquez, R., Rodríguez, M., and Piattini, M. (2023). Calidad en los sistemas ia: adaptación de modelos de procesos y productos. *Actas de las XXVII Jornadas de Ingeniería del Software y Bases de Datos.*

Rahman, A. (2019). Quality consideration for e-learning system based on iso/iec 25000 quality standard.

Rodríguez, M., Oviedo, J. R., and Piattini, M. (2016). Evaluation of software product functional suitability: A case study. *Software Quality Professional*, 18(3).

Romero, J., Medina-Bulo, I., and Chicano, F. (2023). *Optimising the Software Development Process with Artificial Intelligence.* Springer.

Van Oort, B., Cruz, L., Aniche, M., and Van Deursen, A. (2021). The prevalence of code smells in machine learning projects. In *2021 IEEE/ACM 1st Workshop on AI Engineering-Software Engineering for AI (WAIN)*, pages 1–8. IEEE.

Verdugo, J., Oviedo, J., Rodríguez, M., and Piattini, M. (2024). Connecting research and practice for software product quality evaluation and certification: a software laboratory's 25-year journey. *IEEE Software*.

Resultados Iniciais de uma *Rapid Review* sobre Tecnologias de Apoio à Engenharia de Sistemas de Software Quântico

Bruno D. de Paiva, Alexandre C. Esteves, Rafael M. de Mello, Guilherme H. Travassos

Universidade Federal do Rio de Janeiro (UFRJ) - Rio de Janeiro - RJ - Brasil

{bdantas, ght}@cos.ufrj.br, alexandre.cysne@ppgi.ufrj.br, rafaelmello@ic.ufrj.br

Abstract. *According to the SWEBOK, the engineering of software products concerns performing different processes, including requirements and programming, among others. Despite evolving the field's evidence-based technologies, contemporary software systems like quantum software systems usually demand further technologies to tackle their unique challenges. Therefore, this work presents the emerging results of a rapid review of the technologies supporting the engineering of quantum software under the perspective of SWEBOK. The initial sample suggests a significant gap and a lack of comprehensive research elements for creating robust technologies to support the engineering of quantum software systems.*

Resumo. *De acordo com o SWEBOK a engenharia de produtos de software diz respeito à execução de diversos processos, incluindo requisitos e programação, entre outros. Apesar da evolução das tecnologias baseadas em evidência, sistemas de software contemporâneos, incluindo software quântico, geralmente exigem tecnologias adicionais para enfrentar os seus desafios. Portanto, este trabalho apresenta os resultados emergentes de uma rapid review sobre tecnologias que apoiam a engenharia de software quântico sob a perspectiva do SWEBOK. A amostra inicial sugere uma lacuna significativa e uma falta de elementos de investigação abrangentes para a criação de tecnologias robustas para apoiar a engenharia de sistemas de software quântico.*

1. Contexto e Problemática

O ciclo de vida da engenharia de software abrange fases desde a concepção até a descontinuação do produto, sendo aplicado com o intuito de criar produtos inovadores e eficientes, priorizando sua qualidade [Bosch, 2021]. Uma visão consolidada do entendimento sobre o ciclo de engenharia dos produtos de software pode ser encontrada no *Software Engineering Body of Knowledge* (*SWEBOK*[1]), um corpo de conhecimento em Engenharia de Software [Bourque e Fairley, 2014] que se mantêm em contínua atualização.

Porém, ainda que haja um entendimento consolidado das disciplinas e atividades previstas no ciclo de engenharia de produtos de software, faz-se necessária a evolução das práticas e tecnologias de apoio relacionadas, visando atender às características disruptivas de sistemas de software contemporâneos. Dentre tais características, podemos destacar a sensibilidade ao contexto [Amalfitano et al. 2021] e a *computação quântica* [Sing et al. 2023].

[1] https://www.computer.org/education/bodies-of-knowledge/software-engineering

Computação quântica é referida como um paradigma emergente que é construído utilizando os princípios da *mecânica quântica* [Upama, 2022]. A *computação quântica* promove a construção de sistemas de software contemporâneos que oferecem benefícios próprios, mas também apontam para novos desafios a serem enfrentados [Singh et al. 2023]. A necessidade de uma abordagem prática e adaptável destaca a importância de alinhar o progresso técnico com as demandas, garantindo sua integração eficaz em cenários do mundo real e potencializando seu impacto em diversos setores [Singh et al. 2023].

Há grandes expectativas em relação à aplicação da *computação quântica* para o desenvolvimento software em diferentes domínios, incluindo as áreas científica e financeira. No entanto, mesmo diante de perspectivas promissoras, existem os desafios existentes à *engenharia do software quântico* [Moguel et al. 2020], que pode ser definida como o desenvolvimento de sistemas de software que seguem lições e conhecimentos obtidos a partir da engenharia de software na *computação quântica* [Piattini 2020].

Considerando a crescente demanda por *software quântico* e, consequentemente, por sua engenharia, este trabalho apresenta o plano de um estudo secundário baseado em *rapid review* visando *caracterizar o estado da arte da engenharia de software quântico*. Devido a abrangência temática e os desafios de investigação em área emergente e relevante, buscamos neste trabalho também discutir a viabilidade da estratégia de pesquisa e apresentar resultados preliminares da *rapid review* com base na análise de conteúdo de sete estudos primários escolhidos aleatoriamente dentre os selecionados. Os resultados iniciais apontam para a existência de lacunas no conhecimento atual da *engenharia do software quântico* e a falta de elementos que direcionam o desenvolvimento de pesquisa necessários para a criação de tecnologias robustas e apropriadas para apoiar a *engenharia de sistemas de software quântico*, contrastando com as expectativas do *SWEBOK*. Em futuro próximo, esperamos que os resultados da r*apid review* indiquem a viabilidade de aumentar a cobertura de áreas da Engenharia de Software oferecendo *tecnologias de software quântico* baseado em evidência, e, principalmente, apontar as lacunas e oportunidades de pesquisas e desenvolvimento em prol da *engenharia do software quântico*.

2. Plano do Estudo

Este estudo foi influenciado pela estratégia de *rapid review*, que tem como objetivo principal prover evidências em um problema de forma mais rápida e eficiente em termos de recursos quando comparada a uma revisão sistemática de literatura convencional [Cartaxo 2018].

O objetivo desta *rapid review* consiste em *caracterizar as tecnologias de software desenvolvidas com base em evidência que contribuem para a engenharia de software quântico, sob a perspectiva do ciclo de engenharia preconizado pelo SWEBOK*. A motivação para o estudo resulta da expectativa de prover uma investigação abrangente quanto ao suporte existente às diferentes fases do ciclo de desenvolvimento de software, com base no *SWEBOK*. Neste sentido, levamos em consideração as seguintes suposições:

Suposição 1. *O interesse na engenharia de software quântico tem aumentado, porém ainda não foi possível observar eventuais disponibilidades ou adaptações nas atividades essenciais da engenharia de software (como por exemplo engenharia de requisitos) para apoiar a construção de software quântico.*

Suposição 2. *As pesquisas tendem a focar em assuntos específicos da engenharia do software quântico, por exemplo teste de software quântico, sem observar o ciclo de construção como um todo e de que maneira estas tecnologias e práticas podem ser integradas em prol da construção de software quântico de qualidade.*

2.1. Características do Estudo

A fim de compreender a evolução da *engenharia de software na computação quântica*, é essencial analisar como o desenvolvimento de novas tecnologias têm impactado diferentes disciplinas e atividades na área. Por isso, escolhemos fundamentar nosso estudo nas 15 áreas de conhecimento do *SWEBOK*. A Tabela 1 apresenta os principais direcionamentos da r*apid review*, incluindo a pergunta de pesquisa, de onde se derivam os demais. Para a determinação da *string* de busca, foi utilizado o modelo PICO [Santos et al. 2007] focando na população (*Quantum Software*), intervenção (*SWEBOK*) e resultado (*Evidence Based*). Seis critérios de inclusão foram estabelecidos para selecionar os artigos retornados pela *string* de busca na *Scopus,* base escolhida para a seleção dos artigos deste trabalho dada sua notória estabilidade, precisão e abrangência.

Tabela 1. Direcionamentos do Estudo

Pergunta de Pesquisa		**RQ1:** Quais as tecnologias de software apresentam evidência de viabilidade de utilização na construção de software quântico de qualidade considerando o ciclo de engenharia preconizado pelo SWEBOK?
String de Busca	**Inicial**	("QUANTUM PROGRAM" OR "QUANTUM SOURCE") AND ("ENGINEERING" OR "REQUIREMENT*" OR "PROCESS*" OR "DESIGN*" OR "METHOD" OR "CONSTRUCTION" OR "TEST*" OR "VERIFIC*" OR "VALIDAT*" OR "MAINTENANCE")
	Final	("QUANTUM PROGRAM" OR "QUANTUM SOURCE" OR "QUANTUM CODE") AND ("ENGINEERING" OR "REQUIREMENT*" OR "PROCESS*" OR "DESIGN*" OR "METHOD" OR "CONSTRUCTION" OR "TEST*" OR "VERIFIC*" OR "VALIDAT*" OR "MAINTENANCE" OR "EVOLUTION" OR "PRACTICE" OR "MODEL*" OR "PRACTICE*" OR "MANAG*" OR "ECONOMICS" OR "LANGUAGE" OR "COMPILER" OR "FUNDAMENTAL") AND ("PRIMARY STUDY" OR "EMPIRICAL" OR "EXPERIMENT*" OR "CONTROL* STUDY" OR "SURVEY" OR "INTERVIEW" OR "CASE STUDY" OR "FOCUS GROUP" OR "ACTION RESEARCH" OR "OBSERVATION*" OR "ETNOGRAPH*" OR "MAPPING STUDY" OR "RAPID REVIEW" OR "*SYSTEMATIC REVIEW" OR "SYSTEMATIC LITERATURE REVIEW" OR "SECONDARY STUDY" OR "SYSTEMATIC MAPPING")
Critério	**Inclusão**	1. O artigo deve estar no contexto de **engenharia de software quântico**
		2. O artigo deve endereçar ao menos um tópico do **capítulo 1 ao 12 do SWEBOK**
		3. O artigo deve reportar um **estudo empírico**
		4. O artigo deve fornecer dados para **responder à pergunta de pesquisa**
		5. O artigo deve ser escrito na **língua inglesa**
		6. O artigo deve ter sido publicado **antes de 2024**

Todos os direcionamentos do estudo foram devidamente discutidos semanalmente entre os autores deste artigo cujo critério de parada era um consenso mútuo a fim de promover a abrangência e qualidade dos resultados. Como resultado, houve uma considerável evolução da *string* de busca inicial até a sua evolução final (Tabela 1). Os três primeiros critérios de inclusão apresentados na tabela foram aplicados sobre o título, resumo e palavras-chave dos artigos retornados. Os demais critérios foram aplicados com base na leitura completa dos artigos pré-selecionados. Para a organização dos artigos, foi utilizada a ferramenta JabRef[2].

2.2. Processo de extração de dados

Para a extração dos dados dos artigos selecionados após leitura completa, foi elaborado um *formulário de extração* de modo que fosse possível extrair a informação necessária para responder a pergunta de pesquisa com base no texto integral de cada artigo correspondente a cada campo. A Tabela 2 apresenta o extrato dos dados extraídos a partir de um dos artigos selecionados [Khan et al. 2022].

Tabela 2. Extrato do formulário de Extração do artigo de Kahn et al. 2022. Extração completa em: https://bit.ly/qse-rapid-review

Campo	Conteúdo Extraído
SWEBOK Category	Software Engineering Management
Type of Study	Semi-structured Interview
Study Subject	26 practitioners across 10 countries
Study RQ's	RQ1: Do agile practices best suited for developing quantum software?
Study Characteristics	Interview instrument: Following the guidelines by Robinson [45], we developed [...]
Threats to Validity	Internal validity: Internal validity is the extent to which particular factors affect the methodological [...]
Quantum Software Technology	In line with this, Gonzalez and Paradela [22] conceptualised a hybrid project management [...]
Benefits	The QSE processes can benefit from well-developed iterative agile practices for team collaboration, [...]
Problems	Not Mentioned
Challenges	Small portion of the interview participants find themselves underprepared due to lack of a [...]
Strategies	Not mentioned

3. Execução do protocolo

A execução deste protocolo, iniciada em 28 novembro de 2023, se deu seguindo o processo apresentado na Figura 1:

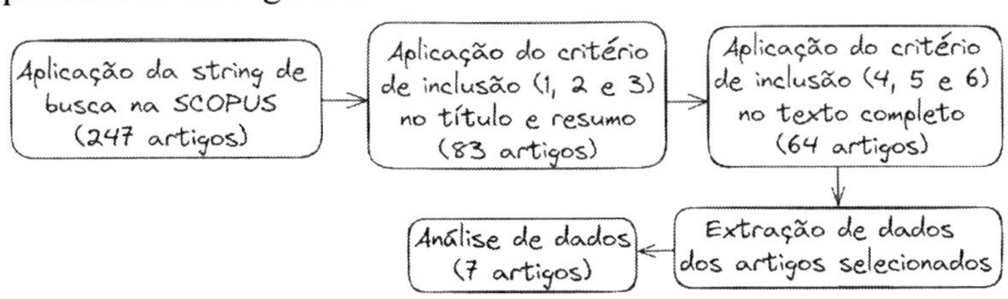

Figura 1. Procedimento de execução do protocolo

Este é um trabalho em progresso em área emergente, por isso o conjunto de artigos a serem analisados foi selecionado aleatoriamente para análise de conteúdo dentre os 64 artigos obtidos após leitura completa, disponível em: *https://bit.ly/qse-rapid-review*. O

---

2 http://www.jabref.org/

objetivo desta análise amostral foi avaliar se a estratégia de pesquisa é viável, considerando a novidade e abrangência da área.

4. Análise de Conteúdo

Realizamos a análise de conteúdo [Strauss e Corbin, 2015] sobre os sete artigos disponibilizados no final da Seção 4. Foi utilizada a ferramenta QDA Miner[3] para auxiliar na codificação e categorização dos textos. O processo de codificação seguiu os princípios de Strauss e Corbin (2015), no qual a etapa de *codificação aberta* foi realizada inicialmente a fim de identificar conceitos, propriedades e dimensões do dado, para posteriormente definir e criar categorias pertinentes ao fenômeno de interesse. Neste estudo, a nomeação das categorias foi baseada nas categorias e conceitos apresentados nos 12 primeiros capítulos do SWEBOK visando garantir consistência na organização temática das tecnologias identificadas.

A Figura 2 exemplifica a codificação de um trecho de um dos artigos selecionados para análise [El Aoun et al., 2021]. O processo de codificação primeiramente permitiu extrair trechos específicos do artigo, e os codificar de forma livre, a fim de compreender o que o trecho selecionado representava (Figura 2.a), como *participantes (subjects), amostra (sample)*, dentre outros. Em seguida, os códigos foram agrupados através da ferramenta em categorias baseadas no *SWEBOK*. Por exemplo, para o *SWEBOK* definições do estudo, como *amostragem*, *objetos de estudo*, *perguntas de pesquisa*, *participantes* se enquadram na categoria de *fundamentos da engenharia* (Figura 2b). Neste sentido, também endereçamos códigos relacionados à *falta de pesquisa* (*lack of research*) a esta mesma categoria, uma vez que se trata de uma categoria relacionada à elementos de pesquisa.

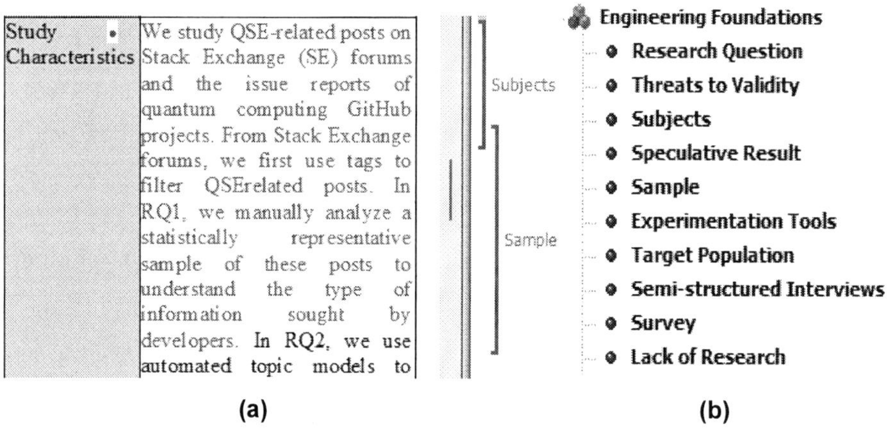

Figura 2. Trecho de codificação do Artigo de El Aoun et al. (2021) (a) e Extrato de códigos da categoria *Engineering Foundations* (b)

4.1 Análise Quantitativa

O processo de análise quantitativa dos códigos e categorias encontrados na amostra analisada foi realizado utilizando a linguagem de programação *Python* por meio do *Google Colab*, tendo como base as codificações realizadas através do *QDA Miner*. Nós

[3] https://provalisresearch.com/products/qualitative-data-analysis-software/freeware/

contabilizamos a frequência de cada código obtido, além do número de casos (artigos) em que estes códigos apareceram, observável na Tabela 3.

Tabela 3. Extrato dos códigos mais frequentes do QDA Miner. A frequência completa se encontra neste site: https://bit.ly/qse-rapid-review

Categoria	Código	Contagem	% Código	Casos	%Casos
Engineering Foundations	Lack of Research	18	10,30%	7	100,00%
Software Engineering Processes	Lack of Proficiency	12	6,90%	5	71,40%
Computing Foundations	Quantum Computing Characteristics	6	3,40%	5	71,40%
Software Construction	Circuit Construction	7	4,00%	4	57,10%
Engineering Foundations	Research Question	10	5,70%	4	57,10%
Engineering Foundations	Threats to Validity	3	1,70%	3	42,90%

A Figura 3 apresenta a distribuição de artigos analisados que cobrem as categorias identificadas na análise. Com base na Tabela 3 e na Figura 3, é possível notar que a categoria com o maior número de casos é a *Engineering Foundations*, responsável por englobar as características de estudos, como amostragem, objetivos, dentre outros.

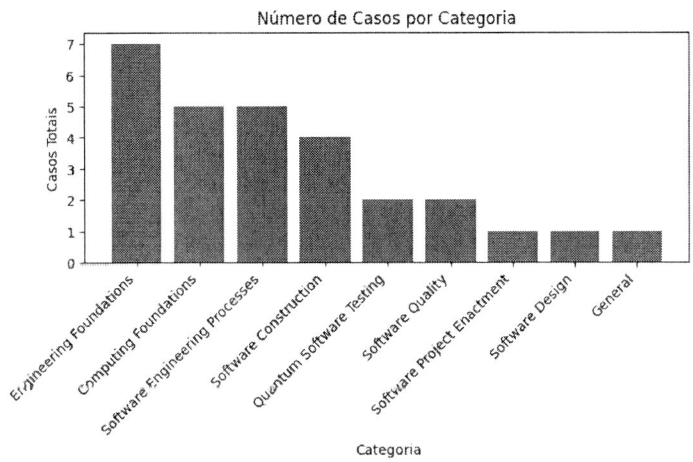

Figura 3. Correlação entre artigos e categorias.

A Figura 4 apresenta a distribuição de artigos analisados por código desta categoria. Apesar de ser uma amostra inicial, chama atenção termos encontrados artigos na área de *engenharia de software quântico* que não possuem uma definição completa dos elementos básicos de um protocolo de pesquisa. De fato, apenas um elemento do protocolo do estudo (questão de pesquisa) é apresentado na maioria dos artigos analisados. O material completo de análise, exemplificado neste artigo, encontra-se disponível em: *https://bit.ly/qse-rapid-review*.

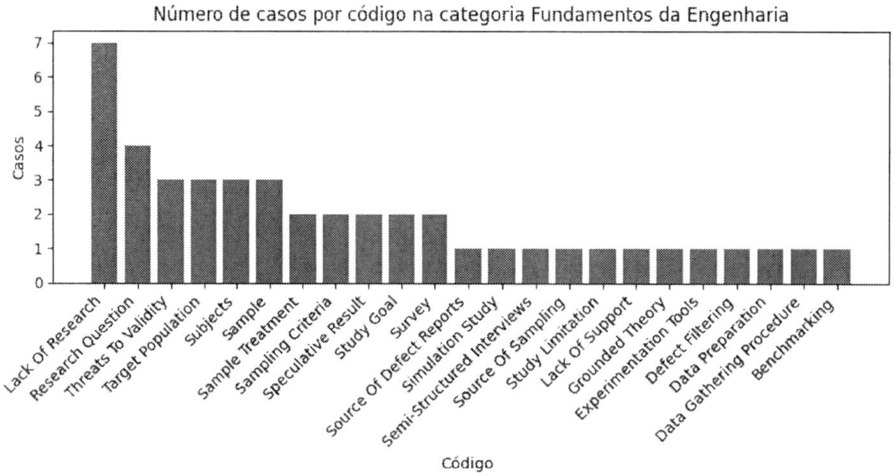

Figura 4. Número de casos por código na categoria Fundamentos da Engenharia.

5. Ameaças à Validade

Para mitigar o viés inerente ao pesquisador, adotamos uma abordagem de revisão em pares, seguida pela validação dos outros pesquisadores. Essa prática não só fortalece a integridade da análise, mas também enriquece a validade dos resultados. Além disso, é importante destacar a dependência das áreas do conhecimento estabelecidas pelo *SWEBOK*, cuja consolidação e atualização recente fornecem uma base sólida para esta pesquisa, que ao serem utilizadas como referência aumenta a consistência e a comparabilidade dos resultados, contribuindo para a robustez da análise.

Quanto à seleção da amostra, é crucial ressaltar que nossa intenção não é apenas obter uma versão mínima dos resultados, mas sim garantir uma representação abrangente e significativa do panorama atual. Para garantir a robustez de nossos achados iniciais, os sete artigos selecionados foram submetidos a uma análise minuciosa realizada por pares de pesquisadores, respeitando os critérios de inclusão e exclusão. Assim, a seleção dos sete artigos e sua análise demonstrou-se adequada para alcançar os objetivos propostos.

6. Considerações Finais

Este artigo apresentou o plano de uma *rapid review* visando *caracterizar o estado da arte em tecnologias para engenharia de software quântico*. Também apresentou uma amostra da análise dos resultados obtidos a partir da execução deste plano. A viabilidade do protocolo se mostra positiva pois foi capaz de mapear toda tecnologia baseada em evidência voltada para *sistemas de software quânticos* em cada artigo analisado.

A leitura dos 64 artigos selecionados indica a existência de ao menos uma tecnologia para *engenharia de software quântico* disponível e de alguma avaliação desta tecnologia, seja experimental ou não. A experiência obtida a partir da análise de dados da amostra de sete artigos indica que o nível de codificação aplicado é adequado, revelando conceitos relevantes da pesquisa e da prática em *engenharia de software*. Além disso, entendemos que os resultados iniciais demonstram que o uso das áreas do *SWEBOK* como critério de categorização dos dados codificados é adequado, ajudando a revelar potenciais lacunas e oportunidades de pesquisa sobre o tema investigado. Apesar das lacunas de conteúdo identificadas nos artigos, todos são cobertos suficientemente por esta categorização. Além disso, os resultados iniciais obtidos sugerem que nossas suposições iniciais podem ser pertinentes.

O próximo passo imediato será, portanto, dar continuidade à análise de conteúdo dos artigos selecionados, permitindo identificar quais áreas do *SWEBOK* têm recebido atenção destacada no apoio tecnológico à *engenharia de software quântico*, bem como o nível de evidência disponível sobre este apoio. Entendemos que a conclusão deste estudo permitirá a identificação de importantes lacunas de pesquisa e fomentar a concepção de novas tecnologias baseadas em evidência para a *engenharia de software quântico*, especialmente para as áreas do *SWEBOK* menos abordadas. No entanto, para alcançar esses objetivos, é crucial enfrentar diversos desafios, como a complexidade inerente dos *sistemas quânticos*, a escassez de profissionais qualificados neste campo e a falta de padrões estabelecidos para a *engenharia do software quântico*. Portanto, é necessário investir em pesquisa e desenvolvimento de tecnologias que possam superar esses desafios e promover avanços significativos na área de *engenharia de software quântico*.

Agradecimentos

Prof. Travassos é Pesquisador CNPq (305701/2022-3) e CNE FAPERJ (E-26/201.170/2021), os quais apoiam esta pesquisa.

Referências

Corbin, J., Strauss, A. 2015. "Basics of Qualitative Research: Techniques and Procedures for Developing Grounded Theory". Sage, 4th Ed.

Wohlin, C., et al. 2012. "Experimentation in Software Engineering", Springer Berlin Heidelberg, Berlin, Heidelberg.

Moguel, E., et al. 2021. "A Roadmap for Quantum Software Engineering: Applying the Lessons Learned from the Classics". CEUR Workshop Proceedings, Volume 2705, pp. 5-13.

Piattini, M., et al. 2020. "The Talavera Manifesto for quantum software engineering and programming," in Proc. Quantum Softw. Eng. Program., pp. 1–5.

Bourque, P. and Fairley, R.E. eds., Guide to the Software Engineering Body of Knowledge, Version 3.0, IEEE Computer Society, 2014.

Santos, C. M., etl al. (2007). The pico strategy for the research question construction and evidence search. Revista Latino-Americana de Enfermagem, 15(3):508–511

Cartaxo, B., Pinto, G., and Soares, S. (2018). The role of rapid reviews in supporting decision-making in software engineering practice. ACM Int. Conf. Proceeding Ser.

Amalfitano, D., Matalonga, S., and Travassos, G. H. (2021). Introduction to the special issue on engineering context-aware software systems. Info and Software Technology, 132:106509.

Bosch, J. (2001). Software product lines: organizational alternatives. In Proceedings of the 23rd International Conference on Software Engineering. ICSE 2001, pp. 91–100.

Singh, J. and Bhangu, K. S. (2023). Contemporary quantum computing use cases: Taxonomy, review and challenges. Arch of Computat Methods in Eng, 30(1):615–638.

Upama, P. B., et al. (2022). Evolution of quantum computing: A systematic survey on the use of quantum computing tools. In 2022 IEEE 46th Annual Computers, Software, and Applications Conference (COMPSAC), pp. 520–529.

Khan, A. A., et al. (2023). Agile practices for quantum software development: Practitioners' perspectives. In 2023 IEEE International Conference on Quantum Software (QSW), pp. 9–20

El aoun, et al. (2021). Understanding quantum software engineering challenges an empirical study on stack exchange forums and github issues. In 2021 IEEE International Conference on Software Maintenance and Evolution (ICSME), pp. 343–354.

Desenvolvendo Jogos por Meio de Linha de Produto Dinâmica

Diego Castro[1,2], **Cláudia Werner**[1]

[1] Programa de Engenharia de Sistemas e Computação
COPPE (Universidade Federal do Rio de Janeiro)
Rio de Janeiro – RJ – Brazil

[2]Centro Federal de Educação Tecnológica Celso Suckow da Fonseca (CEFET)
Rio de Janeiro – RJ – Brazil

{diegocbcastro,werner}@cos.ufrj.br

Resumo. *O desenvolvimento de jogos é um processo que pode envolver vários colaboradores e estágios, fazendo com que muitos títulos e atualizações demorem meses ou até anos para serem lançados. Essa demora no lançamento pode gerar ansiedade e descontentamento na comunidade de usuários, que devido a isso, acabam migrando para outros jogos ou até mesmo criando suas próprias versões dos jogos a partir do original. Algumas empresas já implementaram soluções para mitigar esse problema, permitindo ao usuário final realizar alterações no jogo por meio de kits de desenvolvimento e plataformas visuais. No entanto, essas ferramentas ainda são pouco exploradas permitindo apenas pequenas edições. Linha de Produtos de Software Dinâmica (LPSD) é extensão do conceito de linha de produto tradicional, utilizada para projetar sistemas em larga escala para auto adaptação em relação ao ambiente que está sendo executado, permitindo gerar várias versões de um sistema em tempo real a partir da combinação das características pré-produzidas de um sistema. Com base nisso, o objetivo inicial deste trabalho é utilizar o conceito de LPSD para dar mais autonomia ao usuário final, permitindo que o mesmo consigar criar variadas versões do mesmo jogo que acaba de adquirir, fazendo com que o mesmo tenha mais opções de jogos, diminuindo sua ansiedade. Um protótipo da proposta foi desenvolvido e avaliado, confirmando o vasto potencial de aplicação deste conceito.*

1. Introdução

Os jogos progrediram significativamente ao longo dos anos, tornando-se uma das formas de entretenimento mais populares da atualidade, com lucros e investimentos atingindo bilhões de dólares por ano [Lee et al. 2020]. Com esse aumento contínuo de investimentos, os games se tornaram uma vitrine do ambiente industrial, atraindo fãs de todos os gêneros, idades e gostos, tornando esta indústria ainda maior, com expectativa de arrecadar cerca de 260 bilhões de dólares em 2025 [Beattie 2020].

Apesar da quantidade de dinheiro movimentado / investido e do tamanho da comunidade de usuários, o processo atual de desenvolvimento de um jogo, desde o planejamento até o lançamento, pode ser altamente custoso, demorado e exigir diversos especialistas, fazendo com que alguns títulos ou atualizações demorem meses ou até mesmo anos para serem lançados [Bilińska et al. 2020]. Essa demora pode causar ansiedade e frustração na comunidade, contribuindo para a busca por novos jogos por parte desses usuários [Unger 2012], o que pode acarretar na migração de usuários de um jogo para o outro ou até mesmo na criação de uma nova versão do jogo por algum jogador [Scacchi 2011]. Algumas empresas já estão utilizando estratégias para mitigar essa ansiedade, como a disponibilização de ferramentas para permitir que o jogador edite determinados elementos do jogo utilizando kits de desenvolvimento e interfaces de edição visual [Hofman-Kohlmeyer 2019, Scacchi 2011]. No entanto, esses métodos são bastante limitados, pois permitem que o usuário edite apenas mapas e imagens de personagens, sem possibilitar a edição de partes significativas dos jogos, como regras, comportamentos e mecânicas, como modificação do tipo de ataque, movimentação, opções de jogabilidade, entre outros.

Linha de Produtos de Software (LPS) é uma das abordagems propostas dentro da área de Reutilização de Software (RS), permitindo gerar várias versões de um sistema a partir da combinação de características pré-produzidas. Essas versões podem ser geradas por meio do agrupamento e edição de Pontos de Variação (PVs), que podem ser compreendidos como trechos do software que podem ser alterados [Krueger 1992]. De modo geral, quando um software possui uma série de características semelhantes e algumas novas que podem ser alterados ou adicionados, LPS, por meio de PVs, pode ser utilizada para gerar um novo produto [Krueger 1992].

Alguns softwares específicos necessitam de adaptação em tempo real, e para isso o conceito de Linha de Produtos de Software Dinâmica (LPSD) pode ser introduzido, sendo uma extensão da LPS que permite a modificação em tempo de execução de certos elementos da LPS para auto adaptação em relação ao ambiente que está sendo executado [Ayala et al. 2021].

Com isso, o presente trabalho propõe a utilização de LPS, mais especificamente LPSD, para o desenvolvimento de jogos, visando dar mais autonomia aos usuários finais permitindo-lhes criar variadas versões do mesmo jogo que acaba de adquirir através da seleção dos PVs em tempo de execução, no intuito de diminuir a ansiedade criada pela demora no lançamento de novos títulos. O uso de LPSD foi escolhido para proporcionar uma melhor interação e dinâmismo para o usuário final, possibilitando que o mesma consiga ajustar as mecânicas, regras e opções visuais do jogo em tempo real.

Para avaliar este conceito foi desenvolvida uma LPSD, disponibilizada por meio de um protótipo de um jogo de plataforma no qual o próprio usuário final pode modificar partes da linha, selecionando as características desejadas através de PVs, permitindo assim a criação de múltiplos jogos. O jogo foi validado por meio de avaliação com profissionais e estudantes da área, demonstrando o potencial do uso de LPSD para expansão de jogos.

O restante deste artigo é apresentado da seguinte forma: a Seção 2 apresenta alguns conceitos principais para o bom entendimento do artigo, a Seção 3 descreve e explica como um protótipo foi criado, como prova de conceito da solução proposta, a Seção 4 apresenta uma avaliação inicial e o que foi observado com a criação do protótipo, e a Seção 5 conclui com algumas observações, limitações e trabalhos futuros.

2. Fundamentação Teórica

Os jogos podem conter inúmeras características, onde a complexidade do mesmo pode aumentar proporcionalmente ao número de seus elementos. Portanto, devido a complexidade de um jogo, são necessárias técnicas para organizar esses elementos. Existem inúmeras maneiras de organizar as propriedades e elementos para o desenvolvimento de um jogo e uma das mais conhecidas é a Tétrade Elementar (TE) [Schell 2008] que visa classificar as propriedades de um jogo em quatro categorias principais: **[1] Mecânica:** pode ser interpretada como as regras e as ações que podem ocorrer durante o jogo. **[1.1]Mecânica de segundo nível:** embora as mecânicas de segundo nível não façam parte da TE, elas serão adicionadas neste trabalho para descrever mecânicas que são geradas a partir da combinação de mecânicas primárias. Essa adição foi feita para trazer mais dinamismo à proposta de alteração dos jogos a serem construídos. **[2] História:** descreve o aspecto narrativo do jogo. Neste trabalho a história será modificada através da modificação direta da estética. Neste trabalho, a história é consequência da estéticas e da seleção das características da LPS. **[3] Estética:** são as imagens do jogo, personagens, objetos e mapas. **[4] Tecnologia:** refere-se às ferramentas e aos sistemas usados para implementar a jogabilidade. Neste trabalho esta categoria não é modificada já que a tecnologia utilizada para todos os jogos é a mesma, sempre utilizando Unity [Koulaxidis e Xinogalos 2022] para o desenvolvimento de jogos mobile.

Conforme mencionado na introdução deste trabalho, o principal problema que este estudo visa abordar é reduzir a ansiedade da comunidade de usuários de jogos, que frequentemente precisam esperar meses ou até mesmo anos pelo lançamento de um novo título. Para resolver isso, foi proposta a LPSD para o desenvolvimento de N versões do mesmo jogo. Além disso, foi realizada uma busca da literatura para descrever as lacunas no estado da arte em relação às modificações de jogos [Castro e Werner 2023].

3. Protótipo

Esta seção busca apresentar o protótipo de um jogo que visou disponibilizar uma LPS, mais especificamente, uma LPSD para jogos de plataforma, permitindo aos usuários finais editar ou adicionar novos recursos à linha de jogos disponibilizada em tempo real. O protótipo foi desenvolvido como um jogo devido à sua simplicidade e para dar mais dinamismo à solução proposta, sem a necessidade de instalação de novas ferramentas. Assim, o próprio jogo geraria novos jogos para o usuário com base nas funcionalidades escolhidas.

Como mencionado na Seção 2, os jogos podem possuir muitas características e, devido a isso, existem algumas maneiras de demonstrá-las. Nesse trabalho foi utilizado método da Tétrade Elementar, a seguir o protótipo criado é descrito de acordo com a mesma:

O protótipo proposto visa disponibilizar uma LPSD de um jogo de plataforma onde o protagonista deve completar três tarefas em cada fase. No início do jogo o jogador deve selecionar as características que deseja incorporar ao jogo, através das três árvores de características, uma para cada nível da TE (mecânica, mecânica de segundo nível e estética). A Figura 1 apresenta alguns níveis gerados pelo jogo, a partir dos quais também é possível visualizar os objetivos que foram selecionados. A Figura 2 mostra a LPSD do jogo, onde o usuário pode selecionar as funcionalidades desejadas para o jogo que quer criar. Nela, de cima para baixo, é possível ver: um ícone de chave inglesa que representa a mecânica, um haltere representando a mecânica do segundo nível e um lápis representando a estética do jogo. Por fim, também exibe o menu de regras do jogo, que descreve como jogar.

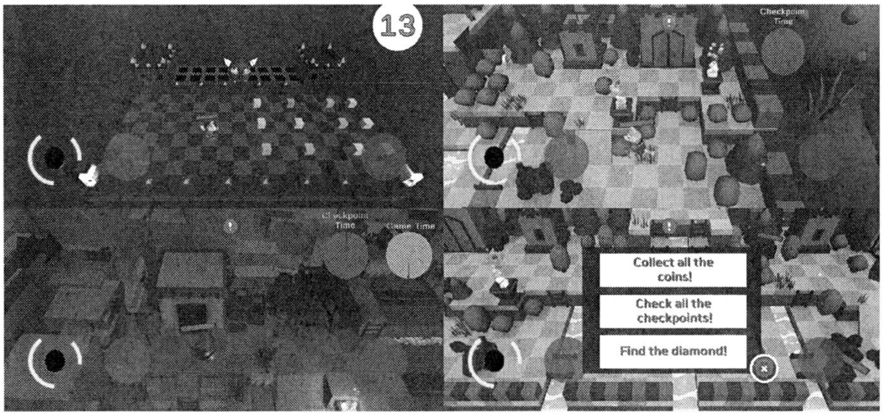

Figura 1. Jogos gerados pela jogo.

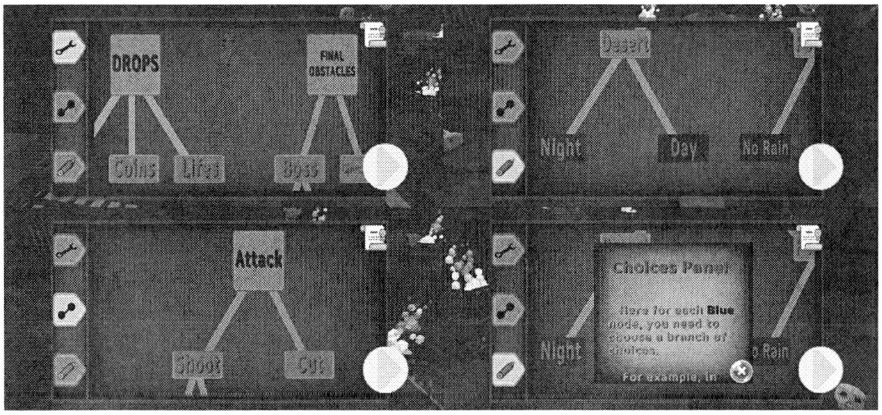

Figura 2. Árvore de seleção de características.

O jogo funciona como uma LPSD onde o jogador pode escolher cada elemento do jogo como: sua mecânica, seus objetivos, seus inimigos e outros elementos. Em cada jogo, o jogador escolherá as características de sua preferência e a própria inteligência da linha criará um jogo com as características selecionadas. A seguir, é descrito cada um dos elementos que podem ser selecionados ou modificados pelo jogo.

Mecânicas: [1] ***Drops*:** na linguagem dos jogos essa palavra pode ser compreendida como o ato de um inimigo proporcionar um item ao usuário ao morrer. Portanto ao selecionar umas dessas características na LPS, o jogador poderá coletar um dos itens listados a seguir. **[1.1] Moedas:** permite o jogador coletar moedas ao matar um inimigo; **[1.2] Vidas:** permite o jogador coletar vidas ao matar determinados inimigos, que ao serem coletadas incrementam a barra de vida do jogador; **[1.3] Poderes:** permite o jogador trocar de arma ao longo do jogo. **[2] Obstáculos:** tarefas a serem superadas pelo jogador ao longo do jogo. **[2.1] Chefe:** escolha se o jogo terá um ou vários chefes (inimigos finais) ao longo da partida. **[2.2] *Check Point*:** obstáculo onde o jogador deve encontrar determinados itens para poder completar a fase. **[3] Objetivo:** objetivo principal do jogo. **[3.1] Salvar cachorro:** o jogador deve resgatar o cachorro que foi preso em uma gaiola pelo vilão principal do jogo. **[3.2] Timer:** escolha se o jogo deve ser vencido antes que o tempo acabe. **[3.3] Encontrar objetos:** selecione os itens que o jogador deve encontrar para resolver um quebra-cabeças.

Mecânica de segundo nível: **[1] Mover:** escolha a mecânica de segundo nível do jogo. **[1.1] Andar:** o personagem só pode andar. **[1.2] Correr:** o personagem poderá ter mais velocidade ao longo do jogo para fugir dos inimigos. **[2] Ataque:** escolha a mecânica de ataque. **[2.1] Shoot:** escolha entre as duas possibilidades de armas, com um tiro de cada vez ou vários tiros. **[2.2] Corte:** escolha uma espada como opção de arma.

Estética: **[1] Ecossistema:** escolha o mapa do jogo, tendo quatro opções de mapa. Os inimigos e imagens do jogo mudam de acordo com o mapa (deserto e floresta) e tempo (dia e noite).

Por fim, para tornar o jogo mais dinâmico e desafiador, uma série de recursos foram adicionados a inteligência da LPSD, incluindo inimigos com níveis de vida variados, diferentes tipos de ataques, um algoritmo A* usado para fazer os inimigos perseguirem o personagem principal, contador de danos e itens que incrementam a vida do personagem quando encontrado.

4. Avaliação e Discussão

4.1. Planejamento

A avaliação buscou verificar a aprovação do desenvolvimento da solução proposta por parte da comunidade, e para isso foram utilizadas algumas questões do modelo de *Technology Acceptance Model* (TAM) [Davis 1993], que coleta dados principalmente sobre a utilidade e usabilidade da solução apresentada, permitindo aos usuários determinar se ela será útil para a comunidade. Porém, como a solução proposta foi implementada através de um jogo, o questionário MEEGA [Petri et al. 2016] também foi utilizado. Este questionário é utilizado principalmente para avaliar a usabilidade e experiência proporcionada por um jogo, porém, neste estudo, foi utilizado para determinar se a usabilidade e experiência do jogo influenciaram ou não na aceitação da solução proposta. Portanto, o questionário MEEGA foi utilizado para avaliar a usabilidade e experiência do jogo, enquanto as questões do TAM foram utilizadas para avaliar a utilidade da ferramenta a ser construída.

O estudo foi composto por duas fases: piloto e estudo final. Para o estudo piloto, apenas um aluno de graduação avaliou o jogo e respondeu o questionário a fim de identificar possíveis problemas. Três grupos de participantes foram escolhidos para o estudo final. Esta divisão de grupos foi criada de forma a dividir os diferentes níveis de experiência dos participantes, envolvendo 46 avaliadores, que se dividiram em: especialistas, que eram profissionais com experiência na área de jogos e Reutilização de Software (RS); alunos do curso de informática que já haviam cursado disciplinas de RS; e a comunidade de entusiastas de jogos que foi composta por usuários de foruns sobre jogos e pesquisadores da área.

O estudo foi realizado remotamente mediante disponibilização dos materiais necessários à execução do mesmo, sendo realizado por meio de uma chamada do *Google Meeting*, fazendo uso do protocolo *think-aloud* [Jääskeläinen 2010]. Esse protocolo foi utilizado para coletar informações adicionais, como se o jogador estava tendo dificuldades e se gostou da solução proposta, entre outras coisas. As principais etapas deste estudo foram: **Descrição do estudo e do jogo:** distribuição de formulário contendo as principais informações necessárias para a realização da avaliação. **Caracterização dos participantes:** questionário utilizado para saber as experiências do avaliador. **Questionário qualitativo:** os questionários TAM [Davis 1993] e MEEGA [Petri et al. 2016] adaptados ao contexto foram disponibilizados a cada um dos participantes. O questionário utilizado pode ser visto com mais detalhes a seguir. **Usabilidade do jogo - MEEGA [Petri et al. 2016]:** **[1]** O *design* do jogo é atrativo (*sprites*, interfaces, gráficos, etc). **[2]** Textos, cores e fontes combinam e são consistentes. **[3]** Aprender a jogar este jogo foi fácil para mim. **[4]** O jogo é fácil de jogar. **[5]** As regras do jogo são claras e fáceis de entender. **[6]** As fontes (tamanho e estilo) utilizadas no jogo são fáceis de ler. **Experiência do jogo - MEEGA [Petri et al. 2016]:** **[7]** As cores usadas no jogo são atrativas e são fáceis de compreender. **[8]** Este jogo é apropriadamente desafiador para mim. **[9]** O jogo oferece novos desafios (obstáculos, situações ou variações) em um ritmo adequado. **[10]** O jogo não se torna monótono à medida que avança. **[11]** Eu recomendaria este jogo aos meus colegas. **[12]** Eu me diverti jogando o jogo. **[13]** Houve algo interessante no jogo que chamou minha atenção. **[14]** Eu estava tão envolvido em minha tarefa de jogo que perdi a noção do tempo. **[15]** Esqueci-me do ambiente ao meu redor enquanto jogava este jogo. **[16]** Os conteúdos do jogo são relevantes para os meus interesses. **Utilidade da ferramenta - TAM [Davis 1993]:** **[17]** Entendi facilmente como usar a abordagem LPS? **[18]** Apliquei a estratégia corretamente? Eu consegui projetar os jogos que queria jogar. **[19]** Entendi o que aconteceu na interação com a ferramenta? **[20]** Percebi como é simples criar um novo jogo usando LPS? **[21]** Eu usaria essa ferramenta para criar / expandir jogos se ela proposta?

4.2. Resultados

omo primeiro ponto de análise dos resultados, é importante destacar que, embora o questionário MEEGA [Petri et al. 2016] tenha sido empregado para coletar informações sobre a usabilidade e a experiência do jogo, essa informação foi obtida apenas para verificar se algum aspecto do jogo, como gráficos e cores, poderia influenciar o resultado final da avaliação. Quanto à usabilidade e experiência do jogo, foi possível observar que não teve efeito direto nos resultados do estudo; entretanto, foram identificadas algumas melhorias que poderiam ser feitas, entre elas: melhorar a movimentação do personagem usando o *joystick*, modificar o nível de dificuldade do jogo e aumentá-lo à medida que os jogos eram criados e adicionar *zoom in* e *zoom out* na tela da árvore de características.

É possível observar um número significativo de avaliadores com respostas positivas, indicando que os usuários conseguiram construir jogos baseados no conceito de LPSD e compreender como o conceito de VPs seria utilizado dentro da árvore de características. Na disponibilização de uma pergunta para respostas abertas, foi possível capturar respostas, como: A possibilidade de derivar jogos a partir da seleção de elementos em uma linha de produto, parece ser uma solução benéfica para a comunidade com aplicação no mundo real; Conceito muito interessante; Consegui criar três jogos totalmente diferentes; Conceito interessante que seria de grande benefício para a comunidade de desenvolvedores de jogos.

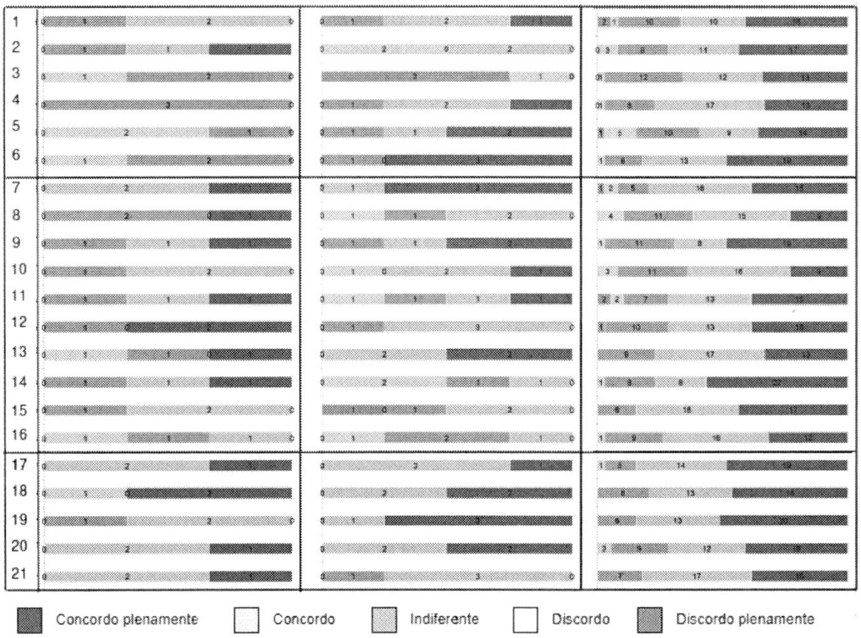

Figura 3. Respostas dos questionários Meega / TAM

Olhando para as respostas de uma forma geral, é possível perceber que mais de 70% das respostas obtiveram resultados positivos (Concordo e Concordo Plenamente) e que aproximadamente 95% dos respondentes deram respostas maiores ou iguais a Indiferente, com apenas 5% das respostas obtiveram nota negativa (Discordo e Discordo Plenamente), num total de 46 participantes. Esse percentual é ainda maior quando se consideram apenas as respostas que discutem a utilidade da ferramenta, com mais de 81% de respostas positivas, mais de 98% de respostas acima de Indiferente e menos de 2% de respostas negativas. A Figura 3 demonstra as respostas quanto à usabilidade, experiência e utilidade da solução proposta proposta. Com isso, é possível demonstrar que a solução tem potencial de utilidade e tem a possibilidade de auxiliar a comunidade de jogos na expansão de seus jogos com maior flexibilidade ao permitir a edição de múltiplos elementos do jogo.

5. Considerações Finais e Trabalhos Futuros

Este trabalho buscou utilizar o conceito de LPSD para dar mais autonomia ao usuário final, permitindo que o mesmo consiga criar variadas versões de um mesmo jogo em tempo real. Para testar a viabilidade da solução proposta, foi desenvolvido um protótipo que visa disponibilizar uma LPSD por meio de um jogo no qual o usuário final pode escolher as características que desejasse, selecionando-as na árvore de características. O protótipo foi avaliado por 46 participantes, onde foi determinado que a solução é interessante e útil para a comunidade de jogos.

A partir da avaliação foi possível perceber que a comunidade acredita no potencial da solução, abrindo a possibilidade de uma expansão da mesma para algo um pouco mais elaborado. Como trabalho futuro, pretende-se ampliar o conceito apresentado pelo protótipo para que seja possível desenvolver uma solução de desenvolvimento de jogos a partir dos conceitos de LPS. A proposta visa o desenvolvimento de duas ferramentas, uma para ser utilizada pela própria empresa desenvolvedora do jogo, para entendimento do domínio do jogo e criação da LPS e dos PVs e outra onde o usuário final consiga editar a LPS do jogo adquirido, permitindo assim que ele consiga criar variadas versões do jogo por meio dos PVs.

Referências

Ayala, I., Papadopoulos, A. V., Amor, M., e Fuentes, L. (2021). Prodspl: Proactive self-adaptation based on dynamic software product lines. *Journal of Systems and Software*, 175:110909.

Beattie, A. (2020). How the video game industry is changing. `https://www.investopedia.com/articles/investing/053115/how-video-game-industry-changing.asp`. Online; accessed 29 May 2022.

Bilińska, K., Dewalska-Opitek, A., e Hofman-Kohlmeyer, M. (2020). To mod or not to mod—an empirical study on game modding as customer value co-creation. *Sustainability*, 12(21):9014.

Castro, D. e Werner, C. (2023). A multivocal review on derivation games. *IARIA Annual Congress on Frontiers in Science, Technology, Services, and Applications*, 1:144 to 149.

Davis, F. D. (1993). User acceptance of information technology: system characteristics, user perceptions and behavioral impacts. *International journal of man-machine studies*, 38(3):475–487.

Hofman-Kohlmeyer, M. M. (2019). Players as content creators. the benefits of game modding according to polish users. *International Scientific Journal News*, 2:8–26.

Jääskeläinen, R. (2010). Think aloud protocol. *Handbook of translation studies*, 1:371–374.

Koulaxidis, G. e Xinogalos, S. (2022). Improving mobile game performance with basic optimization techniques in unity. *Modelling*, 3(2):201–223.

Krueger, C. W. (1992). Software reuse. *ACM Computing Surveys (CSUR)*, 24(2):131–183.

Lee, D., Lin, D., Bezemer, C.-P., e Hassan, A. E. (2020). Building the perfect game–an empirical study of game modifications. *Empirical Software Engineering*, pages 1–34.

Petri, G., von Wangenheim, C. G., e Borgatto, A. F. (2016). Meega+: an evolution of a model for the evaluation of educational games. *INCoD/GQS*, 3:1–40.

Scacchi, W. (2011). Modding as an open source approach to extending computer game systems. *Proceedings of IFIP International Conference on Open Source Systems*, pages 62–74.

Schell, J. (2008). *The Art of Game Design: A book of lenses.* CRC press.

Unger, A. (2012). Modding as part of game culture. *Computer Games and New Media Cultures*, pages 509–523.

A Case Study on Test Case Construction with Large Language Models: Unveiling Practical Insights and Challenges

Roberto F. Lima Jr[1], **Luiz Fernando P. B. Presta**[2], **Lucca S. Borborema**[2], **Vanderson N. Silva**[1], **Marcio L. M. Dahia**[1], **Anderson Santos**[1]

[1]CESAR
Recife, PE, Brazil

[2]CESAR School
Recife, PE, Brazil.

{rflj,vns, mlmd, acss}@cesar.org.br, {lfpbp, lsb}@cesar.school

Abstract. *This study delves into the integration of Large Language Models (LLMs) in test case construction within software engineering, exploring their potential to enhance efficiency and effectiveness in test generation. Leveraging LLMs, known for their sophisticated natural language processing abilities, this research conducts a detailed case study on a representative software application to evaluate the practicality of LLMs in creating detailed and accurate test scenarios. The investigation focuses on the challenges and advantages of LLMs in test case development, assessing their impact on test comprehensiveness, accuracy, and the formulation process. By providing a nuanced understanding of LLMs' role in software testing, this paper aims to inform practitioners and researchers about their potential and limitations, offering insights into their application in real-world testing environments and their contribution to advancing software testing methodologies.*

1. Introduction

Software testing constitutes a critical phase in the software development life cycle, ensuring the delivery of reliable and high-quality software products. In recent years, the advent of advanced technologies, particularly Large Language Models (LLMs), has introduced novel possibilities for automating and enhancing various facets of software engineering. LLMs, exemplified by models such as OpenAI's GPT (Generative Pre-trained Transformer)[OpenAI 2023], exhibit remarkable natural language processing capabilities and have demonstrated applicability in diverse domains. This paper addresses the intersection of LLMs and software testing, focusing specifically on their role in the construction of test cases.

The use of LLMs in software testing holds the promise of increasing the efficiency and effectiveness of test case generation. The ability of these models to understand and generate human-like text prompts paves the way for more natural and expressive articulation of test scenarios. However, the practical implications of integrating LLMs into the nuanced process of test case construction remain under explored. This study seeks to bridge this gap by presenting a detailed case study that investigates the application of LLMs in constructing test cases for a real-world software application.

The case study methodology adopted in this research involves the selection of a representative software application, the formulation of test case construction methodologies leveraging LLMs, and a thorough evaluation of the outcomes. By examining the interplay between LLMs and the complexities inherent in software testing, this study aims to provide insights into the practical advantages, challenges, and considerations associated with their implementation. Through this exploration, the intent is to contribute substantively to the ongoing dialogue surrounding the integration of cutting-edge technologies, such as LLMs, in the pursuit of optimizing software testing practices.

2. Related Work

The intersection of Large Language Models (LLMs) and software engineering has witnessed growing interest in recent literature, reflecting a broader acknowledgment of the transformative potential of these models in many domains. Within the realm of software testing, where the efficacy of test case construction significantly influences software quality, the exploration of LLM applications remains a relatively nascent but promising area.

The preeminent contribution of LLMs to software engineering lies in their ability to comprehend and generate human-like text, a feature that has inspired its application in diverse natural language processing tasks. Prior studies, such as [Brown et al. 2020] showcase the prowess of LLMs, exemplified by models like GPT-3, in understanding context, generating coherent responses, and adapting to diverse language inputs. This linguistic versatility positions LLMs as potentially powerful tools for expressing and formulating test cases in a more natural, context-aware manner.

Taking advantage of LLMs, many Generative AI models have been developed to implement diverse use cases, such as generating documentation for code [Feng et al. 2020], auto-completing code [Kim et al. 2021] and generating unit tests [Tufano et al. 2021].

In the specific context of software testing, recent research by [Wang et al. 2024] summarized the use of LLMs in a diverse set of applications, integrating them with traditional methods such as differential and mutation testing. Despite showing promise, LLMs are recognized as complementary rather than exclusive solutions for software testing. The research also combined LLMs with metamorphic testing, generating test cases based on expected input-output relationships, and explored their role in model-based testing, enhancing model accuracy through natural language descriptions and adapting to system changes.

However, existing literature lacks comprehensive insights into the practical implications, challenges, and considerations associated with integrating LLMs into the intricate task of test case construction for real-world software applications.

3. Approach

This section outlines our approach, consisting of the semi-automated test cases constructions and the evaluation framework for it. First it was explored the integration of LLMs with software specifications for generating test cases and later elucidates our method for qualitatively assess the effectiveness of the generated test cases.

3.1. Test cases construction

To generate test cases from the model, the strategy of prompt engineering was employed. The prompt, which serves as the input for the LLM, comprises a set of instructions and necessary data for task completion. The quality of the model's response improves with clearer and more contextual descriptions provided in the prompt. Another effective strategy for achieving positive outcomes involves allowing the model to engage in reasoning by decomposing the task into intermediate steps [Wei et al. 2022].

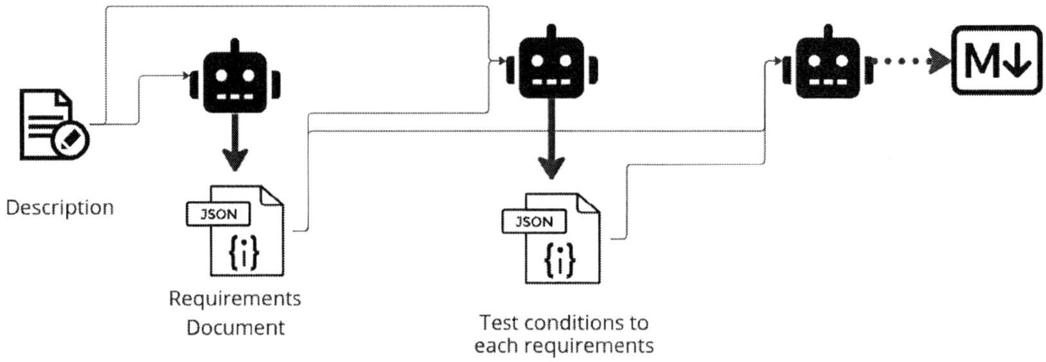

Figure 1. The workflow for building test cases using a Large Language Model (represented as the robot)

An interactive method was devised to derive test cases from the model, as outlined in Figure 1. Initially, engineers used a specially designed template to provide detailed application descriptions efficiently. This template, refined through extensive testing, helps pinpoint the most relevant information for the model to grasp the software context. The model then generates a requirements document, which, combined with the initial description, is used to formulate and produce test cases in the required format.

The OpenAI API was used with the GPT-3.5 Turbo model [OpenAI 2023] together with the Python framework LangChain [LangChain 2023] in order to manage the prompts, insert the context, memory, and handle interactivity. The following subsections details the step by step of this procedure.

3.1.1. Application Description

Providing contextual information is crucial for tailoring the test cases to the specific application at hand and preventing hallucinations, as emphasized by [Lewis et al. 2020]. Crafting this description should not become more challenging than generating the test cases themselves. To balance this trade-off and ensure accurate communication of relevant information, empirical experiments were conducted with various hypothetical software. These experiments involved a qualitative analysis to identify potential gaps or missing information. It was observed that using one template per software feature resulted in significantly better outcomes than attempting to describe all features in a single template file. Consequently, a template has been devised to guide the application description process:

What is the software name? • A single line with the desired name to refer to the software **What is the software's main purpose?** • A brief description with no more than 3 lines **What is the platform type?** • The platform of the software: Web, mobile, ... **Feature description** • An overview of each feature from the software

3.1.2. Prompt Design

In the prompt elaboration, throughout the tests and references about prompt engineering, the input for the model was separated into three parts, with each one complementing the other, reducing the complexity and granting better quality in the responses [Gu et al. 2023]. The prompts use the concept of Role Prompting [Kong et al. 2023], which provides the model context in the way it should interpret the input, thus, contributing into more elaborated responses from the model.

To build the software requirements the prompt is consisted of the role description (Ex.: QA Engineer), the feature description as stated in section 3.1.1 with all information filled according to the under testing software, and the instructions for the expected output:

- `Project name`
- `Project goal`
- `List of the software's non-functional requirements.`
- `The list of the software's functional requirements.`

The first two attributes are used to confirm that the model has accurately absorbed the given context and can succinctly summarize the software's purpose. Additionally the instruction also request to format the output as JSON, enabling its seamless integration as input for subsequent prompts.

The next step is to produce the test conditions. This includes incorporating the role, the software description, and the generated software requirements from the previous step into the prompt. As part of the prompt's instructions, the desired output is specified to be a list of test conditions for each functional requirement, formatted in JSON.

In the final step, test cases are built for each test condition. This process involves looping over the list created in the previous step. Each prompt includes several key elements: the role, the software description, the requirement, and the test condition itself. For the output, markdown format is specified. This choice facilitates the subsequent conversion of the test cases into a PDF document, significantly improving their visualization and organization. The test cases should incorporate several essential attributes: `ID`, `Title`, `Pre-conditions`, `Steps`, `Expected results`, `Test Data`.

3.2. Evaluation setup

To effectively evaluate test case generation, we selected Da.tes, an active web platform with a broad range of features for connecting startups, investors, and businesses, as our study subject. The platform's diverse functionalities facilitated a comprehensive analysis of test case generation effectiveness. Access to Da.tes' existing manual test cases provided a crucial comparison point for our research.

Our evaluation centered on the quality of test case documentation, sidestepping metrics that necessitate code access or historical data, focusing on qualities like Clarity, Correctness, Completeness, Consistency, Understandability, Self-containedness, and Specificity, as outlined in [Barraood et al. 2021a] and [Barraood et al. 2021b].

The study employed an unbiased approach, using anonymous, uniformly formatted sets of 10 AI-generated and 10 manual test cases, assessed by quality assurance engineers to gauge documentation quality effectively.

Two separate forms were created for the evaluation. The first form was designed to focus explicitly on the quality sub-factors of each test case under analysis. To mitigate volunteer fatigue and potential confusion, only the three most critical factors identified by [Lai 2017] were used: **Correctness**, **Completeness**, and **Consistency**. Volunteers were asked to rate each factor for each test case on a scale of 1-5, in accordance with the criteria outlined in Table1.

Score	1	2	3	4	5
Meaning	Very Poor	Poor	Regular	Good	Very Good

Table 1. Scores definition that was used by volunteers to rate the test cases

The second form focused on the implicit quality of the test cases, employing an A/B testing format to gauge preferences. In this setup, two similar test cases—each testing the same path in the software—were presented side by side. Volunteers were given 10 questions, asking them to choose between test A or test B, without knowing which was AI-generated and which was manually crafted. Additionally, a justification field was provided, where they could explain their choice. This feedback, inherently subjective and not based on predefined quality factors like the first form, aims to uncover any discernible differences between the two groups of test cases that may warrant further investigation

4. Results and Discussions

A total of 7 participants completed both forms. While the analysis is based on this limited sample, the consistency in responses and the insightful explanations submitted by participants offer relevant insights. We start our analysis with the quantitative scores for each metric. To provide an overview, the average scores for each group were calculated. Figure 2 shows the comparison between AI and Manual test cases. The total average scores across all three metrics are similar - 4.31 for AI versus 4.18 for Manual - with a slight advantage for the AI-generated process.

The correctness metric revealed the most significant discrepancy between the AI and Manual test groups in our evaluation. A closer examination of individual results indicated that AI-generated tests never received the lowest score. However, the manually written tests did receive the lowest score in a few cases, thereby lowering their average. Despite this, the overall assessment suggests that the AI is capable of generating test cases with a level of correctness comparable to human performance.

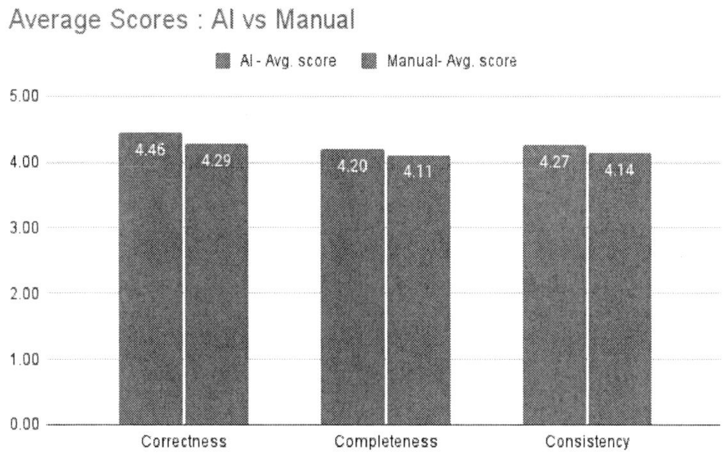

Figure 2. Average rate for AI and Manual test cases group split by quality factors

The same observation applies to the consistency of the test cases, where some instances of very low scores explain the observed gap. Consistency, defined as the degree of uniformity and reliability in test outcomes, reflects the ability of a set of test cases to produce reliable and expected results under varying conditions. In our analysis, it was evident that the test cases created by the AI maintained a consistent level of logic, even though they were generated in separate interactions. This consistency is likely attributable to the specific prompt that guided the output format, ensuring a uniform approach across different test cases.

In the analysis of completeness, we observed that the averages were quite similar between the two groups. However, there was a notable difference in their distributions. The manually created tests received more top scores (35 rated as '5') compared to the AI-generated tests (which received 32 top scores), but they also had a greater number of the lowest scores. Completeness, which refers to the extent to which a set of test cases covers all possible scenarios and functionalities of the software, can vary significantly. This variation in scores can be attributed to the test engineer's personal judgment, particularly in deciding the level of detail needed based on the perceived importance or rarity of a feature.

The second questionnaire provides more insight into the perceptions and preferences regarding the test cases, deliberately avoiding inference of any specific metrics, as it was presented in an A/B testing format. Given the total of the responses for all tests (70 - 7 evaluators and 10 test cases), the overall preference leaned towards the AI-generated cases (58.6%). These results are illustrated in Figure 3.

In analyzing the results on a case-by-case basis, we defined a 'clear win' as a scenario where the preference difference exceeds one vote (e.g., a 4 versus 3 vote count is considered a tie). Applying this criterion, we found that only two AI-generated tests were preferred over their manual counterparts, and similarly, two manual tests were favored over the AI ones. The remaining six test cases resulted in what can be termed as a technical tie.

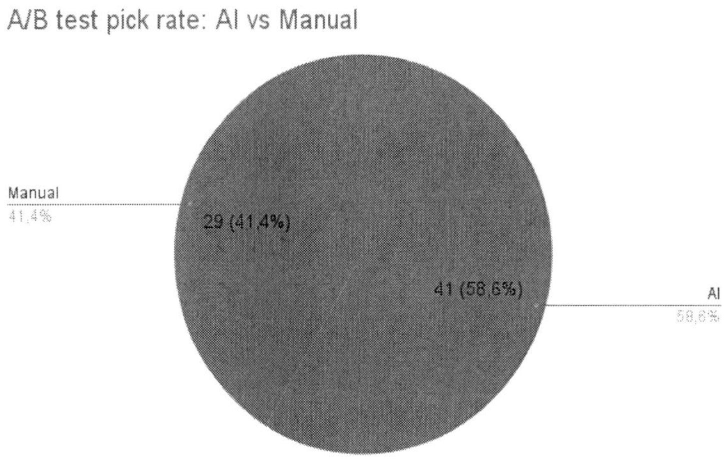

Figure 3. Pick rate for AI and Manual test cases in the A/B test

In delving into the reasons provided when Manual test cases were preferred, common themes emerged around correctness and completeness, with 'clarity' being a frequently cited new factor. Conversely, when AI-generated test cases were favored, the justifications predominantly revolved around the level of detail and completeness. The rationale behind the ties varied, ranging from perceptions of equivalency between the cases to differing opinions on correctness. For example, in the evaluation of the same test case, some evaluators identified a mistake, while others considered it more correct and complete.

Our analysis reveals a complex picture of AI-generated versus manually created test cases, highlighting the trade-offs and potential synergies between the two. Preferences vary, with evaluators considering factors like clarity, correctness, detail, and completeness, challenging the conventional views on automated versus manual testing. These insights, demonstrating the nuanced aspects of test case quality, pave the way for a deeper understanding of AI's role in quality assurance as we delve into the concluding discussions of this paper.

5. Conclusion

This paper explored the use of Large Language Models (LLMs) in generating test cases for software engineering, focusing on a case study with the software application Da.tes. We found that LLMs can create test cases that rival those made by humans in quality, showcasing their potential as tools in test case development, though human input remains crucial for ensuring accuracy and context-appropriateness. While LLMs enhance efficiency and detail in test creation, their effectiveness varies, indicating the need for a combined approach with human expertise. Future research should investigate the broader implications, including cost and time benefits, of integrating LLMs in test case generation. Despite some limitations in handling complex inter-feature tests, enhancing the LLM's understanding of feature interdependencies could significantly improve its applicability in more intricate testing scenarios.

References

Barraood, S., Mohd, H., and Baharom, F. (2021a). Test case quality factors. *Turkish Journal of Computer and Mathematics Education (TURCOMAT)*, 12:1683–1694.

Barraood, S., Mohd, H., and Baharom, F. (2021b). Test case quality factors: Content analysis of software testing websites. *Webology*, 18:75 – 87.

Brown, T., Mann, B., Ryder, N., Subbiah, M., Kaplan, J. D., Dhariwal, P., Neelakantan, A., Shyam, P., Sastry, G., Askell, A., et al. (2020). Language models are few-shot learners. *Advances in neural information processing systems*, 33:1877–1901.

Feng, Z., Guo, D., Tang, D., Duan, N., Feng, X., Gong, M., Shou, L., Qin, B., Liu, T., Jiang, D., et al. (2020). Codebert: A pre-trained model for programming and natural languages. In *Findings of the Association for Computational Linguistics: EMNLP 2020*, pages 1536–1547.

Gu, J., Han, Z., Chen, S., Beirami, A., He, B., Zhang, G., Liao, R., Qin, Y., Tresp, V., and Torr, P. (2023). A systematic survey of prompt engineering on vision-language foundation models. *arXiv preprint arXiv:2307.12980.*

Kim, S., Zhao, J., Tian, Y., and Chandra, S. (2021). Code prediction by feeding trees to transformers. In *2021 IEEE/ACM 43rd International Conference on Software Engineering (ICSE)*, pages 150–162. IEEE.

Kong, A., Zhao, S., Chen, H., Li, Q., Qin, Y., Sun, R., and Zhou, X. (2023). Better zero-shot reasoning with role-play prompting. *arXiv preprint arXiv:2308.07702.*

Lai, S.-T. (2017). Test case quality management procedure for enhancing the efficiency of iid continuous testing. *Journal of Software*, 12(10):794–806.

LangChain (2023). Langchain: Building applications with llms through composability. https://github.com/langchain-ai/langchain.

Lewis, P., Perez, E., Piktus, A., Petroni, F., Karpukhin, V., Goyal, N., Küttler, H., Lewis, M., Yih, W.-t., Rocktäschel, T., et al. (2020). Retrieval-augmented generation for knowledge-intensive nlp tasks. *Advances in Neural Information Processing Systems*, 33:9459–9474.

OpenAI (2023). Openai: Advancing digital intelligence. https://www.openai.com. Accessed on November 21, 2023.

Tufano, M., Drain, D., Svyatkovskiy, A., Deng, S. K., and Sundaresan, N. (2021). Unit test case generation with transformers and focal context. *arXiv preprint arXiv:2009.05617.*

Wang, J., Huang, Y., Chen, C., Liu, Z., Wang, S., and Wang, Q. (2024). Software testing with large language models: Survey, landscape, and vision. *IEEE Transactions on Software Engineering.*

Wei, J., Wang, X., Schuurmans, D., Bosma, M., Xia, F., Chi, E., Le, Q. V., Zhou, D., et al. (2022). Chain-of-thought prompting elicits reasoning in large language models.

Utilizando o GenderMag para aprimorar UX em plataformas educacionais

Kethelen do Carmo Souza, Genildo Gomes, Bruno Gadelha, Tayana Conte

[1]Instituto de Computação – Universidade Federal do Amazonas (UFAM)
Av. Gen. Rodrigo Octávio, 6200, Coroado I, Setor Norte, Campus Universitário
69080-900 – Manaus – AM

kethelen.souza, genildo.gomes, bruno, tayana@icomp.ufam.edu.br

Abstract. *In software development, gender bias can be reflected in products that favor or disadvantage a specific gender. This paper addresses integrating the GenderMag method and Nielsen's heuristics in requirements elicitation for user experience, focusing on gender inclusion in software design, particularly in Learning Management Systems (LMSs). The methodology involves applying the GenderMag method to inspect two LMS platforms, Moodle and Google Classroom, with the adaptation of personas based on this method. Issues identified through GenderMag were analyzed in light of Nielsen's heuristics. As a result, we elicited 6 recommendations based on identifying gender bias in the interfaces, functionalities, and interactions offered by the LMS platforms. The findings underscore the importance of considering user diversity to ensure an inclusive user experience.*

Resumo. *No contexto do desenvolvimento de software, o viés de gênero pode se refletir em produtos que favorecem ou prejudicam um determinado gênero. O artigo aborda a integração do método GenderMag e das heurísticas de Nielsen na elicitação de requisitos para a experiência do usuário, com foco na inclusão de gênero no design de software, especialmente em sistemas de gestão de aprendizagem (LMSs). A metodologia empregada envolve a aplicação do método GenderMag na inspeção de duas plataformas LMSs, o Moodle e o Google Classroom, com a adaptação de personas baseadas nesse método. Os problemas identificados através do GenderMag foram analisados à luz das heurísticas de Nielsen. Como resultado, foram elicitados 6 recomendações derivados da identificação de viés de gênero nas interfaces, funcionalidades e interações oferecidas pelas plataformas LMSs. Os resultados evidenciam a importância de considerar a diversidade de usuários para garantir uma experiência de uso inclusiva.*

1. Introdução

Os Learning Management Systems (LMS) são plataformas *online* que facilitam o ensino remoto, oferecendo uma maneira de gerenciar cursos e possibilitando a comunicação entre professores e alunos. Exemplos dessas plataformas incluem o Moodle e o Google Classroom, que são conhecidas por integrar diversos recursos, como atribuição de atividades, avaliação *online* e fóruns de discussão. No entanto, o uso dessas plataformas pode ser desafiador devido às características específicas de estudantes e professores ao interagir com elas [Tejedor et al. 2012].

A diversidade de gênero é uma das características relevantes dessas plataformas. Clark e Horton (2019) destacam a importância de proporcionar oportunidades equitativas a homens, mulheres e pessoas com diversas identidades de gênero, sem discriminação com base no sexo [Clark and Horton 2019]. Essa diversidade tem impactado decisões de *design*, desenvolvimento de funcionalidades e experiência do usuário (UX) em sistemas de software ao longo do tempo [Moro 2022].

A Experiência do Usuário (UX) se refere aos sentimentos das pessoas em relação a produtos, sistemas e serviços [ISO9241-110 2010]. Em plataformas de aprendizagem *online* como o Moodle e o Google Classroom, uma UX bem projetada é crucial para o sucesso do ensino, simplificando o uso para educadores e melhorando a experiência de aprendizado dos alunos. Avaliações de UX em LMS podem ser feitas através de testes de usabilidade, feedback dos usuários e análise de métricas de interação, proporcionando insights para melhorias na interface e no processo educacional.

A abordagem GenderMag é uma ferramenta proeminente para lidar com vieses de gênero no *design* de software [Burnett et al. 2016b]. Reconhecendo a importância da UX para promover a inclusão em ferramentas, essa abordagem destaca a necessidade de uma análise crítica e específica sobre o viés de gênero nas plataformas utilizadas. Essa análise visa corrigir possíveis desigualdades de gênero, estereótipos ou discriminações nos softwares, promovendo equidade e inclusão para todos os usuários, independentemente de sua identidade de gênero [Barbosa et al. 2021].

Nesse sentido, ao abordar aspectos específicos da usabilidade, é possível incorporar princípios relacionados às Heurísticas de Nielsen [Nielsen and Molich 1990], uma vez que oferecem uma abordagem sistemática para encontrar problemas de usabilidade, contribuindo para uma melhor experiência do usuário. Com isso, a aplicação dessas heurísticas pode ajudar a diminuir os vieses de gênero encontrados via aplicação do GenderMag, apoiando os softwares para que estes atendam de maneira equitativa a todos os usuários, independentemente de sua identidade de gênero.

2. Trabalhos relacionados

O método GenderMag foi projetado para capacitar os profissionais de software a avaliarem seus produtos em relação a preocupações relacionadas à inclusão de gênero [Burnett et al. 2016a]. De acordo com o método, são identificadas as facetas relacionadas ao gênero, permitindo a compreensão dos motivos que afetam a interação do usuário com o software. O GenderMag [1] considera cinco facetas cognitivas para as quais tem-se evidências de diferenças de gênero. Essas facetas são: (1) Motivação para uso da tecnologia, (2) Estilo de Processamento de Informação, (3) Atitude em relação ao risco, (4) Auto-eficácia computacional, (5) Estilo de Aprendizagem. Essas cinco facetas com suas variações por gênero são então incorporadas em diferentes personas. Desse modo, as personas possuem comportamentos únicos, por exemplo, a persona Abby utiliza a tecnologia apenas quando for necessário, prefere ficar em sua zona de conforto. Já a persona Tim adora conhecer novas tecnologias e verificar novas funções da ferramenta. Na sequência, aplicam-se walkthroughs cognitivos para demonstrar a interação das personas com o software, possibilitando a identificação de possíveis problemas.

[1] https://gendermag.org/foundations.php

Na literatura, já existem diversos trabalhos que utilizam o GenderMag. Burnett et al. (2016a) conduzem uma pesquisa sobre a habilidade dos profissionais de software em reconhecer questões de inclusão de gênero utilizando o GenderMag. O trabalho de Marsden e Haag (2016) utiliza personas do GenderMag para analisar como as caracteristicas de gênero em personas de software impactam a percepção dos usuários, especialmente no contexto de *design* de software. Outro exemplo é Chatterjee et al. (2021) que utilizaram o GenderMag para desenvolver uma técnica para prática de inclusão em comunidades Open Source Software (OSS). Adicionalmente, Burnett et al. (2016b) na literatura, também utilizam o GenderMag para mecanismo de verificação ao preconceito de gênero em anúncios de emprego.

Diante dos diferentes trabalhos na literatura que exploraram a aplicação do GenderMag, optou-se por utilizar esse método para avaliar e aprimorar a inclusão de gênero em softwares. Este método possibilita uma maior inclusão feminina digital, a identificação de viés de gênero, correções específicas e melhorias direcionadas nas interfaces de software.

3. Metodologia

Para alcançar o objetivo dessa pesquisa, que consiste em identificar problemas de vieses de gênero em LMSs utilizou-se o método GenderMag e os problemas identificados foram analisados de acordo com as Heurísticas de Nielsen. O método foi utilizado na inspeção de duas plataformas LMSs para análise, o Moodle e o Google Classroom. Buscou-se identificar elementos que pudessem refletir viés de gênero nas interfaces, funcionalidades ou interações oferecidas pelas plataformas.

A aplicação do método GenderMag incluiu 3 etapas: na etapa (i), realizou-se adaptação das personas baseadas no método GenderMag (Tim Maia, Tim Limbo, Abby Lúcia e Abby Joana). As personas foram desenvolvidas com base em uma estrutura predefinida fornecida pelo GenderMag. Baseado nos perfis de usuários de plataformas LMS, estabeleceu-se as personas Abby Joana e Tim Maia como professores, e as personas Abby Lúcia e Tim Limbo como alunos. As personas desenvolvidas para inspeção se encontram no material suplementar [2].

Na etapa (ii), realizou-se a inspeção das plataformas. Primeiro, elaborou-se um roteiro específico para cada plataforma, destinados a professores e alunos. Esses roteiros foram projetados para orientar a interação das personas com o LMS, abrangendo tarefas relevantes do contexto educacional. A elaboração desses roteiros levou em consideração os diferentes papéis desempenhados pelos usuários no ambiente educacional, destacando possíveis áreas onde os viéses de gênero poderiam surgir. Cada persona considerou o subobjetivo em questão como um passo essencial para alcançar o objetivo geral. Para cada ação correspondente a um subobjetivo, a persona possibilitou a avaliação minuciosa de quais facetas eram relevantes para a realização bem-sucedida da tarefa. A análise dos resultados e a formulação de recomendações, correspondentes à etapa (iii), foram conduzidas considerando as razões pelas quais a persona não conseguiu concluir a tarefa ou enfrentou obstáculos durante sua execução.

Para realização da inspeção, foram definidas as seguintes atividades: Em relação ao **Classroom**, para o perfil de **professor**, a tarefa geral consistiu em disponibilizar

[2] https://doi.org/10.6084/m9.figshare.25464364.v2

materiais para uma turma. Para isso, determinou-se as seguintes subtarefas: acessar a plataforma, criar uma nova turma, preencher detalhes da turma, configurar acesso à turma, adicionar alunos, disponibilizar material, enviar material, organizar material em pastas (opcional), definir acesso aos materiais e notificar os alunos. Já em relação ao perfil de alunos, a tarefa geral consistiu em acessar um material disponibilizado para a turma. Logo, os alunos precisam concluir a seguintes subtarefas: acessar à plataforma, localização da turma, entrada na turma, acesso aos materiais e a opção de visualizar ou baixar esses materiais.

Para a plataforma Moodle, para o perfil de professor, como tarefa geral, determinou-se disponibilizar um material na turma. Como isso, as subtarefas foram: o acesso à plataforma, criação de uma turma, acesso à turma, criação de um tópico para disponibilizar o material e adicionar material ao tópico. No que diz respeito aos alunos, estabeleceu-se a seguinte tarefa: acesso a um material disponibilizado na turma. Para isso, os aluno precisava realizar: acesso à plataforma, ingressar na turma designada, acesso ao material disponibilizado e retorno para a tela inicial do curso.

Após criação do roteiro, realizou-se a inspeção nas plataformas. A inspeção ocorreu com duas inspetoras, onde cada inspetora incorporou uma persona do GenderMag. A extensão auxiliava o inspetor a incorporar as personas durante a inspeção, ao gerenciar o resultado das atividades da persona. Durante a inspeção, cada inspetor utilizou as personas de aluno e professor. Para cada tarefa concluída, o inspetor tinha que marcar umas das opções de finalização: Sim, Não ou Talvez, quais facetas eram afetadas e descrever a justificativa de escolha da faceta. Como resultado, obteve-se um relatório contendo as decisões de cada persona em relação a cada atividade. Desse modo, utilizou-se o relatório para alcançar os resultados dessa pesquisa.

Após a obtenção dos resultados, realizou-se a análise das dificuldades das personas em relação às plataformas, para encontrar recomendações para solução dos problemas encontrados. Além disso, realizou-se a identificação de padrões comuns entre as dificuldades relatadas por diferentes personas. Dessa maneira, isso facilitou a categorização e priorização dos problemas, fornecendo insights que pudessem ajudar as personas a obterem uma melhor experiência como usuário.

4. Resultados

Em relação ao perfil de professor, os resultados obtidos da inspeção podem ser observados abaixo na Tabela 1 - A. No classroom, observa-se que o perfil Tim Maia talvez não conseguiria realizar a tarefa 8 (Organizar Material em Pastas) e não conseguiu realizar a atividade 9 (Definir acesso dos materiais). Já o perfil Abby Joana não conseguiu realizar a tarefa 4 (Configurar acesso a turma), talvez não conseguiria realizar a tarefa 8 e não conseguiu realizar a Atividade 9. Em contrapartida, no Moodle, Tim Maia obteve sucesso em todas as suas atividades e Abby Joana talvez não conseguisse realizar a tarefa 4 (Adicionar o material no tópico criado).

Os resultados obtidos revelaram a presença de vieses de gênero, indicando problemas na experiência baseados no gênero das personas pelos olhos das Heurísticas de Nielsen. Os resultados obtidos podem incluir insights sobre como melhorar a experiência do usuário para eliminar ou diminuir os vieses identificados.

Na Tabela 2 - B, são apresentados os perfis dos alunos que usaram as plataformas

A - Professores

Classroom										
Perfil	Atividade									
	1	2	3	4	5	6	7	8	9	10
Tim Maia	S	S	S	S	S	S	S	T	N	S
Abby Joana	S	S	S	N	S	S	S	T	N	S
Moodle										
	Atividade									
Tim Maia	S	S	S	S	S					
Abby Joana	S	S	S	T	S					

B - Alunos

Classroom					
Perfil	Atividade				
	1	2	3	4	5
Tim Limbo	S	S	S	S	S
Abby Lúcia	S	S	S	T	S
Moodle					
Atividade					
Tim Limbo	T	S	S		
Abby Lúcia	N	S	S		

Tabela 1. A Tabela A, corresponde ao resultado dos Professores usando o Classroom e o Moodle. A Tabela B, corresponde ao resultado dos alunos. Foram determinadas as seguintes respostas: S - Sim, N - Não, T - Talvez.

LMSs. No Classroom, o perfil Tim Limbo conseguiu realizar todas as tarefas porém, a Abby Lúcia talvez não conseguiria realizar a atividade 4 (Acessar os materiais). Por outro lado, no Moodle, o Tim Limbo talvez não conseguiria realizar a atividade 1 (Ingressar na turma designada). Simultaneamente o perfil feminino, a Abby Lúcia não consegueria realizar a atividade 1.

Com essas análises das tabelas, foi visto que um dos problemas ocorre na página inicial do Classroom quando, manipulada pelo usuário criador de uma sala de aula, onde existem duas opções de ferramentas com o mesmo símbolo gráfico, conforme mostra a Figura 1, mas finalidades diferentes, o que não deixa claro o padrão de ações. Isso fere a Heurística 4 (Consistência e padrões). Isso pode levar os usuários a se questionarem se essas ferramentas têm diferença significativa entre elas, como aponta a tarefa 4 da Abby Joana na Tabela 1 - A.

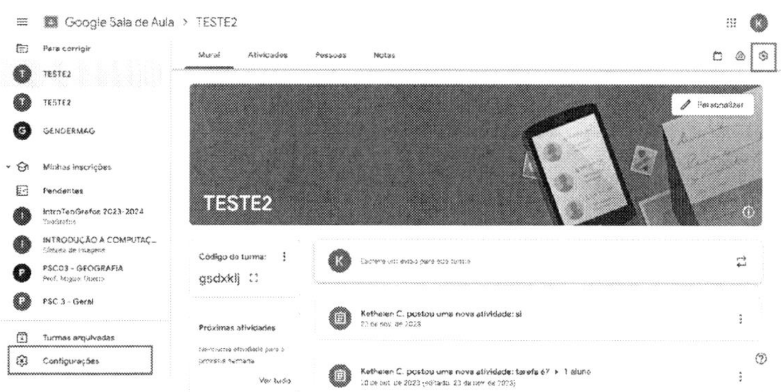

Figura 1. Página inicial do Classroom

O segundo problema que se repetiu muitas vezes, mostrado abaixo, encontrado no Classroom é: O Classroom não torna visível, de maneira clara e acessível, as opções importantes, como editar tarefa ou privar tarefa. Isso fere a Heurística 6 (Reconhecer ao invés de lembrar). A persona demoraria para tornar privado a tarefa especificamente para um aluno, como aconteceu com o Tim Maia e a Abby Joana na tarefa 9. A falta de visibilidade demanda que os usuários explorem extensivamente a página, aumentando a chance de não encontrarem a informação desejada ou se distraindo com outras opções. Essa inadequação pode resultar em frustração e perda de tempo. Conforme pode ser visualizado na Figura 2.

Figura 2. Página de editar tarefas do Classroom

O terceiro problema identificado, porém, encontrado no Moodle é: A barra de busca no final da página é fora dos padrões presentes em site, conforme pode ser observado na Figura 3. A presença de informações desnecessárias, como cursos adicionais, também pode contribuir para a poluição visual. A falta de recursos como guias, tutoriais ou um tour interativo impede que os usuários novos ou inexperientes se familiarizem facilmente com a plataforma. Isso fere as Heurísticas 4 (Consistência e padrões) e 8 (Estética e *design* minimalista). A persona passaria mais tempo analisando outras funções e menus, gastando seu tempo nessas funcionalidades até finalmente encontrar, por meio da exploração, o local para busca de cursos.

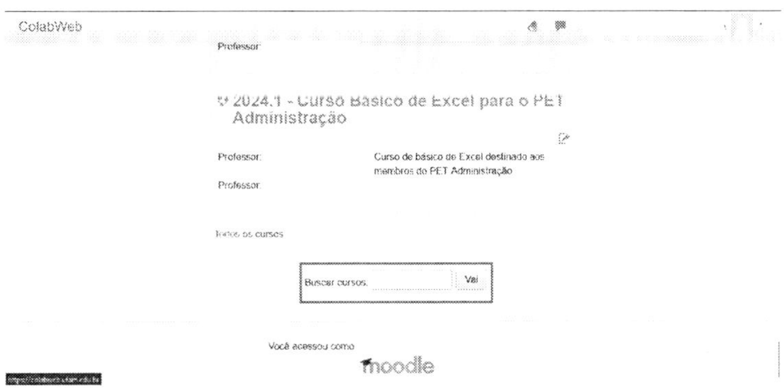

Figura 3. Página inicial do Colabweb

5. Análise dos Resultados e Discussão

Para resolver o primeiro problema e aderir à Heurística 4, a plataforma deve garantir consistência visual e funcional entre ferramentas, usando ícones e cores distintas para diferenciar as opções de forma clara. No contexto da usabilidade, a integração das Heurísticas de Nielsen pode reduzir vieses de gênero identificados pelo GenderMag, promovendo uma experiência mais equitativa para todos os usuários [Nielsen and Molich 1990]. Este estudo propõe recomendações específicas para resolver cada problema identificado. Por exemplo, para o primeiro problema, as recomendações incluem manter o ícone da aba lateral, certificar de que as escolhas de cores e ícones sejam acessíveis a todos os usuários, incluindo aqueles com deficiências visuais pelas diretrizes WCAG; e consistência no *design* dos ícones.

No segundo problema, sugere-se a adoção de um padrão de *design* reconhecível, como uma barra de ferramentas na página de 'Tarefas', facilitando a localização de informações. Recomenda-se também sinalização clara das tarefas para melhorar a usabilidade. Já para o último problema, manter a barra de busca no topo da página e fornecer tutoriais para orientar os usuários na plataforma são soluções propostas. Tais recomendações visam aprimorar a experiência do usuário e reduzir as barreiras de gênero no uso das plataformas educacionais.

A análise das personas revelou que usuários com menos afinidade tecnológica tendem a hesitar mais ao usar a plataforma, devido ao medo de explorar o ambiente virtual. Além disso, a comparação entre perfis masculinos e femininos mostrou desafios específicos enfrentados por cada grupo, evidenciando a importância de considerar a diversidade de gênero no *design* de software educacional. Por exemplo, o problema identificado na página inicial do Classroom, onde existem duas opções de ferramentas com o mesmo ícone, ilustra um desafio para a persona Abby Joana (professora). Essa situação pode ser interpretada como uma barreira de gênero, pois a falta de clareza e consistência na interface pode afetar negativamente a eficiência de uso, especialmente para usuárias.

O GenderMag é uma ferramenta eficaz para identificar vieses de gênero, fornecendo recomendações antes mesmo dos testes com as personas, agilizando o processo de desenvolvimento de software [Stumpf et al. 2020].

6. Conclusão

Partindo do pressuposto da predominância masculina em equipes de desenvolvimento de software, o estudo investigou o viés de gênero em produtos desenvolvidos, analisando dois Learning Management Systems (LMSs), o Moodle e o Google Classroom. Para isso, utilizou-se o método GenderMag, complementado pelas Heurísticas de Nielsen, visando compreender as necessidades específicas das diferentes identidades de gênero ao interagir com plataformas de aprendizado. Essa abordagem enriquece a avaliação heurística ao destacar questões de equidade de gênero, acessibilidade e experiência do usuário, frequentemente omitidas em métodos tradicionais de avaliação. Assim, a integração do GenderMag na geração de recomendações, aliada à análise das heurísticas de Nielsen, representa uma estratégia abrangente para aprimorar o *design* e a usabilidade dos Learning Management Systems. Esse esforço conjunto visa não apenas melhorar a experiência do usuário, mas também garantir uma abordagem mais inclusiva, sensível às diversas identidades de gênero e necessidades dos usuários em ambientes educacionais.

Agradecimentos

O presente trabalho é decorrente do projeto de Pesquisa e Desenvolvimento (P&D) 001/2020, firmado entre a Fundação da Universidade do Amazonas e FAEPI, que conta com financiamento da Samsung, usando recursos da Lei de Informática para a Amazônia Ocidental (Lei Federal nº 8.387/1991), estando sua divulgação de acordo com o previsto no artigo 39.º do Decreto nº 10.521/2020. Adicionalmente, essa pesquisa foi apoiada pela

Universidade Federal do Amazonas (UFAM), CAPES–Código de Financiamento 001, CNPq processo 314797/2023-8, Fundação de Amparo à Pesquisa do Estado do Amazonas–FAPEAM–por meio do projeto POSGRAD 22-23.

Referências

Barbosa, M., Brilhante, I., Andrade, A., Conceição, J. L., Gomes, G., Conte, T., and Gadelha, B. (2021). Diversidade de gênero and elicitação de requisitos: Uso do gendermag como estratégia de identificação de requisitos de usabilidade. In *WER*.

Burnett, M., Peters, A., Hill, C., and Elarief, N. (2016a). Finding gender-inclusiveness software issues with gendermag: A field investigation. In *Proceedings of the 2016 CHI conference on human factors in computing systems*, pages 2586–2598.

Burnett, M., Stumpf, S., Macbeth, J., Makri, S., Beckwith, L., Kwan, I., Peters, A., and Jernigan, W. (2016b). Gendermag: A method for evaluating software's gender inclusiveness. *Interacting with Computers*, 28(6):760–787.

Chatterjee, A., Guizani, M., Stevens, C., Emard, J., May, M. E., Burnett, M., and Ahmed, I. (2021). Aid: An automated detector for gender-inclusivity bugs in oss project pages. In *2021 IEEE/ACM 43rd International Conference on Software Engineering (ICSE)*, pages 1423–1435.

Clark, J. and Horton, R. (2019). What is the lancet doing about gender and diversity? *The Lancet*, 393(10171):508–510.

ISO9241-110 (2010). *Ergonomics of Human-system Interaction: Part 210: Human-centred Design for Interactive Systems*. ISO.

Marsden, N. and Haag, M. (2016). Evaluation of gendermag personas based on persona attributes and persona gender. In *HCI International 2016–Posters' Extended Abstracts: 18th International Conference, HCI International 2016, Toronto, Canada, July 17-22, 2016, Proceedings, Part I 18*, pages 122 127. Springer.

Moro, M. (2022). Lack of diversity: Are you part of the problem or its solution? In *Anais do II Simpósio Brasileiro de Educação em Computação*, pages 261–271, Porto Alegre, RS, Brasil. SBC.

Nielsen, J. and Molich, R. (1990). Heuristic evaluation of user interfaces. In *Proceedings of the SIGCHI conference on Human factors in computing systems*, pages 249–256.

Stumpf, S., Peters, A., Bardzell, S., Burnett, M., Busse, D., Cauchard, J., Churchill, E., et al. (2020). Gender-inclusive hci research and design: A conceptual review. *Foundations and Trends® in Human–Computer Interaction*, 13(1):1–69.

Tejedor, F. J. T., García, A. G.-V. M.-R., et al. (2012). Avaliação da integração de plataformas e-learning no ensino secundário. *Revista Iberoamericana de Educación*, 58(4):1–12.

Towards an AI-based Genomic Medicine of Precision that Integrates Predictive and Explainable Knowledge Dimensions

Óscar Pastor[1], Salvador Navarro[1], Alberto García[1], Mireia Costa[1], Ana León[1]

[1] VRAIN Research Institute, Universitat Politècnica de Valencia, Spain

opastor@dsic.upv.es, sfnava@upv.es, algarsi3@pros.upv.es, micossan@vrain.upv.es, aleon@vrain.upv.es

Abstract. *Understanding the human genome and deciphering the Language of Life is a grand challenge that modern sequencing technologies are making feasible by generating huge amounts of data whose correct interpretation has yet to be accomplished. To do it, two knowledge dimensions must be integrated: the predictive one, Machine Learning-oriented, that obtain accurate information from data, and the explainable one, Conceptual Modeling-based, that uses a symbolic representation to provide meaning to the data in order to understand and explain the semantics behind predictions. This position report discusses the problem, contextualizes it under a Life Engineering perspective, and it proposes how to face the design of AI-based data management platforms that follows the introduced ideas.*

1 Introduction

Deciphering the language of life is a grand challenge that the modern genome sequencing technologies are making more and more feasible. This position paper discusses how combining two dimensions of Knowledge Engineering -a predictive one, Machine Learning (ML)-oriented, and an explainable one, Conceptual Modeling (CM)-based- can guide the process of understanding the genome, using the genomic medicine of precision as working context.

Software Engineering (SE) has made possible to create a software whose final code representation is a binary language represented by millions of 0s and 1s. This binary language is generated by compiling programming languages whose instructions we, Humans, know well because we have invented them. Programs written in these languages are obtained from Conceptual Models that represent the relevant aspects of the domain under analysis. Model-driven Development research and practice is still being developed to show to transform Conceptual Models into executable programs [Pastor and Molina 2007].

Making an analogy with SE, Life Engineering (LE) is exploring how to discover the instructions of the programming language of life that instead of being a binary language of 0s and 1s, is a quaternary, four-letter language (A, C, G, T) with a biological background, where those four letters represent four nucleotides. Millions of them together constitutes a program of life, which is our genomic sequence. A massive data generation process is continuously running thanks to the unstoppable progress of the genome sequencing technology, what is generating more and more data about the genome.

But data without semantics are useless, especially when our final purpose is to understand the genome and discover what are the instructions of the programming language that should guide that understanding process. ML techniques process data and train algorithms that predict valuable information. In our working domain, which is the genome-based medicine of precision this means that if a given patient (person) has a health problem (e.g. colorectal cancer (CRC)). Training a function with a sufficient number of samples from people with and without the considered disease (phenotype), a ML process can solve the predictive knowledge perspective of the game.

But to diagnose a sample with a CRC without explaining why this is the case, is an incomplete result. The explainable knowledge dimension is required. It is incorporated by applying an explainable AI process which is based on the use of a Conceptual Model of the Human Genome (CMHG) that delimits which is the relevant information to be considered to "explain" why the diagnosis is given. Navigating through the CMHG from genotype to phenotype information, the results provided by the ML trained function can be explained. For instance, selecting features related to genome variants that are relevant for the disease, the presence of these variants together with their associated effects in the protein synthesis process and their pathway participation's role can make the wished explanation process feasible.

Through the paper, these ideas are developed in more details. In section 2 we emphasize the analogy between the SE and LE perspectives, characterizing what do we mean by LE as a main process to face the grand challenge of deciphering the language of life. Taking the medicine of precision working domain of reference, and with the goal of articulating what is the valuable knowledge to be considered, Section 3 discusses the predictive knowledge dimension that is associated to a ML-based process, while Section 4 focuses on the explainable dimension, which is guided by the use of a CMHG as the main artefact, and that complements the ML perspective. Section 5 discusses the benefits of combining the predictive and the explainable knowledge dimensions, and how effective software platforms to manage health genomic data can be designed and implemented. Finally, conclusions and references close the work.

2 From Software Engineering to Life Engineering

Figure 1 depicts our comparison between SE and LE. Following a top-down perspective, SE has created programming languages that built programs with which a problem domain is represented. The software production process includes a set of models and models transformations from the conceptual model (that represents the relevant information of the domain under analysis) to the program (using instructions of a selected programming language) and to the code (binary code).

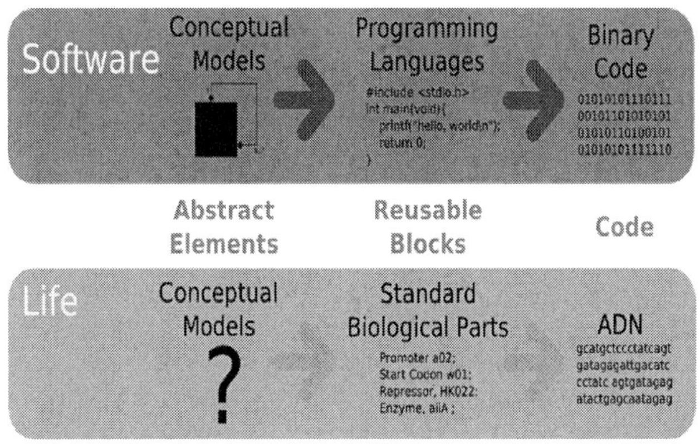

Figure 1: The analogy between Software Engineering and Life Engineering: from models, to programs, to code

LE follows a data-driven, bottom-up perspective. In this case, sequencing technologies allow us to get data and to know the lowest-level code (quaternary code-based), but we don't know yet which are the instructions of the programming language of life that is hidden behind this huge amount of genomic code that we accumulate. In a reverse way, we have to go from code to (biological) programs, and to models of life. Modeling life is still a further goal, but understanding the code of life is the problem that we are already facing. Our big challenge, a scientific challenge for humanity, is how to discover the instructions of that programming language of life. This is what we mean by deciphering the language of life. To do it, the SE analogy provides a useful approach, that has two main steps:

1. Massive data gathering, that is what modern sequencing techniques makes continuously feasible.
2. Discovery of programming patterns that are behind those data.

As it happens in SE, abstraction is an essential mechanism to make the information obtained from data explainable. The genomic-based medicine of precision provides a right working context to progress in that direction. Once a given disease (phenotype) is selected, comparing the genome (code) of healthy and unhealthy people (step 1), it becomes possible to identify programming patterns that are hidden in the data (step 2).

This is what we are doing in our PROS Research Center (within the VRAIN Research Institute at the Universitat Politècnica of València), and what we present here. Our strategy to advance in that direction is based on the need to distinguish clearly the two dimensions of knowledge that we discuss next:

- A predictive knowledge, ML-oriented because once a phenotype is selected, it trains a function with the corresponding clinical data in order to predict if a person is positively diagnosed.
- An explainable knowledge, that is CM-based: using a holistic conceptual model of the human genome, the relevant pieces of information are identified, and explanations associated to a provided prediction are given.

The correct integration of these predictive and explainable knowledge facets can be seen as the two sides of the coin that any AI-based software platform for managing genome data must accomplish. Such a software platform must achieve the combination of i) the adequate use of ML techniques to get a right prediction (predictive knowledge dimension) with ii) a trustworthy explainable AI, based on a conceptual model that provides a common, shared under-standing of the domain in order to establish cause-effect relationships for understanding the biological behavior and explaining a given prediction (explainable knowledge dimension).

3 The Predictive Knowledge Dimension (ML-oriented)

Using ML techniques, what we refer to as "the magic of mathematics" makes possible to train an algorithm with data in order to generate a model that predicts valuable information with a maximum accuracy [Swanson et al. 2023] In clinical terms, this means to follow the process of:

1. Selecting a phenotype of interest.
2. Understanding the task to be performed and selecting the right scope.
3. Creating the datasets by collecting the relevant data and improve its quality.
4. Selecting the appropriate ML technique intended to deliver the most accurate results in the domain under analysis.
5. Informing the final result.

The final result is the prediction provided by the selected ML technique. This predictive knowledge dimension states that a given diagnosis is associated to the patient whose data analytics process has been accomplished. Large initiatives as The Cancer Genome Atlas (TCGA) provides an effective data background to train different ML approaches [Liñares-Blanco et al. 2021]. This knowledge dimension covers the fast-thinking perspective discussed in [Guizzardi et al. 2023], where a clear distinction in made between "fast thinking" (data-driven) and "slow thinking" (theory-driven) characterization. The "fast thinking" side of the coin focuses on learning from data even if a precise conceptual counterpart is lacking. Paraphrasing Immanuel Kant, "Concepts without data are empty; data without concepts are blind": an explainable knowledge dimension is then needed to have the full picture (the "slow thinking" side of the coin).

4 The Explainable Knowledge Dimension (CM-based)

Explaining a prediction requires to use abstraction to understand what concepts are behind data representations, and what causal relationships explain natural effects. To do it well, any sound Explainable AI process must start with getting a shared understanding of the studied domain [Spreeuwenberg [S.d.]]. This is why the explainable knowledge dimension is CM-based: a holistic Conceptual Model of the Human Genome (CMHG) becomes a key artifact to identify relevant concepts that cover how genome, transcriptome and proteome are connected with the functional counterpart that pathways characterize. In several previous works we have presented and evolved such a CMHG, that provides the semantic basis to explain why a given prediction makes sense [Pastor et al. 2021] [Reyes Román et al. 2016] [Pastor 2008].

This explainable dimension is about concepts' identification, about how they relate to each other, and about how previous, reported associations between concepts and effects in the context of a particular disease explain the identification of a precise diagnosis. Additionally, this explainable dimension discovers connections between functional biological effects, and their "code" counterpart. Navigating through the CMHG, it is for instance possible to associate genome variations with functional problems that allow us to infer those programming patterns that lead to the emergence of the programming instructions of the Programming Language of Life, the grand challenge behind the final goal of our long-term research work: deciphering the language of life.

Looking at health problems as "software" bugs that can be first identified, then corrected (by using the recently discovered genome edition techniques, the CRISPR-based approaches) opens a window of opportunity that has never before being possible to reach: to understand and subsequently manipulate the human genome. This is where SE and LE converge: LE-based solutions must now provide methods and tools to advance in how to make explainable the predictive, databased knowledge that is provided through genome sequencing. This is where integrating both types of knowledge with a sound, semantic ground becomes a need for any software platform to be designed and developed.

5 Integration & Discussion

We discuss in this section: i) how to integrate effectively the two knowledge dimensions that we have introduced before (predictive and explainable) in a software platform intended to manage valuable genomic data, and ii) what is our starting experience in developing such a software platform, called the "DELFOS Genome Oracle" [León Palacio et al. 2024](DELFOS in short from now on).

Making a reliable prediction and being able to explain it is the result of the proposed combination. AI-based software platforms that deal with sensitive data as the clinical ones must achieve the needed integration. Reusing the "coin" image for such a software platform, one side of it will provide the ML-based trained models that make accurate predictions, while a CM-based XAI process will articulate the other side of the coin.

Looking at a genome data management software platform from a holistic point of view, three steps conform its design process:

1. Selection of the phenotype (disease)
2. Development of an associated ML-based training model (predictive knowledge dimension)
3. Analysis of the relevant genomic data whose effects have been reported in a genomic data source with a concrete clinical significance (explainable knowledge dimension).

This what we are doing with our DELFOS platform in our Research Center (PROS@Vrain). For an initial set of phenotypes that include cardiopathies and pediatric oncology, with the support of clinical experts of three hospitals of the Valencian Community in Spain -Hospital La Fe and Hospital Clinic in Valencia, Hospital General in Alicante- and one local biotech company, we have developed the DELFOS software platform prototype, under the OGMIOS ResearchProject.

Reusing the DELFOS Oracle Greek mythology metaphor, we envision DELFOS as a platform that includes all the known genomic data for the phenotypes under study. Once a particular disease is selected from an initial set of available diseases, an individual user can enter DELFOS with her relevant information that can include two different types of genomic information:

i) the set of features required by a ML prediction process, that should for instance include gene expression or DNA methylation, and
ii) the information associated to the user' sequenced genome, normally using standard file formats as VCF.

This set of information has a twofold use:

- The first one is used as input for the ML-based model that will give the predictive result, answering the question of "is the user affected by the disease?".
- The second one is used to explain why that prediction is provided. The explanation is based on the information included in the CMHG, whose

concepts and relationships among concepts determine what effects explain why the reported health problem appears.

An initial prototype of DELFOS is being designed to diagnose (using the predictive perspective) and explain (using the explainable perspective) if an individual is affected by a given disease and why. The explanation generates a clinical report that, for the selected disease, states which relevant genomic variants have been identified with which clinical significance.

Several challenges must be addressed as immediate next steps. Firstly, the platform must evolve according to how new genomic knowledge is generated. As the genome understanding is a scientific field which is in continuous development, new information can lead to new knowledge that should automatically update previous clinical reports. Under the explainable dimension, this happens for instance when one new combination of variants is reported to be associated with a particular disease: having the source patient sequence with these variants whose connection was initially unknown, the former clinical report can be timely corrected/updated. Under the predictive dimension, the ML-based model training strategy can lead to datasets that update the set of selected features depending on that new genomic information.

Secondly, under the predictive knowledge dimension the idea is to design a generic, phenotype-independent method for the ML-based training model process. It should provide a template including the steps to be followed when a new predictive genome service (for a new disease) is incorporated in DELFOS, together with the methodological guidance needed to assist in the selection of the right ML technique by characterizing different possible working contexts.

Thirdly, under the explainable knowledge dimension, a XAI-based process is also to be defined. Strictly based on the CMHG, this process is intended to characterize where to search for the right genomic information for a selected phenotype, how to identify the relevant information from the selected data sources, how to make all that relevant information persistent in a DB engine, and what interaction mechanisms have to be provided for access and querying. We have initial results focused on a subset of the CMHG concerning the genomic variation information. A method called SILE (for Search, Identification, Load and Exploitation) [Palacio and López 2018] has been designed in our Research Center, and it has been initially used under a set of practical projects with our clinical partners obtaining positive results [Costa et al. 2022] [Costa et al. 2023].

Finally, coming back to our Grand Challenge of deciphering the language of life, we keep a long-term objective with our proposal: the more data we accumulate in our DELFOS Oracle, the more information can be discovered about those programming patterns that are hidden in the data. Connections among data which is associated to different phenotypes can provide clues to understanding what are those programming language of life' instructions.

6 Conclusions

Modern AI-based data management platforms must combine two essential knowledge dimensions:

- a predictive one, that is databased, and uses ML techniques to infer valid knowledge from data without being able to semantically explain with a precise conceptual ground why a given prediction is provided.
- an explainable one, that getting a shared understanding of a domain with a Conceptual Model, provides a symbolic knowledge with a precise semantics from where concrete explanations can be obtained.

We have shown in this position paper how Life Engineering can be a discipline conceptually equivalent to Software Engineering, where from a reverse engineering perspective we have huge amounts data that need to be understood. To accomplish this challenge, these two knowledges' dimensions (predictive and explainable) must be combined in a holistic software platform, as we are doing with our DELFOS approach. Our further work is oriented to extend our initial results to accumulating more data and generating more and more knowledge from that twofold knowledge integration strategy, having in mind the long-term Grand Challenge of deciphering the language of life with from our AI-based approach.

7 References

Spreeuwenberg, S. ([S.d.]). AIX: Artificial intelligence needs explanation. – Transparency increases the success of AI based decision support systems.

Costa, M., García, A. S. and Pastor, O. (1 dec 2023). The consequences of data dispersion in genomics: a comparative analysis of data sources for precision medicine. BMC Medical Informatics and Decision Making, v. 23, n. 3, p. 1–17.

Costa, M., García S, A. and Pastor, O. (2022). Conceptual Modeling-Based Cardiopathies Data Management. Lecture Notes in Computer Science (including subseries Lecture Notes in Artificial Intelligence and Lecture Notes in Bioinformatics), v. 13650 LNCS, p. 15–24.

Guizzardi, G., Pastor, O., Storey, V. C. and Kruchten, P. (1 nov 2023). Thinking Fast and Slow in Software Engineering. IEEE Software, v. 40, n. 6, p. 139–142.

León Palacio, A., García Simón, A., Reyes Román, J. F. and Costa, M. (mar 2024). The Delfos Platform: A Conceptual Model-Based Solution for the Enhancement of Precision Medicine [acepted for publication].

Liñares-Blanco, J., Pazos, A. and Fernandez-Lozano, C. (12 jul 2021). Machine learning analysis of TCGA cancer data. PeerJ Computer Science, v. 7, p. 1–47.

Palacio, A. L. and López, Ó. P. (27 dec 2018). Smart Data for Genomic Information Systems: the SILE Method. Complex Systems Informatics and Modeling Quarterly, v. 0, n. 17, p. 1–23.

Pastor, O. (2008). Conceptual modeling meets the human genome. Lecture Notes in Computer Science (including subseries Lecture Notes in Artificial Intelligence and Lecture Notes in Bioinformatics), v. 5231 LNCS, p. 1–11.

Pastor, Ó., León, A. P., Reyes, J. F. R., Garciá, A. S. and Casamayor, J. C. R. (18 jan 2021). Using conceptual modeling to improve genome data management. Briefings in Bioinformatics, v. 22, n. 1, p. 45–54.

Pastor, O. and Molina, J. C. (2007). Model-driven architecture in practice: A software production environment based on conceptual modeling. Model-Driven Architecture in Practice: A Software Production Environment Based on Conceptual Modeling, p. 1–302.

Reyes Román, J. F., Pastor, Ó., Casamayor, J. C. and Valverde, F. (2016). Applying conceptual modeling to better understand the human genome. Lecture Notes in Computer Science (including subseries Lecture Notes in Artificial Intelligence and Lecture Notes in Bioinformatics), v. 9974 LNCS, p. 404–412.

Swanson, K., Wu, E., Zhang, A., Alizadeh, A. A. and Zou, J. (13 apr 2023). From patterns to patients: Advances in clinical machine learning for cancer diagnosis, prognosis, and treatment. Cell, v. 186, n. 8, p. 1772–1791.

The use of a shared database for cost reduction with user licenses: An experience report

Carlos C. S. Conde Junior[1], Marcus V. C. Correa[1], Hualter Oliveira Barbosa[1], Tatiany Mafra da Silva[1]

[1]Instituto de Pesquisas Eldorado – IPE
Av. Mário Ypiranga, nº 315, Condomínio The Office, salas 901/902, Adrianópolis, CEP: 69057-070, Manaus – AM – Brazil.

carlos.conde@eldorado.org.br, marcus.correa@eldorado.org.br, hualter.barbosa@eldorado.org.br, tatiany.silva@eldorado.org.br

Abstract. *This article presents an experience report that analyzes the migration of servers to the data center as a solution to reduce financial costs and improve the performance and usability of the Jira tool. The solution adopted by the team resulted in a 70% reduction in costs compared to the option of maintaining the old data process and servers provided by Atlassian. Such works reinforce the need for companies to rethink traditional models, always aiming to reduce costs and process risks. Solutions from research and development (R&D) projects can play an important role in evaluating and testing possible changes in the process without compromising or interrupting production.*

1. Introduction

The accelerated development of new technologies has driven the emergence of new business models, making it imperative for companies using these services to adapt (Sayabek, Z. and Omarova, 2018). According to Sahin, I. and Zahedi, F. (2001), changes to software systems often result in high costs after the changes. Therefore, it is in the organization's interest to keep costs under control.

In this context, there is the sale of licenses and support for web applications (Jira). In order to use these web applications, they need to be installed on a server, which will keep them running constantly. The price of certain business software varies according to the number of customers using it. Software as a service allows software providers to charge the customer based on the number of users or the volume of transactions (Kroenke and Boyle, 2015). Additionally, these software solutions have version limitations, necessitating regular updates and upgrades, so that the system is free of vulnerabilities that do not compromise its use.

This article presents an experience report on the customization of Jira, through changes and improvements made to the migration of Jira instance servers, each instance being a virtual server used to serve the business model. Thus, in the current configuration, it was found that the instances had many users in common, which would represent unnecessary costs for the company in the study. As a result, work is underway to carry out the migration, in which it is already possible to obtain a 70% reduction in possible costs, compared to the old process of five instances.

The aim of this article is the unification of the instances. Through a cost analysis, the solution used was to migrate to a self-managed data center. This option indicated to be a viable alternative to reduce costs, reduce duplicate data and make it possible to maintain the applications contained in each instance. This article presents a possible solution with the unification of these databases, the challenges encountered with the migration and the practices adopted to facilitate this type of process in different contexts.

2. Experience Report

The Instituto de Pesquisas Eldorado currently has projects focused on several areas: including health, oil and gas, energy, agribusiness and information and communication technology. The projects are carried out in collaboration with companies in these sectors, in which problems are identified and ways to solve them are developed through research and development.

In this context, in February 2021, the partner company in the case study had to rethink how it would deal with license changes imposed by Atlassian. The partner company could no longer acquire new licenses for the version it was used to working with. Consequently, Atlassian would cease to develop new features for the old products, potentially posing vulnerability risks for the use of these applications in the Company discussed in this article.

Atlassian provided two options to handle the license changes: the first would be to migrate to the cloud, while the second would be to upgrade to a self-managed data center (Atlassian, 2024). In a cost analysis carried out by the software engineering team, after the cost simulation available at the Atlassian website, in addition, attributes were raised for choosing the solution: security, ease, flexibility for customization.

Therefore, the first option was discarded, due to the restrictions of the partner company's own business requirements in maintaining its product data in a self-managed environment. In addition, cloud migration solutions typically entail higher costs and come with challenges related to workload and ensuring a smooth transition from one environment to another with minimal interruptions (C. Ward et al., 2010). On the other hand, the second option involves hosting the applications on the partner company's own infrastructure. Taking into account the attributes of the cost analysis, the decision was made to proceed with the data center upgrade. The results of this cost analysis may be expected.

However, when mapping the current state, it was identified that the costs of the new move (to the data center) would be higher if no action was taken to get around the problem of the license cost per user. Since the web application used five different instances with separate databases (for production, development and testing), which totaled 15 virtual machines, and with different volumes of users, the largest of which had 4,612 users. In addition, these users could also exist on the other instances for different projects, representing approximately 11,200 users. Therefore, if the migration took place with all these instances and duplicate users, the cost would be in the range of 15,000 users (the number defined by Atlassian for the new data center).

As a way of making the option of migrating to the self-managed data center viable and avoiding high costs, it was decided to eliminate duplicate users by refactoring the source code and comparing duplicates. The aim of the code refactoring was to improve the maintainability of the applications contained in Jira, where it was noticed that some of them were duplicated in other instances. With the migration underway, these duplicate plugins were improved and this ensured that the objectives of the new instances were met.

Another adopted solution was the consolidation of instances. Previously, we operated with five instances, but we transitioned to only two instances (for production, environments, and testing), totaling six virtual machines. This solution was feasible due to the implementation of sanity tests, which helped save time and resources. These tests facilitated the swift detection of potential usability issues during the migration process (Chauhan, 2014).

In order to balance the workload, four-node clustering was adopted, which made it possible to maintain the stability of the instances, especially during the migration process, since in some cases it was necessary to restart the instance due to applications being migrated to the production database. To maintain stability, stress tests were also carried out with a larger amount of data in the indexing, which allowed more users to be active simultaneously.

Once the workload was balanced, because there was always a cluster node available to receive the necessary changes, it was possible to reduce the number of non-existent users and eliminate tools with duplicate logics that existed in the previous process, by validating data conflicts between customized functionalities for each instance.

3. Results

The obtained results indicate that the migration to the data center was the best option for the partner company in the case study. Concerning the analyzed attributes, it is observed that in terms of security, especially when dealing with specific business rules, the preference is to keep the data self-managed by the organization rather than in the cloud environment. Regarding ease of customization, it is evident that in this case, Atlassian would be the better option as it provides technical support services and security updates. However, the team identified this as an opportunity for improvement, and it was in this area that the software engineering team focused their efforts. In terms of flexibility for customization, the optimal choice was to leverage the software engineering team. This allowed new developments to align with the new business rules of the present study's company, resulting in significant improvements in application web performance and usability. In terms of costs, the cloud solution ends up being a more expensive option compared to the self-managed data center.

In this way, the solution adopted by the team with the unification of instances not only reduced financial costs, but also maintained high performance, data security and reliability and ensured that updates to the web application versions were possible. With the actions used, the number of users went from approximately 12,000 to less than 10,000 users, bringing usage into a range with fewer users, which made it possible to work within the range of 10,000 users and also made it possible to improve efficiency and reduce the maintenance of the applications contained in each instance.

Therefore, the solution adopted through a research and development project resulted in a cost reduction of 70% compared to the option of maintaining the old data process and servers provided by Atlassian. Work of this kind reinforces the need for companies to rethink traditional models, aiming to reduce process costs and risks. In addition, solutions from research and development (R&D) projects can play an important role in evaluating and testing possible changes to the process, without compromising or interrupting production.

Expected results for the future include further cost optimization, enhanced data security, improved application performance, task automation, infrastructure scalability, and innovation drive. These objectives aim to streamline processes, ensure regulatory compliance, boost operational efficiency, accommodate future growth, and leverage advanced technologies for continuous improvement in the shared database environment. By achieving these outcomes, the organization can enhance productivity, reduce risks, increase agility, and stay competitive in the dynamic business landscape.

Acknowledgements

This article is the result of a Research, Development and Innovation project carried out by the Instituto de Pesquisas Eldorado with funds provided for in Informatics Law No. 8.387/1991, in accordance with art. 21 of Decree No. 10.521/2020.

References

Sayabek, Z. and Omarova, A. and Doszhan, R. and Saparova, G. and Zharaskyzy, G. (2018). Diversification of R&D results commercialization. Problems and Perspectives in Management. 16. 331-343. 10.21511/ppm.16(4).2018.27.

Sahin, I.; Zahedi, F. Control Limit Policies for Warranty, Maintenance and Upgrade of Software Systems in IIE Transactions 33, 729–745, 2001. https://doi.org/10.1023/A:1010993715340.

Kroenke, David M.; Bolyle, Randall J. Using MIS. 8. ed. Boston: Pearson Education, 2015.

Atlassian. Support for Server products ends on Feb. 15, 2024. Available at < https://www.atlassian.com/migration/assess/journey-to-cloud>. Accessed on: January 08, 2024.

C. Ward et al. Workload Migration into Clouds Challenges, Experiences, Opportunities. In 2010 IEEE 3rd International Conference on Cloud Computing, Miami, FL, USA, 2010, pp. 164-171, doi: 10.1109/CLOUD.2010.84.

Chauhan, Vinod Kimar. Smoke Testing. International Journal of Scientific and Research Publications, Volume 4, Issue 2, India, 2014, ISSN 2250-3153

Especificação de Requisitos em um projeto de Big Data no Setor Público

Alex F. F. Costa[1], Leidiana I. A. Freitas[1], Dafne A. Cavalcante[1], Victória T. Oliveira[1], Valéria Lelli[1], Ismayle S. Santos[1,2], Pedro A. M. Oliveira[1,3], Tales P. Nogueira[1,4], Rossana M. C. Andrade[1]

[1] Federal University of Ceará (UFC), [2] Ceará State University (UECE),
[3] Federal Institute of Education, Science and Technology of Maranhão (IFMA),
[4] University for International Integration of the Afro-Brazilian Lusophony (UNILAB)

Abstract. *The procedures involved in the planning, development and optimization stages of a Big Data project present challenges in the scope of Requirements Engineering (RE), highlighting the difficulties inherent in managing requirements in multidisciplinary teams. Optimizing activities related to requirements processes and processes involving other teams (e.g., Design/UX and Data Science) contributes to the success of these projects. This paper presents an experience report on the difficulties faced in specifying requirements and their solutions in the development of a Big Data platform in the public sector.*

Resumo. *Os procedimentos envolvidos nas etapas de planejamento, desenvolvimento e otimização de um projeto de Big Data apresentam desafios no âmbito da Engenharia de Requisitos (ER), evidenciando as dificuldades inerentes à gestão de requisitos em equipes multidisciplinares. A otimização das atividades relacionadas aos processos de requisitos e os processos que envolvem outros times* (e.g., *Design/UX e Ciência de Dados) contribui para o sucesso desses projetos. Este artigo apresenta um relato de experiência sobre as dificuldades enfrentadas e suas soluções na fase especificação de requisitos no desenvolvimento de uma plataforma Big Data no setor público.*

1. Introdução

Os sistemas *Big Data* compreendem as tecnologias de software escaláveis nas quais grandes quantidades de dados heterogêneos são coletados de múltiplas fontes, gerenciados, analisados e fornecidos aos usuários finais e/ou aplicativos externos [Davoudian and Liu 2020]. Esses sistemas têm trazido diversos desafios no desenvolvimento de software, tais como desafios técnicos relacionados aos 5Vs (Volume, Velocidade, Variedades, Veracidade e Valor) e desafios organizacionais que envolvem o trabalho em conjunto do Engenheiro de Software e do Cientista de Dados para descobrir e maximizar os valores de *Big Data*. Nesse contexto, os sistemas Big Data têm demandado significativas adaptações para a Engenharia de Requisitos (ER).

O processo de ER engloba as atividades de produção dos requisitos (elicitação, análise, especificação e validação) e seu gerenciamento com o intuito de identificar as necessidades das partes interessadas e dar suporte às atividades de desenvolvimento [Kalinowski et al. 2023]. Estudos recentes têm mostrado que as metodologias tradicionais de ER são comumente centradas nos usuários em vez de dados. As atividades tradicionais de ER se concentram nos requisitos que são visíveis para os usuários, em vez dos requisitos obtidos pelos cientistas de dados após a análise de *Big Data*.

Conforme destacado por [Altarturi et al. 2017], a responsabilidade pela tomada de decisão sobre quais dados devem ser mantidos ou descartados deve ser do cientista de dados, visto que essa escolha é crucial para agregar valor ao negócio. Além disso, segundo os autores, na atividade de Elicitação de Requisitos, o cientista de dados deve colaborar com o Engenheiro de Requisitos e com os clientes para identificar os dados nos requisitos de usuários que podem ser usados para aprimorá-los antes de serem documentados.

No caso do setor público, quando o gestor de uma cidade decide investir no uso de Big Data, existe uma série de desafios a serem enfrentados. Por exemplo, há diversas fontes de dados com formatos variados, baixa qualidade dos dados, e poucos estudos que auxiliem o time de requisitos a especificar documentos que contenham dados. Neste relato, são apresentados os problemas bem como suas respectivas soluções no âmbito do projeto da plataforma Big Data Fortaleza[1].

2. Descrição do Processo de Especificação dos Requisitos

A Especificação de Requisitos da plataforma *Big Data Fortaleza* é baseada na metodologia Scrum. A Figura 1 apresenta o processo utilizado no projeto, o qual inicia-se com a identificação de uma necessidade, que pode manifestar-se de três maneiras distintas: i) **Solicitação de Melhoria**, quando *stakeholders* e/ou membros da equipe identificam oportunidades de melhoria no projeto e validam com a gerência; ii) **Solicitação vinda de reunião com os *Product Owners* (POs)**, quando acontecem melhorias provenientes de reuniões regulares com POs para discutir os objetivos do projeto e as necessidades do cliente; e iii) **Solicitação da Gestão**, quando a alta administração ou gestores identificam a necessidade de implementar um novo recurso ou funcionalidade.

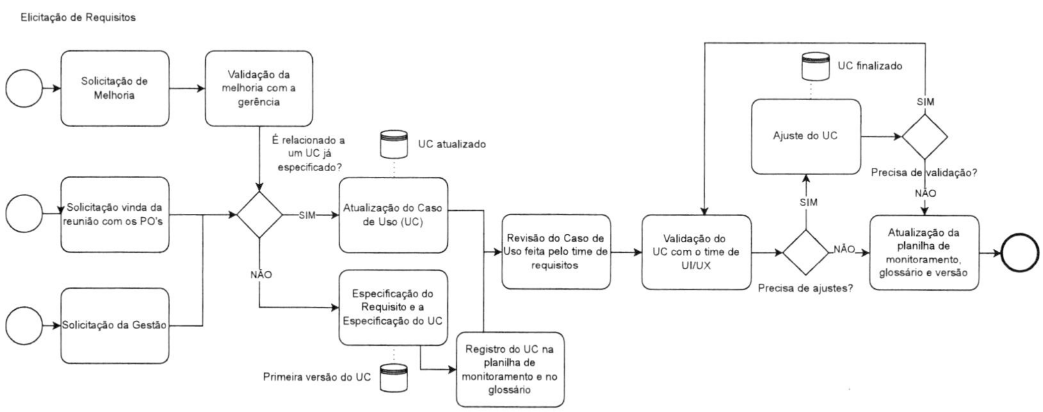

Figura 1. Fluxo do Processo de Especificação dos Requisitos

Após a identificação da necessidade, o analista de requisitos verifica se o Caso de Uso (do inglês, Uses Cases - UC) já foi especificado ou se é necessário a criação de um novo. A partir disso, se o UC já existe ocorre a **Atualização do Caso de Uso (UC)** com base na solicitação. Caso contrário, ocorre a especificação de um novo Requisito Funcional e a Especificação de um novo UC (**Especificação do Requisito e a Especificação do UC**) e o **Registro do UC na planilha de monitoramento e no glossário**.

[1]https://bigdata.fortaleza.ce.gov.br/

Um ponto de convergência no fluxo é a etapa de **Revisão do UC feita pelo time de requisitos**, que é a revisão por pares. Após esta validação pelo próprio time ocorre a **Validação do UC com time de *User Interface/User Experience* (UI/UX)**. Nesta fase, é verificado se ajustes são necessários (**Ajustes do UC**). Em caso de ajustes, o UC é modificado e armazenado, o time de requisitos verifica se o UC necessita novamente de validação, se sim, o fluxo retorna à etapa de **Validação com time de UI/UX**. Caso contrário ocorre a **Atualização da planilha de monitoramento, glossário e versão**, indicando o término do processo.

3. Desafios e Soluções

A plataforma *Big Data Fortaleza* já possui uma versão inicial em produção e continua em desenvolvimento contínuo à medida que os dados de outras secretarias são disponibilizadas. Durante a execução desse projeto, o processo de requisitos passou por uma evolução significativa até atingir o estado atual. A seguir, destacam-se soluções cruciais que tiveram um impacto positivo no processo de requisitos:

Inclusão de uma planilha de monitoramento: a gestão de versões e *status* dos artefatos produzidos pelo time de requisitos era dificultada por ser usada uma ferramenta de gerenciamento de documentos (Google Docs). Esta não era integrada ao sistema de gestão de tarefas do projeto (GitLab). Por este motivo, foi produzida uma planilha na qual a versão e o status dos artefatos eram informados. Para cada artefato, o time de requisitos informava se o artefato ainda estava sendo produzido, se já tinha sido revisado ou concluído. A versão estável do documento era informada na planilha, permitindo que os times de desenvolvimento e testes pudessem identificar qual versão eles poderiam considerar durante a realização de suas atividades. Com essa ação, muitos dos problemas reportados em relação às mudanças constantes nos artefatos puderam ser sanados.

Aperfeiçoamento da interação entre os times de requisitos e UI/UX: a necessidade de um contato direto entre os times de requisitos e UI/UX foi necessária, pois as validações dos requisitos com o cliente ocorriam de uma forma mais fluida quando apresentada em conjunto com os protótipos de alta fidelidade. Por esse motivo, uma reunião semanal entre os times de requisitos e UI/UX foi estabelecida. Nesta reunião eram sanadas todas as dúvidas que surgiam entre os dois times em relação as atividades da *sprint*. Com essa reunião, foi percebida a redução dos questionamentos sobre inconsistências entre os artefatos de UI/UX e requisitos.

Validação dos requisitos com o time de projeto: esta etapa foi adicionada para que o time de requisitos trabalhasse em conjunto com o time de UI/UX com o intuito de apresentar os requisitos e os protótipos das funcionalidades destinadas a serem implementadas nas próximas *sprints*, conforme delineado pelo *roadmap* do projeto. Essa etapa ocorria na semana anterior a próxima reunião com os POs.

Registro de solicitações de melhorias da gestão: como o projeto atendia um grande número de clientes/usuários, ocorriam diversas solicitações de inclusão de novas funcionalidades ou ajustes pontuais. No entanto, essas solicitações eram, geralmente, atendidas de forma *ad hoc*, e a informação de quem ou quando solicitou a melhoria era perdida. Por este motivo, o time de requisitos incluiu no seu processo um tratamento específico para este tipo de solicitação. As solicitações de melhorias eram registradas em um canal de comunicação de forma estruturada, onde informações sobre o solicitante, data da solicitação e motivação do pedido eram apresentados. Essas solicitações eram repassadas para documentos, para que assim ficassem registradas, e atividades para o time de requisitos eram criadas, visando a análise e a atualização dos artefatos necessários para que a solicitação pudesse ser incorporada ao produto final.

Elaboração do diagrama de casos de uso: um débito técnico do time de requisitos era a criação do diagrama de casos de uso. A ausência desse diagrama foi percebida durante a necessidade de definir as limitações de acesso das funcionalidades para o perfil de cada tipo de usuário. Com uma visão macro das funcionalidades do sistema, a partir do diagrama de casos de uso, foi possível então estabelecer, com uma maior precisão, os limites de acesso para cada um dos perfis que o sistema deveria permitir.

Especificação de requisitos de dados: um desafio para o time de requisitos foi a documentação de requisitos de dados. O sistema apresentava funcionalidades que tratavam dados sensíveis e os apresentavam de forma estruturada a partir de visualizações pré-definidas. O dado e o tipo de visualização são variáveis, mas definidos previamente pelo cliente. Essas solicitações foram tratadas como requisitos de dados, pois precisavam da atuação de cientistas de dados para analisar e tratar os dados antes de incorporar ao sistema. No entanto, esse tipo de requisito não era facilmente atendido pelos casos de uso, pois eram cenários genéricos variantes do uso das funcionalidades do sistema. A necessidade de registrar essas solicitações levou a criação de um novo tipo de artefato, denominado "documentos do job". Nestes eram descritos os dados que seriam exibidos, o tipo de visualização, qual a fonte do dados, dentre outras especificações técnicas. Diferente dos outros requisitos, esses tipos de solicitações eram analisadas e especificadas pelos cientistas de dados. Essa ação contribuiu para que este time atuasse de forma mais independente, agilizando o processo de incorporação desses requisitos ao sistema.

4. Conclusão

Este artigo apresentou as principais ações de melhorias no processo de especificação de requisitos realizadas no projeto *Big Data Fortaleza*. A execução desse processo revelou-se um desafio multifacetado, com dificuldades que iam desde a falta de ferramentas especializadas até a complexidade na especificação de requisitos de dados. A superação desses obstáculos demandou esforços adicionais da equipe e destacou a necessidade de abordagens mais adaptadas aos contextos particulares desses ambientes de desenvolvimento com Big Data.

Referências

Altarturi, H. H., Ng, K.-Y., Ninggal, M. I. H., Nazri, A. S. A., and Ghani, A. A. A. (2017). A requirement engineering model for big data software. In *2017 IEEE Conference on Big Data and Analytics (ICBDA)*, pages 111–117.

Davoudian, A. and Liu, M. (2020). Big data systems: A software engineering perspective. 53(5).

Kalinowski, M., Escovedo, T., Villamizar, H., and Lopes, H. (2023). *Engenharia de Software para Ciência de Dados: Um guia de boas práticas com ênfase na construção de sistemas de Machine Learning em Python*. Caso do Código, 1 edition.

Quantum Services Engineering: development, quality, testing, and security (Q-SERV Project)

Enrique Moguel[1], Jose Garcia-Alonso[1], Erik B. Terres-Escudero[2], Danel Arias[2], Pablo García Bringas[2], Ana Díaz Muñoz[3], Moisés Rodríguez Monje[3], Jesús Ramón Oviedo Lama[3] and Juan M. Murillo[1]

[1]Quercus Software Engineering Group,
Universidad de Extremadura, Cáceres, España

[2]Universidad de Deusto, Bilbao, España

[3]Instituto de Tecnologías y Sistemas de Información (UCLM).
C/ de Moledores s/n. 13071 Ciudad Real, España
{enrique, jgaralo, juanmamu}@unex.es,
{erik.terres.es, danel.arias}@opendeusto.es, pablo.garcia.bringas@deusto.es,
ana.diaz8@alu.uclm.es, {Moises.Rodriguez, jesusramon.oviedo}@uclm.es

Abstract. *The new and revolutionary quantum computation aims to advance in important fields such as AI, cybersecurity, and medicine. The development of this technology has encouraged several research centers and companies such as Amazon, IBM, Google or Microsoft to devote considerable efforts to the development of new technologies that bring quantum computing to the market. Currently, access to this technology is provided through the Infrastructure as a Service paradigm and with hybrid systems that combine classical and quantum computing. In order to create these systems, significant advances in service-oriented quantum computing are required to enable developers to create and operate quantum services with the same level of quality and security as their classical counterparts. Therefore, the project presented in this paper is primarily aimed at providing techniques and methodologies for quantum software development by applying the lessons learned from classical software engineering.*

1. Introduction

Quantum computing is rapidly gaining interest in many research areas, from mathematics or physics focused on building more powerful quantum computers or more stable qbits, to economics or healthcare focused on creating new quantum algorithms for specific problems. However, not much research effort is yet devoted to the development of technologies to build future quantum software [Mario Piattini et al. 2020].

Today's information systems are, in general, complex structures composed of simpler parts globally distributed and connected by complex communication infrastructures and protocols. The simpler parts are usually encapsulated as services with clear responsibilities. All this is made possible by different technologies such as service-oriented computing, cloud computing, etc. Building software systems in this way provides advantages such as paying only for the infrastructure used or obtaining high-quality attributes such as increased interoperability, independence, high decoupling, reusability, maintainability, reliability, scalability, security, etc.

The main objective of the project presented in this article (Q-SERV project) is to provide techniques and methodologies for quantum software development by applying the lessons learned from classical software engineering.

2. Q-SERV Project

The Q-SERV project is a coordinated project of the Call 2021 "Knowledge Generation Projects", and its aim is to solve the aforementioned problems by addressing three of the main limitations of current quantum services. Firstly, the subproject led by the University of Extremadura (UEx) focuses on the **development and operation of quantum services**; secondly, the subproject led by the University of Castilla-La Mancha (UCLM) focuses on the **quality and testing of quantum services**; and thirdly, the subproject led by the University of Deusto (UD) focuses on the **security aspects of quantum services**.

2.1. Development and Operation of Quantum Services

In its current form, most of the existing quantum computers can be accessed through the cloud in a model called Quantum Computing as a Service (QCaaS). QCaaS allows developers to access some of the existing quantum computers in the world, however, this access is highly dependent on specific hardware and developers must be highly proficient in quantum computing to benefit from its advantages.

To increase the level of abstraction of QCaaS, there are multiple research efforts underway. However, very few works focus on service engineering for quantum software.

The team at the UEx focuses on the development and exploitation of quantum microservices. More specifically, it focuses on aspects related to the servitization of quantum algorithms and their life cycle (deployment, execution, orchestration, etc).

2.2. Quantum Software Quality and Testing

There are several factors that influence the quality of quantum information systems: the quantum hardware, the quantum software platform, and the quantum software. There are different types of simulators and quantum computers. However, to date, most of them are still buggy, hence the name "*NISQ-Noisy Intermediate-Scale Quantum*". In addition, the underlying technology has a decisive influence on the maturity level of quantum computers. These different technologies exhibit different coherence times, gate latencies, etc.

Additionally, and despite the vast knowledge of software testing, "classical software testing techniques" are not directly applicable to quantum software test cases. Moreover, qubits cannot be "observed" or "measured" during the execution of a program. For these reasons, among others, approaches to software testing as conceived from the classical software point of view are very limited, but some proposals are already appearing on the research horizon [García de la Barrera et al. 2023].

The UCLM team is focused on the development of techniques [Díaz et al. 2024] and tools that guarantee the development of quality quantum software. Quantum Software Engineering needs to establish itself as a body of knowledge, therefore, research in those areas of Quantum Software Engineering that allow activities such as measurement and testing of such software, with the aim of evaluating and improving its quality, is considered crucial.

2.3. Quantum Services Security

Quantum code security must be addressed by design. This is important learning that the fields of Computer Science and Software Engineering have gained and matured after more than two decades of incidents, challenges, and advances in security [Arias et al. 2022].

The current limitations of quantum hardware lead to qubits being more unstable and error-prone than classical bits. These errors are extremely attractive to attackers. Therefore, a security analysis must be performed to ensure the intended operation of the program.

Based on its solid, broad, and deep experience in terms of cybersecurity-oriented software analysis, the UD team focuses on the design and development of new methods and tools to secure current quantum computing paradigms.

3. Results obtained

This project is at the halfway point of its execution and has made significant progress. Firstly, the subproject led by UEx has developed technologies to facilitate developers' access to different quantum service providers [Alvarado-Valiente et al. 2023d]. It has also worked on tools for the development and deployment of quantum services [Romero-Álvarez et al. 2023]; on the orchestration and management of quantum services using DevOps techniques [Alvarado-Valiente et al. 2023c]; on the generation of quantum services using OpenAPI and AsyncAPI; among others.

In addition, the subproject led by the UCLM has achieved the evaluation of the quality of quantum services, focusing for now on the analyzability of these services. During future work, research will be carried out to extend this evaluation to the rest of the characteristics that make up the quality of the software product following ISO 25010.

And finally, the subproject led by the UD has analyzed the security of current quantum software engineering [Arias et al. 2022]. It has also worked on avoiding the potential risks produced by noise on NISQ computers, creating error estimation techniques, and analyzing the effects of noise in data encoding circuits [Terres Escudero et al. 2023]. Additionally, the UD has developed a piece of software to detect bug patterns on quantum circuits in order to avoid known vulnerabilities.

There have also been collaborations between the different promoters as in the work [Alvarado-Valiente et al. 2023b] in which UEx and UCLM propose a process for the generation and deployment of quantum services focused on the quality of services; the work [Alvarado-Valiente et al. 2023a] in which UEx and UD propose a process for error and noise control for the generation of quantum services; the work [Arias et al. 2023] in which UD and UCLM analyze the concerns in the process of achieving secure quantum software engineering.

Acknowledgments. This work is part of the grants PID2021-124054OB-C31, PID2021-124054OB-C32, and PID2021-124054OB-C33 financed by MCIN/AEI/10.13039/50100011033 and FEDER funds. Also funded by the QSALUD project (EXP 00135977/MIG-20201059) in the CDTI action lines; by the Ministry of Science, Innovation and Universities (projects TED2021-130913B-I00 and PDC2022-133465-I00); by the Regional Ministry of Economy, Science and Digital Agenda of the

Regional Government of Extremadura (GR21133); and by EU under the Agreement - 101083667 of the Project "TECH4E-Tech4effiencyEDIH" (DIGITAL-2021-EDIH-01) supported by the European Commission through the Digital Europe Program. And also funded by the Q2SM Project: Quality Quantum Software Model (EXP 13/22/IN/032) financed by the Junta de Comunidades de Castilla-La Mancha and FEDER funds.

References

Alvarado-Valiente, J., Romero-Álvarez, J., Arias, D., Terres, E. B., Garcia-Alonso, J., Moguel, E., García Bringas, P., and Murillo, J. M. (2023a). Improving the quality of quantum services generation process: Controlling errors and noise. In *Hybrid Artificial Intelligent Systems*, pages 180–191. Springer.

Alvarado-Valiente, J., Romero-Álvarez, J., Díaz, A., Rodríguez, M., García-Rodríguez, I., Moguel, E., Garcia-Alonso, J., and Murillo, J. M. (2023b). Quantum services generation and deployment process: A quality-oriented approach. In *Quality of Information and Communications Technology*, pages 200–214. Springer.

Alvarado-Valiente, J., Romero-Álvarez, J., Moguel, E., and García-Alonso, J. (2023c). Quantum web services orchestration and management using devops techniques. In *Web Engineering*, pages 389–394. Springer.

Alvarado-Valiente, J., Romero-Álvarez, J., Moguel, E., García-Alonso, J., and Murillo, J. M. (2023d). Technological diversity of quantum computing providers: a comparative study and a proposal for api gateway integration. *Software Quality Journal*.

Arias, D., García Rodríguez de Guzmán, I., Rodríguez, M., Terres, E. B., Sanz, B., de la Puerta, J. G., Pastor, I., Zubillaga, A., and García Bringas, P. (2023). Let's do it right the first time: Survey on security concerns in the way to quantum software engineering. *Neurocomputing*, 538:126199.

Arias, D., Sanz, B., de la Puerta, J. G., Pastor, I., and Bringas, P. G. (2022). A repeated mistake is a choice: Considering security issues and risks in quantum computing from scratch. In *14th International Conference on Computational Intelligence in Security for Information Systems*, pages 156–166. Springer.

Díaz, A., Rodríguez, M., and Piattini, M. (2024). Towards a set of metrics for hybrid (quantum/classical) systems maintainability. *Journal of Universal Computer Science*.

García de la Barrera, A., García-Rodríguez de Guzmán, I., Polo, M., and Piattini, M. (2023). Quantum software testing: State of the art. *Journal of Software: Evolution and Process*, 35(4):e2419.

Mario Piattini et al. (2020). The talavera manifesto for quantum software engineering and programming m2i formación ramsés gallego quantum world association.

Romero-Álvarez, J., Alvarado-Valiente, J., Moguel, E., and Garcia-Alonso, J. (2023). Quantum web services: Development and deployment. In *Web Engineering*, pages 421–423. Springer.

Terres Escudero, E. B., Arias Alamo, D., Mentxaka Gómez, O., and García Bringas, P. (2023). Assessing the impact of noise on quantum neural networks: An experimental analysis. In *International Conference on Hybrid Artificial Intelligence Systems*, pages 314–325. Springer.

Understanding Productivity of Colombian Development Teams Working on Remote Environments

Alejandro Ahogado[1], Juan Hoyos[1], José Bocanegra[1], Viviola Gómez[2], Kelly Garcés[1]

[1]School of Engineering, Department of Systems and Computing Engineering
Universidad de los Andes
Bogotá – Colombia

[2]School of Social Sciences, Department of Psychology
Universidad de los Andes
Bogotá – Colombia

{a.ahogado,js.hoyosm,j.bocanegra,vgomez,kj.garces971}@uniandes.edu.co

Abstract. *This project is a collaborative effort to understand and address productivity challenges in remote development teams, employing a multifaceted approach that integrates software engineering, psychology, and design thinking methodologies. The initial focus has been on developing a tool for mining GitHub repositories, laying the groundwork for subsequent phases of the research.*

1. Introduction

During the pandemic, the restrictions imposed by health organizations forced software companies to make an accelerated transition from their in-person operations to fully/partial remote environments . The World Health Organization (WHO) declared the end of the global health emergency due to Covid-19 in May 2023. However, remote work has not finished, instead it has become the new "normal" in the software industry.

Although there are several theoretical benefits of remote work, such as flexibility for employees and savings on the normal commuting time to the workplaces [Ipsen et al. 2021], previous work has shown that the productivity [1] of development teams has changed significantly [Almeida et al. 2023, da Mota Silveira Neto et al. 2022, Bao et al. 2022, Smite et al. 2022, Russo D. 2021]. It is worth noting that we did not find a consensus in the literature about which indicators should be considered to evaluate productivity. For example, some works [da Mota Silveira Neto et al. 2022] use indicators that are calculated from repositories/planning tool activity (e.g., commits, pull-requests, issues). In addition, industry companies may use financial indicators such as project profitability.

Despite the efforts made by some software development companies, they recognize that the improvement in productivity is still a challenge and that new approaches are required to create best work environments where employees feel safe, supported, and productive. At the moment, there is a lack of certainty about the factors that caused positive/negative impact on the productivity of the development teams who work in remote

[1]In the context of this project, productivity is understood as the relationship between effectiveness and efficiency, not only evaluating the quantity of contributions but also their quality.

environments. A Colombian company, whose name we are unable to disclose, brought this problem to our research group.

When reviewing the literature, we found various studies [Bao et al. 2022, Ralph et al. 2020] that address this problem at a global level, pointing out that, especially for extensive projects, physical presence in the office favors team cohesion and improves communication, crucial elements for greater productivity. It is likely possible that some of the results found at global level would be applicable to Colombian development teams, but we believe that other factors may appear considering our social/economic/cultural situation.

Given that, we decided to formulate a project where the problem is investigated by industry practitioners and professors/students from the System and Computing Engineering Department and the Psychology Department. The project objectives are: (i) to determine the factors that impact the productivity of development teams in remote environments; (ii) propose a set of new practices to mitigate the impact of the factors identified above.

2. Proposal

The phases of the project are: indicators scoping, mining of software artifacts, focus groups/surveys and co-creation. Such phases are described below.

2.1. Indicators scoping

The purpose of this phase is to select which indicators should be considered to evaluate productivity in remote environments. Each company may have its own indicators but we believe that it is important to reflect on how the remote modality has change software development activities, such as, problem solving, coding, communication, messages management, meetings participation, testing and so on [Russo D. 2021]. As a result, we select indicators from the most relevant activities and explore where these indicators might come from. Some of them may already be available in company systems but others might require mining of software artifacts.

2.2. Mining of software artifacts

We propose mining code repositories or other useful artifacts in the company's development process to have objective information (i.e., KPI's and visualizations) that can be used in the discussion of the ofcus groups and in the design of the survey. For example, based on the repositories, we could analyze team productivity in terms of commits/pull-requests/issues during a time-window of interest (pandemic period with lockdown, post-pandemic period, etc.), taking into account developer experience. Some indicators are given below for illustration purposes:

- The number of commits needed to solve a bug and the number of issues created and resolved will demonstrate the ability of developers to solve problems and to prioritize development activities, which is essential for efficient project management.
- The total number of pull requests will allow us to have a vision of the speed and efficiency of reviewing and merging the code.

- The number of closed pull requests will indicate the degree of team collaboration and the quality of the code review process.
- The time developers have spent in the repository will allow us to evaluate the experience accumulated in the project and their way of acting in the face of different circumstances, such as: their ability to resolve bugs efficiently, the way in which they transmit the knowledge (evaluated through participation in code reviews).

Aforementioned indicators could motivate questions for the focus groups and in the survey. For example, suppose that repository metrics show a decrease in the number of commits that resolve issues. This finding can motivate questions such as: what are the causes of this decreasing behavior since developers are working remotely?

2.3. Focus groups and surveys

In a nutshell, the focus groups and the survey will allow us to collect the perception of development team members regarding the impact of remote work on productivity.

In particular, the objective of the focus group is to improve understanding of the problem and to determine additional elements that can be measured in the study. Different people will be invited to focus groups to have different perspectives on the situation under study, for example, people with the following characteristics: i) living in Bogotá or outside; ii) had having a process of onboarding and work 100% remote; iii) working in the company under a face-to-face modality since before the pandemic; iv) participating in projects with high or low profitability; v) having dependents or not, etc.

For the design of the focus groups, the insights obtained in the *mining of software artifacts* will be taken into account. The information from the focus groups will be transcribed, organized and analyzed to guide the design of the survey.

The survey seeks to collect perceptions through guiding questions that are aligned with the priorities of the research. The surveys are aimed at a wider audience than those who participated in the focus groups in order to have a significant volume of data to analyze.

Both the execution of the focus groups and the application of the survey will be chaired by the University researchers and that the information collected will be disclosed in aggregate form at the project level and not at the individual level, in order to provide a safe environment for participants to share their opinions.

2.4. Strategies co-creation

We propose socialization meetings aimed at all members of the company where the results will be shared and a collective reflection will be made on what strategies could help improve productivity, taking into account the particularities of the stakeholders identified in the study. Finally, the project includes the approach of how to follow up on the strategies that the company decides to implement.

3. Results

So far the project progress has been the development of a tool to mining Github repositories. The reason to choose this kind of artifact is that repositories are one of the main artifacts that shows software development productivity. In addition, they are many open-source Github repositories that can be used to evaluate the tool prototype. The tool architecture consists of the following nodes:

- A client node hosts critical components such as Tableau Desktop and a Web user interface which provides the ability to interact with the data effectively. This node authenticates with Github Authentication API to guarantee a secure interaction with repositories.
- A server node, composed of Uvicorn and FastApi, supports the extraction and transformation of the repositories data which is available by accessing the Github API. In addition, it helps on efficiently delivering the data to the client node.
- A PostgreSQL node stores the extracted data.

The tool has been evaluated in two manners: i) experiments to test that the tool is functional when analyzing different open-source repositories; ii) a survey to evaluate the usability perceived by industry users. The remaining phases of the project are ongoing work.

References

Almeida, A., Cunha, J., and Fernandes, J. (2023). Impact of remote work on portuguese software professionals during the covid-19 pandemic. In *Anais do XXVI Congresso Ibero-Americano em Engenharia de Software*, pages 191–205, Porto Alegre, RS, Brasil. SBC.

Bao, L., Li, T., Xia, X., Zhu, K., Li, H., and Yang, X. (2022). How does working from home affect developer productivity?—a case study of baidu during the covid-19 pandemic. *Science China Information Sciences*, 65(4):142102.

da Mota Silveira Neto, P. A., Mannan, U. A., de Almeida, E. S., Nagappan, N., Lo, D., Singh Kochhar, P., Gao, C., and Ahmed, I. (2022). A deep dive into the impact of covid-19 on software development. *IEEE Transactions on Software Engineering*, 48(9):3342–3360.

Ipsen, C., van Veldhoven, M., Kirchner, K., and Hansen, J. P. (2021). Six key advantages and disadvantages of working from home in europe during covid-19. *International journal of environmental research and public health*, 18(4):1826.

Ralph, P., Baltes, S., Adisaputri, G., Torkar, R., Kovalenko, V., Kalinowski, M., Novielli, N., Yoo, S., Devroey, X., Tan, X., et al. (2020). Pandemic programming: How covid-19 affects software developers and how their organizations can help. *Empirical software engineering*, 25:4927–4961.

Russo D., Hanel P.H.P., A. S. (2021). Predictors of well-being and productivity among software professionals during the covid-19 pandemic. *Journal of Software Engineering*, 26:62.

Smite, D., Tkalich, A., Moe, N. B., Papatheocharous, E., Klotins, E., and Buvik, M. P. (2022). Changes in perceived productivity of software engineers during covid-19 pandemic: The voice of evidence. *Journal of Systems and Software*, 186:111197.

Análise da experiência do consumidor no setor automotivo: um projeto P&D com a Renault do Brasil

Geovany A. D. Cancio[1,2] **, Marcelo Teixeira**[1]**, Diego S. Patriota**[2]

[1] Universidade Tecnológica Federal do Paraná (UTFPR), Pato Branco, Brasil

[2]Renault do Brasil

geovany@alunos.utfpr.edu.br, mtex@utfpr.edu.br

diego.patriota@renault.com

Abstract. *Companies compete for market leadership in the automotive domain based on strategies centered on understand consumers. This understanding generally focuses on specific experiences without considering the chained effect of a set of expectations. The solution proposed in this paper can capture the integrated effect of the consumer's interaction with the company. Through a substantial data engineering effort, a dataset is obtained to computationally expose the integration of user experiences with the company, from which insights are generated and reconfigured to understand better consumption profiles in terms of market vision, intentions and purchasing process. The solution is tested and illustrated by a case study involving real data from Renault.*

Resumo. *No setor automotivo, empresas competem pela liderança de mercado a partir de estratégias centralizadas no entendimento dos consumidores. Em geral, esse entendimento se concentra em domínios específicos da experiência, sem considerar o efeito encadeado de um conjunto de expectativas. A solução proposta neste artigo captura o efeito integrado e multidimensional da interação do consumidor com a empresa. Por meio de engenharia de dados, um dataset é construído para integrar as experiências dos usuários, a partir do qual uma estrutura de insights é gerada com opções de reconfiguração dinâmica para melhor compreender cada perfil de consumo. A solução é testada e ilustrada mediante um estudo de caso envolvendo dados reais da Renault.*

1. Objetivo principal do projeto

Este projeto propõe uma solução de software para a visualização integrada de perfis de consumidores do setor automotivo. A solução visa ultrapassar a abordagem unidimensional na análise de perfis de consumidores, buscando uma compreensão que incorpore diversos aspectos multidimensionais, tais como a análise conjunta de mercado, *leads*, pós-vendas, entre outros. Inicialmente, será apresentado um modelo de mapeamento de dados coletados de fontes e em momento distintos. Na sequência, é introduzido as etapas técnicas que compreendem um processo de engenharia de dados voltado à construção da estrutura de *insights* e à reconfiguração dinâmica com filtros demográficos. Esse modelo generaliza para diferentes empresas automotivas, uma vez que muitos dados são comuns a elas, como pesquisas de mercado, satisfação, dentre outras. Um estudo de caso na montadora de veículos Renault do Brasil é usado para ilustrar a abordagem.

2. Beneficiários da proposta

Este trabalho está vinculado à Renault do Brasil, no polo Design da Experiência do Usuário. O polo atua em projetos que impactam usuários internos e externos da companhia, como *chatbots* de atendimento, sistemas de bonificação de concessionárias, *websites* e toda a cadeia de desenvolvimento de novos modelos de veículos. A empresa mantém cooperação formal com a UTFPR e Fundação Araucária, no contexto de chamadas públicas, em particular a 11/2022. Os pilares impactados pelo projeto contemplam a geração e transferência de produtos tecnológicos, a obtenção de resultados científicos e a formação de recursos humanos qualificados.

3. Tecnologias utilizadas

A Renault dispõe de uma série de ferramentas licenciadas, bem como de metodologias para o desenvolvimento de projeto integradores de dados e design. Isso incluiu os dados relacionados a experiência do consumidor em pontos distintos de contato com a empresa e todo um ecossistema de ferramentas de análise e engenharia de dados.

Os dados incluem a *Pesquisa Geral de Mercado*, conduzida por institutos especializados e que proporciona uma compreensão nacional dos perfis de compra, sendo financiada por várias marcas em parceria; o *Sistema de Gerenciamento do Relacionamento com Clientes* (CRM), que fornece dados relacionados desde a geração de *Leads* até a entrega do veículo; a *Voz do Consumidor* (VOC), que oferece a avaliação da concessionária após a entrega do veículo, e a partir de serviços oferecidos no pós-venda; e dados demográficos que subsidiam a geração de *insights* a partir da configuração de um determinado perfil.

A empresa também dispõe da *Google Cloud Platform* (GCP) através do *Data Warehouse* para o armazenamento dos dados processados pelos *scripts* desenvolvidos em *Python*. A escolha dessa linguagem de programação se deve à sua versatilidade no processamento e integração de dados. O GCP facilita o pré-processamento via *Structure Query Language* (SQL), com o uso do serviço *Bigquery*. Além disso, a plataforma permite a integração com a ferramenta de visualização TIBCO Spotfire, voltada à geração de *insights* e análises dinâmicas com opções de filtragem e personalização de usabilidade através de *JavaScript*, *Cascading Style Sheets* (CSS) e *Hyper Text Markup Language* (HTML). Vale destacar que a empresa possui licenças para o uso do Spotfire e GCP, sendo a escolha dessas ferramentas alinhada com as estratégias tecnológicas vigentes.

4. Resultados alcançados e em andamento

Cada consumidor, desde aqueles que manifestam interesse na marca até os que concluem a compra, percorre diversos pontos de contato com a empresa. Esses pontos de contato são organizados em momentos-chave, como ilustrado na Figura 1.

O momento *Mercado X Consumidor do Futuro* oferece *insights* sobre como se comportam diferentes perfis no mercado nacional. Já o momento *Leads* compila informações desde o primeiro contato do consumidor com a marca via *Internet* até pesquisas realizadas alguns dias após a conclusão da compra e entrega do veículo. Por fim, o momento *Clientes* engloba as informações de pós-venda e coleta o modo de utilização do veículo por meio de sensores. As principais fontes de dados foram descritas na seção 3, enquanto as demais apresentam seus significados com base em seus nomes.

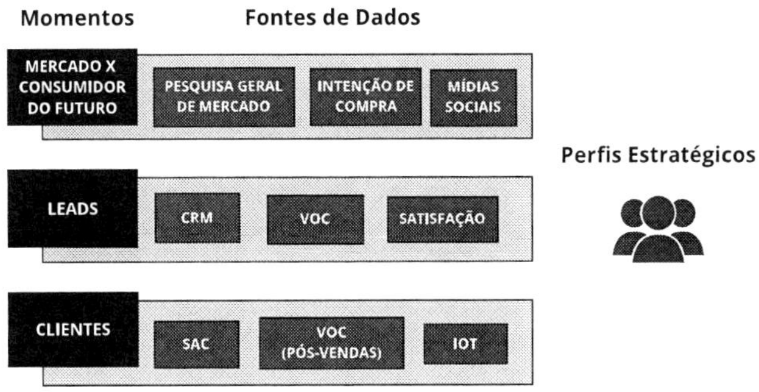

Figura 1. Estrutura de interação para consumidores do setor automotivo.

A construção dos momentos, por si só, já representa um avanço significativo na jornada de CX. No entanto, há um elemento central que, quando integrado aos momentos, possibilita a análise e o aprimoramento das estratégias da empresa automotiva: os perfis estratégicos. Esses perfis representam segmentos distintos de consumidores no mercado nacional, pois todo o processo de desenvolvimento de um modelo de veículo é baseado num perfil previamente escolhido. Essa estrutura também pode ser visualizada na Figura 1.

Os resultados até aqui expressam essencialmente o conceito da empresa, sobre o qual a nossa solução integra engenharia e análise de dados, conforme mostra a Figura 2.

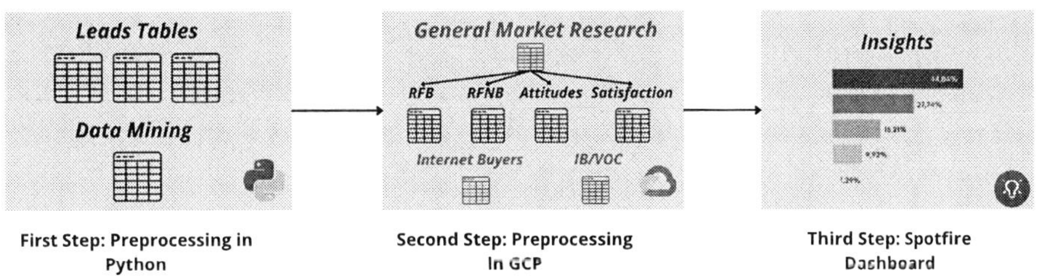

Figura 2. Estrutura técnica da solução.

Os dados, provenientes de pesquisas internas, de mercado, CRM e bancários, são extraídos e processados em *Python* para a devida integração, limpeza e validação das estruturas de dados. O dataset resultante desse processo é transferido para o GCP, de onde é submetido a uma nova fase de processamento, agora sobretudo usando o SQL a fim de reagrupar, fundir ou decompor novas estruturas, que tenham um valor semântico mais representativo e, assim, levar a *insights* mais completos sobre o modelo de negócio da empresa. Por fim, as tabelas processadas alimentam a ferramenta de visualização de dados TIBCO Spotfire, resultando em doze páginas que abrangem insights gerados para o momento de *Mercado* e *Leads*, no qual sua estrutura final é ilustrada na figura 3, cuja configuração com CSS, HTML e JavaScript otimiza a experiência do usuário e atribui um grau de personalização que favorece compreender e comparar momentos.

4.1. Resultados em andamentos e trabalhos futuros

A implementação do momento *Clientes* segue em desenvolvimento devido a recente aquisição dos dados da pesquisa VOC (pós-venda), essencial para a construção deste mo-

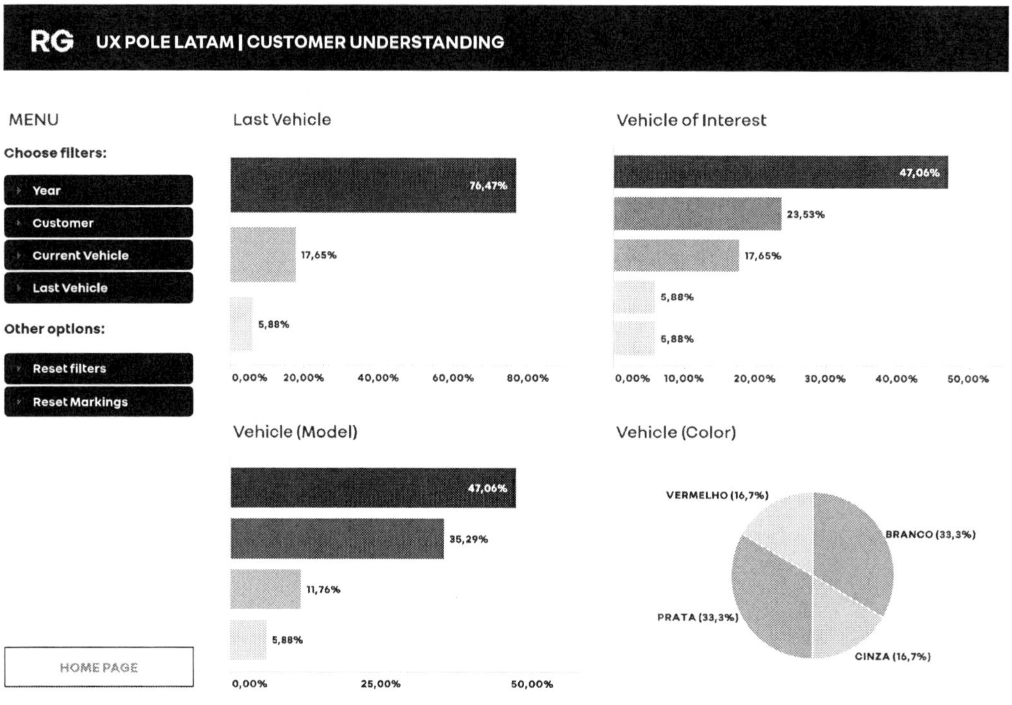

Figura 3. Página de *Insights* gerada no Spotfire.

mento. Outro aspecto em andamento é a construção dos perfis estratégicos, utilizando um algoritmo de aprendizado não-supervisionado para segmentar amostras a partir da Pesquisa Geral de Mercado com compradores de veículos eletrificados. Após a conclusão dessas tarefas em andamento, os dados utilizados neste trabalho, como parte integrante de um processo, serão processados e submetidos à mineração de processos. Nesta tarefa futura, a tabela de *logs* servirá como entrada para ferramentas especializadas na mineração de processos, com o objetivo de identificar a causa raiz dos problemas que levam os consumidores a desistirem de suas compras.

Por fim, os resultados já obtidos resultam em uma análise multidimensional da experiência do consumidor. A conclusão das demais etapas em andamento, concluirá toda a estrutura estabelecida por meio de um estudo interno na Renault voltado a experiência do consumidor. Com os trabalhos futuros, a estrutura estabelecida terá cada vez mais a capacidade de aprimorar não apenas os processos relacionados aos projetos dentro do polo de Design, mas também em outras iniciativas no Brasil e em países da América Latina.

5. Agradecimentos

Os autores agradecem o suporte financeiro da CAPES (código 001), CNPq (bolsa PQ 309946 /2020-4), Fundação Araucária, FINEP e Renault do Brasil.

Fortaleza City Hall Strategic Planning based on Data Analysis and Forecasting

Élcio Batista[1], Rossana M. C. Andrade[2], Ismayle S. Santos[2,3], Tales P. Nogueira[2,4], Pedro A. M. Oliveira[2,5], Valeria Lelli[2], Victória T. Oliveira[2]

[1]Fortaleza City Hall
Fortaleza Planning Institute (IPLANFOR)

[2]Group of Computer Networks, Software Engineering and Systems (GREat)
Federal University of Ceará (UFC)

[3]Ceará State University (UECE)

Fortaleza – CE – Brazil

[4]University for International Integration of the Afro-Brazilian Lusophony (UNILAB)
Redenção – CE – Brazil

[5]Federal Institute of Education, Science and Technology of Maranhão (IFMA)
Pedreiras – MA – Brazil

Abstract. *This paper presents the Big Data Fortaleza platform, which uses Big Data and Machine Learning for providing data analysis and prediction. The platform aims to assist in the strategic planning of solutions for the sustainable urban development of Fortaleza, in line with the activities of the Fortaleza Planning Institute (IPLANFOR). The challenge initially addressed is Early Childhood, once intelligent data management can significantly contribute to decision-making aimed at improving child development. Several exploratory and predictive analyses have been conducted to address critical issues in this domain, identified through discussions with several stakeholders from Fortaleza City Hall.*

Resumo. *Este artigo apresenta a plataforma Big Data Fortaleza que utiliza técnicas de Big Data e Machine Learning para análise de dados e predição. Seu objetivo é auxiliar no planejamento estratégico de soluções para o desenvolvimento urbano sustentável de Fortaleza, em consonância com as atividades do Instituto de Planejamento de Fortaleza (IPLANFOR). O desafio inicialmente abordado é relacionado à Primeira Infância, uma vez que a gestão inteligente de dados contribui significativamente para a tomada de decisões que visam melhorar o desenvolvimento infantil. Até o momento, diversas análises exploratórias e preditivas foram conduzidas para abordar questões essenciais nesse domínio.*

1. Introduction

Smart Cities emerged aiming to evolve cities to the future in which citizens' well-being is prioritized, and industry and urban planning are evaluated from a sustainable perspective [Sánchez-Corcuera et al. 2019]. From this perspective, technologies such as Big Data, Internet of Things (IoT), Cloud Computing, Artificial Intelligence, Software Engineering and Mobile Computing are allies in several Smart City scenarios.

Initially, the city of Fortaleza established a comprehensive urban plan designed to harmonize territorial development with socioeconomic advancement. This plan encompasses a strategic framework with objectives segmented into short, medium, and long-term phases, projecting up to the year 2040. Furthermore, it seeks to foster multifaceted discourse concerning urban development, engaging diverse perspectives, sectors, geographical regions, and governmental levels. Fortaleza 2040[1] presents challenges to overcome low qualifications, youth vulnerability, poverty, and social inequality as well as educational backwardness.

Given these challenges, data collection and analysis as well as machine learning techniques are essential for diagnosing and supporting the decisions of city managers. By analyzing the available data intelligently, it is possible, for example, to improve the quality of services offered to citizens and to anticipate the impact of changes in urban infrastructure.

Thus, this paper presents the Big Data Fortaleza platform, which uses Big Data and Machine Learning techniques for providing, respectively, data analysis and forecasting, as well as cloud computing and software engineering. The platform emerged to support the activities of the mayor, vice-mayor, and secretaries to solve Fortaleza's demands and to assist them in the strategic planning of solutions for the sustainable urban development of Fortaleza city, in line with the activities of the Fortaleza Planning Institute (IPLANFOR)[2]

The challenge initially addressed was Early Childhood, children between the ages of zero and six years old, once intelligent data management can significantly contribute to decision-making aimed at improving child development. The challenges faced in Early Childhood encompasses cross-sectoral areas of action, so we have first focused on children between the ages of zero and four years old and actions in health, education, human rights, and social development. In education, public managers must guarantee access to nurseries and schools for early childhood education. In health, it is crucial to take care of pregnant women by attending prenatal appointments and ensuring that the child receives care after birth, such as appointments and vaccinations. In human rights and social development, it is essential to identify families in a situation of socio-economic vulnerability or homelessness and offer support through social benefits, intending to reduce inequalities in access to goods and services that meet children's rights.

2. BigData Fortaleza Platform

As previously discussed, the BigData Fortaleza platform was designed to assist decision-making in different contexts of the city. Therefore, it was necessary to build a platform capable of adapting to the different data types that each challenge requires. The platform architecture follows the Medallion architecture and was implemented using Amazon AWS services such as S3, Glue, Athena among others [Saxena et al. 2023].

2.1. Workflow

The platform workflow has as its central point the challenge defined by the managers of Fortaleza City Hall (PMF – from Portuguese "Prefeitura Municipal de Fortaleza").

[1]Fortaleza 2040 website: fortaleza2040.fortaleza.ce.gov.br/site/.

[2]Iplanfor website: iplanfor.fortaleza.ce.gov.br.

These challenges can be related to initiatives to reduce social inequalities, as outlined in the Fortaleza 2040 plan. Data scientists then begin to understand the challenge domain, identifying issues in collaboration with PMF stakeholders (for example, using structured meetings) and defining the data products as well as the process of acquiring, processing and analyzing data.

The process begins with the definition of the challenge by public managers and follows with the registration of this challenge on the platform. This registration is crucial for monitoring the activities performed by the data scientists, such as understanding the context, identifying the strategic questions, defining the data products, processing and analyzing data, and validating the answers with Big Data. At the end of the process, the access profiles for the functionalities and the user groups for viewing each analysis are defined, and managers can analyze the data products.

2.2. Platform Development

The platform development follows software engineering principles, including the Scrum methodology, requirements engineering, continuous integration, software testing and validation, and user experience and interface. The platform was developed using the following technologies: React, Spring Boot, Mongo DB, and Amazon Web Services (AWS). Several tests were also conducted using the OWASP ZAP framework to ensure the platform security. In addition, the Brazilian General Personal Data Protection Law (LGPD) was followed throughout the process. Figure 1 shows the platform home page (A) and an example of the system's monitoring panel, where managers can customize and add analytics. (B).

Figure 1. (A) Home page of the BigData Fortaleza platform. (B) Example of analytics on the Early Childhood challenge

3. Platform Impacts and Results

The first challenge of the BigData Fortaleza platform was the "Demand for Daycare Vacancies". Thus, the team launched initiatives to achieve tangible results in the project first six months (from July to December, 2022). During the first quarter of 2023, efforts were directed toward other challenges related to personalized care for pregnant women and vaccination in daycare centers.

The map in Figure 2 (A) shows the current number of pregnant women per neighborhood in Fortaleza. The number of pregnant women per neighborhood can help with future demands for places in daycare centers and personalized health care for pregnant women.

Figure 2. (A) Choropleth map of pregnant women by neighborhood. (B) Geographical Map with Daycare Centers and Missing Vaccination in Children.

The map in Figure 2 (B) shows the integration of education and health data. Each nursery school shown in the map provides information on the number of children enrolled and how many children have missing vaccinations, supporting Fortaleza City Hall in making personalized public policies, such as vaccination campaigns in nurseries.

4. Final Remarks and Acknowledgments

Going beyond conventional analysis platforms, the BigData Fortaleza[3] platform focuses on data visualizations and forecasts to anticipate future demands of the population. PMF managers can obtain customized information to help their decisions on public policies that will allow them to analyze current scenarios accurately and predict future demands more reliably.

Finally, we would like to thank FUNCAP for the project financial support and CNPq for the productivity grant awarded to Rossana M. C. Andrade (306362/2021-0).

References

[Sánchez-Corcuera et al. 2019] Sánchez-Corcuera, R., Nuñez-Marcos, A., Sesma-Solance, J., Bilbao-Jayo, A., Mulero, R., Zulaika, U., Azkune, G., and Almeida, A. (2019). Smart cities survey: Technologies, application domains and challenges for the cities of the future. *International Journal of Distributed Sensor Networks*, 15(6):1550147719853984.

[Saxena et al. 2023] Saxena, M., Sowell, B., Alamgir, D., Bahadur, N., Bisht, B., Chandrachood, S., Keswani, C., Krishnamoorthy, G., Lee, A., Li, B., Mitchell, Z., Porwal, V., Chappidi, M. R., Ross, B., Sekiyama, N., Zaki, O., Zhang, L., and Shah, M. A. (2023). The story of AWS Glue. In *VLDB 2023*.

[3]BigData Fortaleza website: bigdata.fortaleza.ce.gov.br.

Digital Services Integration in Smart Cities: a Trusted Execution Environment Based Solution *

Regis Schuch[1], Rafael Z. Frantz[1], José Bocanegra[2], Fabricia Roos-Frantz[1], Sandro Sawicki[1], Carlos Molina-Jiménez[3]

[1]Unijuí University – Ijuí – Brazil

[2]University of los Andes – Bogotá – Colombia

[3]University of Cambridge – Cambridge – United Kingdom

{regis.schuch, rzfrantz, frfrantz, sawicki}@unijui.edu.br,

j.bocanegra@uniandes.edu.co, carlos.molina@cl.cam.ac.uk

Abstract. *This paper elucidates the use of Trusted Execution Environments as a solution to the challenges of data security and privacy within the context of digital services integration in smart cities. This type of environment is engineered to safeguard sensitive data during execution, thereby guaranteeing that tasks involving such data are performed within isolated memory compartments.*

Keywords*: Privacy. Morello Board. Compartmentalisation.*

A smart city integrates physical, IT, social, and business infrastructures, utilising collective intelligence [Harrison et al. 2010]. To be considered smart, cities must develop three dimensions: people, institutions, and technologies [Nam and Pardo 2011]. This paper focuses on the technological dimension, which includes a rich ecosystem of digital services from both the public and private sectors. These services must be interoperable and integrated to provide new services, thereby supporting business processes. Integration platforms are specialised software tools used to design, implement, and run integration processes. An integration process is designed as a workflow of tasks that implements an integration logic, allowing two or more digital services to exchange data and share functionality. Data that flows within the integration process must be protected against external and unauthorised access, thereby preventing data leaks and preserving privacy.

To circumvent these issues, we propose a hardware-based approach that utilises a TEE to execute the integration process. A TEE is a secure environment within a processor capable of executing code containing confidential data [Sabt et al. 2015]. In our proposal, we have chosen to use the Morello Board [ARM 2022] TEE implementation, as it incorporates Capability Hardware Enhanced RISC Instructions (CHERI) concepts [Watson et al. 2019], enabling fine-grained memory protection. A distinguishing feature of the Morello Board is that a developer can control specific areas in the memory, which is not possible with other TEE implementations on the market. Morello's software ecosystem is compatible with operating systems such as

*Supported by the Coordination for the Improvement of Higher Education Personnel (CAPES) and the Brazilian National Council for Scientific and Technological Development (CNPq) under the following project grants 309425/2023-9, 402915/2023-2, 311011/2022-5.

CheriBSD [Watson and Davis 2023], which incorporates specific features of the CHERI architecture. Library compartmentalisation allows each library to operate in its own protection domain within a compartmentalisation-enabled process [Watson et al. 2023].

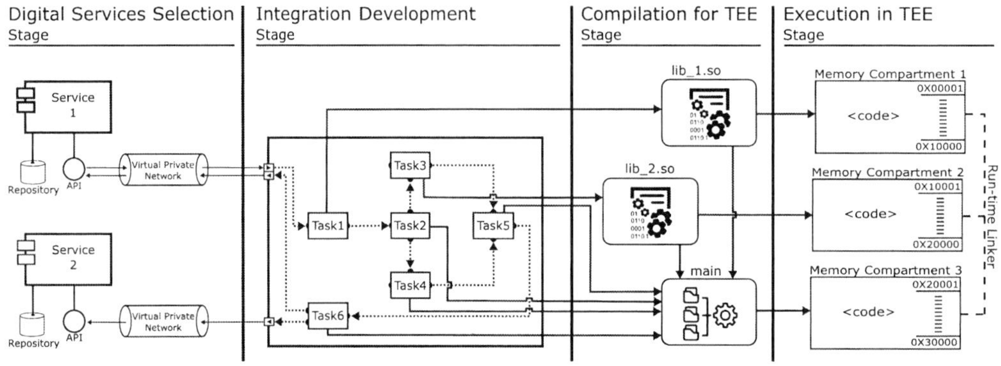

Figure 1. Stages for executing an integration process in a TEE.

Roughly speaking, we divide the process of executing an integration process in a TEE into four stages as illustrated in Figure 1. Digital Services Selection entails analysing data repositories to identify available data, access methods, and protocols, and ensuring data transmission through secure channels like Virtual Private Network (VPN). Integration Development involves creating processes and atomic tasks for data operations. Compilation for TEE involves implementing integration process components as libraries, and deployment in a secure environment requires compilation in CheriBSD. Finally, objects are executed in TEE instantiated in the Morello Board, accessing memory spaces and the run-time linker. The run-time linking process creates compartments for each library, granting and restricting access to resources, and communication between compartments occurs through function calls and passing arguments. We implemented and experimented with this strategy and our view is that it is viable in practice, as it allows for the protection of data flowing through an integration process.

References

ARM (2022). Morello prototype architecture. `https://developer.arm.com/documentation/den0133/0100/?lang=en`. [online: access in 10-jan-2024].

Harrison, C., Eckman, B., Hamilton, R., Hartswick, P., Kalagnanam, J., Paraszczak, J., and Williams, P. (2010). Foundations for smarter cities. *IBM J. of R. and Dev.*, 54(4):1–16.

Nam, T. and Pardo, T. A. (2011). Conceptualizing smart city with dimensions of technology, people, and institutions. In *Proc. 12th Annual Int'l Digital Government Research Conf.: Digital Government Innovation in Challenging Times*, page 282–291.

Sabt, M., Achemlal, M., and Bouabdallah, A. (2015). Trusted execution environment: what it is, and what it is not. In *2015 IEEE Trustcom/BigDataSE/Ispa*, pages 57–64.

Watson, R. N., Moore, S. W., Sewell, P., and Neumann, P. G. (2019). An introduction to cheri. Technical report, University of Cambridge, Computer Laboratory.

Watson, R. N. M. and Davis, B. (2023). Getting started with cheribsd 23.11. `https://ctsrd-cheri.github.io/cheribsd-getting-started/cover/index.html`. [online: access in 11-jan-2024].

Watson, R. N. M., Witaszczyk, K., and Man, J. (2023). Library compartmentalization. `https://www.cheribsd.org/tutorial/23.11/c18n/index.html`. [online: access in 11-jan-2024].

Framework Ágil para Certificação de Software Aeronáutico

Andréia Aparecida Costa[1,2], Johnny Marques[1]

[1]Programa de Pós-graduação em Ciências e Tecnologias Espaciais
Instituto Tecnológico de Aeronáutica (ITA) São José dos Campos – SP – Brasil

[2]EMBRAER S.A.
São José dos Campos – SP – Brasil

andreiaapps@gmail.com, johnny@ita.br

Resumo. *Este artigo resumo apresenta uma proposta de framework para desenvolvimento de software aeronáutico, como proposta de pesquisa de mestrado em andamento, onde esse framework apresenta compliance com a RTCA DO-178C, incorporando os valores e princípios do Manifesto Ágil e uma extensão do Scrum.*

1. Introdução

Tipicamente, os *Software Safety Critical* são desenvolvidos em ambientes regulados por normas e padrões. Exemplos deste tipo de Software são encontrados em domínios, tais como: Aeronáutico, Biomédico, Ferroviário e Nuclear. Segundo Marques et al. (2019), na aviação, o uso de tecnologias avançadas incorporadas aos sistemas, traduz bem a necessidade de Software Aeronáutico que atenda um alto desempenho, combinado com a preocupação em segurança e qualidade.

A RTCA DO-178C [RTCA 2012] fornece recomendações para o desenvolvimento e certificação de software de aviação. Em sua estrutura, os diversos processos do ciclo de vida do software são descritos por meio de atividades e objetivos que devem ser atendidos [Yelisetty et al. 2015]. A RTCA DO-178C contém 71 objetivos que devem ser cumpridos [Marques and Cunha 2017].

O Scrum é um *framework* ágil que utiliza ciclos de trabalho curtos chamados *sprints* para promover a colaboração e a entrega incremental de produtos, incluindo papéis, artefatos e cerimônias [Larman and Basili 2003].

O objetivo geral desta pesquisa é, partindo da norma RTCA DO-178C, identificar pontos que possam comprometer a adoção de métodos ágeis no desenvolvimento de software embarcado de uso aeronáutico e propor adaptações no *framework* Scrum.

2. Metodologia de Pesquisa

A metodologia de pesquisa envolve 4 etapas: (i) Execução de um Mapeamento Sistemático da Literatura (MSL); (ii) Organização dos Requisitos para o *Framework*; (iii) Concepção do *Framework*; e (iv) Avaliação do *Framework* por Grupo Focal de Especialistas e/ou por Experimento. A Figura 1 apresenta um fluxo com as etapas de pesquisa.

3. Framework

A Figura 2 apresenta, de forma visual, a primeira de duas camadas de abstração do *framework*. A operação do *framework* inicia-se com entradas que vão: a) viabilizar a

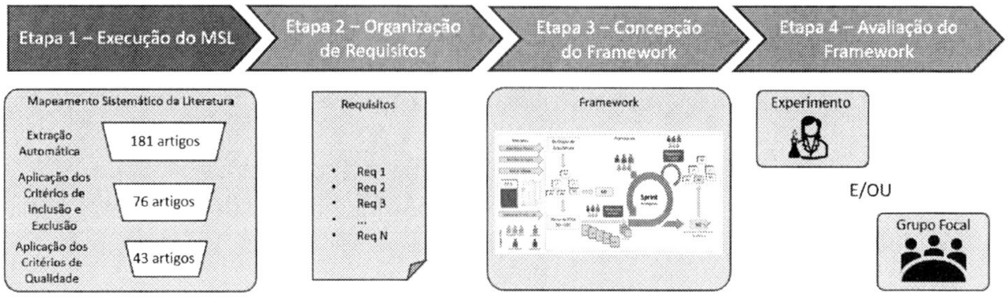

Figura 1. Etapas de pesquisa

construção de uma arquitetura inicial para a aplicação que precisará ser desenvolvida; b) fornecer informações para a escrita dos planos; e c) delinear o modo de execução do Framework.

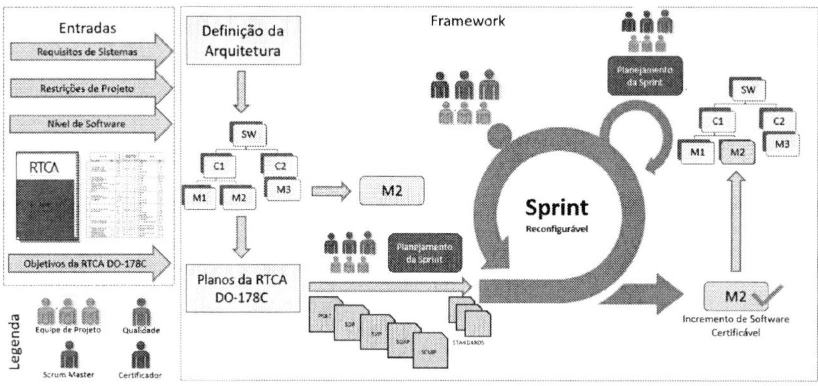

Figura 2. Proposta Inicial do *Framework*

Agradecimentos

O presente trabalho foi realizado com apoio da Coordenação de Aperfeiçoamento de Pessoal de Nível Superior - Brasil (CAPES) - Código de Financiamento 001

Referências

Larman, C. and Basili, V. (2003). Iterative and incremental development: A brief history. *Computer*, 36:47–56.

Marques, J. (2019). Uma análise das características de especificação de requisitos de software em normas de ambientes regulados. In *Anais do WER19 - Workshop em Engenharia de Requisitos*.

Marques, J. and Cunha, A. (2017). Verification scenarios of onboard databases under the rtca do-178c and the rtca do-200b. In *36th IEEE/AIAA Digital Avionics Systems Conference*.

RTCA (2012). *DO-178C - Software Considerations in Airborne Systems and Equipment Certification*.

Yelisetty, S., Marques, J., and Tasinaffo, P. (2015). A set of metrics to assess and monitos compliance with rtca do-178c. In *34th AIAA/IEEE Digital Avionics System Conference*.

AUTHOR INDEX